T0325194

New Technologies in Virtual and Hybrid Events

Sharad Kumar Kulshreshtha
North-Eastern Hill University, India

Craig Webster
Ball State University, USA

A volume in the Advances in
Hospitality, Tourism, and the
Services Industry (AHTSI) Book
Series

Published in the United States of America by
    IGI Global
    Business Science Reference (an imprint of IGI Global)
    701 E. Chocolate Avenue
    Hershey PA, USA 17033
    Tel: 717-533-8845
    Fax: 717-533-8661
    E-mail: cust@igi-global.com
    Web site: http://www.igi-global.com

Library of Congress Cataloging-in-Publication Data

CIP Pending
ISBN: 979-8-3693-2272-7
EISBN: 979-8-3693-2273-4

British Cataloguing in Publication Data
A Cataloguing in Publication record for this book is available from the British Library.

All work contributed to this book is new, previously-unpublished material.
The views expressed in this book are those of the authors, but not necessarily of the publisher.

For electronic access to this publication, please contact: eresources@igi-global.com.

Advances in Hospitality, Tourism, and the Services Industry (AHTSI) Book Series

Maximiliano Korstanje
University of Palermo, Argentina

ISSN:2475-6547
EISSN:2475-6555

MISSION

Globally, the hospitality, travel, tourism, and services industries generate a significant percentage of revenue and represent a large portion of the business world. Even in tough economic times, these industries thrive as individuals continue to spend on leisure and recreation activities as well as services.

The Advances in Hospitality, Tourism, and the Services Industry (AHTSI) book series offers diverse publications relating to the management, promotion, and profitability of the leisure, recreation, and services industries. Highlighting current research pertaining to various topics within the realm of hospitality, travel, tourism, and services management, the titles found within the AHTSI book series are pertinent to the research and professional needs of managers, business practitioners, researchers, and upper-level students studying in the field.

Coverage

- Casino Management
- Health and Wellness Tourism
- International Tourism
- Leisure & Business Travel
- Tourism and the Environment

IGI Global is currently accepting manuscripts for publication within this series. To submit a proposal for a volume in this series, please contact our Acquisition Editors at Acquisitions@igi-global.com or visit: http://www.igi-global.com/publish/.

AI Innovations in Service and Tourism

Titles in this Series

For a list of additional titles in this series, please visit: www.igi-global.com/book-series

Marketing
Vipin Nadda (University of Sunderland, UK) Pankaj Kumar Tyagi (Chandigarh University, India) Amrik Singh (Lovely Professional University, India) and Vipin Singh (Vellore Institute of Technology, India)
Business Science Reference • copyright 2024 • 591pp • H/C (ISBN: 9798369379097) • US $425.00 (our price)

Interlinking SDGs and the Bottom-of-the-Pyramid Through Tourism   ·
Marco Valeri (Niccolò Cusano University, Italy) and Shekhar (University of Delhi, India)
Business Science Reference • copyright 2024 • 315pp • H/C (ISBN: 9798369331668) • US $255.00 (our price)

Special Interest Trends for Sustainable Tourism
Kittisak Jermsittiparsert (University of City Island, Cyprus) and Pannee Suanpang (Suan Dusit University, Thailand)
Business Science Reference • copyright 2024 • 463pp • H/C (ISBN: 9798369359037) • US $345.00 (our price)

Cultural, Gastronomy, and Adventure Tourism Development
Rui Alexandre Castanho (WSB University, Poland) and Mara Franco (University of Madeira, Portugal)
Business Science Reference • copyright 2024 • 407pp • H/C (ISBN: 9798369331583) • US $325.00 (our price)

Dimensions of Regenerative Practices in Tourism and Hospitality
Pankaj Kumar Tyagi (Chandigarh University, India) Vipin Nadda (University of Sunderland, UK) Kannapat Kankaew (Burapha University International College, Thailand) and Kaitano Dube (Vaal University of Technology, South Africa)
Business Science Reference • copyright 2024 • 338pp • H/C (ISBN: 9798369340424) • US $295.00 (our price)

IGI Global
PUBLISHER of TIMELY KNOWLEDGE

701 East Chocolate Avenue, Hershey, PA 17033, USA
Tel: 717-533-8845 x100 • Fax: 717-533-8661
E-Mail: cust@igi-global.com • www.igi-global.com

Editors' dedication to their loving families, who constantly support and encourage us to do good deeds.

This book is to dedicated my Guru Prof. U.N. Shukla and parents Shri. Jiwan Prakash Kulshreshtha (father) & Late Smt. Sushma Kulshreshtha (mother), Sakshi (wife), Atharv (son) & Aashvi (daughter).

- Dr. Sharad Kumar Kulshreshtha

I would also like to dedicate this to my family, including my parents Robert and Carolee Webster, my wife Maria Webster, and my three sons, Paris, Simon, and Scott. In addition, I want to acknowledge the support and love of those who I consider my family, despite a lack of genetic relations. They will always be a part of my family in this life.

- Prof. Craig Webster

Editorial Advisory Board

Table of Contents

Editorial Advisory Board vi

Foreword xxii

Preface xxv

Acknowledgment xxxvi

Introduction xxxviii

Chapter 1
Emerging Technologies in Virtual and Hybrid Events: Major Issues and
Major Drivers 1
    Sharad Kumar Kulshreshtha, North-Eastern Hill University, India
    Craig Webster, Ball State University, USA

Chapter 2
Revolutionizing Events: Exploring the Seamless Integration of Robots in
Hybrid and Virtual Experiences 19
    Anila Thomas, Jyoti Nivas College (Autonomous), Bangalore, India

Chapter 3
Exploring the Use of Virtual and Hybrid Events for MICE Sector: Trends
and Opportunities 47
    Amrik Singh, Lovely Professional University, Punjab, India
    Mildred Nuong Deri, University of Energy and Natural Resources,
        Ghana

Chapter 4
Event-Enabled Mobile Applications: Seamless and Smart Technological
Platforms for Managing Virtual and Hybrid Events and Festivals 71
    Sharad Kumar Kulshreshtha, North-Eastern Hill University, India
    Sunildro S. Akoijam, North-Eastern Hill University, India
    Paramjeet Kumar, North-Eastern Hill University, India
    U. N. Shukla, Institute of Tourism and Hotel Management, Agra, India

Chapter 5
From Connectivity to Immersion: Unleashing the Potential of 5G for
Seamless Virtual Event Experiences 89
Paramjeet Kumar, North Eastern Hill University, India
Wallamkupar Dkhar, North Eastern Hill University, India

Chapter 6
The Interactive Bleisure Event: Gamification and Bibliometric Trends
Transforming Attendee Participation 106
Narendra Kumar, Amity University, Noida, India
Swati Sharma, Amity University, Noida, India
Gaurav Kumar Gupta, JS University, Shikohabad, India

Chapter 7
Emergence of Metaverse: An Innovative Technological Fusion in Indian
Festivals 128
Ruchika Kulshrestha, GLA University, Mathura, India
Ashutosh Pandey, FORE School of Management, New Delhi, India
Abhijeet V. Tiwari, GLA University, Mathura, India

Chapter 8
An Analysis on the Future Usage of Metaverse in the Marketing Event
Industry in India: An ISM Approach 146
Supriya Lamba Sahdev, Alliance University, Bengaluru, India
Chitra Krishnan, Symbiosis Centre for Management Studies, Symbiosis
    International University (Deemed), Pune, India
Amilson Durans, Centro Universitário Santa Terezinha, São Luís, Brazil
Ahdi Hassan, Global Institute for Research Education and Scholarship,
    Amsterdam, The Netherlands
Jugnu Thakur, ISBR Business School, India

Chapter 9
Role of Metaverse in Events Industry: An Empirical Approach 164
Sujay Vikram Singh, Banaras Hindu University, India
Pravin Chandra Singh, MSMSR, Mats University, Raipur, India
Kuldeep Singh, Amity University, Gurugram, India
Akshay Nain, Amity University, Gurugram, India

Chapter 10
Service Automation and Festivals: Technologies and Their Impact Upon
Sustainability of Events 184
Craig Webster, Ball State University, USA

Chapter 11

Leveraging Event Gamification for Event Planning and Creating a
Memorable Experience 198

    Aarti Madan, Atal Bihari Vajpayee School of Management and
        Entrepreneurship, Jawaharlal Nehru University, India
    Vaniki Joshi Lohani, Atal Bihari Vajpayee School of Management and
        Entrepreneurship, Jawaharlal Nehru University, India

Chapter 12

Viral Content in Event Management of Hospitality and Socio-Cultural
Activities 228

    Bovsh A. Liudmyla, State University of Trade and Economics, Ukraine
    Kamel Mouloudj, University of Medea, Algeria
    Alla M. Rasulova, State University of Trade and Economics, Ukraine
    Tetiana Mykhaylivna Tkachuk, State University of Trade and
        Economics, Ukraine

Chapter 13

Hybridized Tourism Education in Hard Times: Pancoe as a Case Study 258

    Maximiliano Emanuel Korstanje, University of Palermo, Argentina

Chapter 14

Transforming Traditions of University Convocations Through Virtual
Platforms: A Case of Amity University India... 278

    Narendra Kumar, Amity University, Noida, India
    Swati Sharma, Amity University, Noida, India

Chapter 15

Virtual Laboratories in the Teaching and Learning Paradigm 295

    Dalamchwami Chen Lyngdoh, North Eastern Hill University, India
    Sarada Prasad Dakua, Hamad General Hospital, Qatar
    Gajendra Kumar Mourya, North Eastern Hill University, India

Chapter 16

The Intervention of New Technology in Traditional Teaching-Learning
Process Through Blended Learning Systematic Literature Review 313

    Ravi Kant Modi, Nirwan University, Jaipur, India
    Aarti Chopra, Poornima University, Jaipur, India

Chapter 17
Enhancing Guest Loyalty in the Hotel Industry Through Artificial
Intelligence-Drive Personalization 335
    Sanjeev Kumar Saxena, Assam University, India
    Vandana Gupta, LM College of Science and Technology, Jodhpur, India
    Sunil Kumar, Institute of Hospitality Management, Kotdwar, India

Chapter 18
Digitally Transforming Learning Campuses While Achieving SDGs 351
    Sanjeev Kumar Ningombam, Indian Institute of Management, Shillong,
        India

Chapter 19
Navigating the Data-Driven Future of Virtual and Hybrid Events 368
    Rajeev Semwal, Amity University Uttar Pradesh, Greater Noida
        Campus, India
    Pankaj Kumar Tyagi, Chandigarh University, India
    Nandita Tripathi, Amity University Uttar Pradesh, Greater Noida
        Campus, India
    Udit Kumar Pandey, Graphic Era Hill University, Haldwani, India

Chapter 20
Virtual Reality Rehabilitation and Artificial Intelligence in Healthcare
Technology 391
    Nitin Sahai, North Eastern Hill University, India
    Prabhat Kumar, University of Pécs, Hungary
    Megha Sharma, Faculty of Health Sciences, University of Pécs, Hungary

Chapter 21
Impacts of COVID-19 on the Customers´ Review Behavior Towards Hotel
and Travel Organizations: A Netnography Approach..................................... 412
    Maximiliano Emanuel Korstanje, University of Palermo, Argentina

Conclusion 427

Compilation of References 429

About the Contributors 496

Index... 504

Detailed Table of Contents

Editorial Advisory Board vi

Foreword xxii

Preface xxv

Acknowledgment xxxvi

Introduction xxxviii

Chapter 1
Emerging Technologies in Virtual and Hybrid Events: Major Issues and
Major Drivers 1
    Sharad Kumar Kulshreshtha, North-Eastern Hill University, India
    Craig Webster, Ball State University, USA

Event management is a fast-growing industry worldwide and there is an expectation that its growth in the short-term and long-term will be substantial. In this industry, technology plays a catalytic role in connecting event stakeholders, enhances the attendee experience, and offers personalized experiences with smart and seamless innovative solutions to the clients and event visitors. Event technology refers to the efficient online event management system or platform, which includes event software applications, mobile based application, innovative electronic devices, wearable technologies, and smart tools for creating immersive event experiences. Such emerging event technologies are not only supporting the design of full-fledged creative events but also customising the event as per the need of the client requirement, budget, time, and ease doing such events. In this context, the event management industry is very much interested to invest in technological research and innovation for getting cost and competitive advantages to more much to make this industry more dynamic and creative to provide more personalised experiences. Virtual and hybrid events offer industry the opportunity to shift platforms and increase cost-effective delivery of events, while keeping participant satisfaction levels high.

Chapter 2
Revolutionizing Events: Exploring the Seamless Integration of Robots in
Hybrid and Virtual Experiences 19
    Anila Thomas, Jyoti Nivas College (Autonomous), Bangalore, India

The rapid progress of technology has introduced a period in which robots are progressively becoming essential contributors in several facets of human life. Amidst the current worldwide pandemic and increasing desire for creative and interactive encounters, facilitating the inclusion of robots into events has become a captivating and transforming trend. In the past few years, hybridized and online gatherings have gained popularity owing to developments in communication technology and the need for flexible audience engagement across various geographical areas. The research explores the many capabilities of robots in event environments, including interactive companionship as well as event logistics and administration. The study also discusses the ethical implications and difficulties that arise from incorporating robots into events, such as concerns around privacy, security, and inclusion, in light of ongoing technological advancements. This chapter pursues to make available valuable perceptions to the present state of robotic technology and its thinkable future advancements.

Chapter 3
Exploring the Use of Virtual and Hybrid Events for MICE Sector: Trends
and Opportunities.. 47
    Amrik Singh, Lovely Professional University, Punjab, India
    Mildred Nuong Deri, University of Energy and Natural Resources,
        Ghana

COVID-19 has fast-tracked the transition to the virtual environment in the global meetings, incentives, conference/convention, and exhibition (MICE) events sector. The present research explores the use of virtual and hybrid events in enhancing the resilience of MICE events. Additionally, these events were found to be essential for information sharing and proved valuable in times of uncertainty. This chapter focuses on how these events provided substantial market opportunities for MICE stakeholders globally. Moreover, several challenges surfaced when hosting such events, including the matter of internet connectivity and the significant capital investments required for their execution. Virtual and hybrid events have emerged as a valuable tool for enhancing the resilience of MICE events to crises, and hybrid events are postulated to become a prominent feature in MICE events offerings in the future. This study focuses on how events provided substantial market opportunities for MICE stakeholders in the country by exploring the opportunities and challenges for MICE sector. Utilizing secondary information available, the study drew conclusions, implications and recommendations are given.

Chapter 4

Event-Enabled Mobile Applications: Seamless and Smart Technological
Platforms for Managing Virtual and Hybrid Events and Festivals 71

Sharad Kumar Kulshreshtha, North-Eastern Hill University, India
Sunildro S. Akoijam, North-Eastern Hill University, India
Paramjeet Kumar, North-Eastern Hill University, India
U. N. Shukla, Institute of Tourism and Hotel Management, Agra, India

Globally, there is a vibrant paradigm shift from physical event management engagements to transforming the event industry through mobile app technology involve leveraging digital tools to enhance the overall event experience for event organizers, attendees, sponsors, and other stakeholders. Nowadays, event mobile apps have become increasingly popular and most indispensable technological tool in the event industry specially after COVID 19 unprecedent and to a variety of reasons to access all event-related information, schedules, and updates, leading to a more convenient and enjoyable experience. Creating an innovative experience through developing mobile apps for events comprises several crucial features and deliberations to ensure a smart, seamless, synchronized, and engaging experience for both host and guest or visitors. A holistic approach of mobile application technology brings positive operational and executional changes in the event industry which focuses on the entire event lifecycle and to cater the diverse needs of all stakeholders. These event mobile apps support proper improvements for future events and festivals, with effective managerial and supervisory functions, engaging both organizers and attendees by offering new event prospects for data-driven decision-making and event sponsorship.

Chapter 5

From Connectivity to Immersion: Unleashing the Potential of 5G for
Seamless Virtual Event Experiences 89

Paramjeet Kumar, North Eastern Hill University, India
Wallamkupar Dkhar, North Eastern Hill University, India

This chapter examines the capacity of 5G technology to transform virtual event experiences through improved connectivity and immersive interactions. The chapter explores the capabilities of 5G networks in terms of delivering faster data speeds, extremely low latency, and expanded network capacity. These advancements enable smooth streaming, real-time communication, and the use of virtual reality applications. Furthermore, it emphasises the influence of 5G on different industries including entertainment, education, and business, demonstrating the capacity to generate virtual environments that accurately simulate the experience of participating in a live event.

Chapter 6

The Interactive Bleisure Event: Gamification and Bibliometric Trends
Transforming Attendee Participation.. 106

Narendra Kumar, Amity University, Noida, India
Swati Sharma, Amity University, Noida, India
Gaurav Kumar Gupta, JS University, Shikohabad, India

This study explores the emerging concept of "bleisure"-the integration of business and leisure- within the context of interactive events, focusing particularly on the role of gamification and provides bibliometric trends in transforming attendee participation. Leveraging the TCCM and using PRISMA technique, the research provides a comprehensive analysis of current literature, offering theoretical insights and practical implications for event organizers. The findings reveal that gamification significantly enhances attendee engagement by introducing elements of competition, reward, and play, thereby creating more memorable and enjoyable experiences. Bibliometric trends indicate a growing interest in interdisciplinary approaches to bleisure events, highlighting the integration of technology, psychology, and business studies. By synthesizing these insights, the study provides a roadmap for future research and practical applications, suggesting that the strategic incorporation of gamification and attention to bibliometric trends can substantially elevate the impact of bleisure events.

Chapter 7

Emergence of Metaverse: An Innovative Technological Fusion in Indian
Festivals 128

Ruchika Kulshrestha, GLA University, Mathura, India
Ashutosh Pandey, FORE School of Management, New Delhi, India
Abhijeet V. Tiwari, GLA University, Mathura, India

This chapter aims to examine how the metaverse has given rise to new interpretations of Indian festivals,which also covers a number of difficulties in establishing connections with the communities. The exploratory study that served as the basis for this chapter aimed to gather factual information regarding the current situation and the emerging metaverse related trends. The actual procedures that stakeholders followed were analysed using a qualitative case study. This research uses secondary data from other scholarly papers and articles to offer the authors' perspective on the metaverse festival blueprint. This chapter focuses on the evolutionary concepts of the metaverse and its implications on intangible ceremonial activities.Since there isn't much previous research published in the literature, there isn't a lot of discussion about metaverse in Indian festivals at the moment.

Chapter 8
An Analysis on the Future Usage of Metaverse in the Marketing Event
Industry in India: An ISM Approach 146

    Supriya Lamba Sahdev, Alliance University, Bengaluru, India
    Chitra Krishnan, Symbiosis Centre for Management Studies, Symbiosis
       International University (Deemed), Pune, India
    Amilson Durans, Centro Universitário Santa Terezinha, São Luís, Brazil
    Ahdi Hassan, Global Institute for Research Education and Scholarship,
       Amsterdam, The Netherlands
    Jugnu Thakur, ISBR Business School, India

The term metaverse has recently attracted much attention and is being widely discussed in various industries around the world, including marketing and events. This research explores future possibilities of the metaverse in the context of the Indian marketing event industry through an ISM analysis. Consequently, the metaverse – an environment that contains interactive digital objects and persons – presents new opportunities for improving the effectiveness of marketing events in terms of interest, accessibility and innovation. Thus, the use of ISM in the context of this research allows to determine the most critical enablers and restraints for the adoption of the metaverse in Indian marketing events. The chapter provides clear tactical implications for using metaverse technologies to enhance traditional formats of events, interact with the audience, and adapt marketing and communication solutions to the Indian market.

Chapter 9
Role of Metaverse in Events Industry: An Empirical Approach........................ 164

    Sujay Vikram Singh, Banaras Hindu University, India
    Pravin Chandra Singh, MSMSR, Mats University, Raipur, India
    Kuldeep Singh, Amity University, Gurugram, India
    Akshay Nain, Amity University, Gurugram, India

The metaverse holds immense potential to transform the event industry, seamlessly blending augmented reality, virtual reality, and internet-based platforms to deliver captivating and engaging experiences. This proposal delves into the profound impact of the metaverse on event organization and participation, showcasing the success of platforms such as Decentraland and Roblox in hosting virtual events. The study explores the various factors that impact the adoption of metaverse, such as performance expectations, ease of use, social influence, and facilitating conditions. The findings highlight the significance of technology that is easy to use, a strong infrastructure, and making use of social networks. This research provides valuable insights for event organizers to improve consumer engagement and adoption rates, ultimately integrating the metaverse into the event industry.

Chapter 10
Service Automation and Festivals: Technologies and Their Impact Upon
Sustainability of Events 184
    Craig Webster, Ball State University, USA

The United Nations' sustainable development goals have created an environment in which the world's population are attempting to link various human activities with improvements in the ways that humans do things to ensure a more sustainable future. In this chapter, the author concentrates upon festivals and other events, focusing upon how various service automation technologies will work to support sustainability in the events industry, a component of SDG 12. The chapter will focus upon how technologies will increase efficiency of operations and reduce energy consumption. The chapter will also highlight some of the major challenges, illustrating what innovations and improvements will need to be made to ensure that festivals can achieve the maximum level of sustainability possible. The chapter ends with a discussion of the externalities of the increased use of automation technologies to show that there will have to be adjustments to not only the way that services are delivered but also to the expectations of the consumers.

Chapter 11
Leveraging Event Gamification for Event Planning and Creating a
Memorable Experience 198
    *Aarti Madan, Atal Bihari Vajpayee School of Management and
        Entrepreneurship, Jawaharlal Nehru University, India*
    *Vaniki Joshi Lohani, Atal Bihari Vajpayee School of Management and
        Entrepreneurship, Jawaharlal Nehru University, India*

This chapter explores the innovative use of game elements and mechanics in event planning to enhance engagement, foster interaction, and create memorable experiences. Beginning with an introduction to gamification concepts and objectives, the chapter delves into the psychology of gamification and various types of gamification techniques. It provides insights into integrating gamification into event planning processes, including pre-event planning, execution, and post-event evaluation. Ethical considerations and challenges, such as ensuring fairness and inclusivity, addressing negative impacts, and mitigating over-competitiveness, are discussed. Additionally, the chapter explores future trends and innovations in event gamification, including emerging technologies, personalization trends, and integration with virtual and hybrid events. The chapter also highlights the power of gamification in transforming event experiences and offers practical insights for event planners and organizers to leverage gamification effectively.

Chapter 12
Viral Content in Event Management of Hospitality and Socio-Cultural
Activities 228
    Bovsh A. Liudmyla, State University of Trade and Economics, Ukraine
    Kamel Mouloudj, University of Medea, Algeria
    Alla M. Rasulova, State University of Trade and Economics, Ukraine
    Tetiana Mykhaylivna Tkachuk, State University of Trade and
        Economics, Ukraine

This chapter examines the determinants of the formation of viral content in the event management of hospitality entities and socio-cultural activities. The methodology covers the assessment of the popularity and potential impact of social networks on marketing and practical opportunities of hospitality entities and socio-cultural activities. The modeling method was applied to create a reference model of the credibility strategy of impression marketing. In the process of forming authenticity and emotional involvement of customers, the technological road map method, which is based on brand marketing approaches, was applied. In addition, the analysis of the involvement of users of social networks was investigated. The selection of key indicators for evaluating the effectiveness of real content and an in-depth review of modern technologies and trends in its creation empirically contributed to the modeling of the strategy of creating real content in the field of event management of hospitality entities and socio-cultural activities.

Chapter 13
Hybridized Tourism Education in Hard Times: Pancoe as a Case Study.......... 258
    Maximiliano Emanuel Korstanje, University of Palermo, Argentina

The present book chapter discusses to what extent hybridized education can be potentiated in the new normal. PANCOE acts to change negative emotions into joy through gamification. Students were subject to looking at pictures containing islands, beaches, and paradisiacal landscapes. The authors denote the term imagined landscape to create a climate of well-being. The present book chapter reflected on the experience of PANCOE, an experiment conducted by the Joy Labs (University of Palermo, Argentina). The aims of this study were twofold. On one hand, it devotes efforts to introduce pleasure to reduce the current academic dropout rates. On another, it looks to standardise academic performance in low-graded or deprived students. Participants –in PANCOE- came from a neighbouring country and lived far away from their friends and families.

Chapter 14

Transforming Traditions of University Convocations Through Virtual
Platforms: A Case of Amity University India.. 278
Narendra Kumar, Amity University, Noida, India
Swati Sharma, Amity University, Noida, India

Covid has brought many challenges to the ceremonial events at educational institutions.
Holding graduating ceremonies or convocations are an integral part of the life of
any graduate, but Covid, like in many other facets of life, has changed the way
convocations were held at the universities. This book chapter presents a detailed case
study on the innovative utilization of virtual platforms to revolutionize convocations
at Amity University, India. Through a lens of transformation, the chapter not only
examines how Amity University has successfully embraced digital technologies to
re-envision its convocation ceremonies, blending tradition with modernity but also
the challenges which the administrative support team has encountered during such a
virtual ceremony. The authors have interviewed administrative staff at the university
who were front-runners in providing such an experience to the post-covid graduates.
The findings of the report have been examined in the light of the chapter theme.

Chapter 15

Virtual Laboratories in the Teaching and Learning Paradigm 295
Dalamchwami Chen Lyngdoh, North Eastern Hill University, India
Sarada Prasad Dakua, Hamad General Hospital, Qatar
Gajendra Kumar Mourya, North Eastern Hill University, India

Laboratories are a fundamental aspect of any academic learning that enables
students to better understand the theoretical concepts of any academic course.
Science, engineering, and medical fields are the main areas of study that heavily
depend on laboratories for demonstrating the practicality of any theory. However,
circumstances may arise where students face challenges in performing practicals
due to insufficient materials, equipment, or the inaccessibility of the laboratory
itself. To counter this challenge, various organizations and institutions have come
forward to develop 'Virtual Laboratories' or 'Virtual Labs'. Virtual laboratories are
platforms where the user can engage in practical sessions without the need to be
present in person. The user can log in anywhere, even remotely, and be able to gain
access to the same setting as in a traditional hands-on laboratory, albeit virtually.
This chapter will detail virtual labs, what they are all about, and the effectiveness
of virtual labs in comparison to traditional labs.

Chapter 16
The Intervention of New Technology in Traditional Teaching-Learning
Process Through Blended Learning Systematic Literature Review 313
    Ravi Kant Modi, Nirwan University, Jaipur, India
    Aarti Chopra, Poornima University, Jaipur, India

An instructional strategy called blended learning mixes virtual or digital components with in-person instruction. The use of computers and other connected devices in the classroom helps students get ready for success in the real world because they are essential for modern business and communication. In blended learning settings, students not only become proficient in the subject matter they are studying, but they also develop advanced technological skills. In the classroom, blended learning has its uses and benefits. This method provides a solid foundation for tying theory and practice together during the teaching process. The methodical blending of online and in-person instruction is known as blended or hybrid learning. The intentional blending of online and in-person components is essential in a blended learning environment. This research study identifies the variables influencing blended learning by conducting an extensive literature review. The literature review aids in the provision of a theoretical framework for this investigation.

Chapter 17
Enhancing Guest Loyalty in the Hotel Industry Through Artificial
Intelligence-Drive Personalization 335
    Sanjeev Kumar Saxena, Assam University, India
    Vandana Gupta, LM College of Science and Technology, Jodhpur, India
    Sunil Kumar, Institute of Hospitality Management, Kotdwar, India

This chapter is a product of the author's extensive first-hand experience gained during their professional journey and as well as their interactions with colleagues who are occupying the role of senior management in various hotels. Personalization has become the key factor for enhancing the experiences of the guest and also to foster loyalty in the hotel industry. The industry has witnessed a significant shift towards artificial intelligence (AI) that plays a pivotal role in providing various opportunities that tailor the guests' preferences accordingly. Through this chapter, the researcher aims to identify the influence of AI on guest loyalty, guest profiling and service customization within the hospitality sector. In addition to examining guest profiling and customized services, this study examines the challenges and ethical considerations related to AI-powered personalization and guest loyalty.

Chapter 18
Digitally Transforming Learning Campuses While Achieving SDGs 351
  *Sanjeev Kumar Ningombam, Indian Institute of Management, Shillong,
    India*

This chapter provides examples of how technology and creative thinking can transform the context of higher education in India. It looks at how technology may bridge the gap between urban and rural communities, increase learning results, and improve access to education. It also emphasises how digital tools and online platforms can offer individualised learning experiences and promote cooperation between teachers and students. By mapping the sustainable development goals, it also aims to address sustainability-related issues. Focus has been made to underline and address the spirit and intent on education reforms as envisaged under the National Education Policy 2020 of India. Students, teachers, and higher education institutions would all benefit from this chapter while planning and creating online courses.

Chapter 19
Navigating the Data-Driven Future of Virtual and Hybrid Events 368
  *Rajeev Semwal, Amity University Uttar Pradesh, Greater Noida
    Campus, India*
  Pankaj Kumar Tyagi, Chandigarh University, India
  *Nandita Tripathi, Amity University Uttar Pradesh, Greater Noida
    Campus, India*
  Udit Kumar Pandey, Graphic Era Hill University, Haldwani, India

Data analytics is transforming virtual and hybrid event planning with quantifiable goals, real-time analytics, and many data sources. Modern technologies like emotional analytics, AI-driven predictive analytics, quantum computing, and others boost customization, engagement, and event immersion. Extended reality (XR) analytics, edge AI, and hyper-personalization provide unmatched participant experiences. An analytical attitude, coordinated leadership, and extensive team training are necessary. Participants' privacy is protected by data security and ethics. Data analytics affects decision-making, customization, innovation, and technology adoption, making virtual and hybrid events more engaging. It signals a shift toward a flexible, life-changing event experience in the data-driven future.

Chapter 20
Virtual Reality Rehabilitation and Artificial Intelligence in Healthcare
Technology 391
Nitin Sahai, North Eastern Hill University, India
Prabhat Kumar, University of Pécs, Hungary
Megha Sharma, Faculty of Health Sciences, University of Pécs, Hungary

The benefit of virtual rehabilitation is that it helps the patient increase their engagement and motivation. Another advantage is that it allows patient specific. A third utility is that the therapist can make the sessions more efficient and productive. A feature of virtual reality (VR) rehabilitation is that it is possible to create virtual environments which are more realistic than those in a video game and in which the patients can perform exercises. As a result, the patients are more immersed and motivated to avoid the boredom from which patients in standard therapy usually suffer. The features of artificial intelligence (AI) in biomedicine are the optimisation of diagnostics, treatment, and patient monitoring. AI allows for the analysis to have the potential to detect subtle deviations. In this chapter, the application of virtual reality and artificial intelligence in healthcare was discussed.

Chapter 21
Impacts of COVID-19 on the Customers´ Review Behavior Towards Hotel
and Travel Organizations: A Netnography Approach 412
Maximiliano Emanuel Korstanje, University of Palermo, Argentina

The COVID-19 pandemic has generated an unparalleled crisis in the circles of tourism industries and beyond. The overcrowded cities associated with the technological revolution applied on transport has contributed directly to disseminating the virus worldwide. The tourism industry has been the main victim and spreader of COVID19. Though originally the consequences of the pandemic remain obscured or at the best uncertain no less true seems to be that scholars have devoted their attention to describing the economic effects in the tourism industry. The cOVID-19 has interrogated deeply the epistemology of tourism alluding to a world without tourists. In this vein, the present chapter discusses the question of entnography a new ethnographic method based on hybridity and hybridized methods of information gathering.

Conclusion 427

Compilation of References 429

About the Contributors 496

Index 504

Foreword

FOREWORD: DIMITRIOS BUHALIS

The future looks bright concerning the revolutionization of new technologies in virtual and hybrid events. The personalization of AI will customize experiences according to the preference of an individual thereby increasing involvement. Augmented reality (AR) as well as virtual reality (VR) lead the industry to immersive environments, bridging the gap between physical and digital experiences. These technologies will make events more interactive, allowing for real-time networking and collaboration. AI-driven personalization will tailor experiences to individual preferences, enhancing engagement. The utilization of artificial intelligence will ensure that each event becomes more interactive enabling live communication plus networking with others instantly throughout meetings. Advanced data analytics will offer valuable insights into attendee behavior, enabling organizers to fine-tune their strategies for maximum impact. Furthermore, advancements in streaming technology will ensure seamless, high-quality broadcasts, making events more accessible to a global audience and redefining the event experience.

This book makes a worthwhile contribution to the current need to understand how the old-fashioned face-to-face industry can make adjustments and cultural changes to meet with the needs of the consumers in the industry. This book is composed of multiple chapters that explain how the industry can incorporate various technologies and change the way of doing things to be more effective in this post-pandemic era in which there is a demand for events but some expectations to having options for virtual and hybrid experiences.

The timing of this book is excellent, offering students, educators, and those in industry to benefit from the insights from researchers from around the world. The knowledge and insights from the various chapters should assist educators in teaching about events in a more thorough and interesting way that is relevant to the current technologies and consumer culture. Those in the tourism and events industries should get insight for how to run their businesses in more effective and profitable ways by learning about the current technologies and how they can be used to satisfy consumer demands. This book will be therefulre interesting, helpful, and useful for anyone working in or studying about the tourism economy. It is appreciated that they put there energies into creating a book on the topic, it needed to be done and it will be of value to anyone interesting in learning about events in the technology enhanced global event industry.

My congratulations to Dr. Sharad Kumar Kulshreshtha, Dr. Craig Webster, and IGI Global for bringing this book into existence. They are a good team to bring this book to fruition at a time when it was needed. As experienced researchers and editors, they were able to assemble a team of authors and a very good time to discuss this important topic.

Thank you very much

Best regards

FOREWORD: STANISLAV IVANOV

Technology is permeating all sectors of the economy. Event management does not make an exception. *New Technologies in Virtual and Hybrid Events* is a pioneering book focusing on the evolving technological landscape of event management. As the global events industry tries to adapt to the changes pushed by digital technologies and the Metaverse, this book is an essential guide for event managers and researchers, presenting innovative strategies and tools that enhance engagement, interaction, and overall event experience.

The book is a balanced mix of chapters that provide a comprehensive overview of various technological solutions for virtual and hybrid events in diverse empirical contexts. The book elaborates on fundamental concepts such as gamification, 5G connectivity, robotics, and the metaverse. The real-world case studies and practical examples illustrate best practices and offer actionable strategies for event planners and organisers.

The book's contribution lies in offering a thorough framework for understanding the various components of virtual and hybrid events. It provides an in-depth analysis of digital technologies and offers practical applications and real-world examples to guide event planners in implementing these tools effectively. The future-oriented perspective of some chapters ensures that readers are prepared for emerging trends and potential challenges in the events industry. The discussions around data analytics, artificial intelligence, robotics and the metaverse highlight the book's relevance in an increasingly data-driven and immersive event landscape.

New Technologies in Virtual and Hybrid Events targets a diverse audience, including event planners and managers, technology enthusiasts, academic researchers, and corporate executives. From a managerial perspective, event professionals will find practical guidance on incorporating new technologies to create engaging and immersive events, while technology enthusiasts will gain insights into the latest technological tools and applications and how they can be utilised for staging events. From a research perspective, the book advances knowledge in important aspects of technology implementation in events management.

Congratulations to the book editors Dr. Sharad Kumar Kulshreshtha, and Dr. Craig Webster, and the chapters' authors for the successful completion of this important book.

Dimitrios Buhalis

The Bournemouth University Business School, U.K.

Stanislav Ivanov

Varna University of Management, Bulgaria

Preface

OVERVIEW

Welcome to *New Technologies in Virtual and Hybrid Events*, a comprehensive exploration into the ever-evolving landscape of event management in the digital age. We, the editors, Sharad Kulshreshtha from the Department of Tourism and Hotel Management at North-Eastern Hill University, and Craig Webster from Ball State University, are delighted to present this timely and forward-looking volume.

The global outbreak of the COVID-19 pandemic has irrevocably transformed the events industry. As physical gatherings became impossible or severely restricted, the world saw a significant shift towards virtual and hybrid event formats. This transition, while borne out of necessity, has also opened up new avenues for innovation and technological integration. Our book delves into these advancements, offering a detailed examination of how the events sector can adapt and thrive in this new paradigm.

This book is designed to serve as a vital resource for scholars, students, and practitioners alike. By providing a thorough analysis of the technological advancements in virtual and hybrid events, we aim to bridge the gap between theory and practice. Our objective is to equip event professionals with the knowledge and tools needed to execute events that are not only effective and engaging but also efficient and profitable.

The chapters in this book cover a wide array of topics essential to the modern event professional, including:

- **Assessment of Platforms**: A critical evaluation of the various platforms available for hosting virtual and hybrid events, highlighting their strengths and weaknesses.

- **Audience Response Systems**: Integration techniques to enhance interactivity and engagement in virtual settings.
- **Virtual Reality**: How VR can be utilized to create immersive experiences.
- **Artificial Intelligence**: Exploring AI's potential in event programming and execution.
- **Robotics**: The role of robots in augmenting event experiences.
- **Ethics**: Addressing the ethical considerations surrounding the use of new technologies in events.
- **Inclusivity**: Overcoming technological barriers to ensure inclusive participation.
- **Future Technologies**: Predicting technological trends and their implications for the event industry.
- **Innovations**: Case studies on transformative technologies in virtual and hybrid events.
- **Livestreaming and Simulive**: Advanced techniques for real-time and recorded event streaming.
- **Event Analytics**: Optimizing data-driven decisions through advanced analytics.
- **Event Apps**: Innovative applications that enhance networking, engagement, and community building.
- **5G Networks**: Leveraging the power of 5G for seamless virtual event experiences.
- **Event Gamification**: Using gamification strategies to plan and create memorable events.
- **Holograms and Beacons**: Cutting-edge applications in event settings.
- **Digital Floor Plans and 3D Renderings**: Enhancing event planning with advanced diagramming tools.
- **RFID and NFC**: Revolutionizing event management with advanced identification technologies.
- **Wearable Technologies**: The impact of wearables on event experiences.
- **Smart and Green Events**: How technology can contribute to more sustainable and intelligent event solutions.
- **Metaverse**: Exploring the potential of the metaverse in the future of events.
- **Best Practices**: Real-world examples of successful hybrid event technologies.

We have curated contributions from leading experts in the field, ensuring that each chapter provides valuable insights and practical guidance. Our aim is to foster a deeper understanding of how technological advancements can be harnessed to create engaging, inclusive, and successful events.

As the events industry continues to navigate the challenges and opportunities presented by virtual and hybrid formats, we hope this book will serve as a crucial reference. We invite you to explore the chapters within, each offering a unique perspective on the intersection of technology and event management.

COVID 19 Crisis and Virtual and Hybrid Events

We are living in an interesting time in history in which the Fourth Industrial Revolution has kicked into gear, the economy is clearly global in scope, and humanity is recovering from the COVID pandemic. These are very interesting times and we can expect that the interaction between technology, culture, and industry will have to adjust to new ways of doing things. In this book, we identified a topic that needed to be more fully investigated because of these radical changes in the world, the ways that technologies will be incorporated into the events industry, since the global COVID pandemic instigated the era of virtual events and we can expect that there will be a sustained demand for virtual and hybrid events, given that consumers are used to using technologies to support events and technologies have developed in ways to make them better at supporting such events.

We felt that we wanted to make a contribution to the literature, since we have lived through the pandemic and have seen a rapid transition from almost entirely face-to-face expectations of events to a greater sense of flexibility. The pandemic brought most of us from the understanding that any event would be done in a face-to-face environment to an understanding that it had to be done in an online format. Post-pandemic, while there seems to be a clear consensus that events are best experienced in a face-to-face format, consumers are often willing to use virtual options and often are quite familiar with the technologies used to participate in online events. So, it seems that the experience of the pandemic was a period in which customers became more familiar with available technologies for virtual conferences and there is some sense that events should be offered in a hybrid way, since many now understand the advantages of technologies.

Emerging Technologies in Virtual and Hybrid Events

This book makes a contribution to this new world that we are now found in in which consumers are knowledgeable about technologies that can allow for us all to communicate in events online. Prior to 2020, there were technologies to allow for virtual events and they were sometimes used, although post-2020, there is a vast swath of the population that is familiar with the technologies of online events and understands the advantages of them.

Apart from the consumer, industry will have to take into account the new customer and the new technologies that have the ability to help transform the industry and revitalize consumer participation. Industry will have to learn to take advantage of this historical period, embracing proven and effective technologies and incorporating them into events. In the new events industry, there is not just changed demand, from a qualitative perspective, but also a change in the abilities and expectations of consumers.

Because of this brave new world of tourism and events, we wanted to gather the best minds who could contribute to this book to inform students, scholars, and industry about our present and future. Hopefully, the chapters in this book will give valuable insight to anyone who has an interest in events, the future of events, and the technologies that will propel the tourism and events industries into the second half of this century. We humbly offer this book to you as food for thought, giving you the chance to learn from the insights and thoughts from a number of scholars who have pondered about the possibilities and future of virtual and hybrid events. We hope that you see the value of this edited book and that you can gain knowledge and food for thought that will help you understand industry, technology, and the changes in culture that have taken place in recent years to be ready for the future. The future is almost here and it is good to be prepared. We hope that this book will help you survive and thrive into the next decades, if even in subtle ways.

OBJECTIVE OF THE BOOK

Since the outbreak of COVID-19 pandemic, an increasing number of events have migrated online to be either virtual or hybrid formats. This book looks to explore the pragmatic and technical aspects of the transition to events into a virtual or hybrid platform and the integration of new technologies from planning and marketing to execution and evaluation of events that are either held entirely virtually or in a hybrid environment. It seeks to be forward-looking and pragmatic, illustrating how new technologies can be used to ensure that virtual and hybrid events can be effective today and how new technologies will enhance such events in the future

In Brief the Book Will Focus on the Following Objectives

1. To cover the new trends and innovations in event management with evolvement of new edge technological applications in various industry globally and locally.

2. To focus the application of smart technology solutions and digital practices for efficient business, education, society, sports, and travel tourism industry practices
3. To emphasis the coverage on the gather ease of doing work, experiences, economy, and environmental impact, due to application this online technology.
4. To explore about new business models, new entrants, innovative practices in the tourism and hospitality, and events sector.

Target Audience

This book also enlightens students, research scholars, academician and industry practitioners, trade professional to acquaint new knowledge and cutting-edge information related with readiness and preparation to survive, sustain and smooth business, education, society, sports and travel tourism industry practices specially in the era of new hybridization of global meetings with rapidly <u>emerging technologies in virtual and hybrid events</u>.

Coverage of the Book

This book covers emerging and cutting edge technologies topics such as event business management and operations, event management, festival management, festival services i.e., travel, tourism, hospitality management, volunteer management, project management, destination marketing, festival entrepreneurship, festive visitor economy, ethnic and cultural festivals, sport event management, environment and sustainability issues for festivals, and global event studies, etc. This book is aimed at scholars, researchers, academicians, festival event policymakers, and tourist industry practitioners who are interested in tourism festivals, events, and festival management.

Organisation of this Book

This book is the collection of 21 diverse chapters from a various domain, i.e., tourism, hospitality and events as an area of expert scholarly contributed from various countries, with various thematic aspects related with *emerging technologies in virtual and hybrid events*. This book offers an interesting fact about the local and global festivals in empirical, qualitative and case study mode with in-depth and systematic manner highlighting current and emerging issues of festivals and destination management study.

Chapter 1: Emerging Technologies in Virtual and Hybrid Events: Major Issues and Major Drivers

Dr. Sharad Kumar Kulshreshtha, North-Eastern Hill University, India and Prof. Craig Webster, Ball State University, U.S.A., this chapter highlights the contemporary global scenario of technologies in virtual and hybrid event industry, focuses on changing event management dynamics with technological transformation comprises in-person event, virtual events, hybrid events, typologies of virtual events and impact of COVID 19 and changing events management dynamics, shifting the focus of virtual and hybrid event technologies. Apart of these this covers on major issues and major drivers of event technologies includes, cost, connectivity, capacity building and skilling, change of old technology, security and data privacy, digital equity, sustainable event management practices and key drivers of emerging technologies in virtual and hybrid events.

Chapter 2: Revolutionizing Events: Exploring the Seamless Integration of Robots in Hybrid and Virtual Experiences

Authored by Anila Thomas from Jyoti Nivas College Autonomous, Bangalore, India, this chapter delves into the transformative role of robots in enhancing hybrid and virtual events. The research investigates the multifaceted capabilities of robots, including interactive companionship and efficient event management, highlighting their growing importance amidst the global pandemic. Ethical considerations such as privacy and security are addressed, providing a comprehensive overview of current robotic technology and its future potential.

Chapter 3: Exploring the Use of Virtual and Hybrid Events for MICE Sector: Trends and Opportunities

Amrik Singh and Mildred Deri examine how virtual and hybrid events have become essential for the resilience of the MICE (Meetings, Incentives, Conferences, and Exhibitions) sector during the COVID-19 pandemic. The chapter highlights the benefits of these events for market opportunities and information sharing, while also addressing challenges such as internet connectivity and capital investments. The authors predict that hybrid events will continue to play a prominent role in the future of the MICE sector.

Chapter 4: Event Enabled Mobile Applications: Seamless and Smart Technological Platforms for Managing Virtual and Hybrid Events & Festivals

Prof. U.N. Shukla, Dr. Bhim Rao Ambedkar University, India, Dr. Sharad Kumar Kulshreshtha. North-Eastern Hill University, India, Dr. Sunildro S. Akoijam, North-Eastern Hill University, India, Mr. Paramjeet Kumar, North Eastern Hill University Shillong, India, this chapter focuses on the dynamics of role of mobile apps in event and festival management, features of event mobile applications, emerging mobile based technologies and innovative event and festival experiences, of attendees through mobile app paradigm for pro-active virtual, hybrid attendee engagements. significant smart and seamless features of event mobile apps, and several challenges and risks which are associated with mobile apps-based event management.

Chapter 5: From Connectivity to Immersion: Unleashing the Potential of 5G for Seamless Virtual Event Experiences

Paramjeet Kumar and Wallamkupar Dkhar from North Eastern Hill University Shillong, India, explore the revolutionary impact of 5G technology on virtual events. The chapter examines 5G's ability to provide faster data speeds, low latency, and expanded network capacity, which enhance real-time communication and the use of virtual reality applications. The authors illustrate how 5G can transform industries like entertainment, education, and business by creating immersive virtual environments that rival live experiences.

Chapter 6: The Interactive Bleisure Event: Gamification and Bibliometric Trends Transforming Attendee Participation

Narendra Kumar, Swati Sharma, and Gaurav Gupta discuss the emerging "bleisure" trend, blending business with leisure, within interactive events. Using gamification and bibliometric analysis, this chapter reveals how competitive and rewarding game elements enhance attendee engagement. The authors provide a roadmap for future research and practical applications, suggesting that gamification and interdisciplinary approaches can significantly elevate the impact of bleisure events.

Chapter 7: Emergence of Metaverse: An Innovative Technological Fusion in Indian Festivals

Ruchika Kulshrestha, Ashutosh Pandey, and Abhijeet V Tiwari investigate how the metaverse is redefining Indian festivals. Through qualitative case studies and secondary data analysis, this chapter explores the challenges and opportunities of integrating metaverse technologies into traditional ceremonial activities. The authors provide a blueprint for future research on the metaverse's impact on cultural events.

Chapter 8: An Analysis on the Future Usage of Metaverse in the Marketing Event Industry in India - An ISM Approach

Supriya Lamba Sahdev, Chitra Krishnan, Amilson Durans, Ahdi Hassan, and Jugnu Thakur use the Interpretive Structural Modelling (ISM) approach to explore the potential applications of the metaverse in India's marketing event industry. The chapter identifies key drivers and barriers to metaverse adoption, offering insights for strategic decision-making and highlighting areas of opportunity and challenge

Chapter 9: Role of Metaverse in Events Industry: An Empirical Approach

Sujay Singh, Pravin Singh, Kuldeep Singh, and Akshay Nain discuss the transformative potential of the metaverse in the events industry. The chapter examines factors influencing metaverse adoption, such as performance expectations and social influence, and provides valuable insights for event organizers to improve consumer engagement and integrate metaverse technologies effectively.

Chapter 10: Service Automation and Festivals: Technologies and their Impact upon Sustainability of Events

Craig Webster from Ball State University focuses on how service automation technologies can support the sustainability of festivals and other events, aligning with the United Nations' Sustainable Development Goals. The chapter discusses how these technologies increase operational efficiency and reduce energy consumption, while also addressing the challenges and necessary innovations for achieving maximum sustainability.

Chapter 11: Leveraging Event Gamification for Event Planning and Creating a Memorable Experience

Aarti Madan and Vaniki Joshi Lohani explore the use of gamification in event planning to enhance engagement and create memorable experiences. The chapter covers the psychology of gamification, integration techniques, and future trends, providing practical insights for event planners on leveraging gamification effectively while addressing ethical considerations and challenges.

Chapter 12: Viral Content in Event Management of Hospitality and Socio-Cultural Activities

Bovsh Liudmyla, Kamel Mouloudj, Alla Rasulova, and T?tiana Tkachuk examine the role of viral content in promoting hospitality, creative industries, and cultural activities. The chapter discusses the benefits and challenges of creating viral content, emphasizing its importance in marketing strategies and event attractiveness. The authors provide a framework for creating effective viral content that ensures sustainability and strategic planning.

Chapter 13: Hybridized Tourism Education In Hard Times: Pancoe as Study-Case

Maximiliano Emanuel Korstanje, University of Palermo, Argentina, this present book chapter discusses to what extent hybridized education can be potentiated in the new normal. PANCOE acts to change negative emotions into joy through gamification. As long as the experiment, participants have been encouraged to dream with preferred destinations while sharing with other students the culinary customs of their countries. students were subject to watch pictures containing islands, beaches and paradisiacal landscapes.

Chapter 14: Transforming Traditions of University Convocations through Virtual Platforms: A Case of Amity University India

Narendra Kumar and Swati Sharma present a case study on how Amity University in India has revolutionized convocation ceremonies using virtual platforms. The chapter explores the blend of tradition and modernity, the challenges faced, and the successful implementation of digital technologies to provide a meaningful experience for graduates in a post-COVID world.

Chapter 15: Virtual Laboratories in Teaching and Learning Paradigm

Dalamchwami Lyngdoh, Sarada Dakua, and Gajendra Mourya discuss the development and effectiveness of virtual laboratories as an alternative to traditional hands-on labs. The chapter explores how virtual labs enable practical learning in science, engineering, and medical fields, addressing challenges such as insufficient materials and remote accessibility, and compares their effectiveness with traditional laboratories.

Chapter 16: The Intervention of New Technology in Traditional Teaching-Learning Process through Blended Learning: A Systematic Literature Review

Ravi Modi and Aarti Chopra conduct a systematic literature review on blended learning, which combines virtual and in-person instruction. The chapter identifies the variables influencing blended learning and provides a theoretical framework for integrating digital components into traditional teaching to enhance technological proficiency and academic outcomes.

Chapter 17: Enhancing Guest Loyalty in the Hotel Industry through Artificial Intelligence-Driven Personalization

Sanjeev Saxena, Vandana Gupta, and Sunil Kumar explore how artificial intelligence (AI) can enhance guest loyalty in the hotel industry through personalized services. The chapter examines the influence of AI on guest profiling, service customization, and the ethical considerations related to AI-powered personalization, providing insights for hoteliers to improve guest experiences and foster loyalty.

Chapter 18: Digitally Transforming Learning Campuses while Achieving SDGs

Sanjeev Kumar Ningombam discusses the digital transformation of higher education campuses in India and its alignment with Sustainable Development Goals (SDGs). The chapter highlights how technology can bridge educational gaps, enhance learning outcomes, and promote sustainability, focusing on the reforms outlined in India's National Education Policy 2020.

Chapter 19: Navigating the Data-Driven Future of Virtual and Hybrid Events

Rajeev Semwal, Pankaj Tyagi, Nandita Tripathi, and Udit Pandey explore how data analytics is revolutionizing virtual and hybrid event planning. The chapter discusses the use of emotional analytics, AI-driven predictive analytics, and other technologies to enhance event customization and engagement. It emphasizes the importance of data security and ethics in protecting participant privacy and highlights the shift towards more flexible and transformative event experiences.

Chapter 20: Virtual Reality Rehabilitation and Artificial Intelligence in Healthcare Technology

Nitin Sahai, Prabhat Kumar, and Megha Sharma investigate the integration of virtual reality (VR) and artificial intelligence (AI) in healthcare rehabilitation. The chapter highlights the benefits of VR for patient engagement and motivation, and the role of AI in optimizing diagnostics, treatment, and patient monitoring, offering a comprehensive overview of these technologies in healthcare

Chapter 21: Impacts of COVID-19 on the Customers´ Review Behaviour towards Hotel and Travel Organization: A Netnography Approach

Maximiliano Emanuel Korstanje, University of Palermo, Argentina, In this vein, the present chapter discusses the question of netnography a new ethnographic method based on hybridity and hybridised methods of information gathering. The COVID-19 pandemic has generated an unparalleled crisis in the circles of tourism industries and beyond. This chapter specially focuses on the tourism industry has been the main victim and spreader of COVID19. Though originally the consequences of the pandemic remain obscured or at the best uncertain no less true seems to be that scholars have devoted their attention to describe the economic effects in the tourism industry.

CONCLUSION

As we draw the curtains on *New Technologies in Virtual and Hybrid Events*, we reflect on the transformative journey this book represents for the events industry. The insights and innovations captured within these pages are a testament to the resilience and creativity that have propelled the sector forward, particularly in the face of unprecedented challenges posed by the global pandemic. This volume, meticulously curated by Sharad Kulshreshtha and Craig Webster, brings together the collective wisdom of leading experts to illuminate the myriad ways in which technology is reshaping event management. From the immersive realms of virtual reality and the seamless connectivity of 5G to the ethical imperatives of AI and the gamification strategies that drive engagement, each chapter offers a window into the future of events.

We hope this book serves as a beacon for scholars, students, and practitioners alike, guiding them through the complexities of virtual and hybrid event technologies. The comprehensive analyses and practical insights provided are designed to bridge the gap between theoretical exploration and practical application, equipping readers with the tools needed to excel in a rapidly evolving landscape. The chapters you have explored underscore the importance of adaptability and innovation. Whether it's the strategic deployment of robotics in event management, the integration of the metaverse in cultural festivals, or the use of AI-driven personalization in hospitality, the future of events is being shaped by those who dare to envision new possibilities.

As the events industry continues to navigate this digital transformation, it is clear that the advancements discussed in this book will play a crucial role in defining the next era of event management. The pandemic may have accelerated the adoption of virtual and hybrid formats, but it has also underscored the enduring need for human connection and meaningful experiences, which technology can uniquely enhance. In closing, we express our deepest gratitude to all contributors who shared their expertise and to the readers who engage with this work. We invite you to continue exploring, innovating, and leading the charge in creating events that are not only technologically advanced but also inclusive, sustainable, and profoundly impactful.

Thank you for joining us on this enlightening journey through the future of events. We look forward to the continued evolution of this vibrant field and the new heights it will undoubtedly reach.

Editors:

Sharad Kumar Kulshreshtha

Department of Tourism and Hotel Management, North-Eastern Hill University, Shillong, India

Craig Webster

Ball State University, USA

Acknowledgment

First of all, our sincere gratitude to divine almighty to his blessings to successfully enable us to complete this book.

Our most sincere thanks to *Professor Dimitrios Buhalis* and *Prof. Professor Stanislav Ivanov* who have given their very insightful and valuable words as 'Foreword' to this book.

We are also immensely grateful to all editorial advisory board members *Professor Dimitrios Buhalis, Professor Maximiliano Korstanje-, Professor Sandeep Kulshreshtha, Professor U.N. Shukla, Professor* Wayne W. Smith, *Professor Ian Yeoman, Professor Ulrike Gretzel, Dr. Sofia Borda de Água de Almeida,* and *Mr. Sanjay Nadkarni.*

Our sincere thanks to all our distinguished contributors as author and co-authors who have shown their interest and enthusiasm with continuous hard work from proposal to final chapter submission of the book project.

We owe an enormous sincere gratitude to all reviewers who gave their constructive in-depth and insight review comments on one or more chapters of this book.

We would like to extend our special thanks to all colleagues *Prof. Saurabh Kumar Dixit, Dr. Punit Gautam and Dr. Benjamin Franklin Lyngdoh,* Head of Department for share their valuable suggestions other university colleagues from Bio-medical Department, NEHU, Dr Nitin Sahai and Dr. Gajendra Maurya for their continuous support this work. Thanks to our research scholars *Ashok, Iadon, Sachin,* Paramjeet, and Balam as well as office staff Kong Bigi and Bah Badap from DTHM NEHU, Shillong

I would like to offer my special thanks to *Lindsay Wertman,* President of IGI Global who has considered this book project on this theme. I am particularly grateful for the assistance given by *Cassandra Martin, Elizabeth Barrantes, Melissa Wagner,* and others as a very supportive team at IGI.

Most importantly, I, Sharad, wish to thank my loving and supportive wife, Sakshi, and my two loving children, Atharv (Son), Aashvi (Daughter), who provide unending inspiration. And I, Craig, would like to thank my wonderful family, Maria, Paris, Simon, and Scott for being so supportive of this project.

Dr. Sharad Kumar Kulshreshtha

Prof. Craig Webster

Editors

Introduction

Technology, social change, economic development, and other factors have worked in ways to bring humanity to the point it now is. Many of us live in a globalized world in which the goods and services that we consume come from all over the world. Many of the foods that we eat may have been grown far away and many of the support systems for the services we consume may be far away. It is not unusual for North American consumers to get support for various technological, financial, or other consumer services from people living as far away as India or the Philippines. But in a similar way, workplace collaboration may also take place from a distance, with people collaborating on projects from throughout the world. We suspect that most of the authors in this book have collaborated on academic projects with people living in other countries and other time zones and have not met their collaborators in a face-to-face way. It seems that we are now living in this century, that the technological capabilities and social environment to support virtual and hybrid events is now firmly in place, especially since the Covid-19 pandemic that normalized online meetings and events. This book is a modest contribution to the field of knowledge on events that are virtual or hybrid in nature.

The book is organized in a way that hopefully makes some sense to readers. The first chapters are devoted to broad and introductory concepts of virtual and hybrid events, largely discussing the issues of the drivers leading to the dissemination of virtual and hybrid events and the major issues linked with the current practices of virtual and hybrid events. Chapter One sets the framework, explaining the drivers and trajectory of virtual and hybrid events. Chapter Two discusses the integration of robots into the virtual and hybrid event environment. Chapter Three delves into the business opportunities of online events for the MICE industry. Chapter Four explores some of the managerial issues involved in dealing with virtual and hybrid events. Chapter Five, as well, discusses some of the more technical and technological concerns of virtual events by discussing the impact of 5G technologies upon virtual events. Chapter Six discusses the use of gamification of events.

The second group of chapters explores the metaverse and discusses how the metaverse will influence and expand possibilities for events. Chapter Seven gives insight into how the metaverse can be incorporated into the expansion of opportunities for festivals in India. Chapter Eight explores the opportunities that the metaverse offers for the marketing of events in India. Chapter Nine analyses the factors associated with the adoption of the metaverse in events.

The third group of chapters highlights a variety of issues linked with virtual and hybrid events with technical and cultural trends. Chapter Ten explores service automation and the way that it influences the sustainability of events. Chapter Eleven analyses opportunities for the gamification of events, a substantial and important topic in the modern event industry. Chapter Twelve discusses viral content and how viral content is important in cultural consumption in the modern era, a good thing to take note of in the modern event industry.

The fourth group of chapters focuses upon educational issues. Chapter Thirteen discusses hybridized tourism education, illustrating the advantages, opportunities, and challenges in hybrid education, with obvious and clear suggestions about online challenges and opportunities for events. Chapter Fourteen also deals with education, concentrating upon a case study from university convocations online. Chapter Fifteen is a thorough discussion of the use of virtual laboratories and their use in educational environments. Chapter Sixteen is an informative systematic literature review of the literature on blended learning.

The fifth, and last group of chapters is a smorgasbord of chapters that focusses upon a number of other issues that are related to virtual and hybrid events. Chapter Seventeen gives insight into how AI can be used to create personalization of services and guest loyalty in hospitality. Chapter Eighteen discusses how digitalization will transform the educational ecosystem in India to support the Sustainable Development Goals. Chapter Nineteen explores how a number of technologies will be increasingly invoked in events with a discussion of the risks and ethics involved in the incorporation of these new technologies. Chapter Twenty explores virtual reality and AI in healthcare, a discussion that should offer some insights into invoking such technologies in the events industry. Finally, Chapter Twenty-one uses a novel ethnographic method to explore how Covid-19 impacted upon the tourism industry with some thoughtful reflection upon how this may influence the event industry.

This book, as you can see, offers a little of something for everyone and can be enjoyed either as a read from front to back or with chapters taken on their own and out of context with the rest of the chapters. For those interested in the broader issues of how the industry is evolving and the drivers of the events industry, some of the first chapters should give a good overview. However, there are also chapters that are a bit more insightful with regards to specific technologies and how we expect that these technologies will be invoked in the events industry in the not-so-distant future and so some of those chapters may be of more interest to those who are more interested in the technological issues. Also, there are a number of chapters that focus upon educational issues and these chapters may be of more interest for those interested in the virtual events and digital technologies in the educational sphere. Finally, there are some chapters that discuss some issues that may seem to be peripheral to virtual events but have a great deal of meaning for virtual events, giving insight into how Covid-19 influenced the environment and how new technologies can be used to encourage greater participation and satisfaction among participants, for example.

We wish you, the reader, a happy reading of this book. We, as the editors, realized that it was time to work to have an edited book that would bring together authors from different countries to use their collective wisdom and insight in order to enable readers throughout the world to benefit. Readers should be able to identify articles that will give specific information for their practical or research needs and also be able to identify chapters that offer food for thought and give insight into future trends and opportunities. It has been a pleasure editing this book for you, the reader, and we hope that you can use the book for your needs. We also hope that the information and ideas in this book can be used by others as a pedestal from which their future writing can be based.

Sharad Kumar Kulshreshtha

Department of Tourism and Hotel Management, North-Eastern Hill University, Shillong, India

Craig Webster

Ball State University, USA

Chapter 1
Emerging Technologies in Virtual and Hybrid Events:
Major Issues and Major Drivers

Sharad Kumar Kulshreshtha
https://orcid.org/0000-0001-7324-8013
North-Eastern Hill University, India

Craig Webster
https://orcid.org/0000-0003-0665-0867
Ball State University, USA

ABSTRACT

Event management is a fast-growing industry worldwide and there is an expectation that its growth in the short-term and long-term will be substantial. In this industry, technology plays a catalytic role in connecting event stakeholders, enhances the attendee experience, and offers personalized experiences with smart and seamless innovative solutions to the clients and event visitors. Event technology refers to the efficient online event management system or platform, which includes event software applications, mobile based application, innovative electronic devices, wearable technologies, and smart tools for creating immersive event experiences. Such emerging event technologies are not only supporting the design of full-fledged creative events but also customising the event as per the need of the client requirement, budget, time, and ease doing such events. In this context, the event management industry is very much interested to invest in technological research and innovation for getting cost and competitive advantages to more much to make this industry more dynamic and creative to provide more personalised experiences. Virtual and hybrid events offer industry the opportunity to shift platforms and increase cost-effective delivery

DOI: 10.4018/979-8-3693-2272-7.ch001

of events, while keeping participant satisfaction levels high.

INTRODUCTION

Event technology has been a cornerstone of the events industry (Brown & Drakeley, 2023) and will be expected to be increasingly integrated into the events industry in the future. The whole world is rapidly transforming from physical to virtual formats as the result of revolutions and inventions of advance information & communication technology with Covid-19 being a catalyst for the process (Pop, Marian-Potra, & Hognogi, 2023). Meetings are the most purposive and interactive exercise normally contacted at particular meeting points, meeting venues of all sorts, depending on the size of gatherings. Meetings previously had done face-to-face, although current and future technologies change the geography of meetings. Virtual meetings are not new phenomena where people connect through digital technology in virtual or online mode with internet facility avail by host and guest, since there are elements of virtual events, one can argue, that have taken place with such "virtual" meetings as conference calls using telephones in recent decades.

Figure 1. Changing event management dynamics with technological transformation

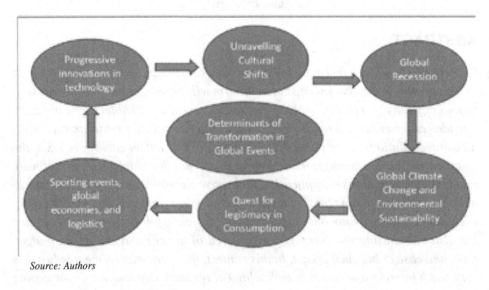

Source: Authors

The figure-1 focuses on changing event management dynamics with techno-logical transformation comprises in-person event, virtual events, hybrid events. In-person event is face to face connect or reconnect at particular place of venue for better networking and people prefer to participate or attend a trade show, conference, seminar, or workshop in person. Virtual events, on the other hand, defy geography, enabling participants to take part in events regardless of where they are in the world (or beyond). Hybrid events, on the other hand, allow for geography to be embraced to allow physical presence of participants while also allowing for virtual participation, regardless of geography. While traditional events were almost entirely face-to-face in the past, recent advances in technologies have allowed for the ability to defy geography to allow for participation over long distances using various communication technologies. Now, there are options for events, from either being stuck in one physical location to being entirely occurring in cyberspace or a mixture of the two.

While there is a substantial literature on the shifting of events from *in situ* events to those that generally defy geography by allowing participation from anywhere, there are types of events that are possible and done for various purposes. Table 1 below lists a number of types of events that may take place in a virtual world. As the table shows, the use of virtual events is applicable to many different businesses and event types and can be used in various ways. While many of the events listed may have seemed odd or novel a few years ago, the covid-19 pandemic normalized such events, such as the advent of online graduation ceremonies.

Table 1. Typologies of virtual events

AI tools contribute to creating more immersive virtual experiences
118 responses

Impact of COVID 19 and Changing Events Management Dynamics

COVID 19 was a major catalyst for virtual and mixed or hybrid event forms, because of concerns for health and safety, as well as government coercion (Pop, Marian-Potra, & Hognogi, 2023). In this context, virtual event technologies played very crucial role to connect people, business, government at local, national, and international level. This digital transformation makes easier of human life, business, industry, services, with more advanced and innovative manner to sustain our future better way.

All information technology companies had tried to revived their services, product quality, service delivery to supply the product and services worldwide. These online virtual platforms made possible to communication, connecting consumers, businesses and governments continuously. During the crisis video conferencing, video calling technologies have greater importance due its unique accessible and user-friendly features, Google Meet, Zoom, Microsoft Team, Webex, were most common virtual platform that time creates these virtual platforms had time utility, place utility, cost utility, and inclusive, intrigued, intelligent, internet driven, internationally connected, virtual platform. Prior to the pandemic, such online platforms were likely not familiar to many people as they are today.

Figure 2. 5 S framework event technologies

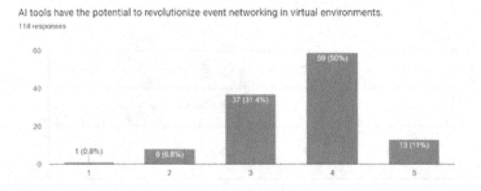

Figure 2'5 S Framework Event illustrates the intentions of smart technologies used in events. The framework illustrates that technological innovations should include a seamless connectivity between user and meeting platforms, servers, internet and databases, strategic alternative solutions, systematic process, and adopt and practice sustainable environmental initiatives for justified the catalytic for efficient event and festival management. Such technologies should also be used in strategic ways and systematic ways in order to encourage successful and profitable events. The expectation, too, is that these technologies can also be used to ensure that events are sustainable and encourage environmental protection and other noteworthy sustainability goals set out by the United Nations and endorsed by political leadership globally.

Webinars: Emerging Online and Virtual Meeting Concept

One of the interesting concepts that has entered the business vernacular in recent years is the concept of the "webinar," which is a concept that deserves a short mention. Webinars was considered an effective online educational tool during COVID-19 (Shal et al., 2024), as a proxy for face-to-face learning/training. The word 'Webinar' acronym as web linked seminar with global reach (Gegenfurtner & Ebner, 2019). Webinars provides kaleidoscope of digital experience (Gegenfurtner & Ebner, 2019a). There are many well-known online meeting applications i.e., Zoom, Google Meet, LiveStorm, (Ismail et al., 2022).

"Webinar" refers to a web-based seminar where small group of members interact, dialogue, share, discuss, and debate urgent issues among the members by common virtual meeting platforms where all attendees have the ability to access those virtual technologies. In this context, webinars are organised or scheduled to connect and communicate the concerned groups of people, societies, business, educations, administration, conducting capacity building and awareness programmes very short notice and ease of join such meeting with average bandwidth of internet speed through normal gadgets i.e., smart phones, laptops, and desktops, e-pads etc. Webinar meeting called by the host who send meeting invitation and start meeting to allow invited attendees or if link is open to all than it will allow as per the limit of the meeting attendees. Webinars includes video and voice interaction, messaging through chat box, real-time virtual interactions, Q&A session, sharing digital documents, videos, PowerPoint Presentation (PPTs) options, other multimedia content with vote of thanks and online feedback.

Key Drivers of Emerging Technologies in Virtual and Hybrid Events

While Covid-19 may have been a catalyst for the increased use of virtual plat-forms for events, there are a number of other drivers that continue to support and encourage the use of virtual platforms for all or a share of the participants in events. Since events are essential phenomena for conducting official, business, commer-cial, political, and social gathering for specific purposes in many businesses, there should be some discussion of what is supporting the growth of virtual and hybrid events when social distancing due to real or perceived health threats is not needed. With the confluence of technological advancements, social change, and political crises, there are some noteworthy drivers that support the growth and development of virtual and hybrid events.

The key drivers are;

1) Emergence of Internet, WiFi,
2) Low cost of Internet data tariff plans
3) High speed internet bandwidths
4) Emergence 5G network technologies
5) Emergence of new millennials, Gen Z
6) Ease of doing events with personalization technologies
7) Seamless and Smart Technologies.
8) Innovations in event management
9) Costing and Return on Investment
10) Customization and higher audience engagement
11) No Transport and Logistic Operation
12) Zero-waste in a virtual environment
13) Instant 24x7 Customer support
14) Rise of Emerging Middle-Class Society in developing countries
15) Increasing Standard of living
16) Event software, and events apps

From these noteworthy drivers, there are a mixture of economic, social, political, and technological changes that work as drivers. Most noteworthy is the advance-ment of technology that has allowed for connection globally to the internet in a continuous and reliable way. If technologies did not exist to allow for reliable virtual meetings of all sorts, virtual events would remain experimental and could not be used widely by private enterprises or government. One critical part of that system of connection to the internet is the provision of services to support users, as well as the continuous improvement of software platforms, allowing for uninterrupted connections and attendance. However, there are other noteworthy developments, specifically in less developed countries in which there is a growth of a skilled and engaged middle class that is educated and feels comfortable using online platforms that support virtual and hybrid events. There are other critical things that are part of the ecosystem that also support the growth of virtual/hybrid events, such as the fact that many younger users now have never lived in an environment in which digital technologies have been a part of the world in which they have lived.

Figure 3. Six keys drivers of hybrid events

What potential benefits do you see in using robots for event management and organization in hybrid and virtual settings?

118 responses

- Automate Large volume and repetitive tasks
- Enhanced Attendee Experience
- Remote Accessibility
- Real-time Data Insights
- Improved Safety protocols and Security measures

Source: Big Maker

According Big Marker Report (Big Marker, 2022), the figure-5 'Six Keys Drivers of Hybrid Events' focuses on contents, connectivity, community, conveniences, customisation and commercial values of manging hybrid events where innovative technological platform create immersive event technological experiences for the event attendees and organiser. So, apart from the social, economic, and other influences for the increased use of virtual and hybrid events, there are also several factors from the consumer and industry side that lead to a greater reliance on the virtual world for the support of events. Some of the key and interesting drivers, from the Big Maker Report is that hybrid events support a sense of community and connectivity. What is interesting about this is that while much of the world has migrated to online/ digital interactions, that online/digital solutions can be used to connect/reconnect humans in ways that apes the ways that face-to-face meetings support a sense of community. The convenience factor is also a major issue, as in global businesses that require meetings from participants from around the world, the cost of physical travel and the need to take the time, energy, and funding to transport people from one part of the world for the purpose of face-to-face meetings can be avoided. That means, in fact, that the use of such platforms not only avoids costs but also serves as a convenience, saving participants in meetings from the investment of substantial amounts of time and energy into travel.

Table 2. Emerging hybrid event platforms

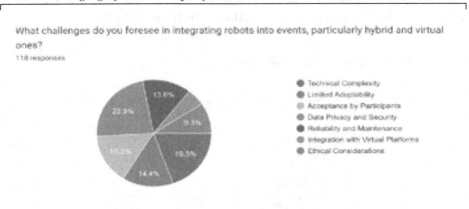

Source: Authors

The interesting thing is that the above table illustrates is that there are many different platforms and commercial services that are available for the supporting of virtual/hybrid events. While some in business ten years ago may have been aware of some of the technological platforms that could support such meetings, there are now a plethora of platforms available and many are likely familiar with a handful of them. While different platforms may be more popular in one part of the world than another, there are likely two or three that many in business or government would feel comfortable using for the purpose of meetings. Additionally, the fact that there are multiple companies involved in the development of such platforms illustrates that there is the perception of a substantial market for such technologies and that commercial enterprises are anxious to produce business solutions that will fill the needs of the market.

REVIEW OF THE ACADEMIC LITERATURE

Because of its importance, there is a substantial and growing literature on virtual and hybrid events. While it is clear what is intended by a virtual event, an onto-logical hybrid comprises artificial and living phenomena, something explained by Diodato (2021). Hanaei et al. (2022) explored the impact of the COVID pandemic globally and the way that it forced events into a virtual world. Event management significances to study the need of the digital age (Rojek, 2020). Some authors have explored online event management systems and their enabling of effective service (Mohana & Anbumani, 2022). Other authors, such as (Mei et al., 2021) explore the development of social media and online events. Others have dealt with other issues such as the changing variables dynamics have affected consumer online experiences (Kharouf et al., 2020), the social interaction in virtual events (Simons, 2019), and the hybrid experience in events (Benet & Pellicer-Valero, 2022).

There are many other academics that have explored many issues linked with the effectivenesss of virtual and hybrid events, innovation issues, the impact of virtual events upon the industry and many other issues (see, for example Bukovska et al., 2021; Prayogi & Michael, 2022; Stefănescu & Papoi, 2020; Iatsyshyn et al., 2020; Alhusban, 2022; Flowers & Gregson, 2012; Sultana et al., 2020; Manas-Alvarez et al., 2023; Duffy & McEuen, 2010; Broderick et al., 2018; Arcos & Smith, 2021; Naraine et al., 2022; Bosse & Pournaras, 2017; Mahadewi, 2023; Talavera et al., 2019). The substantial growth in the literature on virtual and hybrid events that even preceded the pandemic suggest that this is a field that is in growth and this book hopefully contributes in ways to the growth of the literature on the topic.

EMERGING TECHNOLOGIES IN EVENT INDUSTRY

There is also reason to discuss more about technologies and the ways that the event industry can integrate such technologies into virtual and hybrid events. While a few decades ago, discussions regarding new innovations such as online registration systems and payment systems may have been interesting and helpful, now more is needed to be learned about engagement of participants. While there is evidence that there is a preference for face-to-face experiences over other types of events (Ogbeide et al., 2013), there is the question of which types of technologies can be used to keep their attention focused upon the event, since there is good reason to believe that younger generations have a talent for tuning out many messages that are marketed to them (Munsch, 2021). One of the chief obstacles to the new era in virtual/hybrid events will be to ensure that consumers keep their attention focused and see the value in virtual events, since there is good reason to believe that virtual events are seen as convenient in many circumstances but also inferior in terms of the event experience, relative to face-to-face events.

For those who host virtual/hybrid events, there is a need to keep the participants' focus. This means that the technology providers will have to be tasked with providing solutions to event organizers, creating innovative solutions to keep the attention of those who attend online events. The trick will be to not only find technologies that mimic fact-to-face events but also to find technologies that can add value to events to make participants want to attend online events or even prefer them. However, one key issue is that the technologies that are used have to be effective and user-friendly, otherwise such technologies may actually have the antithetical impact, driving consumers away from virtual events.

Figure 4. Shifting the focus of virtual and hybrid event technologies

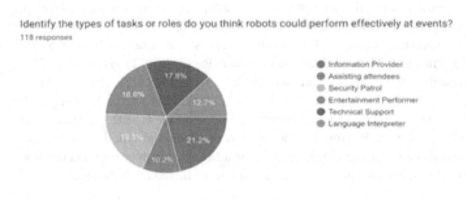

Source: Authors

The figure -4 'Shifting the Focus of Virtual and Hybrid Event Technologies' highlights the application and implementation of technologies in the regular affairs of society and community, friends and relatives by 'socialisation', connecting business and industry, consumers and stakeholders by 'commercialisation', customer care, health and educations, entertainments and leisure by 'personalisation' and holistic approach to combined all in integrated manner by 'virtualisation', The role of shifting the focus of virtual and hybrid event technologies creates new experiences with immersive and augmented and virtual realities, metaverse, blockchains, data analytics etc.

SUSTAINABLE EVENTS AND GREEN TECHNOLOGIES

Sustainability practices are essential to integrate into in all types of events in the current business environment (Nawarathna & Arachchi, 2021). There is an urgent need to move towards sensible resource consumption, efficient use energy, conversion technologies, renewable energy to effectively enable circular economy framework (Nižetić et al., 2019a). Ongoing United Nations' Sustainable Development Goals support for eco- friendly and green sustainable practices for better future of the planet, people and profit illustrate a dedication from global elites for support for various sustainable practices. There are many goals which align towards sustainability and green practices and they can be expected to become increasingly an among various event stakeholders. Event planners are very much conscious to take responsibility to save environment by implementing sustainable practices during the organizing their events and festivals at respective destinations to save water, energy, and conserve the green environment by adopting nature friendly approach through host and guest perspectives.

Green technology plays significant role in attaining sustainable development goals (Guo et al., 2020) and there is no reason to believe that such technologies would not be integrated into a large and quickly-growing industry such as events. Additionally, smart approach and technologies can be expected to support and possibly solve crucial problems of societies (Nižetić et al., 2019) and reduce carbon emissions (Desheng et al., 2021). In addition, there is evidence that even small firms show interest in investing in green technology(Vimala et al., 2022), so it can be expected that even smaller private enterprises may act in ways to invest in technologies that support reductions in environmental damage, including events.

These are some major suggestions for managing green events by applying green technological solutions:

- Selection of sustainable and environmentally-friendly event venues, convention centres, or other venues.
- Promote 3Rs approach reduce, recycle and reuse practices by attendees.
- Use locally grown products and services in events to support local economy.
- Use green transport practices in events i.e., walking, cycling, car-pooling, use battery driven vehicle.
- Prohibited single-use plastic and make sure this event is in plastic free.
- Avoid plastic mineral water bottles and arrange water dispensers for providing drinking water.
- Encourages digital practices among attendees to buy e-tickets for save and promote green initiatives.
- Waste management system

New Virtual World and New Technologies

Table 3 below illustrates a number of different technologies that can be or will be implemented in the events industry. As we can see, there are a number of different technologies that can or will be implemented widely in the event industry in the near future. The implementation of these technologies allow for easier administration of events as well as the running of events. Already, we see that many of these technologies are implemented widely in events, although some are either quickly developing and improving (such as AI) and others are still quite expensive and more rarely used (such as holograms). At any rate, we see that there are multiple existing and developing technologies to support and enhance virtual and hybrid events.

Table 3. Emerging technologies in event industry

Are there any specific features or functionalities you would like to see in robots designed for event experiences?

118 responses

- Interactive Interface
- Guided Navigation
- Multilingual Support
- Entertainment Features
- Event Analytics
- Emergency Response
- Environmental Sensors

Source: Authors

In spite of abundant of technological features, benefits still there have lots of practical challenges to use these event management technologies in day-to-day life of event planners. No doubt there are many challenges of in-person, virtual, and hybrid events. These challenges budget constraints related with investment and cost-benefit analysis of event technologies, training and skilling, upgraded and outdated technologies, data security issues, competition of implementation advancement of technologies in event companies, security and privacy, high speed connectivity issues, and remote location events.

The future of event and festival technologies brought transformation and innovation in event management industry worldwide with immersive and experiential virtual and hybrid events management. The advanced smart and seamless technologies include artificial intelligence (AI), virtual reality (VR) and augmented reality (AR) metaverse, blockchain, data analytics have event management industry in futuristic direction. The blockchain technology has revolutionised the delivery system of event booking, budgeting, parking issues, time and team management. These virtual event technologies supporting event organisers, event attendees, with AI-powered chatbots, personalisation services, seamless and smart technologies with immersive digital settings, development of interactive communication between host and guest experiences. The future scenario of events and festivals management definitely more prosperous and prospective in terms of event innovation, creativity and experiential, social inclusion, technological integration, and following sustainable green event management practices for managing event destination and environment for next generation.

CONCLUSION

The global event management industry is going through rapid transformative path of development and innovations, originally shocked into moving virtual during the recent pandemic but since then continuously pushed into a virtual world because of various social, economic, and political drivers. The emerging technological development in event industry has revolutionised the landscape of event experiences, services, personalisation, professionalism, and service quality delivery of event management industry. The emerging event technologies like augmented reality, virtual reality, artificial intelligence, blockchains, data analytics, event application and software have changed the attendees' experiences, cost, customisation, care and concern of event organisers. These cutting-edge emerging event and festivals technologies are supporting to measure event size, scalability, cost-minimisation, event resource optimisation and rationalisation for and effective decision-making for sustainable event management practices.

However, there are many key challenges of these technologies like cost, connectivity, capacity building and skilling, change of old technology, security and data privacy, digital equity, are some major issues of event and festival technologies. Sustainable Development Goals also emphasis digitalisation practices to make this world more inclusive, integration, intelligence and interactive to deliver quality event services to the clients, stakeholders. With changing dynamics of emerging technologies are shaping prospective green &, clean environmental future of event practices and destination.

The intention of this chapter was to explain the major issues involved in virtual and hybrid events giving an overview of the field before the following chapters that deal with specific issues related to virtual and hybrid events. The following chapters illustrate that virtual and hybrid events are here to stay and that there are many different technologies and managerial practices that will allow them to be a vibrant and growing part of the event ecosystem. This is a growing and vibrant academic field and it is also reflective of a growing commercial field. The topic of virtual and hybrid events should be of interest to many, with the growth of the virtual world. In addition, there should be something of interest to readers as each of the contributors make their own specific contribution, noting social concerns, practical/managerial concerns, technological issues, and other issues. We expect that there is something for everyone in a book with so many broad perspectives. We wish you a good read and wish you the best in this increasingly virtual world.

REFERENCES

Alhusban, H. A. (2022). A Novel Synchronous Hybrid Learning Method: Voices from Saudi Arabia. *Electronic Journal of e-Learning*, 20(4), 400–418. 10.34190/ejel.20.4.2340

Arcos, R., & Smith, H. (2021). Digital communication and hybrid threats. In *Icono14*. 10.7195/ri14.v19i1.1662

Benet, D., & Pellicer-Valero, O. J. (2022). *Metaverse in Ophthalmology: The Convergence of Virtual and Physical Space in Eye Care*. Digital Medicine and Healthcare Technology., 10.5772/dmht.10

Bosse, S., & Pournaras, E. (2017). An ubiquitous multi-agent mobile platform for distributed crowd sensing and social mining. *Proceedings - 2017 IEEE 5th International Conference on Future Internet of Things and Cloud, FiCloud 2017*. IEEE. 10.1109/FiCloud.2017.44

Broderick, M., Bender, S. M., & McHugh, T. (2018). *Virtual Trauma: Prospects for Automediality*. M/C Journal. 10.5204/mcj.1390

Brown, T., & Drakeley, C. (2023). *Designing the virtual and hybrid event experience*. Goodfellow Publishers eBooks. 10.23912/978-1-915097-34-7-5400

Bukovska, G., Mezgaile, A., & Klepers, A. (2021). The pressure of technological innovations in meeting and event industry under the COVID-19 influence. *Vide. Tehnologija. Resursi - Environment, Technology. Resources*, 2, 44–50. 10.17770/etr2021vol2.6623

CVENT. (2024). *Metrics That Matter: 68 Event Statistics You Need to Know in 2024*. CVENT. https://www.cvent.com/en/blog/events/event-statistics

Desheng, L., Jiakui, C., & Ning, Z. (2021). Political connections and green technology innovations under an environmental regulation. *Journal of Cleaner Production*, 298, 126778. 10.1016/j.jclepro.2021.126778

Diodato, R. (2021). Ontology of the Virtual. In *Philosophy of Engineering and Technology*. 10.1007/978-3-030-54522-2_15

Duffy, C., & McEuen, M. B. (2010). *The future of meetings: The case for face-to-face*. Cornell Hospitality Industry Perspectives.

Flowers, A. A., & Gregson, K. (2012). Decision-making factors in selecting virtual worlds for events: Advocacy, computer efficacy, perceived risks, and collaborative benefits. *Event Management*, 16(4), 319–334. 10.3727/152599512X13539583375054

Gegenfurtner, A., & Ebner, C. (2019). Webinars in higher education and professional training: A meta-analysis and systematic review of randomized controlled trials. In *Educational Research Review*. 10.1016/j.edurev.2019.100293

Guo, R., Lv, S., Liao, T., Xi, F., Zhang, J., Zuo, X., Cao, X., Feng, Z., & Zhang, Y. (2020). Classifying green technologies for sustainable innovation and investment. *Resources, Conservation and Recycling*, 153, 104580. 10.1016/j.resconrec.2019.104580

Hanaei, S., Takian, A., Majdzadeh, R., Maboloc, C. R., Grossmann, I., Gomes, O., Milosevic, M., Gupta, M., Shamshirsaz, A. A., Harbi, A., Burhan, A. M., Uddin, L. Q., Kulasinghe, A., Lam, C. M., Ramakrishna, S., Alavi, A., Nouwen, J. L., Dorigo, T., Schreiber, M., & Rezaei, N. (2022). Emerging Standards and the Hybrid Model for Organizing Scientific Events during and after the COVID-19 Pandemic. *Disaster Medicine and Public Health Preparedness*, 16(3), 1172–1177. 10.1017/dmp.2020.40633100253

Iatsyshyn, A. V., Kovach, V. O., Lyubchak, V. O., Zuban, Y. O., Piven, A. G., Sokolyuk, O. M., Iatsyshyn, A. V., Popov, O. O., Artemchuk, V. O., & Shyshkina, M. P. (2020). Application of augmented reality technologies for education projects preparation. *CEUR Workshop Proceedings*. CEUR. 10.31812/123456789/3856

Ismail, S., Salam, A., & Hajriyanti, R. (2022). Event Management System for Webinars and Survey. *International Journal Software Engineering and Computer Science (IJSECS)*. 10.35870/ijsecs.v2i1.761

Kharouf, H., Biscaia, R., Garcia-Perez, A., & Hickman, E. (2020). Understanding online event experience: The importance of communication, engagement and interaction. *Journal of Business Research*, 121, 735–746. 10.1016/j.jbusres.2019.12.037

Mahadewi, N. (2023). *Hybrid Event: Utilization of Digital Technology in Organizing Events during the COVID-19 Pandemic in Indonesia*. MDPI. 10.3390/proceedings2022083053

Manas-Alvarez, F. J., Guinaldo, M., Dormido, R., & Dormido, S. (2023). *Robotic Park: Multi-Agent Platform for Teaching Control and Robotics*. IEEE., 10.1109/ACCESS.2023.3264508

Marker, B. (2022). *6 Keys To Success For Any Hybrid Event*. Big Maker. https://get.bigmarker.com/blog/6-keys-to-success-for-any-hybrid-event

Mei, Z., Shuheng, D., Guofang, L., Yazhen, X., Xinyuan, F., Wei, Z., & Ziqiang, X. (2021). Negativity bias in emergent online events: Occurrence and manifestation. *Acta Psychologica Sinica*, 53(12), 1361. 10.3724/SP.J.1041.2021.01361

Mohana. S, & Anbumani, P. (2022). Online Event Management System. *International Journal of Research Publication and Reviews Journal Homepage.*

Munsch, A. (2021). Millennial and generation Z digital marketing communication and advertising effectiveness: A qualitative exploration. *Journal of Global Scholars of Marketing Science*, 31(1), 10–29. 10.1080/21639159.2020.1808812

Naraine, M. L., Hayduk, T., & Doyle, J. P. (2022). *The Routledge Handbook of Digital Sport Management.* Taylor & Francis. http://books.google.ie/ books?id=gI-CUEAAAQBAJ&pg=PT73&dq=digital+tarnsformation+not+for+profit+sport+organisation&hl=&cd=1&source=gbs_api

Nawarathna, D. B., & Arachchi, D. R. S. S. W. (2021). *A Study on Sustainable Event Management Practices in Sri Lanka; Event Managers' Perspective.* Tourism and Sustainable Development Review. 10.31098/tsdr.v2i1.40

Nižetić, S., Djilali, N., Papadopoulos, A., & Rodrigues, J. J. P. C. (2019). Smart technologies for promotion of energy efficiency, utilization of sustainable resources and waste management. In *Journal of Cleaner Production.* 10.1016/j.jclepro.2019.04.397

Ogbeide, G. C., Fenich, G. G., Scott-Halsell, S., & Kesterson, K. (2013). Communication Preferences for Attracting the Millennial Generation to Attend Meetings and Events. *Journal of Convention & Event Tourism*, 14(4), 331–344. 10.1080/15470148.2013.843480

Pop, A. M., Marian-Potra, A. C., & Hognogi, G. G. (2023). The COVID-19 Pandemic as Catalyst for Virtual Events. *Journal of Settlements & Spatial Planning*, 14(1), 13–23. 10.24193/JSSP.2023.1.02

Prayogi, S. F., & Michael. (2022). Kajian Desain 3D Virtual Exhibition Ruang Pamer Karya Desain Produk Istts. *Prosiding SNADES.*

Rojek, C. (2020). Event Management. In *Routledge Handbook of Leisure Studies.* Routledge. https://doi.org/10.4324/9781003074717-49

Shal, T., Ghamrawi, N., & Ghamrawi, N. A. R. (2024). Webinars for teacher professional development: Perceptions of members of a virtual professional community of practice. *Open Learning*, 1–17. 10.1080/02680513.2023.2296645

Simons, I. (2019). Events and online interaction: The construction of hybrid event communities. *Leisure Studies*, 38(2), 145–159. 10.1080/02614367.2018.1553994

Ştefănescu, D. C., & Papoi, A. (2020). NEW threats to the national security of states ⇓ Cyber threat. *Scientific Journal of Silesian University of Technology. Series Transport.* 10.20858/sjsutst.2020.107.13

Sultana, S., Parvez, M., Khan, R. S., & Jalil, M. S. (2020). PERCEPTION OF EVENT MANAGEMENT COMPANY TOWARDS GREEN EVENT: EVIDENCE FROM BANGLADESH. *Academy of Strategic Management Journal.*

Syah, F., & Rajoendah, M. I. K. (2022). The Role Model of MICE Activities After the COVID-19 Pandemic in Indonesia. *Journal of Tourism Education.* 10.17509/jote.v2i1.48875

Talavera, A. M., Al-Ghamdi, S. G., & Koç, M. (2019). Sustainability in mega-events: Beyond qatar 2022. In *Sustainability (Switzerland).* MDPI. 10.3390/su11226407

Vimala, D., Evangelin, M. R., & Vasantha, S. (2022). Sustainability and Green Technology Innovation. In *Remittances Review.* 10.47059/rr.v7i2.2408

Chapter 2
Revolutionizing Events:
Exploring the Seamless Integration of Robots in Hybrid and Virtual Experiences

Anila Thomas

https://orcid.org/0000-0001-6068-6639

Jyoti Nivas College (Autonomous), Bangalore, India

ABSTRACT

The rapid progress of technology has introduced a period in which robots are progressively becoming essential contributors in several facets of human life. Amidst the current worldwide pandemic and increasing desire for creative and interactive encounters, facilitating the inclusion of robots into events has become a captivating and transforming trend. In the past few years, hybridized and online gatherings have gained popularity owing to developments in communication technology and the need for flexible audience engagement across various geographical areas. The research explores the many capabilities of robots in event environments, including interactive companionship as well as event logistics and administration. The study also discusses the ethical implications and difficulties that arise from incorporating robots into events, such as concerns around privacy, security, and inclusion, in light of ongoing technological advancements. This chapter pursues to make available valuable perceptions to the present state of robotic technology and its thinkable future advancements.

DOI: 10.4018/979-8-3693-2272-7.ch002

INTRODUCTION

The world-wide event business has expanded dramatically in the Western world over the last decade, but Asia Pacific nations such as China and India are catching up quickly. The experience and knowledge economies, in particular, are on the rise, necessitating that business events be considerably more experience and knowledge-oriented. The usage of the internet, mobile technologies, and virtual applications will also have a momentous impression on the occasion of celebration and happenings. With governments throughout the world constantly revising the criteria and the possibility of future pandemic waves, it is becoming increasingly impossible to predict how things will unfold over the next few years. The events segment should be motivated to become accustomed to a new-fangled standard, in which hybrid events will allow the business to resurface. Successful hybrid events might be achieved by combining world-class venue amenities, audience interaction technologies, skilled staff, and health and safety safeguards for all involved.

Today's youngsters will be tomorrow's event participants. Corporations ought to consistently make adjustments on their promotional concepts and methods to this more youthful prioritize demographics that are identified as digital natives, with the goal to smooth the forthcoming millennial transition. Event organizers must not be scared to acquaint with newfangled features besides opportunities primarily on the attendees. The notion of smart networks shows how both participants and organizers may profit from new developments by creating intelligent information networks. On a technological level, virtual assistant systems and humanoid robots can help convert an occasion into a incomparable, individualized involvement of partakers respectively in the impending instances. Furthermore, the utilization of 3D techno-applications converted the schedules into a genuine world with visual, tactile, and audio aspects.

Determinants of Transformation in Global Events

Events are a crucial continuous industry, either because they are required for the everyday operations of businesses and governments, or because they provide large economic rewards. Many studies have been undertaken to assess the utmost imperative stimulus in addition to trials for forthcoming occurrences, as well as the influence on various industries.

Figure 1. Determinants of transformation in global events

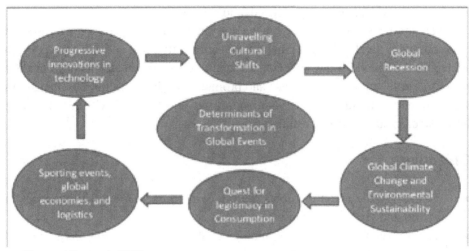

*Source: (Alananzeh, 2022)

Figure 1 summarizes the causes that drove change and new innovations in the realm of global events. Events allow individuals to network, spend time, celebrate, learn about different beliefs, and stimulate originality and cooperation (Quinn, 2009). It brings the local population to life and permits a dwelling to display its experience in the occurrence while also maximizing monetary rewards. Modern event management is a complex and demanding profession. It reflects fundamental functional areas of event management (Bladen, C., et al., 2022), such as promotion, investment, venture supervision, policy-making, procedures, event proposal, and societal possessions, across a wide range of happening circumstances from sports to fundamental proceedings. Bestowing to several research, extraordinary proceedings are exclusive occasions that are commemorated for wide-ranging reasons. Public gatherings are spatial-temporal phenomena, and individually distinct owing to communications among establishment, persons, and administrative structures (Pilipczuk, 2021).

Primeval Outlook on How Technology Has Influenced Events and Festivals

Throughout the course of time, technology has had an impact on events and festivals, from ancient agricultural gatherings to contemporary virtual encounters. Events and commemorations are a portion of social culture since time immemorial, providing as occasions for celebration, community connection, and tradition preservation. Technical applications have had a noteworthy influence on the character and experience of these meetings across millennia. From the birth of the wheel to the digital era, technical innovations have transformed the technique by which events and festivals are prepared, experienced, and remembered.

Over the course of the centuries, technology has been an accelerator in the growth of events and festivals, changing their organisation, diffusion, and experience. From ancient rites to modern-day spectacles, technological advancements have made it easier to create unforgettable events and promote worldwide cultural exchange. As we continue to embrace new technology, events and festivals will become more immersive, inclusive, and revolutionary.

Objectives

- To analyze the effect of robots on improving the experience of attendees in hybrid and virtual procedures.
- To discover and assess the technological obstacles and resolutions associated with the integration of robots.
- To get insights into the viewpoints of event organizers and attendees on the use of robots in events.
- To evaluate the overall influence of robots on the achievement and efficiency of hybrid and virtual events.

RESEARCH METHODOLOGY

An interdisciplinary strategy, combining descriptive and empirical exploratory methodologies, was used. The research design chosen was appropriate for the study's aims. The alternatives included experimental investigations, surveys, case studies, or a mix of these methods. A survey instrument was created to gather quantitative data on attendees' impressions, preferences, and experiences. In addition, qualitative observations were obtained through interviews with event organizers, technical developers, and attendees. Direct observation of hybrid and virtual events, together with robot/AI integration, provided firsthand knowledge. Focus groups were used to facilitate conversations about relevant aspects of robotics/AI integration. Furthermore, key records, such as event reports, were examined to supplement the information gathered.

Sampling

Careful selection of samples ensured the study's legitimacy and relevance. The sample group includes event coordinators, technology specialists, participants in hybrid and virtual events, and businesses that use robotic technologies for events. The sample selection comprised a varied assortment of events from innumerable industries, together with conferences, trade fairs, and displays. Responders are chosen based on their experience with both traditional and hybrid/virtual events, as well as their use of robots. Finding the ideal sample group for the study was a critical challenge. Many aspects were considered during this process, including the required level of accuracy, available resources, and statistical strength. The unplanned selection approach was used to divide the sample group and then choose participants based on specific criteria relevant to the investigation. Industry conferences, social media platforms, professional networks, and collaborations with event organizers were all potential paths of interaction.

Rising Technologies and its impact on the Events and Festivals

Events generate a lot of demand and perform an imperative part in revitalizing the tourism earnings. Technology is essential for event planning, execution, and completion. As technology advances swiftly and tremendously, diverse technical applications are being applied in many industries (Cobanoglu, C., et al., 2021). Today, robots have grown into structures capable of acting autonomously and performing tasks. The number of festivals having a technical focus has amplified in all time. To ensure the success of the festivals, numerous aspects must be considered throughout the scheduling and organizing phases. Once lessons on significant aspects that contribute to festive occasions success are looked into, substances like the ceremony initiatives, the celebration domain, connectivity, insights, workers and supporters, vacation souvenirs, functionality, food choices, and safeguarding become apparent (Dalgic & Birdir, 2021), still nearly few conclusions are available about technical features. There is uncertainty over which industrial operations are featured in the festivities and how they affect participant experiences.

Because of the incredible expansion in the realm of virtual reality, where physical borders disappear from view, interactions are overwhelming and concurrently occurring, and the quantity of individuals who use it rises to staggering levels and moves on getting bigger day by day, mainstream media demonstrations and executions have become insufficient, and operational communication has started to emerge as an essential promotional instrument for the tourist business. Nowadays, social networking is regarded as a highly strong novel publicizing medium for achieving this advertising goal and making marketing efforts more successful (Shih, 2010).

The digitalised programs are modest, straightforward, and quick. These promising possibilities for social media present significant benefits for event organizers in reaching out to more potential attendees.

Recently, there has been an upsurge in the use of increasingly sophisticated technology for different occasions and session arrangement and conception. Emerging technology and apps have revolutionized the professional style of event preparation and implementation (Yen, Wey, & Sullivan, 2016) in several appealing traditions. During 1980s, event organizers used rudimentary automated badge manufacture and accepted reservations over the phone or in person (Boshnakova and Goldblatt, 2017). SpotMe staged the first virtual exhibition, Expo Exchange, in London in 2000 (Cobanoglu, C. et al., 2021). The exhibition allowed guests to view photos and connect to other attendees. Countless machine-driven progressions have been make known to in succeeding years, including wi-fi, iPhone, Skype, Face Time, and others (Aksentyeva et al. 2020).

The overview of the web-based services, event developers began to create comprehensive and deliver crucial and accurate evidence to websites. At that time, they began creating social media profiles to correspond with both stakeholders and guests, resulting in more fruitful event experiences. Online stages helped to design various promotional techniques for the event. Together with the onset of the fourth industrial revolution, revolutionary innovations have entered the corporate world in a variety of appealing and profitable ways (Ryan, W. G., et al., 2020). Many industries, including automotive, medicine, retail, agriculture, and tourism, have begun to use automated processes, The use of Virtual Reality (VR) operations, the application of Augmented Reality (AR), Machine Learning advancement, the Internet of Things (IoT) and detection devices, automated drones, self-driving automobiles and a variety of innovations.

Virtual innovations are being employed at artistic inheritance locations and arts centers to increase tourist interaction (Han, D. I. D., et al., 2019). Contactless orders and payments become feasible because to the Internet of Things (IoT), which is defined as the connectivity of things via internet protocol (Atzori, L., et al., 2017). Wearable technology enables users to track their movements. Unmanned flying items, like as drones, aid in the recording and photography of events and festivals (BR, S.R., 2022). Augmented reality and holographic technology may be experienced during athletic events and concerts.

Information and message networking expertise advancements have had a wide-ranging influence on the event management industry. The academic research on technological innovations and their existing and prospective applications in the event managing has not set aside up with trade expansion. As a result, there are few studies on modern-day and real-world implementations of ICTs to replicate judgmentally on these breakthroughs in the functioning of event business and to enrich professional training on managing events (Thomson, A., et al., 2021). Addressing to similar void in event-related administration, scholarly works is critical from an organization standpoint. ICT projects reveal how to provide a variety of rate savings for session planners and investors, at the same time, improve the standard of involvement and give new and innovative ways to attend events (Slocum & Lee, 2014). It is also critical that we represent ICT improvements in our event education.

Incorporating Robots Into Hybrid and Virtual Events

Robots have grown popular at hybrid and virtual events for a variety of motives, including boosting overall experience quality and expanding participant communication opportunities. The enhanced degree of participation might range from virtual avatars that simulate real-life participants to physical robots that interact with the audience in person. Participants may operate these robots from a distance, which increases engagement.

The event-based services are conventionally depended on on digitization for occurrence orchestrating and production, and the use of *Robotic, Artificial Intelligence, and Service Automation* (RAISA) technology in events has been restricted but has substantial prospects for the future (Ogle & Lamb, 2019). RAISA has the potential to perform a critical technological role in the event's profession. Robotic tools and approaches provide program supervision with tremendous sustainable development capability. Events express human/societal interactions and activities. The smart use of RAISA has the potential to reduce attendance obstacles while also promoting successful marketing and industry sustainability.

AI improves realism in immersive virtual experiences. AI algorithms allow the construction of lifelike surroundings, people, and interactions, blurring the distinction between the virtual and the real. AI-powered graphics engines, for example, may produce extremely detailed landscapes, realistic weather patterns, and lifelike character motions, giving viewers a greater feeling of immersion. AI techniques help to create more immersive virtual experiences by dynamically developing individualized surroundings, improving interactions with virtual characters, and automatically producing different material. By leveraging AI, virtual reality transforms from a simulation to a fully immersive and interactive parallel environment. Artificial intelligence-powered virtual characters, sometimes known as non-player characters (NPCs), enrich virtual interactions (Karaca, Derias, & Sarsar, 2023). AI enables NPCs to comprehend and respond to your verbal and nonverbal signals using Natural Language Processing (NLP) and sentiment analysis, resulting in more realistic and immersive interactions (Westera, et al., 2020). For example, if you display fear or excitement during a virtual meeting, AI algorithms assess your tone and change the NPC's conversation and behaviour appropriately, increasing the sensation of immersion and presence.

AI techniques provide individualized engagement in virtual environments, responding to individuals' specific interests and habits. Natural Language Processing (NLP) methods provide conversational interfaces, which allow users to engage with virtual entities via speech or text input. Furthermore, AI-powered recommendation systems leverage user data and preferences to customize content, proposing suitable experiences, activities, or virtual worlds based on each user's interests, increasing engagement and immersion.

Figure 2. Contribution of AI tools for more immersive virtual experiences

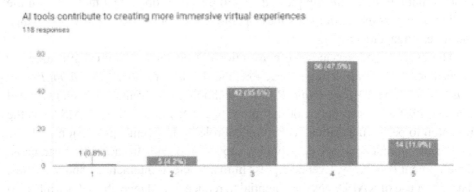

(*Source: Author's observations and findings of the study)

Artificial intelligence technologies with emotional intelligence improve virtual immersion by imitating human-like emotions, expressions, and interactions. Emotion detection algorithms scan facial expressions, gestures, and voice intonations to determine the user's emotional state, allowing virtual entities to respond empathetically and adaptably. Virtual avatars with emotional AI may communicate empathy, pity, and even comedy, building stronger emotional relationships and improving the entire immersive experience.

AI technologies have a revolutionary impact on virtual experiences, leading to greater realism, customized engagement, dynamic adaptability, and emotional intelligence. By leveraging AI, virtual worlds become more immersive, dynamic, and engaging, providing users with unparalleled options for exploration, creativity, and connectivity. In the constantly shifting environment of contemporary events and gatherings, socializing is an integral component of accomplishment. Connecting with like-minded people, industry experts, and possible collaborators is essential for stimulating creativity, promoting company success, and broadening one's professional network. Traditional networking strategies, on the other hand, frequently fail to connect people based on their interests, expertise, and aspirations.

Figure 3. AI tools revolutionizing event networking

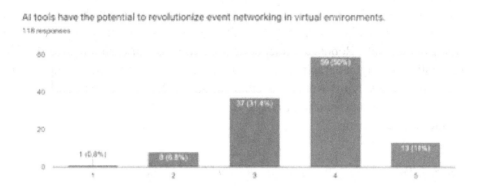

(*Source: Author's observations and findings of the study)

Artificial intelligence-powered platforms have transformed event networking by providing tailored and simplified experiences for attendees, exhibitors, and organizers alike. These systems use automated learning techniques to assess enormous quantities of information gathered, including participant profiles and preferences, event agendas, and past encounters. Conventional social gatherings frequently rely on serendipity, which forces guests to explore busy rooms in search of interesting discussions. AI-powered matching systems, on the other hand, may effectively match individuals with compatible counterparts, increasing the possibility of meaningful connections. These systems may anticipate users' demands by evaluating their behaviour patterns and preferences, and then provide related seminars, workshops, or networking opportunities. This proactive strategy not only increases attendee involvement, but also allows event organizers to create more focused and meaningful events. Furthermore, AI tools enable seamless communication and interaction before to, during, and after events, overcoming the constraints of physical proximity.

Benefits of Using Robots in Hybrid and Virtual Settings

Robot integration into hybrid and virtual environments is becoming more common, transforming a wide range of businesses and areas. In manufacturing, androids furnished by progressive sensing and image structures intensification, assembly precision and speed, resulting in better production outputs and quality control. Robots perform an important role in maintaining safety and risk reduction in hazardous or high-risk areas. Robots improve interaction and collaborative efforts in hybrid and virtual environments by reducing the disparity between remote and on-site participants. Robots use telepresence to offer real-time communication and cooperation among geographically separated teams, boosting synergy and collaborative problem solving. Robots function as intermediates in corporate meetings, academic conferences, and joint research initiatives, allowing for smooth contact and knowledge sharing.

Figure 4. Potential benefits of robots in hybrid and virtual settings

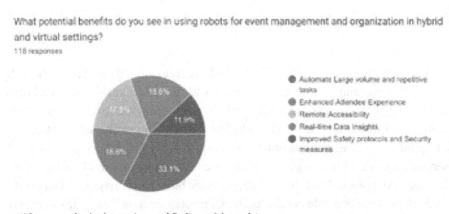

(*Source: author's observations and findings of the study*)

The deployment of robots in hybrid and virtual contexts has several advantages that improve human-computer interaction and spur innovation. Robots have a revolutionary role in defining the future of work, education, healthcare, and other fields, from increased accessibility and efficiency to improved user experience and safety. As we continue to harness the power of robotics technology, the possibilities for building immersive and collaborative environments become limitless, offering a future in which people and robots cohabit peacefully to pursue common goals.

Challenges of Using Robots in Hybrid and Virtual Environment

The emergence of robotics into hybrid and virtual settings presents a slew of problems that must be overcome before these technologies may realize their full potential. While robots have showed exceptional skills in regulated contexts such as factories and warehouses, their performance in hybrid and virtual environments, where they interact with both real and virtual aspects, is continually improving. Indeed, one of the most difficult aspects of employing robots in hybrid and virtual settings is maintaining smooth interaction between the actual and virtual worlds. In these contexts, robots must be able to properly sense and navigate both real and virtual areas. This necessitates cutting-edge sensor technology like LiDAR and depth cameras, as well as sophisticated sensor fusion and perception algorithms.

An additional obstacle is assuring the safety of both robots and people in these settings. Robots working in hybrid and virtual settings must be able to recognize and avoid physical and virtual impediments in order to avoid collisions. Furthermore, robots must be able to interact securely with people, necessitating the discovery of reliable and readily apparent human-robot interaction strategies. Robots functioning in these surroundings must be able to plan and carry out complicated activities that need interaction with both physical and virtual components.

Figure 5. Challenges of using robots in hybrid and virtual events

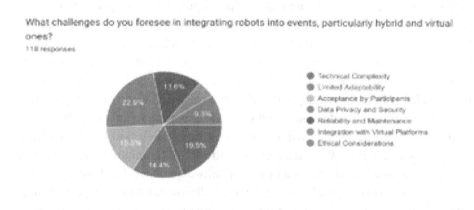

(*Source: author's observations and findings of the study)

In order to solve these problems, researchers are creating new technologies and methodologies that attempt to increase robot capabilities in hybrid and virtual settings. Researchers, for example, are looking at using machine learning and artificial intelligence approaches to improve robot vision and decision-making in these settings. Furthermore, researchers are working on novel sensor technologies, such as touch sensors and 3D cameras, to increase robot sensing.

The Tasks or Roles Performed by Robots at Events

Robots are already playing critical roles in improving the attendance experience, optimizing operations, and expanding the bounds of event management. Improving engagement and interaction is one of the major responsibilities that robots do at hybrid and virtual events. Robots are outfitted with powerful Artificial Intelligence (AI) and Natural Language Processing capabilities, permitting them to interact with guests in meaningful ways. Humanoid robots, for example, can function as virtual hosts, leading guests through the event agenda, answering questions, and making tailored recommendations based on their interests.

Robots also help to streamline event management activities. Robots automate a variety of duties, including registration and check-in, logistics, and crowd management, lowering the workload of event organizers and workers. Automated registration and check-in systems, which use robotic technology, speed up the admission process, reduce waits, and increase attendance satisfaction. Furthermore, robots outfitted with sensors and cameras can monitor crowd density and flow, allowing event organizers to maximize space use and provide attendees with a seamless event experience, whether they are there in person or digitally.

Robots are progressively being used as virtual presenters and performers at online celebrations, pushing the envelope of originality and innovation. These robots, which frequently have expressive facial features and lifelike motions, give lectures, conduct panels, and even execute creative performances, blurring the line between human and machine. Robots also play a crucial part in hybrid and virtual events through delivering technical support and logistical help. Virtual event platforms frequently use AI-powered Chatbots and active supporters to answer participants' technical queries and handle difficulties in real time. These intelligent solutions may help guests navigate the virtual event platform, fix common issues, and give on-demand support, improving the entire attendance experience. Furthermore, robots with remote diagnostic capabilities may remotely discover and resolve technological faults, reducing interruptions and assuring the smooth operation of virtual events.

Figure 6. The tasks or roles performed by robots in hybrid and virtual events

Identify the types of tasks or roles do you think robots could perform effectively at events?
118 responses

● Information Provider
● Assisting attendees
● Security Patrol
● Entertainment Performer
● Technical Support
● Language Interpreter

(*Source: author's observations and findings of the study)

From increasing engagement and involvement to improving event management operations and offering technical assistance, robots help modern events be more efficient, innovative, and dynamic. As technology advances, incorporating robots into events creates limitless possibilities for innovation, personalization, and immersive experiences. The notion of human-machine interaction has attracted a lot to get noticed over the past few decades as a method of attaining blended mechanization in industrial production. When used in assemblage, the requirement for being adaptable, flexible while remaining secure renders constructing and upgrading Human Robot Collaborative (HRC) structures a challenging and susceptible to mistakes task. The employing of time-sensitive perpetual modelling helps create an appropriate online setting for verification and evaluation, making it easier to put together intricate HRC systems.

Conventional simulators, on the other hand, do not provide an immersive environment for end users to experience the future production system. Research investigations were done to investigate the technical advancements in VR for the creation of personalized manufacturing platforms, and an identical structure was built to connect robotic interaction with human beings. The VR replication, which is event-driven, assisted in calculating human-robot sequence intervals, establishing course tactics, outline appraisal, and android regulator plans (Malik & Brem, 2021).

The use of robots into hybrid and virtual events is expected to have a disruptive impact, giving new potential for involvement, efficiency, and innovation. With the continued growth of technology, it is likely that the events industry will shift toward interactive, tailored, and technology-driven experiences.

Strategic Measures to Enhance Virtual Experiences

Instructional sessions for professionals and business executives are encouraged to identify standards of excellence, possibilities and impediments to marketing, as well as to arrange virtual and hybrid meetings (Sox, Crews & Kline, 2014). Best practice guidelines for virtual meetings included collaborating with conference organizers, adding immersive practices, and as well as active professionals. Despite the momentum generated by the COVID-19 epidemic, the event industry, particularly in rural places, has been a idle user of AI, which might contribute an impact on its foreseeable productivity. An entirely novel Exhibition Sector Readiness (ESR) for the artificial intelligence Implementation framework has been proposed (Hradecky, D., et al., 2022) which managers and researchers might utilize to investigate obstacles and drivers for adoption of artificial intelligence (AI), that has been complemented for the current challenges affecting the expo organizing industry.

Numerous researchers were interested in exploring the implication of Artificial Intelligence (AI) in improving the adaptability of industrial operations at the time of COVID-19 pandemic. Similarly, another accomplishment to assist the model based on the combined *Voting Analytical Hierarchy Process* (VAHP) and *Bayesian Network* (BN) method is formed (Dohale, V., et al., 2022). The increasing number of hybrid event forms after the epidemic, such as discussions, agreements, and training sessions, increases attendance' resistance and approachability. To eliminate the disparity, the losconCircles technique integrates collaborative education groups with a merged plan structure. The losconCircles encouraged new relationships, social engagement, and, to an approximate range, collective training among virtual and on-site partakers (Hartmann, 2023).

Recent Advances in Competent Robot Integration in Hybrid and Virtual Events

Robots are being used more and more to improve the recreational value as well as effectiveness of tourism events, especially hybrid (in-person and virtual) and online instances. Robotics in tourism has gained in popularity, providing novel ways to optimize guest experiences, increase functionality, and assure stability. Several case studies have proven and emphasized the productive utilization of robots in hybrid and virtual tourism events. These case studies cover all elements of tourism, from dealing with clients to virtual tours, showcasing the adaptability and influence of robotic technology.

Figure 7. Robotic integration in hybrid and virtual events: Review analysis

Sl. No.	Case-Study	Robotic Implementation	Success Factors	Challenges
1.	Tokyo 2020 Olympics (Russo, E., et.al., 2022)	Robot as guides and also offering hospitality service	Enhanced experience and operational efficiency, remote presence	High cost, technical complexities
2.	Expo 2020 Dubai (Mahanta & Lele, 2022)	Robot as ambassadors, virtual tours guides, offer sanitization assistance	Interactive engagement, safety and hygiene	Integration with existing systems, user acceptance
3.	Seoul Lantern Festival, South Korea (Park, J. S., et.al., 2023; Shih, N. J., et.al., 2020)	Virtual Tour Guides	High-definition video and interactive features, exhibition of cultural and historical legacies	Wide-coverage of festival's distinctiveness, Dissemination of information
4.	Smithsonian National Museum of Natural History, USA (Jadán-Guerrero, et.al., 2023)	Remote-controlled Robot Guides	Telepresence robots to explore exhibits, web interface, accessibility for people with disabilities, educational outreach	Connectivity problems, High initial setup costs
5.	Henn-na Hotel, Japan (Fusté-Forné & Jamal, 2021)	Robots as Receptionists, room service assistants, supporting virtual tours	Contactless service, innovative marketing activities	Maintenance issues, potential over-reliance on technology
6.	ITB Berlin (International Tourism Exchange), Germany (Tempel, P., et.al., 2015; Tuomi, 2021)	Giant cable-driven parallel robots; Humanoid robots (Pepper by SoftBank Robotics)	To greet attendees, provide information, assist with navigation, high interactivity, Streamlined event management	Integration with existing event management systems, High costs of deployment and maintenance.

(*Source: author's observations and findings of the study)

All case examples (Figure 7) emphasize the significance of sophisticated robotics and AI in delivering hassle-free and stimulating experiences. Tokyo's hotel robots provide hospitality services, Korea's virtual tour guides prioritize real-time involvement and Singapore's event robots facilitate hybrid encounters. Robots greatly improve the client's experience by offering competent, customized, and participatory services. This is obvious in Tokyo's hospitality services, Korea's cultural demonstrations, and Singapore's hybrid event experiences. Health and safety have been top priorities, particularly during the outbreak of the disease. Tokyo's contactless services and Singapore's hybrid approach both eliminate physical encounters, which successfully addresses health issues. South Korea's remote tourism program and Singapore's hybrid events demonstrate robots' effectiveness in enabling tourism and events readily available and entertaining to a worldwide audience.

Looking into the aforementioned case studies reveals that robots play a substantial part in revolutionizing the hospitality industry by providing scalable and adaptive solutions for emerging issues and possibilities. Perpetual creativity and revisions are required to retain functionality and appropriateness. While connected to integration and cultural difficulties should be dealt with, the commendable results and concerns obtained through these case studies offer beneficial perspectives for future visitors' implications. The tourism industry can use robotics to generate inventive, enticing, and secured confronts for both hybrid and virtual events by encompassing approaches such as the adoption of advanced technologies, upgraded customer interaction, an organized approach to carrying out health and safety measures, modified and refined ways to make things easier, and further development.

Futuristic Outlook of Using Robots in Hybrid and Virtual Settings

Conventional event planning has evolved in recent years in response to new technology, and we are now existing in an age of digitalised environment, that utilize conventional celebrations with novel technologies such as live telecasting. Online seminars and coaching sessions have also turn out to be ubiquitous; the near-term prospects is in the virtual environment (Pakarinen & Hoods, 2018). Virtual reality, artificial intelligence, and holograms are now being explored in a variety of businesses. Attendees, speakers, and organizers are the primary stakeholders in the event industry.

Figure 8. Expected functionalities of robots in event experience

(*Source: author's observations and findings of the study)

This study design provides a systematic method for conducting a detailed examination of the introduction of robots into hybrid and virtual events. Modifications may be necessary based on the conditions, available resources, and desired goals of the study. Recent research has advocated an innovative immersive environment known as Data-Space, that incorporates a novel grouping of assorted technology and techniques of interface to create a improved collaborative workplace (Cavallo, M., et al., 2019). In particular, the setting provided a unique interactive environment in addition to AR and VR technologies, allowing for the presentation of complicated sorts of data and alleviating the scaling limitations of existing immersive experiences.

In an age where technological advances effortlessly reconcile into our everyday routines, the amalgamation of physical and digital encounters has become a growing trend. This tendency, known as the "phygital" age, is altering industries everywhere, including business events (Bevolo & Amati, 2024). Understanding and embracing the notion of physical experiences is becoming increasingly important as organizations attempt to engage with their consumers in meaningful ways while adjusting to a quickly changing market. "Phygital" refers to the combination of physical and digital components in an event or festival to produce immersive and engaging experiences (Jia, S., 2023). The task reflects a comprehensive strategy that takes advantage of the characteristics of both domains to improve participation, accessibility, and creativity. Phygital experiences blur the distinction between offline and online interactions, providing participants with a continuous journey across numerous touchpoints. To what extent utilizing Augmented Reality (AR), Virtual Reality (VR), live-telecast, or collaborative digital platforms, the goal is to deliver a unified and fulfilling experience that breaks free from traditional boundaries.

CONCLUSION

The coronavirus illness pandemic has had a substantial influence on almost every aspect of human existence since its inception in 2020. Individuals are becoming more addicted to virtual worlds online to make up for the dearth of face-to-face connection, with advantages like as increased inclusion and connectivity, in addition to a smaller carbon footprint. However, emerging web technologies are unable to completely substitute live intellectual gatherings. Meetings held in person are unaffected by poor Internet connectivity and provide new opportunities for connection, teamwork, and shared thoughts. To maintain such activities, a hybrid model for methodical events that includes both in-person and virtual components may be an option (Hanaei, S., et al., 2022). Even though attendees have the flexibility to select how they participate, virtual meetings would be most beneficial to those who are unable to attend in-person owing to constraints.

Festivals, exclusive occasions, and exhibitions are examples of a location's rich cultural assets that enable it to successfully accommodate tourists. Many organizations and towns throughout the world arrange and promote unique events to establish a favourable image of the location while also raising funds for the local community (Backman, K. F., et al., 1995). Although there has been much study on the economic impact of location-specific festivities, nothing has been carried out at the local or regional level to investigate event motives and activities.

Hybrid Intelligence, often known as Human-AI (Artificial Intelligence) cooperation, is an idea that balances the competences of manpower and AI to produce better values than each could do without help (Hemmer, P., 2021). Hybrid intelligence has the potential to significantly improve consumer experience and customization in event promotion. AI can give insights by analyzing consumer data, preferences, and behavior, whereas human judgment may be utilized to develop pertinent and interesting information, recommendations, and collaboration for festivals and other occasions (Haleem, A., et al., 2022). This partnership enables a more personal and individualized approach to event promotion.

Because AI is capable of automating processes, enhance choices, and give perspectives (Huang & Rust, 2022), Hybrid Intelligence knowledge is critical for establishing strategies, analyzing outcomes, and causing achievement. This teamwork leads to well-organized and successful supervision of promotional campaign (Davenport & Ronanki, 2018). Hybrid intelligence can also help handle confidentiality of information and moral encounters (Petrescu & Krishen, 2023). Artificial intelligence may be utilized to comply with event rules, safeguard consumer facts, and identify deception, but anthropological standards ought to assure openness, responsibility, and conviction. This grouping assures that event campaign performs adhere to moral standards and comply with confidentiality requirements. Working together between human intelligence and artificial intelligence provides major benefits to the event marketing area. Event marketing tactics, campaign success, and customer relationships may be improved by integrating mankind perception and inventiveness with AI's computing assistances (Soni, 2023). Hybrid intelligence is a strong idea that has the possibility to convert event marketing, thus it is hazardous to investigate its returns and problems for publicizing tactics and logical aspects.

MICE Tourism produces foreign cash, reassures business and venture, generates occupations, strengthens home-grown financial prudence, and encourages local destinations (Disimulacion, 2020). The key to its attainment is restrictive partnerships with a wide range of interest groups in the traveling, lodging establishment, and recreational businesses who supply facilities and expertise. As a consequence, any disruption to its manufacturing process could culminate in substantial monetary damages for all parties, ranging from administrators, respondents, vendors, investors, and the host communities.

REFERENCES

Aksentyeva, N., Aminov, D. S., Cayenne, J., Foo, J., Kammogne, G., Lum, A., & Zhou, H. (2020). Technology Use in Meetings. NIH.

Al Fararni, K., Nafis, F., Aghoutane, B., Yahyaouy, A., Riffi, J., & Sabri, A. (2021). Hybrid recommender system for tourism based on big data and AI: A conceptual framework. *Big Data Mining and Analytics*, 4(1), 47–55. 10.26599/BDMA.2020.9020015

Alananzeh, O. A. (2022). Drivers and Challenges for Future Events and their Impact on Hotel Industry. *African Journal of Hospitality, Tourism and Leisure*, 11(3), 1273–1287.

Alroy, A., Ben-Shushan, E., & Katz, B. (2022). *Event Success: Maximizing the Business Impact of In-person, Virtual, and Hybrid Experiences*. John Wiley & Sons.

Andronas, D., Kampourakis, E., Papadopoulos, G., Bakopoulou, K., Kotsaris, P. S., Michalos, G., & Makris, S. (2023). Towards seamless collaboration of humans and high-payload robots: An automotive case study. *Robotics and Computer-integrated Manufacturing*, 83, 102544. 10.1016/j.rcim.2023.102544

Atzori, L., Iera, A., & Morabito, G. (2017). Understanding the Internet of Things: Definition, potentials, and societal role of a fast-evolving paradigm. *Ad Hoc Networks*, 56, 122–140. 10.1016/j.adhoc.2016.12.004

Backman, K. F., Backman, S. J., Uysal, M., & Sunshine, K. M. (1995). Event tourism: An examination of motivations and activities. *Festival Management & Event Tourism*, 3(1), 15–24.

Batth, R. S., Nayyar, A., & Nagpal, A. (2018, August). Internet of robotic things: driving intelligent robotics of future-concept, architecture, applications and technologies. In *2018 4th international conference on computing sciences (ICCS)* (pp. 151-160). IEEE. 10.1109/ICCS.2018.00033

Behringer, W. (2006). Communications revolutions: A historiographical concept. *German History*, 24(3), 333–374. 10.1191/0266355406gh378oa

Bevolo, M., & Amati, F. (2024). The future of business events in the "phygital" age: development of a generative tool: A qualitative research project combining Design Research and foresight principles to co-design and develop a futures matrix for potential implementation by business event designers and managers. *World Leisure Journal*, 66(1), 92–115. 10.1080/16078055.2023.2238275

Bignell, J., & Fickers, A. (Eds.). (2008). *A European television history.* Wiley-Blackwell.

Bladen, C., Kennell, J., Abson, E., & Wilde, N. (2022). *Events management: An introduction.* Routledge. 10.4324/9781003102878

Boshnakova, D., & Goldblatt, J. (2017). *The 21st century meeting and event Technologies: Powerful tools for better planning, marketing, and evaluation.* CRC Press.

BR, S. R. (2022). Information and communication technology application in tourism events, fairs and festivals in India. *Technology Application in Tourism Fairs, Festivals and Events in Asia, 209.*

Campbell, M., Greated, C. A., & Myers, A. (2004). *Musical instruments: history, technology, and performance of instruments of western music.* OUP Oxford. 10.1093/acprof:oso/9780198165040.001.0001

Cavallo, M., Dholakia, M., Havlena, M., Ocheltree, K., & Podlaseck, M. (2019, March). Dataspace: A reconfigurable hybrid reality environment for collaborative information analysis. In *2019 IEEE conference on virtual reality and 3D user interfaces (VR)* (pp. 145-153). IEEE. 10.1109/VR.2019.8797733

Cobanoglu, C., Doğan, S., & Güngör, M. Y. (2021). Emerging technologies at the events. In *Impact of ICTs on Event Management and Marketing* (pp. 53–68). IGI Global. 10.4018/978-1-7998-4954-4.ch004

Cudny, W. (2014). The phenomenon of festivals: Their origins, evolution, and classifications. *Anthropos*, (H. 2), 640-656.

da Silva, M. P. (2021). *The Age of Hybrid Events: Amplifying the Power of Culture Through Digital Experiences (Music Festivals Feat. Technology)* [Doctoral dissertation, Instituto Politecnico do Porto, Portugal].

Dagnaw, G. (2020). *Artificial intelligence towards future industrial opportunities and challenges.*

Dalgic, A., & Birdir, K. (2021). Which Key Factors Will Be Effective in the Success of Festivals?: An Evaluation in the Context of Information and Communication Technology. In *Impact of ICTs on Event Management and Marketing* (pp. 1-17). IGI Global.

Davenport, T. H., & Ronanki, R. (2018). Artificial intelligence for the real world. *Harvard Business Review*, 96(1), 108–116.

Diestro Mandros, J., Garcia Mercado, R., & Bayona-Oré, S. (2021). Virtual reality and tourism: visiting Machu Picchu. In *New Perspectives in Software Engineering:Proceedings of the 9th International Conference on Software Process Improvement (CIMPS 2020)* (pp. 269-279). Springer International Publishing. 10.1007/978-3-030-63329-5_18

Disimulacion, M. A. T. (2020). MICE tourism during Covid-19 and future directions for the new normal. *Asia Pacific International Events Management Journal*, 1(2), 11–17.

Dohale, V., Akarte, M., Gunasekaran, A., & Verma, P. (2022). Exploring the role of artificial intelligence in building production resilience: Learnings from the COVID-19 pandemic. *International Journal of Production Research*, 1–17.

Dowson, R., Albert, B., & Lomax, D. (2022). *Event planning and management: Principles, planning and practice*. Kogan Page Publishers.

Estanyol, E. (2022). Traditional festivals and COVID-19: Event management and digitalization in times of physical distancing. *Event Management*, 26(3), 647–659. 10.3727/152599521X16288665119305

Feulner, S., Sedlmeir, J., Schlatt, V., & Urbach, N. (2022). Exploring the use of self-sovereign identity for event ticketing systems. *Electronic Markets*, 32(3), 1759–1777. 10.1007/s12525-022-00573-935965736

Fremdling, R. (1997). Industrial revolution and scientific and technological progress. *Jahrbuch für Wirtschaftsgeschichte/Economic History Yearbook, 38*(2), 147-168.

Fusté-Forné, F., & Jamal, T. (2021). Co-creating new directions for service robots in hospitality and tourism. *Tourism and Hospitality*, 2(1), 43–61. 10.3390/tourhosp2010003

Glennie, P., & Thrift, N. (2009). *Shaping the day: a history of timekeeping in England and Wales 1300-1800*. OUP Oxford. 10.1093/acprof:oso/9780199278206.001.0001

Goldblatt, J. (2010). *Special events: A new generation and the next frontier* (Vol. 13). John Wiley & Sons.

Haleem, A., Javaid, M., Qadri, M. A., Singh, R. P., & Suman, R. (2022). Artificial intelligence (AI) applications for marketing: A literature-based study. *International Journal of Intelligent Networks*, 3, 119–132. 10.1016/j.ijin.2022.08.005

Hall, M. A. (2015). *Radio After Radio: Redefining radio art in the light of new media technology through expanded practice* [Doctoral dissertation, University of the Arts London].

Han, D. I. D., Weber, J., Bastiaansen, M., Mitas, O., & Lub, X. (2019). Virtual and augmented reality technologies to enhance the visitor experience in cultural tourism. *Augmented reality and virtual reality: The power of AR and VR for business*, 113-128.

Hanaei, S., Takian, A., Majdzadeh, R., Maboloc, C. R., Grossmann, I., Gomes, O., Milosevic, M., Gupta, M., Shamshirsaz, A. A., Harbi, A., Burhan, A. M., Uddin, L. Q., Kulasinghe, A., Lam, C.-M., Ramakrishna, S., Alavi, A., Nouwen, J. L., Dorigo, T., Schreiber, M., & Rezaei, N. (2022). Emerging standards and the hybrid model for organizing scientific events during and after the COVID-19 pandemic. *Disaster Medicine and Public Health Preparedness*, 16(3), 1172–1177. 10.1017/dmp.2020.40633100253

Hartmann, I. (2023). *Bridging the hybridity gap: connecting online and onsite participants through peer learning circles at hybrid events.*

Hashimoto, S. (2022). Technology Application in the Asian Tourism Industry: The Future. In *Handbook of Technology Application in Tourism in Asia* (pp. 1299–1310). Springer Nature Singapore. 10.1007/978-981-16-2210-6_59

Heaton, H. (2017). Industrial revolution. In *The causes of the industrial revolution in England* (pp. 31–52). Routledge. 10.4324/9781315172163-2

Hemmer, P., Schemmer, M., Vössing, M., & Kühl, N. (2021). Human-AI Complementarity in Hybrid Intelligence Systems: A Structured Literature Review. *PACIS*, 78.

Hernandez, F., Birke, J., & Bullinger, A. C. (2023, July). The Tribrid-Meeting-Setup–Improving Hybrid Meetings Using a Telepresence Robot. In *International Conference on Human-Computer Interaction* (pp. 347-361). Cham: Springer Nature Switzerland. 10.1007/978-3-031-34609-5_26

Hill, D. (2013). *A history of engineering in classical and medieval times*. Routledge. 10.4324/9781315800110

Hoggenmüller, M. (2022). *Urban Robotic Interfaces: Designing for Encounters with Non-Humanoid Robots in Cities* [Doctoral dissertation, The University of Sydney].

Hradecky, D., Kennell, J., Cai, W., & Davidson, R. (2022). Organizational readiness to adopt artificial intelligence in the exhibition sector in Western Europe. *International Journal of Information Management*, 65, 102497. 10.1016/j.ijinfomgt.2022.102497

Huang, M. H., & Rust, R. T. (2022). A framework for collaborative artificial intelligence in marketing. *Journal of Retailing*, 98(2), 209–223. 10.1016/j.jretai.2021.03.001

Huff, T. E. (2010). *Intellectual curiosity and the scientific revolution: a global perspective*. Cambridge University Press. 10.1017/CBO9780511782206

Hutson, J., & Hutson, P. (2024). Immersive Technologies. In *Inclusive Smart Museums: Engaging Neurodiverse Audiences and Enhancing Cultural Heritage* (pp. 153–228). Springer Nature Switzerland. 10.1007/978-3-031-43615-4_5

Jadán-Guerrero, J., Mendoza, M., & Alvites-Huamaní, C. (2023). Redefining the Museum Experiences in the Virtual Age. In *Intelligent Sustainable Systems: Selected Papers of WorldS4 2022* (Vol. 1, pp. 459–469). Springer Nature Singapore. 10.1007/978-981-19-7660-5_39

Jia, S., Chi, O. H., Martinez, S. D., & Lu, L. (2023). When "Old" Meets "New": Unlocking the Future of Innovative Technology Implementation in Heritage Tourism. *Journal of Hospitality & Tourism Research (Washington, D.C.)*, 10963480231205767. 10.1177/10963480231205767

Jones, M. (2017). *Sustainable event management: A practical guide.* Routledge. 10.4324/9781315439723

Karaca, Y., Derias, D., & Sarsar, G. (2023). AI-Powered Procedural Content Generation: Enhancing NPC Behaviour for an Immersive Gaming Experience. *Available at SSRN* 4663382. 10.31234/osf.io/8pt4q

Mahanta, N. R., & Lele, S. (2022). Evolving Trends of Artificial Intelligence and Robotics in Smart City Applications: Crafting Humane Built Environment. *Trust-Based Communication Systems for Internet of Things Applications*, 195-241.

Malik, A. A., & Brem, A. (2021). Digital twins for collaborative robots: A case study in human-robot interaction. *Robotics and Computer-integrated Manufacturing*, 68, 102092. 10.1016/j.rcim.2020.102092

Malik, A. A., Masood, T., & Bilberg, A. (2020). Virtual reality in manufacturing: Immersive and collaborative artificial-reality in design of human-robot workspace. *International Journal of Computer Integrated Manufacturing*, 33(1), 22–37. 10.1080/0951192X.2019.1690685

Martin, V., & Cazarré, L. (2016). *Technology and Events: Organizing an engaging event.* Goodfellow Publishers Ltd.

Morey, Y., Bengry-Howell, A., Griffin, C., Szmigin, I., & Riley, S. (2016). Festivals 2.0: Consuming, producing and participating in the extended festival experience. In *The festivalization of culture* (pp. 251-268). Routledge.

Mulder, J. (2013). *Making things louder: Amplified music and multimodality* [Doctoral dissertation, OPUS].

Ogle, A., & Lamb, D. (2019). The role of robots, artificial intelligence, and service automation in events. In *Robots, artificial intelligence, and service automation in travel, tourism and hospitality* (pp. 255–269). Emerald Publishing Limited. 10.11 08/978-1-78756-687-320191012

Pakarinen, T., & Hoods, J. (2018). *From hybrid events to the next generation-interactive virtual events: Viewed from three different stakeholders' point of view.* Research Gate.

Palmer, M. (2005). Industrial archaeology: Constructing a framework of inference. In *Industrial archaeology: Future directions* (pp. 59–75). Springer US. 10.1007/0-387-22831-4_3

Park, J. S., Kim, K. H., Hong, J., Jeong, S. H., Kim, S. D., Nduhura, D., & Mumporeze, N. (2023). *ICT Innovation and Korean Society: Industry*. Media, and Culture.

Pearlman, D. M., & Gates, N. A. (2010, November). Hosting business meetings and special events in virtual worlds: A fad or the future? [). Taylor & Francis Group.]. *Journal of Convention & Event Tourism*, 11(4), 247–265. 10.1080/15470148.2010.530535

Petrescu, M., & Krishen, A. S. (2023). Hybrid intelligence: human–AI collaboration in marketing analytics. *Journal of Marketing Analytics*, 11(3), 263–274. 10.1057/s41270-023-00245-3

Pilipczuk, O. (2021). A Conceptual Framework for Large-Scale Event Perception Evaluation with Spatial-Temporal Scales in Sustainable Smart Cities. *Sustainability (Basel)*, 13(10), 5658. 10.3390/su13105658

Quinn, B. (2009). Festivals, events and tourism. *The SAGE handbook of tourism studies*, 483-503. Sage.

Ramos, C. M., Henriques, C., & Lanquar, R. (2016). Augmented reality for smart tourism in religious heritage itineraries: Tourism experiences in the technological age. In *Handbook of research on human-computer interfaces, developments, and applications* (pp. 245–272). IGI Global. 10.4018/978-1-5225-0435-1.ch010

Richert, A., Shehadeh, M. A., Müller, S. L., Schröder, S., & Jeschke, S. (2016, July). Socializing with robots: Human-robot interactions within a virtual environment. In *2016 IEEE Workshop on Advanced Robotics and its Social Impacts (ARSO)* (pp. 49-54). IEEE. 10.1109/ARSO.2016.7736255

Rieple, A., DeFillippi, R., & Schreiber, D. (2023). Trans formational Innovation in Ephemeral Experiences. *Transformational Innovation in the Creative and Cultural Industries*, 152.

Russo, E., Figueira, A. R., & Kogut, C. S., & Mello, R. D. C. D. (2022). The Tokyo 2020 Olympic Games: Impacts of COVID-19 and digital transformation. *Cadernos EBAPE.BR*, 20, 318–332. 10.1590/1679-395120210150

Ryan, W. G., Fenton, A., Ahmed, W., & Scarf, P. (2020). Recognizing events 4.0: The digital maturity of events. *International Journal of Event and Festival Management*, 11(1), 47–68. 10.1108/IJEFM-12-2019-0060

Schipper, F. (2008). *Driving Europe: Building Europe on roads in the twentieth century* (Vol. 3). Amsterdam University Press.

Shih, C. (2010). *The Facebook era: Tapping online social networks to market, sell, and innovate*. Pearson Education.

Shih, N. J., Diao, P. H., Qiu, Y. T., & Chen, T. Y. (2020). Situated ar simulations of a lantern festival using a smartphone and lidar-based 3d models. *Applied Sciences (Basel, Switzerland)*, 11(1), 12. 10.3390/app11010012

Slocum, S. L., & Lee, S. (2014). Green ICT practices in event management: Case study approach to examine motivation, management and fiscal return on investment. *Information Technology & Tourism*, 14(4), 347–362. 10.1007/s40558-014-0019-3

Smil, V. (2005). *Creating the twentieth century: Technical innovations of 1867-1914 and their lasting impact*. Oxford University Press. 10.1093/0195168747.001.0001

Soni, V. (2023). Adopting Generative AI in Digital Marketing Campaigns: An Empirical Study of Drivers and Barriers. *Sage Science Review of Applied Machine Learning*, 6(8), 1–15.

Sox, C. B., Crews, T. B., & Kline, S. F. (2014, April). Virtual and hybrid meetings for generation X: Using the Delphi method to determine best practices, opportunities, and barriers. []. Routledge.]. *Journal of Convention & Event Tourism*, 15(2), 150–169. 10.1080/15470148.2014.896231

Spracklen, K. (2015). *Digital leisure, the internet and popular culture: Communities and identities in a digital age*. Springer. 10.1057/9781137405876

Strohm, R. (2005). *The rise of European music, 1380-1500*. Cambridge University Press.

Tempel, P., Schnelle, F., Pott, A., & Eberhard, P. (2015). Design and programming for cable-driven parallel robots in the German Pavilion at the EXPO 2015. *Machines (Basel)*, 3(3), 223–241. 10.3390/machines3030223

Thomson, A., Proud, I., Goldston, A. L., & Dodds-Gorman, R. (2021). Virtual reality for better event planning and management. In *Impact of ICTs on event management and marketing* (pp. 177–198). IGI Global. 10.4018/978-1-7998-4954-4.ch011

Tuomi, A. I. (2021). *Designing Restaurants of the Future: Integrating Robots into Hospitality Service* [Doctoral dissertation, University of Surrey].

Valipour, M., Krasilnikof, J., Yannopoulos, S., Kumar, R., Deng, J., Roccaro, P., Mays, L., Grismer, M. E., & Angelakis, A. N. (2020). The evolution of agricultural drainage from the earliest times to the present. *Sustainability (Basel)*, 12(1), 416. 10.3390/su12010416

Van Winkle, C., & Bueddefeld, J. (2020). Information and communication technology in event management. *Handbook of e-Tourism*, 1-22.

Wang, Y. C., & Uysal, M. (2024). Artificial intelligence-assisted mindfulness in tourism, hospitality, and events. *International Journal of Contemporary Hospitality Management*, 36(4), 1262–1278. 10.1108/IJCHM-11-2022-1444

Wenzlhuemer, R. (2013). *Connecting the nineteenth-century world: The telegraph and globalization*. Cambridge University Press.

Westera, W., Prada, R., Mascarenhas, S., Santos, P. A., Dias, J., Guimarães, M., Georgiadis, K., Nyamsuren, E., Bahreini, K., Yumak, Z., Christyowidiasmoro, C., Dascalu, M., Gutu-Robu, G., & Ruseti, S. (2020). Artificial intelligence moving serious gaming: Presenting reusable game AI components. *Education and Information Technologies*, 25(1), 351–380. 10.1007/s10639-019-09968-2

Xie, T., Wang, X., Cifuentes-Faura, J., & Xing, Y. (2023). Integrating immersive experience into hybrid education: A case study in fintech experimental education. *Scientific Reports*, 13(1), 22762. 10.1038/s41598-023-50259-138123646

Xie, X., Siau, K., & Nah, F. F. H. (2020). COVID-19 pandemic–online education in the new normal and the next normal. *Journal of information technology case and application research, 22*(3), 175-187.

Yen, T. H., Wey, P. S., & Sullivan, K. (2016, May). Classification of Event and Meeting Technology. In *International Interdisciplinary Business-Economics Advancement Conference* (p. 88).

Yeoman, I., Robertson, M., & Smith, K. (2014). A futurist's view on the future of events. In *The Routledge handbook of events* (pp. 518–536). Routledge.

Zagorski-Thomas, S. (2016). The Influence of Recording Technology and Practice on Popular Music Performance in the Recording Studio in Poland between 1960-1989. *Polish Sociological Review*, 196(4), 531–548.

Zhao, Z., Ma, Y., Mushtaq, A., Rajper, A. M. A., Shehab, M., Heybourne, A., Song, W., Ren, H., & Tse, Z. T. H. (2022). Applications of robotics, artificial intelligence, and digital technologies during COVID-19: A review. *Disaster Medicine and Public Health Preparedness*, 16(4), 1634–1644. 10.1017/dmp.2021.933413717

Chapter 3
Exploring the Use of Virtual and Hybrid Events for MICE Sector:
Trends and Opportunities

Amrik Singh
https://orcid.org/0000-0003-3598-8787
Lovely Professional University, Punjab, India

Mildred Nuong Deri
https://orcid.org/0000-0003-1564-4880
University of Energy and Natural Resources, Ghana

ABSTRACT

COVID-19 has fast-tracked the transition to the virtual environment in the global meetings, incentives, conference/convention, and exhibition (MICE) events sector. The present research explores the use of virtual and hybrid events in enhancing the resilience of MICE events. Additionally, these events were found to be essential for information sharing and proved valuable in times of uncertainty. This chapter focuses on how these events provided substantial market opportunities for MICE stakeholders globally. Moreover, several challenges surfaced when hosting such events, including the matter of internet connectivity and the significant capital investments required for their execution. Virtual and hybrid events have emerged as a valuable tool for enhancing the resilience of MICE events to crises, and hybrid events are postulated to become a prominent feature in MICE events offerings in the future. This study focuses on how events provided substantial market opportunities for MICE stakeholders in the country by exploring the opportunities and challenges for MICE sector. Utilizing secondary information available, the study drew conclusions, implications and recommendations are given.

DOI: 10.4018/979-8-3693-2272-7.ch003

INTRODUCTION AND BACKGROUND

In an era shaped by unprecedented challenges and dynamic changes, the landscape of Meetings, Incentives, Conferences, and Exhibitions (MICE) events has undergone a profound evolution. The integration of virtual and hybrid events has emerged not just as a response to global disruptions but as a transformative strategy to enhance the resilience of MICE initiatives. Virtual and hybrid events offer a robust framework that transcends geographical boundaries, enabling seamless connectivity and participation from diverse global audiences. By leveraging advanced digital platforms, these formats empower organizers to adapt swiftly to uncertainties, ensuring continuity and engagement even amidst unpredictable circumstances.

However, virtual and hybrid events amplify accessibility, fostering inclusivity by accommodating varied preferences and needs of participants. They provide flexibility in attendance, allowing individuals to join remotely without compromising on the quality of interaction or content delivery. This versatility not only broadens the reach of MICE events but also enriches the overall attendee experience through personalized engagement opportunities. These innovative event formats promote sustainability by reducing carbon footprints associated with travel and logistics, aligning with global efforts towards eco-conscious practices. They offer cost-effective solutions without compromising on the caliber of presentations or networking possibilities, thereby optimizing resource utilization and enhancing operational efficiencies. In essence, the strategic adoption of virtual and hybrid events represents a pivotal shift towards resilient MICE practices, capable of navigating uncertainties while fostering innovation and inclusivity. By embracing these technologies, organizers can future-proof their events, ensuring continuity, accessibility, and sustainability in an ever-evolving landscape.

Events are dynamic platforms that enable MICE stakeholders to generate revenue, expand their networks, enhance brand visibility, showcase expertise, stimulate local economies, foster innovation, and gain valuable market insights. By effectively leveraging these opportunities, stakeholders can maximize their impact and sustain long-term success in the competitive MICE industry.

Hybrid events are not something new, since they have existed for more than a decade, nor are they a simple anecdote, because their future is undeniable. They were discussed by all event professionals when the covid-19 pandemic changed the rules of the MICE sector. It is important first that we are clear about what hybrid events are NOT. They do not refer to the mere broadcasting of a face-to-face event so that other people can follow it online. Nor is it an event that takes place in different places simultaneously (multi-site event). A hybrid event is one that takes place in a physical venue with a limited number of in-person attendees and another part. The fundamental thing, therefore, to determine if an event is really hybrid, is that online attendees must have the opportunity to participate in the event in a way that is as close as possible to that of face-to-face attendees (Singh & Bathla, 2023; Sharma & Singh, 2024; Bhalla et al., 2023; Deri et al., 2024; Francis et al., 2024; Singh & Hassan, 2024). It is true that they will hardly participate in the catering of the event, for example, but technology advances so that there are more and more possibilities for them to interact just as any other attendee.

In other words, the line between face-to-face and online attendees is much more blurred in these types of events. In a hybrid event, all attendees can ask questions, vote, play games, arrange meetings, visit stands, read communications, complete tests, make a presentation, take part in a debate, etc., regardless of whether they are at the venue itself, at its home or in an office. The organizer is, therefore, with the great challenge of engagement (Singh & Bathla, 2023; Sharma & Singh, 2024; Bhalla et al., 2023; Deri et al., 2024; Francis et al., 2024; Singh & Hassan, 2024). Through their growth in the postmodern and capitalist-oriented economies, "meetings", all forms of MICE events (Meetings, Incentives, Conventions, Exhibitions) represent purely quantitative, ever more comprehensive, resource-consuming gatherings. Such a development does not only increase the complexity of the business gatherings in terms of their global economic importance, but also in terms of increasing CO_2 emissions.

In recent years there has been a response to this development and new potentials for a sustainable meeting industry has been created, driven also by the megatrend of digitalisation, and the innovations related to it. Although sustainability of meetings have already been discussed more from the perspective of environmentally friendly or resource-conserving use (Singh & Bathla, 2023; Sharma & Singh, 2024; Bhalla et al., 2023; Deri et al., 2024; Francis et al., 2024; Singh & Hassan, 2024).

The technological innovation in web-based applications, platforms and mobile applications, have changed the business event industry, specifically meetings and conferences, enabling event professionals to create more meaningful event experiences, reach wider audiences and increase returns on investment. The research discusses the context of business events in relation to the evolution, development and benefits of virtual and hybrid events. It particularly examines the impact of COVID-19 on the event industry and the responding pivot to online events with designing virtual and hybrid experiences. It posits that hybrid events will be a cornerstone of this new event landscape, providing a lifeline for event professionals and increasing the sustainable practices with green shoots that provide some optimism for the future of the event industry.

Despite, there is a gap in the academic perspective and lack of research on virtual events and particularly hybrid events, the research methodology examine and explore the benefits and best practice approaches for this new event context, that discussed as emerging from the pandemic crisis. As a result of the rapid spread of the Coronavirus pandemic across the globe in early 2020, all governments worldwide implemented strict measures to limit the movements of their populations to prevent and limit increase in infections. These restrictions included regional and national lockdownswhich severely restricted personal activities, with all but essential workers urged to work remotely from home, schools and universities closed and moved online. Many businesses and economies were affected by the lockdowns, travel, tourism, hospitality, and event industry most severely affected with collapse of international travel and tourism (Maga.C., 2020; Singh & Bathla, 2023; Sharma & Singh, 2024; Bhalla et al., 2023; Deri et al., 2024; Francis et al., 2024; Singh & Hassan, 2024).

The traveling for Meetings, Incentives, Conferences and Exhibitions defined as MICE tourism and Events area global industry and in most places, events were postponed or cancelled following announcement of a health emergency that presents an existential crisis threatening lives and businesses around the world which may take years to recover. Further, events are considered as one of the biggest transmission sources of infectious disease Therefore, cancellation or postponement of the events is always mandatory decision when it comes to a pandemic situation (Ahmed & Memish,2020; McCloskey et al., 2020; Singh & Bathla, 2023; Sharma & Singh, 2024; Ansari & Singh, 2023).

Research suggests that the MICE sector plays a crucial role in the global economic recovery following the COVID-19 pandemic (International Congress and Convention Association [ICCA], 2020; Orthodoxou et al., 2022). This study focuses globally as identified as pivotal in the tourism development strategy (Rogerson, 2019). Globally, MICE stands out as a leading sector and holds a competitive position (Weru & Njoroge, 2021; Zhou, 2021). Furthermore, this sector is seen as instrumental in driving the recovery of tourism (Rogerson & Baum, 2020). Given its significance, it is essential to explore its accelerated development phase brought about by the pandemic.

This study aligns with the viewpoint of Sox et al. (2017) that ongoing research is necessary due to the emergence of rapidly evolving technological advancements in the MICE sector. Despite existing research on virtual and hybrid MICE events, the utilization of secondary data is limited. Hence, this study focuses on how events provided substantial market opportunities for MICE stakeholders globally by exploring the opportunities and challenges for MICE sector.

LITERATURE REVIEW

The MICE industry, which stands for Meetings, Incentives, Conferences, and Exhibitions, has witnessed a significant transformation in recent years. Technology has played a crucial role in elevating this industry by providing innovative solutions to enhance the overall experience of attendees and organisers. One of the most significant contributions of technology to the MICE industry is the introduction of virtual events (Bhalla et al., 2023; Deri et al., 2024; Francis et al., 2024; Singh & Hassan, 2024; Singh & Bathla, 2023; Ansari & Singh, 2023). Virtual events have gained immense popularity in recent times due to the Covid-19 pandemic, which has made it difficult to organise physical events. Virtual events have not only allowed organisers to reach a broader audience but have also reduced costs significantly. With the help of technology, virtual events can be as engaging and interactive as physical events. Attendees can participate in virtual events from the comfort of their homes and still have a personalised experience.

The importance of technology in the MICE industry cannot be overstated, as it has revolutionised the way events are organised and executed. MICE events are created in order to foster and drive business-to-business interactions, with the available literature showing that there are several reasons for the attendance of such events, including social networking, education and opportunities to learn new trends within a particular sector (Cassar et al., 2020; Huang, 2016; Jung & Tanford, 2017; Kim et al., 2020; Lee et al., 2010; Bhalla et al., 2023; Deri et al., 2024; Ansari & Singh, 2023; Francis et al., 2024; Singh & Hassan, 2024; Singh & Bathla, 2023). Henderson (2015) conceptualises MICE events as sites for social and intellectual activity. Networking is one of the most highly rated motivations for attending business events, with Jung and Tanford (2017) explaining how networking includes building professional relationships, interacting with colleagues, friends, and individuals in the same professional space, and seeking opportunities to grow careers.

Similarly, MICE events, particularly exhibitions and trade shows, have traditionally been places where major advancements and product developments have also been introduced (Lee et al., 2010; Rittichainuwat et al., 2020; Ansari & Singh, 2023; Tinnish & Mangal, 2012; Singh & Bathla, 2023; Sharma & Singh, 2024; Bhalla et al., 2023; Deri et al., 2024; Francis et al., 2024; Singh & Hassan, 2024). Huang (2016) continued to add that exhibitions also offer the opportunities for exhibitors to further extend their relationships with their clients. The past few decades have been marked by remarkable advancements in technological developments, particularly those related to information and technology (Locke, 2010; Shi et al., 2021; Sox et al., 2014). As a result, MICE event organizers have looked for ways to incorporate more technology into these events (Sox et al., 2014). Typically, the MICE sector has incorporated technology in event planning and staging, as well as in enhancing the attendees' experience pre, during, and post-the event (Simons, 2019; Solaris, 2018; Sox et al., 2014; Talantis et al., 2020; Tanford et al., 2012; Bhalla et al., 2023; Deri et al., 2024; Francis et al., 2024; Singh & Hassan, 2024). Regarding the former of the uses, Pearlman and Gates (2010) explained that technology offers organisers the ability to reduce costs, extend the event brand, build an event community and enable better tracking (of attendees) and data management. Regarding the event experience, research has slowly begun examining the use of virtual reality, augmented reality, and mobile applications and attendees' acceptance of such technologies (Ansari & Singh, 2023; Cassar et al., 2020; Locke, 2010; Simons, 2019; Talantis et al., 2020; Singh & Bathla, 2023; Sharma & Singh, 2024; Bhalla et al., 2023; Deri et al., 2024; Francis et al., 2024; Singh & Hassan, 2024). For a long time, technology had been used to enhance the in-person event experience (Chuang, 2020; Sox et al., 2014). As opined by Cassar et al. (2020) and Talantis et al. (2020), the inclusion of event technology has now become a differentiating factor that could enhance the competitiveness of the event and host destination.

Meetings

Meetings are usually a single-day event held in hotel conference rooms or at convention centres. They can vary in size from only a small group of senior executives to larger gatherings like annual shareholder meetings. The purpose is to bring together people from one company, industry, or project to address challenges, discuss plans, and set goals. Catering is often kept simple and there's rarely an entertainment program.

Incentives

Incentives are probably the most fun part of the MICE segment. They include all types of travel rewards a company offers to individual staff, teams, or partners (e.g. affiliates). In this context, the goal of an incentive is to thank people for their great performance, boost morale, or increase employee loyalty. Incentives can take different forms depending on the company organising them. Some may send their team for an all-inclusive weekend trip to an out-of-town resort. Others might plan a variety of activities closer to home to encourage staff to bond in an informal setting.

Conferences

Think of conferences as supersized meetings. They often last more than one day and can vary in size, but usually they have more attendees than meetings (Singh & Bathla, 2023; Sharma & Singh, 2024; Bhalla et al., 2023; Deri et al., 2024; Francis et al., 2024; Singh & Hassan, 2024). As with incentives, conferences can look very different depending on the organisers and the industry behind them.

Common activities at conferences include one, a mix, or all of the below:

- Panels: A group of experts discusses a topic and presents new findings. A moderator asks questions, ensures good flow, and may take questions from the audience.
- Presentations: At a company conference, senior leaders may present the latest successes or results of the business. At public industry conferences, thought leaders may be invited as guest speakers to share the newest trends and insights. Presentations often rely on props, slides, or other visual elements.
- Speeches: Also known as keynotes, speeches often mark the beginning or end of a conference. Sometimes it's the host or organiser welcoming or thanking attendees for joining. Other times an industry leader may address an important issue and share ideas for solutions.
- Discussions: They can be part of a panel. In this case, a select group talks about a topic while the audience listens. Some organisers use breakout rooms to encourage active debate among small groups of attendees.
- Workshops: A small group of participants works on a specific problem case or researches a certain topic. This approach is a great way to offer attendees an interactive learning experience.

The purpose of conferences varies, but usually, they're meant to address and find solutions to challenges in a business or industry (Ladkin, 2006). Sharing new insights and research is a big part of that. So are networking and team-building activities.

Exhibitions

Also referred to as trade shows, exhibitions are usually massive events that draw thousands of visitors and exhibitors from around the world. They can last anywhere from several days to a week. Exhibitions are usually very industry-specific and have a well-defined target market. Exhibitors go to trade shows to present and promote their product or service, drive business, and liaise with existing and potential partners (Singh & Bathla, 2023; Sharma & Singh, 2024; Bhalla et al., 2023; Deri et al., 2024; Francis et al., 2024; Singh & Hassan, 2024). Industry professionals go to network, find clients or jobs, and discover new ways to solve problems.

Common activities at exhibitions can include one, a mix of, or all of the activities present at conferences, as well as:

- Networking events: Trade shows often have networking parties for subgroups among their attendees. This is a great place to meet potential partners, discuss collaborations, and exchange thoughts on current trends.
- Awards: An award show is part of many exhibitions and honours industry leaders for their achievements. It also gives winners quite a PR and marketing

push. Even if you're not up for an award, it's worth checking out the nominees for inspiration.

- New business pitches: Since trade shows want to promote growth and innovation in their industry, there's often a dedicated event for new business pitches. It's great for start-ups to gain visibility, funding, clients, and job applicants.

MICE is an important source of business for many hotels. First, exhibitors and attendees fill many rooms at properties with meeting facilities or close to convention centres. Second, a study from Hong Kong found that on average MICE guests pay 17.5% more than leisure guests. This is partly because having large events in town leads to high demand and the chance to charge premium room rates. Hotels that host on-site meetings or conferences may offer slightly discounted rates to organisers. However, they can drive additional revenue from meetings and F&B packages. Finally, MICE can be a reliable source of recurring revenue. Many conferences and trade shows happen at set intervals, so hotels plan their annual budgets with these events in mind. MICE technology has developed by leaps and bounds in the past years (Singh & Bathla, 2023; Sharma & Singh, 2024; Bhalla et al., 2023; Deri et al., 2024; Francis et al., 2024; Singh & Hassan, 2024; Ansari & Singh, 2023)

Opportunities for MICE

In addition to attracting a substantial number of delegates, MICE events significantly boost national economies as attendees typically spend more time and money compared to leisure tourists (Wan, 2011). This results in considerable revenue for sectors such as transportation, accommodation, entertainment, advertising, and leisure (Spencer & Bavuma, (2018); Ratajczak-Mrozek, 2014), while also creating numerous business opportunities across the tourism sector and related industries (Whitfield et al., 2012). Because MICE events often take place during off-peak seasons, they help alleviate seasonality within host destinations. Furthermore, successful MICE events can enhance a destination's reputation (Wee, Mustapha & Anas, (2021); Munjal et al., 2014). Exhibitions associated with MICE events attract a large number of attendees, offering substantial exposure for products and services to potential buyers. Participation in conventions also facilitates networking opportunities with industry peers. MICE events contribute to the exchange of ideas, knowledge, and insights, benefiting both host countries and participants. They play a crucial role in disseminating information and expertise across borders swiftly and comprehensively. Consequently, due to the significant economic impact of MICE events on host destinations, many countries are actively enhancing their national services, facilities, infrastructure, and safety standards to meet international benchmarks (Lau, 2009).

Challenges Facing MICE

There are numerous challenges confronting the MICE industry, which can be outlined as follows: (a) Safety and security considerations are paramount in organizing MICE events. (b) Addressing the needs of travelers with disabilities. (c) Enhancing services, facilities, venue design, and IT infrastructure (Hotel Mule, 2010). (d) Providing adequate training and education for industry professionals. (e) Addressing the lack of comprehensive data on MICE tourism, including insights into key markets, buyer decision-making processes, market trends, and the overall impact—both positive and negative—of MICE events (Korstanje, Gowreesunkar & Maingi, 2024). (f) Enhancing customer satisfaction by offering leisure activities, scheduling ample free time during conferences and meetings, choosing accessible routes, and incorporating relaxation exercises and classes at venues. (g) Mitigating negative environmental impacts such as pollution, greenhouse gas emissions, excessive energy consumption, increased waste generation, and intensified traffic. This requires strict adherence to environmental regulations and ethical practices by organizers and participants alike (Tsyvinskaya, 2011).

MATERIALS AND METHODS

Existing literature on MICE events was carried out using content analysis. Content analysis is used to analyze and interpret the content of various forms of communication, such as text documents. It involves systematically examining the characteristics, themes, and patterns within the content to derive meaningful insights and draw conclusions. (Sousa & Rocha, 2018, Law et al., 2018). According to Adeyinka-Ojo, (2018) content analysis is quite helpful when analyzing a variety of literary works and a big number of articles. This method was used to analyze literature related to "use of Virtual and Hybrid Events for MICE Sector", to identify key themes and trends. In reference to hospitality and tourism research, content analysis is commonly employed (Fathiyah, Roszilah, Azrul, & Mohamad, 2019).

Scholarly works published in journals with a focus on the Use of Virtual and Hybrid Events for MICE Sector were used as references for the literature review. A single search engine, Google Scholar, was used to search large data bases like Web of Science, Scopus, Taylor and Francis. According to Law et al., (2018), these are the biggest search engines and online databases. This process is in line with earlier studies (Adeyinka-Ojo, Lee, Abdullah, Teo, 2020; Law et al., 2018) that used several databases to examine data for analysis.

In addition, keywords searched for were Virtual events; Hybrid events; MICE tourism; Hospitality; Technology, Innovation. These approaches were based on earlier research that combined related phrases (Adeyinka-Ojo, et al., 2020; Fathiyah, et al., 2019). This current review supports previous studies on the Use of Virtual and Hybrid Events for MICE Sector (Bailenson, 2021). Due to the study's emphasis on the Use of Virtual and Hybrid Events for MICE Sector in emerging hospitality and tourism environment. A deductive approach was utilized.

DISCUSSION AND INTERPRETATION

The Meetings, Incentives, Conventions, and Exhibitions (MICE) industry is considered the fastest growing tourism sector (Ansari & Singh, 2023; Bhalla et al., 2023; Deri et al., 2024; Francis et al., 2024; Singh & Hassan, 2024). MICE generate foreign exchange, increases trade and investments, provide employment, boost local economies, and promote destinations. The major key to its success is the strong collaboration with the travel, hospitality, and leisure sectors that provide products and services for the industry. Therefore, any disruption along its value chain may lead to significant losses for its stakeholders: organizers, participants, suppliers, sponsors, and host destinations

Streamlining the Processes

Technology has also enabled event organisers to streamline their operations, making them more efficient and cost-effective. With the help of event management software, organisers can manage various aspects of an event, such as registration, ticketing, marketing, and logistics, from a single platform. This not only saves time but also reduces the risk of errors and ensures that everything runs smoothly.

Enhanced Experiences

Furthermore, technology has also enhanced the overall attendee experience at events. For example, the use of augmented reality and virtual reality technologies has allowed attendees to experience events in a more immersive and interactive way. Augmented reality can be used to create interactive displays and games, while virtual reality can provide a fully immersive experience that transports attendees to different locations (Singh & Bathla, 2023; Sharma & Singh, 2024; Bhalla et al., 2023; Deri et al., 2024; Francis et al., 2024; Ansari & Singh, 2023; Singh & Hassan, 2024).

Capitalizing Data

Another important contribution of technology to the MICE industry is the use of data analytics. Data analytics can provide valuable insights into attendee behaviour and preferences, allowing organisers to tailor their events to meet their needs better. For example, by analysing attendee data, organisers can determine which sessions were the most popular, which speakers were the most engaging, and which topics generated the most interest. This information can be used to improve future events and make them more appealing to attendees (Francis et al., 2024; Singh & Hassan, 2024; Singh & Bathla, 2023; Sharma & Singh, 2024; Bhalla et al., 2023; Deri et al., 2024).

Improved Security

The use of technology has also enabled organisers to enhance event security. With the help of facial recognition technology and other biometric solutions, organisers can ensure that only authorised personnel have access to restricted areas. Moreover, technology can also be used to monitor crowds and detect potential security threats, ensuring that everyone at the event remains safe and secure. The popularity of hybrid events is growing at a faster-than-expected pace. A hybrid event is an event that takes place at a physical venue while allowing the audience to engage in interaction on its virtual platform as well. This new type of events is rising as a potential breakthrough for the MICE industry, which has been feeling the deep impacts of the coronavirus pandemic for the past few months (Ansari & Singh, 2023; Bhalla et al., 2023; Deri et al., 2024; Francis et al., 2024; Singh & Hassan, 2024).

MICE companies are now actively turning to hybrid events, combining them with digital marketing options like social media, VR, and IoT. Many players in the MICE sector have been pursuing hybrid events for the last decade. These events are called "hybrid" as they welcome visitors to their physical venues while livestreaming the event to engage audience on their online platform as well (Francis et al., 2024; Singh & Hassan, 2024; Singh & Bathla, 2023; Sharma & Singh, 2024; Bhalla et al., 2023; Deri et al., 2024; Ansari & Singh, 2023). Hybrid events are fundamentally different from virtual events in that the latter takes place online only. The advancement of meeting technology led to a gradually rising popularity of hybrid events.

Although hybrid events were not as much at the center of attention as some new technologies, the widespread pandemic of COVID-19 put the kind under the spotlight. Naturally, digital marketing events are among the quickest to turn to going hybrid. DIGIMARCON Midwest 2021, a digital marketing conference and exhibition scheduled to take place in Chicago in June 2021, is already open for registration, welcoming audience from a wide spectrum of industries. MozCon, another digital marketing conference, decided to go fully virtual this year. It was a change of course after continuously combining online components such as posting promotion videos online. More theatrical performances and fashion shows are also livestreaming for their audience.

Why Pay for an Online Event?

The answer is simple. It's lucrative. Considering that enabling human interaction is a core mission of the MICE industry, no wonder why many experts in the sector are not sure about whether hybrid or virtual events without face-to-face meetings could attract a large audience who are willing to pay for the event. The recent dramatic growth of online events in the U.S. might shine a light on such suspicion. A recent USA Today article, "The future of conference: Will events remain virtual after lockdowns?" showed the U.S.'s online event industry has seen growth of 1100% year-on-year. The CEO of Socialive, a video broadcasting tool maker, said their customer base has grown by 90% and their revenue has grown 146% since the beginning of March when the pandemic started to spread throughout the world. USA Today said many hotels and event planners are trying to combine virtual and in-person experiences, which consumers are willing to pay for.

According to the recent Global Tourism Dashboard released by the World Tourism Organization (UNWTO), the global tourism industry witnessed a year-on-year growth rate of -22.4%. The figure plunged to a staggering -57%, the lowest on record, in March when the coronavirus outbreak started to sweep the world. The UNWTO stated that this translates into a loss of 67 million international arrivals and about US$80 billion in receipts (Francis et al., 2024; Singh & Hassan, 2024; Singh & Bathla, 2023; Sharma & Singh, 2024; Ansari & Singh, 2023; Bhalla et al., 2023; Deri et al., 2024). It also pointed out that the current scenarios point to possible declines in arrivals of 58% to 78% for the year. Hybrid events might be the only solution that could save the MICE industry. Mayank Chowdhary, the founder of a large business event platform called 10Times.com, shared his thoughts on hybrid events in his article for the Financial Express. "Industry players can consider adopting the hybrid model to tide through the pandemic. At the same time, when the crisis is over and physical events are back on track, the added virtual dimension can function as a critical revenue generation supplement. Until then, organizers who are thinking of cancelling or postponing their events can instead consider virtual or hybrid models as viable alternatives."

Technology Application in MICE

- Proposal management: Modern proposal management systems allow you to automate proposal creation. They also let you set up interactive microsites which are easier for clients to go through than cumbersome PDFs.
- Supplier networks: Venues can be listed on these networks — like the Cvent Supplier Network™ — and get notifications when an organiser posts a request for an event proposal (RFP). The benefit for event locations is that they can respond quickly to new RFPs and have access to international planners.
- Event diagramming tools: They allow organisers to carefully plan their venue's setup and floor plan. Every chair, table, booth, and hand sanitizer station can be included and mapped out. Especially in light of COVID-19, this is important to guarantee events comply with all local safety regulations.
- Room block management: Tools like Cvent Passkey® make it easier for hotels to manage event room blocks, all without endless rooming spreadsheets. They allow properties to provide organisers with a private booking link that feeds attendee bookings directly into the hotel's reservation system.

MICE Technology at the Event

- Facial recognition: This technology can be used to grant admission to registered attendees on Day 1 of the event. It also does away with the need for IDs or tickets since people entering can simply have their faces scanned (Francis et al., 2024; Singh & Hassan, 2024; Singh & Bathla, 2023; Sharma & Singh, 2024; Bhalla et al., 2023; Deri et al., 2024).
- Augmented, mixed, and virtual reality: As these technologies evolve, they create new chances for more immersive and engaging events. Especially for product demonstrations, presentations, or entertainment, AR and VR are opening endless new doors in the MICE industry.
- Internet of Things: Web-based access control (think digital keys), thermostats, speakers, and lighting controlled via the internet: The Internet of Things makes it all possible and creates new ways for venues to tailor their service to the client's needs.
- Virtual event platforms: The increased demand for hybrid and virtual events created the need for sophisticated virtual platforms. Cvent's Virtual Event Platform addresses that by offering an online space where organisers and attendees can network, engage, and interact.

Starting a Career in the MICE Field

As you can tell from previous sections, the MICE industry is a diverse industry that encompasses a wide variety of jobs. They all have one thing in common though: They're demanding, require a high degree of flexibility, resourcefulness, communication skills, and resilience. And in many cases, they come with long hours and shifts on weekends or holidays.

MICE Jobs at a Hotel Level

At a hotel level, the sales and marketing teams take care of a lot of the organisational tasks related to MICE. They handle incoming inquiries, create offers, and liaise with other departments to realise the client's vision for their event. Banquet managers look after the operational side of things. They plan set-up and tear-down, schedule the staff, and work with suppliers to ensure everything runs smoothly on the day (Ansari & Singh, 2023).

MICE Jobs at an Event Location

Account and event managers at a concert hall or a convention centre look after a set of clients to support them in planning their events. They call in suppliers, get quotations, and participate in planning every detail. Depending on the event, they may attend to make sure everything runs smoothly.

MICE Jobs With Large Companies

Large companies that regularly host events often have an in-house events team. They take care of all the organisational tasks like outlining and planning events and communicating with the venues. Inviting guests and planning entertainment is also their job, but they may call in an external planner to help with the latter. And of course, they'll be on-site during the event to oversee the overall operation.

Virtual and Hybrid Events Trends

The COVID-19 pandemic has brought significant changes to the events industry, with virtual and hybrid events becoming the norm. As the world begins to adapt to the new normal, it is crucial to stay up-to-date with the latest trends in virtual and hybrid events.

1. Personalisation

Personalisation is key in virtual and hybrid events. Tailor your event to your audience's needs and preferences by incorporating personalised content and interactive experiences.

2. Accessibility

Ensure that your virtual and hybrid event is accessible to all attendees, including those with disabilities. Consider providing closed captioning, sign language interpretation, and other accessibility features.

3. Engagement

Keep attendees engaged throughout the event by incorporating interactive elements such as live polls, Q&A sessions, and gamification.

4. Networking

Facilitate networking opportunities for attendees by incorporating virtual networking lounges, breakout rooms, and other opportunities for attendees to connect with one another.

5. Production Value

Invest in high-quality production value, including professional lighting, sound, and video equipment to ensure a seamless and professional experience for attendees.

6. Sustainability:

Incorporate sustainable practices into your virtual and hybrid event, such as reducing paper waste and using eco-friendly materials for promotional items.

7. Data Collection

Collect data on attendee engagement, satisfaction, and feedback to help improve future virtual and hybrid events.

8. Security

Ensure the security of your virtual and hybrid event by using secure platforms and implementing measures such as two-factor authentication.

9. Hybrid Experience

Create a seamless hybrid experience by incorporating features such as live streaming, interactive chat, and virtual reality experiences for both virtual and in-person attendees.

10. Flexibility

Be flexible and adaptable to changes in the industry and attendee needs. Incorporate feedback from attendees to improve future virtual and hybrid events.

Virtual and hybrid events have become an integral part of the events industry, and it is essential to stay up-to-date with the latest trends to create successful events. By incorporating personalization, accessibility, engagement, networking, production value, sustainability, data collection, security, hybrid experiences, and flexibility, you can create a memorable and impactful event for your attendees.COVID-19 pandemic has accelerated the adoption of virtual and hybrid events in the MICE industry (Francis et al., 2024; Ansari & Singh, 2023; Singh & Hassan, 2024; Singh & Bathla, 2023; Sharma & Singh, 2024; Bhalla et al., 2023; Deri et al., 2024). As we move towards a post-pandemic world, it's important to explore the future of virtual and hybrid events and how they will shape the MICE industry.

This article delves into the trends and technologies driving the growth of virtual and hybrid events and their potential impact on the MICE industry.The pandemic has forced the Meetings, Incentives, Conferences and Exhibitions (MICE) industry to adapt to new ways of organising events. Virtual and hybrid events have become increasingly popular as the future of MICE industry and experts predict that they will continue to play a significant role in the future of the MICE industry (Francis et al., 2024; Singh & Hassan, 2024; Singh & Bathla, 2023; Sharma & Singh, 2024; Bhalla et al., 2023; Deri et al., 2024; Ansari & Singh, 2023). Virtual events refer to meetings, conferences, and exhibitions that are conducted entirely online, while hybrid events combine virtual and in-person elements. Hybrid events allow for a larger audience by providing virtual access to the event while also accommodating a limited number of attendees in person.

Virtual and Hybrid Events

One of the biggest advantages of virtual and hybrid events is the ability to reach a global audience. Event organisers can now bring together attendees from all over the world without the constraints of physical distance and travel restrictions. This also opens up new opportunities for collaboration and networking between attendees from different countries and regions. Moreover, virtual and hybrid events offer a more cost-effective solution than traditional in-person events. The costs of travel, accommodation, and venue rental can be significantly reduced, making it easier for small businesses and start-ups to participate in events and reach a larger audience. Virtual and hybrid events also provide a more flexible and convenient experience for attendees. With virtual events, attendees can participate from the comfort of their own homes or offices, without the need for expensive travel and accommodation. Hybrid events provide the best of both worlds, allowing attendees to participate in person or virtually, depending on their preferences and needs (Ansari & Singh, 2023; Singh & Bathla, 2023; Sharma & Singh, 2024; Bhalla et al., 2023; Deri et al., 2024; Francis et al., 2024; Singh & Hassan, 2024).

The use of technology is a key factor in the success of virtual and hybrid events. Advanced audio and visual technologies allow for high-quality live streaming, webinars, and virtual exhibitions, creating an immersive and engaging experience for attendees. Interactive features such as real-time polls and Q&A sessions also allow for increased engagement and participation. The popularity of virtual and hybrid events is expected to continue even after the pandemic subsides. Event organisers are likely to continue to explore the potential of these formats, given the cost savings, convenience, and reach they provide. Hybrid events are particularly promising, as they offer the best of both worlds – the engagement and personal connections of in-person events, combined with the flexibility and accessibility of virtual events.

Moreover, virtual and hybrid events are also more sustainable than traditional in-person events (Singh & Bathla, 2023; Sharma & Singh, 2024; Bhalla et al., 2023; Deri et al., 2024; Francis et al., 2024; Singh & Hassan, 2024). They significantly reduce the carbon footprint associated with travel and accommodation, and minimise waste generated from event materials and infrastructure. This aligns with the growing trend towards sustainable practices in the MICE industry. However, there are challenges associated with virtual and hybrid events that must be addressed. For example, virtual events may struggle to create the same level of engagement and personal connections as in-person events (Ansari & Singh, 2023; Francis et al., 2024; Singh & Hassan, 2024; Singh & Bathla, 2023; Sharma & Singh, 2024; Bhalla et al., 2023; Deri et al., 2024). It can be more challenging to network and build relationships with other attendees in a virtual environment. Hybrid events may also be more complex to organise, requiring advanced technology and logistics to ensure a seamless experience for both in-person and virtual attendees.

Another potential challenge is the issue of accessibility. While virtual and hybrid events provide greater accessibility for attendees who cannot travel or attend in person, they may also create barriers for those who lack the necessary technology or reliable internet access (Singh & Bathla, 2023; Ansari & Singh, 2023; Sharma & Singh, 2024; Bhalla et al., 2023; Deri et al., 2024; Francis et al., 2024; Singh & Hassan, 2024). This highlights the need for event organisers to ensure that virtual and hybrid events are accessible to everyone, regardless of their location or resources. Virtual and hybrid events are likely to play a significant role in the future of the MICE industry. They offer a cost-effective, flexible, and sustainable solution for event organisers and attendees, and provide opportunities for collaboration and networking on a global scale. While there are challenges associated with these formats, the benefits they provide make them a promising option for the MICE industry moving forward.

As the MICE industry continues to evolve and adapt to new challenges and opportunities, the adoption of virtual and hybrid events is likely to accelerate. The success of these formats depends on the effective use of technology. Another benefit of virtual and hybrid events is that they can be recorded and shared for future use. This means that the event's content can be accessed and utilised by a wider audience, even after the event has ended (Singh and Bathla, 2023; Sharma and Singh, 2024; Bhalla et al., 2023; Deri et al., 2024; Francis et al., 2024; Singh and Hassan, 2024; Ansari & Singh, 2023). This is especially useful for educational events, as the recorded sessions can be used as learning resources for students or professionals who were unable to attend the live event. Moreover, virtual and hybrid events can provide cost savings for both event organisers and attendees. With virtual events, there are no expenses related to travel, accommodation, or venue rental. This can result in significant cost savings for both event organisers and attendees, making it a more accessible option for individuals or organisations with limited budgets.

CONCLUSION

Virtual and hybrid events also present challenges that must be addressed for the industry to fully embrace them. One major challenge is the lack of face-to-face interaction, which can limit networking opportunities and lead to a less engaging experience for attendees. Additionally, technical issues such as poor internet connectivity or insufficient equipment can negatively impact the virtual event's quality. The MICE industry has been significantly impacted by the COVID-19 pandemic, leading to the rise of virtual and hybrid events. The future of the industry will likely continue to include these types of events, even as in-person events resume. The benefits of virtual and hybrid events, such as accessibility, cost savings, and environmental sustainability, make them an attractive option for event organisers and attendees alike. However, challenges related to engagement and technical issues must be addressed for virtual and hybrid events to reach their full potential. As the MICE industry continues to evolve and adapt, it will be important for event organisers to consider the role of virtual and hybrid events in their overall event strategy. This is where the integration of must-have conference gadgets comes into play. Additionally, the industry can work towards more sustainable practices by reducing the carbon footprint of events and embracing technologies that minimise waste and promote environmental.

Practical Implications

The MICE sector has been significantly transformed by advancements in technology, leading to the rise of virtual and hybrid events. These new formats have become essential, especially in response to global events such as the COVID-19 pandemic, which restricted travel and large gatherings. Virtual and hybrid events offer innovative solutions to traditional challenges faced by the MICE industry, providing new opportunities for engagement, cost efficiency, and global reach. By understanding these implications, stakeholders in the MICE industry can better navigate the evolving landscape and capitalize on the advantages of virtual and hybrid event technologies. Some practical implications for using virtual and hybrid events in this sector are Cost efficiency: reduced travel and accommodation costs: Virtual and hybrid events minimize the need for participants to travel, reducing overall expenses for travel, accommodation, and meals. Lower Venue Costs: Virtual events eliminate the need for physical venues, while hybrid events may require smaller venues, leading to cost savings on renting large spaces.

Increased Accessibility and Reach: Global Audience: Virtual and hybrid events allow for greater geographical reach, enabling participants from around the world to join without the need for travel. Inclusive Participation: These formats can be more accessible for individuals with disabilities or those with time constraints, allowing a more diverse range of attendees. Flexibility and Convenience: On-Demand Content: Sessions can be recorded and made available for later viewing, allowing participants to access content at their convenience. Flexible Scheduling: Organizers can schedule sessions at times that are convenient for different time zones, maximizing participation.

Environmental Impact: Reduced Carbon Footprint: With less travel and fewer physical resources required, virtual and hybrid events are more environmentally friendly. Sustainable Practices: The reduction in physical waste and resource consumption aligns with growing sustainability goals within the industry. Technological Requirements: Reliable Infrastructure: Successful virtual and hybrid events require robust internet connections, reliable software platforms, and technical support. Cybersecurity: Ensuring the security of the virtual platforms and protecting the data of participants is crucial.

The shift towards virtual and hybrid events presents both opportunities and challenges for the MICE sector. By leveraging the benefits of these formats, such as cost efficiency, increased reach, and enhanced data insights, and addressing the associated challenges, event organizers can create successful and impactful events that meet the evolving needs of their audiences.

Recommendations

The MICE sector is continually evolving, with virtual and hybrid events emerging as key components in its transformation. These formats have become increasingly essential, particularly in the wake of global disruptions like the COVID-19 pandemic, which have highlighted the need for flexibility and innovation in event planning. Virtual and hybrid events offer a range of benefits, including cost efficiency, broader reach, and enhanced engagement. However, to fully capitalize on these advantages, it is crucial for stakeholders to implement strategic recommendations tailored to these new formats. This paper provides a comprehensive set of recommendations for effectively utilizing virtual and hybrid events within the MICE sector, aiming to help event planners and organizers navigate the complexities and maximize the potential of these dynamic event solutions. To effectively leverage virtual and hybrid events within the Meetings, Incentives, Conferences, and Exhibitions (MICE) sector, stakeholders should consider the following recommendations:

Invest in Reliable Technology and Infrastructure: Choose robust virtual event platforms that offer stable performance, user-friendly interfaces, and a wide range of interactive features. Ensure round-the-clock technical support to address any issues promptly and maintain a seamless experience for participants. Prepare contingency plans for potential technical failures, including backup internet connections and alternative platforms.

Ensure Data Security and Privacy: Use secure virtual event platforms that comply with data protection regulations to safeguard participant information. Implement data encryption and other cybersecurity measures to protect sensitive information from breaches. Clearly communicate privacy policies to attendees, explaining how their data will be used and protected.

Promote Sustainability: Emphasize the environmental benefits of virtual and hybrid events, such as reduced travel and lower carbon footprints (Gowreesunkar, Maingi & Korstanje, 2024). Incorporate sustainability into all aspects of event planning, from virtual materials to digital communications.

Innovate with Emerging Technologies: Explore the use of VR and AR to create immersive and interactive event experiences. Leverage artificial intelligence and automation to streamline event management processes and enhance attendee experiences. By implementing these recommendations, stakeholders in the MICE sector can maximize the benefits of virtual and hybrid events, creating engaging, cost-effective, and sustainable experiences for participants.

REFERENCES

Ansari, A. I., & Singh, A. (2023). Application of Augmented Reality (AR) and Virtual Reality (VR) in Promoting Guest Room Sales: A Critical Review. Z. Tučková, S. Dey, H. Thai, & S. Hoang. (Ed.) *Impact of Industry 4.0 on Sustainable Tourism.* Emerald Publishing Limited, Leeds. 10.1108/978-1-80455-157-820231006

Bailenson, J. N. (2021). Nonverbal Overload: A Theoretical Argument for the Causes of Zoom Fatigue. *Technology, Mind, and Behavior*, 2(1). 10.1037/tmb0000030

Basurto-Cedeno, E., & Pennington-Gray, L. (2018). An Applied Destination Resilience Model. *Tourism Review International*, 22(3), 293–302. 10.3727/1544272 18X15369305779092

Bhalla, A., Singh, P., & Singh, A. (2023). Technological Advancement and Mechanization of the Hotel Industry. In Tailor, R. (Ed.), *Application and Adoption of Robotic Process Automation for Smart Cities* (pp. 57–76). IGI Global. 10.4018/978-1-6684-7193-7.ch004

Bhamra, R., Dani, S., & Burnard, K. (2011). Resilience: The Concept, A Literature Review and Future Directions. *International Journal of Production Research*, 49(18), 5375–5393. 10.1080/00207543.2011.563826

Bueno, A. R., Urbistondo, P. A., & Martínez, B. A. (2020). The MICE Tourism Value Chain: Proposal of a Conceptual Framework and Analysis of Disintermediation. *Journal of Convention & Event Tourism*, 21(3), 177–200. 10.1080/15470148.2020.1740851

Burnard, K., Ran, B., & Christos, T. (2018). Building Organisational Resilience: Four Configurations. *IEEE Transactions on Engineering Management*, 65(3), 351–362. 10.1109/TEM.2018.2796181

Cakir, A. E. (2002). Virtual Communities – A Virtual Session on Virtual Conferences. *Behaviour & Information Technology*, 21(5), 365–371. 10.1080/0144929021000048439

Cassar, J., Whitfield, J., & Chapman, A. (2020). Contemporary Factors Influencing Association Conference Attendance. *Journal of Convention & Event Tourism*, 21(1), 57–90. 10.1080/15470148.2020.1719948

Chetty, K., & Motala, S. (2021). Working from Anywhere: Is South Africa Ready? *HSRC Review*, 19(1), 14–16.

Dahles, H., & Susilowati, T. P. (2015). Business Resilience in Times of Growth and Crisis. *Annals of Tourism Research*, 51, 34–50. 10.1016/j.annals.2015.01.002

Deri, M. N., Zaazie, P., & Singh, A. (2024). Digital Future of the Hospitality Industry and Hospitality Education Globally. In Sharma, A. (Ed.), *International Handbook of Skill, Education, Learning, and Research Development in Tourism and Hospitality. Springer International Handbooks of Education.* Springer. 10.1007/978-981-99-3895-7_14-1

Dillette, A., & Ponting, S. S. (2021). Diffusing Innovation in Times of Disasters: Considerations for Event Management Professionals. *Journal of Convention & Event Tourism*, 22(3), 197–220. 10.1080/15470148.2020.1860847

Do, H., Budhwar, P., Shipton, H., Nguyen, H.-D., & Nguyen, B. (2022). Building Organisational Resilience, Innovation through Resource-Based Management Initiatives, Organisational Learning and Environmental Dynamism. *Journal of Business Research*, 141, 808–821. 10.1016/j.jbusres.2021.11.090

Duchek, S., Raetze, S., & Scheuch, I. (2020). The Role of Diversity in Organisational Resilience: A Theoretical Framework. *Business Research*, 13(2), 387–423. 10.1007/s40685-019-0084-8

Elston, K., & Draper, J. (2012). A Review of Meeting Planner Site Selection Criteria Research. *Journal of Convention & Event Tourism*, 13(3), 203–220. 10.1080/15470148.2012.715269

Francis, R. S., Anantharajah, S., Sengupta, S., & Singh, A. (2024). Leveraging ChatGPT and Digital Marketing for Enhanced Customer Engagement in the Hotel Industry. In Bansal, R., Ngah, A., Chakir, A., & Pruthi, N. (Eds.), *Leveraging ChatGPT and Artificial Intelligence for Effective Customer Engagement* (pp. 55–68). IGI Global. 10.4018/979-8-3693-0815-8.ch004

Gowreesunkar, V. G., Maingi, S. W., & Korstanje, M. E. (2024). Introduction: The Interplay Between Tourism Resilience and Sustainability in the New Normal. In *Tourist Behaviour and the New Normal, Volume II: Implications for Sustainable Tourism Development* (pp. 1-6). Cham: Springer Nature Switzerland.

Korstanje, M. E., Gowreesunkar, V. G., & Maingi, S. W. (2024). Conclusion: Tourist Behavior in the New Normal—Emerging Frontiers Toward Tourism Resilience. In *Tourist Behaviour and the New Normal, Volume I: Implications for Tourism Resilience* (pp. 273-278). Cham: Springer Nature Switzerland.

Ladkin, A. (2006). Conference tourism–MICE market and business tourism. In *Tourism business frontiers* (pp. 56–66). Routledge. 10.1016/B978-0-7506-6377-9.50014-6

Lekgau, R. J., & Tichaawa, T. M. (2022). Exploring the Use of Virtual and Hybrid Events for MICE Sector Resilience: The Case of South Africa. *African Journal of Hospitality, Tourism and Leisure*, 11(4), 1579–1594. 10.46222/ajhtl.19770720.310

Marais, M., Du Plessis, E., & Saayman, M. (2017). Critical Success Factors of a Business Tourism Destination: Supply Side Analysis. *Acta Commercii*, 17(1), 1–12. 10.4102/ac.v17i1.423

Neate, R. (2020). Zoom Booms As Demand For Video-Conferencing Tech Grows. *The Guardian*. https://www.theguardian.com/technology/2020/mar/31/zoom-booms -as-demand-for-video-conferencing-tech-grows-in-coronavirus-outbreak

Orthodoxou, D. L., Loizidou, X. I., Gavriel, A., Hadjiprocopiou, S., Petsa, D., & Demetriou, K. (2022). Sustainable Business Events: The Perceptions of Service Providers, Attendees, and Stakeholders in Decision-Making Positions. *Journal of Convention & Event Tourism*, 23(2), 154–178. 10.1080/15470148.2021.1964666

Pearlman, D. M., & Gates, N. A. (2010). Hosting Business Meetings and Special Events in Virtual Worlds: A Fad or the Future? *Journal of Convention & Event Tourism, 11*(4).

Rogerson, C. M. (2019). Business Tourism Under Apartheid: The Historical Development of South Africa's Conference Industry. *Urbani Izziv*, 30(30, Supplement), 82–95. 10.5379/urbani-izziv-en-2019-30-supplement-006

Rogerson, C. M., & Baum, T. (2020). COVID-19 and African Tourism Research Agendas. *Development Southern Africa*, 37(5), 727–741. 10.1080/0376835X.2020.1818551

Rogerson, C. M., & Rogerson, J. M. (2021). COVID-19 and Changing Tourism Demand: Research Review and Policy Implications for South Africa. *African Journal of Hospitality, Tourism and Leisure*, 10(1), 1–21. 10.46222/ajhtl.19770720-83

Sharma, M., & Singh, A. (2024). Enhancing Competitive Advantages Through Virtual Reality Technology in the Hotels of India. In Kumar, S., Talukder, M., & Pego, A. (Eds.), *Utilizing Smart Technology and AI in Hybrid Tourism and Hospitality* (pp. 243–256). IGI Global. 10.4018/979-8-3693-1978-9.ch011

Singh, A., & Bathla, G. (2023). Fostering Creativity and Innovation: Tourism and Hospitality Perspective. In P. Tyagi, V. Nadda, V. Bharti, & E. Kemer (Eds.), *Embracing Business Sustainability Through Innovation and Creativity in the Service Sector* (pp. 70-83). IGI Global. 10.4018/978-1-6684-6732-9.ch005

Singh, A., & Hassan, S. C. (2024). Service Innovation Through Blockchain Technology in the Tourism and Hospitality Industry: Applications, Trends, and Benefits. In Singh, S. (Ed.), *Service Innovations in Tourism: Metaverse, Immersive Technologies, and Digital Twin* (pp. 205–214). IGI Global. 10.4018/979-8-3693-1103-5.ch010

Spencer, J. P., & Bavuma, Z. (2018). *How important are mice to the tourism economy?* The Business and Management Review.

Wee, H., Mustapha, N. A., & Anas, M. S. (2021). Characteristic of green event practices in mice tourism: A systematic literature review. *International Journal of Academic Research in Business & Social Sciences*, 11(16), 271–291. 10.6007/IJARBSS/v11-i16/11234

Chapter 4
Event–Enabled Mobile Applications:
Seamless and Smart Technological Platforms for Managing Virtual and Hybrid Events and Festivals

Sharad Kumar Kulshreshtha
https://orcid.org/0000-0001-7324-8013
North-Eastern Hill University, India

Sunildro S. Akoijam
North-Eastern Hill University, India

Paramjeet Kumar
https://orcid.org/0000-0002-3824-2289
North-Eastern Hill University, India

U. N. Shukla
Institute of Tourism and Hotel Management, Agra, India

ABSTRACT

Globally, there is a vibrant paradigm shift from physical event management engagements to transforming the event industry through mobile app technology involve leveraging digital tools to enhance the overall event experience for event organizers, attendees, sponsors, and other stakeholders. Nowadays, event mobile apps have become increasingly popular and most indispensable technological tool in the event industry specially after COVID 19 unprecedent and to a variety of reasons to access all event-related information, schedules, and updates, leading to a more convenient and enjoyable experience. Creating an innovative experience through developing

DOI: 10.4018/979-8-3693-2272-7.ch004

mobile apps for events comprises several crucial features and deliberations to ensure a smart, seamless, synchronized, and engaging experience for both host and guest or visitors. A holistic approach of mobile application technology brings positive operational and executional changes in the event industry which focuses on the entire event lifecycle and to cater the diverse needs of all stakeholders. These event mobile apps support proper improvements for future events and festivals, with effective managerial and supervisory functions, engaging both organizers and attendees by offering new event prospects for data-driven decision-making and event sponsorship.

INTRODUCTION

Today, mobile app technology has become an integral part of event industry where it provides event owners and organizers, as well as event attendees, with a variety of exciting and inventive tools and options for building a smarter and better event. one of the important advantages of having a mobile app for event is that it facilitates getting the event attendee more engaged and having it more customised and personal. Mobile Apps can serve both informative needs with personalized (Cheng et al., 2020). The Android app displays a user-friendly interface (Bhanot, et al., 2024). Personalization techniques to keep users engaged (Grau et al., 2022). The significance and seamless power of mobile based event apps technology has become very faster, feasible and favourable for event attendees, organisers, and attached event service providers. In the present year of 2024, the smart and seamless mobile revolution has brought transforms and innovations in the shaping and creative design and manging experiential events and conferences worldwide. The event managers and attendees are very much convenient and feel ease doing event management operations and routine event work activities as well as both are pleased to adopting these advance technological tools which has completely changed the event management scenario. With the hybrid, virtual, and innovative events being expected for the coming years (Werner et al., 2022). COVID-19 has rapidly changed virtual environment in the global events sector (Lekgau & Tichaawa, 2022). The technological innovation in applications and platforms for web and mobile, have changed the business tourism and event industry (Rady Mohamed, 2022)

The attendee can view inside the app, event schedules, maps, speakers' information, and even advanced interesting options that can set a more participatory experience with gamification and augmented reality, as well as giving them direct feedback for their satisfaction and involvement (Aggarwal and Ansari, 2014). In comparison with the before period of having mobile apps for events, event organisers and owners can analyse and use the app at the post event phase to gather useful data about attendee behaviour and patterns, and also use these data to fix and control some business decisions for the coming events.

Another one is how the mobile app technology plays a crucial part in shaping the future of even management. Currently, more and more people tend to see the importance of mobile app technology in the event management, in particular the virtual even and the hybrid even. Recent catastrophic COVID-19 pandemic has changed the business practice scenario worldwide, the event management market was also affected very much and brought major technological transformation in event management system. The traditional even such as onsite even, conference and meeting have to be given a way to the virtual even or hybrid even for the epidemic has had a serious impact on our personal health safety. In recent years, more and more mobile applications were developed to facilitate the virtual even and the hybrid even for attendees can register, access the meeting content information, talk to each other, even take part in different interactivity from our comfort zone such as home PC or mobile phones.

This has also opened up the doors to new forms of contextual marketing – the ability to personalise an attendee experience by engaging with them at the right time and in the right place (based on an attendee's location, behaviour or preferences) – for increased value and relevancy to sponsors and exhibitors. The implementation of Artificial Intelligence (AI) in the mobile applications will have a major impact on the nature of experiences and value formation of event. Transcending the 'enabling' capacity of current information and communication technologies (Buhalis et al. 2019), AI serves as a game changer in that it becomes a key autonomous resource creating a new level of human to non-human interaction (Gidhagen et al. 2017).

CONCEPTUAL FRAMEWORK OF EVENT MOBILE APPLICATIONS

The rise of mobile apps has proven to be an important, if not indispensable, part of the event industry's infrastructure. Entire platforms now exist that specialize in hosting event apps, offering various features and functionalities to all interested parties (organisers, attendees, sponsors, etc). Mobile app specifically developed and designed through software technology for effective and efficient events management functions and operations support to make team-based coordination, communication, control of event service providers with pro-active participation attendees in events.

A framework for the conceptualization of mobile apps could be outlined by the following elements includes: innovative solutions, artificial intelligence, attendees: interest, participation, real time tracking, personalisation: 24/7 support & ready, interactive experience, engagement, innovative functions of event mobile apps.

innovative solutions, artificial intelligence, attendees: interest, participation, real time tracking, personalisation: 24/7 support & ready, interactive experience, engagement, innovative functions of event mobile apps.

Figure 1. Features of event mobile app

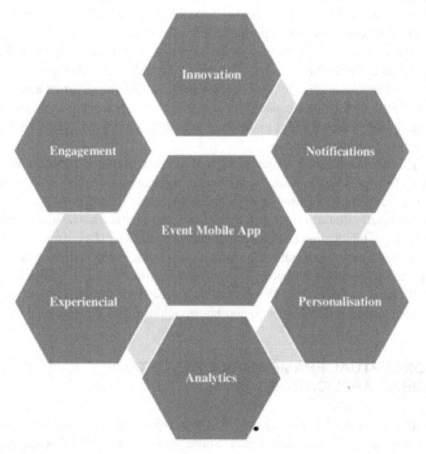

Source: Authors

Innovative: Mobile Innovative Application

Artificial Intelligence: Artificial Intelligence (AI) can significantly enhance the functionality and user experience of a mobile event app.

Personalisation: Personalization in mobile event apps can significantly enhance attendee engagement and satisfaction.

Attendees: the audience (people registered to attend your event using the app or those who interact with the app when it happens). They both make or break a mobile event app.

Experience: With experiential features in a mobile event app attendee participation can be enhanced with memories.

Engagement: If people are using the app, they will have more satisfaction with the event and feel like they've gotten more out of it.

Real time updates: These should be given to keep audiences informed during the event.

Accessible on other devices: with mobile event apps like this one, attendees stay in sync and stay connected.

Personalisation: In the context of the mobile event app, personalisation refers to the customisation of an app's functionality and content to suit the specific needs and tastes of an event organiser or attendee.

REVIEW OF LITERATURE

The research literature on the potential benefits of mobile apps to event management domain presents us a whole list of benefits to organisers, attendees and sponsors. The overall design and performance attributes of event apps might be the crucial factors for attendee engagement and event satisfaction. Fang et al. reported a study in 2017 that the app design dimensions (such as personalisation and social interaction) and app performance dimensions (eg, how responsive and reliable the app is) could be significant factors that affect 'behavioural engagement' of mobile travel app users. Another study into music festivals and the role mobile apps can play in this context identified that consumer-focused app design that addresses event anticipation, scheduling and personalisation can improve the overall event experience and mobile apps design, functionality and impact (Luxford and Dickinson, 2015). Garcia Revilla et al. (2023) stated that event management mobile applications enhanced the process of learning, skills acquisition and provided advantages for event planning which has practical implications for overall hospitality industry. Bran et al. (2022) introduced a platform for creating event related applications that supported seamless management of virtual and hybrid events through modular design tools and mixed reality elements. Mansouri (2022) discussed the application of technology in event tourism with focused on a local food festival in Thailand reflecting its impact on overall event management. Pasi et al. (2018) also highlighted the development of an android based event management app for organising various educational, medical and social events that will enhance the event planning through mobile apps.

Chen and Lu (2017) stated that there is a growing trend of event planners using mobile applications for the purpose of task management, communication with various stakeholders and logical coordination. These applications are significant in optimizing workflows and mitigating challenges normally faced in the process of event planning. Smith et al. (2018) put the emphasis on how mobile application for event planners must have especially robust communication functionality and features, which must allow event organisers to collaborate with different stakeholders and coordinate it in real time to smooth event execution. In the same context, Task management features are very important for event mobile application allowing the organisers to manage tasks in event plan efficiently as mentioned by Jones and Johnson, (2019). These applications will help the organisers to drive event management focused and orderly. Moreover, these mobile tools help organisers in managing budgets and tracking expenses also. Brown and Davis (2020) also showed how mobile event planning application need to have some financial management features allowing the organisers to monitor budgets, track expenses and generate invoices seamlessly. As such this will improve financial transparency and accountability. Lee and Kim (2021) highlighted the importance of user experience design, with focus on making interfaces intuitive and simple for users to navigate and improve the number of satisfied users. Having the knowledge of user needs are crucial to optimise the design and functionality of mobile event application.

Mobile event apps also offer real value in supporting the back-of-house logistics and operations of an event, and the ability to make data-centric decisions.

One study on event-based mobile social networks details the capabilities of mobile apps to offer event information, event scheduling, and attendee networking – all of which can facilitate event operations and planning more effectively and efficiently (Ahmed at al., 2014). Secondly, these apps can harvest valuable attendee behaviour and preferences data that can be leveraged by event organisers to optimise event programming, sponsorship opportunities, and broader strategic decision-making.

RESEARCH QUESTIONS

1. What are the emerging mobile event apps available for attendee engagement in the event market?
2. What are the unique features and innovation of mobile event apps for smart decision-making for an event?
3. How these innovative seamless mobile apps can be effective for quality marketing and sponsorship for event?

4.   How does mobile event apps enable the virtual and hybrid event experience,

OBJECTIVES

1.   To study the contemporary practices of mobile event apps event apps to enabling the virtual and hybrid event experience
2.   To review the unique features and innovation of mobile event apps for smart decision-making for an event
3.   To evaluate the role of innovative seamless and smart event mobile apps for effective event and festivals operations, marketing and sponsorship

METHODOLOGY

This study is based on systematic review of literature augmented by secondary source of data analysis to investigate this problem 'Event Enabled Mobile Applications: Seamless and Smart Technological Platforms for Manging Virtual and Hybrid Events & Festivals.' The literature review follows a rigorous search strategy across databases such as Scopus, Scient Direct, Web of Science and includes studies published between 2015 and 2024. Inclusion criteria encompass transformation of event and festival dynamics through technologies i.e., smart event apps, with a focus on [event apps, event and festivals management, smart and seamless technologies. Secondary data, sourced from repute tourism, hospitality, event management-based journals, books, magazine and well-established event management-based companies' websites have extracted and synthesized to identify key findings and trends. Data synthesis employs thematic analysis to uncover recurring themes and theoretical insights. The methodology ensures robustness through quality assessment of included literature and critical evaluation of secondary data sources, thereby providing a comprehensive understanding of event enabled mobile applications. Ethical considerations encompass confidentiality and data protection measures. There are some limitations including limited published research on event and festival apps, time and money. This approach offers insights into event enabled mobile applications. and lays groundwork for future research directions.

EMERGING PARADIGMS OF INNOVATIVE EVENT TECHNOLOGIES

Transformative Mobile Applications (Luxford & Dickinson, 2015). Attendee Mobile Applications (Ahmed et al., 2014) Sponsor Mobile Applications (Guerreiro et al., 2020). Exhibitor Mobile Applications (Aggarwal & Ansari, 2014). Global event consumers are primed and ready to adopt different forms of technology that enhance the overall event ecosystem – enabling event organizers to execute more effectively and efficiently, enabling event attendees to enjoy the experience in a richer manner, and enabling event sponsors/exhibitors to realise enhanced returns on event investments. In actuality, event applications have indeed started to have a transformative impact.

At the centre of this paradigm shift is the ubiquity of the smartphone, and the increasing reliance of event attendees on mobile technologies to navigate and engage in the experience at the event. Indeed, the mobile revolution and the growing prominence of the smartphone have created an opportunity for event organisers to utilise the mobile application to connect with their audiences, enhance the operational effectiveness of an event, and facilitate more personalised branded sponsorships.

A major area of mobile event app innovation has been in attendee experience. Research reveals that mobile event app design and performance attributes such as personalisation, social interaction and reliability are key drivers of group outcome measures such as attendee engagement and satisfaction. Features that can address attendees' anticipatory, scheduling and personalisation needs – such as exhibitor floor plans, personalised schedules and online networking features – can greatly augment the attendee experience.

Going beyond the intent of improving the experience of attendees, the mobile apps have become a tool for event organisers to improve the logistics, operations and data-driven decision-making during events. Mobile apps can serve as the central spot for the attendees to find out about the event, schedule and network with other delegates and can also help the event organisers in collecting data on attendees' behaviour and preferences, which can be utilised as tactical inputs for taking strategic decisions – from planning the event programme to increasing the chances of securing expensive sponsorship (Ahmed et al, 2014; Aggarwal and Ansari, 2014).

Moreover, the contextual marketing functionality of mobile event apps mean that they offer new opportunities for event organisers and sponsors to engage with attendees in more contextual and focused ways. For example, location-based services can be used to send specific promotional offers and coupons based on the location of the attendee in relation to the event, contextual brand activations can be triggered in the app when the attendee is close to a specific booth, and sponsorship of events, trains and buses can all be facilitated through mobile apps. All this adds up to greater engagement from attendees, with an added bonus that all stakeholders, organisers, sponsors and exhibitors, benefit from increased revenue.

The event market will increasingly be shaped by the ability of mobile applications to reshape the way events are experienced by participants, and to offer new ways of measuring impact, improving operational efficiency and creating new commercial opportunities.

FEATURES OF EXPERIENTIAL EVENT MOBILE APPLICATION

Mobile Application is fastest growing area of technologies where more focus have given on the customer personalisation, smart and seamless digital interface, services, safely, security. Therefore, these are some insightful reviews of event based mobile app features includes: a) Mobile Event App Attendees Engagement; b) Experiential Technological Features of Event Mobile Apps; c) Event App Personalization; d) Event App Attendees; e) Artificial Intelligence (AI) -Driven Event App; f) Innovative Event App.

Some Significant Smart and Seamless Features of Event Mobile Apps

1. **Event Program:** App provide custom agenda to attendees, event service providers, and before the starting the meeting, workshop, seminar and conferences.
2. **Event Notifications:** This app help to send push notifications to Send reminders, updates and alerts about upcoming classes, schedule changes or announcements.
3. **Event Networking:** Event App support to connect attendees with other attendees to communicate, consult, convey message to each other.
4. **Event Venue: GPS Enabled Location Maps:** Event App updates GPS enabled real time information about event program, venue and locations times of various technical sessions, exhibitor booths, restrooms and other points of interest.
5. **Event Live Chat & Instant Opinion Polls:** Mobile event apps have very unique and interactive feature to Integrate live question answer session and conduct opinion polling during the sessions.
6. **Event Gamification:** Gamification is the immersive features of this event app which provides access to live, online and exited updated various gaming platforms to play and experience.
7. **Integration of Social Media Platforms:** This mobile event apps have well connected and integrated with social media networks, including Facebook, LinkedIn. X, Instagram etc.

8. **Event Feedbacks:** This feature of the app provides proper option to give ratings for event and events services by the attendees as speakers, participants for the betterment of future event management.
9. **Immersive Experiential Technologies:** These two immersive virtual technologies engage with AR/VR experiences to the audiences and attendees, all such immersive experiences create virtual event experiences, virtual tours, virtual games as part of experiential such gadgets and VR devices.
10. **Live Streaming Apps:** These live streaming apps provides easy to connect, quality audio-visual interaction with host and guest (meeting convenor and attendees) high quality data analytics, with many privacy protection layers etc. Live Stream Apps provides real time video broadcast of events, activities through various online platforms, social media platforms like YouTube, Facebook, Instagram, Twitch Vimeo etc.
11. **Digital Contents.** The app provides with lots of relevant digital contents in the form of audios, visuals, documents, digital repository as e-resources for the support of event management.
12. **In-App Messaging:** In-App messaging allow attendees to directly message each other for networking and business purposes.
13. **Chatbots and Virtual Assistants:** AI-powered chatbots to provide help on-demand, and answer simple questions and provide virtual assistants to the attendees.
14. **Facial Recognition Check-in:** Implement facial recognition technology for attendee check-in at the event venue to make it faster and more secure
15. **Behavioural Analytics:** Read attendee behaviour and interactions in the app to gather insights about how to achieve better event planning, content delivery and attendee satisfaction.
16. **Predictive Analytics:** Use AI to forecast attendance levels of different participant types and sessions, as well as resource and infrastructure requirements, so as to enable organisers to optimise logistics and reduce inefficiencies in use of resources.
17. **Blockchain:** Blockchain for ticketing and security deploy smart systems for ticket sales, building better customer relationships.
18. **Smart Badge Integration:** Use smart badges or wearable technology to integrate networking, attendee check-ins and related features with the app, enabling networking conversations and strengthening session engagement.
19. **Voice Commands:** Make the app voice-command-enabled so that attendees can navigate the app with hands-free voice commands and get info and interact with it via voice prompts.

CHALLENGES AND RISKS ACCOSIATED WITH MOBILE APP INTEGRATION IN EVENT MANAGEMENT

There are several challenges and risks which are associated with mobile apps-based event management. These can be broadly analysed under three categories:

Security Issues: A mobile app may involve user sensitive data such as personal records, bank information, medical records etc. while processing. If these data are used in a secure manner, it may lead to serious breaches issues. Authentication and authorization are another security issue may emerge. There is a need for effective implementation of robust authentication mechanism and authorization controls to protect user accounts and data. Integration with third party Application programming Interface (API) may expose the mobile app to security issues. In this regard, proper validation, encryption of data in transit as well as securing the handling of API keys are crucial. Lastly, the mobile apps may be exposed to SQL injection, cross site scripting, secure storage of data and other common software vulnerabilities. For this purpose, security testing and code reviews should be performed on regular intervals.

Privacy concerns: The users should be informed clearly about the data, the mobile app will be collecting, storing and using. These should comply with some of the regulations that are put in place. In many of the apps, there may be a need to use sensitive information about one' s location and unique identifiers of one's device. The user should be ensured that such sensitive data will also be used for the designated purpose and it will be kept secure. Whenever there is a case of integration with third party services, there is a chance of sharing the user data with these third parties. In such cases, there is a need to adhere to the privacy practices and regulations against unlawful disclosure of the data.

User Accessibility issues: Mobile apps need to function seamlessly across different devices and versions. Therefore, testing for compatibility and optimizing user interfaces and user experience is necessary. Integration with third party can also have impact on the performance of the app which may lead to issues like slow loading times, crashes or even battery drain. In this regard, there is a need for performance testing and optimization to maintain a smooth user experience. The mobile apps should also ensure its usability and accessibility for person with disability with vision impairments and motor disorder. For this purpose, accessibility standards and usability tests with variety of users can also be employed to ensure compliance.

Ministry of Electronics and Information Technology (MEITY), Government of India is very much vigilant to review such apps have threat for national cyber security and prevent operation of such fraud mobile application and protect citizen of India by creating awareness and taking strict actions against such mobile apps. Although, time to time government monitor such activities Recently the government had blocked 59 apps in 29th June, 2020, 188 apps in 2nd September, 2020 and

43 mobile apps in 24ᵗʰ November 2020 issued order for block of these mobile apps under Section 69A of the Information Technology Act, 2000 for the access safe and secure digital operation through such mobile applications (Source: Press Information Bureau, Govt of India press released on dated 24ᵗʰ November 2020).

DISCUSSIONS AND OUTCOMES

The mobile event apps have transformed the landscape of event industry in its planning and management thereby giving benefits to organisers, attendees, exhibitors and all stakeholders. There are numerous event apps introduced by global companies across the globe. Most of these apps have innovative features that address various issues and make the event a memorable experience for all stakeholders. Some of the notable features included in these apps are:

i) **Customised schedules & agendas:***It enables the attendees to customise and adjust their schedule to only those sessions which they like to attend or are interested. It has increased the satisfaction level of the attendees making the event meaningful and interactive for them.*

ii) **Real time notifications & updates:***It helps the attendees to get time to time notifications and updates related to events on real time basis. It enables them to do the necessary changes to ensure that they can attend the event with in effective manner with prior information and preparation.*

iii) **Seamless event registration & check ins:***With this feature, the attendees can get the detailed information about the registration and its process. The interested attendees can proceed with the registration process on their own through the seamless process and also do the check in process on their own through it hassle free.*

iv) **Interactive navigation tools and maps:***This feature is integrated with advanced navigation tools which can help the attendees find the venue of the events very easily. It further enables the attendees to locate various destinations or spots within the venue itself thereby reducing the efforts and time to attend the event.*

v) **User friendly interface:***It provides the user-friendly platform to the attendees to get detailed information and the process for accessing the event in a very convenient manner. It takes care of attendees with different technological knowledge to use it comfortably.*

vi) **Networking tools for attendees:***It serves one of the important purposes for attending the event i.e. networking. It provides the detailed information of attendees thereby providing an opportunity to create strong bond and socialisation during the events.*

vii) **Live polls:** It provides the attendees to express their opinions regarding the management of the events on real time basis. It makes the event interactive and alive for the attendees.

viii) **Q&A:** The attendees normally have many queries or doubts that need to be clarified for attending the event. This feature act as a platform for attendees to put forward their queries or doubts that will make the decide whether to attend or not attend the event and guide them how to attend the event in the most productive and effective way.

ix) **Event analytics:** This feature provides data on attendee engagement, popular sessions and overall apps usage rate which may be useful to various attendees to make future decisions in terms of whether to attend such kinds of events or what things they should take care of when they organise similar kinds of events.

x) **Sponsors & exhibitor visibility:** It provide data on the sponsors and exhibitors which may be of interest to the attendees thereby increasing visibility and engagement.

xi) **Interactive feedback:** This feature enables the attendees to provide instant and interactive feedback to the organisers which are important so that the attendees' issues and problems are taken care of instantly.

xii) **Gamification features:** With the incorporation of such feature in event apps, the attendees' participation have increased significantly. It results in active and enjoyable engagement of the attendees with the event.

All these features provide immense benefits to the attendees in many ways. With the addition of more such features and functions in the event apps, the attendees' engagement and interest with events will increase significantly.

The use of event apps for organising events provide the insightful data that are crucial for making crucial decision. In the process of event planning and management, some of the features and functions of these apps enable the organisers to get accurate data on various dimensions that will help in improving future events planning and management. The various features and functionality of mobile event apps help in effective management of logistics, operations and data driven decision making in the following ways:

i) **Efficient logistic & operation:** By having access to these real time data through these features of apps, the event organisers can also analyse the ongoing events and bring out any shortcoming that can be addressed spontaneously during the event. With the use of these features and functions, the apps enable the organiser to identify real time issues and resolve it resulting in effective control of the operation of the event. With the continuous monitoring of data in real time including traffic flow, resource usage, attendee distribution, organisers can also effectively engage in optimum resource allocation. Moreover, the organiser can use real time data to identify some of the potential safety issues which can be addressed promptly with prior necessary alternative arrangements. As a result, it helps in effective and timely decision making that will affect the overall management of the event.

ii) **Data driven decision making:** It provides the real time data of the attendees in terms of their attendance, interactions and networking during the event. It will help the organiser to manage a better event experience. Data analytics through event mobile apps help the organisers make informed decisions for improving any future events.

The mobile event apps are the carrier of event related context that provides users with multi-dimensional contextual experience that brings the attendees closer to the organiser. These apps give most needed information and services to the users when they need it for making important decisions thereby providing the ultimate experience. Through the use of these apps, the organises are able to create attendee friendly environment whereby the attendee can attend the event, enjoy and fulfil their desired goals with some memorable experience. The organisers collect and analyse contextual data to make important decisions related to events and any potential needs of the attendees in the future. Based on the contextual information, the organisers are able to predict attendees' behaviour and accordingly they come out with the strategies to provide the value-added service for the attendees. The information related to location and timing of the event are very crucial for attendees which can be provided or responded in an efficient manner through these apps.

The mobile event apps also provide numerous scope and opportunities to the sponsors also in contextual marketing and sponsorship opportunities. It can help the brand of sponsors get high brand exposure in many ways. The app can provide much needed information for its customers such as name, tagline and the specialisation they are in. It will also enhance their visual branding process that will improve brand awareness. The audience engagement data can be retrieved from such apps that will provide the accurate data on how many attendees visited the sponsorship section of the app which is an effective way to reinforce the value of sponsorship. Through the use of apps, the sponsors get the leverage of attendees' visit to their websites directly.

The literature indicates that the technology is influenced by the success of virtual adaptions and cyber enablement for sustaining events and making destinations resilient during challenging times. With the presence of advanced technologies, the exclusive in-person events are now being eliminated as the technology has overtaken the event management post COVID seamlessly (Carswell et al. 2023). A pertinent example in this regard is the increased adoption of mobile event apps as the enablers of both virtual and hybrid event experiences. In a study about the 2018 edition of Roland Garros (the French Tennin Premier tournament), researchers exhibited how the use of mobile apps is becoming a key feature that has the ability to provide the ultimate level of experience to the fans, (Schut & Glebova, 2022). Similarly, the case of Kaamatan Festival in Sabah in Malaysia also emphasized on the role of social media to advertise itself during pandemic in response to COVID 19 that minimized the cancellation or postponement of in-person activities (Francis et al., 2023). The event organisers in Kuching, Sarawak also realised the need for hybridisation of events to serve their audiences post pandemic era (Paul & Ali Amaran, 2023). Some of these case studies emphasized that the appropriate mobile event app and digital event platform can enhance viability and attendee experience. As the event industry has been undergoing unique transformation, there is a requirement of the ability to leverage smart advanced technology apps for effective sustainable event management.

CONCLUSION

The emergence of the innovative mobile app for event management has changed the landscape and transformed the way how the events are organised in a very pro-active manner. It serves as a boon for the event organisers, attendees, sponsors as well as other stakeholders involved in this business. Global event consumers are adopting various forms of advanced technology that enhance the overall experience of the attendees in the event. Among these technologies, the use of mobile app for pro-active virtual, hybrid and in-person events enable the attendees to engage themselves in much richer experience. The mobile app is also a boon for the event organisers too. It enables the organisers to plan and organise the event in a more systematic approach. It creates a platform for effective connection and networking between the organiser and the attendees thereby enabling the organisers to understand the attendees' behaviour, expectations and their problems. The increasing functionality and add on in these mobile apps will provide enormous opportunities to the event organisers and also change the paradigm of how various events are organised in a more contextual and focused manner for the attendees to give them a lifetime memory. Despite all these advantages and opportunities, there are several challenges and risks associated with use of mobile apps in event management. In order to leverage on such opportunities and minimise the impact of such risks, there is a need for understanding these risks and taking proactive measure while using these apps. As a result, it will be being a transitional change in the growth and development of event industry in the near future.

REFERENCES

Aggarwal, V., & Ansari, N. (2014). *Emerging trends: apps in event management.* ACM. 10.1145/2593761.2593767

Ahmed, A. M., Qiu, T., Xia, F., Jedari, B., & Abolfazli, S. (2014). Event-Based Mobile Social Networks: Services, Technologies, and Applications. *IEEE Access : Practical Innovations, Open Solutions*, 2, 500–513. 10.1109/ACCESS.2014.2319823

Bhanot, L., Shyam, R., Khan, M. A., Bahadur, P., & Ali, S. (2024). Even to: An Android App for Event Planners. *International Research Journal of Modernization in Engineering Technology and Science.* 10.56726/IRJMETS53489

Bran, E., Nadoleanu, G., & Popovici, D. M. (2022). Towards an Accessible Platform for Multimodal Extended Reality Smart Environments. *Information (Basel)*, 13(9), 439. 10.3390/info13090439

Brown, A., & Davis, M. (2021). The role of financial management tools in event planning applications: A user perspective. *Proceedings of the IEEE International Conference on Computer Vision*, (pp. 486-499). IEEE.

Buhalis, D., Harwood, T., Bogicevic, V., Viglia, G., Beldona, S., & Hofacker, C. (2019). Technological disruptions in services: Lessons from tourism and hospitality. *Journal of Service Management*, 30(4), 484–506. 10.1108/JOSM-12-2018-0398

Carswell, J., Jamal, T., Lee, S., Sullins, D. L., & Wellman, K. (2023). Post-Pandemic Lessons for Destination Resilience and Sustainable Event Management: The Complex Learning Destination. *Tourism and Hospitality*, 4(1), 91–140. 10.3390/tourhosp4010007

Chen, Y., & Lu, H. (2018). Leveraging AI in event planning applications: Opportunities and challenges. *International Conference on Human-Computer Interaction*, (pp. 482-495). Research Gate.

Cheng, Y., Sharma, S., Sharma, P., & Kulathunga, K. M. M. C. B. (2020). Role of Personalization in Continuous Use Intention of Mobile News Apps in India: Extending the UTAUT2 Model. *Information (Basel)*, 11(1), 33. 10.3390/info11010033

Fang, J., Zhao, Z., Wen, C., & Wang, R. (2017). Design and performance attributes driving mobile travel application engagement. *Elsevier BV*, 37(4), 269-283. 10.1016/j.ijinfomgt.2017.03.003

Francis, R., Wan Zainodin, W. H., Saifuddin, A. H., & Ahmadrashidi, N. (2023). The Role of Social Media Platforms in Promoting Kaamatan Festival During Covid-19 Pandemic. *International Journal of Academic Research in Business & Social Sciences*, 13(5). 10.6007/IJARBSS/v13-i5/16729

García Revilla, R., Martinez Moure, O., & Einsle, C. S. (2023). Advances in event management using new technologies and mobile applications. *International Journal of Event and Festival Management*, 14(1), 56–72. 10.1108/IJEFM-05-2022-0039

Gidhagen, M., Helkkula, A., Löbler, H., Jonas, J., Sörhammar, D., & Tronvoll, B. (2017). Human-to-nonhuman value co-creation and resource integration: parasocial actors in a service ecosystem. In E. Gummesson, C. Mele, & F. Polese (Eds.), *Service Dominant Logic, Network and Systems Theory and Service Science: Integrating three Perspectives for a New Service Agenda*. Youcanprint Self-Publishing.

Grua, E. M., De Sanctis, M., Malavolta, I., Hoogendoorn, M., & Lago, P. (2022). An evaluation of the effectiveness of personalization and self-adaptation for e-Health apps. *Information and Software Technology*, 146, 106841. 10.1016/j.infsof.2022.106841

Guerreiro, C., Wang, Z., & Nguyen, H. (2020). *New Avenues in Mobile Tourism*. IEEE. 10.1109/IJCNN48605.2020.9207561

Jones, K., & Johnson, L. (2019). Task management features in event planning applications: A usability study of [Your Application Name Here]. *International Journal of Usability Studies*, 14(2), 87–101.

Lee, S., & Kim, E. (2021). User experience design in event planning applications: A comparative study of [Your Application Name Here] and similar apps. *Journal of User Experience Design*, 8(1), 45–60.

Lekgau, R. J., & Tichaawa, T. M. (2022). Exploring the Use of Virtual and Hybrid Events for MICE Sector Resilience: The Case of South Africa. *African Journal of Hospitality, Tourism and Leisure*. 10.46222/ajhtl.19770720.310

Lindström, S., & Pettersson, M. (2010). *Supporting ad-hoc re-planning and share-ability at large-scale events*. 10.1145/1880071.1880113

Luxford, A., & Dickinson, J. E. (2015). The Role of Mobile Applications in the Consumer Experience at Music Festivals. *Event Management*, 19(1), 33–46. 10.3727/152599515X14229071392909

Mansouri, S. (2022). Technology Application in Tourism Events: Reflections on a Case Study of a Local Food Festival in Thailand. In *Digital Transformation and Innovation in Tourism Events*. 10.4324/9781003271147-10

Medini, K., Wiesner, S., Poursoltan, M., & Romero, D. (2020). Ramping Up Customer-Centric Modular Design Projects: Mobile App Development for Pandemic Relief. *Systems*, 8(4), 40. 10.3390/systems8040040

Pasi, S. A., Altaf, P., Shah, T., Amol, P., & Kasture, B. (2018). A Study and Implementation of Event Management System Using Smartphone. *International Journal of Innovative Research in Engineering & Multidisciplinary Physical Sciences*, 6(5).

Paul, N. I., & Ali Amaran, M. (2023). The music events in Kuching, Sarawak post-pandemic times: Changes and perception. *International Journal of Applied and Creative Arts*, 6(1), 01–11. Advance online publication. 10.33736/ijaca.4825.2023

Rady Mohamed, S. (2022). *Technological Innovation in Tourism and Events industry: A hybrid future of Events*. International Journal of Tourism, Archaeology and Hospitality., 10.21608/ijtah.2023.185020.1027

Reinartz, W., Wiegand, N., & Imschloss, M. (2019). The impact of digital transformation on the retailing value chain. *International Journal of Research in Marketing*, 36(3), 350–366. 10.1016/j.ijresmar.2018.12.002

Schut, P. O., & Glebova, E. (2022). Sports Spectating in Connected Stadiums: Mobile Application Roland Garros 2018. *Frontiers in Sports and Active Living*, 4, 802852. 10.3389/fspor.2022.80285235368418

Smith, J. (2018). Enhancing communication and collaboration in event planning through mobile applications: Insights from [Your Application Name Here]. *Journal of Event Technology and Communication*, 5(1), 18–32.

Werner, K., Junek, O., & Wang, C. (2022). Event Management Skills In The Post-Covid-19 World: Insights From China, Germany, And Australia. *Event Management*, 26(4), 867–882. 10.3727/152599521X16288665119558

Zheng, X., Lin, F., & Cai, X. (2021). Exploration of Contextual Marketing Model Based on Mobile Apps. *Proceedings of the 6th Annual International Conference on Social Science and Contemporary Humanity Development (SSCHD 2020)*. Atlantis Press. 10.2991/assehr.k.210121.017

Chapter 5

From Connectivity to Immersion:
Unleashing the Potential of 5G for Seamless Virtual Event Experiences

Paramjeet Kumar
https://orcid.org/0000-0002-3824-2289
North Eastern Hill University, India

Wallamkupar Dkhar
North Eastern Hill University, India

ABSTRACT

This chapter examines the capacity of 5G technology to transform virtual event experiences through improved connectivity and immersive interactions. The chapter explores the capabilities of 5G networks in terms of delivering faster data speeds, extremely low latency, and expanded network capacity. These advancements enable smooth streaming, real-time communication, and the use of virtual reality applications. Furthermore, it emphasises the influence of 5G on different industries including entertainment, education, and business, demonstrating the capacity to generate virtual environments that accurately simulate the experience of participating in a live event.

DOI: 10.4018/979-8-3693-2272-7.ch005

INTRODUCTION TO 5G AND VIRTUAL EVENT EXPERIENCES:

As a result of COVID-19, events related to entrepreneurship and innovation are increasingly being held virtually, and even after the restrictions of the pandemic end, there is an expectation that they will remain a popular choice with above-mentioned features (Jauhiainen, 2021). It has become popular to use this sort of virtual event platform as a perfect substitute for real events, which have an easy and engaging platform for participants. These systems have made great use of 5G technologies to provide better platform connection, where participants can interact on an instant communication analytics and interactive analytics. Such innovations are made possible due to the features of 5G technologies including massive connection and smart bandwidth.

5G technologies grant opportunities for unusual innovations in the experience of online events. While these technologies are quickly emerging, they are becoming more commonplace and their benefits understood. As a result, they are already impacting dramatically on the experience of virtual event participants. An example of this is natural user interfaces and user experiences, many of which rely in part on 5G technology.

It could be said that virtual reality and augmented reality are leading the paradigm shift on these innovations. Elbamby et al. argue in the journal Arab Journal of Business and Management Review that virtual reality will be one of the major applications in the 5G network expected to change the experience of events.

'It allows for participants to interact in an extremely realistic and immersive environment, virtually through the senses. The ability to transmit data via 5G networks due to its high speed and low transmission time will enhance properties of new technologies such as augmented reality and virtual reality.'

Onwuegbuzie (2022) suggests that 5G augments the potentials of various areas of application of AR/VR technologies. This suggests that AR/VR technologies depend on the characteristics of 5G networks, which include high transmission speed, high transmission bandwidth, high network signal quality, low network delay, the number of connections, and many more.

5G can satisfy real-time task requirements with low latency and high speed. The combination of 5G and AR/VR technologies enables a more realistic and diverse interactive experience during event activities.

5G's Role in Enhancing Virtual Event Experiences

The integration of features of 5G in virtual event platforms can be the answer to its development, as Salih et al suggest that 'future smart city as well as intelligent transportation systems are underpinned by the 5G technology'. Further, 'the smart cities and smart transportation concept can serve as an organisational framework for the design of virtual events'. 5G features such as low latency, high bandwidth and network slicing, can be the answer and key for real-time interactions, high-quality seamless virtual experiences and personalized environment tailored to the user and the specific situated necessities. For instance, 'the low latency characteristic of 5G networks permits quick completion of tasks without noticeable lag time inherent in VEPs (virtual event platforms)(Kumar, Mehta, and Pindoriya, 2020)'. Besides, the high bandwidth of 5G networks will allow the transmission of high-quality video and audio data that can be streamed in real-time. Additionally, another 5G technology can enable a virtual-only network: network slicing (also known as network virtualisation). Network slicing creates multiple isolated virtual networks within a single physical network that operate at the same time. These isolated networks can be created to support specific applications, including virtual events. For example, to ensure reliable, secure and quality-focused experience of participating, event traffic can be isolated and independent from other traffic.

Technical Challenges and Considerations

But while 5G-powered virtual events to some extent could potentially resolve this access issue, technical obstacles need to be overcome before its use could be implemented. Of significant importance is the fact that the virtual and physical worlds need to be connected in a way that enables interoperability and compatibility between the virtual or digital worlds and the physical worlds. As Tripathi et al indicate: 'A truly merged experience will require the inundation of the virtual elements with the physical world such that both are indistinguishable. Security and privacy then become matters of primary concern. Virtual event platforms must be built in a way that guarantees protection of user and attendee data, and the confidentiality of all information.

Other important issues are resource management and the scalability of virtual event platforms. Tripathi et al note that 'due to humongous demand for virtual events in the future, if they [these platforms] are required to handle such an extremely large number of users, their processing needs might exceed the computing resources available.' The growing social media backbone will add to the potential of these virtual events, which need to be designed in an optimised manner such that the processing, storage, networking and financial strategies are capable of handling this accelerated growth. Adoption of artificial intelligence-based approaches can play a pivotal role in enabling global-scale platforms for virtual events as discussed by Tripathi et al. AI-based strategies will require further research and development to be integrated with 5G-powered virtual events, since they are still in their infancy.

5G's Impact on Virtual Event Experiences

The integration of 5G has enabled virtual event experiences with new capabilities. One capability example of 5G is network slicing, which provides the means to create dedicated and isolated network environments per catered to the requirements of virtual event applications. This allows for specific envisioned capabilities required by virtual event participants, organisers and service provides, including dedicated slices for domestic and international roaming, and aids in enabling seamless broadcasting of events across different time zones. Network slicing also provides the ability to orchestrate virtual network functions to enable the virtual event infrastructure to scale to meet demand dynamic changes. Coupled with the ultra-low latency of 5G networks, it allows for real-time interactions and feedback enabling 'presence' – a primary component of shared, meaningful and believable immersive experiences that allow us, for virtual events, to experience and communicate as if we were together in the same physical space. This also requires very low latency – a delay of more than 20 milliseconds can cause dissonance in our perception of immersion and make us feel like watching a YouTube video rather than feeling fully present in the VR experience. These also allow higher-bandwidth, higher-quality video and multimedia to be delivered over 5G networks, adding rich visual and sensory piazze features to the experience and creating an opportunity for people to feel more present together. Furthermore, the massive connectivity of 5G networks permit hosting more users in an immersive event with no degradation of the experience. This makes it easier for organisers of virtual events to appeal to a broader audience and reach new audiences.

CHALLENGES AND CONSIDERATIONS

(Mitra Marina 2021) Although the use of 5G technology in virtual experience events gives immense benefits there are some challenges and issues that should be considered. (Giordani et al., 2019)(Kumar Pindoriya, 2020)(Mitra Marina, 2021) Perhaps the most pressing concern is the need to ensure strong cyber security to secure virtual event ecosystem. There is a need to safeguard the event at which thousands of people will be prospective bidders for the auction targeted. Given greater connectivity and prominence of mobile devices, the 5G enabled virtual events represent a new category of attack vectors. There is a greater menace to privacy, safety and security due to integration of a large number of devices and technologies in 5G networks. Hence, it is vital to design robust security protocols and measures to address the security and privacy threats. As Agiwal et al. points out in Mitra & Marina (2021): 'In 5G networks, network agility, capability to connect billions of smart devices, use of machine learning (ML) models and open-source software (OSS) makes them more vulnerable to a new dimension of security as well as of privacy threats.' Thus, virtual event organisers must strive to closely work with security experts to ensure all round cyber security of the event. A further issue might lie with unequal access to 5G technology for participants located in regions with limited infrastructure or resources – generating a digital gap, whereby individuals absent from the bonafide 5G route might not be able to fully partake in the immersive 5G experience of virtualised events, while rendering them unable to partake in the event.

Finally, merging 5G and next-generation technology, such as immersive augmented reality and virtual reality, may demand substantial investment in hardware and software infrastructure, training and user education. As Dang et al noted, 'the interaction between the physical world and the virtual world has to be [comprehensively] investigated and standardised before the feeling of presence, being in the metaverse, is achieved'. Moreover, due to the information-processing demands associated with scaling up virtual events for 5G functionality – as well as the operational needs for consistency and integration – it may become increasingly necessary to adopt AI-supported approaches, as advocated by Dang et al, which may bring a new set of data management, algorithm-creation and ethical constraints.

Overview of Connectivity Trends: An Explanation of 5G

The fifth-generation mobile network known as 5G will eventually transform wireless communications in a way that will greatly improve the experience of virtual events by providing improved communication speeds and bandwidth, as well as higher throughput. Ahmad et al. (2021) describe 5G as follows: 5G technology … will provide high-speed communication, higher capacity, and higher throughput. 5G enables efficient mobile broadband, is able to minimise latency for data transmission, and guarantees reliability of communication while supporting a vast number of machine-to-machine communication services. As a consequence, attendees can experience better video streaming, immediate interaction and instant access to the virtual events platforms. On the other hand, the 5G enables the virtual events platforms to include features such as virtual reality, augmented reality and hologram projections to have a better immersive XR experiences for attendees. 5G enhances the performance of the virtual events, removing many limitations, providing a more complete delivering of the event, serving more attendees and incorporating different types of multimedia techniques that raboscobe. 5G enhances performance of the virtual events platforms: enhances streaming performance, instantiation in milliseconds, endless number of attendees, removing geographic restrictions, virtual reality, augmented reality, and holographic projections, multimedia techniques Immersive XR experiences: instant, on demand, video streaming, collaboration, interaction, haptic, instantiation and representation, rendering Virtual events platforms of the future: better-quality events, more attendees, platform evolution, evolution of XR technology, virtual reality, computer vision, artificial intelligence Giordani, E., Sotiropoulos, K., Papadopoulos, G. and Zhou, L., 2019. 3D Reconstruction Data Streaming With Multi-Resolution Coding for Mixed Reality Content. IEEE Transactions on Multimedia.31(7), pp.2362-2372.DOI: 10.1109/TMM.2018.2881109You, K., Jesionowski, J., Aiello, S. and Bajcsy, R., 2018. Event data analytics and planning for interactive live experiences. IEEE Transactions on Visualization and Computer Graphics. DOI: 10.1109/TVCG.2018.2836935 Conversely, legacy wireless generations (eg, 4G) did not have the necessary bandwidth, latency and connectivity to facilitate the emergence and delivery of virtual events and associated immersive technologies at scale (Giordani et al., 2019),(Le et al., 2016). The technological affordances associated with 5G – eg, network slicing, beamforming and massive MIMO – are now powering a paradigm shift in the use of virtual events.

Potential Benefits of 5G for Virtual Events

(Kumar & Pindoriya, 2020) (Giordani et al., 2019) (Huynh-The et al., 2023) (Mitra & Marina, 2021) It is believed that the incorporation of 5G to the virtual events platforms provides a large scope of the advantages that are useful to virtual event participants, organisers and service providers in multiple ways. Another clear advantage is the higher level of connectivity and network performance achieved with 5G. According to Bartoli and Bevilacqua: 5G networks feature very low latencies, high reliability, and massive device connectivity – all functional enablers for supporting real-time interactions, accurate synchronisation and seamless user experiences such as those required in virtual events.5G Technology Revolution (2017). On the other hand, the low latency and high bandwidth of 5G networks are a prime enabler of event. Case in point, for application services that require immediate reaction for optimal experience, 5G has direct benefits such as 'interactive sessions, screen-taking, remote-working, live QA', allowing 'remote participants to perform a real live discussion, screen-taking, sharing and co-creating without significant asynchrony as latency', as reported by Guidotti et al in 2019. Furthermore, the higher number of devices that can be connected and the scalability of 5G networks allow for more participants to be placed in virtual events, while maintaining the quality of the experience. This allows virtual event organisers to appeal to larger and more diverse audiences in their events. The incorporation of the 5G technology also paves the way for more immersive experiences via augmented reality (AR) and virtual reality (VR). According to Dang et al., 5G's ability to support a high-bandwidth along its low-latency communication is deliberately built for enabling more responsive and immersive experiences during immersive, virtual events. On-site participants at such events can feel more navigable through the virtual world, enabled to interact with interactive holograms or see more three-dimensional content than today, thus leading to greater engagement and presence. Additionally, 5G's features include capabilities called network slicing, which will allow an operator to create secure and reliable 'virtual lanes' within a single network. For example, some VN security and network slicing capabilities might be made available to stage an event requiring secure communications, among other capabilities, and establishing reliable and secure video conferencing, providing network slicing, or assigning different participants different bandwidth quotas for their VN links. VNs are easy to customise for serving virtual events to make them more secure, reliable and of higher quality of service than provided for today's events.

Emerging Technologies Enabled by 5G for Virtual Events

The implementation of this technology for e-events could be more evident if it would be connected with the new technologies including virtual reality (VR), or augmented reality (AR). As this technology uses the virtual environment to provide realistic and immersive experiences for the users, and they would be able to perceive different sensory objects virtually and interact with them in the real world – they will be able to "see, hear, move or feel" in the 3D virtual environment, by stimulating different sensory organs of their body – like touch, smell, hear and see (3d effect) – this technology is considered one of the highest use cases that we would be using on the 5G networks (Elbamby et al., 2019). 5G networks with very low latency, enough bandwidth and reliable connectivity play an instrumental role in electrifying the applications of virtual reality, especially for online conferences, creating an immersive experience for participants. Likewise, overlaid on these real-world views is augmented reality, which includes digital information layered over the real world. Because of the low latency and high bandwidth of 5G networks that support the real-time rendering of augmented reality, event participants in the virtual space can interact with the virtual elements in a natural and responsive manner. Second, the large bandwidth of 5G networks allows the incorporation of an extensive number of IoT devices and sensors into the smart and reactive virtual event environments. These smart environments can be adapted to participant preferences, respond to input on events, adjust lighting, acoustics, et cetera, and can automate event management tasks for a memorable and efficient experience of virtual event. All of these are expected to enhance the event of event such as virtual events, via the powerful combination of 5G technology with these new technologies. More specifically, the ultra-high connectivity, ultra-low latency and high bandwidth that 5G can bring are essential enablers of these transformative technologies for more immersive, interactive and responsive virtual events. References– Huynh-The, K.A.T through

Kim Nguyen. Augmented Reality: Potential for Integration With 5G Technology and Security Concerns. Education. Special Issue: Future of Higher Education: Technology Trends and Strategy. Mobile Learning Using Augmented Reality: Present and Future Prospects. Wireless Communications and Mobile Computing (Huynh-The et al., 2023) (Le et al., 2016) (Kumar & Pindoriya, 2020).

The Significance of 5G in Virtual Events

The effect of 5G is essential in virtual events because it transmits a fine immersive experience to the virtual participants. Using the ability to Virtualise and divide network functions, 5G can guarantee the improved transmission and processing of data, which makes little delay in data communication and reliable communication possible. (Tang, 2022) "5G technology enhances mobile users' broadband experience regarding data connection and communication speed, with reliability and little delay. Moreover, it supports massive connection services for diverse applications. "Since the development of virtual events is essentially the virtual interconnection of the staff and participants, the most critical part is to ensure connectivity. 5G provides sound base for the development of connection, making sure each be participant can participate and communicate actively in the virtual events. What's even better is the fact that 5G offers greater bandwidth capacity, which is essential for the distribution of top-quality multimedia content (virtual reality and augmented reality experiences especially).Thanks to the wide bandwidth capacity of the 5G networks, high-quality, ultra-high-definition, eye-popping video and multimedia content can be delivered for enhanced virtual online events where experience is boosted to the optimum levels, visually and audio-wise. Furthermore, 5G's low latency is also a key driver with important implications for virtual live events, because it can monitor and track real-time interactions and reactions between real people in the virtual space with almost no disruption or delay. In strong contrast to the 300 ms latency that Zoom experiences, 5G raises the possibility of virtual events that can be as interactive as a real-life concert or conference where synchronous, real-time dialogues that properly register the virtual conversations of hundreds or thousands of users within a single event can be supported. Many popular live events, such as some types of panel discussions, workshops or live question-and-answer sessions, demand the intelligence of enabling real-time interactions between participants. To conclude, the inclusion of 5G in virtual events will afford a new paradigm for a live feel to virtual event participants by integrating an enhanced networking infrastructure that significantly promised the business and adoption trajectory for immersive, high resolution, and responsive multimedia and applications experiences within the 5G networks domains (Guidotti et al., 2019)(Giordani et al., 2019)(Guevara Cheein, 2020)(Kumar Pindoriya, 2020).

The Evolution from Connectivity to Immersion: A Progression

The more immersive your event experience, the more memorable it will be With virtual reality and augmented reality (VR/AR) technology, people can be immersed in the details of an event. VR/AR technologies let people feel like they are there and can take users to a virtual world that is almost real. The outstanding speed of 5G can help to open up the full potential of virtual event experience. Another is augmented and virtual reality technologies. VR and AR technologies are a ubiquitous source of excellence as they help people experience uniqueness. For instance, they allow contemplating places that are not feasible in person – being at every planet in the solar system; hearing a concert play by the best seat in the house; visiting an archaeological site of historic landmarks. However, the real-time data transmission required on a large scale for VR and AR technologies may not be achieved by 5G networks. Hence our research is focused subsequently on building more robust network architecture to enable a reliable dedication of data for VR/AR events. For example, virtualisation of network functions allows making more effective use of network resources and makes it possible to adjust capacity in real-time according to the needs of virtual events. This will enhance the capacity of 5G to transmit data and ensure that virtual events have good connections with low delay, stable and high enough capacity to provide immersive experiences. The combined capability of 5G networks and VR/AR technologies will make a comprehensive difference to the experience of virtual events. It goes far beyond the function of connecting people and could potentially bring the 'virtual' experience to a whole new level of immersion and interactivity.

The Convergence of 5G, VR/AR, and IoT for Transformative Virtual Events

By combining 5G, virtual/augmented reality and the Internet of Things (IoT), traditional virtual events could become much more conducive to real-world interactions Celebrities would be able to disseminate video footage, captured with 5G high-bandwidth and low-latency streams, that could be delivered to an audience's VR headsets using 5G. Such content would encompass the five senses and have high resolution. Additionally, audience members could be equipped with wearable IoT devices to capture further data on, for example, heart rate and keystrokes – all unobtrusively. The interconnected devices to enhance the overall virtual event experience.

For example, in virtual events, IoT sensors and devices can be used to monitor the reaction and sentiment of participants in real time, as well as to provide personalised recommendations based on that data to improve the experience. Moreover, 5G, VR/ AR and IoT would support such innovative features as remote collaboration, holographic displays or virtual items 'published' in the physical space, which might even become a part of the real world – participants will be able to visit a virtual workshop, meeting or teambuilding together as if kind of teleported, using, manipulating and annotating digital 3D models, performing other digital tasks in synchronised real-time. Together, these transformative technologies promise to usher us into the next wave of virtual events with features that go well beyond those delivered by Zoom-style online meetings and webinars. This convergence makes it possible for event organisers to create new forms of immersion, interactivity and interconnectivity, affording them new ways for participants to engage like never before.

Enhancing Immersive Experiences With 5G

Event organisers in cyberspace can use 5G functionality to provide the highest immersive experiences for attendees. By enabling new use cases and scenarios in the areas of enhanced mobile broadband communications, ultra-reliable and low-latency communication, and massive machine-type communications, 5G promises faster communication, higher bandwidth and improved throughput. Participants would be able to enjoy full-length HD (or even full 8K quality video) streaming, with high interactivity and low latency, as well as additional features such as haptic feedback and advanced spatial audio. AR and VR are considered both spatial services in these networks (Kitanov et al., 2021). However, due to the current physical data transmission constraints in the 5G network, specific applications may surpass the capacity and latency limits, such as remote surgery, haptic technologies and meeting room VR eXperiences. Nevertheless, constant improvement in 5G would help overcome the barriers and release the full potential for a more immersive VE experience. Thanks to 5G, VEs would be able to truly eliminate the constraints of traditional events and create a real environment. 5G would help VE organisers to completely transform the way participants encounter the VE. One of the key features presented by 5G is haptic technology. Participants are able to perceive a 3D virtual environment through senses other than just their eyes or ears. These virtual attendants can experience the VE through their skin, another sense that can be more immersive and alluring. A study conducted by Wu et al (2021) found that, by combining conventional sensory modalities of VR experiences, participants experienced higher immersion. When haptic feedback is added, the overall sense of immersion is significantly elevated. Through 5G haptic technology, participants can have a more realistic sense of VE. Another great feature presented by 5G is its low latency transmission capability, which helps with data transfer speed, minimal delays and smooth user interaction during VE participation. For example, an online event can involve 100 participants from different countries showing an animation film to viewers worldwide. 5G can serve all the viewers by promptly delivering small video clips and allowing interaction between participants and viewers. The use of 5G CMi (cloud mobile internet) not only accelerates the transmission speed and reduces communication cost, but also brings AR-assisted interventions. Combining 5G and AR provides immersive mixed reality (MR) experiences. Participants can build a 'mixed' AV environment not only communicate with virtual objects, but also share these objects with the actual physical environment. Embodied perception is no longer limited in being 'in-between' physical and virtual space. These features offer tremendous possibilities for event organisers to envisage original and attractive events. For instance, they can create VE halls where participants are able to walk into virtual booths and check different products. For educational events, they can come up with VE classrooms where participants can interact, ask questions and solve problems cooperatively through the powerful interactive school-based educational platform Meet. Based on the wide bandwidth of 5G and rate of rapid data transmission, in VE cooperation and communication can be achieved instantaneously (Liang et al., 2023). Both participants and viewers can talk to each other in real time, exchange data or presentations and conduct cooperation activities without any lag.

The Transformative Capacity of 5G in Revolutionising Virtual Events

5G has the power to transform virtual event experience 5G offers several distinct capabilities that can enhane virtual event experience. Faster transmission speed and higher signal transmission bandwidth make 5G capable of drastically improving the experience of virtual event. Also, due to the low delay on 5G networks, those virtual event attendees should have better experience that will not be dropped going online and can connect more easily, because of the high transmission bandwidth of 5G networks that can allow up to 20,000 times per second. Additionally, 5G can enable approximately 1 milliseconds of latency, which allows new features, such as smooth action for computer-controlled objects on a two-dimensional screen, for example in a game. An experienced gamer can easily notice any latency that differs from zero or close to it. A two-dimensional virtual tour can also be quality assured on a 5G network. Low latency is a critical parameter in virtual events. It ensures that the data transmission to the user does not delay in a way that a participant can notice. Low latency is the characteristic that differentiates wired internet from wireless 5G service For a seamless and immersive experience, 5G can serve as a pipeline for the rapid and effective transmission of large amounts of video information or intricate virtual environments while offering good quality. Low latency networks also allow the transmission of haptic feedback. This is the transmission of sensations that can enhance a virtual reality experience. Haptic feedback can enrich the physical sensation of the immersive experience and thus heighten the level of engagement and saturation it can offer. In a virtual exhibition or conference, an immersive visitor can enjoy the benefits of haptic feedback. This technology allows visitors to feel more lifelike through the sensations provided by computer-controlled objects. Besides sight and hearing, participants can touch and feel a multisensorial three-dimensional experience that distinguishes well from the perceived reality.

Overcoming the Limitations of 5G in Virtual Events

(5G Technology Revolution, 2017) (Giordani et al., 2019)(Guidotti et al., 2019) Despite the numerous advantages of 5G, the technology might not yet be sufficient for delivering all the features demanded by the lifelike experiences of the virtual environment, thus raising some limitations. In line with (Bui et al., 2023), a major hurdle that 5G cannot surmount is scaling the size of the virtual environments while maintaining the distributed consistency such as keeping a consistent spatial awareness of a virtual space where many users interact at the same time. Additionally, inherent limitations of 5G such as mainly outdoor signal propagation that cannot penetrate indoor walls, appearing only on camera view and unable to be seen through obstructions or high-density users/objects like in the metaverse might also hinder delivering a lifelike experience of virtual events (Bui et al., 2023). Future research on 6G networks may be able to fill in the gaps. Artificial intelligence-based solutions may potentially help optimise the network processing, storage and networking to mitigate the cost and resource constraints of the metaverse and virtual environments for virtual meeting planners and meeting attendees. Through the resolution of these limitations, we believe that 5G and beyond could optimally deliver unprecedented, immersive and interactive experiences for the participants of the virtual events. (Huynh-The et al., 2023) (Bui et al., 2023)

Unleashing the Potential: 5G and Seamless Virtual Events

While we are planning 5G for live events, it is important to respect the numerous critical enablers that underpin its features. The obvious one will be the 5G infrastructure: 5G base stations and network infrastructure required to provide wide area 5G coverage and connectivity. There's also a chance to improve how virtual events perform on existing platforms and apps as quickly as 5G networks develop. This involves coding and developing content to exploit the low latency and high data speeds of 5G. Moreover, it involves the implementation of edge computing and content delivery networks to cut latency and provide seamless streaming of the content of virtual events. Furthermore, 5G capabilities should be incorporated in virtual events only through cooperation between network providers, virtual event organisers and content developers. This is a key aspect of effective implementation of 5G capabilities for virtual events. Lastly, hardware and software for user devices are critically important to ensuring smoother operation of virtual events on 5G networks. For instance, most headsets and phones today would not be able to cope with the levels of hardware and software demands for smoothly running VR and AR immersive technologies. Moreover, their speeds and connections must be able to cope with 5G as a network. All of these factors listed here for users are important in the use of 5G for smooth virtual events. However, all of the factors listed above are important to making 5G suitably usable for running virtual events. It is important to recognise that 5G has the capability to revolutionise virtual event experiences via the provision of continuous connectivity and the use of interactive media tools like VR and AR (Chamola et al., 2020).

Case Studies: Successful Deployments of 5G in Virtual Events

Now let's delve into some case studies showing how 5G technology can be integrated in virtual events.

1.The 2021 Tokyo Olympics demonstrated 5G at its finest for engagement with virtual events. Organisers used 5G to give viewers across the world an immersive viewing experience. This technology played a major role in making the virtual experience feel as real as possible by enabling spectating virtually. Spectators were able to use 5G, a wireless connection with ultra low latency and high capacity, to provide virtually an immersive experience. This was done through streaming VR video without a hitch.

2. Mobile World Congress, the major annual industry event of the mobile business, welcomes thousands of attendees from all over the world every year. For the 2022 edition, its organisers have chosen to partner with a leading telecommunications operator to provide a 5G network throughout the event. This allowed the MWC to enhance the virtual experience for guests at its first hybrid edition, thanks to the deployment of a specific 5G network. This network featured broadcasting of virtual reality information in real time, interactive discovery experiences in augmented reality, and also tools for collaboration for networking purposes as well as business meetings. This is one of many examples of the use of 5G in virtual events.

They demonstrate the potential of 5G to transform virtual event experiences by providing nearly lag-free connectivity, immersive technologies and better interactivity for guests. It isn't surprising that virtual reality video is being heralded as the perfect use case for 5G wireless connectivity at virtual events. This is because it can provide an immersive viewing experience while offering the low-latency high-bandwidth network requirements.

Difficulties and Advantages in Enforcing 5G for Virtual Events

However, despite the potential that 5G technology shows to render virtual events flawless, there are still caveats that should be considered on the way to get there. The obstacle that is essential to tackle when considering the use of 5G for immersive technologies is its capacity to transfer high amounts of live data. This serves as a foundation to harness the potential included in the 5G network's theory for immersive virtual events, as applications such as haptic technologies, virtual reality or augmented reality might overstep it at one point. Likewise, another actual example shows another caveat implied in using 5G for virtual events: extremely minimal delay that might need to be considered for applications such as remote surgery or bean counter technology. Haptic headset, Osuit, 2020. At the same time, these caveats for technology notwithstanding, there are also prospects for innovation and for enhanced progress in the utilization of 5G. The main focus must be on inventing new technologies and solutions that would allow further increases of network capacity and for more and more decreased latency. Likewise, there are several benefits that may be obtained when 5G technology is utilized in virtual events: Benifits of 5G for immersive virtual events:- Increased speed of data transfer sites and decreased latency: this is one of the main goals achieved when enabling faster and more performant telecommunication through the usage of 5G networks.- Unstopped streaming: the benefits of fast data speeds are that virtual events can be streamed in high-definition and in real-time, without any minimizing modifications through data packages or any interferences during the live event- Increased immersion through he interaction and the engagement into active participation: the tiny delay achieved by the extremely small latency of 5G also enables real-time interaction and co-creation within virtual events, which is considered to be the main focus behind any truly immersive experience.- More chances through increasing accessibility: the huge presence offered by 5G networks makes it possible to reach more people than ever and to achieve equal access to virtual events for any human, without the need of access to specialized technologies or advanced devices. In conclusion, there are several benefits that may be obtained through the implementation of 5G technology within virtual events and the way towards making the use of such technologies flawless seems to start also now.

There are challenges remaining to overcome, of course, but with advancements in connected events, wider availability of non-stop streaming, immersive experiences and accessibility, 5G functionally promises the technology to help make virtual events part of the future as we know it, not an add-on. Event organisers and technology providers need to work together to help solve the barriers that currently exist and use the capabilities to deliver successful and captivating virtual event experiences.

CONCLUSION: THE PROSPECTS OF 5G AND VIRTUAL EVENT EXPERIENCES

The prospects for 5G and virtual experience is also very exciting. 5G technology can enrich the development of virtual event experience, how it happens will be talked in details. The advantages of 5G can be shown in following points: 1)5G can guarantee a seamless connectivity. 2)A larger â€canvasâ€™ allow organisers to build more engaging experience. 3)With immersive techniques such as low-latency and high-speed data transmission, as well as large capacity, 5G can create ultimate viewing experiences. This also makes the audience and attendees of a convention able to listen and interact seamlessly. One of the key advantages of 5G is its capacity for transporting large amounts of data in real-time. It could support demanding real-time applications, with lower latency and higher bandwidth, which makes it possible to use virtual reality video as the ultimate use case for virtual events (Liu et al., 2020). The development of 5G will also arouse some new applications and use cases. For example, Cardiac surgery done at a distance, Haptic technologies through 5G network, Virtual online conference rooms. 5G will make the experience of virtual event richer than ever. 5G technology can enrich the experience of virtual events through several aspects including connectivity, low latency and immersive techniques. In order to achieve a smooth incorporation of 5G technology in experience of virtual events, there are still several obstacles to overcome that related to the massive capacity, low latency and large bandwidth allowing real-time data transport. Overcoming these obstacles and by saving the potential of 5G, virtual events organisers can may also generate truly smooth, seamless and immersed experience for their attendees. To conclude, the potential of 5G in providing smooth virtual experience is unlimited. 5G technology has the chance offer ultralow latency and ultrahigh security. This can benefit virtual and augmented reality application and help to change the way how the virtual events are being organised.

REFERENCES

Ahmad, H., Islam, M. Z., Ali, R., Haider, A., & Kim, H. S. (2021). Intelligent stretch optimization in information centric Networking-Based tactile internet applications. *Applied Sciences (Basel, Switzerland)*, 11(16), 7351. 10.3390/app11167351

Bui, V., Pandey, S. R., Chiariotti, F., & Popovski, P. (2023, January 1). Game Networking Principles for Real-Time Social Networking in the Metaverse. Cornell University. https://doi.org//arxiv.2302.0167210.48550

Chamola, V., Hassija, V., Gupta, V., & Guizani, M. (2020). A Comprehensive Review of the COVID-19 Pandemic and the Role of IoT, Drones, AI, Blockchain, and 5G in Managing its Impact. *IEEE Access : Practical Innovations, Open Solutions*, 8, 90225–90265. 10.1109/ACCESS.2020.2992341

Giordani, M., Polese, M., Mezzavilla, M., Rangan, S., & Zorzi, M. (2019, January 1). Towards 6G Networks: Use Cases and Technologies. Cornell University. https://doi.org//arxiv.1903.1221610.48550

Guevara, L., & Cheein, F. A. (2020, August 11). The Role of 5G Technologies: Challenges in Smart Cities and Intelligent Transportation Systems. *Sustainability (Basel)*, 12(16), 6469–6469. 10.3390/su12166469

Guidotti, A., Vanelli-Coralli, A., Conti, M., Andrenacci, S., Chatzinotas, S., Maturo, N., Evans, B., Awoseyila, A., Ugolini, A., Foggi, T., Gaudio, L., Alagha, N., & Cioni, S. (2019, March 1). Architectures and Key Technical Challenges for 5G Systems Incorporating Satellites. *IEEE Transactions on Vehicular Technology*, 68(3), 2624–2639. 10.1109/TVT.2019.2895263

Huynh-The, T., Gadekallu, T R., Wang, W., Yenduri, G., Ranaweera, P., Pham, Q., Costa, D B D., & Liyanage, M. (2023, June 1). *Blockchain for the metaverse: A Review*. Elsevier. 10.1016/j.future.2023.02.008

Jauhiainen, J. S. (2021). Entrepreneurship and Innovation Events during the COVID-19 Pandemic: The User Preferences of VirBELA Virtual 3D Platform at the SHIFT Event Organized in Finland. *Sustainability (Basel)*, 13(7), 3802. 10.3390/su13073802

Kitanov, S., Petrov, I., & Janevski, T. (2021). 6G MOBILE NETWORKS: RESEARCH TRENDS, CHALLENGES AND POTENTIAL SOLUTIONS. *Journal of Electrical Engineering and Information Technologies*, 6(2), 67–77. 10.51466/JEEIT2162186067k

Kumar, D., & Pindoriya, N M. (2020, December 17). *A Review on 5G Technological Intervention in Smart Grid*. 10.1109/NPSC49263.2020.9331759

Le, N T., Hossain, M A., Islam, A., Kim, D., Choi, Y., & Jang, Y M. (2016, January 1). *Survey of Promising Technologies for 5G Networks*. IOS Press. 10.1155/2016/2676589

Liang, X., Liu, F., Wang, L., Zheng, B., & Sun, Y. (2023). Internet of Cultural Things: Current research, challenges and opportunities. *Computers, Materials & Continua*, 74(1), 469–488. 10.32604/cmc.2023.029641

Liu, Z., Li, Q., Chen, X., Wu, C., Ishihara, S., Li, J., & Ji, Y. (2020). Point Cloud Video Streaming in 5G Systems and Beyond: Challenges and Solutions. IEEE Network. 10.36227/techrxiv.13138940.v1

Mitra, R N., & Marina, M K. (2021, January 26). *5G Mobile Networks Security Landscape and Major Risks*, 1-23. Wiley. 10.1002/9781119471509.w5GRef145

Onwuegbuzie, I. U. (2022). 5G: next generation mobile wireless technology for a fast pacing world. [JPAS]. *Journal for Pure and Applied Sciences*, 1(1), 1–9. 10.56180/jpas.vol1.iss1.57

Park, J., & Bennis, M. (2018). URLLC-eMBB Slicing to Support VR Multimodal Perceptions over Wireless Cellular Systems. *IEEE Conference on Global Communications (GLOBECOM)*. IEEE. 10.1109/GLOCOM.2018.8647208

Tang, Q., Yu, F. R., Xie, R., Boukerche, A., Huang, T., & Liu, Y. (2022). Internet of Intelligence: A survey on the enabling technologies, applications, and challenges. *IEEE Communications Surveys and Tutorials*, 24(3), 1394–1434. 10.1109/COMST.2022.3175453

You, X., Zhang, C., Tan, X., Jin, S., & Wu, H. (2018, October 26). AI for 5G: Research directions and paradigms. *Springer Nature*, 62(2), 1589–1602. 10.1360/N112018-00174

Chapter 6

The Interactive Bleisure Event:
Gamification and Bibliometric Trends Transforming Attendee Participation

Narendra Kumar
https://orcid.org/0000-0002-3325-3448
Amity University, Noida, India

Swati Sharma
https://orcid.org/0000-0003-2949-2363
Amity University, Noida, India

Gaurav Kumar Gupta
JS University, Shikohabad, India

ABSTRACT

This study explores the emerging concept of "bleisure"-the integration of business and leisure- within the context of interactive events, focusing particularly on the role of gamification and provides bibliometric trends in transforming attendee participation. Leveraging the TCCM and using PRISMA technique, the research provides a comprehensive analysis of current literature, offering theoretical insights and practical implications for event organizers. The findings reveal that gamification significantly enhances attendee engagement by introducing elements of competition, reward, and play, thereby creating more memorable and enjoyable experiences. Bibliometric trends indicate a growing interest in interdisciplinary approaches to bleisure events, highlighting the integration of technology, psychology, and business studies. By synthesizing these insights, the study provides a roadmap for future

DOI: 10.4018/979-8-3693-2272-7.ch006

research and practical applications, suggesting that the strategic incorporation of gamification and attention to bibliometric trends can substantially elevate the impact of bleisure events.

INTRODUCTION

The word 'bleisure' has gained much attention within the domain of event management. Bleisure events, which are a mix of professional and recreational activities, offer a unique platform where participants engage in work-related pursuits and leisure experiences. This is done to enhance attendee satisfaction, improved networking opportunities, and increasing overall engagement of the participants. Day by day, with the advent of new technologies and innovative strategies, such events are continually evolving. Transforming attendee participation during the event is one of the most important contributors to the success of any such event.

The traditional boundaries between work and leisure are increasingly getting blurred due to changing work styles, available technology and cultural shift among the different generations. The rise of staycation and digital nomadism has contributed to this trend immensely and has enabled youth to go for work with a travel part into it. Thus, the concept of bleisure has become more prominent not only for employers but also for employees with its potential to enhance productivity and job satisfaction.

Bleisure events cater to this trend by integrating elements of leisure into business meetings. These events are designed to provide attendees a more conducive environment for learning and networking with enough opportunities to relax and enjoy. The inclusion of leisure activities not only enhances the overall experience but also encourages longer participation. In this process, attendees are more likely to extend their stay when both work and fun are mixed.

Gamification in Bleisure Events

Gamification has become one of the sought-after tools for attendee engagement in business events these days and event organisers are trying to create more interactive and immersive experience by bringing elements like points, badges, challenges and leaderboards. One of the main objectives of gamification in business events is to enhance attendee engagement with enjoyable and rewarding experience. There are many research manuscripts that show significant increase in motivation, participation, and satisfaction among attendees with these gamification tools. For instance, incorporating a scavenger hunt into a conference can encourage attendees to explore the venue, interact with exhibitors, and network with peers, all while competing for prizes. This achieves dual purpose of the event, making events more dynamic and achieving business objectives more effectively.

The literature on business events and attendee participation is diverse and covers various aspects related to different fields. (Tawfeeq & Alabdullah, 2023) focused on the role of audit committees in Omani business contexts and their impact on the financial performance of non-financial companies, particularly in the post-COVID-19 period. The study examined the profitability of the Muscat Securities Market non-financial sector in relation to specific audit committee features. On the other hand, (SenthilKumar et al., 2023) explored student leadership development initiatives for medical students, specifically transitioning to virtual modalities. The study assessed the feasibility and participation in a virtual student organization focused on leadership training, as well as the importance of leadership perceptions among students.

Business events play a crucial role in providing attendees with valuable opportunities for networking, business interactions, and knowledge exchange. (Bauer et al., 2008) has reported that attendees are primarily motivated by business and networking opportunities when participating in mega-business events. (Inoue & Havard, 2014) also suggested that the perceived social impact of a sport event can also influence attendees' experiences and satisfaction, highlighting the importance of generating social benefits for host communities. (Mody et al., 2016) revealed that the destination and product images can significantly impact attendees' perceived benefits and overall experience at conventions and exhibitions. Moreover, (Jung et al., 2016) has shown the incorporation of sustainable practices in the MICE industry while enhancing attendee engagement and satisfaction. (Colombo & Marques, 2020) also studied that understanding attendee motivations is essential for event organizers because different motivations influence the overall event experience. For instance, (Dimitrovski et al., 2021) studied that senior participants attending business events at spa destinations may have varying push and pull motivations, which can be segmented based on destination personality. In times of uncertainty, such as the COVID-19 pandemic, event organizers have emphasized the importance of innovation and resilience in building transformative event environments (Dragin-Jensen et al., 2022). Digital technologies have been utilized to enhance attendees' experiential platforms and expand business potential, rather than just serving as makeshift solutions. This highlights the need for event management research to explore innovative strategies for building a resilient event sector in a post-COVID world.

Bibliometric analysis provides valuable insights into the scholarly trends within a particular field (Kumar & Sharma, 2024). We can highlight emerging trends and identify key areas of focus by analysing publication patterns, citation networks, and current research trends.

In the context of gamification in bleisure events, bibliometric analysis can reveal how the concept has evolved over time, the disciplines that are contributing to its development, and the key themes that are being explored. This information is crucial for researchers and practitioners alike, as it helps them stay updated of the latest developments and identify opportunities for innovation and collaboration.

LITERATURE REVIEW

The concept of bleisure (a combination of business and leisure) has become one of the major areas of research among the researchers of business tourism. Broader changes in work patterns, technology, and cultural attitudes toward work-life balance can be seen. Bleisure events, which integrate professional and recreational activities, offer a unique value proposition by enhancing attendee satisfaction and engagement. Here, we have drawn theoretical framework from multiple disciplines, including tourism, business management, psychology, and technology. From a tourism perspective, the incorporation of leisure into business travel is seen as a strategy to enhance the overall travel experience and increase traveller satisfaction.

Psychological theories like self-determination theory suggests combining leisure activities into professional events can enhance overall well-being and motivation. Such theories reveal that satisfying intrinsic needs for autonomy, competence, and relatedness can get more engagement from the attendees. By offering leisure activities that fulfil these needs, bleisure events can create a more engaging and satisfying experience for attendees. Contextual factors like the location of the event, nature of the business activities, and the availability of leisure options including gamification determine the success of any business event. Research indicates that destinations with a strong appeal for leisure tourism are particularly well-suited for bleisure events, as they offer a wide range of recreational opportunities enhancing the overall experience of the attendees.

The nature of the business activities also plays a crucial role. Events that involve high levels of interaction, creativity, and networking are more likely to benefit from the integration of leisure activities. For instance, business meetings that include team-building exercises or social events can foster stronger relationships among attendees and enhance mutual knowledge transfer.

The effectiveness of any bleisure event depends on the associated activities, the duration of the event and the type of attendees attending it. Different types of activities, pre and post event tours (cultural tours to wellness programs), gamification of the event, can determine the overall success of any business event. For any event to be leisure-oriented, duration of the event plays a significant role. Events that have longer duration, can club leisure activities without compromising the main objective of the event. Even the short duration events, if planned strategically, can benefit attendees with meaningful breaks from there professional activities and thus make such events success. The profiles of the attendees also matter. Events targeting younger professionals, for instance, may benefit more from gamified elements and technology-driven leisure activities, as these demographics are generally more receptive to such innovations.

The methodological approaches used in studying bleisure events are diverse, ranging from qualitative case studies to quantitative surveys and experimental designs. Qualitative methods, such as interviews and focus groups, are valuable for exploring the subjective experiences of attendees and gaining in-depth insights into their motivations and satisfaction (Adu-Ampong & Dillette, 2024; Bassyiouny & Wilkesmann, 2023; Hazira et al., 2022; Tsaur & Tsai, 2023). Quantitative methods, such as surveys and experiments, are useful for measuring the impact of specific interventions, such as gamification, on attendee engagement and satisfaction. These methods can provide robust data that can be generalized across different contexts and populations (Andresen & Bergdolt, 2021; Flavián et al., 2024; Liu-Lastres et al., 2024).

Mixed-method approaches, which combine qualitative and quantitative techniques, offer a comprehensive way to study bleisure events. By integrating the strengths of both approaches, researchers can gain a deeper understanding of the complex dynamics at play (Lichy & McLeay, 2018; Pinho & Marques, 2021; Unger et al., 2019).

Research indicates that gamification can significantly increase motivation, participation, and satisfaction among attendees. For instance, a study by (Hamari et al., 2014) found that gamified elements in educational settings led to higher levels of engagement and improved learning outcomes. Similar effects have been observed by Richter et al. (2015) in the context of professional events, where gamified activities can encourage networking, knowledge sharing, and active participation.

Moreover, gamification can help achieve business objectives by driving specific behaviors. For example, a gamified scavenger hunt at a conference can encourage attendees to visit different booths, interact with exhibitors, and collect information, thereby enhancing their overall experience and increasing the value of the event for sponsors (Wood & Reiners, 2014).

Several studies have focused on the economic impact of the tourism sector in various countries, particularly those in the Mediterranean region (Üyesi Gonca et al., 2019). The COVID-19 outbreak has significantly affected travel behavior and modes of traveling in South Asian countries, as evidenced by a study that collected data from 256 respondents through an online survey (Deyshappriya, 2020). In the Yangtze River Delta, daily intercity mobility dynamics have been analyzed using big data to understand the spatial-temporal patterns of population movements, including different travel purposes such as business trips and leisure activities (Cui et al., 2020). Senior tourism has also been a subject of interest, with a study using SWOT analysis to identify strengths, weaknesses, opportunities, and threats in the senior tourism business sector (Mangunsong, 2020). Factors influencing interest in revisiting tourist destinations have been examined, revealing new factors that impact visitors' perspectives on returning to specific locations. Additionally, camel genetic resources conservation through tourism has been explored as a sociocultural approach to leisure activities, highlighting the importance of customer satisfaction and loyalty in this tourism segment (Pastrana et al., 2020). The COVID-19 pandemic has brought about significant changes in the tourism industry, leading to the concept of "tourism in quarantine" and new challenges for the sector. Different types of tourism based on the purpose of the journey have been studied. Furthermore, the launch of motivation and sports tourism has been investigated through empirical data and regression analysis to understand the factors influencing participation in sports-related tourism activities (Yang, 2021). These studies provide valuable insights into the economic, social, and cultural aspects of business travel and leisure activities, highlighting the importance of understanding travel behavior, tourism trends, and customer satisfaction in the evolving landscape of the tourism industry.

RESEARCH METHODOLOGY

Initial Search

Our review was focused on the database extracted from Scopus. The year range was from 2014-2024 (for ten years). We concentrated on the title, abstract, and keywords fields of the chosen databases to find appropriate papers. The key search phrases were TITLE-ABS-KEY (" Business Travel" OR "business events" OR "Gamification in events" OR " Attendee Participation") AND PUBYEAR > 2013 AND PUBYEAR < 2025 AND (LIMIT-TO (PUBSTAGE, "final")) AND (LIMIT-TO (SUBJAREA, "BUSI") OR LIMIT-TO (SUBJAREA, "SOCI")) AND (LIMIT-TO (DOCTYPE, "ar") OR LIMIT-TO (DOCTYPE, "ch")) AND (LIMIT-TO (LANGUAGE, "English")). Following the inclusion criteria, this initial literature search produced 1361 items in total. Further screening, choosing, and assessing the research items were carried out on the basis of relevance and quality of the document.

PRISMA Technique

PRISMA (Preferred Reporting Items for Systematic Reviews and Meta-Analyses) technique has been used to ensure the selection of relevant and high-quality articles for our study. It is a standardized way of conducting systematic reviews and meta-analyses with a clear scope of identifying, screening, and inclusion of related studies (Moher et al., 2009).

The PRISMA technique involved several key steps for our study. First of all, we did a comprehensive search of academic databases available on Scopus so that we can identify potential articles related to our study. Keywords related to bleisure, gamification, and business tourism were used to identify a wide range of relevant studies. The database was searched keeping following keywords in mind. " Business Travel" OR "business events" OR "Gamification in events" OR " Attendee Participation". Then after, we screened the articles on the basis of predefined inclusion and exclusion criteria. The PRISMA diagram below shows our exclusion and inclusion. This we did to ensure that we include only studies that meet the research objectives. Then, the screened articles were further examined for their relevance, quality, and contribution to the field. This step helped us in filtering out studies that do not provide significant insights or are methodologically flawed. Then the final set of documents (N=234) were obtained which were put for synthesizing a comprehensive overview of the current state of research on gamification in bleisure events.

Figure 1. PRISMA flow chart

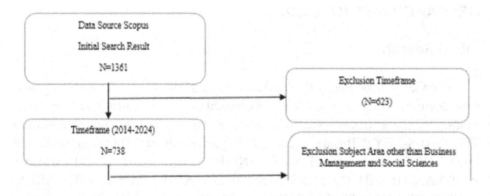

Theoretical Framework: TCCM Approach

To systematically examine the literature on gamification in bleisure events, this study employed the TCCM (Theory, Context, Characteristics, Methodology) framework. The TCCM approach provides a structured way to review and categorize existing research, ensuring a comprehensive and balanced analysis (Paul & Shrivatava, 2016). The TCCM framework has been utilized in various studies to systematically review literature and outline future research agendas (Gaur & Kumar, 2018; Kahiya, 2018; Palmatier et al., 2018; Rugman et al., 2011). The TCCM framework has been instrumental in providing a structured approach to reviewing literature and setting the stage for future research in various fields such as service innovation, marketing standardization/adaptation, organizational ambidexterity, international business, and the impact of external factors like the COVID-19 pandemic. In our study also, we have used TCCM framework that has four of its core approaches. The theoretical foundation of bleisure events encompasses various theories including Theory of Planned Behaviour, Random Utility Theory, Values-Attitudes-Behaviour (VAB) Theory, Social Identity Theory, Social Practice Theory, Institutional Theory (IT), Diffusion of Innovations Theory (DIT), Social Practice Theory, Social Capital Theory and Travel Motivation Theory. By synthesizing these various theories, businesses can create a holistic approach to travel that not only meets operational needs but also supports strategic objectives and enhances the overall employee experience. Different theories used in the extracted database of Scopus were employed by the articles and provided substantial base for conducting this study. The context is another significant area while applying TCCM framework. Bleisure events are planned and decided by the location, the nature of the business activities, and the leisure options available. By examining different contexts, we can identify best practices and potential challenges. For our study, we have identified geographical location as the context. Companies operating in globally dispersed markets must navigate the complexities of time zones, varying climate conditions, and regional infrastructure capabilities, which all affect travel schedules and costs. For instance, traveling to remote or hill area with minimum transport options often demands carefully plalned events and associated activities as arranging them could incur higher expenses compared to well-connected urban business centres. United States, United Kingdom, Australia, China, Germany, Spain, South Africa, India, New Zealand, Malaysia, Italy, Finland and Japan are the countries where research related to business travel has higher frequency. Another crucial factors in TCCM framework is the characteristics of bleisure events as this helps in designing more effective and appealing events. Scavenger hunts, networking games, and knowledge-based quizzes at conferences and trade shows are some of the tools that can transform passive attendees into active participants through gamification. Overall event value can also be increased by encouraging involvement of the attendees and this can be done by rewarding behaviors such as attending sessions, visiting exhibitor booths, or participating in workshops. The methodological approaches used in studying bleisure events vary widely, from qualitative case studies to quantitative surveys and experimental designs. By reviewing the methodologies, we can assess the robustness of the findings and identify gaps in the literature. Adopting a mixed-method approach, combining quantitative surveys with qualitative interviews or focus groups, offers a comprehensive understanding of the multifaceted dimensions of bleisure travel. Surveys can provide quantitative data on the prevalence, motivations, and preferences of bleisure travelers, offering valuable insights into demographic trends and travel behaviours. Meanwhile, qualitative methods allow for a deeper exploration of the psychological, social, and cultural factors driving bleisure decisions, shedding light on the experiential aspects and emotional dynamics of blending work and leisure activities. Additionally, employing longitudinal or cross-sectional designs enables researchers to track changes in bleisure practices over time and compare variations across different regions or industries. By adhering to robust methodological principles, researchers can generate credible and actionable findings that inform business strategies, policy decisions, and marketing initiatives aimed at tapping into the growing bleisure market.

Table 1. TCCM framework

Theory	Context	Characteristics	Methodology
• Theory of Planned Behaviour • Random Utility Theory • Values-Attitudes-Behaviour (VAB) Theory • Social Identity Theory • Social Practice Theory • Institutional Theory (IT) • Diffusion of Innovations Theory (DIT) • Social Practice Theory • Social Capital Theory • Travel Motivation Theory	• United States • United Kingdom • Australia • China • Germany • Spain • South Africa • India • New Zealand • Malaysia • Italy • Finland • Japan	• Reward • Competition • Recognition • Gamification • Business Travel • Business Events	• on-site survey • Qualitative Research • Mixed Method Approach • Face to Face interviews • Structured Questionnaire Survey • Quantitative Survey Method • two-stage case-study methodology • PLS-SEM methodology • Digital Content Analysis

BIBLIOMETRIC ANALYSIS OF EVENT GAMIFICATION

Co-Authorship Analysis

Co-authorship analysis examines the collaborative relationships between authors based on their co-authored publications. The main purpose of finding co-authorship analysis is to identify research groups or collaborations between authors; to analyze the strength and structure of these collaborative networks and to discover prominent authors and collaborative hubs in the field of our study. In our study, we have chosen minimum two articles and 10 citations of any author as threshold limit. Of the 522 authors, we found only 48 authors meeting the threshold criteria. For each of the 48 authors, the total strength of co-authorship links with other authors was calculated and the authors with greatest total link strength was selected for further analysis. Figure 1 shows the authors' collaborative work in the field of business events and associated activities that can motivate the attendee's engagement in the business events. We could find very limited studies that could talk about the role of gamification in the motivation of attendees that means there is still lot to be researched and analysed with regard to gamification in the business events. Interesting to note here that one of highly contributed author in the field of business travel, Liisa Mäkelä from the Finland has discussed at length about the personal well-being of the business travellers (Mäkelä et al., 2014, 2015, 2021a, 2021b; Mäkelä & Kinnunen, 2018). We can see that with these kind of mental and health related problem with the business travellers, gamification can provide relaxed environment and a positive business environment can be created. Two clusters (cluster 1 and cluster 2) are visible with three prominent authors (Kinnunen Ulla, Mäkelä Liisa, Tanskanen jussi and Bergbom Barbara, Saarenpää Kati, Suutri Vesa) in each cluster who have collaborated in the field of business travel. It is notable that great scope lies in the field of business travel and associated gamification in events.

Overlay Visualization of Co-Author Analysis

Figure 2. Overlay visualization of co-author analysis

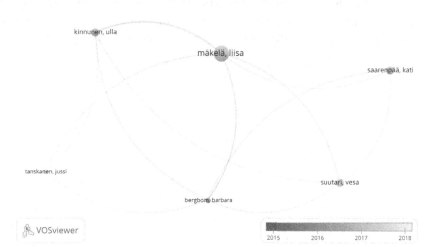

Overlay Visualization of Country-Wise Collaboration

Overlay visualization of country-wise collaboration is a valuable tool for understanding research trends and partnerships between different nations. In a bibliometric analysis of business events, the use of overlay visualization maps country-wise collaborations, providing insights into the global research landscape. Overlay visualization of network analysis includes a country-wise co-authorship analysis, demonstrating the collaborative efforts between countries in this area of research. The visualization of collaborative efforts between countries can help interpret research trends and highlight areas of strong international cooperation. By utilizing overlay visualization techniques, we gain a better understanding of the distribution of research output and collaborations across different countries. While analysing country collaboration, we kept a threshold of minimum 2 documents of a country. The most collaborative countries were United Kingdom, Australia, United States, China, Germany, South Africa, Malaysia, Finland and Spain with 43,32,22,19, 13, 12 11,10 and 10 documents respectively. This shows that research collaboration is in nascent stage in most of the developing countries with regard to business tourism and a lot of collaboration is required to increase the contribution from these countries. Funding for research could also be possibly one of the reasons why these developing countries are lacking behind in terms of research on business tourism. When we talk about the gamification in the event business, countries like UK, US and Australia have prioritised the research in this area too.

Figure 3. Overlay visualization of country-wise collaboration

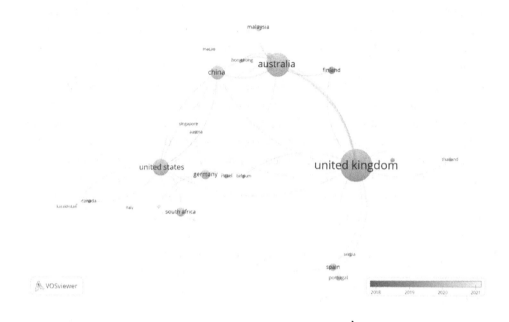

Co-Citation Analysis

Co-citation analysis in tourism is a valuable method for understanding the interconnectedness of research within the field. Sustainable tourism management, digital transformation, tourism forecasting, immersive technology, digital tourism, smart hotels, and e-commerce in tourism are some the trends that have shaped the recent studies in the field of smart tourism. These studies demonstrate the importance of bibliometric analysis in understanding trends, developments, and future research directions. Co-citation analysis has been utilized in various studies to explore different aspects of business and tourism. (Arcese et al., 2021) conducted a systematic literature review to investigate the role of the family business model as an innovation driver in the tourism sector. (Teixeira et al., 2020) also employed co-citation analysis to map and analyze the intellectual knowledge on research into family firms in Asian contexts, focusing on their unique characteristics and succession management. (Santos et al., 2020) utilized co-citation analysis to understand the scientific production in frugal innovation, highlighting the different perspectives and scattered nature of the concept. Furthermore, (Kraus et al., 2020) conducted co-citation analysis in the sharing economy research, identifying themes related to the tourism industry such as public acceptability and social connection. (Shekhar et al., 2022a) used co-citation networks to map the development of research on family business in tourism and hospitality, recognizing key contributors, major themes, and suggesting future research directions. Additionally, (Binh Nguyen et al., 2023) focused on tourism content marketing research, revealing themes such as the impact of electronic word of mouth (eWOM) and social media on business performance through co-citation analysis. Overall, co-citation analysis has proven to be a valuable tool in understanding various aspects of business and tourism research (Kumar et al., 2022), from family business models to frugal innovation and content marketing. By identifying key contributors, major themes, and research trends, co-citation analysis provides insights that can guide future research directions in these fields.

In our study here, we have analysed co-citation analysis on the basis of cited references. The threshold (minimum number of citations of a cited references) selected for this co-citation analysis was 5. Of the 11506 cited references, we found 49 meeting the threshold. One article had no link strength and hence was not included in clusters. We found 4 clusters with cluster 1 (16 items in red), cluster 2 (14 items in green), cluster 3 (12 items in blue) and cluster 4 (6 items in olive).

Figure 4. Co-Citation analysis

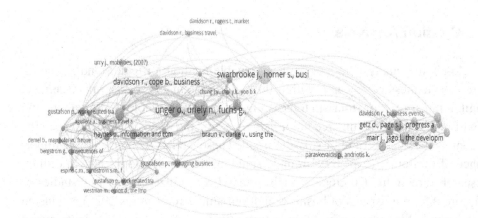

Bibliographic Coupling of Sources

The intersection of innovation, entrepreneurship, and knowledge in the business scientific field has been recognized as crucial for economic competitiveness and growth (Piñeiro-Chousa et al., 2020). Through bibliometric studies utilizing co-citation and bibliographic coupling, researchers have been able to analyze ongoing studies in various business-related fields, such as business schools and family business in tourism and hospitality (Shekhar et al., 2022b). These studies have provided insights into key contributors, major themes, and future research directions within these areas. The impact of external factors, such as the coronavirus health crisis, on the business and tourism sector has also been explored through bibliographic methodologies. By conducting surveys among small and medium-sized companies in the tourism sector, researchers have aimed to understand the social and economic implications of such crises on businesses. Furthermore, the use of bibliometric analysis has extended to other fields, such as flood management (Kusuma et al., 2021), management international review (Mukherjee et al., 2021), entrepreneurship in tourism studies (Ochoa Jiménez et al., 2022) and Netnography in business research (Bansal et al., 2023). These studies have contributed to understanding the research landscape, identifying key trends, and suggesting future research directions within their respective domains. Bibliographic coupling of sources helps in understanding how closely different journals are related in terms of the references they cite. This is particularly useful in fields like business tourism, where the literature can be multidisciplinary, spanning areas such as business management, tourism studies, and hospitality. In our study, the threshold that we have taken, is minimum 02 documents from a source and minimum 20 citations of a source. Of the 130 sources, we found only 22 meeting the threshold criteria. *"Event Management"* has topped the list with 21 documents with meeting criteria. *"Journal of Convention and Event Tourism"* has 7 document and *"Tourism Management"*, and *"Journal of Global Mobility"* has 5 documents each. In terms of citation counts, *"Tourism Management"*, "Event *Management"* and "Annals *of Tourism Research"* are the top three journal sources that have dominated the citation count.

Figure 5. Bibliographic coupling of sources

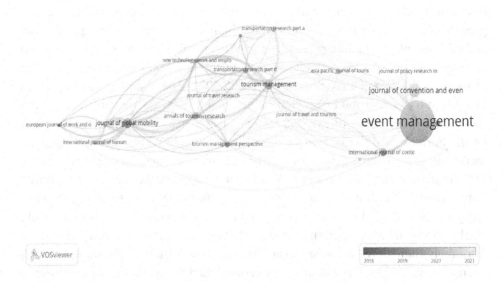

Limitations and Future Scope of the Research

While this study provides valuable insights into the integration of gamification and bibliometric trends in bleisure events, several limitations must be acknowledged to contextualize the findings and guide future research. The scope of the research is limited to the examination of bleisure events through the lens of gamification and bibliometric analysis. While these two areas offer significant potential for enhancing attendee participation and satisfaction, they represent only a subset of the broader spectrum of factors that influence the success of bleisure events. Other elements, such as event design, cultural influences, and individual attendee preferences, also play critical roles and warrant further investigation.

Additionally, the findings of this study may not be fully generalizable across all types of bleisure events. Different industries and professional contexts might exhibit unique characteristics and requirements that affect the applicability of gamification and bibliometric insights. For example, a medical conference might have different engagement dynamics compared to a tech industry summit. The study relies heavily on existing literature and secondary data obtained through bibliometric analysis. While this approach provides a broad overview of research trends and developments, it may not capture the most recent or unpublished innovations in the field of bleisure events. The quality and reliability of the findings are dependent on the rigor and comprehensiveness of the studies included in the analysis. Moreover, bibliometric analysis often focuses on quantitative metrics such as citation counts and publication frequencies, which may not fully reflect the qualitative impact or practical relevance of the research. High citation counts can sometimes be driven by factors unrelated to the quality or applicability of the research, such as the prominence of the authors or journals.

The rapid pace of technological advancement presents both an opportunity and a challenge for research in bleisure events. Technologies such as virtual and augmented reality, artificial intelligence, and mobile applications are continually evolving, offering new ways to enhance the bleisure experience. However, this rapid evolution can also render existing research quickly outdated, necessitating continuous updates and adaptations of theoretical models and practical frameworks. The study may not fully account for the latest technological innovations or their potential impacts on bleisure events. Ongoing research and real-time data collection are essential to keep pace with these developments and ensure the relevance of the findings.

CONCLUSION

The integration of gamification and bibliometric trends in bleisure events presents a rich field for ongoing research and innovation. Several promising avenues can be explored to deepen our understanding and enhance the practical applications of these concepts. Future research can delve deeper into the design and implementation of advanced gamification strategies tailored specifically for bleisure events. This includes exploring various game mechanics and dynamics, such as narrative storytelling, personalized challenges, and real-time feedback systems. Researchers can investigate how different gamification elements impact attendee engagement, learning, and satisfaction across diverse event formats and industries (Sailer et al., 2017).

Moreover, longitudinal studies can examine the long-term effects of gamification on attendee behavior and business outcomes. By tracking participants over multiple events, researchers can assess how sustained engagement with gamified activities influences networking, knowledge retention, and career development. The rapid advancement of emerging technologies such as virtual reality (VR), augmented reality (AR), artificial intelligence (AI), and blockchain presents new opportunities for enhancing bleisure events. Future research should explore how these technologies can be integrated with gamification to create immersive and interactive experiences. For example, VR and AR can be used to create virtual environments for networking and collaboration, while AI can provide personalized recommendations and adaptive learning experiences (Kim et al., 2018).

Personalization is a key trend in many industries, and bleisure events are no exception. Future research can explore how data analytics and machine learning algorithms can be used to personalize bleisure experiences based on individual preferences, behaviors, and feedback. Personalized agendas, customized leisure activities, and tailored networking opportunities can significantly enhance attendee satisfaction and engagement (Smith et al., 2020). Researchers can also examine the ethical implications of personalization, particularly in terms of data privacy and security. Ensuring that attendees' personal information is handled responsibly and transparently will be crucial for building trust and fostering positive experiences.

As bleisure events become more global, understanding the cultural nuances that influence attendee preferences and behaviors is essential. Future research should conduct comparative studies across different cultural and regional contexts to identify how cultural factors affect the design and effectiveness of gamified bleisure activities. This can include examining differences in work-life balance attitudes, leisure activity preferences, and receptiveness to gamification (Hofstede et al., 2010). By identifying culturally specific strategies, event organizers can create more inclusive and adaptable bleisure experiences that resonate with diverse audiences. This research can also inform the development of culturally sensitive gamification frameworks that enhance engagement and participation across different regions.

Comprehensive evaluation methods are needed to assess the impact of bleisure events on both attendees and organizers. Future research should develop and validate robust evaluation frameworks that capture a wide range of outcomes, including attendee satisfaction, knowledge transfer, networking effectiveness, and business ROI. Mixed-method approaches that combine quantitative surveys, qualitative interviews, and behavioral analytics can provide a holistic understanding of the event's impact (Creswell & Creswell, 2017).

Furthermore, longitudinal studies can track the long-term effects of bleisure events on professional development, career advancement, and organizational performance. This research will provide valuable insights into the enduring benefits of integrating business and leisure activities and inform the continuous improvement of bleisure event strategies.

REFERENCES

Adu-Ampong, E. A., & Dillette, A. (2024). Commemoration and commodification: Slavery heritage, Black travel and the #YearofReturn2019 in Ghana. *Tourism Geographies*, 26(1), 120–139. 10.1080/14616688.2023.2275731

Andresen, M., & Bergdolt, F. (2021). Individual and job-related antecedents of a global mindset: An analysis of international business travelers' characteristics and experiences abroad. *International Journal of Human Resource Management*, 32(9), 1953–1985. 10.1080/09585192.2019.1588349

Arcese, G., Valeri, M., Poponi, S., & Elmo, G. C. (2021). Innovative drivers for family business models in tourism. *Journal of Family Business Management*, 11(4), 402–422. 10.1108/JFBM-05-2020-0043

Bansal, R., Martinho, C., Pruthi, N., & Aggarwal, D. (2023). From virtual observations to business insights: A bibliometric review of netnography in business research. *Heliyon*, 10(1), e22853. Advance online publication. 10.1016/j.heliyon.2023.e2285338163120

Bassyiouny, M., & Wilkesmann, M. (2023). Going on workation – Is tourism research ready to take off? Exploring an emerging phenomenon of hybrid tourism. *Tourism Management Perspectives*, 46, 101096. 10.1016/j.tmp.2023.101096

Bauer, T., Law, R., Tse, T., & Weber, K. (2008). Motivation and satisfaction of mega-business event attendees: The case of ITU Telecom World 2006 in Hong Kong. *International Journal of Contemporary Hospitality Management*, 20(2), 228–234. 10.1108/09596110810852195

Binh Nguyen, P. M., Pham, X. L., & To Truong, G. N. (2023). A bibliometric analysis of research on tourism content marketing: Background knowledge and thematic evolution. *Heliyon*, 9(2), e13487. 10.1016/j.heliyon.2023.e1348736816254

Colombo, A., & Marques, L. (2020). Motivation and experience in symbiotic events: An illustrative example grounded in culture and business events. *Journal of Policy Research in Tourism, Leisure & Events*, 12(2), 222–238. 10.1080/19407963.2019.1657437

Cui, C., Wu, X., Liu, L., & Zhang, W. (2020). The spatial-temporal dynamics of daily intercity mobility in the Yangtze River Delta: An analysis using big data. *Habitat International*, 106, 102174. 10.1016/j.habitatint.2020.102174

Deyshappriya, N. P. R. (2020). Dynamics of Travel Behaviour and Mode of Travelling during COVID-19 Outbreak. Evidence from South Asian Countries. SSRN *Electronic Journal*. https://doi.org/10.2139/SSRN.3725681

Dimitrovski, D., Seočanac, M., & Luković, M. (2021). Business events at a spa destination: An insight into senior participant motivation. *International Journal of Tourism Cities*, 7(1), 13–31. 10.1108/IJTC-04-2019-0054

Dragin-Jensen, C., Kwiatkowski, G., Hannevik Lien, V., Ossowska, L., Janiszewska, D., Kloskowski, D., & Strzelecka, M. (2022). Event innovation in times of uncertainty. *International Journal of Event and Festival Management*, 13(4), 387–405. 10.1108/IJEFM-07-2021-0063

Flavián, C., Ibáñez-Sánchez, S., Orús, C., & Barta, S. (2024). The dark side of the metaverse: The role of gamification in event virtualization. *International Journal of Information Management*, 75, 102726. 10.1016/j.ijinfomgt.2023.102726

Gaur, A., & Kumar, M. (2018). A systematic approach to conducting review studies: An assessment of content analysis in 25 years of IB research. *Journal of World Business*, 53(2), 280–289. 10.1016/j.jwb.2017.11.003

Hamari, J., Koivisto, J., & Sarsa, H. (2014). Does gamification work? - A literature review of empirical studies on gamification. *Proceedings of the Annual Hawaii International Conference on System Sciences*, (pp. 3025–3034). IEEE. 10.1109/HICSS.2014.377

Hazira, M. N., Alagas, E. N., Amin, M., Zamzuri, N. H., & Zairul, M. M. (2022). The best practice of marketing strategies for the Malaysian business event industry from experts' perspective. *Journal of Hospitality and Tourism Insights*, 5(2), 413–434. 10.1108/JHTI-09-2020-0178

Inoue, Y., & Havard, C. T. (2014). Determinants and Consequences of the Perceived Social Impact of a Sport Event. *Journal of Sport Management*, 28(3), 295–310. 10.1123/jsm.2013-0136

Jung, S., Kim, Y. S., Malek, K., & Lee, W. (2016). Engaging attendees in environmental sustainability at trade shows: Attendees' perceptions and willingness to participate. *Anatolia*, 27(4), 540–542. 10.1080/13032917.2016.1193758

Kahiya, E. T. (2018). Five decades of research on export barriers: Review and future directions. *International Business Review*, 27(6), 1172–1188. 10.1016/j.ibusrev.2018.04.008

Kraus, S., Li, H., Kang, Q., Westhead, P., & Tiberius, V. (2020). The sharing economy: A bibliometric analysis of the state-of-the-art. *International Journal of Entrepreneurial Behaviour & Research*, 26(8), 1769–1786. 10.1108/IJEBR-06-2020-0438

Kumar, N., & Sharma, S. (2024). *Demystifying the Technology Adoption by the Asian Cargo Industry*. 10.4018/979-8-3693-1602-3.ch006

Kumar, N., Tandon, R., & Misra, N. (2022). Emotional Intelligence as Intangible Class Content for Effective Communication in Managing University Classes: A Bibliometric Analysis. *Journal of Content. Community and Communication*, 16(8), 26–36. 10.31620/JCCC.12.22/03

Kusuma, R. R., Widianingsih, I., Ningrum, S., & Myrna, R. (2021). Five clusters of flood management articles in Scopus from 2000 to 2019 using social network analysis. *Science Editing*, 8(1), 85–92. 10.6087/kcse.234

Lichy, J., & McLeay, F. (2018). Bleisure: Motivations and typologies. *Journal of Travel & Tourism Marketing*, 35(4), 517–530. 10.1080/10548408.2017.1364206

Liu-Lastres, B., Bufkin, A., & Cecil, A. (2024). Developing a risk profile of female business travellers in pandemic times. *Routledge handbook on gender in tourism: Views on Teaching, Research and Praxis*, 178–192. 10.4324/9781003286721-18

Mäkelä, L., Bergbom, B., Saarenpää, K., & Suutari, V. (2015). Work-family conflict faced by international business travellers: Do gender and parental status make a difference? *Journal of Global Mobility*, 3(2), 155–168. 10.1108/JGM-07-2014-0030

Mäkelä, L., Bergbom, B., Tanskanen, J., & Kinnunen, U. (2014). The relationship between international business travel and sleep problems via work-family conflict. *Career Development International*, 19(7), 794–812. 10.1108/CDI-04-2014-0048

Mäkelä, L., & Kinnunen, U. (2018). International business travelers' psychological well-being: The role of supportive HR practices. *International Journal of Human Resource Management*, 29(7), 1285–1306. 10.1080/09585192.2016.1194872

Mäkelä, L., Tanskanen, J., Kangas, H., & Heikkilä, M. (2021a). International business travelers' job exhaustion: Effects of travel days spent in short-haul and long-haul destinations and the moderating role of leader-member exchange. *Journal of Global Mobility*, 9(3), 434–455. 10.1108/JGM-10-2020-0066

Mäkelä, L., Tanskanen, J., Kangas, H., & Heikkilä, M. (2021b). International business travelers' job exhaustion: Effects of travel days spent in short-haul and long-haul destinations and the moderating role of leader-member exchange. *Journal of Global Mobility*, 9(3), 434–455. 10.1108/JGM-10-2020-0066

Mangunsong, F. (2020). SENIOR TOURISM AND CHANCE FOR TOURISM BUSINESS PLAYERS. *Journal of Tourism, Hospitality and Environment Management, 5*(19), 01–13. 10.35631/JTHEM.519001

Mody, M., Gordon, S., Lehto, X., So, S. I., & Li, M. (2016). The Augmented Convention Offering: The Impact of Destination and Product Images on Attendees' Perceived Benefits. *Tourism Analysis*, 21(1), 1–15. 10.3727/108354216X145374 59508739

Mukherjee, D., Kumar, S., Donthu, N., & Pandey, N. (2021). Research Published in Management International Review from 2006 to 2020: A Bibliometric Analysis and Future Directions. *MIR. Management International Review*, 61(5), 599–642. 10.1007/s11575-021-00454-x34658534

Ochoa Jiménez, S., García García, A. R., Valdez del Río, S., & Jacobo Hernández, C. A. (2022). Entrepreneurship in Tourism Studies in the 21st Century: A Bibliometric Study of Wos and Scopus. *SAGE Open*, 12(2). 10.1177/21582440221102438

Palmatier, R. W., Houston, M. B., & Hulland, J. (2018). Review articles: Purpose, process, and structure. *Journal of the Academy of Marketing Science*, 46(1), 1–5. 10.1007/s11747-017-0563-4

Pastrana, C. I., González, F. J. N., Ciani, E., Baena, S. N., & Bermejo, J. V. D. (2020). Camel Genetic Resources Conservation through Tourism: A Key Sociocultural Approach of Camelback Leisure Riding. *Animals (Basel)*, 10(9), 1–23. 10.3390/ani1009170332962294

Paul, J., & Shrivatava, A. (2016). Do young managers in a developing country have stronger entrepreneurial intentions? Theory and debate. *International Business Review*, 25(6), 1197–1210. 10.1016/j.ibusrev.2016.03.003

Piñeiro-Chousa, J., López-Cabarcos, M. Á., Romero-Castro, N. M., & Pérez-Pico, A. M. (2020). Innovation, entrepreneurship and knowledge in the business scientific field: Mapping the research front. *Journal of Business Research*, 115, 475–485. 10.1016/j.jbusres.2019.11.045

Pinho, M., & Marques, J. (2021). The bleisure tourism trend and the potential for this business-leisure symbiosis in Porto. *Journal of Convention & Event Tourism*, 22(4), 346–362. 10.1080/15470148.2021.1905575

Richter, G., Raban, D. R., & Rafaeli, S. (2015). Studying gamification: The effect of rewards and incentives on motivation. *Gamification in Education and Business*, 21–46. 10.1007/978-3-319-10208-5_2

Rugman, A. M., Verbeke, A., & Nguyen, Q. T. K. (2011). Fifty Years of International Business Theory and Beyond. *MIR. Management International Review*, 51(6), 755–786. 10.1007/s11575-011-0102-3

Santos, L. L., Borini, F. M., & Oliveira Júnior, M. (2020). In search of the frugal innovation strategy. *Review of International Business and Strategy*, 30(2), 245–263. 10.1108/RIBS-10-2019-0142

SenthilKumar, G., Sommers, K. C., He, Y., Stark, K., Craig, T., Keval, A., Shah, N., Patel, K., & Meurer, J. (2023). Student Leadership Development Initiative for Medical Students: Lessons Learned From Transitioning to Virtual Modalities. *Journal of Medical Education and Curricular Development*, 10, 23821205231200731. 10.1177/23821205231200731137692559

Shekhar, G., Gupta, A., & Valeri, M. (2022a). Mapping research on family business in tourism and hospitality: A bibliometric analysis. *Journal of Family Business Management*, 12(3), 367–392. 10.1108/JFBM-10-2021-0121

Shekhar, G., Gupta, A., & Valeri, M. (2022b). Mapping research on family business in tourism and hospitality: A bibliometric analysis. *Journal of Family Business Management*, 12(3), 367–392. 10.1108/JFBM-10-2021-0121

Tawfeeq, T., & Alabdullah, Y. (2023). THE ROLE OF AUDIT COMMITTEES IN OMANI BUSINESS CONTEXT: DO THEY AFFECT THE PERFORMANCE OF NON-FINANCIAL COMPANIES. *JOURNAL OF HUMANITIES, SOCIAL SCIENCES AND BUSINESS*, 2(4), 643–659. 10.55047/jhssb.v2i4.707

Teixeira, S., Mota Veiga, P., Figueiredo, R., Fernandes, C., Ferreira, J. J., & Raposo, M. (2020). A systematic literature review on family business: Insights from an Asian context. *Journal of Family Business Management*, 10(4), 329–348. 10.1108/JFBM-12-2019-0078

Tsaur, S. H., & Tsai, C. H. (2023). Bleisure travel experience: Scale development and validation. *Journal of Travel & Tourism Marketing*, 40(1), 21–37. 10.1080/10548408.2023.2199773

Üyesi Gonca, Ö., Davras, M., Uygulamalı, I., Üniversitesi, B., Fakültesi, T., Üyesi, Ö., Baykul, A., & Yüksekokulu, I. M. (2019).. . *Türk Turizm Araştırmaları Dergisi ARAŞTIRMA MAKALESİ Akdeniz Ülkelerinde Turizm Sektörünün Ekonomik Etkinliğinin Değerlendirilmesi.*, 2019(3), 791–804. 10.26677/TR1010.2019.192

Wood, L. C., & Reiners, T. (2014). *Gamification*. IGI Global. 10.4018/978-1-4666-5888-2.ch297

Yang, D. (2021). RETRACTED: Online sports tourism platform based on FPGA and machine learning. *Microprocessors and Microsystems*, 80, 103584. 10.1016/j.micpro.2020.103584

Chapter 7
Emergence of Metaverse:
An Innovative Technological Fusion in Indian Festivals

Ruchika Kulshrestha
GLA University, Mathura, India

Ashutosh Pandey
FORE School of Management, New Delhi, India

Abhijeet V. Tiwari
GLA University, Mathura, India

ABSTRACT

This chapter aims to examine how the metaverse has given rise to new interpretations of Indian festivals,which also covers a number of difficulties in establishing connections with the communities. The exploratory study that served as the basis for this chapter aimed to gather factual information regarding the current situation and the emerging metaverse related trends. The actual procedures that stakeholders followed were analysed using a qualitative case study. This research uses secondary data from other scholarly papers and articles to offer the authors' perspective on the metaverse festival blueprint. This chapter focuses on the evolutionary concepts of the metaverse and its implications on intangible ceremonial activities.Since there isn't much previous research published in the literature, there isn't a lot of discussion about metaverse in Indian festivals at the moment.

DOI: 10.4018/979-8-3693-2272-7.ch007

INTRODUCTION

The vibrancy and diversity of Indian festivals have long been celebrated as integral components of the country's cultural fabric, reflecting a rich tapestry of traditions, beliefs, and rituals (Shah P.et al., 2023). From Diwali's illuminating festivities to Holi's kaleidoscopic splendour, these annual celebrations serve as occasions for communal bonding, spiritual reverence, and artistic expression. However, in an increasingly digitised world characterised by technological advancements and virtual interactions, the question arises: how can Indian festivals adapt and thrive in the metaverse?The metaverse has created a stir in the business sector because to its capacity to remodel an ecosystem for new goods, services, and developing synthetic consumer experiences. However, there is a dearth of information about the metaverse and its potential for use by scholars and practitioners worldwide (Buhalis et al., 2023).

The metaverse, a phrase popularised by science fiction and currently gaining prominence in technical discussions, denotes a shared virtual realm where individuals can engage, generate, and investigate in real-time (Bibri,SE.et al., 2022). The convergence of immersive technologies like virtual reality (VR), augmented reality (AR), and other technologies creates for consumers a smooth integration of digital and physical lives (Dwivedi, Y. K., et al., 2022). Festival celebrations may change dramatically as the metaverse permeates many sectors, including entertainment, education, commerce, and social networking.

A major effect of the COVID-19 pandemic has been on the travel and tourist sector. In response, a lot of travel agencies have included Metaverse technologies in their offerings to satisfy customers (Chen, 2021). A digital revolution is now taking place in the industry in response to the emergence of digital platforms (Cuomo et al., 2021). Traditional travel models can no longer satisfy consumers who want personalised experiences and deep connections. More clever and efficient tourism services must therefore be developed (Zhou et al., 2019).

This technology also addresses challenges related to limited mobility, expensive travel expenses, and environmental considerations. Prominent travel companies and large technological firms are currently investigating the potential of Metaverse tourism. A number of companies have already launched Metaverse platforms. With the progression of Metaverse technology, it will become indispensable to the tourism industry, expanding the horizons of travellers (Go and Kang, 2023).

The metaverse is a combination of several technologies that are rapidly evolving. The objective is to comprehend the potential impacts of integrating the metaverse into Indian festival culture through ongoing discussions, case studies, and previous academic papers. Developing a fully immersive metaverse that accurately renders visually stunning settings for millions of users will require significant work, spanning several years.The metaverse enabling technologies are:

Table 1. Metaverse enabling technologies in present and in progress/prospective

Technological Innovations	Present	In Progress/Prospective
User Devices	Smartphones Laptops/PC Virtual Reality (VR) Headsets Augmented Reality (AR) Headsets	Digital Senses and Touch
Internet of Things (IoT)	Standardisation Industrial cases	The complete metaverse necessitates a minimum of 6G connectivity with nearly imperceptible latency.
Computing Power	Edge/cloud computing	AI chips (rapid development) Quantum computing (prototype stage)
Communication Networks	5G WiFi 6/6E High-speed fiber	Big Data analytics (still maturing) Security (e.g. distributed technology attacks)
Block chain	Non Fungible Tokens/digital assets Digital currency	Smart contracts Enhanced efficiency Power use
Artificial Intelligence	Computer vision, sensory perception, Machine learning, Natural language processing, Intelligent voice	
3D Real time technology	A 3D engine Graphics in real-time. Space visualisation	Reducing expenses to enhance availability

Source: Adapted from Deloitte, The Metaverse Overview: Vision, Technology, and Tactics, 2022

These festivals, which have strong linkages to religious beliefs, historical narratives, and social behaviours, play a huge part in the lives of millions of people across the Indian subcontinent and beyond. However, in this era that is defined by rapid technological improvements and shifting social conventions, the traditional means of celebrating festivals are being rethought and adapted through technological innovations such as the metaverse. Conventional methods of celebrating festivals are being reimagined and updated. The objective is to evaluate and comprehend the complex nature of this ever-evolving ecosystem by utilising a multidisciplinary approach that integrates cultural studies, technology, and sociology. This will allow us to appreciate the potential of this environment better.This chapter aims to explore the relationship between Indian festivals and the metaverse, aiming to uncover fresh perspectives and identify recurring patterns in this transformative domain.

LITERATURE REVIEW

Metaverse as a Concept

Technology has facilitated the advancement of new business models and modernising service delivery in the tourism industry (Standing et al., 2014). These advancements play a vital role in addressing the issues of sustainability in tourism (Go and Kang, 2023) and their impact on both tourism demand and the environment (Puertas Medina et al., 2022). VR and metaverse have the potential to revolutionise tourism by offering lifelike immersive experiences that do not require physical presence (Ball, 2022). These technologies enable engaging visitor experiences without the necessity of physical travel. This study showcases the global rise of virtual tourism in recent years. It has revolutionised how people interact with tourist destinations by allowing them to virtually visit and experience locations and attractions without leaving their homes. This technology has overcome the limitations of physical and financial barriers (Hollensen et al., 2022). Recent advancements in technology allow for a high level of immersion in artificial settings that closely resemble reality. Virtual reality (VR), augmented reality (AR), and mixed reality have transformed customer interactions by blending physical and virtual components (Yang et al., 2023), leading to substantial alterations in the entire customer experience.

Upon analysing its literature, it is evident that considerable effort is being dedicated to studying and clarifying the concept of the metaverse. This has enhanced prospective stakeholders' comprehension of the metaverse's important elements and potential opportunities. Therefore, it was predictable that this idea would captivate the attention of businesses, especially multinational organisations. However, it was very astonishing to observe Facebook undergoing a rebranding process, renaming itself as Meta, which signifies its strong commitment to advancing the metaverse. The act of transforming this moniker has significantly enhanced the widespread recognition of the metaverse and has been continuously assessed on a worldwide level (Damar, 2021).

Conceptual Frameworkof Metaverse
Experiences and Innovation Modalities

The existing body of study in management and marketing has changed its focus from making things to people who buy the metaverse experiences. This movement has helped us learn more about the customer experience and create and provide goods and services that make customers feel good on all levels (mental, emotional, and behavioral). Technology and design are very important subjects to study because they have a big impact on how tourist goods are made. They work hand-in-hand

and are major factors in the creation of tourist attractions (Fesenmaier and Wang, 2017; Shin et al., 2022).

Putting the metaverse together with real and virtual places is best for making highly engaging settings, which are thought to be a more advanced form of virtual experiences (Ball, 2022). The literature that has already been written has accepted that second life, which is a virtual world, has an effect on the whole tourist experience. However, when compared to traditional virtual platforms, the metaverse shows a greater level of fidelity (Richter & Richter, 2023). As Yang K.et al.(2023) explain, the digital twin in travel is the technology that makes it possible to make a true copy of a place in the metaverse. So, the creation of a digital-twin platform is a very important factor in how people experience the metaverse. Our tourism research is based on design science, and our goal is to learn more about how platform features affect people.

Obstacles in the Process of Transforming Events Into a Futuristic Format

Several authors have expressed their dissent towards the metaverse or highlighted the associated issues. Challenges such as data privacy and security (Huang et al., 2023), digital inequality (Wang et al., 2023), potential harm to physical tourism sites (Allam et al., 2022), and ethical concerns (Monaco and Sacchi, 2023) are among the difficulties faced. According to Kuntsman and Miyake (2019), spending a long time in virtual settings might cause the distinction between the real world and the virtual world to become unclear, resulting in emotions of being disconnected and lonely. Hence, it is imperative to assess the metaverse's impact on the hotel and tourism industry from a well-rounded standpoint, acknowledging both its favourable and unfavourable aspects. Collecting designer viewpoints is essential for determining the display and control of the metaverse. Their expertise and viewpoint can be extremely important in ensuring that the metaverse is constructed with ethical considerations and accountability in mind, while also being enjoyable and user-friendly.

Research Gaps

While the metaverse has grown considerably, there is still a need for further research on how to effectively manage and construct the metaverse to enhance the overall visitor experience (Gursoy et al., 2022).

While the metaverse concept is gaining popularity, further research is required to properly understand the management and structure of many domains, particularly with regards to the customer experience in the travel and lodging industry. It is imperative to analyse the most efficient strategies for managing and organising the metaverse to enhance the overall user experience, while also considering the integration of festivals. This entails understanding how potential travelers might be motivated and captivated during the pre-trip stage by utilising the metaverse to explore virtual destinations, accommodation choices, and recreational opportunities. Furthermore, it is crucial to take into account the viewpoints of all stakeholders in the metaverse ecosystem (Chen et al., 2023). Employing developers to construct applications for the metaverse can provide valuable insights into the technological and design aspects necessary for constructing intuitive and user-friendly virtual environments. To summarise, while there is an increasing amount of information on managing and constructing the metaverse in relation to the traveler's experience, further research is needed to address current deficiencies and discover novel insights.

Research Questions

Indian festivals are characterised by their vibrancy, cultural richness, and strong adherence to tradition. They promote social cohesion, cultivating a feeling of solidarity and collective cultural legacy. The metaverse, an amalgamation of virtually improved physical reality and physically persistent virtual reality provides novel opportunities for immersing oneself in these celebrations. Integrating Indian festivals into the metaverse has the potential to revolutionise the way cultural events are celebrated, experienced, and conserved.

1. How did audience perceive the Indian celebration in the metaverse compared to traditional celebrations?
2. What are the key factors influencing the adoption of Metaverse platforms for celebrating Indian festivals

Metaverse: An Innovative Strategy to Entice the Festival's Visitors

Many businesses, including Metaform and XP&DL (a company dealing in metaverse and innovative technologies), tried to create products and businesses tied to the metaverse as soon as the idea gained traction, such as the Durga Pooja festival(Fu, 2022). Museums and art galleries are significant locations for both leisure and business activity in urban tourism(Antchak& Adams, 2020). During the coronavirus pandemic, meta devotion—using virtual reality environments and avatars for religious worship and community—became more common in Christian congregations. Without a doubt, metaverse in festival tourism will enable visitors to co-create life-changing experiences.

Figure 1. Tata Tea premium

Source: Tech Desk, 2022

Tata Tea Premium: An esteemed Indian tea firm ventures into the metaverse realm by organising a unique Holi celebration on the platform in 2022. Wavemaker India has designed and implemented a technologically advanced virtual platform to commemorate the Holi festival, establishing the brand as the pioneer in this global event. Upon accessing the platform, patrons are granted the opportunity to select their desired avatars and engage in an assortment of enthralling Holi activities, accompanied by a vivid exhibition of hues. To heighten the ambiance, the celebration will showcase an exclusive festive performance by the esteemed Indian musician, lyricist, and composer.

The event was adeptly depicted the lively customs of Uttar Pradesh's Lathmaar Holi and Delhi's Rangwali Holi, which are flawlessly captured on Tata Tea Premium's limited edition holiday packaging. Customers have the opportunity to participate in the holi party by clicking on the provided link. Ultimately, the metaverse has emerged as an innovative strategy to attract attendees to festivals, and it is expected to enhance the prospects of festival tourism in the future. Nevertheless, unresolved concerns still need to be addressed when integrating festival tourism with the metaverse. The problems are shifts in tourist behavior and preferences, control and dissemination of data, and the development of intellectual property related to metaverse tourism. Future studies should prioritise the investigation of these potential concerns and conduct a more thorough analysis of them (Zhang J. &Quoquab F,. 2023)

Practices of Metaverse Festival Experience

Cultural Reelection Through Metaverse:
Case of Deepavali Festivals

The metaverse, an online environment where users communicate through avatars, is becoming into a thriving cultural hub rather than just a place for gamers to play or businesses to have board meetings. The Metaverse's Deepavali serves as evidence of this. Imagine a virtual environment where avatars wearing traditional clothing come together to celebrate, and the streets are decked with vibrant, digital diyas (lamps). Geographical barriers vanish in this place, enabling individuals from all over the world to participate in the celebrations.

Rebuilding well-known Indian locations is essential to Deepavali celebrations in the metaverse. The digital representations of majestic palaces in Jaipur or the riverfront steps in Varanasi offer a distinctive experience that effortlessly combines heritage and advanced technology. Virtual fireworks have become essential to Deepavali celebrations, brightening the virtual sky without the usual environmental pollution accompanying real festivities. Furthermore, interactive components are of great significance. Avatars can actively participate in virtual puja ceremonies, partake in traditional games, and witness live performances by digital artists. The celebration is augmented by using haptic gloves and VR headsets, offering a heightened level of interactivity and sensory immersion.

The metaverse facilitates the reexamination of Deepavali narratives. Deepavali is a celebration that celebrates legendary stories, such as the account of Lord Ram's homecoming to Ayodhya, which may be experienced through an immersive 3D presentation. This educational presentation educates folks on the cultural significance of the occasion while also providing entertainment, especially for the younger audience.

Deepavali, within the metaverse, possesses the power to unite geographically apart groups. The Deepavali celebrations among the dispersed Indian diaspora often elicit yearning and wistfulness for the festivities back in their native land. The metaverse serves as a virtual space that allows individuals to experience the same joy and enthusiasm as they would in their homes, thus bridging the gap between the two realms.This online event also acts as a focal point for merging multiple cultures. Within the metaverse, individuals from various backgrounds who cannot physically participate in Deepavali can nevertheless participate in the festivities. Deepavali is celebrated worldwide, not just in India, as a festival that represents enlightenment and joy while promoting cultural interchange and understanding. Furthermore, the metaverse provides a comprehensive setting for persons who cannot engage in traditional celebrations owing to health or mobility constraints. People from diverse backgrounds are encouraged to participate in the celebrations at this venue, overcoming any restrictions given by physical obstacles.

Also, the festival's unique feature of dynamic markets is replicated in the metaverse through community-led events, like as virtual bazaars, where artists and traders can sell products related to Deepavali. These marketplaces enhance the whole experience by serving as a focal point for community engagement and trade, facilitating the exchange of customs and stories. The relocation of Deepavali celebrations to the metaverse has led to the compelling metamorphosis of ancient rites into a digital format. The metaverse combines conventional traditions with modern digital elements, making them more easily accessible and engaging, especially for the younger, technologically skilled population.

A prime illustration is the virtual Lakshmi Puja. During this event, attendees are given the chance to engage in a communal religious ceremony overseen by a virtual priest. By including interactive elements that surpass physical constraints, such as displaying virtual flowers or burning virtual candles, the overall experience is enhanced and the appeal of the ritual is intensified. Another element involves the integration of Rangoli, a technique for producing vibrant patterns on the ground. Within the metaverse, individuals possess the capability to generate and trade three-dimensional Rangoli designs, so an enhanced dimension is introduced to this form of artistic representation. These digital artworks possess the added advantage of being transient and readily adaptable, hence fostering increased creativity and involvement. Virtual representations can possess the same degree of complexity and liveliness as their physical counterparts. Furthermore, the metaverse has profoundly revolutionised the manner in which Christmas stories are conveyed. Interactive storytelling sessions augment the significance and allure of these age-old narratives by enabling avatars to traverse digitally reconstructed settings from epics like the Ramayana. By participating in this activity, the cultural legacy is both conserved and modified to appeal to a worldwide audience that is knowledgeable in utilising the internet.

The observance of Deepavali in the metaverse is a groundbreaking idea and a model for future reimagination of traditional festivities. This exemplifies how customs can be preserved and improved through the utilisation of technology in a swiftly changing society. In the future, the potentialities seem boundless. Imagine augmented reality (AR) experiences that seamlessly integrate virtual and real elements by superimposing virtual celebrations onto real-world surroundings. Furthermore, AI can customise celebrations according to individual preferences, augmenting sentiments of inclusiveness and joy. This has the potential to lead to a rise in interactive and personalised events. Furthermore, within the metaverse, the environmental effects of celebrations like Deepavali, which frequently lead to worries about waste and pollution, can be greatly reduced. Virtual celebrations provide an opportunity to participate in festivals while ensuring the preservation of our planet's health. They exhibit both creativity and durability.

The metaverse offers supplementary channels for enterprises and craftsmen and prospects for economic growth through virtual marketplaces and experiences. The digital economy linked to festival celebrations has the potential to make a substantial contribution to innovation and the conservation of culture.The celebration of Deepavali in the metaverse signifies the commencement of a novel age, whereby customs and technology converge to establish a lively, all-encompassing, and environmentally conscious approach to honouring one of the globe's most cherished festivals. These technological breakthroughs are thrilling and essential as we navigatethe digital era, safeguarding the uninterrupted development and preservation of our cultural legacy. The metaverse provides limitless possibilities for redefining our events, making them more accessible, sustainable, and globally impactful. The observation and interaction during holidays like Deepavali will naturally change with time, reflecting the dynamic nature of our cultures in a society that relies more and more on technology.

Revealing the presence of a deity in the virtual reality world: A celebration of Durga Puja

The Durga Puja religious festival, held annually in India, is the most significant in the country. During the week-long celebrations in October, it draws a staggering number of people, reaching up to 250 million. The purpose of the festival is to commemorate the triumph of the mother-goddess Durga over evil. Indians who couldn't physically attend the UNESCO-listed Durga Puja celebrations were able to experience it virtually without the need for goggles. This was made possible through the use of a smartphone or computer and the 3D social network called Spatial, thanks to Indian start-ups XP&Dland and Metaform.

Source: ML Lifestyle (2022)
https://manslife.in/lifestyle/maa-durga-marks-her-entry-into-the-metaverse-with-metapujo/

The puja has now been incorporated into large-scale cultural events on Web3. It is fitting to start with Durga Puja, as it is the most important and often held human gathering worldwide. Users can create an avatar and then enter a virtual world where they can explore and interact with digital versions of "pandals," which are temporary structures resembling temples or churches located in various locations in India and are used as homes for goddesses.

The major obstacle to the objectives is obtaining reliable high-speed internet access in the Indian areas(Kshetri, N. et al.2024).According to research conducted by the British Council in 2019 on behalf of the local government, the Durga Puja festival in the region has an estimated economic value of US$4.53 billion, which represents approximately 2.58% of the state's GDP. The research report "Mapping the Creative Economy around Durga Puja 2019" examines 10 creative industries that contribute to Durga Puja, considered one of the largest public art festivals in the world. This collective endeavour to comprehend the significance of a particular festival delineates a potential plan for states nationwide - whether it be Diwali in the North, Pongal in the South, Ganesh Puja in the West, or Bihu in the Northeast - to fully acknowledge the economic and cultural advantages that these splendid festivals bestow upon their communities. By providing quantifiable evidence of the influence of arts and cultural organisations, enterprises, and government, informed decisions may be made regarding public and private investments in the creative industry.

The metaverse has the capacity to generate novel marketplaces and enterprises while also expanding employment prospects (Yemenici, A. D.,2022).This metaverse pilot programme in India was conducted with four Durga Puja organisersin the year 2022 in the eastern Indian state of West Bengal. The team developed digital representations of the four pandals and distributed the god's 16,000 non-fungible tokens (NFTs) through internet platforms.

It was also suggested that online viewers should be able to buy souvenirs, photographs, or artworks in the future. "The metaverse approach enables individuals with health issues or residing at a significant distance to participate in the Durga Puja festivities online,"The people who do not want to forego the opportunity due to the lack of time and can not visit West Bengal,also got the chance to visit the Durga Puja due to the metaverse.

MANAGERIAL IMPLICATIONS

In India, the metaverse tourism industry is currently in its initial phases, and the information and expertise acquired from Indian Festival tourism can substantially impact the metaverse's future development on a global scale. The convergence of metaverse and festival tourism in India is attracting more attention from travellers, especially those who are not residents of India. Given the growing demand, the government and practitioners must address significant problems by developing suitable solutions. Festival tourism managers should recognise the metaverse's potential and its ability to provide travellers with immersive and interactive experiences (Brown and Drakeley, 2023). This acknowledgement should encompass government agencies and tourism operators. It is advisable for them to explore ways to incorporate metaverse technology into their goods and leverage them to attract and engage visitors. Ensuring a fair competitive environment is of utmost importance in the advancement of metaverse tourism, necessitating the government and industry players to actively prevent monopolies. This can entail the development of immersive metaverse experiences, utilising digital models to replicate festivals and capture the essence of celebratory atmospheres. Simultaneously, the government and professionals can investigate the integration of other components in metaverse tourism, with the assistance of technical experts, to offer tourists more innovative and unique experiences.

CONCLUSION

The metaverse is poised to challenge and disrupt the tourism sector, transforming tourist behaviour and industry operations and modifying human perspectives.The choice to participate or abstain from the metaverse festive environment, the actions taken upon arrival, and the methods of sustaining involvement will remain clouded by several uncertainties regarding its expansion, CSR, governance, and regulation. The focus should be on continuous advancement,anticipating advancements in future applications that provide exceptional spatial experiences for socialising, entertaining, and commerce. This critical reflection intends to provide a complete evaluation of how the metaverse can revolutionise the industry based on a review of existing literature. It will clarify the changes brought about by this revolutionary technology and define the opportunities and challenges it presents. In addition, this chapter includes potential areas of research that might serve as a direction for both academia and festival tourism players to fully utilise their capabilities.This gives rise to the prime market for the adoption of the next iteration of the internet. The metaverse presents an opportunity to significantly transform major economies of the region, and vice versa making a meaningful impact on how the metaverse take shape globally.

FUTURE RESEARCH FOR METAVERSE IN INDIAN FESTIVALS TOURISM

The metaverse-integrated Indian festival tourism study could change tourists' perceptions towards cultural events. This new field connects technology, heritage, and travel, showing enormous promise. With immersive technologies like VR and AR, Indian festivals can reach people from diverse locations and offer dynamic cultural activities. The metaverse allows global accessibility, immersive narrative, cultural preservation, money production, and tourism marketing innovation. Festivals can reach a global audience via Metaverse technology, fostering cultural diversity and inclusivity. The immersive nature of VR and AR technologies allows for deep engagement in festival rituals and traditions. This enhances participants' sense of presence and connection to Indian culture. Metaverse experiences, as digital archives, can preserve indigenous knowledge, rituals, and art. Virtual ticket sales, product sales, and sponsorships can assist event organisers and local communities in attaining economic security. Festivals boost socio-economic progress in host regions (Alston, 2024). Tourism marketers can also use metaverse-enabled events to differentiate locations and attract tech-savvy tourists seeking unique and immersive experiences. The metaverse's incorporation into Indian festival tourism is a pioneering frontier that can revolutionise cultural celebrations, tourism experiences, and socio-economic advancement. By acknowledging and overcoming the challenges and embracing metaverse technology, individuals and organisations can plan for a future where virtual festivals are vibrant centres of cultural interaction, innovation, and global connectivity, enhancing Indian heritage and tourism for future generations.

REFERENCES

Allam, Z., Sharifi, A., Bibri, S. E., Jones, D. S., & Krogstie, J. (2022). The metaverse as a virtual form of smart cities: Opportunities and challenges for environmental, economic, and social sustainability in urban futures. *Smart Cities*, 5(3), 771–801. 10.3390/smartcities5030040

Alston, E. (2024). When Digital Carnival? Distributed Control of the Metaverse Asset Layer to Enable Creative Digital Expression to Flourish. In *Defining Web3: A Guide to the New Cultural Economy* (pp. 105-113). Emerald Publishing Limited. 10.1108/S0733-558X20240000089009

Antchak, V., & Adams, E. (2020). Unusual venues for business events: Key quality attributes of museums and art galleries. *International Journal of Tourism Cities*, 6(4), 847–862. 10.1108/IJTC-09-2019-0156

Ball, M. (2022). *The metaverse: and how it will revolutionise everything*. Liveright Publishing Corporation. www.matthewball.vc/all/forwardtothemetaverseprimer

Barrera, K. G., & Shah, D. (2023). Marketing in the metaverse: Conceptual understanding, framework, and research agenda. *Journal of Business Research*, 15, 113420. 10.1016/j.jbusres.2022.113420

Bibri, S. E. (2022). The social shaping of the metaverse as an alternative to the imaginaries of data-driven smart Cities: A study in science, technology, and society. *Smart Cities*, 5(3), 832–874. 10.3390/smartcities5030043

Brown, T., & Drakeley, C. (Eds.). (2023). *Virtual Events Management: Theory and Methods for Event Management and Tourism*. Goodfellow Publishers Ltd. 10.23912/978-1-915097-03-3-4967

Buhalis, D., Leung, D., & Lin, M. (2023). Metaverse as a disruptive technology revolutionising tourism management and marketing. *Tourism Management*, 97, 104724. 10.1016/j.tourman.2023.104724

Chen, C. F. (2023). Literary Theory and Cultural Practice of "Metaverse" in China. *Critical Arts*, 1–15. 10.1080/02560046.2023.2269238

Chen, S., Chan, I. C. C., Xu, S., Law, R., & Zhang, M. (2023). Metaverse in tourism: Drivers and hindrances from stakeholders' perspective. *Journal of Travel & Tourism Marketing*, 40(2), 169–184. 10.1080/10548408.2023.2227872

Chen, Z. (2024). Beyond boundaries: Exploring the metaverse in tourism. *International Journal of Contemporary Hospitality Management*. 10.1108/IJCHM-06-2023-0900

Cheng, X., Zhang, S., Liu, W., & Mou, J. (2023). *Understanding visitors' metaverse and in-person tour intentions during the COVID-19 pandemic: A coping perspective.*

Cuomo, M. T., Tortora, D., Foroudi, P., Giordano, A., Festa, G., & Metallo, G. (2021). Digital transformation and tourist experience co-design: Big social data for planning cultural tourism. *Technological Forecasting and Social Change*, 162, 120345. 10.1016/j.techfore.2020.120345

Dwivedi, Y. K., Hughes, L., Baabdullah, A. M., Ribeiro-Navarrete, S., Giannakis, M., Al-Debei, M. M., Dennehy, D., Metri, B., Buhalis, D., Cheung, C. M. K., Conboy, K., Doyle, R., Dubey, R., Dutot, V., Felix, R., Goyal, D. P., Gustafsson, A., Hinsch, C., Jebabli, I., & Wamba, S. F. (2022). Metaverse beyond the hype: Multidisciplinary perspectives on emerging challenges, opportunities, and agenda for research, practice and policy. *International Journal of Information Management*, 66, 102542. 10.1016/j.ijinfomgt.2022.102542

Dwivedi, Y. K., Hughes, L., Wang, Y., Alalwan, A. A., Ahn, S. J., Balakrishnan, J., Barta, S., Belk, R., Buhalis, D., Dutot, V., Felix, R., Filieri, R., Flavián, C., Gustafsson, A., Hinsch, C., Hollensen, S., Jain, V., Kim, J., Krishen, A. S., & Wirtz, J. (2023). Metaverse marketing: How the metaverse will shape the future of consumer research and practice. *Psychology and Marketing*, 40(4), 750–776. 10.1002/mar.21767

Dwivedi, Y. K., Kshetri, N., Hughes, L., Slade, E. L., Jeyaraj, A., Kar, A. K., Baabdullah, A. M., Koohang, A., Raghavan, V., Ahuja, M., Albanna, H., Albashrawi, M. A., Al-Busaidi, A. S., Balakrishnan, J., Barlette, Y., Basu, S., Bose, I., Brooks, L., Buhalis, D., & Wright, R. (2023). "So what if ChatGPT wrote it?" Multidisciplinary perspectives on opportunities, challenges and implications of generative conversational AI for research, practice and policy. *International Journal of Information Management*, 71, 102642. 10.1016/j.ijinfomgt.2023.102642

Fesenmaier, D. R., & Xiang, Z. (2017). *Design Science in Tourism: Foundations of Destinations Management.* Springer. 10.1007/978-3-319-42773-7

Filimonau, V., Ashton, M., & Stankov, U. (2022). Virtual spaces as the future of consumption in tourism, hospitality and events. *Journal of Tourism Futures.*

Florido-Benítez, L. (2024). Metaverse cannot be an extra marketing immersive tool to increase sales in tourism cities. *International Journal of Tourism Cities.*

Go, H., & Kang, M. (2023). Metaverse tourism for sustainable tourism development: Tourism agenda 2030. *Tourism Review*, 78(2), 381–394. 10.1108/TR-02-2022-0102

Gursoy, D., Malodia, S., & Dhir, A. (2022). The metaverse in the hospitality and tourism industry: An overview of current trends and future research directions. *Journal of Hospitality Marketing & Management*, 31(5), 527–534. 10.1080/19368623.2022.2072504

Hollensen, S., Kotler, P., & Opresnik, M. O. (2022). Metaverse–the new marketing universe. *The Journal of Business Strategy*, 44(3), 119–125. 10.1108/JBS-01-2022-0014

Huang, X., Wu, Y., Kang, J., Nie, J., Zhong, W., Kim, D. I., & Xie, S. (2023). Service reservation and pricing for green metaverses: A Stackelberg game approach. *IEEE Wireless Communications*, 30(5), 86–94. 10.1109/MWC.014.2300095

Huang, X. T., Wang, J., Wang, Z., Wang, L., & Cheng, C. (2023). Experimental study on the influence of virtual tourism spatial situation on the tourists' temperature comfort in the context of metaverse. *Frontiers in Psychology*, 13, 1062876. 10.3389/fpsyg.2022.106287636687952

Kim, D. Y., Lee, H. K., & Chung, K. (2023). Avatar-mediated experience in the metaverse: The impact of avatar realism on user-avatar relationship. *Journal of Retailing and Consumer Services*, 73, 103382. 10.1016/j.jretconser.2023.103382

Kshetri, N., Dwivedi, Y. K., & Janssen, M. (2024). Metaverse for advancing government: Prospects, challenges and a research agenda. *Government Information Quarterly*, 41(2), 101931. 10.1016/j.giq.2024.101931

Kshetri, N., Dwivedi, Y. K., & Janssen, M. (2024). Metaverse for advancing government: Prospects, challenges and a research agenda. *Government Information Quarterly*, 41(2), 101931. 10.1016/j.giq.2024.101931

Kuntsman, A., & Miyake, E. (2019). The paradox and continuum of digital disengagement: Denaturalising digital sociality and technological connectivity. *Media Culture & Society*, 41(6), 901–913. 10.1177/0163443719853732

Monaco, S., & Sacchi, G. (2023). Travelling the metaverse: Potential benefits and main challenges for tourism sectors and research applications. *Sustainability (Basel)*, 15(4), 3348. 10.3390/su15043348

Richter, S., & Richter, A. (2023). What is novel about the metaverse? *International Journal of Information Management*, 73, 102684. 10.1016/j.ijinfomgt.2023.102684

Ruban, A. (2023). *The role of the government in metaverse development in China and South Korea: A Comparative Analysis.*

Shah, P., Agrawal, S., Joby, J., Ansari, S., Bhandari, R., & Bhatt, I. (2023). Prevalence of Indian Culture over Western Culture in 21st Century. *Integrated Journal for Research in Arts and Humanities*, 3(5), 230–239. 10.55544/ijrah.3.5.21

Shin, H. H., Jeong, M., So, K. K. F., & DiPietro, R. (2022). Consumers' experience with hospitality and tourism technologies: Measurement development and validation. *International Journal of Hospitality Management*, 106, 103297. 10.1016/j.ijhm.2022.103297

Tsai, S. P. (2022). Investigating metaverse marketing for travel and tourism. *Journal of Vacation Marketing*, 13567667221145715.

Yang, K., Zhang, Z., Tian, Y., & Ma, J. (2023). A secure authentication framework to guarantee the traceability of avatars in metaverse. *IEEE Transactions on Information Forensics and Security*, 18, 3817–3832. 10.1109/TIFS.2023.3288689

Yemenici, A. D. (2022). Entrepreneurship in the world of Metaverse: Virtual or real? *Journal of Metaverse*, 2(2), 71–82. 10.57019/jmv.1126135

Zhang, J., Quoquab, F., & Mohammad, J. (2024). Metaverse tourism and Gen-Z and Gen-Y's motivation: "will you, or won't you travel virtually?". *Tourism Review*, 79(2), 304–320. 10.1108/TR-06-2023-0393

Zhou, Y., Huang, H., Yuan, S., Zou, H., Xie, L., & Yang, J. (2023). Metafi++: Wifi-enabled transformer-based human pose estimation for metaverse avatar simulation. *IEEE Internet of Things Journal*, 10(16), 14128–14136. 10.1109/JIOT.2023.3262940

Chapter 8
An Analysis on the Future Usage of Metaverse in the Marketing Event Industry in India:
An ISM Approach

Supriya Lamba Sahdev

Alliance University, Bengaluru, India

Chitra Krishnan

https://orcid.org/0000-0003-1135-8852

Symbiosis Centre for Management Studies, Symbiosis International University (Deemed), Pune, India

Amilson Durans

https://orcid.org/0000-0003-1656-4356

Centro Universitário Santa Terezinha, São Luís, Brazil

Ahdi Hassan

https://orcid.org/0000-0003-1734-3168

Global Institute for Research Education and Scholarship, Amsterdam, The Netherlands

Jugnu Thakur

ISBR Business School, India

ABSTRACT

The term metaverse has recently attracted much attention and is being widely dis-

DOI: 10.4018/979-8-3693-2272-7.ch008

cussed in various industries around the world, including marketing and events. This research explores future possibilities of the metaverse in the context of the Indian marketing event industry through an ISM analysis. Consequently, the metaverse – an environment that contains interactive digital objects and persons – presents new opportunities for improving the effectiveness of marketing events in terms of interest, accessibility and innovation. Thus, the use of ISM in the context of this research allows to determine the most critical enablers and restraints for the adoption of the metaverse in Indian marketing events. The chapter provides clear tactical implications for using metaverse technologies to enhance traditional formats of events, interact with the audience, and adapt marketing and communication solutions to the Indian market.

INTRODUCTION

The term metaverse is an idea of the next step beyond current online access, which provides an integration of the virtual world and the physical plane into one common virtual environment. This emergent model has far-reaching implications for numerous sectors, pre-empting imminent changes in how corporations interact with customers and other interested parties.

However, there is one issue that the marketing event industry in India will encounter in the near future, and that is the influence of the metaverse. This sector can be described as very competitive and always on the lookout for new ways to capture the consumer's attention. The metaverse offers unique value propositions for generating immersive and engaging experiences that are not in the physical or digital realm (Wang et al., 2023).

With the help of virtual and augmented realities in the metaverse, marketing events have the potential to go to the next level in terms of audience engagement. People can interact with products and brand experiences in a way that was nearly unimaginable before, thereby fostering loyalty and long-term effects (Smith et al., 2023). On the other hand, well-calibrated engagements not only enhance brand commitment but also have a strong effect on consumer behavior regarding purchase intentions and brand attitudes (Mainardes et al., 2022).

Nonetheless, using metaverse as part of marketing events in India has its disadvantages. Some potential issues that can be considered include the readiness of technology in developing and delivering such experiences, users' acceptance and resistance to the metaverse platforms, and the probable legal frameworks that may influence the use of the metaverse in teaching and learning (Chandiwala, et al., 2023). Addressing these challenges requires a systematic approach that can help one identify interrelationships between these factors and inform strategic decision making. On this front, Interpretive Structural Modelling (ISM) could be applied.

This chapter also aims at providing a descriptive illustration of how the metaverse can be used in the marketing event industry in India using the ISM matrix. Having identified the factors that support and hinder the adoption of the metaverse, this study seeks to offer insights that can help decision-makers in the industry avoid both the excessive enthusiasm and the outright rejection of the metaverse technologies. Ultimately, this study should contribute to the development of the industry and promote the use of the metaverse concept and the possibilities of digital transformation for re-thinking the strategies of marketing events in India.

BACKGROUND

The concept of the metaverse has recently received increased attention in scientific publications and business innovations in the course of the advancement of digital technologies in the last decade (Wang, et al., 2023). Studies have also been made on metaverse technologies in the marketing event business, particularly on how the latter can transform usual event experiences, making them more attractive and engaging. This change is often attributed to the growth in the use of virtual and augmented reality, which enables engagement with brands more innovatively.

It has been found that the metaverse offers certain advantages in the realm of event marketing, including the possibility of customization and longer event involvement (Kumar, et al., 2023). More people have embraced the use of virtual, especially during the COVID-19 period, which confirmed their viability as they do not limit participation based on location (Elçi & Abubakar, 2021). This trend will persist in the future as more companies discover that virtual event solutions are cost-effective and can be increased as needed.

For instance, the marketing event industry in India has experienced remarkable growth because of the increasing middle class and advancement in digital technology (Chandiwala et al., 2023). The development of this sector has proved that metaverse technologies are quite effective in creating new and exciting experiences for the consumers of this sector (Singh et al., 2022). Nevertheless, there are some factors that cannot be disregarded such as insufficient technological support and varying levels of user preparedness (Gupta, 2023).

According to Sharma and Verma (2022), some of the trends that have been found in the use of metaverse in marketing include virtual product launches and immersion branding. These papers address the importance of integrating metaverse elements into campaigns and related topics, including data privacy (Durans et al., 2021a, 2023a).

In conclusion, according to the previous literature, the future of the metaverse in the marketing event industry of India appears to be bright if the important players in the industry can navigate around the potential problems and seize the opportunities of this new technology. As such, this research seeks to add to this emerging literature by examining the chosen factors that enable and hinder the adoption of metaverse in the Indian marketing event sector through the ISM model.

RESEARCH METHODOLOGY

This research work adopts the exploratory research paradigm to examine the possibility of the metaverse on the marketing event industry in India. Starting with an extensive literature search and analysis of both academic papers industry reports and case studies is the initial step. This review seeks to compile the current information on the metaverse, virtual and augmented reality, and their uses in marketing events. The findings derived will help in the definition of key variables and factors that impact adoption.

The data will be collected in the form of interviews with event planners, technology creators, and regulatory experts. These interviews will focus on the trends, challenges, and opportunities of integrating metaverse technologies in marketing events in India. Data gathered from interviews will enhance the literature review part by presenting real-life suggestions and cases.

As the aim of the study is to establish the relationship between the variables under consideration, ISM has been chosen. ISM is a formalized model that helps to represent the hierarchical relationships between factors that can affect the use of the metaverse. This analysis will also determine which of these factors are the drivers and which ones are dependent as well as the role each factor plays in the adoption process.

The research will also involve the analysis of Indian marketing event companies that have adopted metaverse technologies. These case studies will include real examples of approaches used, problems encountered, and lessons learned. It will also be useful to look at examples of successful and failed metaverse technologies to gain insight into the potential of such technologies.

The following top ten variables have been identified in the order of their contribution to the future usage of the metaverse in the marketing event industry in India:

1. Technological Infrastructure: Interacting with the metaverse involves using current technology and a good internet connection (Gupta, 2023).

2. User Acceptance: This shows that the acceptance level of the consumers and the participants in the events shall greatly determine the success of metaverse technologies (Kaur et al., 2024).

3. Regulatory Environment: For this reason, government policies should be clear and supportive regarding data privacy, security, and digital transactions to enable the integration of the metaverse (Durans et al., 2021a, 2023a; Chandiwala et al. , 2023).

4. Investment and Funding: It is imperative to call for enough funding for metaverse research and development along with the metaverse solutions that can be sustained in the future (Kumar et al, 2023).

5. Content and Experience Design: Consumers will accept and be content with the high-quality content and experiences aimed to be delivered to the segment (Singh et al., 2022).

6. Market Demand: By the consumer and business view, there will be more innovation in Virtual events/immersive experiences (Wang et al., 2022).

7. Collaboration and Partnerships: The various stakeholders including event organisers, technology companies, and others can exchange information and develop better solutions (Durans et al., 2021b; Sharma et al., 2022; Durans et al., 2023b).

8. Cost and Accessibility: Metaverse technologies must continue to be cheap for the populace and available to as many people as possible (Sahoo et al., 2022).

9. Security and Privacy: Protecting users' data privacy and security is the key to credibility in metaverse applications (Chandiwala, 2023; Durans et al., 2021a, 2023a).

10. Scalability and Flexibility: Metaverse scalability of types and sizes of events is just as crucial to meet the need (Kaur et al., 2024).

These are important in establishing the likelihood of future adoption of the metaverse for the Indian marketing event industry and are the foundation of analysis and suggestions in this paper.

The Reachability Matrix

Among the tools used in the Implementation of ISM, the reachability matrix is one major technique that is crucial for the modeling of structures due to its role in identifying the relationships in variable hierarchism. This matrix is built on a base of linear algebra, using 1s and 0s only, where the value '1' indicates that a variable within a system affects another variable, and the value '0' expresses no influence. The use of a reachability matrix makes it easier to evaluate the interaction of the variables in a given sequence since the impact of one variable depends on the result produced by another variable. For instance:

- Technological Infrastructure: This variable can have implications for other variables such as willingness to accept technology, cost issues and availability, and questions about growth and portability. Superior technological implementation which includes; internet connectivity and device capabilities will help boost the user adoption of metaverse technologies by providing the user with seamless and quality interaction. In addition, as business technology becomes more solidified, it may become less expensive in the long term and is often more adaptable to the varying demands of a show and the size of the audience.

- Regulatory Environment: Privacy and information security laws, as well as other communication and electronic and digital transaction laws or regulations, help to position metaverse technologies significantly. The applicable legislation which embraces the provision of a legal foundation for metaverse promotes investment and funding of research and development in metaverse solutions. This also helps adhere to security and privacy measures that are required to protect consumers and their data, thereby boosting the confidence of users and other stakeholders in the organization. Further, friendly regulations enable easier scalability and flexibility in the implementation of metaverse applications across various event possibilities and real-life regulatory barriers that need not be a limiting factor.

- Market Demand: Market demand, which correlates with the desire for fully encompassing, multi-sensory experiences, affects multiple factors, such as the content and the approach to delivering the experience, price, opportunity for widespread implementation, and modularity. Consumers' demand for live-like virtual events, performances, and ceremonies is a key reason behind the passion for creative and immersive content. Meeting market demand helps to guarantee people's adoption of metaverse technologies since, in most cases, they aim to remain affordable products. Furthermore, the presentation of results in a manner that meets market demands is significant for scalability considering the variety of audiences and event types.

These relations clarify how variables intertwine with each other within the context of the marketing event industry in India. The reachability matrix thus lays down a strategic map that enables the identification of drivers and dependences to enhance decision-making as well as enable easier integration of metaverse technology to support the intended marketing events.

Table 1. The reachability matrix for the top ten variables according to the ISM approach

		User			Content and			Cost and		
	0	1	0	0	0	0	0	1	0	1
User	0	0	0	0	1	1	0	0	1	0
Regulatory	0	0	0	1	0	0	0	0	1	1
Investment and Funding	0	0	0	0	0	0	1	0	0	0
Content and Experience Design	0	0	0	0	0	1	0	0	0	0
Market Demand	0	0	0	0	0	0	0	1	0	1
	0	0	0	0	1	0	0	0	0	0
Cost and	0	0	0	0	0	0	0	0	1	1
Security and Privacy	0	0	0	0	0	0	0	1	0	0
Scalability and Flexibility	0	0	0	0	0	0	0	0	0	0

In the context of ISM, the reachability matrix is the primary instrument for mapping the relationships between variables and identifying their positions in the hierarchy. Here's how the reachability matrix is constructed and its significance in ISM analysis: below mentioned is how the reachability matrix is constructed and its significance in ISM analysis:

Constructing the Reachability Matrix

- Variables Identification: Based on their potential impact and relevance, the following are the top ten variables that affect the future usage of the metaverse in the marketing event industry in India.
- Binary Representation: Each variable is a row and a column in the matrix. The matrix consists of cells which are filled with either 1 or 0.
- Influence Assessment: A value of 1 is assigned where one variable (row) has a direct impact on another variable (column). A score of 0 means that there is no direct relationship between the two variables in question.

Interpreting the Reachability Matrix

- Identifying Influences: A value of 1 in the matrix means that the variable in the particular row affects the variable in the particular column.

- Hierarchical Structure: As a result, the matrix helps to identify the hierarchy of variables. Control variables that affect other variables but are not affected by them are usually located at higher levels of the hierarchy.
- Insight Generation: The matrix helps to determine which variables are critical to changes or effects within the system of variables being analyzed.

Foundation for ISM Analysis

- Structural Understanding: The reachability matrix is the initial step of ISM analysis that depicts the direct relationships and interdependencies of the mentioned variables.
- Hierarchy Identification: It assists in identifying clusters of variables and their hierarchical relationships ranging from drivers to influenced variables.
- Strategic Insights: With the help of this matrix, ISM can identify strategic inputs like which variables to target for intervention, possible constraints, and ways to manage the adoption and integration of metaverse technologies in marketing events.

Therefore, the reachability matrix in ISM is used to systematically analyze and map the interdependencies of the factors that determine the future use of the metaverse in the Indian marketing event industry. It is a valuable instrument for tracing dependencies, determining power relations, and supporting decision-making processes.

The MICMAC Analysis

The MICMAC analysis in ISM is used to classify the variables according to their driving power and dependence power in a system.

MICMAC Analysis Categorization

1. Independent Variables:

All these variables have high driving power but low dependence power. These are core and form the basis of the system.
Examples:

- Technological Infrastructure (Driving Power: 3. 0, Dependence Power: 0. 0)
- User Acceptance (Driving Power: 3. 0, Power of dependency: 1. 0)
- Regulatory Environment (Driving Power: 3. 0, Dependence Power: 0. 0)

Explanation: Dependent variables are those which are affected by independent variables and do not have much effect on other variables. They are important for defining the direction of the system and its reliability.

2. Linkage Variables:

All these variables have high driving power and high dependence power. They are aware of the change and can affect the system in any way.
Example:

- Market Demand (Driving Power: 2. 0, Dependence Power: 2. 0).

Explanation: The linkage variables are important because a change in the linkage variable will have a consequential effect on other variables. It is vital in the management of the system and the overall responsiveness of the system.

3. Dependent Variables:

All these variables have low driving power but high dependence power. It is also important to note that they are very much determined by other variables.
Examples:

- Content and Experience Design (Driving Power: 1. 0, Dependence Power: 2. 0
- Cost and Accessibility (Driving Power: 1. 0 Dependence Power: 3. 0
- Security and Privacy (Driving Power: 1. 0 (Dependence Power: 2. 0).
- Scalability and Flexibility (Driving Power: 0. 0, Dependence Power: 4. 0, 5. 0.

Explanation: Dependent variables heavily depend on other variables in the system to achieve their functioning and changes. They are important but may not always have the power to effect significant changes on their own.

4. Autonomous Variables:

These variables have low driving power and low dependence power. They are fairly autonomous and do not have a significant effect on the system.
Examples:

- Collaboration and Partnerships (Driving Power: 1. 0, Dependence Power: 1. 0
- Investment and Funding (Driving Power: 1. 0, Dependence Power: 1. 0).

Explanation: The autonomous variables have little impact on other variables and are least likely to be affected by changes in the system. Generally, they work on their own and do not have a major impact on the system's behavior.

Significance of MICMAC Analysis

- Strategic Insights: This also assists in determining the variables that require strategic management such as the independent and linkage variables as opposed to the dependent and autonomous variables that require support.
- Risk Assessment: Outlines factors that could be potentially problematic if not properly addressed such as high dependence variables.
- Decision Making: Aids in the decision-making process by indicating key factors and interrelations of the system, which can be valuable for optimizing the use of resources and controlling the system's development.

The classification of variables in MICMAC analysis facilitates the systematic view of the roles and interdependencies of various variables in the adoption of metaverse technology in the Indian marketing event industry. The above analysis provides a roadmap for stakeholders to know where to channel their efforts and resources to achieve the desired outcomes in the metaverse.

The Interpretive Structural Modelling (ISM) Approach

In the ISM approach, the preference matrix is a critical instrument for ranking the variables based on their driving and dependence power. The preference matrix enables identification of which variables are important for the future adoption of metaverse in the marketing event sector in India. It can help to establish which variables are most important and need to be analysed in detail and which ones can be left aside for the moment.

Based on the driving power and the dependence power calculated from the MICMAC analysis, the preference matrix is developed. Variables with higher driving power have more influence and should be accorded more attention. On the other hand, variables with high powers of dependence can be considered as potentially sensitive to the influence of other variables and may require control.

In the next section, the researchers will utilize the MICMAC analysis presented in this chapter to develop the preference matrix that ranks the ten critical factors discussed in this chapter.

To construct a preference matrix, it is required to rank the variables depending on their driving and dependence abilities. Variables that have a higher driving power should impact the system more and therefore should be ranked higher. High-dependence power variables are more likely to be affected by other variables and might need to be closely watched.

- Assign Priority: These variables are assigned higher priority because they are seen to have a stronger influence on the system.
- Sort Variables: We rank the variables in descending order according to their driving power. In the case of ties, we can use dependence power as a secondary criterion.
- Establish Preference: The variables that have high priority are positioned above the variables that have low priority in the preference matrix.

Below is table 2, where the study has constructed the preference matrix based on the top ten variables, their driving power, and dependence power, as identified in this chapter and previous analysis.

Table 2. Preference matrix

Priority	Variable	Driving Power	Dependence Power	Category
1	Regulatory Environment	3	0	Independent
2	Technological Infrastructure	3	0	Independent
3	User Acceptance	3	1	Independent
4	Market Demand	2	2	Linkage
5	Collaboration and Partnerships	1	1	Autonomous
6	Investment and Funding	1	1	Autonomous
7	Content and Experience Design	1	2	Dependent
8	Security and Privacy	1	2	Dependent
9	Cost and Accessibility	1	3	Dependent
10	Scalability and Flexibility	0	4	Dependent

The preference matrix ranks the variables according to their driving power and dependence power and groups them into independent, linkage, autonomous, and dependent variables. This allows for clear direction and allocation of resources to effectively capitalize on the metaverse in the marketing event sector in India.

The Normalized Matrix

The normalized matrix in the ISM approach is derived from the reachability matrix. Normalization helps to make relationships between the attributes more explicit and remove any transitive relationships. In the normalized matrix, a value of 1 shows that two variables are directly related while a value of 0 shows that the two variables are not related. To create the normalized matrix:

- Start with the reachability matrix: This matrix depicts the connections between the variables, with the value of 1 signifying that one variable affects another.
- Perform transitive reduction: In this step, you remove any links that are inferred from other links in the matrix. This means stripping away all the indirect relationships to only keep the direct ones.
- Create the normalized matrix: After transitive reduction, the non-zero elements in the matrix correspond to direct connections between the variables.

Table 3 showcases, the normalized matrix based on the reachability matrix and the ISM approach:

Table 3. Normalized matrix

		User			Content and			Cost and		
	0	1	0	0	0	0	0	1	0	0
User	0	0	0	0	1	1	0	0	1	0
Regulatory	0	0	0	1	0	0	0	0	1	1
Investment and Funding	0	0	0	0	0	0	1	0	0	0
Content and Experience Design	0	0	0	0	0	1	0	0	0	0
Market Demand	0	0	0	0	0	0	0	1	0	0
	0	0	0	0	0	0	0	0	0	0
Cost and	0	0	0	0	0	0	0	0	1	0
Security and Privacy	0	0	0	0	0	0	0	1	0	0
Scalability and Flexibility	0	0	0	0	0	0	0	0	0	0

The normalized matrix shows only the direct relations between variables and does not include any intermediate links. A value of 1 in this matrix indicates that the variable in the row has an impact on the variable in the column while a value of 0 shows that there is no impact between the two variables. This matrix is an important component of the ISM approach and it helps in visualizing the interconnections between elements of the system.

RECOMMENDATIONS AND SUGGESTIONS

- Invest in Technological Infrastructure: There are other aspects that organizations should also consider, including how they will invest in new technologies like better and faster internet connection, strong servers, and data centers. Such investments are important to ensure that the metaverse is well-maintained and continues to function as expected.

- Focus on User Acceptance: It is especially important to improve the level of satisfaction of users. To do this, companies need to carry out certain surveys that will determine the perception and willingness of users in the metaverse applications. For instance, one can use educational communication campaigns and live presentations to this end.

- Monitor Regulatory Environment: This means that other legal frameworks about digital matters must also be adhered to by firms and this includes data protection and security laws as well as digital transactions legal framework. These are the measures that should be followed because they help in developing confidence and ascertaining the sustainability of business.

- Leverage Market Demand: Heighten the awareness of the market and consumer appreciation of the experiential and the involvement of experiences.

- Enhance Content and Experience Design: This should be centered on the production of useful and engaging content that will encourage users and make their experience worthwhile. To change the perception of a brand, it is crucial to create a good environment that will make people get interested and be committed to the change.

- Address Cost and Accessibility: Consequently, the metaverse experiences should be made as affordable and accessible to the public as much as possible. The following is the objective; ascertain the pricing models that can be within the reach of users of different economic status.

- Prioritize Security and Privacy: It is recommended that there is a provision of proper measures that will protect the user information as required by the data privacy clauses in the metaverse domains. This aspect of data handling ensures that the users develop trust and thus they are more confident in the system.

- Seek Collaboration and Partnerships: Interact with stakeholders, including vendors and content owners, to collaboratively work and exchange information and resources. Strategic partnerships may also help speed up the rate of innovation and improve the market position of actors in the metaverse ecosystem.
- Consider Scalability and Flexibility: Explain how metaverse can be applied to different kinds of events of different sizes. This makes it possible to implement the system in various types of marketing events without much problem.
- Encourage Investment and Funding: Going out to look for funds for the research and development and deployment of metaverse technologies in the form of capital investments. This sector is still growing and that is why it is crucial to have financial backing to grow further and develop.

Scholarly Suggestions

- Further Research on User Behaviour: Carry out a consumer behavior study in the metaverse so that marketing strategies can be improved and the satisfaction of metaverse users can be increased.
- Study Regulatory Impact: Explain how the integration of the metaverse and its application in the marketing event could be influenced by such changes. Understand the implications of compliance on operational strategies and costs for technology investment.
- Explore Technological Advances: Learn more about the current technologies that can be incorporated into the metaverse including Artificial Intelligence (AI), Augmented Reality (AR), and Virtual Reality (VR) to increase the interactivity of the metaverse.
- Assess Economic Viability: Conduct cost-benefit analysis, cost-utility analysis, and other economic assessments, such as the ROI assessment to assess the revenue generation from metaverse marketing events.
- Examine Cross-Industry Applications: Identify the possible uses of metaverse technologies in various sectors and how these uses can shape the future of marketing events and strategies.
- Investigate Ethical Considerations: The following are the aspects of Ethical Conduct about user information, content moderation, and handling of user information in the metaverse. Advocates for the right behavior that is most suitable for the user.
- Analyse Long-Term Trends: Propose further research on longitudinal designs to evaluate the evolution and effects of metaverse on the marketing event

business. Recognize trends and try to predict the changes that may occur in the future.

- Collaborate with Industry: Suggest a framework for the collaboration of two or more disciplines that can serve to transfer knowledge from the academic community to the industry community in an attempt to determine research gaps in the area of marketing events and metaverse technologies.
- Promote Interdisciplinary Research: Promote the infusion of engineering, business, behavioral sciences, and law into one curriculum. This can thus provide a holistic understanding of the different effects of the use of metaverse.
- Develop Standardized Metrics: Define how the success, ROI, and results of metaverse marketing events can be quantified. Such metrics can be easily compared and assessed, particularly about the levels of effectiveness.

The following recommendations and suggestions are made to guide the stakeholders on how best to overcome the various risks that may arise in the course of integrating metaverse technologies in marketing events in India. This paper focuses on the technological, legal, user, and academic aspects of the metaverse and how companies can use and benefit from the metaverse.

CONCLUSION

The chapter explains how and why implementing metaverse technologies in the marketing event industry in India can be beneficial or not. In this study, therefore, the ISM approach is adopted to systematically identify and evaluate the drivers for future use of the metaverse in this industry. The following conclusions can therefore be deduced from the analysis of the above. Namely, the metaverse is a great chance for the marketing event industry in India as it has the potential to let consumers engage meaningfully, interactively, and interestingly. From the ISM approach, there are a number of variables that are essential in integrating metaverse in marketing events among which include technological infrastructure, user acceptance, regulatory environment, and market demand. Technological infrastructure is considered a resource since it supports the theory that the metaverse requires effective and robust technological foundations to function. It is also imperative that the industry gains insight on the attitudes of the users towards it in order to capture the market, address their concerns and gain more users. The legal and compliance factors are risks and opportunities that need to be adequately addressed to ensure that an entity is operating according to the new laws and regulations. Thus, the market lies in presenting consumers with new and exciting events based on their preferences because consumers are already interested in such metaverse experiences. The ISM approach also enhances the capacity to take into account security, privacy, and cost in the actualisation of metaverse. These aspects can be tackled in order to enhance the consumer's trust and, as a result, enhance the experience that metaverse offers.

To sum up, the research indicates that the application of the metaverse in the marketing event industry in India in the future has great potential. Thus, the companies that focus on technology, user-centric approach, and compliance will be able to benefit from the metaverse. Future research and partnership between the business and the academic sector will also help in the continued acceptance and development of metaverse technologies in the marketing event apparatus.

REFERENCES

Chandiwala, M., Patel, P., & Mehta, A. (2023). Advertising and branding with Metaverse. *Dogo Rangsang Research Journal*, 13(6), 95–99.

Durans, A. de A., d'Angelo, M. J., Macedo, C. J. T., & Vale, C. (2021b). *Líder, você é a força motriz da sua organização? Como a responsabilidade social e os comportamentos contraproducentes podem impactar o desempenho dos colaboradores e das organizações. 1.* Appris.

Durans, A. de A., Macedo, C. J. T., Vale, C., Cisneiros, G. P. O., & Patwardhan, A. A. (2021a). Boas e más práticas da privacidade de dados pessoais na visão dos consumidores do Brasil e da Índia. *XLV EnANPAD*. https://anpad.org.br

Durans, A. de A., Silva, F. P. B., Costa, K. C. S., Franco, J. P., & Kran, F. S. (2023b). Satisfação e insatisfação no trabalho: Estudo de caso com trabalhadores brasileiros. *Revista Saúde, Ambiente. Sustentabilidade & Tecnologia*, 1(1), 90–108. 10.5281/zenodo.10042373

Durans, A. de A., & Sousa, W. S de., Costa, N. P. de M., Vale, C., & Macedo, C. J. T. (2023a) Novo petróleo mundial? Guia de aplicação prática em privacidade de dados pessoais. *3° Business Technology Congress* (B-TECH). https://fucape.br/btechcongress

Gupta, P. (2023). *International Conference on Business, Innovation and Sustainability in Digital Era*. Research Gate.

Kaur, G., Pande, R., Mohan, R., Vij, S., Agrawal, P., Shobhane, P., & Bagane, P. (2024). A Comprehensive Review of Metaverse: Taxonomy, Impact, and the Hype around It. *Engineering Proceedings*, 62(1), 9.

Kumar, A., Shankar, A., Shaik, A. S., Jain, G., & Malibari, A. (2023). Risking it all in the metaverse ecosystem: Forecasting resistance towards the enterprise metaverse. *Information Technology & People*. 10.1108/ITP-04-2023-0374

Mainardes, E. W., Cisneiros, G. P. de O., Macedo, C. J. T., & Durans, A. de A. (2022). Marketing capabilities for small and medium enterprises that supply large companies. *Journal of Business and Industrial Marketing*, 37(1), 47–64. 10.1108/JBIM-07-2020-0360

Renieris, E. M. (2023). *Beyond data: Reclaiming human rights at the dawn of the metaverse*. MIT Press. 10.7551/mitpress/14119.001.0001

Sahoo, N., Gupta, D., & Sen, K. Metaverse: The Pursuit to Keep the Human Element Intact in the Media and Entertainment Industry. In *The Business of the Metaverse* (pp. 156-167). Productivity Press.

Sharma, S. K., Dwivedi, Y. K., Metri, B., Lal, B., & Elbanna, A. (Eds.). (2023). Transfer, Diffusion and Adoption of Next-Generation Digital Technologies. *IFIP WG 8.6 International Working Conference on Transfer and Diffusion of IT, Proceedings, Part I* (Vol. 697). Springer Nature.

Singh, A., Yadav, B., Kaushik, A., Raj, A., Yadav, J., & Hari, P. B. (2022). *3D Virtual Modelling and Its Future Scope-Metaverse.*

Smith, C. H., Molka-Danielsen, J., Rasool, J., & Webb-Benjamin, J. B. (2023). *The world as an interface: exploring the ethical challenges of the emerging metaverse.*

Wang, J., Makowski, S., Cieślik, A., Lv, H., & Lv, Z. (2023). Fake news in virtual community, virtual society, and metaverse: A survey. *IEEE Transactions on Computational Social Systems.*

Wang, W. X., & Zhou, F., Wan, Y. L., & Ning, H. S. (2022). A survey of metaverse technology. *Chinese Journal of Engineering*, 44(4), 744–756.

Chapter 9
Role of Metaverse in Events Industry:
An Empirical Approach

Sujay Vikram Singh
https://orcid.org/0000-0002-7113-2698
Banaras Hindu University, India

Pravin Chandra Singh
https://orcid.org/0000-0002-6002-0703
MSMSR, Mats University, Raipur, India

Kuldeep Singh
https://orcid.org/0000-0002-7999-1585
Amity University, Gurugram, India

Akshay Nain
https://orcid.org/0000-0002-0003-2542
Amity University, Gurugram, India

ABSTRACT

The metaverse holds immense potential to transform the event industry, seamlessly blending augmented reality, virtual reality, and internet-based platforms to deliver captivating and engaging experiences. This proposal delves into the profound impact of the metaverse on event organization and participation, showcasing the success of platforms such as Decentraland and Roblox in hosting virtual events. The study explores the various factors that impact the adoption of metaverse, such as performance expectations, ease of use, social influence, and facilitating conditions. The findings highlight the significance of technology that is easy to use, a strong infrastructure, and making use of social networks. This research provides valuable

DOI: 10.4018/979-8-3693-2272-7.ch009

insights for event organizers to improve consumer engagement and adoption rates, ultimately integrating the metaverse into the event industry.

INTRODUCTION

The event industry is on the brink of being revolutionized with the advent of the metaverse, it is going to affect how the events are scheduled, arranged, and taken place. A metaverse uses a mix of augmented, virtual and web-based platforms to establish a collaborative virtual space, offering users distinctive and immersive experiences. The innovative sector goes further than just progresses in technology and it revolutionises human contact, accessibility and elevates the overall experience of attending an conveyance. On the metaverse, we can go the other way by creating experiences and engaging people in multisensory environments (Jun, 2020). Virtual reality events have found application opportunities in places like Decentraland and Roblox, which have demonstrated successful hosting of everything from groovy concerts to business conferences. Participants will navigate through active 3D environments to interact with others in scheduled actives. By moving to the virtual, we can start to remove these constraints, for example in terms of location and size, and make events more accessible and wider-reaching for a global audience. Hybrid events combine physical and virtual experiences to allow for an integrated experience for those attending in person along with those attending virtually, the power of the metaverse. Solutions: The demand for such flexible event formats that cater to all the preferences is higher as COVID only expedited the virtual events shift (Davis *et al.*, 2009; Arpaci *et al.*, 2022). Hybrid events provide the best of all worlds, incorporating interactive elements such as live polls, Q&As, and networking. From an economic perspective, new revenue channels can be generated with the metaverse including virtual ticketing, merchandise sales, sponsorships and branded experiences. These virtual marketplaces within the metaverse span many different types of digital assets, from VR gear to digital art to exclusive goods (Choi & Choi, 2020). It also verifies who owns a digital asset which builds the trust and transparency in the virtual economies. Blockchain is a technology that ensures secure transactions. The metaverse can also be a place to harness user data and offer analytics to further enrich the user experience and economic value. VR and the metaverse offer event organizers a level of detail in user behaviors and interactions that remains unmatched in even the most detailed digital event in reality(Wang & Shin, 2022; Alvarez-Risco *et al.*, 2022). It likes the third sock and it helps all other organizations to ensure that best content, marketing strategies, and participant engagement make for better events by validating decisions prior to going live. Performance expectancy, Effort expectancy, Social influence and Facilitating Conditions have a significant effect on the adoption of metaverse technology in the event industry. Performance Expectancy - This would believe in the potential of the metaverse to add value to event experiences and/or event outcomes. Effort expectancy - referring to the ease of use of metaverse platforms as experienced by stakeholders. It is an essential part of social norms to emulate society's approval of metaverse adoption when peers participate in it, as well as the socio-cognitive endorsement of more influential entities. Facilitators: Enabling the metaverse to get seamlessly integrated are key technical and organizational infrastructural preconditions (Akour *et al.*, 2022; Shen *et al.*, 2021). Those factors together influence the dependent factor - consumers' intention to adopt the metaverse for the event industry, which in the end form the picture of the future of metaverse in event industry. The metaverse really is changing the world of events by providing new and innovative experiences that offer unparalleled immersion, interaction and engagement which cannot be delivered by a traditional physical setup. Event planners can schedule concerts, conferences, and trade shows in a virtual 3D environment from platforms such as Decentraland or Roblox (O' Brien and Elliott, 2022). 1Attendees are provided with an opportunity to interact with one another in real-time and provide the event with a personal and all-immersive feeling. This shift from real to virtual tackles multiple problems of traditional conferences like physical place constraint and boundaries thus giving equal rights to participate and making it Global (Huggett, 2020). In addition, shader support (the advertiseable availability of powerful image processing), the metaverse can offer an augmented reality (AR) or virtual reality (VR) supported world leading to a sense rich virtual experience equivalent to that of physical events. In addition, hybrid events that mix physical and virtual should benefit from metaverse in collaboration with diversified choices of the audiences. Especially essential in the post-pandemic present, as Cirisano (2020) writes, is, the flexibility in event formats. Digital platforms are used by hybrid events to combine real events with things like live polls, Q&As and networking to maintain high levels of engagement (Lau et al., 2024). The metaverse has also economic perspectives as it provides more earning opportunities - people can earn additional income through selling virtual tickets and sponsorships or even by creating branded experiences (Kim, 2021). It employs blockchain technology to ensure safe transactions and certification of digital assets that creates more trust and transparency. A single metaverse can offer seamless data collection and analytics quickly and effortlessly achieved by getting to the bottom of user behavior and understandings that will inevitably improve the event planning and its operation.

LITERATURE REVIEW AND HYPOTHESIS DEVELOPMENT

Performance Expectancy

In technology adoption models such as the Unified Theory of Acceptance and Use of Technology (UTAUT), performance expectancy (the degree to which an individual believes that using technology will help them improve their job performance) has emerged as an important driver. The expected performance could considerably influence customer's intention to use the new invention; as an example, it is considered, in the metaverse, in the events industry of metaverse, that the performance expected will influence customer use intention (Alkhwaldi, 2023). Research has shown that end users are increasingly likely to engage and adopt new technologies when they perceive clear benefits with potential improved productivity, improved communication and simply better use experience (Pillai, et.al, 2024). One example is the truly immersive nature of the metaverse that will bring massive interactive and individual experiences to the real world -experiences which some consumers might find beneficial to experience over a standard event format. Additionally, technology-driven studies in the events domain recommend that technology readiness (TR), which is associated with improving the experience of users and the expectations for their satisfaction, shapes the aspirations of individuals to adopt it. If so, the metaverse, with the potential to provide genuine simulations of worlds and live presentations in a digital environment, seems to be up to the task. The greater the value the metaverse is perceived to provide the average consumer in the form of smoother networking, better content engagement, and innovative new features that traditional 2D platforms simply cannot achieve, the more quickly it will be adopted. This relationship again underscores performance expectancy as a salient individual factor in the consumer decision-making process of metaverse adoption for events. Thus, understanding and enhancing performance expectancy of the metaverse might be crucial for event planners looking to increase consumer adoption rates.

H1: Performance Expectancy has a significant effect on consumer intention to adopt metaverse in the event industry.

Effort Expectancy

Effort expectancy i.e., the degree to which an individual will perceive the use of technology as easy in the case of metaverse adoption by individuals in the context of event industry is pivotal. According to the UTAUT model, consumers are more likely to adopt technologies that they believe are easy to use. When it comes to the metaverse itself, this does improve the user-friendliness in forms of clear and easy interfaces and easy ability to quickly navigate through virtual worlds - yes! Previous research has found that the easier consumers perceive a technology to be, the more likely they are to adopt it in their everyday lives (Hennig-Thurau et al., 2024; Nguyen et al., 2023; Kumar et al., 2023). For example, a future where metaverse platforms made for events which prioritize convenience and ease of use decreases the friction and gives the lowest cognitive barrier to entry for consumers likewise, would have higher chance of adoption. In addition, elusive proof maintains the role of effort expectancy as a predictor of user acceptance along with adoption intentions across various technology landscapes inclusive of virtual reality as well as online platforms (Al-adwan & Al-debei, 2013). According to Xi et al. (2024) as well as Aburbeian et al. (2022), perceived ease of use in the event context, where immersive and interactive experiences are possible, plays a large role in consumer intentions to adopt the technology, causing consumers to use the metaverse technology for events, when they believe that it is easy to access, navigate, and utilize its features (see Shukla et al., 2024; Corne et al., 2023). Therefore, more comfortable interactions and better support also contribute to increased perceptions of effort expectancy, therefore enhancing the user experience in that regard. From this we can expect greater use of the metaverse in sectors like events.

H2: Effort Expectancy has a significant effect on consumer intention to adopt metaverse in the event industry.

Social Influence

When establishing the consumer intent to adopt the metaverse in the event industry, the belief of others in the use of a specific technology is a key determinant. The UTAUT model emphasizes that social influence is considered critical for user acceptance on the new technologies, specifically for the early stages of adoption. The acceptance and perceived value of the metaverse can be widely enhanced if it enjoys support from the researchers, industry influencers, and administrators (Al Kfairy et al, 2024; Hadi et al., 2024). If they are seeing respected and powerful members of their social groups joining the party and benefiting from the metaverse for events people are more likely to favourably view this as a technology for them to utilise as well. It is believed that social influence is an important driver that influences user perception and behavior in adopting technology: a number of recent studies evidenced that social influence reshapes (1) technology attitude (Lee & Kim 2022), (2) user adoption behavior (Pillai et al., 2024), and (3) psychological norms (Park, 2024). In the events business, the success of the metaverse will be based on how well it can replicate and upgrade these social dynamics (Teng et al., 2011; Lee et al., 2011), as networking and socializing are fundamental. People are encouraged to participate in things metaverse when they feel that their social circles approve of their participation in metaverse events. Furthermore, integrated community features and social validation mechanisms within metaverse platforms can drive social influence and reinforcing loops improving adoption rates (Sritong et al., 2024; Arpaci et al., 2022). Therefore, the effective promotion of the metaverse as a viable hosting and event attendance avenue will require the use of social influence via well-executed marketing and community engagement activities.

H3: Social Influence has a significant effect on consumer intention to adopt metaverse in the event industry.

Facilitating Conditions

Resource and support devises that need to be available to use a technology, also known as facilitating conditions, have a high level of significance towards influencing the intent to adopt the metaverse by event consumers. The Unified Theory of Acceptance and Use of Technology (UTAUT) model similarly highlights the role of enabling conditions in influencing user acceptance and sustained use of interventions (David & Chalon 2023: Ooi et al, 2023; Simova et al, 2024). Facilitation Conditions are the various elements that ensure a smooth user experience in the metaverse. Some of these factors include reliability of internet connectivity, hardware compatibility with VR or AR technology, technical support, and user training programs (Jo, 2023; Sim, 2023). These are resources that will make the metaverse more accessible for researchers to get quickly started without having to spend a lot of work to support the userinterface and related tools for metaverse interaction. The explanation to this line of reasoning is that stronger facilitating conditions will result in a higher confidence level of consumers using the technology which will eventually create an intention to adopt (Albaom et al., 2022). Support on the facilitation conditions have been found empirically to be an important driver for new technologies adoption in several industries, and also - in the events industry (Anwar *et al.*, 2024). In particular, the following facilitating conditions within the metaverse are likely instrumental in addressing potential user concerns surrounding the complexity and reliability of this type of technology, as originally noted. With this being said, these are conditions that make the integration of the metaverse more seamless with existing infrastructure and make technical support more readily available: Hence, when meeting conditions that enable consumers embrace the metaverse more likely when it comes with its better experiential and interactive designs (Vieira & Medeiros, 2023). This indicates the importance of investing resources in infrastructure and support systems for the metaverse to be integrated as commonplace among event industry.

H4: Facilitating Conditions have a significant effect on consumer intention to adopt metaverse in the event industry.

Figure 1. Conceptual framework

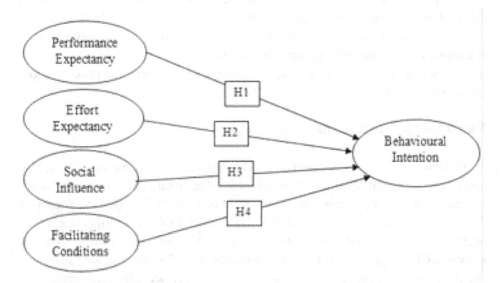

RESEARCH METHODOLOGY

Data Collection

To collect the required information, a closed-ended questionnaire was created, which included a 5-point Likert scale. The questionnaires were prepared in the English language and disseminated to possible participants through electronic channels, notably via email. The study has a sample size of 330, and the data was obtained using convenience sampling.

Construct Measures

The items for Performance Expectancy, Effort Expectancy, Social Influence, Facilitating Conditions, and Behavioural Intention were adopted from the following sources (Table 1).

Table 1. Measurement Instruments

Constructs	No of Items	Source
Performance Expectancy	3	(Pham & Thi Nguyet, 2023)
Effort Expectancy	3	(Chang et al., 2022; Jain et al., 2022)
Social Influence	3	(Venkatesh & Davis, 2000)
Facilitating Conditions	3	(Chang et al., 2022)
Behavioural Intention	3	(Khalilzadeh et al., 2017)

Respondent's Profile

The respondents for this study were from Raipur, Chhattisgarh. The demographic characteristics of the respondents are as follows: The proportion of male and female participants in this study were 58% and 42%, respectively. The target age range for this research was 18–60 years old consumers and majority of participants were between the ages of 25 and 35 years.

Table 2. KMO and Bartlett's test

Kaiser-Meyer-Olkin Measure of Sampling Adequacy.		.834
Bartlett's Test of Sphericity	Approx. Chi-Square	4128.502
	Df	105
	Sig.	.000

DATA ANALYSIS AND FINDINGS

Reliability Test

We used Cronbach's alpha reliability analysis to check how reliable the whole construct was. (Table 3) shows that the total construct under evaluation has a Cronbach's alpha larger than 0.70. (Cavana, R., Delahaye, B. & Sekeran, 2001), this suggests that the structure is good for further investigation.

Validity Test

The value of KMO was determined to be 0.834, as shown in **(Table 2)**. The Bartlett's test of sphericity produced a statistically significant result (P=0.000); with 105 degrees of freedom for all correlations within the matrix. These results suggest that factor analysis was appropriate for the investigation. After doing principal component analysis and varimax rotation, it was shown that all constructs had eigenvalues exceeding 1 **(Table 4)**, suggesting statistical significance. The components exhibit significant variances, which suggest their high level of explanatory capability. Regarding convergent validity, the factor loadings for each construct surpass the criterion of 0.50 **(Table 3)**.

Table 3. Factor loading and Cronbach alfa

Constructs	Items	Factor Loading
Performance Expectancy (Cronbach's α = 0.866)		
PE1	Metaverse allows me to improve the events experience	0.783
PE2	Metaverse helps me to access events information more accurately	0.861
PE3	Metaverse helps me in avoiding misinformation about events	0.868
Effort Expectancy (Cronbach's α = 0.791)		
EE1	Metaverse is easy to use	0.705
EE2	The use of metaverse is reliable and saves time in the events management	0.572
EE3 .	Metaverse simplifies the decision-making process regarding events management.	0.878
Social Influence (Cronbach's α = 0.942)		
SI1	People whose opinions I appreciate would prefer that I use metaverse for events management, rather than other innovative technologies	0.887
SI2	People who can influence my decision motivate me to use metaverse for events management	0.861
SI3	If many people in my community or my friends use metaverse for events management, I will also use this technology	0.868
Facilitating Conditions (Cronbach's α = 0.941)		
FC1	I think I have the resources (technological devices) to use metaverse for events management	0.870
FC2	I think I have the required expertise to use metaverse for events managements	0.889
FC3	I believe it is easy to manage events through metaverse technology	0.875
Behavioural Intention (Cronbach's α = 0.832)		
BI1	I intend to adopt metaverse within 3 years	0.738
BI2	I expect to use the metaverse for events management	0.806
BI3	I will recommend the use of metaverse to friends and acquaintances for events management	0.752

Source: Analysis Output

Table 4. Total variance explained

Component	Initial Eigenvalues			Extraction Sums of Squared Loadings			Rotation Sums of Squared Loadings		
	Total	% of Variance	Cumulative %	Total	% of Variance	Cumulative %	Total	% of Variance	Cumulative %
1	7.074	47.157	47.157	7.074	47.157	47.157	3.030	20.198	20.198
2	1.699	11.327	58.484	1.699	11.327	58.484	3.021	20.140	40.338
3	1.432	9.544	68.028	1.432	9.544	68.028	2.447	16.316	56.653
4	1.230	8.202	76.230	1.230	8.202	76.230	2.122	14.146	70.799
5	1.022	6.810	83.040	1.022	6.810	83.040	1.836	12.241	83.040
6	.789	5.257	88.297						
7	.389	2.593	90.890						
8	.269	1.793	92.684						
9	.237	1.583	94.267						
10	.225	1.502	95.769						
11	.167	1.110	96.879						
12	.143	.956	97.835						
13	.125	.831	98.666						
14	.107	.713	99.379						
15	.093	.621	100.000						

Extraction Method: Principal Component Analysis.

Table 5. Model summary

Model	R	R Square	Adjusted R Square	Std. Error of the Estimate
1	.659	.434	.427	3.70809

Predictors: (Constant), Performance Expectancy, Effort Expectancy, Social Influence, Facilitating Conditions.

The correlation coefficient, represented as 'R', was calculated to be 0.659. This score signifies a statistically significant level of predictability for consumer behavioural intention towards metaverse adoption in event industry. The R^2 value of 0.434 **(Table 5)** indicates that 43.04% of the variability in the dependent variable (consumer behavioural intention towards metaverse adoption in event industry) can be explained by the independent variables i.e. Performance Expectancy, Effort Expectancy, Social Influence, Facilitating Conditions.

Table 6. ANOVA

Model		Sum of Squares	Df	Mean Square	F	Sig.
	Regression	3234.064	4	856.016	62.256	.000
1	Residual	4468.724	325	13.750		
	Total	7892.788	329			

Predictors: (Constant), Performance Expectancy, Effort Expectancy, Social Influence, Facilitating Conditions.

The regression model was assessed and analysed using **(Table-6)** to establish its appropriateness for the data. The independent factors included in **(Table-6)** show statistical significance, showing their potential to predict consumer behavioural intention towards metaverse adoption in event industry. The analysis reveals that the dependent variable is significantly influenced by these factors, as evidenced by the F statistic (4, 330) =62.256, with a significance level of $P < 0.05$. Therefore, we may deduce that the regression model mentioned above is a suitable match for the given data.

The regression model was assessed and analysed using **(Table-6)** to establish its appropriateness for the data. The independent factors included in **(Table-6)** show statistical significance, showing their potential to predict consumer behavioural intention towards metaverse adoption in event industry. The analysis reveals that the dependent variable is significantly influenced by these factors, as evidenced by the F statistic (4, 330) =62.256, with a significance level of $P < 0.05$. Therefore, we may deduce that the regression model mentioned above is a suitable match for the given data.

Table 7. Coefficients

Model		Unstandardized Coefficients		Standardized Coefficients	t	Sig.
		B	Std. Error	Beta		
	(Constant)	2.137	.713		2.998	.003
	Performance Expectancy	.182	.050	.173	3.613	.000
1	Effort Expectancy	.283	.053	.277	5.382	.000
	Social Influence	.117	.047	.129	2.468	.014
	Facilitating Conditions	.249	.047	.273	5.308	.000

a. Dependent Variable: Consumer Behavioural Intention towards Metaverse Adoption in Event Industry

We can see the p-value of 0.000, which is much less than the alpha value of 0.05 for Performance Expectancy, Effort Expectancy, Social Influence, and Facilitating Conditions. So, there very little room to reject any of the alternative hypotheses (H1 to H4) As such, this research study contributes to scientific knowledge by detecting that Performance Expectancy, Effort Expectancy, Social Influence and Facilitating Conditions have a significant and positive impact on Consumer Behavioural Intention towards Metaverse Adoption in the Event Industry. Thus, the multiple regression equation for this study will be:

Consumer Behavioural Intention towards Metaverse Adoption in Event Industry= 2.137 + 0.283 Effort Expectancy + 0.249 facilitating conditions + 0.182 performance expectancy + 117 social influences.

The (**Table-7**) makes clear that Consumer Behavioural Intention towards Metaverse Adoption in Event Industry and effort expectancy are strongly correlated (strongest relationship) serving as one of the primary antecedents of consumer behaviour intention towards adoption of a metaverse in the event industry, followed by facilitating conditions, performance expectancy and social influence.

DISCUSSION

The research concludes with a set of significance discovered in the analysis of the study that indicates the correlation among the variables and consumers 'behavioral intention to adopt the metaverse in the event industry. The demographic profile of the respondents indicates a balanced mix of both the genders and The dominance of age group 25 to 35years. This generation is more technology-driven and receptive to creative event management solutions. The statistical tests conducted etc., on the sample used and data collected suggest that there is factorial validity for most of the findings. Thus, the strong mean scale scores combined with high Cronbach's alpha values for each constructs demonstrate high internal consistency and hence reliability of the measures used.

Multiple regression analysis yielded the results showing which factors are associated with consumer behavioral intention toward metaverse adoption in the event industry (Xu et al., 2024). Performance Expectancy, Effort expectancy, Social Influence & Facilitating Conditions. The R-square value of the model allows us to understand to what extent these factors explain the behavior of the consumer (from the quick view of the chart, we can get a good idea), but still interesting to put the data in the context of model. Notably, the predictor that emerged as most salient was Effort Expectancy, emphasizing the criticality of user-friendliness for adoption. It shows if event organizers want more people to jump onto the metaverse bandwagon, then they better get busy engineering the tech to be more user friendly, support it with resources and influencers.

Deeper investigation of the study discovered Facilitating Conditions plays a major role in consumer intention towards metaverse in the event industry. We see that simply consumers can be more confident in using these metaverse technologies if they had access to the right resources: technology, support systems etc. Together with the strong factor loadings and a significant Cronbach's alpha for Facilitating Conditions in this study, it underscores the crucial role that infrastructural support and user expertise have in advancing metaverse adoption. This result reflects the importance of perceived ease of access and support systems in technology acceptance as identified in previous research (Venkatesh et al., 2003). This leads to a situation where event leading bodies would be logically obliged to develop an enabling environment having all necessary resources and training being available, to harness the metaverse in full effect.

The importance of social dynamics in the adoption of technology is again underscored with the effect of social influence on consumer behavioral intention. As we see, the adjustment in metaverse technologies individual intentions seems to be deeply rooted by the recommendations from influential individuals and community adoption which is noted by the significant effect on forming the intentions to use (positive correlation). Thus, the findings demonstrate the importance of social networks and influential individuals to support the uptake of novel technologies in the event industry (Ünlü et al., 2023). Through endorsements by reputable faces of popular culture or testimonials from the veritable pioneers of the metaverse advocates can significantly increase the desirability and trustworthiness of the metaverse and hence catalyzed to achieve this acceptation by the general public (Cavana, R., Delahaye, B. & Sekeran, 2001). As an area for future exploration, we could investigate the effect of social influence further considering demographic and culture peculiarities to tailor more specific strategies to the promotion of the metaverse.

IMPLICATIONS

Theoretical Implications

This study clearly contributes to the technology adoption literature by focusing on the technology within the event sector. The use of metaverse also is strongly dependent on metaverse. It is expected to have significance resources and user self-efficacy, the Facilitating Conditions, to have also significant with consumer intention to adopt this technology further shows the importance of this constructs for technology acceptance models such as the Unified Theory of Acceptance and Use of Technology (UTAUT) (Wu and Lin, 2022; Avvari and Guy, 2016). This study enhances UTAUT by validating its constructs in metaverse adoption for events, and underlines the significance of infrastructural and social contexts in this process. Besides, the study also acknowledges the notion of social networks and an influential based society, which ultimately determines the behaviour of the consumer (Jo, 2023). This gives a more thorough account of what is energizing the metaverse adoption.

Managerial Implications

For event organizers, the study's findings represent another piece of the puzzle as they figure out how the metaverse fits into their event strategies. The impending nature of Facilitating Conditions means that organisers should be putting their resources into making sure that the tech is robust and each of the users are confident, equipped and supported to access the metaverse. Further, the strong impact of Social Influence also shows that marketers need to resort to endorsements from key opinion leaders and local community leaders to create trust and credibility in technologies of metaverse. By building a fostering environment as well as creating a social network effect where users influence one another, event organizers are able to maximise user engagement and adoption, ensuring a full integration into the event industry of the metaverse (Singh, 2018).

Limitations and Future Scope

Even though the study provided perspectives to metaverse, it had couple of constrains. The sample was narrowed down to responses from Raipur, Chhattisgarh, which might limit its generalization to other regions or countries. Future studies may extend the geographical reach and population composition to add externally valid aspects to the findings (Singh, 2017). In addition, the use of self-report data also leaves the present study open to other biases such as social desirability and poor introspection. It manages to provide a deeper look into metaverse adoption due to inserting objective technology usage and behavior as outcomes. In so doing, the study focused on certain constructs of Technology Acceptance Model: Performance Expectancy, Effort Expectancy, Social Influence and Facilitating Conditions. Future studies can further explore several important factors to better understand consumer behavioral intentions to adopt the metaverse in the event industry. Such factors may include perceived fun, fear of consequences, or economic concerns (Cheng,

2023). These additional elements will help reveal a more complete picture of the determinants of consumer behavior in this context and more.

Going forward, there are plenty of fascinating directions for further research. The long-term implications metaverse adoption has on post-event satisfaction and loyalty of event attendees is a fascinating research bin. Longitudinal studies provide the ability to examine the full spectrum of adoption through engagement on the platform. Moreover, conducting, how technology has improved the ability to take advantage of VR and AR can offer an advantageous view to those and event organizers who aim to assess ways to keep themselves ahead in the competition (Atrakchi-Israel, B., & Nahmias, Y., 2022). Researching the numerous uses of the metaverse technologies in different industries was another intriguing research path. Considering all the parts of the four frameworks and how this technology is developing moreover having a brief impact in training, retail, medical care, and occasion industry (Brossillon & Ferjani, 2023). By comparing contexts between different metaverse scenarios, this can shed surprisingly compelling insights into the possible challenges and indeed opportunities for metaverse adoption.

CONCLUSION

The metaverse is revolutionizing the event industry with immersive, engaging and accessible experiences. We also propose two hypotheses, theory based on empirical approach which is theoretical development via quantitative analysis and predict that Performance Expectancy significantly impacts perceived benefits of metaverse events. Widespread Adoption Effort Expectancy: ease for use Social influence: getting stakeholders to buy in it. Enabling Integration and Facilitate Conditions to integration like Infrastructure (requirement for enabling seamless system integration) etc. all of this drives Behavioural Intention, taking the metaverse event into mainstream success and acceptance.

REFERENCES

Aburbeian, A. M., Owda, A. Y., & Owda, M. (2022). A technology acceptance model survey of the metaverse prospects. *AI*, 3(2), 285–302. 10.3390/ai3020018

Akour, I. A., Al-Maroof, R. S., Alfaisal, R., & Salloum, S. A. (2022). A conceptual framework for determining metaverse adoption in higher institutions of gulf area: An empirical study using hybrid SEM-ANN approach. *Computers and education: artificial intelligence, 3*, 100052.

Al-Adwan, A. S., & Al-Debei, M. M. (2023). The determinants of Gen Z's metaverse adoption decisions in higher education: Integrating UTAUT2 with personal innovativeness in IT. *Education and Information Technologies*, 1–33.37361794

Al-Kfairy, M., Alomari, A., Al-Bashayreh, M., Alfandi, O., & Tubishat, M. (2024). Unveiling the Metaverse: A survey of user perceptions and the impact of usability, social influence and interoperability. *Heliyon*, 10(10), 1–16. 10.1016/j.heliyon.2024. e3141338826724

Albaom, M. A., Sidi, F., Jabar, M. A., Abdullah, R., Ishak, I., Yunikawati, N. A., Priambodo, M. P., Nusari, M. S., & Ali, D. A. (2022). The moderating role of personal innovativeness in tourists' intention to use web 3.0 based on updated information systems success model. *Sustainability (Basel)*, 14(21), 13935. 10.3390/su142113935

Alkhwaldi, A. F. (2023). Understanding learners' intention toward Metaverse in higher education institutions from a developing country perspective: UTAUT and ISS integrated model. *Kybernetes*, ●●●, 1–12. 10.1108/K-03-2023-0459

Alvarez-Risco, A., Del-Aguila-Arcentales, S., Rosen, M. A., & Yáñez, J. A. (2022). Social Cognitive Theory to Assess the Intention to participate in the Facebook Metaverse by citizens in Peru during the COVID-19 pandemic. *Journal of Open Innovation*, 8(3), 142. 10.3390/joitmc8030142

Anwar, M. S., Alhalabi, W., Choi, A., Ullah, I., & Alhudali, A. (2024). Internet of metaverse things (IoMT): Applications, technology challenges and security consideration. In *Future Communication Systems Using Artificial Intelligence, Internet of Things and Data Science* (pp. 133–158). CRC Press.

Arpaci, I., Karatas, K., Kusci, I., & Al-Emran, M. (2022). Understanding the social sustainability of the Metaverse by integrating UTAUT2 and big five personality traits: A hybrid SEM-ANN approach. *Technology in Society*, 71, 102–120. 10.1016/j. techsoc.2022.102120

Atrakchi-Israel, B., & Nahmias, Y. (2022). Metaverse, Competition, and the Online Digital Ecosystem. *Minnesota Journal of Law, Science & Technology*, 24, 235.

Brossillon, B., & Ferjani, C. (2023). Metaverse and Video Game: Brand Development in the Sport Industry. In *Digital Marketing in Sports* (pp. 252-272). Routledge.

Cavana, R., Delahaye, B., & Sekeran, U. (2001). *Applied business research: Qualitative and quantitative methods*. John Wiley & Sons.

Chang, M., Walimuni, A. C. S. M., Kim, M., & Lim, H. (2022). Acceptance of tourism blockchain based on UTAUT and connectivism theory. *Technology in Society*, 71, 102027. 10.1016/j.techsoc.2022.102027

Cheng, S. (2023). Metaverse. In *Metaverse: Concept, Content and Context* (pp. 1–23). Springer Nature Switzerland.

Choi, U., & Choi, B. (2020). The effect of augmented reality on consumer learning for search and experience products in mobile commerce. *Cyberpsychology, Behavior, and Social Networking*, 23(11), 800–805. 10.1089/cyber.2020.005732799542

Cirisano, T. (2020). Getting in the game: With his record-setting (and eye-popping) performance in Fortnite, Travis Scott proved that limitless creative potential—and a captive, merch mad audience could make video games the most lucrative new frontier for the live music business. *Billboard*, 132(11), 36–43.

Corne, A., Massot, V., & Merasli, S. (2023). The determinants of the adoption of blockchain technology in the tourism sector and metaverse perspectives. *Information Technology & Tourism*, 25(4), 605–633. 10.1007/s40558-023-00263-y

David, B., & Chalon, R. (2023, July). Digitalization and Virtual Assistive Systems in Tourist Mobility: Evolution, an Experience (with Observed Mistakes), Appropriate Orientations and Recommendations. In *International Conference on Human-Computer Interaction* (pp. 125-141). Cham: Springer Nature Switzerland. 10.1007/978-3-031-35908-8_10

Davis, A., Murphy, J., Owens, D., Khazanchi, D., & Zigurs, I. (2009). Avatars, people, and virtual worlds: Foundations for research in metaverses. *Journal of the Association for Information Systems*, 10(2), 90–117. 10.17705/1jais.00183

Gursoy, D., Malodia, S., & Dhir, A. (2022). The metaverse in the hospitality and tourism industry: An overview of current trends and future research directions. *Journal of Hospitality Marketing & Management*, 31(5), 527–534. 10.1080/19368623.2022.2072504

Hadi, R., Melumad, S., & Park, E. S. (2024). The Metaverse: A new digital frontier for consumer behaviour. *Journal of Consumer Psychology*, 34(1), 142–166. 10.1002/jcpy.1356

Hennig-Thurau, T., Herting, A. M., & Jütte, D. (2024). EXPRESS: Adoption of Virtual-Reality Headsets: Role of Metaverse Trials for Consumers' Usage and Purchase Intentions. *Journal of Interactive Marketing*, 1–54. 10.1177/10949968241263353

Hossain, M. I., Jamadar, Y., Alam, M. K., Pal, T., Islam, M. T., & Sharmin, N. (2024). Exploring the Factors Impacting the Intention to Use Metaverse in the Manufacturing Industry Through the Lens of Unified Technology Acceptance Theory. In *Research, Innovation, and Industry Impacts of the Metaverse* (pp. 43-61). IGI Global. 10.4018/979-8-3693-2607-7.ch003

Huggett, J. (2020). Virtually real or really virtual: Towards a heritage metaverse. *Studies in digital heritage, 4*(1), 1-15.

Jain, G., Kamble, S. S., Ndubisi, N. O., Shrivastava, A., Belhadi, A., & Venkatesh, M. (2022). Antecedents of Blockchain-Enabled E-commerce Platforms (BEEP) adoption by customers–A study of second-hand small and medium apparel retailers. *Journal of Business Research*, 149, 576–588. 10.1016/j.jbusres.2022.05.041

Jo, H. (2023). Tourism in the digital frontier: A study on user continuance intention in the metaverse. *Information Technology & Tourism*, 25(3), 307–330. 10.1007/s40558-023-00257-w

Jun, G. (2020). Virtual reality church as a new mission frontier in the metaverse: Exploring theological controversies and missional potential of virtual reality church. *Transformation (Durban)*, 37(4), 297–305. 10.1177/0265378820963155

Khalilzadeh, J., Ozturk, A. B., & Bilgihan, A. (2017). Security-related factors in extended UTAUT model for NFC based mobile payment in the restaurant industry. *Computers in Human Behavior*, 70, 460–474. 10.1016/j.chb.2017.01.001

Kim, J. (2021). Advertising in the metaverse: Research agenda. *Journal of Interactive Advertising*, 21(3), 141–144. 10.1080/15252019.2021.2001273

Kumar, A., Kumar, D. V. S., Khetarpal, M., & Megha, R. U. (2023). Customer Experience in the Magic World of Metaverse: Conceptual Framework of Customer Adoption of Metaverse. In *Immersive Technology and Experiences: Implications for Business and Society* (pp. 99–126). Springer Nature Singapore.

Lau, J. X., Ch'ng, C. B., Bi, X., & Chan, J. H. (2024). Exploring attitudes of gen z towards metaverse in events industry. *International Journal of Sustainable Competitiveness on Tourism*, 3(01), 49–53.

Lee, S. G., Trimi, S., Byun, W. K., & Kang, M. (2011). Innovation and imitation effects in Metaverse service adoption. *Service Business*, 5(2), 155–172. 10.1007/s11628-011-0108-8

Lee, U. K., & Kim, H. (2022). UTAUT in metaverse: An "Ifland" case. *Journal of Theoretical and Applied Electronic Commerce Research*, 17(2), 613–635. 10.3390/jtaer17020032

Nguyen, L. T., Duc, D. T. V., Dang, T. Q., & Nguyen, D. P. (2023). Metaverse Banking Service: Are We Ready to Adopt? A Deep Learning-Based Dual-Stage SEM-ANN Analysis. *Human Behavior and Emerging Technologies*, 2023(1), 1–23. 10.1155/2023/6617371

Ooi, K. B., Tan, G. W. H., Al-Emran, M., Al-Sharafi, M. A., Arpaci, I., Zaidan, A. A., & Iranmanesh, M. (2023). The metaverse in engineering management: Overview, opportunities, challenges, and future research agenda. *IEEE Transactions on Engineering Management*.

Park, E. (2024). Examining metaverse game platform adoption: Insights from innovation, behavior, and coolness. *Technology in Society*, 77, 102594. 10.1016/j.techsoc.2024.102594

Pham, C. T., & Thi Nguyet, T. T. (2023). Determinants of blockchain adoption in news media platforms: A perspective from the Vietnamese press industry. *Heliyon*, 9(1), e12747. Advance online publication. 10.1016/j.heliyon.2022.e1274736685429

Pillai, R., Sivathanu, B., Rana, N. P., Preet, R., & Mishra, A. (2024). Factors influencing customers' apparel shopping intention in metaverse. *Journal of Computer Information Systems*, 1–16.

Shen, B., Tan, W., Guo, J., Zhao, L., & Qin, P. (2021). How to promote user purchase in metaverse? A systematic literature review on consumer behavior research and virtual commerce application design. *Applied Sciences (Basel, Switzerland)*, 11(23), 11087. 10.3390/app112311087

Shukla, A., Mishra, A., Rana, N. P., & Banerjee, S. (2024). The future of metaverse adoption: A behavioral reasoning perspective with a text-mining approach. *Journal of Consumer Behaviour*, ●●●, 1–21. 10.1002/cb.2336

Sim, A. J. X. (2023). *A study of metaverse acceptance among Malaysian undergraduate media students based on the technology acceptance model* [Doctoral dissertation, UTAR].

Šímová, T., Zychová, K., & Fejfarová, M. (2024). Metaverse in the virtual workplace. *Vision (Basel)*, 28(1), 19–34. 10.1177/09722629231168690

Singh, S. V. (2018). Study on impact of factors in employee retention and turnover in hospitality industry with special reference to hotels in Varanasi. *Development of Aspects in Tourism and Hospitality Sector*, 190-201.

Singh, S. V. (2018). An Analysis of Tourist Satisfaction in Varanasi as Destination Perspective through Important Performance Analysis. *Avahan. Journal of Hospitality and Tourism.*

Sritong, C., Sawangproh, W., & Teangsompong, T. (2024). Unveiling the adoption of metaverse technology in Bangkok metropolitan areas: A UTAUT2 perspective with social media marketing and consumer engagement. *PLoS One*, 19(6), e0304496. 10.1371/journal.pone.030449638848432

Teng, Z., Cai, Y., Gao, Y., Zhang, X., & Li, X. (2022). Factors affecting learners' adoption of an educational metaverse platform: An empirical study based on an extended UTAUT model. *Mobile Information Systems*, 2022(1), 5479215. 10.1155/2022/5479215

Ünlü, S., Yaşar, L., & Bilici, E. (2023). Metaverse as a Platform for Event Management: The Sample of the Metaverse Türkiye E-Magazine. *TRT Akademi*, 8(17), 122–143. 10.37679/trta.1202057

Venkatesh, V., & Davis, F. D. (2000). Theoretical extension of the Technology Acceptance Model: Four longitudinal field studies. *Management Science*, 46(2), 186–204. 10.1287/mnsc.46.2.186.11926

Vieira, E., & Medeiros, F. (2023). Feasibility of immersive environments in the metaverse for remote practical education in computer networks. In *ICERI2023 Proceedings* (pp. 7301-7310). IATED. 10.21125/iceri.2023.1815

Wang, G., & Shin, C. (2022). Influencing factors of usage intention of metaverse education application platform: Empirical evidence based on PPM and TAM models. *Sustainability (Basel)*, 14(24), 17037. 10.3390/su142417037

Xi, N., Chen, J., Gama, F., Korkeila, H., & Hamari, J. (2024). Acceptance of the metaverse: A laboratory experiment on augmented and virtual reality shopping. *Internet Research*, 34(7), 82–117. 10.1108/INTR-05-2022-0334

Xu, Y., Liu, W., He, T., & Tsai, S. B. (2024). Buzzword or fuzzword: An event study of the metaverse in the Chinese stock market. *Internet Research*, 34(1), 174–194. 10.1108/INTR-07-2022-0526

Chapter 10
Service Automation and Festivals:
Technologies and Their Impact Upon Sustainability of Events

Craig Webster

https://orcid.org/0000-0003-0665-0867

Ball State University, USA

ABSTRACT

The United Nations' sustainable development goals have created an environment in which the world's population are attempting to link various human activities with improvements in the ways that humans do things to ensure a more sustainable future. In this chapter, the author concentrates upon festivals and other events, focusing upon how various service automation technologies will work to support sustainability in the events industry, a component of SDG 12. The chapter will focus upon how technologies will increase efficiency of operations and reduce energy consumption. The chapter will also highlight some of the major challenges, illustrating what innovations and improvements will need to be made to ensure that festivals can achieve the maximum level of sustainability possible. The chapter ends with a discussion of the externalities of the increased use of automation technologies to show that there will have to be adjustments to not only the way that services are delivered but also to the expectations of the consumers.

DOI: 10.4018/979-8-3693-2272-7.ch010

INTRODUCTION

The tourism and hospitality industries are industries that are consume a great deal of materials, energy, water, construction materials, and produce waste. While nearly any human activity will include the use of various inputs and result in a number of wastes, the added element of transportation and intercontinental aspects of transportation for tourism and events are quite wasteful and have a noteworthy impact upon the environment (Ahmad et al., 2019; Sharpley, 2021). While it would be impossible to eliminate all negative social, economic, and environmental externalities from hospitality, tourism, and events, there may be ways in which current and future technologies may reduce waste, minimize the impact up resources, and generally decrease the negative consequences associated with tourism, hospitality, and related industries.

There is a history associated with concerns with environmental protection and sustainability. During the late 1960s there was a growing movement that focused upon the protection of the environment and this developed into our new sense of "sustainability." In 1968, Paul and Anne Ehrlich (1968) published their groundbreaking book, *The Population Bomb*, in which they discussed the concern that the Earth is overpopulated and made predictions about future environmental collapse. It was also the same year that the Club of Rome was founded as an informal organization concerned with important global issues, one of which is environmental issues. By 1970, societal concerns with environmental issues had grown a great deal, enough that the first Earth Day was declared. By the 1980s, there was increased concern and institutionalization of environmental concerns with the production of the Brundtland Report (WCED, 1987). The most massive and most global institutionalization of environmental concerns is the UN's 17 Sustainable Development Goals (SDGs), having been put into place in 2016 as a list of goals and indicators towards environmental, economic, and social goals to be met by 2030.

So, while tourism is a massive part of the economy globally, one of the globe's major industries, we also see that the tourism economy is projected to expand. By 2033, it is estimated that the global tourism industry will be worth $15.5 trillion economy with the US component of the economy being worth $3 trillion (Girma, 2023). With the expansion of the tourism economy, a person would expect that the negative external impacts of the economy would be increased in size. However, this is an opportunity for the use of automation technologies to play a role in improving the efficiency of the use of energy and raw materials in tourism-related businesses. In this chapter, we will first discuss what is meant by "sustainability," showing that it is often a word used in conjunction with tourism and tourism-related industries. Then, we will illustrate the ways in which we expect that automaton technologies will be used in ways to assist in making events (a subset of the tourism and hospitality industries) more effective and efficient, with the hopes of increasing the sustainability of events in the future.

Sustainability as a Concept

The word "sustainability" is one that is frequently used in conjunction with a myriad of different human enterprises globally and it is attached to many different desired outcomes. Merriam-Webster (2024) defines this concept in two different ways, one referring to "capable of being sustained" and the other "relating to, or being a method of harvesting or using a resource so that the resource is not depleted or permanently damaged." As such, it seems that both of these concepts are related in that they project that there are different ways of doing things that have a different type of trajectory, one being capable of continuing for a reasonable period of time into the future and another that can not be carried out for a longer period of time into the future. It seems that the original concerns from the late 1960s was related to purely environmental/ecological concerns, although there is reason to believe that the concept of sustainability has been adapted and expanded to all sorts of activities that are not directly linked with environmental concerns.

The latest and most bombastic expression of the values associated with sustainability is the United Nations Sustainable Development Goals (SDGs). The goals of this project contain seventeen different goals related to the concept of sustainability of development (UN, 2022). These goals are listed in abbreviated titles in Table One below.

Table 1. SDG goals and direct relevance to environmental protection

SDG	Abbreviated Goal Title	Direct Relevance with Environmental Protection?
1	No poverty	No
2	Zero hunger	No
3	Good health and well-being	No
4	Quality education	No
5	Gender equality	No
6	Clean water and sanitation	Maybe
7	Affordable and clean energy	Maybe
8	Decent work and economic growth	No
9	Industry, innovation and infrastructure	Maybe
10	Reduced inequalities	No

continued on following page

Table 1. Continued

SDG	Abbreviated Goal Title	Direct Relevance with Environmental Protection?
11	Sustainable cities and communities	Maybe
12	**Responsible consumption and production**	**Yes**
13	Climate action	**Yes**
14	Life below water	Maybe
15	Life on land	Maybe
16	Peace, justice, and strong institutions	No
17	Partnerships for the goals	No

What is noteworthy about the SDGs upon closer look is that while they are to a large extent embraced by much of the world, they are especially relevant for developing countries. For example, developed countries have largely eradicated poverty (depending upon what is considered poverty) and have more issues with overindulgence with food than issues linked with hunger. So, it seems, that a good deal on this list is most critical as goals for developing countries, despite the acute interest in developed countries for the attainment of these goals. Additionally, in terms of linking how directly these goals are linked with environmental protection, there seems to be only a few goals (SDG12 and SDG13) that are directly and acutely linked with environmental protection. So, while an argument can be made in this world that everything is related to everything, there seems to be two specific goals for the SDGs that are clearly and unequivocally linked with environmental protections. SDG12 is linked with the ways that humans consume and produce goods and SDG13 includes goals linked with mitigating and preventing anthropogenic climate change.

While in some ways there are many of us who associate "sustainability" with trajectories of social and economic systems that are long-term, there is no reason that some of the goals listed in the SDGs do not really have to be achieved in order to have environmental protections and a long-term functioning global system. For example, the first five SDGs need not be achieved to have environmental/ecological conditions that have a positive long-term trajectory. Gender and other inequalities do not have to be linked in positive ways, necessarily, for the environment to be protected. In fact, it seems that the SDGs are largely a set of goals that are utopian (and I do not mean to refer to this in a pejorative way) and create a world in which some would prefer humanity to inhabit.

While the utopian goals of the SDGs may be a good moral compass for this discussion of technology and sustainability in events, I would like to take the narrower discussion of sustainability, that of a concern with the limiting of environmental stress done by the process of human consumption and production of goods and services.

This narrower discussion of sustainability, as discussed in more depth by Glavič (2021) deals with the very real stresses that economic production and consumption places upon our home planet. SDG12, then, is the focus of this discussion, since it focussed upon a very limited part of what is referred to in discussions of sustainability. The SDG12 goals are composed of a number of specific goals, even if the goals themselves may be less than specific such as 12.5 "By 2030, substantially reduce waste generation through prevention, reduction, recycling and reuse." While there are is some vagueness in terms of measurement, the intent of the goal is quite clear and it can easily be imagined that technology could play a role in reaching such a goal, regardless of the sector of the economy.

Research in tourism and hospitality has embraced not only the SDG goals but also the language of sustainability. For example, in terms of language, it is easy to see that the SDGs have been very influential in terms of influencing the titles of various academic articles as well as the research agendas of researchers. Alonso-Muñoz et al, (2023) link the SDGs with increased sustainability in tourism. But there are many other articles in recent years that reference sustainability or make sustainability the central focus of the research (see, for example; Alarcón, & Cole, 2019; Boluk, et al., 2019; Elshaer, et al., 2021; Majid et al., 2023; Martin-Rios, et al., 2020; Schönherr et al., 2023).

In terms of technology's specific contribution to attaining the SDG goals for tourism industries, there is a growing literature. Ivanov (2023) and Ali et al. (2020) illustrate how all the SDGs can be linked with technology improvements tourism and its related industries to help improve outcomes and lead to a sustainable future. Specifically, it seems that only one scholarly article (Ivanov et al., 2024) has focussed specifically on SDG12, illustrating how this specific goal can and will influence tourism-related industries.

Automation of Tourism Services

There has been an impressive incorporation of various automation technologies into industry in general as well as tourism and hospitality outlets. Many automation technologies have been integrated into the tourism and hospitality ecosystem in recent years and the academic literature has reflected upon this (see, for example, Buhalis & Moldavska, 2022; Ivanov, et al., 2017; Rastegar et al., 2021; Song et al., 2023). The most relevant to our discussion of events and festivals is linked with the work of Ivanov et al. (2017) that separates the concept of the automation of events into two categories, one category is the general concept of "service automation" while the other is "robots." The robots are the physical expression of a machine, while service automation may include other technologies (such as AI) that is software rich and thus not necessarily the physical representation of technology in a tangible form.

At the time of writing, the authors noted the current and future capabilities of such technologies for events and they included for those capabilities at the time of writing:

- Mobile telepresence (service automation)
- Self-service check in kiosks (service automation)
- Self-service mobile check in (service automation)
- Mobile service requests (service automation)
- Booth attendants (robots)
- Concierge robots (robots)
- Robot bartenders (robots)
- Robot baristas (robots)
- Robot servers (robots)
- Entertainment (robots)
- Delivery robots (robots) (Ivanov et al., 2017)

However, the authors also suggested that there would be two major capabilities in the future, including the fully mobile telepresence and an interactive booth attendant (Ivanov et al., 2017). These various technologies, as a whole work in ways to limit the amount of labour used in the provision of goods and services, for the most part, by replacing the labour with capital, whether software or hardware (in the case of the robot). There are two major reasons for the incorporation of such automation technologies into various enterprises. One major reason is that there is a major explosion of capabilities that is referred to as the Fourth Industrial Revolution, so just the presence of the technical ability to implement automation technologies is a factor. However, there is the other major reason, the demographic decline in almost all developed countries (Webster, 2021). The long-term demographic decline that is a major factor in almost all developed countries is a significant driver, forcing almost all industries to look at ways of using less human labor, since less human labor is available to draw from.

SDG12 and Events

While there has been some attention given to the question of sustainability of events recently (Cavallin Toscani et al., 2024), none has focused specifically upon the issue of SDG12 ("Responsible consumption and production") and its relationship or potential relationship with the events industry. To begin with, this goal has two major components (and we will not deal with the very specific measures of the subgoals here), one of an improvement of the qualities of consumption and the other with the qualities of production. From this, there is the idea that there should be changes from the demand as well as the supply side of the equation. Here, we should indicate how each side of the equation can be used in conjunction with technologies in order to improve sustainability.

First, in terms of the consideration of consumption patterns can be altered in ways that foster a more sustainable ecological system, there is some role for technologies to influence patterns that are favourable to the promotion of SDG12. Most notably, the push factor can be utilized in order to encourage behaviours that are measured and deemed to be more supportive of consumption patterns that are favourable (Webster, 2022). Automation technologies driven by AI can manipulate and influence choices by the consumers in ways that will give the appearance of a market choice, but will be able to suggest choices that are determined to be more sustainable and even adjust prices in some ways to encourage practices that are considered more favourable. For example, while it is common for airlines to offer carbon offsets as a purchase that a conscientious consumer may choose to purchase when checking out, AI may be used at various points in the purchase process to remind consumers of the environmental costs of particular options and may even educate consumers. In the end, many consumers will have expectations of sustainable products in the events industry (as well as all other industries) but various automation technologies will be used to influence choices and purchases in ways that give consumers choices while also nudging them to make decisions that are in line with how AI can design these choices to be made.

Second, and most importantly, there is the issue of how the industry will produce events in ways that are more in line with sustainability. One of the major ways that this will take place is that AI technologies will increase efficiencies and decrease some of the silly mistakes made due to the emotionality of humans. Humans trying to make estimates of what resources will be needed to make an event run will be no match for the computing technologies of even present computing technologies (Giddings, 2008). Additionally, taking the human element out of the production side of events may also be helpful since humans are likely to make mistakes influenced by emotional issues or informed by irrational thinking, such as hunches (Lerner *et al.*, 2015).

Additionally, there is the direct influence of just having fewer people running festivals, since automation will reduce human labour massively. Humans require a substantial organization framework to support their labour (human resources, payroll, management) and they also have biological needs (air, food, rest) while producing biological waste. Replacing human labour with automated labour will have some savings in terms of ecological issues but they will also introduce some other issues. For example, the present lithium battery is toxic and is not entirely safe (Nedjalkov et al., 2016; Liu et al., 2021), so the use of such common batteries to power many automation technologies are not particularly earth-friendly nor safe. Additionally, many tangible automation technologies will include plastics that are quite toxic by nature at present (Verma et al., 2016).

Generally, the increased use of service automation in events will require increased use of technologies largely out of necessity, since labour supply (at least in developed countries) will be increasingly an issue for employers. However, there are massive technological and practical things that will have to be solved to ensure that events are increasingly ecologically friendly. Consumers will have to be more educated about what they are consuming and what they consume, although technologies will influence their choices to be more consistent with ecologically-favourable outcomes. The producers of events will have to use technologies that ensure that events are managed in ways to ensure a reduction in negative externalities. One key issue in this is the question of the progress of technology, since current technologies can be either not entirely effective (Liu et al., 2023) or are toxic or dangerous. So, a major leap in the performance of technologies is needed, as well as the development of automation technologies that use little energy and are generally earth-friendly and safe around humans.

CONCLUSION

We expect in the near future to live in an economy that is robonomic in nature, being almost entirely run by automation technologies in nearly all industries (Ivanov, 2021) and there is no reason that the events industry would somehow be exempt from this. While many may wonder about the possibility of having robonomic events, we see that the growth of the capabilities of technologies paired with the massive dearth of labour in developed countries means that it is a necessity to automate much more. It may largely be our biases and people who have grown up with the conception that service industries require a great deal of human contact that may make us question whether it is possible to automate events. Necessity, though, as they say is the mother of invention.

There are some social implications associated with the increased automation of events. For example, there may be a bifurcation of the workforce with a highly skilled workforce engaged in the economy with another part of the workforce that can not be well-integrated into the workforce. Because of this, one would expect that there would be a Luddite reaction to the introduction of service automation into industries, with some workers being seemingly opposing automation with robo-phobic attitudes, as some have envisioned (Webster and Ivanov, 2021). However, it may simply be that some technologies are more accepted than others, as some have found (Leung, et al., 2023). So, it may not be some sort of blanked rejection of new technologies but specific technologies that employees either embrace or reject.

Consumers, on the other hand, may reject some technologies, although a certain subset may embrace them either because of the perception about the advantages of the technologies. One of the key issues that the previous research has shown, is that consumers expect a cost savings Ivanov & Webster, 2021), when automation technologies are integrated into operations.

From the consumption side, we expect that there will be a culture shift in the consumer. The culture shift will be a result of the education of consumers who have high expectations for sustainability of events that has been cultivated over decades through formal educational systems in schools but also from an ethos that surrounds them in their cultural environment. In this way, the future consumer will be socialized from a young age into concern with ecological issues. Various technologies, including AI, with work in ways to ensure that the consumer makes choices that are consistent with the desired outcomes of sustainability. To this end, there will be a need to ensure that the ideology of sustainability is part and parcel of the industries programming the software and that the ideology is programmed into the regulatory frameworks, although the regulatory frameworks may also have to compete against different ideological frameworks and different levels of institutions (Webster & Cain, 2024).

From the production side, various technologies have the most potential to influence improvements in the production of events. First and foremost, AI promises to identify problems and ensure that there is increased efficiencies in terms of the use of energy and other inputs into the production of events. Also, there will be a reduction of humans needed for labour and since human labour will require resources (water, food, and space) while producing biological waste and creating bureaucratic issues (payments, human resource issues…), there should be a substantial reduction in terms of the stresses that events place upon the ecology. However, there is also an issue that current technologies are not quite earth-friendly yet.

For the future, we can expect that there will be no reduction in the human demand for events. We know that there will be all sorts of externalities that are social in nature, including the reshaping of employment and the exclusion of a large percentage of the workforce. There will have to be all a number of different social, economic, and political innovations to deal with the externalities, ensuring a more sustainable future both environmentally and socially. However, we also see that the way that events will be experienced will be different. First, and foremost, there will be less of a human presence in terms of the provision of services to support the events because technologies will continue to be viable and effective and because of reductions of the supply of labour in developed countries. Second, we expect that the consumer will be different, first of all because of the way that they have been socialized, as well as the way that AI and other technologies will nudge the consumer to consume in ways that are determined to be more sustainable. Finally, we will see an increased use of automation technologies in order to staff events, even using such technologies as holograms and robots to entertain participants.

REFERENCES

Ahmad, F., Draz, M. U., Su, L., & Rauf, A. (2019). Taking the bad with the good: The nexus between tourism and environmental degradation in the lower middle-income Southeast Asian economies. *Journal of Cleaner Production*, 233, 1240–1249. 10.1016/j.jclepro.2019.06.138

Alarcón, D. M., & Cole, S. (2019). No sustainability for tourism without gender equality. *Journal of Sustainable Tourism*, 27(7), 903–919. 10.1080/09669582.2019.1588283

Ali, A., Rasoolimanesh, S. M., & Cobanoglu, C. (2020). Technology in tourism and hospitality to achieve sustainable development goals (SDGs). *Journal of Hospitality and Tourism Technology*, 11(2), 177–181. 10.1108/JHTT-05-2020-146

Alonso-Muñoz, S., Torrejón-Ramos, M., Medina-Salgado, M.-S., & González-Sánchez, R. (2023). Sustainability as a building block for tourism – future research: Tourism Agenda 2030. *Tourism Review*, 78(2), 461–474. 10.1108/TR-12-2021-0568

Boluk, K. A., Cavaliere, C. T., & Higgins-Desbiolles, F. (2019). A critical framework for interrogating the United Nations Sustainable Development Goals 2030 Agenda in tourism. *Journal of Sustainable Tourism*, 27(7), 847–864. 10.1080/09669582.2019.1619748

Buhalis, D., & Moldavska, I. (2022). Voice assistants in hospitality: Using artificial intelligence for customer service. *Journal of Hospitality and Tourism Technology*, 13(3), 386–403. 10.1108/JHTT-03-2021-0104

Cavallin Toscani, A., Vendraminelli, L., & Vinelli, A. (2024). Environmental sustainability in the event industry: A systematic review and a research agenda. *Journal of Sustainable Tourism*, 1–35. 10.1080/09669582.2024.2309544

Ehrlich, P., & Ehrlich, A. (1968). *The Population Bomb*. Sierra Club/Ballantine Books.

Elshaer, I., Moustafa, M., Sobaih, A. E., Aliedan, M., & Azazz, A. M. (2021). The impact of women's empowerment on sustainable tourism development: Mediating role of tourism involvement. *Tourism Management Perspectives*, 38, 100815. 10.1016/j.tmp.2021.100815

Giddings, G. (2008). Humans versus computers: Differences in their ability to absorb and process information for business decision purposes — and the implications for the future. *Business Information Review*, 25(1), 32–39. 10.1177/0266382107088211

Girma, L. L. (2023). Travel Will Represent a $15.5 Trillion Economy by 2033. *Bloomberg News*. https://www.bloomberg.com/news/articles/2023-08-21/global-travel-and-tourism-will-represent-a-15-5-trillion-economy-by-2033

Glavič, P. (2021). Evolution and current challenges of sustainable consumption and production. *Sustainability (Basel)*, 13(16), 9379. 10.3390/su13169379

Ivanov, S. (2021). Robonomics: The rise of the automated economy. *ROBONOMICS: The Journal of the Automated Economy*, 1, 11. https://journal.robonomics.science/index.php/rj/article/view/11

Ivanov, S., Duglio, S., & Beltramo, R. (2023). Robots in tourism and Sustainable Development Goals: Tourism Agenda 2030 perspective article. *Tourism Review*, 78(2), 352–360. 10.1108/TR-08-2022-0404

Ivanov, S., Seyitoğlu, F., & Webster, C. (2024), Tourism, automation and responsible consumption and production: a horizon 2050 paper, *Tourism Review*. 10.1108/TR-12-2023-0898

Ivanov, S., & Webster, C. (2021). Willingness-to-pay for robot-delivered tourism and hospitality services – an exploratory study. *International Journal of Contemporary Hospitality Management*, 33(11), 3926–3955. 10.1108/IJCHM-09-2020-1078

Ivanov, S., Webster, C., & Berezina, K. (2017). Adoption of Robots and Service Automation by Tourism and Hospitality Companies. *Revista Turismo & Desenvolvimento*, 27/28, 1501-1517., Available at *SSRN*: https://ssrn.com/abstract=2964308

Lerner, J. S., Li, Y., Valdesolo, P., & Kassam, K. S. (2015). Emotion and decision making. *Annual Review of Psychology*, 66(1), 799–823. 10.1146/annurev-psych-010213-11504325251484

Leung, X. Y., Zhang, H., Lyu, J., & Bai, B. (2023). Why do hotel frontline employees use service robots in the workplace? A technology affordance theory perspective. *International Journal of Hospitality Management*, 108, 103380. 10.1016/j.ijhm.2022.103380

Liu, D., Li, C., Zhang, J., & Huang, W. (2023). Robot service failure and recovery: Literature review and future directions. *International Journal of Advanced Robotic Systems*, 20(4), 17298806231191606. 10.1177/17298806231191606

Liu, F., Wang, T., Liu, X., & Fan, L. Z. (2021). Challenges and recent progress on key materials for rechargeable magnesium batteries. *Advanced Energy Materials*, 11(2), 2000787. 10.1002/aenm.202000787

Majid, G. M., Tussyadiah, I., Kim, Y. R., & Pal, A. (2023). Intelligent automation for sustainable tourism: A systematic review. *Journal of Sustainable Tourism*, 31(11), 1–20. 10.1080/09669582.2023.2246681

Martin-Rios, C., Hofmann, A., & Mackenzie, N. (2020). Sustainability-oriented innovations in food waste management technology. *Sustainability (Basel)*, 13(1), 210. 10.3390/su13010210

Nedjalkov, A., Meyer, J., Köhring, M., Doering, A., Angelmahr, M., Dahle, S., Sander, A., Fischer, A., & Schade, W. (2016). Toxic Gas Emissions from Damaged Lithium Ion Batteries—Analysis and Safety Enhancement Solution. *Batteries*, 2(1), 5. 10.3390/batteries2010005

Rastegar, N., Flaherty, J., Liang, L., & Choi, H. C. (2021). The adoption of self-service kiosks in quick-service restaurants. *European Journal of Tourism Research*, 27, 2709. 10.54055/ejtr.v27i.2139

Schönherr, S., Peters, M., & Kuščer, K. (2023). Sustainable tourism policies: From crisis-related awareness to agendas towards measures. *Journal of Destination Marketing & Management*, 27, 100762. 10.1016/j.jdmm.2023.100762

Sharpley, R. (2021). On the need for sustainable tourism consumption. *Tourist Studies*, 21(1), 96–107. 10.1177/1468797620986087

Song, X., Li, Y., Leung, X. Y., & Mei, D. (2023). Service robots and hotel guests' perceptions: Anthropomorphism and stereotypes. *Tourism Review*, 79(2), 505–522. 10.1108/TR-04-2023-0265

United Nations. (2022). *Fast Facts – What is Sustainable Development?* UN. https://www.un.org/sustainabledevelopment/blog/2023/08/what-is-sustainable-development/

Verma, R., Vinoda, K. S., Papireddy, M., & Gowda, A. N. S. (2016). Toxic pollutants from plastic waste-a review. *Procedia Environmental Sciences*, 35, 701–708. 10.1016/j.proenv.2016.07.069

WCED. (1987). *Our Common Future*. Oxford University Press.

Webster, C. (2021). Demography as a Driver of Robonomics. *ROBONOMICS: The Journal of the Automated Economy, 1*, 12. https://journal.robonomics.science/index.php/rj/article/view/12

Webster, C. (2022). War of the Default Settings. *ROBONOMICS: The Journal of the Automated Economy, 3,* 38. https://journal.robonomics.science/index.php/rj/article/view/38

Webster, C. & Cain, L. (2024) Regulation, Automated Technologies, and Competitiveness in the Hospitality Industry. *Journal of Hospitality and Tourism Research*. OnlineFirst.

Webster, C., & Ivanov, S. (2021). Attitudes towards robots in tourism: robophobes vs. robophiles. In Farmaki, A., & Pappas, N. (Eds.), *Emerging Transformations in Tourism and Hospitality* (pp. 66–82). Routledge. 10.4324/9781003105930-6

Chapter 11
Leveraging Event Gamification for Event Planning and Creating a Memorable Experience

Aarti Madan

https://orcid.org/0000-0002-6293-092X

Atal Bihari Vajpayee School of Management and Entrepreneurship, Jawaharlal Nehru University, India

Vaniki Joshi Lohani

https://orcid.org/0009-0006-6097-2137

Atal Bihari Vajpayee School of Management and Entrepreneurship, Jawaharlal Nehru University, India

ABSTRACT

This chapter explores the innovative use of game elements and mechanics in event planning to enhance engagement, foster interaction, and create memorable experiences. Beginning with an introduction to gamification concepts and objectives, the chapter delves into the psychology of gamification and various types of gamification techniques. It provides insights into integrating gamification into event planning processes, including pre-event planning, execution, and post-event evaluation. Ethical considerations and challenges, such as ensuring fairness and inclusivity, addressing negative impacts, and mitigating over-competitiveness, are discussed. Additionally, the chapter explores future trends and innovations in event gamification, including emerging technologies, personalization trends, and integration with virtual and hybrid events. The chapter also highlights the power of gamification in transforming event experiences and offers practical insights for event planners and

DOI: 10.4018/979-8-3693-2272-7.ch011

organizers to leverage gamification effectively.

INTRODUCTION TO EVENT GAMIFICATION

Gamification is the application of game-design elements and principles in non-game contexts to engage and motivate people towards specific goals (Deterding et al., 2011). It uses psychological features of games, such as competition, achievement, and reward systems, to motivate desired actions and outcomes. In the context of event planning, gamification involves cfxjeincorporating game-like elements, mechanics, and experiences into the event design to enhance attendee engagement, participation, and overall satisfaction. At its core, gamification taps into fundamental human motivations, such as the desire for mastery, autonomy, social interaction, and recognition. By leveraging these innate drives, event organizers can create dynamic and engaging events that engage attendees and leave an enduring impression.

The concept of gamification extends beyond traditional notions of games and entertainment. It encompasses a wide range of strategies, including point systems, challenges, leaderboards, badges, rewards, and storytelling elements, all aimed at making the event experience more enjoyable, interactive, and memorable (Santhanam et al., 2016). Moreover, gamification is not limited to physical events but can also be applied to virtual and hybrid events, leveraging digital platforms and technologies to create engaging experiences in online environments.

In today's fast-paced and digitally connected world, event planners face the challenge of capturing and maintaining the attention of increasingly distracted and discerning attendees. Traditional event formats, such as lectures, seminars, and exhibitions, often struggle to sustain engagement and foster meaningful interactions. This is where gamification plays a pivotal role. By infusing elements of play and competition into the event experience, gamification transforms passive spectators into active participants, driving higher levels of engagement and interaction. Attendees are motivated to explore, compete, collaborate, and immerse themselves fully in the event proceedings.

Gamification has become a game-changer in event planning, reshaping how organizers engage participants and craft immersive experiences. By infusing game elements into event design, gamification holds significant importance in boosting attendee engagement, encouraging interaction, and ultimately, ensuring event success (Sisson & Whalen, 2021). It's instrumental in transforming passive attendees into active participants (Liu et al., 2019), whether through interactive quizzes, scavenger hunts, or collaborative challenges, fostering a vibrant event atmosphere that keeps participants invested. Moreover, gamification facilitates networking and community-building by breaking the ice and encouraging meaningful connections

(Araújo & Pestana, 2017). It incentivizes participation and attendance through rewards and recognition systems, driving overall engagement (Hyun & Jordan, 2019). Gamification also improves the process of learning by making it more participatory and memorable, ensuring attendees leave with valuable insights. Importantly, it helps events stand out by creating unique, branded experiences that resonate with attendees. Additionally, gamification provides valuable insights into participant behavior through analytics, enabling organizers to fine-tune strategies for future events. In sum, gamification is a cornerstone of modern event planning, elevating engagement, interaction, and overall attendee experience.

The utilization of gamification in events serves a multifaceted set of objectives aimed at enhancing attendee engagement, fostering interaction, and achieving specific outcomes. Primarily, gamification seeks to elevate attendee engagement (Suh et al., 2017) and participation by infusing game elements like challenges, quests, and rewards into event activities. This approach creates a dynamic and interactive event environment that encourages attendees to actively engage with content and experiences, resulting in higher levels of satisfaction. Additionally, gamification serves as a powerful tool for fostering interaction and networking among attendees. By providing opportunities for collaboration, team-based competitions, and gamified networking activities, organizers can facilitate meaningful connections and relationship-building opportunities, enriching the overall event experience (Talantis et al., 2020). Moreover, gamification enables organizers to drive desired behaviors among attendees by offering incentives, rewards, and recognition for specific actions aligned with event objectives. Whether it's encouraging participation in sessions, booth visits, or surveys, gamification motivates attendees to take desired actions, maximizing the impact of the event. Furthermore, gamification enhances learning and knowledge retention by transforming educational content into interactive and engaging experiences. Through gamified learning activities, simulations, and challenges, organizers can facilitate skill development, reinforce key concepts, and promote deeper learning among attendees. Additionally, gamification serves branding and differentiation purposes by creating distinctive event experiences aligned with brand identity and messaging. By incorporating branded gamified elements, organizers can strengthen brand recognition and leave a lasting impression on attendees. Finally, gamification makes data gathering and analysis easier, providing useful insights into attendee conduct, inclinations, and participation levels. Using gamification analytics, event organizers may assess the efficacy of methods, find areas for development, and make data-driven decisions to enhance future event experiences. Overall, the goals of using gamification in events are diverse and complementary, with each contributing to the event's success and impact. This chapter aims to explore gamification and its potential to revolutionize the event planning industry. Gamification, which incorporates game aspects and mechanics into event design, can increase audience engagement, develop meaningful interactions, and create memorable moments. This chapter seeks to provide a thorough overview of gamification, its benefits, and practical ways for successfully implementing it in a variety of events.

UNDERSTANDING THE PSYCHOLOGY OF GAMIFICATION

Gamification has become a prevalent strategy in various fields, including education (Landers & Landers, 2014), marketing (Hamari, 2017), healthcare (Jones et al., 2014), and workplace management (Fernandes et al., 2012). At its core, gamification leverages principles of psychology to motivate and engage individuals towards specific goals or behaviors. Understanding the psychology behind gamification is crucial for designing effective and impactful experiences that capture and sustain participants' attention and enthusiasm.

Motivation and Engagement

Motivation and engagement are fundamental concepts in the psychology of gamification. Motivation refers to the driving force behind individuals' actions, while engagement pertains to the level of involvement and interaction in an activity. In gamification, these concepts are intertwined, as motivating individuals to engage with a task or experience is essential for achieving desired outcomes.

Motivation can be divided into intrinsic and extrinsic types. Intrinsic motivation comes from within, driven by personal interest, enjoyment, and the satisfaction gained from the activity itself (Ryan & Deci, 2000a). On the other hand, extrinsic motivation originates from external rewards or incentives, such as points, badges, or prizes. Effective gamification balances both intrinsic and extrinsic motivators to sustain engagement over time, recognizing that while extrinsic rewards can provide initial incentives, intrinsic motivators are essential for fostering long-term engagement and enjoyment (Ryan et al., 2006).

Furthermore, gamification leverages various psychological principles to enhance motivation and engagement, including progression, challenge, social interaction, autonomy, and meaningful goals (Hanus & Fox, 2015). By incorporating these elements into the design of gamified experiences, practitioners can create dynamic and immersive environments that captivate participants and drive desired behaviors.

Behavioral Psychology in Gamification

Gamification draws heavily from behavioral psychology principles to influence and shape participant behavior. One fundamental notion is operant conditioning, which holds that the consequences of behavior influence it. In gamification, this translates into designing reward systems and feedback mechanisms that reinforce desired behaviors and discourage undesirable ones.

Reinforcement plans, such as fixed ratio, variable ratio, fixed interval, and variable interval, are widely used in gamification to schedule rewards and keep players engaged. For example, intermittent reinforcement, where rewards are delivered unpredictably, tends to be more effective in sustaining behavior than continuous reinforcement.

Additionally, gamification leverages principles of intrinsic and extrinsic rewards to motivate behavior. Intrinsic rewards are inherently satisfying and enjoyable, such as a sense of accomplishment or mastery, while extrinsic rewards are external incentives provided to motivate behavior, such as points, badges, or prizes (Davis & Singh, 2015). By strategically designing reward systems that tap into both intrinsic and extrinsic motivators, gamification can effectively stimulate engagement and participation (Sailer et al., 2017).

Moreover, gamification incorporates cognitive biases and heuristics to influence decision-making and behavior. For example, the scarcity heuristic, which suggests that people place greater value on scarce resources, can be used to create a sense of urgency or exclusivity in gamified experiences, driving engagement and participation.

Intrinsic vs. Extrinsic Motivation

Intrinsic and extrinsic motivation play distinct roles in gamification, each contributing to the overall engagement and enjoyment of participants. The intrinsic drive stems from internal reasons like individual curiosity, delight, and satisfaction with the activity itself. It is driven by the inherent pleasure and fulfilment individuals experience when engaging in activities that align with their values, interests, and goals.

In contrast, extrinsic drive is derived from external benefits or rewards (Ryan & Deci, 2000a), such as points, badges, or prizes. These rewards serve as tangible recognition for achievements and milestones, providing participants with extrinsic reinforcement and motivation to continue engaging in the activity.

Effective gamification strikes a balance between intrinsic and extrinsic motivation (Deci et al., 2001), leveraging both types of rewards to create a dynamic and engaging experience. By aligning game mechanics with participants' intrinsic values and aspirations while providing meaningful extrinsic incentives, gamification can stimulate motivation and engagement over time.

Elements of Effective Gamification

Effective gamification relies on several key elements that work together to engage and motivate participants, ultimately enhancing their overall experience. Let's look at each of these features to discover their importance and how they impact the effectiveness of gamified experiences.

1. Clear Goals:

Establishing clear and meaningful goals is essential in gamification to provide participants with a sense of direction and purpose. These goals serve as targets for participants to strive towards, guiding their actions and efforts throughout the experience. Clear goals help to focus participants' attention, motivate them to take specific actions, and provide a sense of accomplishment when achieved. Whether it's completing challenges, earning rewards, or reaching milestones, well-defined goals create a sense of progression and achievement that keeps participants engaged and motivated.

2. Feedback Mechanisms:

Feedback is extremely important in gamification since it provides participants with timely and relevant information about their progress and performance (Werbach, 2014). Feedback mechanisms, such as progress bars, notifications, and leaderboards, help participants track their accomplishments, understand their strengths and weaknesses, and make informed decisions about their next steps (Peng et al., 2012). Positive feedback reinforces desired behaviors, while constructive feedback offers opportunities for improvement and growth. By incorporating effective feedback mechanisms, gamified experiences can maintain motivation, encourage participation, and drive continuous improvement among participants.

3. Progression Systems:

Progression systems are designed to provide participants with a sense of advancement and achievement as they navigate through the gamified experience. These systems typically include incremental challenges, levels, and rewards that become progressively more challenging as participants progress (Werbach & Hunter, 2012). By offering a structured path for advancement, progression systems create a sense of accomplishment and mastery that motivates participants to continue engaging with the experience (Sailer et al., 2013). As participants overcome obstacles and achieve milestones, they feel a sense of satisfaction and fulfillment, further fueling their motivation to succeed (Rigby & Ryan, 2011).

4. Social Interaction:

Incorporating social elements into gamified experiences, such as collaboration, competition, and peer feedback, fosters a sense of community and belonging among participants (Schöbel et al., 2020). Social interaction enhances motivation by providing opportunities for connection, support, and recognition from peers (Suzuki et al., 2020). Collaborative challenges encourage teamwork and cooperation, while competitive elements add excitement and engagement (Santhanam et al., 2016). Peer feedback and recognition validate participants' efforts and achievements, reinforcing their sense of belonging and motivating them to continue participating. By leveraging social interaction, gamified experiences can create a sense of camaraderie and community that enhances motivation and enjoyment (Kapp, 2012).

5. Customization and Personalization:

Customizing the gamified experience to individual tastes and interests enhances engagement and relevance for participants. Customization and personalization allow participants to choose their own paths, set their own goals, and engage with content that aligns with their interests and abilities. By offering options for customization, such as avatar customization (Buckley & Doyle, 2017), difficulty levels, and personalized challenges, gamified experiences empower participants to take ownership of their experience and make it uniquely their own. Personalization also enhances motivation by making participants feel valued and respected, ultimately increasing their investment in the experience (Jahn et al., 2021).

6. Immersive Storytelling:

Integrating narrative elements and storytelling techniques into gamified experiences captivates participants' attention and creates emotional connections that enhance their overall experience (Kapp, 2012). Immersive storytelling adds depth, context, and meaning to the gamified experience, making it more engaging and memorable. By weaving narratives into challenges, quests, and rewards, gamified experiences create a sense of adventure and intrigue that motivates participants to actively participate and explore (Nicholson, 2014). Immersive storytelling also evokes emotions and creates lasting impressions, increasing participants' enjoyment and satisfaction with the experience.

Effective gamification relies on clear goals, feedback mechanisms, progression systems, social interaction, customization and personalization, and immersive storytelling to engage and motivate participants. By incorporating these key elements into gamified experiences, organizers can create engaging, rewarding, and memorable experiences that captivate participants' attention, foster motivation, and drive desired behaviors. Ultimately, effective gamification enhances the overall participant experience, leading to increased engagement, satisfaction, and success.

TYPES OF GAMIFICATION IN EVENTS

Gamification offers event planners a versatile toolkit to enhance attendee engagement, foster interaction, and create memorable experiences. By incorporating game-like elements and mechanics into event design, organizers can transform passive participants into active contributors, driving higher levels of participation and satisfaction. There are several types of gamification strategies that event planners can leverage to achieve specific objectives and cater to different audiences. These include competitive games, collaborative games, exploratory games, and interactive presentations and workshops.

Competitive Games

Competitive games are centered around challenges and competitions that pit individuals or teams against each other in pursuit of victory. They are a cornerstone of gamification, harnessing participants' competitive drive and desire for achievement to create engaging and thrilling experiences. Whether in the form of team-based challenges, head-to-head competitions, or leaderboard rankings, these games fuel excitement and motivation among participants. By pitting individuals or teams against each other in pursuit of victory, competitive games foster a dynamic and energetic atmosphere that captivates participants' attention and encourages active participation. Participants are driven to push their limits, showcase their skills, and outperform their peers, resulting in heightened engagement and a memorable event experience. These games capitalize on participants' competitive spirit and desire for achievement, driving engagement and excitement throughout the event (Morschheuser et al., 2019). Some examples of competitive games commonly used in events include:

Team-based Challenges: Organizers can divide attendees into teams and assign them various challenges or tasks to complete within a specified time frame. These challenges can range from physical activities, such as scavenger hunts or obstacle courses, to mental puzzles and problem-solving challenges. Team-based challenges promote collaboration, communication, and teamwork, fostering a sense of camaraderie among participants.

Leaderboards and Rankings: Implementing leaderboards and rankings allows participants to track their progress and compare their performance with others in real-time. Leaderboards can be built around a variety of measures, including points earned, activities done, and accomplishments unlocked. By displaying leaderboards prominently at the event venue or through a mobile app, organizers can instill a sense of competitiveness and incentive in attendance to advance through the ranks and achieve recognition.

Competitive games are effective for energizing the event atmosphere, encouraging participation, and fostering friendly rivalry among attendees (Vegt et al., 2014). However, it's essential to ensure that competition remains healthy and inclusive, avoiding overly competitive environments that may alienate certain participants.

Collaborative Games

Collaborative games emphasize teamwork, cooperation, and collective achievement, creating a feeling of belonging and shared objectives among participants while motivating them to work collectively to achieve common goals. (Salen & Zimmerman, 2003). By leveraging each other's strengths and abilities, attendees collaborate to overcome challenges, solve puzzles, and achieve success as a group. Collaborative games promote communication, trust, and camaraderie among participants, creating bonds and connections that extend beyond the event. Examples of collaborative games suitable for events include team-based challenges, group problem-solving activities, and cooperative quests. These games not only enhance engagement and interaction but also reinforce the importance of collaboration and teamwork in achieving collective success. Some examples of collaborative games suitable for events include:

Cooperative Tasks and Quests: Organizers can design collaborative tasks or quests that require participants to work together to overcome obstacles, solve puzzles, or achieve specific objectives. These tasks often involve a series of challenges that must be completed sequentially, encouraging teamwork and coordination among participants (Morschheuser et al., 2019). Collaborative tasks can be incorporated into various event formats, such as team-building activities, workshops, or interactive exhibits.

Group Challenges and Achievements: Group challenges challenge participants to achieve collective milestones or objectives through coordinated efforts. These challenges can range from community service projects, such as volunteering or fundraising activities, to creative endeavors, such as group art projects or performances. By emphasizing collective achievement, group challenges promote a sense of unity and collaboration among attendees, fostering meaningful connections and shared experiences (Vegt et al., 2014).

Collaborative games are effective for promoting teamwork, communication, and mutual support among participants. They encourage attendees to collaborate, share ideas, and pool resources to achieve common goals, fostering a sense of belonging and camaraderie.

Exploratory Games

Exploratory games encourage participants to explore their surroundings, discover hidden treasures, and engage with the event environment in new and exciting ways. These games capitalize on participants' innate curiosity and thirst for adventure, motivating them to explore and engage with various facets of the event space. From scavenger hunts that lead participants on a quest to uncover clues scattered throughout the venue to interactive challenges that prompt attendees to interact with installations or exhibits, exploratory games offer an immersive and dynamic experience. By encouraging participants to actively explore their surroundings and discover new discoveries, these games foster a sense of excitement, discovery, and engagement, transforming the event into an adventure-filled journey of exploration and discovery. Some examples of exploratory games suitable for events include:

Scavenger Hunts: Scavenger hunts challenge participants to find and collect a series of items or clues scattered throughout the event venue. These items can be physical objects hidden in various locations or digital clues accessible through a mobile app. Scavenger hunts promote exploration, discovery, and active engagement with the event environment, encouraging participants to interact with exhibits, sponsors, and other attendees (Hutzler et al., 2017).

Interactive Maps and Exhibits: Interactive maps and exhibits allow participants to navigate the event venue and discover points of interest, activities, and attractions. These maps can be enhanced with interactive features, such as clickable icons, augmented reality overlays, or gamified challenges. Interactive maps and exhibits provide attendees with a personalized and immersive experience, allowing them to explore and engage with event content at their own pace.

Exploratory games are effective for encouraging participants to explore and engage with event content, venues, and activities. They provide attendees with opportunities for discovery, adventure, and serendipitous encounters, enriching the overall event experience.

Interactive Presentations and Workshops

Interactive presentations and workshops leverage gamification techniques to enhance audience engagement, participation, and retention. These sessions incorporate interactive elements, such as quizzes, polls, simulations, and role-playing activities, to actively involve attendees in the learning process. Some examples of interactive presentations and workshops suitable for events include:

Quizzes and Polls: Quizzes and polls allow presenters to gauge audience knowledge, opinions, and preferences in real-time. These interactive activities can be integrated into presentations or workshops to assess understanding, spark discussion, and gather feedback from participants. Quizzes and polls promote active participation and engagement, keeping attendees attentive and involved throughout the session (Yasin et al., 2021).

Simulations and Role-Playing: These activities engage participants in realistic scenarios or situations, allowing them to explore different perspectives, practice skills, and apply knowledge in a secure and regulated setting. These interactive activities could be used to simulate real-world challenges, decision-making processes, or interpersonal interactions, fostering experiential learning and skill development among participants (Yasin et al., 2021).

Interactive presentations and workshops are effective for transforming passive audiences into active participants, fostering collaboration, and facilitating meaningful learning experiences. By incorporating gamification techniques, presenters can create dynamic and interactive sessions that captivate attendees and leave a lasting impression.

Thus, gamification offers event planners a versatile toolkit for enhancing attendee engagement, fostering interaction, and creating memorable experiences. By leveraging competitive games, collaborative games, exploratory games, and interactive presentations and workshops, organizers can cater to diverse audiences and achieve specific objectives. Whether it's energizing the event atmosphere, promoting teamwork and collaboration, encouraging exploration and discovery, or facilitating learning and skill development, gamification can enrich the overall event experience and leave a lasting impression on attendees.

INTEGRATING GAMIFICATION INTO EVENT PLANNING

Gamification has become a vital strategy for event planners to enhance attendee engagement, foster interaction, and create memorable experiences. Whether it's a conference, trade show, or corporate event, gamification can transform the event landscape by infusing game-like elements and mechanics into various aspects of planning, execution, and evaluation. We'll explore how to integrate gamification into event planning across three major phases: prior to the event planning, event execution, and post-event assessment.

Prior to the Event Planning

Setting Targets: The success of any gamification initiative hinges on clearly defined objectives and goals (Hamari, 2013). Before diving into the specifics of gamification mechanics and design, event planners must first identify what they hope to achieve through gamification. Are the objectives to increase attendee engagement, promote networking, drive booth traffic, or enhance learning and knowledge retention? Setting defined, measurable and attainable objectives ensures that gamification efforts align with broader event goals and contribute to overall success.

Choosing the Right Gamification: Mechanics With objectives in mind, the next step is to choose the right gamification mechanics to achieve desired outcomes. Gamification mechanics encompass a range of elements and rules that define the structure and dynamics of the game experience. Common gamification mechanics include points, badges, leaderboards, challenges, rewards, levels, and quests. Event planners must carefully select mechanics that resonate with their target audience and support event objectives. For example, a competitive leaderboard may be suitable for driving engagement in a sales conference, while collaborative challenges might be more appropriate for fostering teamwork at a team-building event.

Designing Game Elements and Rules: Once objectives and mechanics are established, event planners can proceed to design game elements and rules that govern the gamified experience (Sailer et al., 2017). This involves defining the objectives, rules, rewards, and progression pathways of the game. What actions will participants take to earn points or badges? How will progress be tracked and rewarded? Will there be individual or team-based challenges? By establishing clear game mechanics and rules, event planners can design a controlled and rewarding experience that promotes engagement and competitiveness.

During the Event Execution

Deploying Technology and Tools: Technology plays a crucial role in implementing gamification during event execution, enabling event planners to track participant activity, deliver real-time feedback, and administer rewards. Event management platforms, mobile apps, gamification software, and RFID/NFC technology are valuable tools for integrating gamification into event planning. These tools facilitate registration, check-ins, activity tracking, leaderboard updates, and reward distribution, enhancing the efficiency and effectiveness of gamified experiences.

Monitoring and Managing Game Progress: Throughout the event, event planners must monitor and manage game progress to ensure a seamless and engaging experience for participants. This involves tracking participant activity, updating leaderboards in real-time, addressing technical issues promptly, and providing support and guidance to participants as needed. By keeping a tight check on game progress, event planners can detect bottlenecks or obstacles and make changes on the fly to improve the gamification experience.

Facilitating Engagement and Participation: Beyond technology and tools, event planners play a crucial role in facilitating engagement and participation during the event. This may involve hosting live challenges, organizing interactive workshops, or creating opportunities for social interaction and collaboration. Event staff should be trained to encourage participation, answer questions, and provide assistance to participants throughout the event. By fostering a supportive and inclusive environment, event planners can maximize engagement and ensure that participants have a positive gamification experience.

Post-Event Evaluation

Analyzing Participant Feedback: Once the event is over, event planners should collect and analyze participant feedback to gain insights into the effectiveness of the gamification initiative. Interviews, focus groups, and surveys offer useful insights into the experiences of respondents, their choices, and recommendations for change. Listening to participant input allows event planners to assess the gamification strategy's strengths and flaws and make informed decisions about future events.

Measuring Success Metrics: In addition to participant feedback, event planners should measure success metrics to evaluate the impact of gamification on event outcomes (Looyestyn et al., 2017). Key performance indicators (KPIs) such as rate of participation, levels of engagement, rate of completion, and satisfaction ratings can provide quantifiable information about the gamification initiative's effectiveness. By comparing KPIs against pre-defined benchmarks and objectives, event planners can assess the success of the gamification strategy and discover chances of improvements.

Iterating and Improving for Future Events: Finally, event planners should use insights from participant feedback and success metrics to iterate and improve the gamification strategy for future events. This may involve refining game mechanics, adjusting rules and rewards, or exploring new gamification tactics based on lessons learned from previous events. By continuously iterating and improving the gamification strategy, event planners can enhance the overall event experience and drive greater attendee satisfaction and engagement in future events.

Thus, integrating gamification into event planning requires careful consideration of objectives, audience preferences, technology requirements, and logistical considerations across the above discussed three key phases. By setting clear objectives, choosing the right gamification mechanics, designing game elements and rules, deploying technology and tools, monitoring and managing game progress, facilitating engagement and participation, analyzing participant feedback, measuring success metrics, and iterating and improving for future events, event planners can create dynamic and immersive experiences that captivate participants and drive desired behaviors. With strategic planning and execution, gamification can elevate events to new levels of excitement, participation, and success.

SUCCESSFUL IMPLEMENTATION OF GAMIFICATION IN EVENTS

Gamification has been successfully implemented in various events across industries, leading to increased attendee engagement, enhanced participation, and memorable experiences (Manu Melwin Joy & Merry Joe Chiramel, 2017). Let's explore some case studies highlighting successful gamification implementations:

Dreamforce

Dreamforce, Salesforce's annual conference, is known for its innovative use of gamification to drive attendee engagement. The event features a gamified mobile app that encourages participants to complete challenges, attend sessions, and interact with sponsors. Points are awarded for each completed task, and participants can track their progress on a leaderboard. Dreamforce's gamification strategy incentivizes attendees to explore the event, engage with content, and connect with peers, resulting in higher levels of participation and satisfaction.

Cisco Live

Cisco Live, an annual technology conference hosted by Cisco Systems, incorporates gamification to enhance the attendee experience and promote learning. The event features a gamified learning environment called the "Cisco Campus," where participants can earn points and badges by attending sessions, completing quizzes, and participating in hands-on labs. Cisco Live's gamification strategy encourages attendees to explore different learning opportunities, engage with subject matter experts, and earn recognition for their achievements, driving deeper engagement and knowledge retention.

IBM Think

IBM Think, IBM's flagship conference, leverages gamification to foster networking and collaboration among attendees. The event features a gamified networking platform that encourages participants to connect with each other based on shared interests and goals. Attendees earn points for initiating conversations, exchanging contact information, and collaborating on projects. IBM Think's gamification strategy facilitates meaningful connections and interactions, helping attendees expand their professional networks and derive value from the event.

Insights Gained from Practical Applications

Real-world implementations of gamification in events provide valuable insights:

Know Your Audience

Considering your target audience's interests, motivations, and habits is critical to creating great gamification experiences. Tailor gamification mechanics and activities to resonate with the interests and preferences of attendees, ensuring maximum engagement and participation.

Balance Competition and Collaboration

Strike a balance between competition and collaboration in gamification design. While competition can drive engagement and excitement, collaboration fosters teamwork and community building. Incorporate both competitive and collaborative elements to cater to different participant preferences and encourage diverse forms of interaction.

Provide Clear Goals and Feedback

Clearly define objectives, rules, and rewards to guide participant behavior and provide feedback on progress. Transparency and clarity are essential for motivating participants and maintaining their interest in the gamified experience.

ETHICAL CONSIDERATIONS AND CHALLENGES

Gamification has become known as a significant tool for event planning, offering opportunities to boost engagement, foster interaction, and create memorable experiences. However, along with its benefits, gamification brings ethical considerations and challenges that event organizers must navigate to ensure fairness, inclusivity, and mitigate potential negative impacts.

Ensuring Fairness and Inclusivity

Fairness and inclusivity are essential principles that underpin the successful implementation of gamification in events. Here are key strategies to ensure fairness and inclusivity:

Clear Rules and Guidelines

Event organizers must establish clear rules and guidelines for gamification activities. Participants should understand the criteria for earning points, rewards, and achieving success. Clear communication of rules and guidelines helps prevent misunderstandings and ensures that all participants have an equal opportunity to participate and succeed.

Avoiding Bias and Discrimination

Gamification mechanics and activities ought to be intended to minimize prejudice and discrimination based on age, ethnic background, gender, or socioeconomic position. Organizers must make sure that gamification programs are inclusive and accessible to all guests, regardless of their history or situations. Activities should promote diversity and equity, fostering a welcoming and inclusive environment for all participants.

Accommodating Different Abilities

Consider the diverse abilities and preferences of participants when designing gamification activities. Ensure that activities are accessible to individuals with disabilities and provide alternative participation options where necessary. Avoid activities that may disadvantage certain individuals or groups based on physical or cognitive abilities, ensuring that everyone can fully participate and enjoy the gamified experience.

Addressing Potential Negative Impacts

Gamification can boost participation and motivation, but it also carries the risk of potential negative impacts if not implemented thoughtfully. Here are key considerations to address potential negative impacts:

Disengagement and Burnout

Over-reliance on gamification mechanics may lead to participant disengagement or burnout if not balanced effectively. Constant challenges, rewards, and incentives can feel overwhelming and detract from the overall event experience. Event organizers must strike a balance between gamification and other forms of engagement to prevent participant fatigue and ensure sustained interest throughout the event (Flavián et al., 2023).

Exclusion and Alienation

Gamification activities that are overly competitive or exclusive may alienate certain participants, leading to feelings of exclusion or inadequacy. Events should create a supportive and inclusive environment where all participants feel welcome and valued. Avoid activities that promote elitism or create barriers to entry, prioritizing inclusivity and diversity in gamification design (Flavián et al., 2023).

Ethical Dilemmas

Gamification initiatives may raise ethical dilemmas related to privacy, consent, and data protection (Dwivedi, 2022). For example, collecting personal data for leaderboard rankings or rewards may raise concerns about privacy and consent. Event organizers should follow moral guidelines and legal regulations for data collection and usage, to ensure that participants' rights are respected and protected.

Mitigating Risks of Over-Competitiveness

Over-competitiveness can undermine the collaborative spirit and positive atmosphere of an event. Here are strategies to mitigate the risks of over-competitiveness:

Emphasize Collaboration

Shift the focus from individual competition to collaborative achievements by incorporating team-based challenges and group activities. Encourage participants to work together towards common goals, fostering a sense of camaraderie and shared success.

Promote Sportsmanship

Encourage sportsmanship and fair play among participants by promoting respect, integrity, and honesty in all gamification activities. Discourage unsportsmanlike behavior such as cheating, sabotage, or gloating, and emphasize the importance of ethical conduct in competitive environments.

Provide Alternative Engagement Options

Recognize that not all participants may enjoy or excel in competitive activities. Provide alternative engagement options such as networking opportunities, interactive exhibits, or creative workshops for participants who prefer non-competitive forms of interaction. By offering diverse engagement options, event organizers can cater to different preferences and ensure that everyone feels included and valued.

Ethical considerations and challenges are integral aspects of integrating gamification into event planning. By ensuring fairness and inclusivity, addressing potential negative impacts, and mitigating the risks of over-competitiveness, event organizers can create gamification experiences that are engaging, enjoyable, and ethically responsible. By prioritizing the well-being and satisfaction of participants, event planners can harness the power of gamification to enhance the overall event experience and create lasting memories for attendees.

FUTURE TRENDS AND INNOVATIONS IN EVENT GAMIFICATION

As event planning continues to evolve, so too does the landscape of gamification. Moving forward, different trends and developments are influencing the future of event gamification. In this section, we will explore emerging technologies and platforms, personalization and customization trends, and the integration of gamification with virtual and hybrid events.

Emerging Technologies and Platforms

Augmented Reality (AR) and Virtual Reality (VR)

AR and VR technologies are transforming event experiences by offering immersive and interactive environments (Rauschnabel et al., 2022). AR and VR can be leveraged to gamify various aspects of events, from scavenger hunts and interactive exhibits to virtual networking and product demonstrations. These technologies create opportunities for attendees to engage with content in new and exciting ways, omproving event experience (Silva et al., 2021).

Artificial Intelligence (AI) and Machine Learning (ML)

AI and ML technologies are employed to customise gamification experiences and provide real-time insights into participant behavior (Tayal et al., 2022). AI-powered chatbots and virtual assistants can deliver tailored recommendations, answer questions, and facilitate engagement throughout the event. ML algorithms can analyze participant's information to optimize gamification mechanics and tailor challenges to individual preferences, driving higher levels of participation and satisfaction (Pérez-Juárez et al., 2022).

Wearable Technology

Wearable technology such as fitness trackers, smartwatches and RFID/NFC-enabled badges are becoming increasingly popular in event gamification. Wearables can track attendee activity, monitor engagement levels, and facilitate seamless interactions with gamification elements. For example, attendees can earn points or rewards by participating in activities tracked by their wearable devices, enhancing the gamified experience.

Personalization and Customization Trends

Adaptive Gamification

Adaptive gamification involves dynamically adjusting game elements and challenges based on individual preferences, behavior, and performance. By personalizing gamification experiences, organizers can create tailored experiences that resonate with each participant (Pakanen et al., 2022). Adaptive gamification algorithms analyze participant data in real-time to deliver personalized challenges, rewards, and incentives, maximizing engagement and motivation (Davis et al., 2009).

Interactive Storytelling

Interactive storytelling combines gamification elements with narrative-driven experiences to create immersive event journeys. Attendees become active participants in the event storyline, making choices and solving challenges that impact the outcome. Interactive storytelling engages participants on an emotional level, fostering deeper connections and memorable experiences.

User-Generated Content

User-generated content is increasingly being integrated into event gamification to encourage participation and creativity (Suzuki et al., 2020). Attendees can contribute photos, videos, or social media posts related to gamification activities, earning points or rewards for their contributions. User-generated content fosters community engagement and enables attendees to discuss their impressions with others, so increasing the visibility and impact of gamified events.

Integration With Virtual and Hybrid Events

Virtual Event Platforms

With the rise of virtual and hybrid events (Hassan & Hamari, 2020), gamification is being integrated into virtual event platforms to enhance engagement and interaction. Virtual event platforms offer gamification features such as virtual badges, leaderboards, and interactive challenges to replicate the excitement of in-person events in a digital environment. Gamification encourages attendees to explore virtual spaces, attend sessions, and network with peers, driving higher levels of engagement and participation.

Hybrid Event Experiences

Gamification is bridging the gap between physical and virtual event experiences in hybrid events (Yung et al., 2022). Attendees can participate in gamification activities both onsite and online, earning points and rewards regardless of their location. Hybrid event gamification encourages collaboration and connectivity among attendees, regardless of whether they are attending in person or remotely.

Gamified Networking

Networking is a key component of both virtual and hybrid events, and gamification is being used to facilitate meaningful connections among attendees. Gamified networking platforms match participants based on shared interests and goals, encouraging interactions through challenges, icebreakers, and virtual meetups. Gamified networking enhances attendee engagement and fosters relationship-building in both virtual and hybrid event environments.

The prospects of event gamification seems promising, with growing technology, customization trends, and the incorporation of gamification into virtual and hybrid events fueling innovation and creativity. Using these trends and advancements, event organizers can create dynamic and immersive experiences that engage attendees, encourage connection, and leave a lasting impression. As the events business evolves, gamification will become increasingly crucial in designing event experiences.

CONCLUSION AND FUTURE RESEARCH DIRECTIONS

The power of gamification in event planning cannot be overstated. Throughout this chapter, we've explored the different ways in which gamification transforms traditional events into dynamic, engaging experiences that captivate participants and drive success. From its ability to enhance attendee engagement to fostering interaction, driving participation, and facilitating learning, gamification has emerged as a transformative strategy that revolutionizes the event landscape.

At its core, gamification appeals to basic human impulses for success, recognition, and social engagement. By incorporating game-like elements and mechanics into event design, organizers can harness these innate motivations to create immersive experiences that resonate with participants on a deeper level (Manu Melwin Joy & Merry Joe Chiramel, 2017). Whether through competitive games that ignite participants' competitive spirit, collaborative challenges that foster teamwork and cooperation, or exploratory quests that encourage exploration and discovery, gamification offers endless possibilities for engagement and interaction.

One of the primary benefits of gamification is its capacity to increase participant engagement.

Traditional events often struggle to maintain participants' interest and attention, leading to passive engagement and lackluster experiences. Gamification addresses this challenge head-on by transforming attendees into active participants who are fully immersed in the event experience. Through interactive challenges, quests, and competitions, gamification captivates attendees' interest and motivates them to actively engage with event content and activities, resulting in higher levels of satisfaction and enjoyment.

Furthermore, gamification serves as a powerful tool for fostering interaction and networking among attendees. Gamification allows players to interact, share experiences, and form meaningful relationships by introducing social components like cooperation, competition, and peer criticism (Zadro et al., 2004). Whether through team-based challenges, gamified networking activities, or interactive icebreakers, gamification reduces barriers and develops a sense of community and belonging among event attendees, hence improving the entire networking experience.

In addition to enhancing engagement and fostering interaction, gamification drives participation and attendance at events. By offering incentives, rewards, and recognition for participation, gamification motivates attendees to actively seek out opportunities for involvement and engagement (Sorrentino et al., 2020). Whether it's earning points, badges, or exclusive rewards, participants are incentivized to participate in sessions, workshops, and exhibits, leading to higher levels of engagement and overall event success.

Moreover, gamification enhances learning and knowledge retention at events. By transforming educational content into interactive and engaging experiences, gamification makes learning fun, accessible, and effective. Whether through gamified learning activities, simulations, or challenges, participants are heavily involved in the learning process, resulting in a better grasp and recall of crucial topics. As a consequence, attendees leave events with useful insights and practical skills to use in their personal and professional life.

Another significant benefit of gamification is its ability to differentiate events and enhance branding. In present-day cutthroat event market, events must stand out and provide memorable experiences that resonate with attendees. Gamification offers a unique opportunity for organizers to create distinctive event experiences that align with their brand identity and messaging. By incorporating branded gamified elements, themes, and narratives, organizers can create immersive and cohesive event experiences that leave a lasting impression on attendees, strengthening brand recognition and loyalty.

Furthermore, gamification provides significant insights into audience preferences and engagement patterns, enabling planners to analyze the performance of gamification tactics, discover areas for development, and make decisions based on data to maximize future event experiences. Using gamification analytics and tracking technologies, organizers can acquire significant insights about participant behavior, preferences, and engagement levels, allowing them to constantly enhance and develop their gamification techniques. (Pearlman & Gates, 2010).

Gamification has the power to transform events by creating immersive, interactive, and memorable experiences for attendees. By leveraging game-like elements and mechanics, event planners can capture the attention of participants, foster engagement, and drive desired behaviors. From scavenger hunts and interactive challenges to personalized rewards and immersive storytelling, gamification offers endless possibilities for creating memorable event experiences that leave a lasting impression on attendees.

As event planners and organizers, it is essential to recognize the potential of gamification in enhancing event experiences and driving desired outcomes. Embrace gamification as a strategic tool for engaging attendees, fostering interaction, and creating memorable experiences. Experiment with different gamification mechanics, platforms, and strategies to explore which methods are most effective for your target audience and event objectives. Stay informed about emerging trends and innovations in event gamification, and be active in modifying and adapting your strategy to meet the changing needs and expectations of attendees.

In conclusion, power of gamification in event planning lies in its ability to enhance engagement, foster interaction, drive participation, and facilitate learning. By integrating game-like themes and dynamics into event design allows organizers to create vibrant and absorbing experiences that engage participants and leave a lasting impact. As events continue to evolve in the digital age, gamification will undoubtedly remain a key tool in the event planner's arsenal.

Key Takeaways

The analysis reveals several significant findings regarding the impact of gamification on event planning:

- Gamification enhances attendee engagement by transforming passive participation into active involvement.
- It fosters improved networking and interaction among attendees through gamified activities.
- Gamification serves as a powerful motivator for participation and attendance, with rewards and recognition systems driving higher involvement.
- It enhances learning experiences by making educational content interactive and memorable.
- Gamification helps differentiate events and strengthens brand recognition.
- Valuable data and insights into participant behavior are provided through gamification analytics.

Future research in gamification for event planning holds promising avenues for enhancing engagement, understanding effectiveness, and addressing ethical considerations. Firstly, investigating various gamification mechanics like points, badges, leaderboards, and quests can shed light on which elements are most impactful for different event types and attendee demographics. Secondly, exploring the effectiveness of personalized and customized gamification experiences can offer insights into tailoring gamified elements to individual preferences and interests. Longitudinal studies tracking participant engagement post-event could reveal the long-term effects of gamification on attendee retention and engagement. Furthermore, examining the impact of gamification on learning outcomes at events can inform strategies for enhancing knowledge acquisition and skill development among participants. Ethical considerations, including fairness, inclusivity, and privacy, require further exploration to develop responsible gamification practices. Integrating emerging technologies such as AR, VR, and AI into gamified event experiences offers opportunities for innovation and enhanced immersion. With the rise of hybrid and virtual events, researching how gamification can be effectively adapted to these formats is crucial for engaging remote participants. Lastly, conducting cross-cultural studies can provide insights into the effectiveness and acceptance of gamified event experiences across diverse cultural contexts, informing global event planning strategies. Overall, future research in gamification for event planning has the potential to advance our understanding of engagement strategies, inform ethical practices, and leverage emerging technologies to create more immersive and impactful event experiences.

REFERENCES

Araújo, J., & Pestana, G. (2017). A framework for social well-being and skills management at the workplace. *International Journal of Information Management*, 37(6), 718–725. 10.1016/j.ijinfomgt.2017.07.009

Buckley, P., & Doyle, E. (2017). Individualising gamification: An investigation of the impact of learning styles and personality traits on the efficacy of gamification using a prediction market. *Computers & Education*, 106, 43–55. 10.1016/j.compedu.2016.11.009

Davis, A., Murphy, J., Owens, D., Khazanchi, D., & Zigurs, I. (2009). Avatars, People, and Virtual Worlds: Foundations for Research in Metaverses. *Journal of the Association for Information Systems*, 10(2), 90–117. 10.17705/1jais.00183

Davis, K., & Singh, S. (2015). Digital badges in afterschool learning: Documenting the perspectives and experiences of students and educators. *Computers & Education*, 88, 72–83. 10.1016/j.compedu.2015.04.011

Deci, E. L., Ryan, R. M., Gagné, M., Leone, D. R., Usunov, J., & Kornazheva, B. P. (2001). Need Satisfaction, Motivation, and Well-Being in the Work Organizations of a Former Eastern Bloc Country: A Cross-Cultural Study of Self-Determination. *Personality and Social Psychology Bulletin*, 27(8), 930–942. 10.1177/0146167201278002

Deterding, S., Dixon, D., Khaled, R., & Nacke, L. (2011). From game design elements to gamefulness. *Proceedings of the 15th International Academic MindTrek Conference on Envisioning Future Media Environments - MindTrek '11, 11*, (pp. 9–15). ACM. 10.1145/2181037.2181040

Dwivedi, Y. K. (2022). Metaverse beyond the hype: Multidisciplinary perspectives on emerging challenges, opportunities, and agenda for research, practice and policy. *International Journal of Information Management, 66*(66), 102542. Sciencedirect. 10.1016/j.ijinfomgt.2022.102542

Fernandes, J., Duarte, D., Ribeiro, C., Farinha, C., Pereira, J. M., & da Silva, M. M. (2012). iThink: A Game-Based Approach Towards Improving Collaboration and Participation in Requirement Elicitation. *Procedia Computer Science*, 15, 66–77. 10.1016/j.procs.2012.10.059

Flavián, C., Ibáñez-Sánchez, S., Orús, C., & Barta, S. (2023). The dark side of the metaverse: The role of gamification in event virtualization. *International Journal of Information Management*, 102726. 10.1016/j.ijinfomgt.2023.102726

Hamari, J. (2013). Transforming homo economicus into homo ludens: A field experiment on gamification in a utilitarian peer-to-peer trading service. *Electronic Commerce Research and Applications*, 12(4), 236–245. 10.1016/j.elerap.2013.01.004

Hamari, J. (2017). Do badges increase user activity? A field experiment on the effects of gamification. *Computers in Human Behavior*, 71(71), 469–478. 10.1016/j. chb.2015.03.036

Hanus, M. D., & Fox, J. (2015). Assessing the effects of gamification in the classroom: A longitudinal study on intrinsic motivation, social comparison, satisfaction, effort, and academic performance. *Computers & Education*, 80, 152–161. 10.1016/j. compedu.2014.08.019

Hassan, L., & Hamari, J. (2020). Gameful civic engagement: A review of the literature on gamification of e-participation. *Government Information Quarterly*, 37(3), 101461. 10.1016/j.giq.2020.101461

Hutzler, A., Wagner, R., Pirker, J., & Gütl, C. (2017). MythHunter: Gamification in an Educational Location-Based Scavenger Hunt. *Communications in Computer and Information Science*, 725, 155–169. 10.1007/978-3-319-60633-0_13

Hyun, M., & Jordan, J. S. (2019). Athletic goal achievement: A critical antecedent of event satisfaction, re-participation intention, and future exercise intention in participant sport events. *Sport Management Review*. 10.1016/j.smr.2019.01.007

Jahn, K., Kordyaka, B., Machulska, A., Eiler, T. J., Gruenewald, A., Klucken, T., Brueck, R., Gethmann, C. F., & Niehaves, B. (2021). Individualized gamification elements: The impact of avatar and feedback design on reuse intention. *Computers in Human Behavior*, 119, 106702. 10.1016/j.chb.2021.106702

Jones, B. A., Madden, G. J., & Wengreen, H. J. (2014). The FIT Game: Preliminary evaluation of a gamification approach to increasing fruit and vegetable consumption in school. *Preventive Medicine*, 68, 76–79. 10.1016/j.ypmed.2014.04.01524768916

Joy, M. M., & Chiramel, M. J. (2017). *Fun is The Future*. Educreation Publishing.

Kapp, K. (2012). *The gamification of learning and instruction: Game-based methods and strategies for training and education*. Wiley.

Landers, R. N., & Landers, A. K. (2014). An Empirical Test of the Theory of Gamified Learning. *Simulation & Gaming*, 45(6), 769–785. 10.1177/1046878114563662

Liu, C.-R., Wang, Y.-C., Huang, W.-S., & Tang, W.-C. (2019). Festival gamification: Conceptualization and scale development. *Tourism Management*, 74, 370–381. 10.1016/j.tourman.2019.04.005

Looyestyn, J., Kernot, J., Boshoff, K., Ryan, J., Edney, S., & Maher, C. (2017). Does gamification increase engagement with online programs? A systematic review. *PLoS One*, 12(3), e0173403. 10.1371/journal.pone.017340328362821

Morschheuser, B., Hamari, J., & Maedche, A. (2019). Cooperation or competition – When do people contribute more? A field experiment on gamification of crowdsourcing. *International Journal of Human-Computer Studies*, 127, 7–24. 10.1016/j.ijhcs.2018.10.001

Nicholson, S. (2014). A RECIPE for Meaningful Gamification. In *Gamification in Education and Business* (pp. 1–20). Springer. 10.1007/978-3-319-10208-5_1

Pakanen, M., Alavesa, P., van Berkel, N., Koskela, T., & Ojala, T. (2022). "Nice to see you virtually": Thoughtful design and evaluation of virtual avatar of the other user in AR and VR based telexistence systems. *Entertainment Computing*, 40, 100457. 10.1016/j.entcom.2021.100457

Pearlman, D. M., & Gates, N. A. (2010). Hosting Business Meetings and Special Events in Virtual Worlds: A Fad or the Future? *Journal of Convention & Event Tourism*, 11(4), 247–265. 10.1080/15470148.2010.530535

Peng, W., Lin, J.-H., Pfeiffer, K. A., & Winn, B. (2012). Need Satisfaction Supportive Game Features as Motivational Determinants: An Experimental Study of a Self-Determination Theory Guided Exergame. *Media Psychology*, 15(2), 175–196. 10.1080/15213269.2012.673850

Pérez-Juárez, M. A., Aguiar-Pérez, J. M., Alonso-Felipe, M., & Del-Pozo-Velázquez, J. (2022). Exploring the Possibilities of Artificial Intelligence and Big Data Techniques to Enhance Gamified Financial Services. Next-Generation *Applications and Implementations of Gamification Systems*. IGI Global. 10.4018/978-1-7998-8089-9.ch010

Rauschnabel, P. A., Babin, B. J., tom Dieck, M. C., Krey, N., & Jung, T. (2022). What is augmented reality marketing? Its definition, complexity, and future. *Journal of Business Research*, 142(1), 1140–1150. 10.1016/j.jbusres.2021.12.084

Rigby, S., & Ryan, R. M. (2011). *Glued to games how video games draw us in and hold us spellbound*. Praeger. 10.5040/9798400658105

Ryan, R. M., & Deci, E. L. (2000a). Intrinsic and Extrinsic motivations: Classic Definitions and New Directions. *Contemporary Educational Psychology*, 25(1), 54–67. 10.1006/ceps.1999.102010620381

Ryan, R. M., & Deci, E. L. (2000b). Self-determination theory and the facilitation of intrinsic motivation, social development, and well-being. *The American Psychologist*, 55(1), 68–78. 10.1037/0003-066X.55.1.6811392867

Ryan, R. M., Rigby, C. S., & Przybylski, A. (2006). The Motivational Pull of Video Games: A Self-Determination Theory Approach. *Motivation and Emotion*, 30(4), 344–360. 10.1007/s11031-006-9051-8

Sailer, M., Hense, J., Mandl, H., & Klevers, M. (2013). Psychological Perspectives on Motivation through Gamification. *Interaction Design and Architecture(S)*, 19(19), 28–37. 10.55612/s-5002-019-002

Sailer, M., Hense, J. U., Mayr, S. K., & Mandl, H. (2017). How Gamification motivates: An Experimental Study of the Effects of Specific Game Design Elements on Psychological Need Satisfaction. *Computers in Human Behavior*, 69(69), 371–380. 10.1016/j.chb.2016.12.033

Salen, K., & Zimmerman, E. (2003). *Rules of Play: Game Design Fundamentals*. The Mit Press.

Santhanam, R., Liu, D., & Shen, W.-C. M. (2016). Research Note—Gamification of Technology-Mediated Training: Not All Competitions Are the Same. *Information Systems Research*, 27(2), 453–465. 10.1287/isre.2016.0630

Schöbel, S. M., Janson, A., & Söllner, M. (2020). Capturing the complexity of gamification elements: A holistic approach for analysing existing and deriving novel gamification designs. *European Journal of Information Systems*, 29(6), 1–28. 10.1080/0960085X.2020.1796531

Silva, F., Ferreira, R., Correia, A., Pinto, P., & Ramos, J. (2021). Experiments on Gamification with Virtual and Augmented Reality for Practical Application Learning. *Springer EBooks*, 175–184. 10.1007/978-3-030-86618-1_18

Sisson, A. D., & Whalen, E. A. (2021). Exploratory study on the perceptions of event gamification on positive behavioral outcomes. *Journal of Hospitality and Tourism Insights*. 10.1108/JHTI-04-2021-0085

Sorrentino, A., Fu, X., Romano, R., Quintano, M., & Risitano, M. (2020). Measuring event experience and its behavioral consequences in the context of a sports mega-event. *Journal of Hospitality and Tourism Insights*, 3(5), 589–605. 10.1108/JHTI-03-2020-0026

Suh, A., Cheung, C. M. K., Ahuja, M., & Wagner, C. (2017). Gamification in the Workplace: The Central Role of the Aesthetic Experience. *Journal of Management Information Systems*, 34(1), 268–305. 10.1080/07421222.2017.1297642

Suzuki, S., Kanematsu, H., Barry, D. M., Ogawa, N., Yajima, K., Nakahira, K. T., Shirai, T., Kawaguchi, M., Kobayashi, T., & Yoshitake, M. (2020). Virtual Experiments in Metaverse and their Applications to Collaborative Projects: The framework and its significance. *Procedia Computer Science*, 176, 2125–2132. 10.1016/j.procs.2020.09.249

Talantis, S., Shin, Y. H., & Severt, K. (2020). Conference mobile application: Participant acceptance and the correlation with overall event satisfaction utilizing the technology acceptance model (TAM). *Journal of Convention & Event Tourism*, 21(2), 100–122. 10.1080/15470148.2020.1719949

Tayal, S., Rajagopal, K., & Mahajan, V. (2022). Virtual Reality based Metaverse of Gamification. *2022 6th International Conference on Computing Methodologies and Communication (ICCMC)*, 1597–1604. 10.1109/ICCMC53470.2022.9753727

Vegt, N., Visch, V., de Ridder, H., & Vermeeren, A. (2014). Designing Gamification to Guide Competitive and Cooperative Behavior in Teamwork. *Gamification in Education and Business*, 513–533. 10.1007/978-3-319-10208-5_26

Werbach, K. (2014). (Re)Defining Gamification: A Process Approach. *Persuasive Technology*, 266–272. 10.1007/978-3-319-07127-5_23

Werbach, K., & Hunter, D. (2012). *For the win: how game thinking can revolutionize your business*. Wharton Digital Press.

Yasin, N., Majid Gilani, S. A., & Nair, G. (2021). "Dump the paper quiz"—The PERI model for exploring gamification in student learning in the United Arab Emirates. *Industry and Higher Education*, 095042222110550. 10.1177/09504222211055067

Yung, R., Le, T. H., Moyle, B., & Arcodia, C. (2022). Towards a typology of virtual events. *Tourism Management*, 92, 104560. 10.1016/j.tourman.2022.104560

Zadro, L., Williams, K. D., & Richardson, R. (2004). How low can you go? Ostracism by a computer is sufficient to lower self-reported levels of belonging, control, self-esteem, and meaningful existence. *Journal of Experimental Social Psychology*, 40(4), 560–567. 10.1016/j.jesp.2003.11.006

KEY TERMS AND DEFINITIONS

Adaptive Gamification: A dynamic approach to gamification that adjusts game elements and challenges based on individual preferences, behavior, and performance, often used to deliver personalized experiences and maximize engagement.

Gamification: The process of incorporating game elements and mechanics into non-game contexts, such as events, to engage participants and drive desired behaviors.

Gamified Networking: A gamification strategy that encourages networking and collaboration among event participants, often using challenges, icebreakers, and virtual meetups to facilitate interactions and relationship-building.

Hybrid Events: Events that combine both in-person and virtual elements, allowing participants to engage either onsite or remotely, often requiring innovative approaches to gamification and engagement.

Inclusivity: Ensuring that gamification activities and experiences are accessible and welcoming to all participants, regardless of background, ability, or circumstances.

Metrics: Quantifiable measures used to assess the effectiveness and impact of gamification, such as participation rates, engagement levels, completion rates, satisfaction scores, and return on investment (ROI).

Personalization: Tailoring gamified experiences to individual preferences, characteristics, and behavior, often achieved through adaptive algorithms or customization options.

Chapter 12
Viral Content in Event Management of Hospitality and Socio–Cultural Activities

Bovsh A. Liudmyla
https://orcid.org/0000-0001-6044-3004
State University of Trade and Economics, Ukraine

Kamel Mouloudj
https://orcid.org/0000-0001-7617-8313
University of Medea, Algeria

Alla M. Rasulova
State University of Trade and Economics, Ukraine

Tetiana Mykhaylivna Tkachuk
https://orcid.org/0000-0001-8657-2621
State University of Trade and Economics, Ukraine

ABSTRACT

This chapter examines the determinants of the formation of viral content in the event management of hospitality entities and socio-cultural activities. The methodology covers the assessment of the popularity and potential impact of social networks on marketing and practical opportunities of hospitality entities and socio-cultural activities. The modeling method was applied to create a reference model of the credibility strategy of impression marketing. In the process of forming authenticity and emotional involvement of customers, the technological road map method, which is based on brand marketing approaches, was applied. In addition, the analysis of

DOI: 10.4018/979-8-3693-2272-7.ch012

the involvement of users of social networks was investigated. The selection of key indicators for evaluating the effectiveness of real content and an in-depth review of modern technologies and trends in its creation empirically contributed to the modeling of the strategy of creating real content in the field of event management of hospitality entities and socio-cultural activities.

INTRODUCTION

With the emergence of the COVID-19 epidemic, the hospitality industry suffered from a decline in demand, causing a decline in revenues (Bouarar et al., 2023), so most hospitality entities turned to digital technology to find practical solutions (Bovsh et al., 2023). In practice, in order to improve business performance, digital transformation has been widely adopted across most industries (Bouarar et al., 2022), including the hospitality industry. In this context, event management becomes a key tool for the promotion and development of hospitality and socio-cultural activities, as it allows you to diversify the product and create profitable package offers, in particular, in the organization of conferences, exhibitions, family events, corporate events, and festivals. In fact, innovative approaches to the implementation of inventive activities, marked by Industry 5.0 and digital technologies, create new opportunities in the services marketing (Bouarar et al., 2023; Bovsh et al., 2023; Oliveira et al., 2024). Now, when the competition in the field of hospitality and socio-cultural activities is intensifying, the formation of authentic content is becoming an important element of marketing strategies and attracting the attention of the target audience. In this sense, real content that conveys the uniqueness of events in the field of hospitality and socio-cultural activities has great potential for attracting attention and attracting new customers. In a consumer society where people share their lives on social media, effective, honest content can spread faster than any other form of advertising. Therefore, the study of its features and the effectiveness of its use in the marketing of hospitality entities and socio-cultural activities is relevant.

The goals of this research are to study the academic field regarding the theoretical categories "virality", "event content", "viral content", their meaningful characteristics in the development of event management of hospitality entities and socio-cultural activities. We also explore the importance of content viralization in the current advertising scenario and the use of emotional intelligence for the perception and distribution of content about events offered by hospitality entities and socio-cultural activities. This research insight forms scientific approaches to the promotion of information and activation of sales of events (event services). The goal is to confirm that authentic content, which conveys the uniqueness of events in the hospitality and socio-cultural sphere, has great potential for attracting attention and attracting new customers.

The basis of the conducted this research is the hypothesis of the importance of measuring the credibility of content that is distributed about innovative services and events in hospitality entities and socio-cultural activities. Accordingly, H1. Viral content that conveys the uniqueness of events in the hospitality and socio-cultural sphere has great potential for attracting attention and attracting new customers. H2. Communities in social networks are becoming an ideal platform for promoting events. The second hypothesis suggests that interactivity, short videos and the ability to create interest are key elements that help event managers create authentic content. H3. Viral content about innovative services helps increase brand awareness. If the event becomes an object of discussion and dissemination on the Internet, it helps to increase brand awareness and creates a positive image for the hospitality entities and socio-cultural activities.

The practical value of the research lies in the elaboration of the theoretical background and practical insights of the real contents of the event management of the hospitality entities and socio-cultural activities. Focused on the formation of real content in event management, the research can become an interesting source of information for industry specialists, marketers, event managers and everyone who is interested in the development of the event space in the context of the globalization of digital marketing.

LITERATURE REVIEW

In the focus of the problems of this study are interrelated multi-aspects: event management, marketing, digital strategies, the field of hospitality and socio-cultural activities, which outline the relevant academic field. Thus, the theoretical foundations for understanding event management are covered in the scientific literature at the levels of strategic management (Wickham et al., 2021; Celuch et al., 2023), project management (Pappas, 2019; Peralta et al., 2021; Salama et al., 2021), operational business processes (stakeholder management as a model of joint organization of events) (Kristiansen et al., 2021; Wallace et al., 2023), and organization of events and social entrepreneurship (Ratten, 2023). Valuable are the approaches of anti-crisis management of the inventive activities of business entities, which are relevant in times of constant threats and challenges of the environment, covered in the studies of Hyatt, 2010; Ragab et al., 2021; Estanyol, 2022).

At the same time, in the conditions of global spread of digitalization, the use of online platforms in communications and brand promotion is gaining relevance (Bouarar et al., 2022; Bouarar et al., 2023; Bovsh et al., 2023). Thus, the mechanism of online content virality has been considered by many scientists. For example, Berger (2012) in his work investigated the psychological connection between emotions and the social transmission of positive and negative online content. Knossenburg et al. (2016) investigated the viral aspects of online video advertisements. Furthermore, Torres (2021) analyzed the use of TikTok "as a tool to spread public health messages during the COVID-19 pandemic." Silver and Rumsey (2022) explored the emotional factors for reaching consumers and virality of media content. As well as the study of Malek et al. (2018) were devoted to evaluating the effectiveness of events on alternative platforms. Recently, Oliveira et al. (2024) investigated the impact of content marketing on SMEs in the Brazilian health industry.

The sphere of hospitality and socio-cultural activities, as the key object of our research, require a more detailed coverage of the literature review. Thus, the study of the influence of viral marketing on the choice of tourist and hospitality organizations is reflected in the works of Daif and Elsayed (2019); use of content created in social media in the article of Tsiakali (2018). Qualitative and quantitative approaches to content analysis in hospitality and tourism were used in the work of Çakar (2022). An important object of event management research is the study of digital communications by Bravo et al. (2021), which focuses on gamification as a motivational process that motivates people to create content on online platforms. Unfortunately, little attention has been paid to the socio-cultural sphere in recent years. Most works have been mainly devoted to the positioning of leisure as a socio-cultural phenomenon (Tkachenko et al., 2019), the potential of socio-cultural animation (Kalaur et al., 2021), processes of digital transformation in the socio-cultural sphere (Bondar et al., 2021), and theoretical aspects of the management of socio-cultural activities (Vychivskyi et al., 2023).

Thus, the scientific sources used in the review are connected by a similar goal - the justification of directions for the formation and distribution of content in social media and other platforms, which for hospitality entities and socio-cultural activities is a tactical task of ensuring the effectiveness of inventive services.

The formation of viralcontent in the event management of hospitality and socio-cultural entities is sufficiently reflected in scientific studies, the relevance of which is enhanced by the processes of total digitalization of the economy and the formation of Industry 5.0. This determines the need for identification of channels and means of effective communications that shape the dissemination of information and promote the sale of innovative services, creating competitive advantages and a positive reputation for the subjects of hospitality entities and socio-cultural activities.

Unresolved Issues

The integration of social networks into the marketing activities of business entities is actively reflected in scientific studies, the relevance of which is enhanced by the involvement of consumers in the online environment and the growth of the volume of online purchases. For hospitality entities and socio-cultural activities, where tangible and intangible services are provided, social networks contribute to the conversion of customers. At the same time, thanks to content about inventive services, lead magnets and sales funnels are created. This determines the need for identification of channels and means of effective communications that shape the dissemination of information and promote sales of innovative services, creating competitive advantages and a positive reputation for hospitality entities. At a time when the formation of viral content in the event management of hospitality entities is sufficiently covered by the scientific focus, the socio-cultural sphere has been out of scientific attention in recent years, therefore both theoretical and practical aspects of the event management of socio-cultural activities need practice, and, in particular, the use social networks for its branding and strategic development as a whole.

MATERIALS AND METHODS

This work examines the research of the determinants of the formation of viral content of inventive services of hospitality and socio-cultural subjects, which are conceptual in their orientation, and the proposed basis is based on the existing literature. Theoretical approaches and operational definitions are formulated on the basis of empirical research. Unit economics approaches were used to assess the virality and potential impact of digital innovations on the formation of the content of pages (blogs and podcasts) in social networks. In turn, modeling was used to create a reference model of SMM management. In the process of forming content marketing in social networks, the technological road map method is applied, which allows to form modules for the formation of virality of event content in social networks.

RESULTS AND DISCUSSION

Semantic Review of key Components of Hospitality Entities and Socio-Cultural Activities

In recent years, society has faced global problems of oversaturation of the information space, which reveals problems for the branding of business entities and its economic security. The aggravation of information wars, the emergence of new social networks and digital innovations in the promotion of content and marketing analytics, the development and total integration of artificial intelligence (AI) - this is a partial list of challenges for the hospitality entities and socio-cultural activities in the formation of offers thanks to social networks.

The gaps in theoretical approaches identified in the scientific literature justify the need to develop key definitions and constructions of the objects of research - hospitality establishments and the socio-cultural sphere. Moreover, the interpretations of the terms "hospitality" and "socio-cultural sphere" should semantically fit into the content of social networks, carry the appropriate emotion and be formed in the consumer's mind as a certain usefulness and value of organized leisure and recreation.

Comparativism of scientific sources allows us to define hospitality as a sphere of economic activity (Filimonau and Brown, 2018; Melissen, 2019; Oskam and Zandberg, 2019), where the social property of the subject or community (hospitableness) is manifested: willingness, desire to receive guests and treat them (Josephi, 2019; Slova, 2024). Thus, the field of hospitality encompasses various activities aimed at providing comfort, service and meeting the needs of tourists and guests (Bouarar et al., 2023).

In turn, the socio-cultural sphere is the activity of economic entities that creates conditions and organizes the consumption of social (education, training, library and cultural funds) and cultural (historical assets, art, sports, religious and ethno-cultural projects, social initiatives), and services etc.

We will demonstrate the key components of the hospitality and socio-cultural sphere, as well as their points of contact (Figure 1).

Figure 1. Component structure of hospitality entities and socio-cultural activities

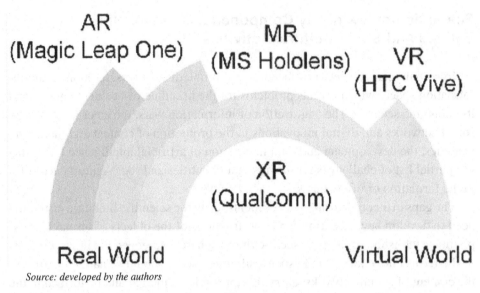

Source: developed by the authors

As we can see, these types of activities interact and create a socio-cultural and hospitality infrastructure, which contributes to the achievement of both an economic effect (making a profit from the sale of hospitality products and socio-cultural activities) and a social effect (the development of culture, communities and the satisfaction of various socio-cultural needs of local communities and customers (tourists).

The field of hospitality and socio-cultural activities is quite dynamic and constantly developing, adding new concepts and approaches to providing convenience and satisfying the moral (spiritual, emotional, gaining experience) and physical (rest, treatment, rehabilitation, etc.) needs of consumers, which with the development of digital technologies is deepening by means virtual reality, artificial and emotional intelligence. Gastrofestivals of national cuisine give a powerful impetus to the development of communities, urban and rural areas, certain regions and locations. And a significant role in the communications of the consumer and subjects of hospitality and socio-cultural activity belongs to social networks, where access to content does not depend on the time and space frame.

Since the key object of research is content in event management, it is important to specify the definition. Considering that content is any information posted on a certain resource (Dictionary, 2024), and event management is a process that defines a standard and sequential procedure for managing the lifecycle of events (Tambral-li, 2021), content in event management (or event content) will be defined in our research as information that formalizes an event (event service) and actualizes its consumer value on a certain resource (platform), and is also the result of integration and correlation efforts of the management system to manage the life cycle of events (event services) and the quality of communications (own interpretation).

Event Management in the Hospitality and Socio-Cultural Activities

As is known, event management is a process of planning, organizing, coordinating and implementing certain events as a complex product. From figure 2, we can see that the event service is a component of business and in the process of creating and implementing a certain event, it can use the resources and products of other components of the sphere of hospitality and socio-cultural activities, forming certain communication links (Figure 2).

Figure 2. Patterns of interdisciplinary adaptations of the event service of hospitality entities and socio-cultural activities

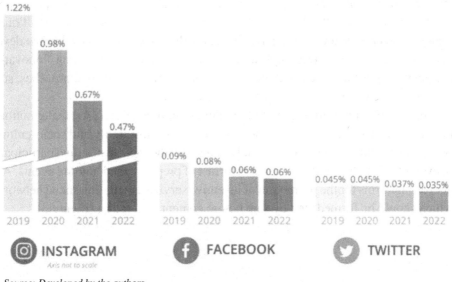

Source: Developed by the authors

Since the goal of event management is the successful implementation of projects that meet certain goals and requirements of the customer or the organizer of the event, taking into account the described patterns in strategizing the activities and products of subjects in the field of hospitality and socio-cultural activities is a priority. Patterns of cross-industry adaptations of the event service may include various strategies and approaches aimed at ensuring sustainability and efficiency in a dynamic business environment. Thus, digital transformation involves the use of modern technologies to improve the organization and conduct of events, from virtual conferences to the use of mobile applications for interaction with participants. Diversification of products is aimed at expanding the range of services offered by hospitality entities and socio-cultural activities. In particular, if the main activity is aimed at the organization of conferences, business meetings, family events or corporate parties, diversification can rely on the experience of the event brand and offer business mentoring: consulting on event organization, training, market research and other additional services that may be valuable for customers. Strategic partnership has two sides. On the one hand, it provides a corporate partnership for the organization of events both for the partner on a long-term basis, and can include event services in the partner's product (concerts, exhibitions, promotional actions, social initiatives, etc. in a restaurant/hotel). On the other hand, it is strategically important to cooperate with stakeholders in the organization and holding of events (e.g., providers of services and products; artistic, cultural or educational institutions/centers; cultural and artistic figures; local communities, city and state authorities; investors; consulting and IT companies ; and meta search companies and providers). In addition, in view of the 2019-2023 coronavirus pandemic and the war in Ukraine, issues of ensuring safety and hygiene in the conduct of events, as well as the development of new formats (e.g., hybrid and virtual events) are important. Innovative financial models take into account the use of innovative financial approaches, such as cryptocurrency or crowdfunding, to finance events.

Special attention will be paid to the integration of artificial (AI) and emotional intelligence (EI) in event management in the field of hospitality and socio-cultural activities, which can bring numerous advantages for the organization and participants of events both offline and in the hybrid format of preparing and holding events. And also on platforms for the promotion of inventive services, including social networks, which should be formed step by step before content generation (Figure 3).

Figure 3. Algorithmization of event management of hospitality entities and socio-cultural activities in social networks

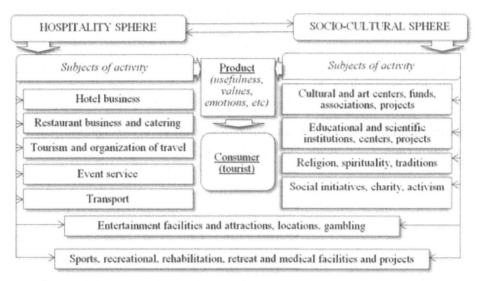

Source: Developed by Cherednichenko (2020); Kalaur and Maksymyak (2021)

As you can see, event management requires flexibility, creativity, organizational skills, and often the ability to work effectively in conditions of limited time, resources, and uncertain environment.

In today's world, event management is becoming a key tool for the promotion and development of hospitality and socio-cultural activities, as it is a significant source of income. For many of them, events determine the specialization of the establishment: business hotel, retreat hotel, club hotel, night club, art restaurant, restaurant-theater, event halls, art center, and cultural foundation, …etc. In addition, in the off-season, innovative services are a lead magnet and reduce low occupancy rates, particularly in accommodation facilities. Gastroevents contribute to the attraction of customers to a restaurant, affect activity in social networks, increase profits, the popularity of the chef/owner, the establishment as a brand and the project in general. Events attract new guests, who later become regulars (Cherednichenko, 2020).

Thus, in the conditions of intensifying competition between subjects of hospitality and socio-cultural activities, event management is a significant source of income from business diversification. At the same time, in the oversaturated information business space, the formation of viral content becomes an important element of marketing strategies and attracting the attention of the target audience, which will depend on the economic and social efficiency of hospitality entities and socio-cultural activities.

Research Insights and Trends in the Creation of Viral Content

Social media are websites and applications used for social communication. They include both online media and communication platforms. Moreover, communications can be conducted both with the help of integrated AI (chat-bot) and live: streams, rails, and podcasts, etc. In any case, content that can meaningfully go viral and quickly spread to the target audience is important. For this purpose, various platforms are used to distribute content (Figure 4).

Figure 4. Key platforms for content distribution in the event management system of hospitality entities and socio-cultural activities

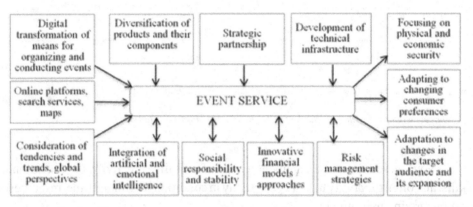

Source: Developed by the authors

Forming a content strategy for event activities, the subject of the hospitality and socio-cultural sphere must choose communication platforms and draw up a content plan to attract users to events. The content plan is not only a schedule that indicates the dates of publications, agendas and performers, it is also about a qualitative approach to the organization of the process of disseminating information and attracting consumers to certain events: not only interest, but also acquisition of participation in these events.

Let's explore the most popular social communication platforms in terms of their use for the promotion and sales of events by hospitality and socio-cultural entities.

Thus, the analysis of communications on the Internet shows that consumers of hospitality and socio-cultural products are interested precisely through social networks (Spoladore et al., 2023). The role of social media and its influence on consumer behavior is quite significant, because the content inspires the appropriate emotions to participate in a certain event, and the reviews of tourists, bloggers and famous people who have received customer experience convince of the feasibility of outreach with an event service company. Taking into account the annual growth of active users of social media (+3.0% in 2022 compared to 2021), the number of which according to Digital 2023: Global Overview Report is about 59.9% of the world's population (Kemp, 2023), it can be stated that it is not easy a communication tool, and a powerful means of viral interaction of hospitality and socio-cultural entities with potential clients of event services.

Each country has its own characteristics of online communications and advantages in choosing platforms, which is confirmed by the dynamics of user engagement (Figure 5).

Figure 5. Dynamics of user engagement in social networks, 2019-2022

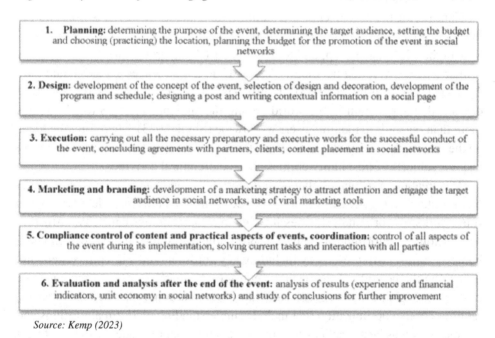

1. **Planning**: determining the purpose of the event, determining the target audience, setting the budget and choosing (practicing) the location, planning the budget for the promotion of the event in social networks

2. **Design**: development of the concept of the event, selection of design and decoration, development of the program and schedule; designing a post and writing contextual information on a social page

3. **Execution**: carrying out all the necessary preparatory and executive works for the successful conduct of the event, concluding agreements with partners, clients; content placement in social networks

4. **Marketing and branding**: development of a marketing strategy to attract attention and engage the target audience in social networks, use of viral marketing tools

5. **Compliance control of content and practical aspects of events, coordination**: control of all aspects of the event during its implementation, solving current tasks and interaction with all parties

6. **Evaluation and analysis after the end of the event**: analysis of results (experience and financial indicators, unit economy in social networks) and study of conclusions for further improvement

Source: Kemp (2023)

However, a deeper study shows that the highest user engagement is in 2023 inFacebook, Instagram, TikTok, and YouTube (Table 1).

Table 1. User Engagement in Social Networks (2023)

Platform	Facebook	Instagram	TikTok	YouTube
Monthly active users (billion)	2,91	2	1	2,56
Middle age	25-34	16-24	18-24	25-34
Average time, (minutes)	52	31	139	112
Content	Text, images, videos, live streams	Text, images, live streams, reels	Video longer than 2 minutes	YouTube Shorts
Advertising	Targeted advertising	Targeted advertising, bloggers advertising	Targeted advertising, bloggers advertising, branded challenges	Google ADS, bloggers advertising

Source: Porobanyuk (2024)

Considering the need to choose a platform for content strategy, it is worth noting that Facebook is used more by the older generation (31% of people aged 15-24, 84% in the 35-44 age group, and 87% in the 55-64 age group), while Instagram is primarily used by young people: 84% aged 15 to 25, 58% aged 25 to 34, and only 22% aged 55-64 (Somova, 2023). In turn, TikTok became in 2022-2023 the most downloaded application in the world among the audience aged 18 to 24 and has more than one billion monthly users worldwide (Shkil, 2023). Therefore, the focus on the specified social media as channels for the promotion of events is an important task for subjects of hospitality entities and socio-cultural activities.

The creation of a content plan is an important component of the event management content strategy of a hospitality and socio-cultural entity, as it details the main frameworks of work and priorities for creating, maintaining regularity, attracting new customers, informing about events, promoting and selling them and, ultimately helps to improve SEO results by including keywords and links in viral content and improving the position of the business entity in the search engine, attracting more customers. Running regular events, including hotel and conference hall conferences, requires content optimization that includes understanding platform algorithms and trends, as well as best practices for creating content that resonates with your target audience. In addition, it includes understanding the different types of content that can be used, such as videos, images, stories and advertisements (Post-up, 2023). In light of the above, let's analyze the infographic of the latest research on the timeframe when content gains the greatest possible reach (Table 2).

Table 2. Optimizing the posting timeframe in social networks

Timeframe / Platform	The best time to post		The worst time to post	The best day to post	The worst posting day ever
Facebook	3.00-10.00	12.00-13.00	21.00-00.00	Monday, tuesday, wednesday	Saturday sunday
Instagram	7.00-9.00	18.00-21.00	9.00-18.00	Tuesday wednesday thursday	Monday
TikTok	6.00-12.00	19.00-23.00	10.00-16.00	monday-sunday	Does not matter
Telegram	10.00-12.00	17.00-19.00	9.00-18.00	Tuesday, wednesday, thursday, friday	monday

Source: Kuznetsova (2023)

At the same time, finding the optimal time for posting event content by hospitality entities and socio-cultural activities is the key to interacting with the target audience and promoting the brand (event, destination, business entity itself) in social networks. Therefore, to increase the reach of viral content in social networks, it is also worth using hashtags, which are a reliable way to spread the content of the content to a larger audience by displaying the publication in search results. Hence, based on the definition of content in event management, we suggest creating a content plan for hospitality entities and socio-cultural activities according to the following structure (Figure 6).

Figure 6. Hash table of coordination of event management functions in the content plan of hospitality entities and socio-cultural activities

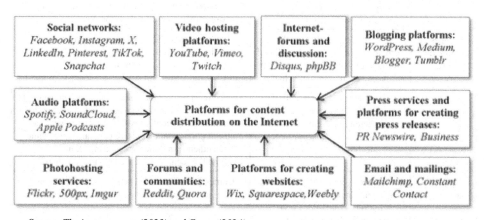

Source: The instapreneurs (2023) and Canva (2024)

In general, the structure of the content plan resembles a calendar that helps to optimize ideas and organize productive creation of publications. A plan is also needed to find a balance between informative, entertaining, promotional and branded content, which helps prevent creative chaos, as content is managed from a thematic perspective. Event content works specifically with branded (reputational) posting and, according to the recommendations of experts (Canva, 2024), should make up about 30%. Therefore, event content should include case studies, testimonials, news, progress reports, feedback processing, and collaborations with thought leaders. This contributes to the development of the profile of the business entity and, in particular, the events (event services) organized by it, content conversion and lead generation - the processes of finding and attracting potential customers. The creation of viral content provides an opportunity for hospitality entities and socio-cultural activitiesto go beyond the traditional advertising approach. If the event becomes an object of discussion and distribution on the Internet, it helps to increase brand awareness and creates a positive image.

Thus, to acquire the properties of virality, the content must correspond to the trends of online communications (Table 3).

Table 3. Trendbook of event content virality

Virality marker	The defining components	Trends and tendencies
Posting format	Text, video, audio or infographics	The largest share of clickability and reposts falls on music and short videos, live streaming and video formats in Stories.
Emotional engagement	Cognitive tools of marketing impressions: admiration, fear, surprise, need for possession, emotional support, etc.	The most common materials cause strong emotional reactions: 17% - positive emotions and laughter, 15% entertaining content; creating emotionally engaging contentthat is perceived personally; storytelling
Headlines and hashtags	Short and expressive headlines with an emphasis on the benefits of participating or watching the event; hashtags are relevant, actual	Use of popular and unique hashtags; creation of a unique identifier; use of branded headlines and hashtags of event content
Tone of Voice	Communication styles: official, friendly, humorous, mixed; authenticity, inclusiveness, curiosity, eco-consciousness, technical orientation	Speech must be on-brand and engaging with the target audience: humorous elements greatly increase the likelihood that content will be shared; rejection of editorial perfection, increasing popularity of openness to authentic and incomplete content, including "behind the scenes" and "life behind the scenes", etc.
Ease of sharing	Design, ease of access, usefulness, having a "share" or "recommend" button, social interaction, encouraging interaction, network effect, mobile optimization	Content is easily shared and disseminated through social media, email or other communication channels
Interactivity	Surveys, voting and questionnaires, gaming	Interaction and participation of viewers or participants in the event contribute to the spread of viral content
Actuality, value	Actual events, topics or trends	Increased demand for content that celebrates meaningful values, diversity and social responsibility

continued on following page

Table 3. Continued

Virality marker	The defining components	Trends and tendencies
Influence	Podcasts, interviews, recommendations from influencers and buyers, etc	The inclusion of famous or influential people can increase interest in the event and promote its dissemination

Source: Developed by the authors

At the same time, the use of event content virality in the activities of hospitality and socio-cultural entities requires a detailed review of possible risks that may lead to the opposite effect - the outflow of customers and their demotivation to distribute content. First, the naturalness of the photo content of the planned or held event. In the era of global digitalization, the active involvement of social networks in the virality of event content of hospitality and socio-cultural activities and, as a result, their high competition in the market, establishments focus on creating "ideal" content for consumers due to excessive photo editing, which causes the brand to lose authenticity and disappoint consumers in the real world. Secondly, the viral trends of unregulated demonstration of photo and video content of events can lead to their excessive popularization and, as a result, the risk of exceeding the capabilities of the destination of the event to receive an unpredictable number of visitors, which in fact causes a negative experience of their stay and demotivates in the distribution of content the event

Let's dwell in more detail on the marker of simplicity of the queue, which depends on whether users will want to share event content with their audience. The ease of sharing in the context of social networks has several key components that need to be integrated into the content strategy of a hospitality and socio-cultural entity:

1) Pleasant design: the content should have an attractive and simple design that is able to draw attention and be easily perceived by users. In this case, the event is positioned in the form of trending formats of a video overview of the location of the event, the "menu" of the event (business event - participants, topics of their reports; holistic event - poster), etc.;
2) Easy access: it should be easy for users to access the content: online registration and purchase of a ticket, online reservation of a location;
3) Obvious benefit: people are more inclined to share something they find useful, funny or interesting. Therefore, the content should look so that there is a great benefit from its distribution (for example, a business event - reputational benefit, a holistic event - consumer value (spiritual, physical) or promising partnership interaction, etc.);

4) Simplified sharing process: ensuring a simple and fast sharing process: integrated "share", "recommend" buttons allow users to easily distribute content and attract the user's target audience to the event, in particular in social networks;

5) Social interaction: content that encourages comments, likes and interaction often gets more attention and can become the object of active sharing;

6) Mobile optimization: since many users browse social networks on mobile devices, content must be optimized for mobile use and easy sharing;

7) Encouraging interaction: creating event content that actively encourages interaction (commenting) and sharing: questions, challenges or other elements that lead the user to interaction;

8) Network effect: facilitating the creation of content that spreads through the network effect, that is, each new "step" of sharing adds new participants.

As we can see, the formation of viral content creates advantages for the event management of the subject of hospitality entities and socio-cultural activities. However, intense competition, the need for resilience, and the risks associated with virality require careful analysis and strategic planning. This necessitates the development of new strategies and creative concepts.

Evaluation of Event Content Virality Parameters of Hospitality Entities and Socio-Cultural Activities

Measuring the virality of event content is a complex task, as there are various metrics and approaches that can help evaluate its effectiveness. At the same time, the following tools are used (EUAM, 2020): Google + Google TrendI; SensortoweN; AppAnniV; Facebook Audience InsightI; CrowdtanglV; BuzzsumX; and Facebook Ad Library, ...etc. At the same time, the following KPIs and metrics are studied (Table 4).

Table 4. Goals and key aspects of evaluating the virality of event content of hospitality entities and socio-cultural activities

Aspect	Characteristic	Application result
Metrics	"Pure" data on the published event content / held event with reference to the date: income, expenses, number of leads/new applications, processing status of new leads, marketing indicators (number of held events/published articles/comments for mass media/youtube recordings (if any)/recordings of podcasts (if any)/posts/stories in corp/persons Fb or Inst/BD events, lead time, etc.)	Simply shows numbers that give an assessment of the actual state of the object and what is happening with the company in strategic or short-term matters
KPI	Show business analytics on an operational dashboard reviewed weekly, monthly and at the end of the year, as well as trends formed by the dynamics of indicators over several years	Allow you to monitor work through the prism of agenda execution

continued on following page

Table 4. Continued

Aspect	Characteristic	Application result
OKR (Objectives and Key Results)	A performance management system designed to establish, report and monitor organizational goals and results; intended to form a transparent event management system and align development goals	Replaces the annual performance review process with real-time performance tracking, goal setting and feedback
	On the macro- and micro-level, identifying markers of change, creating a scenario of probable and unlikely, dangerous for development and supporting development, events in event management and post-event (event services), feedback and commenting, reputational compliance	Prediction of threats/risks; allows you to manage the development of events by influencing the areas in which compliance is broken or may be broken

Source: EUAM (2020) and Microsoft.Com (2024)

Let's specify some described in the table. 3 metrics that are most relevant:

- Lead time, measuring how long it takes to develop event content (from the idea to the release);
- HR Flow Efficiency is a metric that shows the speed of the team's work on the creation of an SMM product (page, content), taking into account the stages of development, testing and release. It is calculated according to the following formula:

$$HR\ Flow\ Efficiency = Work / (Work + Wait) \times 100\%$$
(1)

where Work is the time spent on the task;
Wait is the time the specialist waited to receive the task;
Regarding KPI, it is worth highlighting ROI (Return on Investment), the return on investment ratio:

$$ROI = (Revenue - OI) / OI \times 100$$
(2)

where OI is the volume of investments.

In turn, OKR (Objective and Key Results) in the context of event content can help event organizers specify their goals and define key results to measure success (see Figure 7).

Figure 7. Tree of OKR virality of content in event management of hospitality entities and socio-cultural activities

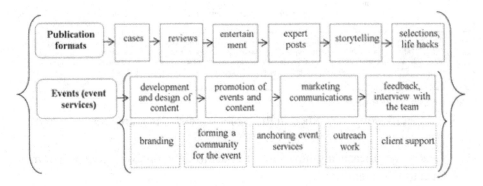

Source: Developed by the authors

So, as you can see, evaluating the virality of event content is quite a difficult task, since it is not always possible to express the quantitative effect obtained due to marketing activities in social networks. In addition, an important aspect of event content in social networks is the issue of compliance - compliance with the requirements of the social platform. For this, all information is checked in accordance with the GDPR (General Data Protection Regulation) and CCPA (California Consumer Privacy Act) protocols, which concern the protection of user privacy.

Directions for Increasing the Virality of Event Content of Hospitality Entities and Socio-Cultural Activities

A reasoned approach to the selection of viral content distribution tools causes a lightning reaction in the audience and promotes self-distribution without additional intellectual and financial costs. The undisputed headliner to look out for in the event content is virtual reality (VR) - technology for creating an artificial world that is broadcast to the brain through all six senses and, ideally, does not differ from reality. The range of applications is represented by many variations: from video games, gambling, feature films, immersive performances to documentary 3D tours of socio-cultural objects (historical monuments, museums, libraries, 3D tours of hotels, …etc), as well as 3D - simulations of educational modules.

The virality of VR technology lies in the neuroconcept of the interaction of event content with human senses, making them aware of the artificial world: vision generates a three-dimensional image; hearing recognizes a three-dimensional sound picture thanks to HRTF (Head-Related transfer function) technology; neuroreceptors come closer to reality through the use of odor generators (immersive cinemas) or speakers that can transmit odors while watching movies or playing games, spraying the aroma through special cartridges that mix and transmit up to 60 aromas; tactility can be recreated through developed gloves or suits with many sensors that can simulate touching any objects in the virtual world; vestibularity (sense of balance) is achieved by mechanized suspensions and seats, etc.

In turn, AR (augmented reality) allows users to see both real scenes right in front of them and virtual objects that do not exist in the real world. AR devices use optical couplers and display components to combine real and virtual objects. AR-glasses can be used in professional activities by planners, designers, surgeons and repairmen. The mass use of AR-glasses will open new niches for viral content in the online environment, including social networks.

It is worth noting such promising concepts for the virality of event content as MR (mixed reality – a combination of virtual and physical reality) and XR (augmented reality). MR-digital objects can not only complement, but also replace real ones. This can improve the user experience and make it more realistic in terms of possibilities for architects and designers (absent the constraints of the laws of the physical world); new types of activities (sports and entertainment); opportunities for advertising; training based on the simulation of certain actions in a real area or a real object. XR is a completely new and forward-looking concept that can encompass VR, AR, and MR technologies, creating a so-called "metaworld" involving the merging of reality, augmented reality, and the virtual world. With XR devices, users can freely switch between different modes, including VR, AR and MR (Figure 8). The introduction of XR elements can affect many sectors of the economy and culture, completely changing the appearance of our world, creating new approaches in the generation and distribution of event content.

Figure 8. Differences among VR, AR, MR, and XR

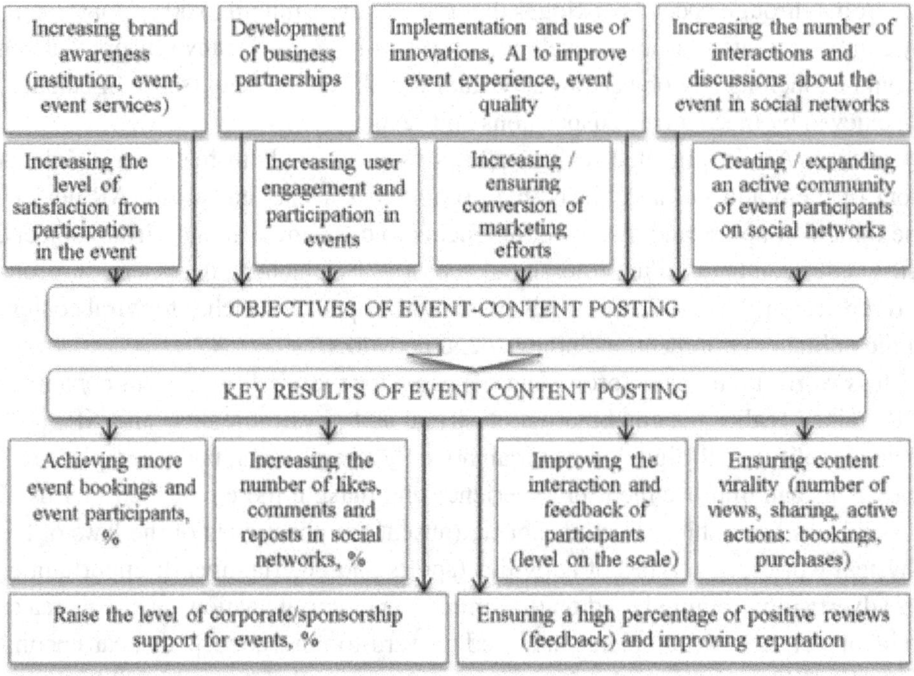

Source: He et al. (2019, p.75).

A comparison of these concepts is given in the table 5.

Table 5. Comparison of VR, AR, MR, and ER

Technology	VirtualContents	RealContents	Interactivity
Virtual reality (VR)	High	Low	Middle
Augmented reality (AR)	Low	High	Middle
Mixed reality (MR)	Middle	High	High
Extended reality (XR)	Switchable	Switchable	Switchable

Source: He et al. (2019, p.75).

Thus, the value created by the VR/AR industry will mainly focus on four aspects: high-quality display technologies, high-performance processors, motion tracking systems and haptic feedback devices (Bellini, 2016).

At the same time, the integration of artificial (AI) and emotional intelligence (EI) allows you to create more personal, impressive and interactive event content, which increases the likelihood of its virality in social networks. Yes, AI analyzes user behavior and interests to deliver personalized content that better meets their needs. In addition, the use of intelligent chatbots facilitates 24/7 communications, providing information, answering questions and interacting with event participants in real time. An innovative direction is the use of AI-based virtual assistants to navigate participants around the "location" of the event and provide them with useful information.

Emotional intelligence, in turn, also contributes to the virality of content in social networks, in particular by determining the emotional tone of the audience, the emotional response to certain aspects of the content event, and feedback on event products. A trend insight is the use of holography technologies to create emotionally charged impressions and performances at the event, which is also integrated into the content of postings in social networks.

The above allows us to state that various types of virality are united by the same common feature: users will want to recommend the event-product to others, and, accordingly, most users will learn about it. But this virality must first be built into the mechanics of the offer and the marketing strategy.Accordingly, when generating event content and distributing it through social networks, in our opinion, it is worth relying on existing technologies and techniques that contribute to the virality of content, which means the branding of events (event services) of hospitality entities and socio-cultural activities (Figure 9).

Figure 9. The reference model of the virality strategy of event content impression marketing in social networks

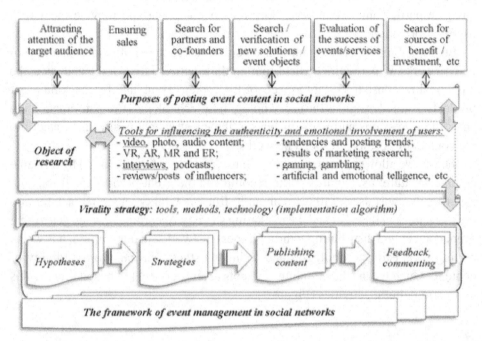

Source: Developed by the authors

In the process of forming the authenticity and emotional involvement of customers, which contribute to the creation of viral content, it is important to maintain the branding of the event/event service and the subject of hospitality and the socio-cultural sphere. For this purpose, we will apply the technological road map method, which is based on brand marketing approaches (Table 6).

Table 6. Designing a technological road map of content virality in social networks

Module	Action scenarios / technical options	Result
Marketing	Conducting marketing research on content virality trends and tendencies, optimizing channels and the timeframe of publications in social networks	Choice of posting format: text, video, audio or infographic; formation of Customer Analytics History, communication with leads and development of ICP & Buyer Personas
Technologies	Analysis of published content of events/event services (own and key competitors)	Compliance with the authenticity and branding of projected content, use of virality technical tools

continued on following page

Table 6. Continued

Module	Action scenarios / technical options	Result
Programs	Analysis of brand development strategies and tactics in social networks	Strategy and tactics of ensuring virality of event content in social networks
Resources	Resource needs analysis	ASsessment of resource costs for content development, posting, ensuring virality and feedback/commenting, as well as monetization sources
Time	Analysis of the importance and urgency of generating and posting event content	Content plan of events / event services
Risks	Analysis of external and internal brand environment	Event content branding and identification plan
Monitoring	Analysis of cyber threat probabilities and reputation risks; control over reactions and active actions of users; assessment of content virality; active feedback and commenting	Conversion rate: CR (Connection Rate), RR (Replay Rate), PRR (Positive Replay Rate), Lead time, HR Flow Efficiency, ROI; control over cyber threats and reputational risks, their manifestation and countermeasures

Source: Developed by the authors based on Artjukhov (2019) and Verezomska et al.(2022)

The given road map demonstrates the step-by-step content formation and operationalization of its virality in social networks due to the synchronous use of modules that help hospitality entities and socio-cultural activities to make adequate decisions regarding the branding of event content.

CONCLUSION

The conducted research confirmed the relevance of scientific studies of viral content issues in the event management of hospitality and socio-cultural entities, as it allows to study and scientifically substantiate the directions of promotion of events and event services in social networks. The scientific works used in this study confirm the importance of using social networks as channels of communication with potential clients, partners and investors, which contribute to the development of innovative activities of hospitality and socio-cultural entities.

It has been argued that the virality of event content is the basis of attracting the attention of the target audience, promoting the event product to the market, managing loyalty and customer behavior through the branding of content posted and distributed in social networks. The section examines the concepts of "viral content", "event content", and "social networks", which created the operational base of the study.

In the course of the research, the hypothesis of the importance of measuring the virality of content that spreads about innovative services and events in hospitality establishments and socio-cultural activities was empirically worked out. So, viral content, which conveys offers to participate in an event or event organization and relies on trending material for posting, has great potential for attracting attention and attracting new customers. In addition, communities in social networks become an ideal platform for popularizing events, because relevant and interesting content gathers a lot of user reactions and share virally in the online space. Research on trends and trends in social media content posts confirmed the assumption that inter-activity, short videos and the ability to generate interest help event managers create viral content. It was also found that the trend in postings on social networks is the use of branding, which contributes to increasing the involvement of users and their loyalty to events/event services of hospitality entities and socio-cultural activities, creates a positive image for it.

A technological road map of the virality of content in social networks is proposed, which helps hospitality entities and socio-cultural activitiesto make adequate decisions regarding the branding of event content. In addition, a reference model of the virality strategy of marketing impressions of event content in social networks has been formed, which reflects the single-vector nature of achieving the strategic goal, i.e. increasing the involvement of the target audience and increasing sales of event products. Finally, we can claim that evaluating the results of approbation the proposed reference model for a viral strategy for marketing event content impressions in social networks is promising for further research.

ACKNOWLEDGMENT

This research received no specific grant from any funding agency in the public, commercial, or not-for profit sectors.

REFERENCES

Artjukhov, A. (2019). Roadmap for the development of education quality assurance systems in higher education institutions: educational and socio-economic aspects. *Prychornomorsjki Ekonomichni Studiji, 37*, 243-247. http://bses.in.ua/journals/2019/37_2019/48.pdf

Bellini, H., Chen, W., Sugiyama, M., Shin, M., Alam, S., & Takayama, D. (2016). Virtual & Augmented Reality: Understanding the race for the next computing platform. *Profiles in Innovation*, 1-58. https://www.gspublishing.com/content/research/en/reports/2016/01/13/eb9acad9-3db9-485c-864d-321372a23726.pdf

Berger, J. (2012). What makes online content viral? *Strategic Direction*, 28(8). 10.1108/sd.2012.05628haa.014

Bondar A., Komarovsky, V., Shobik, V., & Yatsenko, V. (2021). Management of digital transformation processes in socio-cultural sphere. *Actual problems of Public Administration, 3*(84), 66-72. _[in Ukrainian]10.35432/1993-8330appa3842021246259

Bouarar, A. C., Mouloudj, S., & Mouloudj, K. (2022). Digital Transformation: Opportunities and Challenges. In Mansour, N., & Ben Salem, S. (Eds.), *COVID-19's Impact on the Cryptocurrency Market and the Digital Economy* (pp. 33–52). IGI Global. 10.4018/978-1-7998-9117-8.ch003

Bouarar, A. C., Stojczew, K., & Mouloudj, K. (2023). An Analytical Study on Digital Transformation in the Poland Hospitality Industry. In Fernandes, G., & Melo, A. (Eds.), *Handbook of Research on Innovation, Differentiation, and New Technologies in Tourism, Hotels, and Food Service* (pp. 32–50). IGI Global. 10.4018/978-1-6684-6985-9.ch002

Bovsh, L. A., Hopkalo, L. M., & Rasulova, A. M. (2023). Digital Relationship Marketing Strategies of Medical Tourism Entities. In Bouarar, A., Mouloudj, K., & Martínez Asanza, D. (Eds.), *Integrating Digital Health Strategies for Effective Administration* (pp. 133–150). IGI Global. 10.4018/978-1-6684-8337-4.ch008

Bravo, R., Catalán, S., & Pina, J. M. (2021). Gamification in tourism and hospitality review platforms: How to R.A.M.P. up users' motivation to create content. *International Journal of Hospitality Management*, 99, 103064. 10.1016/j.ijhm.2021.103064

Çakar, K. (2022). The Use of Qualitative Content Analysis in Hospitality and Tourism. In Okumus, F., Rasoolimanesh, S. M., & Jahani, S. (Eds.), *Contemporary Research Methods in Hospitality and Tourism* (pp. 143–155). Emerald Publishing. 10.1108/978-1-80117-546-320221010

Canva, (2024). How best to make a content plan: instructions, templates and examples. Available at: https://surl.li/pkrrw

Celuch, K., & Neuhofer, B. (2023). Towards Transformative Event Experiences: State of the Art and Future Research. *Event Management*. Advance online publication. 10.3727/152599523X16990639314792

Cherednichenko, A. (2020). *Invited dinners, press brunches, gastronomic apartments and restaurant festivals*. SURLI. https://surl.li/pkrrw

Daif, R., & Elsayed, K. (2019). Viral marketing impact on tourism and hospitality industry. *International Journal of Research in Tourism and Hospitality*, 5(3). 10.20431/2455-0043.0503004

Estanyol, E. (2022). Traditional Festivals and Covid-19: Event Management And Digitalization in Times of Physical Distancing. *Event Management*, 26(3), 647–659. 10.3727/152599521X16288665119305

EUAM. (2020). *Посібник з питань використання соціальних мереж*. EUAM. https://surl.li/ewfil

Filimonau, V., & Brown, L. (2018). 'Last hospitality' as an overlooked dimension in contemporary hospitality theory and practice. *International Journal of Hospitality Management*, 74, 67–74. 10.1016/j.ijhm.2018.02.019

He, Z., Sui, X., Jin, G., & Cao, L. (2019). Progress in virtual reality and augmented reality based on holographic display. *Applied Optics*, 58(5), 74–81. 10.1364/AO.58.000A7430873963

Hyatt, C. (2010). Facilitating quality in event management. In Mallen, C., & Adams, L. (Eds.), *Sport, Recreation and Tourism Event Management* (pp. 181–196). Routledge. 10.4324/9780080878768-15

Josephi, S. (2019). Adding value to the hospitality experience. *Hospitality Experience*, 38–65. 10.4324/9781003023814-2

Kalaur, S. M., & Maksymyak, B. (2021). The potential of sociocultural animation in the organization of socio-pedagogical prevention of aggressive behavior of school-children. *Social work: today's challenges: a collection of scientific works based on the materials of the 10th International Scientific and Practical Conference.* Ternopil: TNPU named after V. Hnatyuka. https://surl.li/pbncf

Kemp, S. (2023). *Digital 2023: Global Overview Report.* Data Reportal. https://datareportal.com/reports/digital-2023-global-overview-report

Knossenburg, Y., Nogueira, R., & Chimenti, P. (2016). Contagious Content: Viral Video Ads Identification of Content Characteristics that Help Online Video Advertisements Go Viral. *Revista Brasileira de Marketing*, 15(4), 448–458. 10.5585/remark.v15i4.3385

Kristiansen, E., Solem, B. A. A., Dille, T., & Houlihan, B. (2021). Stakeholder Management of Temporary Sport Event Organizations. *Event Management*, 25(6), 619–639. 10.3727/152599521X16106577965080

Kuznetsova, A. (2023). *Why is posting time important for social media?* Web-promo. https://web-promo.ua/ua/blog/najkrashij-chas-dlya-postingu-u-socialnih-merezhah-u-2023-roci/

Malek, K., Tanford, S., & Baloglu, S. (2018). Evaluating event effectiveness across alternate platforms. *Event Management*, 22(2), 135–151. 10.3727/152599518X15173355843307

Melissen, F. (2019). The concept of hospitality. *Hospitality Experience*, 10–36. 10.4324/9781003023814-1

Microsoft. (2024). What are OKRs (Objectives and Key Results)? Definition of methodology of OKR. Microsoft. https://www.microsoft.com/uk-ua/microsoft-viva/what-is-okr-objective-key-results

Oliveira, Z., Teixeira, S., Teixeira, S., & Pratas, J. M. (2024). The Use of Social Media: Influence of Content Marketing for Brazilian Health Industry SMEs. In J. Remondes, P. Madeira, & C. Alves (Eds.), *Connecting With Consumers through Effective Personalization and Programmatic Advertising* (pp. 243-267). IGI Global. 10.4018/978-1-6684-9146-1.ch013

Oskam, J., & Zandberg, T. (2019). The hospitality industry. *Hospitality Experience*, 66–96. 10.4324/9781003023814-3

Pappas, N. (2019). Crisis Management Communications For Popular Culture Events. *Event Management*, 23(4), 655–667. 10.3727/152599519X15506259855652

Peralta, A., & Salama, M. (2021). *Sustainable business model innovation for event management.* Event Project Management., 10.23912/9781911635734-4771

Porobanyuk, V. (2024). *SMM 2024: improving strategies and latest trends.* Web-promo. https://surl.li/pnrnl

Post-up. (2023). *Content strategy for Instagram in 2023.* Post-Up. https://www.postup.com.ua/kontent-strategiya-dlya-instagram-v-2023/

Ragab, H., & Salama, M. (2021). *Advanced Technology for Event Management.* Event Project Management. 10.23912/9781911635734-4774

Ratten, V. (2023). Event Management and Social Entrepreneurship: An Overview. *Event Management,* 27(8), 1127–1134. 10.3727/152599523X16847420514782

Shkil, L. (2023). 63% of people are online now. *The Big Digital 2022 Report on Internet Users.* AIN. https://ain.ua/2022/04/30/zvit-digital-2022/

Silver, D., & Rumsey, L. (2022). Going viral: Limited-purpose public figures, involuntary public figures, and viral media content. *Communication Law and Policy,* 27(1), 49–76. 10.1080/10811680.2021.2014297

Somova, O. (2023). *How the rating of social networks in Ukraine and the world has changed: current statistics after February 24, 2022.* SURLI. https://surl.li/echar

Spoladore, E., Geri, M., & Widmann, V. (2023). Strategic Communication in a Transnational Project—The Interreg Alpine Space Project HEALPS2. In Spoladore, D., Pessot, E., & Sacco, M. (Eds.), *Digital and Strategic Innovation for Alpine Health Tourism. Springer Briefs in Applied Sciences and Technology* (pp. 117–127). Springer. 10.1007/978-3-031-15457-7_8

Tambralli, K. (2021). Event Management. ITSM. https://www.itsm-docs.com/blogs/itil-concepts/itsm-event-management

The Instapreneurs. (2023). *We generate ideas: How to create a content plan and why it is needed.* The Instapreneurs. https://www.theinstapreneurs.com.ua/blog-posts/how-to-create-a-content-plan

Tkachenko, V., & Tkachenko, K. (2019). Leisure as the area of socio-cultural activity. *Bulletin of the Cherkasy National University named after Bohdan Khmelnytskyi.* https://ped-ejournal.cdu.edu.ua/article/view/3460

Torres, K. P. (2021). A virus and viral content: The Vietnam government's use of TikTok for public health messages during the COVID-19 pandemic. In Hutchins, A. L., & Tindall, N. T. (Eds.), *Public Relations and Online Engagement* (pp. 70–77). Routledge. 10.4324/9780429327094-10

Tsiakali, K. (2018). User-generated-content versus marketing-generated-content: Personality and content influence on traveler's behavior. *Journal of Hospitality Marketing &amp. Journal of Hospitality Marketing & Management*, 27(8), 946–972. 10.1080/19368623.2018.1477643

Verezomska, I., Bovsh, L., Baklan, H., & Prykhodko, K. (2022). Cyber protection of hotel brands. *Restaurant and Hotel Consulting.Innovations*, 5(2), 190–210. 10.31866/2616-7468.5.2.2022.270089

Vychivskyi, P., Malanyuk, T., Orlova, V., & Drychak, S. (2023). Modern approaches to understanding the essence of socio-cultural activity management in scientific literature. *Scientific Perspectives*, 4(34), 204–214. 10.52058/2708-7530-2023-4(34)-204-214

Wallace, K., & Michopoulou, E. (2023). Building Resilience and Understanding Complexities of Event Project Stakeholder Management. *Event Management*, 27(4), 499–517. 10.3727/152599522X16419948695143

Wickham, M., Donnelly, T., & French, L. (2021). Strategic Sustainability Management in the Event Sector. *Event Management*, 25(3), 279–296. 10.3727/152599519X15506259856318

KEY TERMS AND DEFINITIONS

Event Management: It is the planning, implementation, and evaluation of public events (such as conferences, exhibitions, and sports games) or private events for social purposes (such as creating awareness of a specific issue) or commercial purposes (such as building the organization's reputation).

Viral Content: Refers to content (such as videos and photos) that spreads quickly on social media networks and and has the ability to attract the attention of a large number of users of these networks.

Viral Marketing: Is a contemporary marketing strategy that involves creating creative content that increases awareness of a service, product, brand, or company by generating positive word of mouth online.

Chapter 13
Hybridized Tourism Education in Hard Times:
Pancoe as a Case Study

Maximiliano Emanuel Korstanje
https://orcid.org/0000-0002-5149-1669
University of Palermo, Argentina

ABSTRACT

The present book chapter discusses to what extent hybridized education can be potentiated in the new normal. PANCOE acts to change negative emotions into joy through gamification. Students were subject to looking at pictures containing islands, beaches, and paradisiacal landscapes. The authors denote the term imagined landscape to create a climate of well-being. The present book chapter reflected on the experience of PANCOE, an experiment conducted by the Joy Labs (University of Palermo, Argentina). The aims of this study were twofold. On one hand, it devotes efforts to introduce pleasure to reduce the current academic dropout rates. On another, it looks to standardise academic performance in low-graded or deprived students. Participants –in PANCOE- came from a neighbouring country and lived far away from their friends and families.

INTRODUCTION

The tourism education has entered in a state of crisis which was aggravated by the recent COVID-19 pandemic. This virus outbreak not only became in global pandemic that left millions of victims, but also it paralyzed the tourism industry as never before (Lapointe 2020; Yeh 2021; Fotiadis, Polyzos & Huan 2021). Among the devastating effects on the pandemic, one must add the rise of student drop out in

DOI: 10.4018/979-8-3693-2272-7.ch013

higher tourism education as well as many implicit problems aggravated by COVID-19 (Sigala 2021; Prayag, 2020). This irreversible crisis anyway left pedagogic lessons. Some studies focused on the positive effects of pandemic regarding virtual learning or e-learning. Digital technologies applied to higher tourism education has offered a good opportunity for some nations while others experienced a rise in the student drop-out rate (Zuccoli & Korstanje 2023a; 2023b). What is equally important, the recent innovation in the fields of augmented reality and Artificial intelligence is not only changing the morphology of tourism but also applied tourism research (Tavakoli & Wijesinghe, 2019; Buhalis 2019).

Having said this, new virtual or hybridized events have come to stay in the new normal. These hybridized events include virtual tours, or virtual festivals, hybridized conferences or congress, and of course e-learning and virtual education (only to name a few) (Westmattelmann, et al. 2021; Remmel, 2021). These considerations need further debate revolving around the essence and evolution of what an event means. As Elisenda Estanyol (2022) puts it, the COVID-19 pandemic, as well as the regulations in the new normal asked for the reorganization of classic events, above all in circumstance when physical distance is needed. The obtained results reveal how some events were certainly postponed or delayed whereas others have taken place through the use of digital technologies like live-streaming or virtual tours. Per her viewpoint the pandemic re-signified a clear enhancement for virtualization and event digitalization. Digital technologies are offered a good solution to transform festivals and events during the pandemic. The author identifies three clear founding moments that boosted digital technology in human history. At a first glimpse, she mentions the increase of digital literacy among the new generation. Secondly, the demands of society for embracing new sustainable practices and ultimately, the technological advances and proliferation of mobile services, the 5G network and the number of consumers engaged with these devices. In a near future, events should tend to hybridized forms which combine some protocoled measures to avoid the pandemic with the natural presence of visitors. The goals of this book chapter are double-fold. On one hand, it explores the potential of technology to create hybridized method earlier and during the pandemic to reduce the students´ dropout rates. On another, it refreshes the current literature with the obtained results of PANCOE, a successful experiment headed by the University of Palermo, Argentina. This experiment deals with pleasurable and wellbeing experiences to potentiate the students´ performance. The question of hybridized method occupies a central position in PANCOE as main study-case.

Tourism Education in Crisis

The turn of the twentieth century has witnessed a deep crisis for higher education. The current rise of student dropout rates is certainly associated to low academic performance as well as the lack of time in professional researchers to serve
as professors. Of course, higher tourism education seems not to be an exception
(Airey, 2013; Hsu 2018). Additionally, metric studies applied in the tourism fields
is wreaking havoc the discipline as never before. Many professional researchers are
pressed to publish leaving their class rooms in amateur colleagues. The genesis and
evolution of tourism curricula needs at the best an updating. As it was originally
denounced by Tribe, the managerial gaze (perspective) has monopolized the knowledge production as well as the curricula in higher tourism education. As a result
of these, other alternative voices are debarred to a peripheral position (Tribe 1997;
2000; 2001). The present section interrogates on the problems of higher tourism
education in pre and post pandemic context. Last but not least, tourism research
has roots in the functioning of the industry as well as in tourism management. The
curriculum was drawn in a moment when the discipline was in its infancy. Now,
the industry is facing serious global risks that press policy makers to update the
curricula (Jafari & Ritchie 1981; Du 2003; Sheldon, Fesenmaier & Tribe 2011).
Cooper & Shepherd (1997) call the attention on the tension-filled dialogue between
the industry and tourism research. Needless to say that both parties, scholarships
and the industry share the same interests and benefits. However, the method here
differs. While policy-makers look the best course of action for the tourism industry,
scholars adopt an experiential (scientific) perspective. Tourism education centers on
the delivery of stakeholders´ expectancies while human sciences look for general
models to explain tourist behavior and its impact in society. This has plausibly led to
a grid-lock. This dissociation has implicitly generated a divide between curricula and
the national policies (Amoah & Baum, 1997), or an academic indiscipline based on
dispersed knowledge production and the lack of a shared (coherent) epistemological
guideline (Airey & Tribe, 2006; Airey et al 2015). In certain consonance with this,
the specialized literature interrogates the future of higher tourism education in two
directions. On one hand, to what extent tourism research gives fresh answer to the
problems of the industry as well as methodologies to enhance curricula. On another,
it punctuates on the current crisis of higher tourism education. At a closer look, we
found in the Cartesian dualism a fresh answer to these problems. Cartesian dualism
not only has monopolized the curricula content but also adopted exclusively for
positive reasoning. This has led to the over-valorization of metrics and quantitative
methods while displacing qualitative ones into a peripheral position. In the fields of
tourism research, positivism has articulated in view of two dynamics: the economic
centered paradigm that said tourism should be defined as an economic (integrated)

system, so to more complex than the sum of its part and the tourist-centricity (Xin, Tribe & Chambers, 2013; Korstanje, Mustellier & Herrera 2016). The economic based paradigm educates next generation not only to serve as professionals but also to protect the interests of the industry. In this process, disciplines as marketing and management occupy a central position. The problem with this managerial perspective is its focus on profits and business while other disciplines are overlooked. Tourist-centricity is a methodological paradigm that enthralls the figure of the tourist as the key player of the game. As a result of this, fieldworkers are trained to believe the tourist is the only agent reliable to knowledge production. Both combined paradigms, which ushered higher education in a conceptual gridlock, seems to be hand-tied to resolve the dilemmas posed on the industry in a new century (Ateljevic, Morgan & Pritchard, 2013; Caton 2014). The recent COVID-19 pandemic is one of those challenges that rearticulated the curricula (Zuccoli, Seraphin & Korstanje 2022; Korstanje & Zuccoli 2023). Additionally, some studies have called attention on the professional pressures on researchers who are imbued in the publish or perishing culture. Most of them leave their classrooms to amateur professors.

Tourism Education and COVID-19

As stated, the COVID-19 pandemic has brought devastating effects not only for the industry but for the entire educational system. The current student dropout rates have triplicated in view of the higher levels of uncertainty to stop the virus propagation. Some academicians have proclaimed for the end of tourism, at least as we know it (Koh, 2020). Other voices applauded for a re-start or reconfiguration of more sustainable forms of tourism consumption (Higgins-Desbiolles, 2020; Becken & Loehr 2022). In this grim context, Tiwari, Seraphin & Chowdhary (2021) offer a lucid analysis of the effects of pandemic in higher tourism education. Per their outcome, the pandemic affected not only various levels of the industry but also the stakeholder collaboration and the shared trust. A radical transformation of the curricula is at least necessary to educate the next generations. Seo & Kim (2021) estimated that crisis accelerated by the pandemic affected the life of 1.6 million students worldwide. Students faced greater levels of distress for excessive online classes as well as burden in new forms of class delivery. In hybridized forms, anyway, tourism education has opened to new solutions and opportunities for online class rooms and virtual group projects. The same technology that mediates in the student-professor´s relationship can be re-used to serve in the host-guest interaction. They put the example of front desk robots, or AI to resolve the problems of new guests avoiding any risk of contagion. In this respect, Yeh & Law (2021) present a local study-case (centered on Hong Kong). Digital technologies is considered obtrusive or an instrument of mass-surveillance, but applied in correct context, it boosts tourism education. Per their estimation, more than 200 Chinese students returned safely to schools and universities. The lessons given by COVID-19 can be utilized for new crisis or virus outbreaks in a near future. Qui, Li & Li (2021) call the attention to digital technologies as a precondition to minimize negative impacts of COVID-19. Distance education, and online teaching worked effectively for students to enhance their programs and careers in China. As they put it, the Chinese experience can be extrapolated to other countries. Rather, other experiences in developing nations show how digital technologies have created contradictory results (Adam 2019; Rogerson & Rogerson, 2021). Zuccolli & Korstanje (2023a; 2023b) alert that technology should be conceived as a double-sword edge. Based on a caustic critique on Cartesian dualism and positivism, which in history dissociated pleasure from reasoning, or emotions from cognitive reasoning, these specialists argue that Cartesian dualism has gravitated further not only in tourism education but in curricula. Students are over-saturated with information which will be never applied in their career. In other contexts, emotionality and joy are regarded as obstacles towards the student´s performance. Technology, far from resolving the problem, reaffirms a long-dormant student-professor dependency because it activates standardized modes of learning and teaching. However, digital technologies can be re-applied to context of friendship and shared trust which very well potentiates students´ performance. Joy opens the endorphins captivating more attention as well as the lateral reasoning, as experts agree. Per their obtained finding, students who have been affected to pleasurable experiences during their learning process obtained better qualifications and transversally the dropout rate decreased.

Hybridized Methods in the COVID-19 Pandemic

In the turn of the century, as it was discussed in earlier sections, not only the tourism industry but also tourism higher education institutions faced an unparalleled crisis. The Pandemic opened the doors to new problems, negotiations (among students and professors) and opportunities. To date, new skills developed by the use of Augmented reality and IA (artificial intelligence) are paving the ways for new situation in higher education system. These technological breakthroughs are generating new forms of tourism, which confronts with classic definitions. For example, virtual tourism or stay-cation is a good (self-explanatory) example how these technologies embody new forms of tourism where physical displacement is not required any-longer. The opposite is equally true, digital tech created hybridized methods that potentiated the students´ performance (Hayes & Tucker, 2021; Mokoena & Hattingh, 2024). Let´s clarify readers that a hybrid method –applied in higher education- should be defined by a set of combined techniques –most probably two or more- redirected to prioritize better results than classic methods. A hybrid method is often excluded from the classic higher education curricula. Hybrid method often utilizes artificial intelligence to create a stage or climate of gamification or simply to stimulate students at the online classes. Some studies have focused on the concept of *blended learning with interesting results* (Kallou & Kikilia, 2021). As the evidence is presented, these outcomes suggest that there would be different attributes associated to hybrid (blended) learning environment that potentiates students´ resilience and engagement. Other works emphasizes the students feel safer in hybrid contexts (Meepron & Fakfare, 2023; Luong et al. 2023).

PANCOE as a Successful Study-Case

Research Objectives

Although the literature in tourism higher education has advanced a lot in the recent years, less attention was given to the role played by emotionality in students´ academic performance. This means that educators and above all policymakers in education turned their attention to structural variables which include curricula, private funding or over-seas exchange instead of students´ inner-world. To fill the gap, this book chapter synthetizes the main obtained results from an innovative and successfully project baptized as PANCOE. This project has been led by Alejandra Zuccoli at the University of Palermo, Argentina for more than one decade. The experiment was originally designed to cover the deficiencies of students as well as reducing their dropout rates. The experiment alternated digital technologies with gamification theory as well as the implementation of social networks. The experiment consisted in creating not only pleasurable experiences but also activities and tasks that engaged students´ performance. As declared in the introductory sections, we hold the thesis that pleasure –far from being a disruptive emotion- enhances the quality of tourism education. PANCOE is a project aimed at stimulating the learning skills of the first undergraduate (UG)) students reported on a Bachelor in Tourism and Hospitality Bachelors. Those participants taking part in this experiment came from neighbouring countries such as Ecuador, Bolivia, Brazil, Chile, Venezuela and Colombia (only to name a few).

Samples and New Potential Skills

Described as a study case, this chapter stresses the role played by pleasure (joy) as an optimiser of learning abilities as well as skills whilst giving an innovative technique to overcome the current barriers in tourism education. Students were encouraged to engage with different team-building activities like baking pieces of bread, food tasting, and cooking. Centred on Cartesian dualism, the tourism curricula do not include these types of activities in programs. What is more important, the figure of pleasure is relegated to a marginal position in the higher education system. PANCOE situates as a pioneering program main based on the Joy Labs to motivate deprived and low-ranked students. The experiment was conducted on basis of two different samples (formed by 10-20 participants in each one). The main goal of PANCOE is strictly associated with the stimulation of creativity of students with the support of AI (Artificial intelligence) and the use of social digital networks such as Twitter. In addition, Joy Labs explores the importance of smart ideas created by the configuration of safe social networks. The study centered on collective intelligence to connote a rapid optimization of learning potentiating students´ skills for tests and exams. The sample was formed by 870 participants who regularly use Twitter ((Twitter-@holapancoe). The sample splits into two, active and passive participants. Whereas the former signals to tourism undergraduate students who take part of PANCOE (almost 40 students), the latter refers to students coming from other universities or areas but excluded from the experiment (830 students). The involved age cohort oscillates from 18 to 26 years old. Originally, the sample was formed by students taking the course of Integracion emocional, ambientacion y communicacion (Communication, environmentalism and emotional integration). It is not otiose to say that PANCOE seeks to integrate the senses in a different direction directly with emotions and academic performance. Digital platforms occupy a central place transforming negative feelings like frustration and fear into positive ones (i.e. trust and joy).

The main learning objectives are as follows:

- To accelerate the inclusion of foreign students who are joining a course as year 1 students in tourism and hospitality careers.
- To potentiate the student learning experience, alongside reducing the rate of students who drop out.
- To make effective innovative methods to improve traditional tourism education, using tourism marketing case studies

Study-Case Description

PANCOE is part of 18 encounters lasting 90 minutes each one. In turn, participants were pre-graduate students well-skilled in tourism marketing and management. PANCOE is not a method but a set of different techniques combined to stimulate students` academic performance whilst reducing the dropout rates. The study examines the figure of pleasure as an innovative strategy to fill the gaps in classic tourism higher education. The obtained results show not only who students who participated in PANCOE have higher degrees but also how endorphins liberated from positive and pleasurable feedback pave the way towards better academic performances. As a promising technique, PANCOE supports directly the learning process of foreign and deprived students whilst outcomes suggest its application in other new universes, for example in the post-COVID19 context. The experiences inserts in the world of new technologies and virtual experiences –derived from virtual (blended) methods-.

The Obtained Results and New Research Perspectives

In the constellations of tourism, many pre-graduate students simply fail to finish their careers or simply leave the university because of high competence and an emerging sentiment of psychological frustration. The literature suggests that once earned their degree the young professionals are subject to excessive working hours associated with low-paid salaries. There is a gap between students` ideals and the reality of the marketplace in the West. With basis on the importance of pleasure (wellness) to stimulate the student cognitive attention, PANCOE which is based on the Joy Labs (laboratory of Joy) at the University of Palermo, Argentina combines different techniques oriented to reduce the student drop-outs as well as improving academic performance. Having said this, PANCOE centres efforts on the role played by pleasure and wellness in the education process. Interesting lines of research can be applied –following this methodology- in Asian universities. PANCOE recycles a climate of extreme competence which is often a source of distress and frustration, in valuable cooperation (gamification) marked in a constructive cooperation process. It is safe to say that the figure of play is vital to understand the PANCOE`s success.

PANCOE is an innovative method that incurs pleasure as a catalyst towards a better academic performance in pre-graduate tourism students. Methodologically speaking, the sample was drawn with two groups, A group which formed with students who took a personal experience with PANCOE, and a group B formed with students who did not take place in the experiment. Having said this, PANCOE has some strengths and weaknesses. Their results are not only promising but also categorical in the sense they exhibit a clear tendency. Students taking part in the experiment have not only better grades but also experienced fewer dropout rates. Amongst the weaknesses, PANCOE is very hard to be measured using the classic standardised pedagogical techniques. For that, we disposed of classic exams (equally applicable for those students in groups A and B). This means that students who were subject to PANCOE showed better cognitive skills in their exams than other samples. A second addition problem was the ratio marked by grade point average. In this respect, some commissions are former by larger than 50 students whilst others only are limited to 25 students. This suggests that ratios will considerably vary without showing a direct correlation between performance and learning skills. To solve this, we used a technique based on the average of students who successfully approved their elective year. Each elective year is based on 8 courses that should be successfully approved.

In 2015, 82% of students who have taken part in PANCOE (Group A) approved the elective year whilst only 68% of students (group B) passed the year. Three years later, in 2018 to be exact, Group A (PANCOE) successfully approved the year with 83% of their students in comparison with 69% in the group (B). The rise of the COVID-19 pandemic, doubtless, affected the performance of all students even in A group, but what is more important; for 2021, group A (Pancoe) showed how 75% of the students approved the year whereas only 67% applies for B group. All this evidence suggests important achievement in the fields of pedagogy with basis on PANCOE method. The results are detailed in Table 1-

Table 1. Performance of Students in Years 2015, 2018, 2021.

Year	PANCOE - A	Group B
2015	82%	68%
2017	80%	65%
2018	83%	69%
2021	75%	67%

Source, self elaboration, PANCOE, 2012-2021

The following tables and pictures shown below validate how effective PANCOE is even in times of COVID-19.

Table 2. Student performance

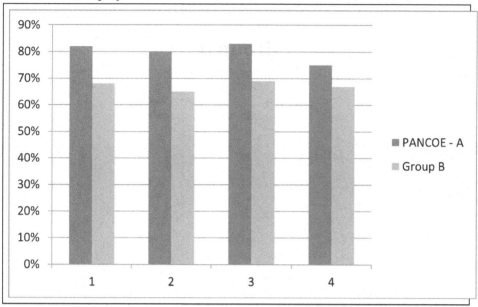

Source: self elaboration, PANCOE Method.

Table 3. Circular performance

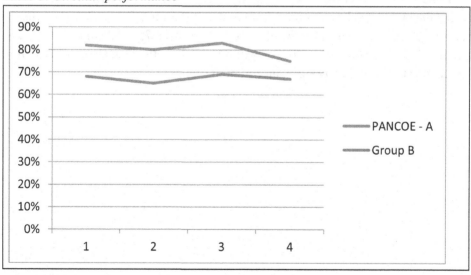

Source: Self elaboration, PANCOE method

In group B the average rate never surpasses the 70% of students approving their respective elective year. The case is notably different with PANCOE who shows rates more than 80%.

Figure 1. Performance of Group B

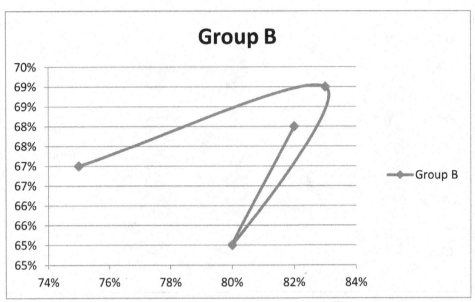

Source: Self-elaboration, PANCOE Method.

Table 2/3 represent the academic performance of B group only whereas comparing the higher and lower points of saturation of B group. This variance oscillates between 65 and 69% whilst PANCOE group ranges from 75 to 82%. Doubtless, this amply evidences not only the efficiency of PANCOE method but also how COVID-19 reduced the academic performance in both groups.

Table 4. Comparison academic performance, Group A/B

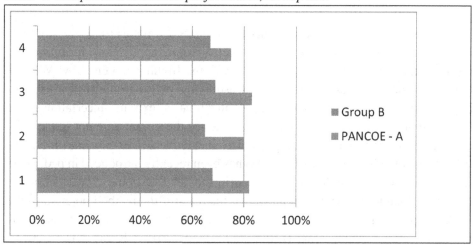

Source: self elaboration, PANCOE Method

In table 4 let`s remind readers that each tier represents an elective year, tier 1 is for 2015, tier 2 is for 2018, two years earlier the COVID-19 pandemic. The tier 3 which notably decreases in performance is for 2021 year, a period fraught by restrictive measures and online-education. Despite the performance has been reduced, those students taking part of PANCOE have better grades than other groups.

Figure 2. Elective years approved

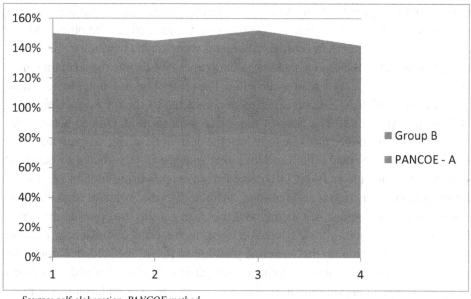

Source: self-elaboration, PANCOE method.

Managerial Perspective and Limitations

To here, we have exposed comments and remarks revolving around the strengths and weaknesses of PANCOE method, as well as future applications for improving tourism higher education. In consonance with the findings obtained by Wellness tourism, we hold the thesis the figure of pleasure (joy) plays a leading role in expanding the current academic performance even in climate of extreme uncertainness and fear –like the COVID-19 pandemic period-. Since the samples are not statistically constructed, results cannot be extrapolated to other universes. At the same time, since the concept of hybrid or blended method has been recently introduced in pedagogy, further empirical research is also needed in the years to come. Some detractors of hybrid (blended) learning acknowledge that even if the method potentiates the students´ performance, they alert on the risks of psychological distress caused by the gamification or competence (Liminiou & Hands, 2019; Cheung & Hew, 2011).

CONCLUSION

We have discussed the main outcomes derived from PANCOE even in pandemic days. As the experiment showed, PANCOE instrumentlized the cognitive reserve of endorphins to get further grades in students´ performance. PANCO is based on virtualized –hibridized- events connecting creativity with digital technologies as well as artificial intelligence. Having said this, PANCOE acts to change negative emotions into joy through gamification. As long as the experiment, participants have been encouraged to dream with preferred destinations while sharing with other students the culinary customs of their countries. Students were subject to watch pictures containing islands, beaches and paradisiacal landscapes. We denote the term imagined landscape to create a climate of well-being. The present book chapter reflected on the experience of PANCOE, an experiment conducted by the Joy Labs (University of Palermo, Argentina). The aims of this study were twofold. On one hand, it devotes efforts to introduce pleasure to reduce the current academic dropout rates. On another, it looks to standardise academic performance in low-graded or deprived students. Participants –in PANCOE- came from a neighbouring country –and lived far away from their friends and families-. Although classic tourism education has taken from Cartesian dualism its traction, this case goes in the opposite direction. PANCOE not only jolts classic education from any lingering complacency but also brings some reflection on the power of pleasure to potentiate students´ cognitive attention. The outcomes notably indicate that participants have better degrees than those who have no opportunity to take part of PANCOE. The endorphins liberated by positive feedback paved the way for new advances in gamification theory. Of course, more research is needed to understand how pleasure helps overcome the pitfalls of classic tourism higher education. Although promising the outcomes cannot be extrapolated to other universes or backgrounds simply because the sample was non-statistically representative. PANCOE, last but not least, evinces promising results even in contexts of extreme deprivation and distress like the COVID-19 pandemic. Of course, though the academic performance in students notably decreased in 2021 –in virtual online education- no less true seems to be that PANCOE group has better scoring than B group.

REFERENCES

Adam, T. (2019). Digital neocolonialism and massive open online courses (MOOCs): Colonial pasts and neoliberal futures. *Learning, Media and Technology*, 44(3), 365–380. 10.1080/17439884.2019.1640740

Airey, D. (2013). Forty years of tourism education and research. *Poznan university of economics review, 13*(4), 1-15.

Airey, D., & Tribe, J. (Eds.). (2006). *An international handbook of tourism education*. Routledge. 10.4324/9780080458687

Airey, D., Tribe, J., Benckendorff, P., & Xiao, H. (2015). The managerial gaze: The long tail of tourism education and research. *Journal of Travel Research*, 54(2), 139–151. 10.1177/0047287514522877

Amoah, V. A., & Baum, T. (1997). Tourism education: Policy versus practice. *International Journal of Contemporary Hospitality Management*, 9(1), 5–12. 10.1108/09596119710157531

Ateljevic, I., Morgan, N., & Pritchard, A. (Eds.). (2013). *The critical turn in tourism studies: Creating an academy of hope* (Vol. 22). Routledge. 10.4324/9780203806586

Becken, S., & Loehr, J. (2022). Asia–Pacific tourism futures emerging from COVID-19 recovery responses and implications for sustainability. *Journal of Tourism Futures*, 9(1), 35–48. 10.1108/JTF-05-2021-0131

Buhalis, D., Harwood, T., Bogicevic, V., Viglia, G., Beldona, S., & Hofacker, C. (2019). Technological disruptions in services: Lessons from tourism and hospitality. *Journal of Service Management*, 30(4), 484–506. 10.1108/JOSM-12-2018-0398

Caton, K. (2014). Underdisciplinarity: Where are the humanities in tourism education? *Journal of Hospitality, Leisure, Sport and Tourism Education*, 15, 24–33. 10.1016/j.jhlste.2014.03.003

Cheung, W. S., & Hew, K. F. (2011). Design and evaluation of two blended learning approaches: Lessons learned. *Australasian Journal of Educational Technology*, 27(8), 1–15. 10.14742/ajet.896

Du, J. (2003). Reforms and development of higher tourism education in China. *Journal of Teaching in Travel & Tourism*, 3(1), 103–113. 10.1300/J172v03n01_07

Estanyol, E. (2022). Traditional festivals and COVID-19: Event management and digitalization in times of physical distancing. *Event Management*, 26(3), 647–659. 10.3727/152599521X16288665119305

Fotiadis, A., Polyzos, S., & Huan, T. C. T. (2021). The good, the bad and the ugly on COVID-19 tourism recovery. *Annals of Tourism Research*, 87, 103117. 10.1016/j.annals.2020.10311733518847

Hayes, S., & Tucker, H. (2021). Using synchronous hybrid pedagogy to nurture a community of inquiry: Insights from a tourism Master's programme. *Journal of Hospitality, Leisure, Sport and Tourism Education*, 29, 100339. 10.1016/j.jhlste.2021.100339

Hsu, C. H. (2018). Tourism education on and beyond the horizon. *Tourism Management Perspectives*, 25, 181–183. 10.1016/j.tmp.2017.11.022

Jafari, J., & Ritchie, J. B. (1981). Toward a framework for tourism education: Problems and prospects. *Annals of Tourism Research*, 8(1), 13–34. 10.1016/0160-7383(81)90065-7

Kallou, S., & Kikilia, A. (2021). A transformative educational framework in tourism higher education through digital technologies during the COVID-19 pandemic. *Advances in Mobile Learning Educational Research*, 1(1), 37–47. 10.25082/AMLER.2021.01.005

Koh, E. (2020). The end of over-tourism? Opportunities in a post-Covid-19 world. *International Journal of Tourism Cities*, 6(4), 1015–1023. 10.1108/IJTC-04-2020-0080

Korstanje, M. E., Mustelier, L. C., & Herrera, S. (2016). Understanding the in-discipline of tourism: A radical critique to the current state of epistemology. In *Global dynamics in travel, tourism, and hospitality* (pp. 208–221). IGI Global. 10.4018/978-1-5225-0201-2.ch012

Limniou, M., & Hands, C. (2019, November). A critique of blended learning: Examples from an undergraduate psychology program. In *Proceedings Of The 18th European Conference On E-Learning (ECEL 2019)* (*Vol. 2019*, pp. 320-328). ACPI.

Luong, T. T., Huynh, V. N., & Kim, E. (2023). A Hybrid Use of Soft Systems Methodology for Developing a Framework of Evidence-Based Teaching for Hospitality and Tourism Instructors in Vietnam. *Systemic Practice and Action Research*, 36(2), 241–274. 10.1007/s11213-022-09609-936032693

Meeprom, S., & Fakfare, P. (2023). Blended learning: Examining must-have, hybrid, and value-added quality attributes of hospitality and tourism education. *Journal of Hospitality & Tourism Education*, ●●●, 1–15. 10.1080/10963758.2023.2172419

Mokoena, P., & Hattingh, C. (2024, March). Unlocking the Potential of Hybrid Learning: Tourism Student Voices in South African Universities of Technology. In *International Conference on Tourism Research* (Vol. 7, No. 1, pp. 232-238). 10.34190/ictr.7.1.2184

Prayag, G. (2020). Time for reset? COVID-19 and tourism resilience. *Tourism Review International*, 24(2-3), 179–184. 10.3727/154427220X15926147793595

Qiu, H., Li, Q., & Li, C. (2021). How technology facilitates tourism education in COVID-19: Case study of Nankai University. *Journal of Hospitality, Leisure, Sport and Tourism Education*, 29, 100288. 10.1016/j.jhlste.2020.10028834720752

Remmel, A. (2021). Scientists want virtual meetings to stay after the COVID pandemic. *Nature*, 591(7849), 185–187. 10.1038/d41586-021-00513-133654258

Rogerson, C. M., & Rogerson, J. M. (2021). The other half of urban tourism: Research directions in the global South. *Urban Tourism in the Global South: South African Perspectives*, 1-37.

Seo, S., & Kim, H. J. (2021). How COVID-19 influences hospitality and tourism education: Challenges, opportunities, and new directions. *Journal of Hospitality & Tourism Education*, 33(3), 147–147. 10.1080/10963758.2021.1929531

Sheldon, P. J., Fesenmaier, D. R., & Tribe, J. (2011). The tourism education futures initiative (TEFI): Activating change in tourism education. *Journal of Teaching in Travel & Tourism*, 11(1), 2–23. 10.1080/15313220.2011.548728

Sigala, M. (2021). A bibliometric review of research on COVID-19 and tourism: Reflections for moving forward. *Tourism Management Perspectives*, 40, 100912. 10.1016/j.tmp.2021.10091234804787

Tavakoli, R., & Wijesinghe, S. N. (2019). The evolution of the web and netnography in tourism: A systematic review. *Tourism Management Perspectives*, 29, 48–55. 10.1016/j.tmp.2018.10.008

Tiwari, P., Séraphin, H., & Chowdhary, N. R. (2021). Impacts of COVID-19 on tourism education: Analysis and perspectives. *Journal of Teaching in Travel & Tourism*, 21(4), 313–338. 10.1080/15313220.2020.1850392

Tribe, J. (1997). The indiscipline of tourism. *Annals of Tourism Research*, 24(3), 638–657. 10.1016/S0160-7383(97)00020-0

Tribe, J. (2000). Indisciplined and unsubstantiated. *Annals of Tourism Research*, 27(3), 809–813. 10.1016/S0160-7383(99)00122-X

Tribe, J. (2001). Research paradigms and the tourism curriculum. *Journal of Travel Research*, 39(4), 442–448. 10.1177/004728750103900411

Westmattelmann, D., Grotenhermen, J. G., Sprenger, M., & Schewe, G. (2021). The show must go on-virtualisation of sport events during the COVID-19 pandemic. *European Journal of Information Systems*, 30(2), 119–136. 10.1080/0960085X.2020.1850186

Xin, S., Tribe, J., & Chambers, D. (2013). Conceptual research in tourism. *Annals of Tourism Research*, 41, 66–88. 10.1016/j.annals.2012.12.003

Ye, H., & Law, R. (2021). Impact of COVID-19 on hospitality and tourism education: A case study of Hong Kong. *Journal of Teaching in Travel & Tourism*, 21(4), 428–436. 10.1080/15313220.2021.1875967

Yeh, S. S. (2021). Tourism recovery strategy against COVID-19 pandemic. *Tourism Recreation Research*, 46(2), 188–194. 10.1080/02508281.2020.1805933

Zuccoli, A., & Korstanje, M. E. (2023a). The Future of Tourism Education Just after the COVID-19. In *The Role of Pleasure to Improve Tourism Education* (pp. 93–107). Springer International Publishing. 10.1007/978-3-031-21580-3_6

Zuccoli, A., & Korstanje, M. E. (2023b). *The Role of Pleasure to Improve Tourism Education*. Springer Nature. 10.1007/978-3-031-21580-3

Zuccoli, A., Seraphin, H., & Korstanje, M. (2022). The Role of Pleasure (Joy) in Enhancing Pregraduate Students' Creativity. In *Strategic Entrepreneurial Ecosystems and Business Model Innovation* (pp. 113–123). Emerald Publishing Limited. 10.1108/978-1-80382-137-520221008

ADDITIONAL READING

Fidgeon, P. R. (2010). Tourism education and curriculum design: A time for consolidation and review? *Tourism Management*, 31(6), 699–723. 10.1016/j.tourman.2010.05.019

Gowreesunkar, V. G., Maingi, S. W., Roy, H., & Micera, R. (Eds.). (2021). *Tourism destination management in a post-pandemic context: Global issues and destination management solutions*. Emerald Publishing Limited. 10.1108/9781800715110

Korstanje, M. E. (2012). Reviewing education concerns. *Journal of Hospitality, Leisure, Sport and Tourism Education*, 11(1), 83–85. 10.1016/j.jhlste.2012.02.006

Korstanje, M. E., Séraphin, H., & Maingi, S. W. (Eds.). (2022). *Tourism through troubled times: Challenges and opportunities of the tourism industry in the 21st century*. Emerald Publishing Limited. 10.1108/9781803823119

Lam, T., & Xiao, H. (2000). Challenges and constraints of hospitality and tourism education in China. *International Journal of Contemporary Hospitality Management*, 12(5), 291–295. 10.1108/09596110010339643

Séraphin, H. (2008). Tourism in the era of globalization of education. *Espaces. Tourisme & Loisirs*, (255), 48–52.

Seraphin, H. (2020). Responsible tourism education of younger consumers: The role of mini-clubs in mountain resorts. *Worldwide Hospitality and Tourism Themes*, 12(4), 409–419. 10.1108/WHATT-05-2020-0022

Seraphin, H., Bah, M., Fyall, A., & Gowreesunkar, V. G. (2021). Tourism education in France and sustainable development goal 4 (quality education). *Worldwide Hospitality and Tourism Themes*, 13(1), 139–147. 10.1108/WHATT-08-2020-0083

Seraphin, H., Yallop, A. C., Seyfi, S., & Hall, C. M. (2022). Responsible tourism: The 'why' and 'how' of empowering children. *Tourism Recreation Research*, 47(1), 62–77. 10.1080/02508281.2020.1819109

Zuccoli, A., & Korstanje, M. E. (2023). PANCOE: A fresh alternative to post-covid-19 challenges in education: The case of tourism education. In *Moving higher education beyond covid-19: Innovative and technology-enhanced approaches to teaching and learning* (pp. 53-63). Emerald Publishing Limited.

Zuccoli, A., & Korstanje, M. E. (2023). The Future of Tourism Education Just after the COVID-19. In *The Role of Pleasure to Improve Tourism Education* (pp. 93–107). Springer International Publishing. 10.1007/978-3-031-21580-3_6

KEY TERMS AND DEFINITIONS

Emotions: Physical and mental states linked to the survival of the organism.

PANCOE: A new pedagogic method innovated by the University of Palermo, Argentina designed to enhance the students' performance through the experience of pleasurable moments.

Students Performance: The extent a student, teacher or group meets the institutional long-term education aims.

Tourism Education: It is a technique oriented to educate the next workforce or professionals to be inserted in the tourism industry.

Tourism: A commercial activity or industry mainly associated to services and leisure consumption.

Chapter 14
Transforming Traditions of University Convocations Through Virtual Platforms:
A Case of Amity University India

Narendra Kumar
https://orcid.org/0000-0002-3325-3448
Amity University, Noida, India

Swati Sharma
https://orcid.org/0000-0003-2949-2363
Amity University, Noida, India

ABSTRACT

Covid has brought many challenges to the ceremonial events at educational institutions. Holding graduating ceremonies or convocations are an integral part of the life of any graduate, but Covid, like in many other facets of life, has changed the way convocations were held at the universities. This book chapter presents a detailed case study on the innovative utilization of virtual platforms to revolutionize convocations at Amity University, India. Through a lens of transformation, the chapter not only examines how Amity University has successfully embraced digital technologies to re-envision its convocation ceremonies, blending tradition with modernity but also the challenges which the administrative support team has encountered during such a virtual ceremony. The authors have interviewed administrative staff at the university who were front-runners in providing such an experience to the post-covid graduates. The findings of the report have been examined in the light of the chapter theme.

DOI: 10.4018/979-8-3693-2272-7.ch014

INTRODUCTION

The COVID-19 pandemic brought unexpected challenges to various sectors including the field of education (Alina et al., 2021; Langston, 2020; Mehla et al., 2021; Sing Yun, 2023). As physical distancing measures and lockdowns became the new normal, educational institutions worldwide were forced to rethink and reshape traditional academic practices (Gómez-Rey et al., 2021; Jyotsna & Madkaikar, 2020). At this time only, virtual platforms came into full existence, ensuring that academic practices do not hamper at any level. With video-conferencing tools and technologies around, the disruptions caused by the pandemic were reduced and the academic processes continued to support teaching- learning environment. Almost overnight, educators had to adapt their pedagogical approaches to virtual environments, utilizing video conferencing tools, learning management systems, and collaborative platforms (Chen, 2020; Fatima Samer et al., 2023). The use of virtual platforms during the COVID-19 pandemic also extended to non-academic aspects of student life. Virtual counseling services (Roberts et al., 2023), career guidance sessions (Choi et al., 2021), and extracurricular activities (Semiz & Čutović, 2023) helped address the holistic needs of students. Social connection platforms and virtual clubs provided avenues for students to engage with their peers, fostering a sense of community even when physical interactions were limited. Live virtual classes became the lifeline of education, allowing students to connect with their teachers and peers in real-time. Through platforms like Zoom, Microsoft Teams, and Google Meet, lectures, discussions, and even group projects were conducted virtually, fostering a sense of continuity amidst the physical isolation imposed by the pandemic. To some extent, these virtual classrooms brought normalcy to academic delivery in those tough times. Beyond the classroom academic activities, these virtual environments also provided a great chance of conducting other academic activities like online conferences, webinars, and virtual convocations as well. Virtual platforms like Zoom, Microsoft Teams, Google Meet provided great scholars with a place to exchange their ideas and knowledge. These virtual platforms helped continue academic discourse and networking opportunities in a virtual space. Faculty members, researchers, and students could participate in and organize events, ensuring that intellectual engagement persisted despite the challenges posed by the Covid.

Conducting events like convocations in hybrid mode offered a range of benefits that blend tradition with innovation, providing a dynamic and inclusive experience for participants. Hybrid convocations allow participants from around the world to join the final day of their college or university. Graduates and their families could actively participate regardless of geographical constraints due to ongoing pandemic. This also fostered the making of a truly global community. The hybrid model of university convocations also helped individuals who might have faced challenges attending physically due to health concerns, travel restrictions, or other reasons. Graduates and attendees have the flexibility to choose their preferred mode of participation—either physically attending the ceremony or joining virtually. This flexibility accommodates diverse preferences and ensures that all participants can engage in a way that suits their needs. One more specific feature of hybrid events is that these events can also save cost for both the organizers and participants. Virtual attendance eliminates travel and accommodation expenses for remote participants, making it a more affordable option while maintaining the ceremonial significance of the event. Hybrid convocations provide a resilient solution that can adapt to changing circumstances, such as unexpected travel restrictions, public health issues, or other unexpected challenges. This flexibility ensures that the event can proceed smoothly, regardless of external factors. Another significant benefit of hybrid events is that it results in increased overall attendance. Because of no barriers related to distance and time zones, virtual participation encourages a larger number of participants to join and celebrate the achievements of graduates. By incorporating technology such as livestreams, virtual reality, and interactive platforms, hybrid convocations leverage the advantages of modern tools. This not only enhances the virtual experience but also provides opportunities for innovation and engagement. Also, environmentally, hybrid events contribute to sustaining the environment by reducing the carbon footprint associated with travel (McCullough et al., 2023). Virtual participation decreases the need for long-distance commuting, aligning with broader efforts to promote eco-friendly practices. Virtual platforms in hybrid convocations can be tailored to offer personalized experiences for participants. Customizable avatars, interactive features, and personalized spaces within virtual environments enhance the overall experience, creating a memorable and unique celebration for each individual. The virtual dimension of hybrid convocations facilitates extended networking opportunities. Graduates, faculty, and attendees can connect with peers, mentors, and professionals from around the world, fostering a global network that extends beyond the physical boundaries of the event.

While there are numerous benefits to conducting events like convocations in hybrid mode, there are also some drawbacks and challenges associated with such events. Technical issues like poor internet connectivity, glitches in the virtual platform, and other unexpected technical problems are common among the virtual platforms. We have seen memes on usage of virtual platforms like "Can you hear me" and many other such memes among the students' community (Huang & Zhi, 2023). These challenges caused a hindrance to the seamless execution of the hybrid events including virtual convocations, impacting the experience for both physical and virtual participants. Another important aspect of using virtual platforms is the digital divide that may result in inadequate access to the virtual events by many of these participants, hampering the overall process (Huang & Zhi, 2023; Huizinga et al., 2022) . This can lead to disparities in the quality of experience for those attending virtually, potentially creating feelings of exclusion (Chua & Bong, 2022; Liu et al., 2022; van Brakel et al., 2023) . One of the drawbacks of hybrid convocations is the diminished sense of physical presence and interaction (Bradaric & Tresselt, 2022). The absence of face-to-face engagement may reduce the emotional impact of the event and the ability to create a personal connection between attendees and organizers. Security and privacy concerns, such as unauthorized access, data breaches, or disruptions are also major concerns of conducting virtual events. Protecting sensitive information and ensuring a secure environment for virtual participants is crucial but can be challenging to manage effectively. The hybrid model may compromise the ceremonial atmosphere that is typically associated with in-person convocations. The grandeur, symbolism, and emotional impact of traditional ceremonies may be diluted in a virtual setting, impacting the overall experience for all stakeholders. The cultural aspect of holding virtual convocations may also get diluted as there will be no or very less attention from the student communities. Symbolic rituals, handshakes, or the physical act of receiving a diploma may lose some of their significance in a hybrid model. Relying heavily on technology poses the risk of technical failures that could disrupt the flow of the event. Graduates and attendees might feel disconnected if technology becomes a hindrance rather than a facilitator. Coordinating an event that accommodates participants across different time zones can be complex. Scheduling ceremonies to suit various regions may result in inconvenient timings for some participants, impacting their ability to fully engage in the celebration. Emotional connection is created by the physical presence of friends, family, and faculty which is missed in virtual convocations whereas physical convocations contribute to these emotional bonding.

LITERATURE REVIEW

The integration of virtual platforms in university convocations has become a significant trend in modern academia. This integration has reshaped traditional convocation ceremonies with enhancing accessibility and engagement. Several scholars have explored this transformation, shedding light on the benefits and challenges associated with virtual graduation ceremonies. Rajan et al. (2021) discussed the intersection of critical theory and Indian ethos that provides insights into the cultural implications of adopting virtual platforms in educational institutions. They also suggested that technological advancements must be balanced with cultural values so that meaningful transition of virtual convocations can be ensured. Awad et al. (2021) discussed the evolving relationship between technology and education, highlighting the role of virtual platforms in fostering global connections and inclusivity in academic events.

Furthermore, Hossain (2008) explored the extent of disclosure in annual reports of banking companies, drawing parallels between transparency in financial reporting and the transparency facilitated by virtual platforms in educational ceremonies. Hossain's research offers a unique perspective on the impact of virtual convocations on communication and information dissemination within academic institutions. Chikusvura et al. (2022) examined the dynamics of collaborative learning in virtual environments and emphasized the potential benefits associated with using virtual platforms to enhance student engagement and interaction during convocations. Their study emphasizes the importance of technology in fostering a sense of community and shared experiences in virtual graduation ceremonies.

The traditional convocation ceremony, with its solemn procession, ceremonial robes, and the crossing of the stage to receive a diploma, has long been a symbol of academic achievement. But due to pandemic like covid, these ceremonies have experienced a transformative. This paradigm shift in how we celebrate academic achievements on a global scale signifies the resilience, adaptability, and inclusive nature of the academic community.

In this era of interconnectedness, the hybrid mode of convocations transcends borders, enabling graduates from every corner of the globe to partake in the celebration (Mehla et al., 2021). In physical ceremonies, a graduate would come to the stage to receive a degree in front of peers, faculty, and families making it a memorable event of their lives. Many of us still have that one picture of holding a degree in our hands and getting clicked on that special day. Those memories are for a lifetime as they take us back to our college days. At the same time, these virtual convocations allow us to be included despite travel restrictions and physical attendance. Technological advancements have made it possible to bridge the gap between two different types of models. High-quality livestreams, virtual reality experiences, and interactive platforms have created a seamless connection between the physical and virtual worlds. Graduates joining remotely are not mere spectators. They actively participate in the ceremony, sharing in the momentous occasion with their peers and loved ones.

Ansah et al. (2023) discussed the unique advantages like flexibility in attendance of hybrid events. Graduates, faculty, and attendees can join from various time zones, breaking down geographical barriers. Chikusvura et al. (2022) examined the virtual facilitates like global networking opportunities, peer connectivity and connectivity with the professionals from around the world. Such a connectivity fosters a sense of community that extends beyond the physical confines of a traditional ceremony. Moreover, the hybrid approach ensures that the essence of a convocation ceremony is not lost in the digital translation. Kumar et al. (2022) discussed the emotional moments attached with such ceremonies which could be captured through virtual gatherings. Graduates have the opportunity to share personal reflections and messages, creating a tapestry of diverse experiences that enrich the overall celebration (Perumal, 2008).

Pre- Requisites for Hybrid Convocation

Conducting virtual convocations require careful planning and effective integration of both physical and virtual components to ensure an inclusive and engaging experience for all stakeholders. Table 1 briefs about the pre-requisites for conducting such virtual convocations.

Table 1. Pre-Requisites for conducting hybrid convocations

Steps	Description
1. Define Objectives and Audience	Clearly outline the objectives of the event, whether it's a convocation, conference, or other gathering.
	Identify the target audience and consider their preferences and needs, both for in-person and virtual participation.
2. Choose a Suitable Venue	Select a physical venue that accommodates the expected number of attendees while adhering to safety guidelines.
	Ensure the venue is equipped with reliable internet connectivity and technology infrastructure for virtual participants.
3. Invest in Technology	Use high-quality audio-visual equipment for both physical and virtual components.
	Set up cameras and microphones to provide an immersive experience for virtual attendees.
	Test the technology in advance to identify and resolve potential issues.
4. Hybrid Platform Selection	Choose a reliable virtual platform for live streaming and interaction (e.g., Zoom, Microsoft Teams).
	Ensure the virtual platform allows for easy interaction between in-person and remote participants (Q&A, chat).
5. Registration and Communication	Implement a unified registration system for both physical and virtual attendees.
	Provide clear communication regarding the event format, schedule, and any technical requirements.
	Share guidelines for virtual participants to ensure a smooth experience.
6. Virtual Engagement Strategies	Incorporate interactive elements for virtual participants, such as live polls, Q&A sessions, and breakout rooms.
	Utilize social media and event hashtags to encourage online engagement and create a sense of community.
7. Professional Moderation	Appoint experienced moderators who can facilitate smooth transitions between physical and virtual segments.

continued on following page

Table 1. Continued

Steps	Description
	Ensure that moderators are familiar with the technology and can troubleshoot issues as they arise.
8. Design Engaging Content	Develop content that caters to both in-person and virtual audiences, avoiding exclusive references to physical locations.
	Use multimedia presentations and visuals to enhance engagement for virtual attendees.
9. Hybrid Networking Opportunities	Facilitate networking opportunities for both physical and virtual participants.
	Use dedicated platforms or features within the virtual platform to enable networking sessions.
10. Safety Protocols for In-Person Attendees	Implement and communicate safety measures such as social distancing, mask requirements, and sanitation protocols.
	Provide a hybrid experience for those preferring virtual attendance due to health concerns.
11. Post-Event Accessibility	Make event recordings and materials accessible to all participants after the event.
	Collect feedback from both physical and virtual attendees to evaluate the success of the hybrid model.

Table 1 describes the prerequisites of conducting any virtual event including virtual convocations so that both physical and virtual attendees have a meaningful and engaging experience during such events.

Use of Hybrid Mode in Convocations Globally

Various universities globally adapted hybrid convocation models in response to the COVID-19 pandemic. Universities such as the University of Toronto and Stanford University in 2020, and others like the University of Sydney, Oxford, and the National University of Singapore in 2021, integrated both in-person and virtual elements to their ceremonies. These institutions utilized advanced technologies, including livestreaming, virtual reality, and augmented reality, to create inclusive and immersive experiences, ensuring participation from graduates and families worldwide regardless of geographical and health-related constraints. Table 4 includes the years when these universities implemented their hybrid convocation approaches, highlighting their commitment to innovation and inclusivity during the COVID-19 pandemic.

Table 2. Global hybrid convocations

University	Country	Year	Hybrid Convocation Approach
University of Toronto	Canada	2020	Embraced a hybrid model with both in-person and virtual components. Utilized livestreams and interactive platforms to connect both audiences.
Stanford University	USA	2020	Implemented a hybrid convocation with personalized virtual experiences. Provided customizable avatars and VR technology to enhance immersion.
University of Sydney	Australia	2021	Combined traditional elements with advanced livestreaming technology. Hosted a physically distanced ceremony and a simultaneous virtual event with live chat and interactive ceremonies.
University of Oxford	United Kingdom	2021	Accommodated both local and international participants through a sophisticated virtual platform. Facilitated real-time interactions and seamlessly integrated physical and virtual experiences.
National University of Singapore	Singapore	2021	Organized hybrid ceremonies with physical gatherings and virtual participation. Employed advanced livestreaming technology and virtual spaces for graduates and families to share the celebration.
University of Cape Town	South Africa	2021	Prioritized accessibility with a user-friendly virtual platform, including real-time translation services. Enabled global participation and fostered a sense of unity.
University of Tokyo	Japan	2021	Created a seamless experience using augmented reality (AR) for both physical and virtual participants. They also created 3D models of the campus for better engagement.
University of Auckland	New Zealand	2021	Incorporated Maori cultural traditions into both physical and virtual ceremonies. They used livestreams and virtual reality to allow international participants witness traditional ceremony and ensured inclusive participation.

These examples highlight the diverse approaches taken by universities globally to embrace hybrid convocations. Whether through advanced technology, virtual reality, or inclusive virtual platforms, these institutions have demonstrated a commitment to ensuring that the celebration of academic achievements are beyond physical barriers and welcomes participants from around the world.

Amity University as a Case Study

Amity University Uttar Pradesh India also were affected due to pandemic and there was a challenge to hold such virtual convocation. The IT team from the university accepted this challenge and created their own virtual platform to organize such a convocation on a global scale. They employed a thoughtful and inclusive approach in designing the platform and integrating all required steps. They used advanced technology to create such a platform and held such a successful event. Despite this, there were some challenges that remained till the end.

Figure 1. Virtual page of Amity University convocation

(www.amity.edu)

To hold virtual convocations, Amity created a user-friendly virtual platform that integrated with the physical ceremony. This platform had many virtual rooms which were available to participants from across the globe. Each of these virtual rooms had features like live streaming, interactive elements, and virtual networking opportunities for each of the participants. The convocation proceedings were available online and were broadcasted through high-quality livestreams so that every participant felt that they were sitting just in front of the stage. Multiple camera setups were capturing key moments so that each attendee felt the same experience as they would have felt during a physical event. Virtual reality elements were incorporated to enhance the experience of the attendees. Such VR technology allowed virtual attendees to immerse themselves in a 360-degree view of the ceremony, creating a more engaging and immersive experience that goes beyond traditional livestreams. The virtual convocation gave attendees a platform to participate from different countries at the same time. Each year, amity university has graduates from African countries who would come from long distance in case of a pure physical event. But this time they had the opportunity to attend it from wherever they were. Lot of cost was saved by these participants in attending such virtual convocation. Interactive elements such as live chat, Q&A sessions, and virtual applause were also integrated into the platform to enhance engagement. Virtual attendees could actively participate in the ceremony, ask questions, and share their thoughts in real time. This gave them the real feeling of attending it. Prior to the convocation, Amity conducted extensive testing of technology infrastructure to identify and address any potential issues. Although such testing may analyze the potential challenges during the main event but since nothing can be assured of the functioning of technology at the last moment, this could have been the case here too. Although the technical team from the university was available to assist virtual participants so that a smooth and glitch-free experience could be provided. This virtual convocation allowed all attendees to participate in a real time manner with a sense of active participation. Once the event was over, all event recordings were kept safe so that future events could be planned accordingly. With such initiatives, Amity successfully created a virtual convocation that not only preserved the ceremonial traditions but also embraced the opportunities presented by technology, fostering a global community of graduates united in their academic achievements.

RESEARCH METHODOLOGY

The present chapter focuses on conducting virtual convocations in universities which involves careful planning and execution to ensure a seamless and meaningful experience for graduates. Some of the key considerations in conducting virtual convocations involve the availability of technological infrastructure, engaging virtual environment, interactive features, global accessibility and participant support. By addressing these considerations, universities can successfully transition traditional convocations into engaging and memorable virtual experiences for graduates and their families. At the same time, conducting virtual convocations in universities comes with its share of challenges, despite the advantages of accessibility and flexibility. Some challenges like platform reliability, connectivity problems, lack of personal interaction, limited networking opportunities, digital divide and emotional impact remain unattended. Addressing these challenges requires careful planning, innovative solutions, and continuous improvement based on feedback from participants. Universities need to find a balance between the benefits of virtual convocations and the inherent challenges to ensure a meaningful experience for graduates.

A purposive sampling strategy has been employed to select participants who have experience with virtual convocations. This has ensured that the data collected is rich and relevant to the following research questions.

1. What was your role in organizing Amity University virtual convocation?
2. What are some of the key administrative tasks involved in planning and executing virtual convocations?
3. From your perspective, what are the main challenges faced when transitioning from traditional convocations to virtual formats?
4. How do you ensure effective communication and coordination among different administrative teams involved in virtual convocation planning?

5. What technological hurdles have you encountered in organizing virtual convocations, and how do you address them?
6. In what ways do virtual convocations impact administrative workload compared to traditional in-person ceremonies?
7. Have you faced any specific challenges related to participant registration, attendance tracking, or data management in virtual convocations?
8. How do you handle the logistics of distributing certificates or diplomas to participants in a virtual convocation setting?
9. Can you discuss any difficulties encountered in ensuring the security and integrity of virtual convocation proceedings?
10. From your experience, what strategies have been effective in overcoming administrative challenges associated with virtual convocations?
11. How do you gather feedback and evaluate the success of virtual convocations from an administrative perspective?
12. What are your thoughts on the long-term sustainability of virtual convocations as a replacement or complement to traditional ceremonies?
13. What recommendations would you give to improve administrative processes for virtual convocations based on your experiences?

The authors have interviewed administrative staff at the university who were front runners in providing such an experience to the post-covid graduates. The findings of the report have been examined in the light of the chapter theme. The responses provided by them have been analysed through Nvivo software and results have been discussed in the light of the chapter theme. Thematic analysis has been used to analyze the data. This process involves coding the data, identifying themes, and interpreting the findings.

RESULTS & DISCUSSIONS

Transformation of convocations through virtual platforms brings challenges and opportunities. Amity University's example highlights the importance of strategic planning and technology investment for successful hybrid and virtual ceremonies. The responses as challenges faced and opportunities in conducting convocation in hybrid mode are presented in the table 3.

Table 3. Summery of responses

Challenges	Details
Technological Infrastructure	**Requirement:** Establish robust infrastructure for virtual convocations. **Challenge:** Ensuring seamless connectivity and quality. **Response:** 81% respondents mentioned that Amity University invested in technology upgrades.
Participant Engagement	**Requirement:** Active engagement of the participant **Challenge:** Overcoming lack of physical presence. **Response:** 75% respondents mentioned the use of interactive elements like live chats and VR.
Logistical Coordination	**Requirement:** Coordinating logistics for such virtual events. **Challenge:** Synchronizing components for smooth operation. **Response:** 96% respondents mentioned the detailed planning and rehearsals were conducted before the hybrid convocation.
Inclusivity and Accessibility	**Requirement:** Ensuring accessibility for diverse audiences. **Challenge:** Address time zones, languages, and special needs. **Response:** 75% respondents mentioned the provision of translation services and customizable avatars.
Opportunities	**Responses from administrative staff of Amity University**
Global Reach	**Opportunity:** Expand reach beyond geographical constraints. **Implementation:** Enabled global participation via virtual platforms.
Cost Efficiency	**Opportunity:** Reduce costs associated with physical events. **Implementation:** Virtual convocations were more cost-effective for the university and participants.
Innovative Engagement	**Opportunity:** Use technology for innovative experiences. **Implementation:** Employed AR and VR for immersive ceremonies.
Sustainability	**Opportunity:** Promote environmental sustainability. **Implementation:** Reduced travel-related emissions by conducting virtual and hybrid convocations.

The transformation of university convocations through virtual platforms presents a mix of challenges and opportunities. Amity University, India, serves as a prime example of how educational institutions can adapt to changing circumstances by leveraging technology and innovative approaches. While there are significant challenges to overcome, the potential benefits of global reach, cost efficiency, innovative engagement, and sustainability make the shift towards hybrid and virtual convocations a valuable endeavor. This chapter discusses the importance of strategic planning and investment in technology to successfully navigate the future of university ceremonies.

Future Scope of the Study

Virtual graduation ceremonies emerged as a prominent solution during the COVID-19 pandemic, providing a way for educational institutions to celebrate their students' achievements despite social distancing measures (Gao & Lyu, 2023). As we look to the future, several trends and possibilities for virtual graduation ceremonies can be anticipated. Many institutions may adopt a hybrid model, combining in-person and virtual elements (Xu, 2023). This allows for the inclusivity and accessibility of virtual ceremonies while retaining the traditional experience for those who can attend in person. The future of virtual graduation ceremonies will likely be characterized by innovative uses of technology, a focus on inclusivity, and hybrid models that blend the best of both virtual and physical worlds. These ceremonies will continue to evolve, offering unique and memorable ways to celebrate academic and professional achievements.

Also, virtual ceremonies are likely to leverage advanced technologies to create more engaging and immersive experiences. These technologies can offer immersive environments where graduates and attendees feel as though they are part of a real ceremony. Holographic representations of graduates or speakers could enhance the sense of presence. Customizable avatars, interactive chat rooms, and networking lounges can simulate the social aspects of in-person ceremonies.

Virtual ceremonies enable participation from a global audience, including international students, distant relatives, and friends who may not have been able to attend otherwise. This inclusivity will likely continue to be a significant benefit. For many institutions, virtual ceremonies are more cost-effective than traditional ones. They eliminate the need for large venues, catering, and other logistical expenses, making them an attractive option for budget-conscious organizations. Graduates might be able to tailor their virtual ceremony experience, choosing different virtual backgrounds, music, and other elements. Virtual ceremonies have a lower environmental footprint compared to traditional ceremonies, as they reduce the need for travel and physical resources. This aligns with increasing awareness and efforts toward sustainability. Beyond educational institutions, virtual graduations could extend to corporate settings, celebrating milestones such as completion of training programs, promotions, or retirements.

CONCLUSION

The COVID-19 pandemic has undeniably reshaped the landscape of education, compelling institutions worldwide to embrace virtual platforms as a means of ensuring continuity in learning and academic engagement. Educators had to adapt rapidly, leveraging video conferencing tools, learning management systems, and collaborative platforms to deliver educational content in virtual environments, while also addressing the holistic needs of students through virtual counseling services, career guidance sessions, and extracurricular activities. Live virtual classes emerged as the lifeline of education, facilitating real-time interactions between students and educators, and virtual platforms played a pivotal role in hosting a myriad of virtual events, conferences, seminars, and convocations, enabling the seamless continuation of academic discourse and networking opportunities in a virtual space. The widespread adoption of virtual platforms in education during the COVID-19 pandemic has demonstrated the resilience and adaptability of educational institutions and highlighted the transformative potential of technology in ensuring continuity, fostering community, and facilitating intellectual exchange in times of crisis.

REFERENCES

Alina, D. M., Miguel, F. L., Marian, N., Mihail, B., & Vanesa, V. M. (2021). The Challenges of the Higher Education Sector. The Impact of COVID-19 Crisis on the Educational Process—Case of Romania. *Springer Proceedings in Business and Economics*, 37–58. Springer. 10.1007/978-3-030-86641-9_3

Ansah, A. A., Vivacqua, A. S., Zhong, S., Boll, S., Constantinides, M., Verma, H., El Ali, A., Lushnikova, A., Alavi, H., Rintel, S., Kun, A. L., Shaer, O., Cox, A. L., Gerling, K., Muller, M., Rusnak, V., Machado, L. S., & Kosch, T. (2023). Reflecting on Hybrid Events: Learning from a Year of Hybrid Experiences. *Extended Abstracts of the 2023 CHI Conference on Human Factors in Computing Systems*, (pp. 1–4). ACM. 10.1145/3544549.3583181

Awad, I., Salah, R., & Saleh, R. (2021). Using virtual platforms in architectural education to manage the Corona virus crisis: An applied study on the Microsoft platform at Horus University - Egypt. *Journal of Architecture, Arts and Humanities*. 10.21608/mjaf.2020.44838.1885

Bradaric, B. D., & Tresselt, D. B. (2022). Factors influencing undergraduate education in an expanding virtual world during COVID-19. *Education and Information Technologies*, 27(9), 11991–12002. 10.1007/s10639-022-11104-635645596

Chen, L. (2020). Online Education in the Post-epidemic Era. *International Journal of Social Science and Education Research*, 3(10), 332–335. 10.6918/IJOSS-ER.202010_3(10).0052

Chikusvura, N., Nkomo, S., & Sibanda, L. (2022). Transition to Virtual Graduation: Experiences of 2021 University Graduates in Zimbabwe. *Randwick International of Education and Linguistics Science Journal*, 3(3), 497–503. 10.47175/rielsj.v3i3.537

Choi, J.-S., Kim, D.-M., Kim, Y., Jin, S., & Ha, J.-Y. (2021). An Analysis of College Students. *Journal of the Korea Academia-Industrial Cooperation Society*, 22(7), 68–76. 10.5762/KAIS.2021.22.7.6834762060

Chua, K. H., & Bong, W. K. (2022). Providing inclusive education through virtual classrooms: A study of the experiences of secondary science teachers in Malaysia during the pandemic. *International Journal of Inclusive Education*. 10.1080/13603116.2022.2042403

Fatima Samer, S., Jahan, Y., & Abrar Hassan, M. (2023). A STUDY ON CHANGE IN LEARNING PATTERN FROM OFFLINE TO ONLINE MODE DURING COVID-19 PANDEMIC. *International Journal of Advanced Research*, 11(02), 636–642. 10.21474/IJAR01/16291

Gao, Z., & Lyu, X. (2023). Planet Anima: A virtual graduation experience in the metaverse. *Digital Creativity (Exeter)*, 34(3), 248–263. 10.1080/14626268.2023.2254750

Gómez-Rey, P., Fernández-Navarro, F., & Vázquez-De Francisco, M. J. (2021). Identifying Key Variables on the Way to Wellbeing in the Transition from Face-to-Face to Online Higher Education due to COVID-19: Evidence from the Q-Sort Technique. *Sustainability (Basel)*, 13(11), 6112. 10.3390/su13116112

Hossain, M. (2008). The extent of disclosure in annual reports of banking companies: The case of India. *European Journal of Scientific Research.*

Huang, X., & Zhi, H. (2023). Factors Influencing Students' Continuance Usage Intention with Virtual Classroom during the COVID-19 Pandemic: An Empirical Study. *Sustainability 2023, Vol. 15, Page 4420, 15*(5), 4420. 10.3390/su15054420

Huizinga, T., Lohuis, A., Zwerver-Bergman, J., & van der Meer, R. (2022). Student and teacher perceptions of community of inquiry in hybrid virtual classrooms. *Heliyon*, 8(12), e12549. Advance online publication. 10.1016/j.heliyon.2022.e1254936619452

Jyotsna, J., & Madkaikar, S. (2020). Educational Repercussions due to Covid-19 in Hospitality Institutes. *JOURNAL OF TOURISM AND HOSPITALITY MANAGEMENT*, 8(2). 10.15640/jthm.v8n2a4

Kumar, N., Tandon, R., & Misra, N. (2022). Emotional Intelligence as Intangible Class Content for Effective Communication in Managing University Classes: A Bibliometric Analysis. *Journal of Content. Community and Communication*, 16(8), 26–36. 10.31620/JCCC.12.22/03

Langston, C. (2020). Entrepreneurial educators: Vital enablers to support the education sector to reimagine and respond to the challenges of COVID-19. *Entrepreneurship Education*, 3(3), 311–338. 10.1007/s41959-020-00034-4

Liu, R., Wang, L., Koszalka, T. A., & Wan, K. (2022). Effects of immersive virtual reality classrooms on students' academic achievement, motivation and cognitive load in science lessons. *Journal of Computer Assisted Learning*, 38(5), 1422–1433. 10.1111/jcal.12688

McCullough, B. P., Collins, A., Roberts, J., & Villalobos, S. (2023). Sport Events and Emissions Reporting: An Analysis of the Council for Responsible Sport Standard in Running Events. *Sustainability, 15*(19), 14375. 10.3390/su151914375

Mehla, L., Sheorey, P. A., Tiwari, A. K., & Behl, A. (2021). Paradigm shift in the education sector amidst COVID-19 to improve online engagement: Opportunities and challenges. *Journal of Global Information Management*, 30(5), 1–21. 10.4018/JGIM.290366

Perumal, J. (2008). Student resistance and teacher authority: The demands and dynamics of collaborative learning. *Journal of Curriculum Studies*, 40(3), 381–398. 10.1080/00220270701724570

Rajan, S., Bindu, G. V., & Mukherjee, S. (2021). Adopting Evolving Technologies to Aid Cognitive Abilities in Classroom Learning-Teaching. *Neuro-Systemic Applications in Learning*, 483–506. 10.1007/978-3-030-72400-9_24

Roberts, A., Goodman-Scott, E. C., & Edirmanasinghe, N. A. (2023). The Experiences of School Counselors Providing Virtual Services During COVID-19: A Phenomenological Investigation. *Professional School Counseling*, 27(1), 2156759X231199738. 10.1177/2156759X231199738

Semiz, M., & Čutović, M. (2023). Extracurricular activities during the COVID-19 pandemic: Teachers' experiences and lessons. *Zbornik Radova Pedagoskog Fakulteta Uzice*, 25(25), 165–182. 10.5937/ZRPFU2325141S

Sing Yun, W. (2023). Digitalization challenges in education during COVID-19: A systematic review. *Cogent Education*, 10(1), 2198981. 10.1080/2331186X.2023.2198981

van Brakel, V., Barreda-Ángeles, M., & Hartmann, T. (2023). Feelings of presence and perceived social support in social virtual reality platforms. *Computers in Human Behavior*, 139, 107523. 10.1016/j.chb.2022.107523

Xu, X. (2023). To social with social distance: A case study on a VR-enabled graduation celebration amidst the pandemic. *Virtual Reality (Waltham Cross)*, 27(4), 3319–3331. 10.1007/s10055-022-00646-235464641

Chapter 15
Virtual Laboratories in the Teaching and Learning Paradigm

Dalamchwami Chen Lyngdoh
North Eastern Hill University, India

Sarada Prasad Dakua
https://orcid.org/0000-0003-2979-0272
Hamad General Hospital, Qatar

Gajendra Kumar Mourya
https://orcid.org/0000-0003-0585-4964
North Eastern Hill University, India

ABSTRACT

Laboratories are a fundamental aspect of any academic learning that enables students to better understand the theoretical concepts of any academic course. Science, engineering, and medical fields are the main areas of study that heavily depend on laboratories for demonstrating the practicality of any theory. However, circumstances may arise where students face challenges in performing practicals due to insufficient materials, equipment, or the inaccessibility of the laboratory itself. To counter this challenge, various organizations and institutions have come forward to develop 'Virtual Laboratories' or 'Virtual Labs'. Virtual laboratories are platforms where the user can engage in practical sessions without the need to be present in person. The user can log in anywhere, even remotely, and be able to gain access to the same setting as in a traditional hands-on laboratory, albeit virtually. This chapter will detail virtual labs, what they are all about, and the effectiveness of virtual labs in comparison to traditional labs.

DOI: 10.4018/979-8-3693-2272-7.ch015

INTRODUCTION

Laboratories have been a core part of education. Academic fields such as science, engineering and medicine require students to have a hands-on approach, familiarizing them with the process. This in turn helps students to grasp the theoretical concepts via practical sessions. Laboratories also foster a sense of teamwork and intelligence when students interact with each other to solve a problem. However, there are certain drawbacks to traditional laboratories. They require a physical area for keeping equipments so that students can carry out experiments in person. Laboratories require lots of maintenance and updation as per the updated curriculums, so it is also expensive, especially for students with no proper access to laboratories that are well-equipped (Ocaña et al., 2018). The next point is the physical presence of the students is required to finish the experiments, which makes it a challenge for every student to get the same opportunity (Serrano-Perez et al., 2023). Another point is that laboratories of departments such as chemistry, biochemistry and biomedical sciences contain various dangerous and hazardous materials that could lead to accidents like explosions or chemical burns (Olewski & Snakard, 2017). These types of labs require stringent safety guidelines (Juergensmeyer & Adetunji, 2022). Finally, there is also the issue of lab size. It could arise that a small lab could not properly host all the students of a class, thereby making some of the students miss out on crucial demonstrations due to the constraint on the size of the lab. In recent times though, technological advancements have greatly impacted the educational sector. Classes have been conducted virtually and study materials have been made available in a digital format. Massive Open Online Courses or MOOCs by institutions such as Massachusetts Institute of Technology (MIT), USA and Indian Institute of Technology (IIT), India was another form of distance and virtual learning that allowed students to complete various courses that may not be available in their institution's curriculum. This furthermore gives rise to the idea of virtual laboratories – labs that are available in a simulation format and can be accessed virtually. Virtual laboratories are aimed to alleviate the issues encountered in traditional laboratories. With time, virtual laboratories have also become part of the academic curriculum. This was not comprehensible in the last decades as one would have thought that virtual classrooms and virtual laboratories could not compete with traditional learning systems. Regardless, this would all change with the COVID-19 pandemic.

COVID-19 and the Rise of Online Education

From 2020 to 2021, the spread of the SARS-CoV-2 virus caused the COVID-19 pandemic that led to the halting of all forms of activities, from public gatherings to social events. Among these activities were all academic and learning activities.

Therefore, as all places where large numbers of people gather were prohibited, schools and institutions also had to shut down. Final-year students of both schools and universities were stuck in an uncertain situation where their future career perspectives remained unclear. The unclear duration of the pandemic would greatly affect the education process for all students (Butnaru et al., 2021). This massive disruption in the completion of various courses made learning institutions and schools come up with alternative solutions to circumvent this issue. Before the pandemic, online learning has already been deployed such as distance learning courses or MOOCs. The pandemic pushed even general platforms meant only for social media and networking to be used as mediums for the continuation of education. Tools such as private messaging apps and calls between two people or multiple participants were commonly utilized during that time (Favale et al., 2020). Various platforms for connecting between teachers and students were also introduced. Zoom and Google Meet platforms for conducting online live classes for students became popular. Microsoft Teams, another online platform, found its place as another source for conducting online classes. Other forms of online learning through platforms such as Coursera and Udemy were also sought after during the pandemic. Thus, smartphones and internet access transformed the learning and teaching paradigm of education. Social networking applications that were utilized in everyday life brought about changes in approaches to teaching and learning, thereby improving the learning process of the students.

Of course, the sudden switch from traditional 'face-to-face' learning to virtual learning took a rough turn, though it took less time for students to get comfortable with this type of learning. Using these tools, they could learn just as when physically attending classes, though tasks such as assessments and tests posed a challenge for teachers (Gonzales et al., 2020). Despite this, many research articles reported positive impacts of online education during the pandemic that continued even post-COVID-19. Rajhans et al conducted a survey to uncover the changes in Indian optometry education during COVID-19. Since April 2020, they observed that most of the optometric institutes have transitioned to online learning for the learning process. A questionnaire that contained a combination of both open and close-ended questions was used in their survey. They found that 73 out of the 78, i.e., 93.58% of the optometric teachers were able to easily transition to online learning in less time. Classes were conducted through Google Meet, Zoom, Microsoft Teams, etc and assessments were done through platforms such as Google Classroom (Rajhans et al., 2020). Gonsalez et al evaluated the performance of the students in self learning in higher education during the COVID-19 confinement. 458 students were included from three different subjects at the Universidad Auto´noma de Madrid in Spain. The students were divided into two groups – the first group that was students from the academic years 2017 to 2019 and the second group was students from the academic year 2019 to 2020, and the contrast in their assessments was examined. They found that the COVID-19 confinement had a favourable effect on the performance of the students. This was found in students with an increased assessment workload and students with the same workload. When students did not change the format of their workload post-confinement, they still observed a positive effect, and it is significant in students with more workload and students with the same workload. They concluded that COVID-19 confinement inculcated a continuous habit of studying in the students (Gonzales et al., 2020). Kummitha et al in their study aimed to examine the methods taken by Higher Educating Institutions (HEIs) to minimize the problems faced at the time of the COVID-19 pandemic by introducing online learning. Their study incorporated a cross-sectional study of 281 academic professionals who work in Higher Educating Institutions across India and Ethiopia. Their study highlighted a division in digital implementation decisions and insufficient preparation to be the challenges for the facilitation of online learning. They also mentioned that training for the faculties in utilizing online learning services was limited (Kummitha et al., 2021). Hence, it can be said that with more implementation of digital services and online platforms, Higher Educational Institutions would experience a more enhanced form of learning process and improved performance in the students.

From these few studies it was seen how with the onset of the pandemic, online learning had a significant impact and favourable effect on the learning process in students. Online learning has distinct merits such as increased flexibility, easily accessible learning materials, familiarity with various types of learning environments, courses and even online communities between faculty and students (Butnaru et al., 2021). Another form of online learning that is now accessible to students is virtual laboratories. Similar to online classes, virtual labs provide not only a platform for classes but also for performing simulations of their experiments as well as completing assigned tasks and assessments. Therefore, the COVID-19 pandemic has also helped establish the pathway for the incorporation of virtual labs into academic curriculums.

What Are Virtual Laboratories?

As online learning has now become a common part of the curriculum in academics, this introduces new ways of effectively learning, like virtual laboratories. Virtual labs enable students to perform their experiments without the need to be present physically to operate the equipment (Van den Beemt et al., 2023). Virtual laboratories are usually deployed for various science courses (Reece 2015). For example, the smart science lab (https://www.smartscience.online/) is a virtual lab dedicated to educating science through visuals like text, videos and images along with an interactive user experience to simulate the theoretical information taught by teachers. Various opportunities become open to students who have limited access to traditional laboratories (Birkeland et al., 2022). Thus, this is a creative way to provide practical experience to students as a solution to the problems encountered with traditional labs. Additionally, virtual labs offer a safe environment for students to perform practicals without the need to maintain safety guidelines, thus avoiding any injury to themselves or equipment damage (Aljuhani et al., 2018). For instance, virtual labs for chemistry are used in simulating experiments that involve chemical reactions or titrations, thus avoiding any accidents that could be dangerous. Considering these advantages, hence there has been an increased utilization of these virtual labs over the years (López-Pernas et al., 2022).

Another platform called V-Lab was initially employed to teach biology to students and visualize various topics such as cells and DNA (Dyrberg et al., 2017). V-Lab introduced students to possibilities for understanding the environment, phenomena and objects around them (Udin & Ramli, 2020). An example of a virtual lab can be seen in Figure 1. Here, the virtual lab can be composed of a Graphical User Interface (GUI) that possesses login buttons, whereby the student can create an account by registering his or her name, batch number, identification details, and so on. The virtual lab will contain a virtual display of the laboratory environment of a particular subject. Suppose a student wants to perform physics lab practicals, then they can select and choose the physics laboratory that would contain all the experiments for a particular grade. If a student wants to perform chemistry practicals instead, they can simply select and choose the lab they want.

Figure 1. An example of a graphical user interface (GUI) for virtual laboratories

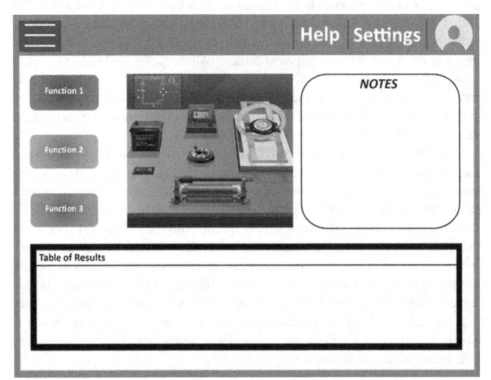

Virtual labs are more applicable to science, technology and engineering courses. This is because these courses heavily rely on the practical simulation of theoretical knowledge. As technology-based training is increasing in various areas, education also shares the same experience. Virtual simulations to improve the capabilities of trainees, and their skills in solving problems and management have been utilized by organizations (Dalgarno, Bishop & Bedgood, 2003; Richard et al., 2006). Virtual labs provide the prospect of practicing any experiment many times, sometimes at a student's own pace. This allows the student to practice without any fear of harming themselves or damaging the equipment or subjects (Elmoazen et al., 2023). Hence, the same virtual equipment may be utilized by many students at the same time.

Types of Virtual Laboratory Environments

Online learning has undergone a considerable transformation with the growing development of the technology and internet (Biasutti, 2017). Teachers, tutors and students can utilize various Online learning platforms for conducting and attending classes (Biasutti, 2017; Molins-Ruano, 2014). Now with the incorporation of virtual laboratories into the mix, this has made E-learning even more effective. In this section, a few examples of virtual laboratories that are available for E-learning will be discussed.

Many organizations have developed different types of virtual labs that are usually available as open-source software. Go-Lab is a project that constitutes a great collection of virtual labs which are highly interactive. Teachers can create inquiry learning spaces via a combination of these virtual labs and applications. Hence, teachers and students can share the learning space to develop and test various hypotheses (Dziabenko & Budnyk, 2019). The Library of Labs or 'LiLa' is another initiative that aimed at developing a framework for virtual experimentations. It aids participants in gaining communication and social skills with each other as well as teachers, apart from gaining scientific knowledge (Richter et al., 2011). In recent years, the Indian Institutes of Technology (IITs) along with other academic institutions under the National Mission on Education through Information and Communication Technology (NMEICT) of the Ministry of Education, Government of India have developed a platform called Virtual Labs (https://www.vlab.co.in/). Various institutes such as IITs and other government institutions were involved. These platforms provide students with a plethora of labs for practicing various experiments. Students from scientific and engineering backgrounds such as core sciences, computer science engineering, biotechnology and biomedical sciences, electronics and communication engineering, mechanical engineering, etc. can register and log in to this portal to attend the labs of their choice. For example, in Figure 2 is an example of a simulation of a thresholding experiment under the image processing lab of the computer science engineering course. Here, we see the entire user interface that displays buttons, radio options and windows to display the processed images. The buttons include the 'Select Image' for choosing the image of our choice, the 'Reset' button removes the image and all the functions applied to it, and the 'Run' button is for applying the image processing techniques on the image. The radio options contain operations such as Single or Double Thresholding, Otsu Thresholding and Region Growing. Once we select the operation of our choice, we can see the result in the second window. This is just one example of the various lab simulations that are available in the category list of Virtual Labs.

Figure 2. Image segmentation experiment under the image processing lab of computer science engineering course

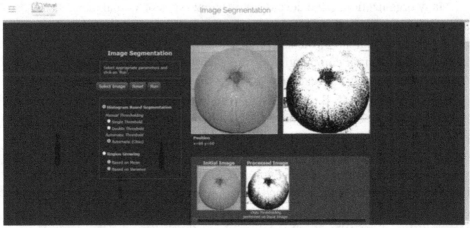

Virtual Labs (https://www.vlab.co.in/)

Apart from these virtual labs, there are still some more platforms available. Laboratory Virtual Instrument Engineering Workbench (LabVIEW) is a virtual platform developed by National Instruments, Texas. This platform allows engineering students to design various circuits and perform these experiments through simulations. Multiple models of electronic components such as resistors, potentiometers, oscillators, etc., and other signal processing elements in this platform help students easily understand and apply theoretical information in practical form. Physics Education Technology or PhET developed by the University of Colorado Boulder, USA is another platform that enables students to do various experiments from the science courses through simulations. Although at first it was initially developed only for conducting physics experiments, other science courses such as chemistry, biology, mathematics and earth sciences were introduced on this platform. PhET simulations offer education based on an interactive and game-like environment. This way, students learn about the scientific principles by exploring the environment. For example, in Figure 3, we see the experiment "Gravity Force Labs: Basics" where students are presented with two masses, mass 1 and mass 2. They can drag either of the masses away or toward the other mass to see how force changes with respect to each mass. They can change the weight of each mass or keep them constant. These features allow the student to individually explore and understand the theoretical concepts easily. LabXchange Harvard is an online environment providing students with a platform to collaborate, share and learn. High-quality study materials and content along with simulations and assessments are offered in various science courses like physics, chemistry, biology and earth sciences. In this platform, students can choose either interactive mode or simulation mode. In interactive mode, students can use the scroll button which will uniquely display the educational content along with graphical representations such as diagrams and answer multiple-choice questions along the way to test their understanding. Simulation mode allows the student to adjust parameters for a particular experiment to see the outcome of those adjustments. PraxiLabs is a virtual lab that offers students access to various types of experiments from physics, chemistry, and biology. Categories are subdivided into sub-disciplines for each subject, thereby making it more effective and time-saving when searching for experiments related to a particular sub-field. In PraxiLabs, students can choose from among the different experiments and perform their practicals through simulations.

Figure 3. Gravity force labs simulation in physics education technology (PhET)

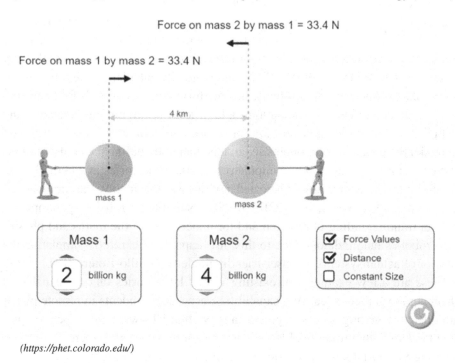

(https://phet.colorado.edu/)

Virtual labs are also being utilized in higher educational courses such as engineering. The Virtual CVD Learning Platform is developed by the Chemical Engineering Department of Oregon State University. This platform allows students to perform simulations for chemical vapor deposition (CVD), and provides students with the pinnacle of experience in incorporating the scientific and statistical principles in engineering (Koretsky et al., 2008). The reactor can be simulated based on the principles of mass transfer and chemical reaction. This platform contains features such as a 3D GUI, an instruction interface integrated with tools for assessment and a server database. The Virtual Electric Machine Laboratory developed at Firat University, Turkey was aimed at providing students with the opportunities to perform various experiments related to electrical machines. The platform was designed through HyperText Markup Language (HTML), Active Server Pages (ASP) and Borland C++ builder. Through this, the effect of the synchronous motor loading, supply voltage changes, or any changes made by the students with respect to the parameters can be observed by them. Virtual applications on the various motors can be observed by changes made to the parameters such as simulation time, sampling frequency and voltage, with the output being visualized graphically (Tanyildizi & Orhan, 2009). ROBOMOSP or Robotics Modeling and Simulation Platform is a virtual lab that was created by Robotics and Automation Group (GAR) of the Pontificia Javeriana University, Cali, Colombia. It exhibits a 3D multi-platform with Computer Aided Design (CAD) system. This platform has a novel characteristic in that, the environment for simulating the robot manipulators and other functions, is unique as compared to other robotic software present. The issue with multibody dynamics is tackled by ROBOMOSP by automatically calculating the robot multi-bodies' mass properties. Additionally, this platform consists of tools for analyzing the dynamic and kinematic simulations, a high-level programming language, and an application interface that is in-built for incorporation of added functions. Users can model the physical components separately, manually define the configurations for the kinematics of the robot manipulators, spatial trajectories in a both discrete and continuous manner, and sophisticated motion tasks that involve the components' interaction inside a workspace. ROBOMOSP is suitable for robotic operators currently in training, aiding in research and for understanding the maths and physics of the robotics manipulators. Due to this, it is capable of carefully simulating the behavior of actual systems in a user-friendly mode (Jaramillo-Botero et al., 2006).

These are a few examples of existing virtual laboratories that are capable of enhancing the student's learning capabilities, especially students in remote places with difficulty getting access to proper labs. Virtual labs were developed to operate in tandem with a traditional lab and not meant to be a replacement. Therefore, including virtual labs in the curriculum alongside traditional labs helps enhance the student's learning process.

Effectiveness of Virtual Laboratories

Virtual laboratories have no doubt been a boon to academia and even industries when it comes to teaching and simulation of experiments. However, in terms of the capability of the students to familiarize themselves with the experimental setup and the time taken to learn, can they compete with traditional laboratories? It is a crucial problem that is required to be analyzed when implementing online learning and virtual laboratories. Hence, a few examples of research addressing this issue have been done to compare the efficiency and performance of virtual laboratories against traditional hands-on laboratories.

Radhamani et al analyzed the potential of virtual labs in biotechnology using the virtual platform developed by Amrita Vishwa Vidhyapeetham University under the Ministry of Education, Government of India. The learning process targeted schools and other institutions for students within the age ranges of 12-15 years and 17-24 years. With the help of feedback reports from students for both online and hands-on labs, they found out that 90% of the students who utilized the virtual biotechnology labs were able to quickly familiarize themselves with the experiment and all the participants were able to score more than 70% in the post-tests (Radhamani et al 2015). Kapichi et al compared the effects of combining both virtual laboratories and traditional laboratories for 7th grade students in the learning process about circuits. They found that virtual laboratories are just as efficient when compared to traditional laboratories, but that incorporating both virtual and traditional laboratories would enhance the student's learning process even more as compared to only virtual or hands-on separately (Kapici et al., 2019). Elmoazen et al, on the other hand, proposed that research on the productiveness of virtual laboratories is still required as there is no standard protocol to assess the efficiency of virtual laboratories (Elmoazen et al., 2023). Mamata Pal conducted an experiment through pre-test and post-test procedures to study the students' enhanced learning process when using Physics Education Technology (PhET). It was found that virtual labs enabled active learning which was greatly effective in the students' learning process (Pal, 2024). Rustana et al in their research examined the impact of online learning through PhET platform on a sample of students from the Science and Mathematics Group, Students of Public High School, Jakarta. Pre and post-test results of the participants who were studying Harmonic Movement was determined to be 47.42 and 73.55 respectively with an N-gain of 0.51. Based on these results, they found that the online learning of harmonic motions to the level of mastering the concept had a significant impact when PhET simulation was utilized for the learning process. The analysis found that the students (Rustana et al., 2021). Banda & Nzabahimana also studied the effects of PhET simulations on the students who were learning about waves and oscillations in Malawi and how it impacted their academic performance. About 280 students were selected from four schools in the Blantyre district of Malawi and divided into two groups – one group was exposed to PhET learning and the control group only used conventional learning. After pre and post-tests were conducted, it was found that the group that was exposed to PhET simulations for learning had improved academic performance in oscillations and waves. They also displayed more positive behavior toward their academic and achievement goals and were more open to online learning (Banda & Nzabahimana, 2023). Nanto et al in their study evaluated the difference between the virtual lab LabXchange and the traditional lab with respect to practicals on the pendulum. However, they discovered that there was not much difference between LabXchange and the traditional lab (Nanto et al., 2022). Yassin studied a sample of 105 students from the Irhaba Secondary School for Boys, out of which 32 utilized the PhET learning platform, 41 students utilized the PraxiLabs virtual laboratory and the remaining 32 students were only on conventional learning. From the analysis, it was found that there is a noteworthy difference between students who used the PhET and PraxiLabs for learning and those exposed only to conventional learning. It was also found that the group that studied from PraxiLabs were slightly performing better than those using PhET. However, it can be concluded that students with PraxiLabs or PhET learning were performing better than those with conventional learning (Yassin, 2022).

From these examples, it can be said that virtual laboratories have their advantages as compared to traditional laboratories. Virtual labs are more cost-efficient, easy to access, save a lot of time, and are environmentally friendly (Ali & Ullah, 2020). Hence, the pros of virtual labs can be summarized as follows –

1. They are cost-efficient for schools and other educational institutions and enable for organization of quality laboratory work for the science, engineering and technology fields.
2. Virtual labs permit more flexibility in conducting experiments as the several components within an experimental setup can be easily generated.
3. The ability for multiple students to access a particular lab or equipment without the need to wait in a queue.
4. The option to change certain parameters that are usually not possible to be done in a physical laboratory. For instance, in a robotic simulation users may modify the robotic links, substitute motors, or other components of a robotic setup.
5. In another robotic simulation example, there could be damage to the physical parts of the robotic equipment due to falls or collisions with the surrounding objects. Overloading damage, that is, damage due to the issue with moving objects with weights more than the capacity of the robotic arm can cause damage to the motors, thus risking damage to the robotic equipment. However, in a virtual setting, such damage will not happen because instead, an error could be displayed and the entire simulation is reset again, with no cost in damage.
6. Usually, it can be unfeasible to open the cover of an equipment in a laboratory as it may cause contamination or may interfere with its functioning, thereby reducing the accuracy and precision of the results. Other times it could be that the covers are shut tightly which may cause damage if not opened correctly.

Thus, it is not easy to open up the equipment for observing its inner components. In a virtual lab, however, this problem is not an issue because the students can easily open the virtual components to view the virtual equipment's inner parts, without causing any problems with the functioning of the experiment. For example, equipment such as the biochemistry analyzer may be opened to see the inner components without affecting the equipment (Potkonjak et al., 2016).

A limitation of the virtual labs is that they do not provide a similar experience for group tasks and interaction between students (Lynch & Ghergulescu, 2017). Thus, the cons of virtual labs are as follows –

1. The challenging aspect of developing dynamic 3D models and CAD models of objects. This is because of the complexity of the integration of these models in the virtual environment.
2. The next limitation arises from the virtual laboratory's nature. As the environment and the objects within the environment are only virtual, this means that they are not real. Because of this, nothing bad will come out of it. This may induce an attitude of negligence in the student when it comes to safety regulations in a lab. It may also bring about a lack of responsibility and seriousness in the student.
3. The final drawback is that, although virtual labs easily help understand the experiment just as a traditional lab does, however, the expertise in actually handling the equipment and getting a feel of the apparatus physically will enable the students to be more prudent and efficient (Potkonjak et al., 2016).

Virtual labs, because of their easy access from any remote place, tend to create an isolated environment. This in turn could also negatively impact the critical thinking and analysis skills of a student that are usually gained through social interactions between students in hands-on lab sessions. Nevertheless, it cannot be determined which type of laboratory triumphs over the other, as each of them possesses its own merits and demerits. However, instead of deciding one over the other, as Kapici et al. have suggested, if virtual labs can be incorporated alongside traditional labs, then the students will benefit a lot from this as not only will they get hands-on experience with the experiments, but they can also fine-tune their skills by constant practice using the virtual labs.

Based on these discussions, it would seem that all educational institutions should follow this pattern. However, there is still a long road ahead to reaching this goal for academia due to certain barriers that hinder this process. According to Deriba et al, the four challenges are technology, infrastructure, pedagogical and culture. The complexity of the technical setup of these virtual labs may discourage some educators from continuing this type of approach, especially individuals who are not technically adept. Sometimes unreliable or flaws in the designs of the virtual objects become limitations in gauging the accurate and exact behavior of the scientific principles, which may dissuade participants from utilizing the virtual lab again. Other times, virtual labs may still face a challenge in being implemented into the curriculum simply because some institutions still prefer the conventional way of education (Deriba et al., 2023). Nevertheless, it was observed that these barriers were overcome in times of crisis like the COVID-19 pandemic which saw schools and educational institutions across the globe transition to online learning platforms to circumvent the obstacle imposed by the pandemic. Hence, the pandemic helped smoothen the way for the implementation of virtual laboratories through the introduction of online learning platforms such as Google Classrooms, Google Meet, Zoom, Microsoft Teams, etc. Therefore, there is much future scope for the adaptation of virtual labs into the academic curriculums.

CONCLUSION

Virtual Laboratories are a boon in the academic curriculum, especially with the exponential growth in technology. They have been largely deployed during the Covid-19 pandemic as an alternative response, but have found their footing even after the pandemic due to their various merits. Their easy accessibility, user-friendly interface, time-saving aspect and cost efficiency have, in a way, given them an edge over traditional hands-on laboratories. It was observed in some research articles how E-learning and virtual laboratories have paved the way for a new approach in academics. Though they hold a high preference in recent years, it cannot be entirely concluded that virtual laboratories triumph over traditional laboratories as they are unable to provide an environment to develop social and communication skills unlike traditional labs due to their online nature. However, if virtual labs and traditional labs are combined in academics, together they can further enhance the learning process of the students and even the teachers.

REFERENCES

Ali, N., & Ullah, S. (2020). Review to analyze and compare virtual chemistry laboratories for their use in education. *Journal of Chemical Education*, 97(10), 3563–3574. 10.1021/acs.jchemed.0c00185

Aljuhani, K., Sonbul, M., Althabiti, M., & Meccawy, M. (2018). Creating a virtual science lab (VSL): The adoption of virtual labs in Saudi schools. *Smart Learn Environ*, 5(1), 16. 10.1186/s40561-018-0067-9

Banda, H. J., & Nzabahimana, J. (2023). The impact of physics education technology (PhET) interactive simulation-based learning on motivation and academic achievement among malawian physics students. *Journal of Science Education and Technology*, 32(1), 127–141. 10.1007/s10956-022-10010-336569225

Biasutti, M. (2017). A comparative analysis of forums and wikis as tools for online collaborative learning. *Computers & Education*, 111, 158–171. 10.1016/j.compedu.2017.04.006

Birkeland, H., Khalil, M., & Wasson, B. (2022). *Learning analytics in collaborative online lab environments: A systematic scoping review.*

Butnaru, G. I., Ni ă, V., Anichiti, A., & Brînză, G. (2021). The effectiveness of online education during covid 19 pandemic–a comparative analysis between the perceptions of academic students and high school students from romania. *Sustainability (Basel)*, 13(9), 5311. 10.3390/su13095311

Dalgarno, B., Bishop, A., & Bedgood, D. (2003). The potential of virtual laboratories for distance education science teaching: reflections from the initial development and evaluation of a virtual chemistry laboratory. In *Improving Learning Outcomes Through Flexible Science Teaching Symposium* (pp. 90-95). Uniserve Science, University of Sydney.

Deriba, F., Saqr, M., & Tukiainen, M. (2023). Exploring Barriers and Challenges to Accessibility in Virtual Laboratories: A Preliminary Review. In *Proceedings of the Technology-Enhanced Learning in Laboratories CEUR workshop (TELL 2023)*, (Vol. 27). IEEE.

Dyrberg, N. R., Treusch, A. H., & Wiegand, C. (2017). Virtual laboratories in science education: Students' motivation and experiences in two tertiary biology courses. *Journal of Biological Education*, 51(4), 358–374. 10.1080/00219266.2016.1257498

Dziabenko, O., & Budnyk, O. (2019). Go-Lab ecosystem: Using online laboratories in a primary school. In *EDULEARN19 Proceedings* (pp. 9276-9285). IATED.

Elmoazen, R., Saqr, M., Khalil, M., & Wasson, B. (2023). Learning analytics in virtual laboratories: A systematic literature review of empirical research. *Smart Learning Environments*, 10(1), 23. 10.1186/s40561-023-00244-y

Favale, T., Soro, F., Trevisan, M., Drago, I., & Mellia, M. (2020). Campus traffic and e-Learning during COVID-19 pandemic. *Computer Networks*, 176, 107290. 10.1016/j.comnet.2020.10729038620622

Gonzalez, T., De la Rubia, M. A., Hincz, K. P., Comas-Lopez, M., Subirats, L., Fort, S., & Sacha, G. M. (2020). Influence of COVID-19 confinement on students' performance in higher education. *PLoS One*, 15(10), e0239490. 10.1371/journal.pone.023949033035228

Jaramillo-Botero, A., Matta-Gomez, A., Correa-Caicedo, J. F., & Perea-Castro, W. (2006). Robomosp. *IEEE Robotics & Automation Magazine*, 13(4), 62–73. 10.1109/MRA.2006.250572

Juergensmeyer, M., & Adetunji, S. A. (2022). Safety in Chemical and Biomedical Laboratories: Guidelines for the Use of Head Covers by Female Muslim Scientists. *Applied Biosafety : Journal of the American Biological Safety Association*, 27(1), 1–6. 10.1089/apb.2021.001536032321

Kapici, H. O., Akcay, H., & de Jong, T. (2019). Using hands-on and virtual laboratories alone or together–which works better for acquiring knowledge and skills? *Journal of Science Education and Technology*, 28(3), 231–250. 10.1007/s10956-018-9762-0

Koretsky, M. D., Amatore, D., Barnes, C., & Kimura, S. (2008). Enhancement of student learning in experimental design using a virtual laboratory. *IEEE Transactions on Education*, 51(1), 76–85. 10.1109/TE.2007.906894

Kummitha, H. R., Kolloju, N., Chittoor, P., & Madepalli, V. (2021). Coronavirus disease 2019 and its effect on teaching and learning process in the higher educational institutions. *Higher Education for the Future*, 8(1), 90–107. 10.1177/2347631120983650

López-Pernas, S., Munoz-Arcentales, A., Aparicio, C., Barra, E., Gordillo, A., Salvachúa, J., & Quemada, J. (2022). Educational Data Virtual Lab: Connecting the Dots Between Data Visualization and Analysis. *IEEE Computer Graphics and Applications*, 42(5), 76–83. 10.1109/MCG.2022.318955736194698

Lynch, T., & Ghergulescu, I. (2017). Review of virtual labs as the emerging technologies for teaching STEM subjects. *INTED2017 proceedings*, 6082-6091.

Molins-Ruano, P., Sevilla, C., Santini, S., Haya, P. A., Rodríguez, P., & Sacha, G. M. (2014). Designing videogames to improve students' motivation. *Computers in Human Behavior*, 31, 571–579. 10.1016/j.chb.2013.06.013

Nanto, D., Agustina, R. D., Ramadhanti, I., Putra, R. P., & Mulhayatiah, D. (2022). The usefulness of LabXChange virtual lab and PhyPhox real lab on pendulum student practicum during pandemic. []. IOP Publishing.]. *Journal of Physics: Conference Series*, 2157(1), 012047. 10.1088/1742-6596/2157/1/012047

Ocaña, M., Khosravi, H., & Bakharia, A. (2019). *Profiling language learners in the big data era*. ASCILITE Publications.

Olewski, T., & Snakard, M. (2017). Challenges in applying process safety management at university laboratories. *Journal of Loss Prevention in the Process Industries*, 49, 209–214. 10.1016/j.jlp.2017.06.013

Pal, M. (2024). Effect of Virtual Lab-Enabled Active Learning Method on Academic Achievement of Secondary Stage Students in Physics. *Educational Administration: Theory and Practice*, 30(2), 709–717.

Potkonjak, V., Gardner, M., Callaghan, V., Mattila, P., Guetl, C., Petrović, V. M., & Jovanović, K. (2016). Virtual laboratories for education in science, technology, and engineering: A review. *Computers & Education*, 95, 309–327. 10.1016/j. compedu.2016.02.002

Radhamani, R., Sasidharakurup, H., Kumar, D., Nizar, N., Achuthan, K., Nair, B., & Diwakar, S. (2015, November). Role of Biotechnology simulation and remotely triggered virtual labs in complementing university education. In *2015 International Conference on Interactive Mobile Communication Technologies and Learning (IMCL)* (pp. 28-32). IEEE. 10.1109/IMCTL.2015.7359548

Rajhans, V., Memon, U., Patil, V., & Goyal, A. (2020). Impact of COVID-19 on academic activities and way forward in Indian Optometry. *Journal of Optometry*, 13(4), 216–226. 10.1016/j.optom.2020.06.00232703749

Reece, A. (2015). *An Investigation of the Impacts of Face-to-Face and Virtual Laboratories in an Introductory Biology Course on Students' Motivation to Learn Biology*.

Richard, E., Tijou, A., Richard, P., & Ferrier, J. L. (2006). Multi-modal virtual environments for education with haptic and olfactory feedback. *Virtual Reality (Waltham Cross)*, 10(3-4), 207–225. 10.1007/s10055-006-0040-8

Richter, T., Boehringer, D., & Jeschke, S. (2011). Lila: A european project on networked experiments. In *Automation, Communication and Cybernetics in Science and Engineering 2009/2010* (pp. 307-317). Springer Berlin Heidelberg. 10.1007/978-3-642-16208-4_27

Rustana, C. E., Khalifah, S. N., & Sugihartono, I. (2021). The effect of the use of harmonic movement phet interactive simulation in online learning process on mastering the concept of high school students. *Journal of Physics: Conference Series*, 2019(1), 012022. 10.1088/1742-6596/2019/1/012022

Serrano-Perez, J. J., González-García, L., Flacco, N., Taberner-Cortés, A., García-Arnandis, I., Pérez-López, G., Pellín-Carcelén, A., & Romá-Mateo, C. (2023). Traditional vs. virtual laboratories in health sciences education. *Journal of Biological Education*, 57(1), 36–50. 10.1080/00219266.2021.1877776

Tanyildizi, E., & Orhan, A. (2009). A virtual electric machine laboratory for synchronous machine application. *Computer Applications in Engineering Education*, 17(2), 187–195. 10.1002/cae.20133

Udin, W. N., Ramli, M., & Muzzazinah, . (2020, April). Virtual laboratory for enhancing students' understanding on abstract biology concepts and laboratory skills: A systematic review. []. IOP Publishing.]. *Journal of Physics: Conference Series*, 1521(4), 042025. 10.1088/1742-6596/1521/4/042025

Van den Beemt, A., Groothuijsen, S., Ozkan, L., & Hendrix, W. (2023). Remote labs in higher engineering education: Engaging students with active learning pedagogy. *Journal of Computing in Higher Education*, 35(2), 320–340. 10.1007/s12528-022-09331-435974997

Yassin, A. A. B. (2022). The Effect of Using Interactive Simulation (Phet) and Virtual Laboratories (Praxilabs) on Tenth-Grade Students' Achievement in Physics. *Britain International of Linguistics Arts and Education (BIoLAE). Journal*, 4(2), 58–72.

Chapter 16
The Intervention of New Technology in Traditional Teaching–Learning Process Through Blended Learning Systematic Literature Review

Ravi Kant Modi
https://orcid.org/0009-0005-3951-2534
Nirwan University, Jaipur, India

Aarti Chopra
https://orcid.org/0000-0002-9068-0155
Poornima University, Jaipur, India

ABSTRACT

An instructional strategy called blended learning mixes virtual or digital components with in-person instruction. The use of computers and other connected devices in the classroom helps students get ready for success in the real world because they are essential for modern business and communication. In blended learning settings, students not only become proficient in the subject matter they are studying, but they also develop advanced technological skills. In the classroom, blended learning has its uses and benefits. This method provides a solid foundation for tying theory and practice together during the teaching process. The methodical blending of online and in-person instruction is known as blended or hybrid learning. The intentional blending of online and in-person components is essential in a blended learning

DOI: 10.4018/979-8-3693-2272-7.ch016

environment. This research study identifies the variables influencing blended learning by conducting an extensive literature review. The literature review aids in the provision of a theoretical framework for this investigation.

INTRODUCTION

Blended learning combines traditional face-to-face classroom instruction with e-learning experiences. This style of learning is becoming more and more well-liked in numerous globally recognised colleges as a means of raising exam passing rates, enhancing time flexibility, and lowering barriers related to distance. Blended learning is more beneficial because of the multi-delivery strategy to maximise learning outcomes and reduce content delivery costs. The transitional phase between receiving teaching in-person in the classroom and receiving the entire curriculum online is known as blended learning. An instructional strategy called blended learning mixes virtual or digital components with in-person instruction (Tayebinik & Puteh, 2013; Hrastinski, 2019).

The use of computers and other connected devices in the classroom helps students get ready for success in the real world because they are essential for modern business and communication. In blended learning settings, students not only become proficient in the subject matter they are studying, but they also develop advanced technological skills. In-person training from teachers is essential to the blended learning approach. Just as important to a student's development as visual and kinesthetic skills are listening comprehension. While there is some degree of student control over the time, location, path, and pace of their education with blended learning, in-person teacher and student presence is still required. In order to improve both content and delivery techniques, computer-mediated activities are combined with in-person instruction even while teachers are still present in traditional classroom settings. (Moskal, et al., 2013).

When it comes to teaching clinical skills and medical education, blended learning has its uses and benefits. This method provides a solid foundation for tying theory and practice together during the learning process. The methodical blending of online and in-person instruction is known as blended or hybrid learning. The intentional blending of online and in-person components is essential in a blended learning environment. Blending tools, techniques, and technologies with the intention of achieving educational goals is known as purposeful blending. Some academics distinguish blended learning environments based on delivery medium, teaching location, teaching kind, and synchronisation factors (Moskal, et al., 2013). The delivery medium specifies if a teacher or technology is delivering the instruction. The teaching location indicates whether instruction is provided online or in a classroom. Furthermore, there is consensus that blended learning is a hybrid of in-person and online learning approaches that depend on technology-mediated instruction and occasionally divide all participants due to distance, according to a 2015 meta-analysis that reviewed a thorough examination of evidence-based research studies on the subject (Gecer & Dag, 2012).

A teaching strategy known as blended learning allows some students to participate online from home while others physically attend courses. Many colleges began implementing remote and hybrid learning strategies after the outbreak. Since its initial appearance, the coronavirus disease 2019 (Covid-19) pandemic has spread quickly to become a genuinely worldwide occurrence. There is concern that additional semesters may be lost in the near future as a number of universities across the globe are impacted. Universities were forced by the threat to make difficult choices about how to continue offering education while safeguarding their staff, students, and society from this public health disaster. Online learning has exploded in popularity as a result of several universities closing their traditional campuses (Bordoloi, et al., 2021). Online education is therefore a means of halting the spread of contagious viruses like Covid-19. The use of modern information and communication technologies (ICT) and digital learning tools may be encouraged by this pandemic. In this regard, the Covid-19 epidemic forces the pedagogy profession to reconsider teaching by putting the known into practice and exploring untapped educational possibilities (Kumar, et al., 2021). According to studies, implementing blended learning in the classroom can have a favourable impact. It is imperative to underscore the significance of meticulous preparation and deliberate deliberation regarding the most effective pedagogical approaches (Dey & Bandyopadhyay, 2019).

Since technology is always changing and affecting every part of our life, it is important to learn about and educate ourselves on these new technologies. It's critical to keep in mind that "evolving" means advancing to the next stage without completely destroying the previous one, or utilising the best aspects of both worlds—the benefits of the new and the advantages of the old. We refer to this in the context of education as blended learning. The best components of traditional face-to-face learning are combined with eLearning in blended learning to meet the evolving needs of modern learners. Education can now take place outside of the classroom by utilising both online and offline resources thanks to blended learning (Kundu, et al., 2021). Students with different learning styles, such as those who study best in a typical classroom setting or those who benefit from computer-based, semi-autonomous training, will find learning more engaging as a result. You can get the finest results from both offline and online training methods when you combine them. Comparing blended learning to a single-method approach reveals how versatile and adaptive it is. All learners are catered to, regardless of their preference for in-person instruction, virtual learning, or a combination of the two. Through the use of cutting-edge technology and the advantages of traditional classroom instruction, blended learning makes learning more engaging, contextual, and real-time. Professional development training and general classroom offerings for various educational programmes across disciplines in global communities are clear examples of blended learning. A growing number of professional development training organisations, departments, and units at universities and colleges are using blended learning as an additional educational instrument to be used in the delivery of instructional and managerial services due to money and time restrictions. In both traditional higher education institutions and other organisations, blended learning is a rapidly expanding trend (Hilliard, 2015; Graham, 2018). According to an online learning survey, blended learning is growing at a rate of at least 46% annually on a global scale. Upon gaining comfort with blended learning applications, instructional faculty members and organisational facilitators at universities and colleges are typically highly motivated to investigate new and improved methods of utilising blended learning for managerial training activities or instructional services.

BACKGROUND

The world is always changing, and these changes have an impact on all the different domains. Not even in the field of education is there an exception. The advancement of digital learning platforms has had a significant impact on educational establishments, ultimately pushing traditional approaches to the back burner. Both conventional learning methods and technology are still in demand, though. Due to this, the term "Blended Learning" refers to the skill of fusing digital learning resources with face-to-face instruction in a regular classroom (Dangwal, 2017). BL refers to a carefully thought-out fusion of worthwhile activities in both face-to-face and online forms. It is not just a combination of the two. A number of aspects must be taken into account when implementing the mix, with a primary emphasis on learning outcomes and the learner-centred instructional environment. Studies suggests using blended learning models in light of the rise of digital technologies and the growing significance of using technology for teaching and learning at all levels, from elementary school to higher education (). The value of in-person, face-to-face instruction is acknowledged, even as digital learning and education are encouraged. As a result, several successful blended learning models will be found and appropriately replicated for various subject areas (Virani, et al., 2023).

Blended learning is difficult to conceptualise generically because it is largely context dependent. Some authors claim that the difficulty in defining blended learning precisely has hindered efforts to assess its effectiveness. According to Hrastinski (2019), blended learning is commonly defined as combining online and in-person training, with the online component acting as a productive substitute for in-person contact time rather than as an addition to it. Students' performance as well as their social and cognitive presence are enhanced by blended learning strategies. Nonetheless, there is a moderate degree of student satisfaction. It has also been noted that tactics and elements that could raise student satisfaction levels need to be identified (Kumar et al. 2021). The strategies that were put into place were able to meet the demands of the COVID-19 pandemic, enhance student engagement and performance, and identify procedures, techniques, and resources for adopting distant learning in the event of future emergencies, pandemics, and other circumstances (Demillo 2019).

For students, especially adults, having the ability to organise and oversee a customised learning path is essential. Knowledge acquisition is not the only, or even the most important, task that employees and students perform. People's lives are multifaceted, consisting of several aspects such as employment, hobbies, family, and friends. Learning shouldn't get in the way of these things. Theoretical content can be difficult, if not dull. It is one thing for students to sit through numerous hours of lectures (Kaur, 2013). The experience is drastically altered when people study the same material through button-clicking, game-like courses, dialogue simulations, and other methods. Acquiring new knowledge may be pleasurable, and blended learning provides several resources to facilitate this. Blended learning necessitates a particular level of digital competency because it involves professors developing online courses, assigning them to students, monitoring their progress, and much more. Some eLearning platforms have a steep learning curve, and not all teachers have the time or willingness to learn a new piece of equipment (Picciano, et al., 2013).

Since technology is always evolving and influencing every aspect of our lives, it is critical that we educate ourselves on these new developments. It's critical to keep in mind that "evolving" means either using the finest aspects of both worlds—the advantages of the new and the benefits of the old—or moving on to the next phase without completely eliminating the previous one. We refer to this in the educational environment as blended learning.

Blended learning has gained popularity in recent years, and learning experts have hailed its benefits (Ranjan, 2020). Through the use of cutting-edge technology and conventional classroom education, blended learning improves engagement among learners, contextualization, and real-time learning.

Since the Covid-19 epidemic, there has been a discernible rise in interest in blended learning. This has spurred a number of studies in this area of research. Because of this, this systematic study will help identify the domains in which research has been conducted as well as the numerous facets of blended learning.

MATERIALS AND METHODS

Sources

The most recent literature was thoroughly examined utilising predetermined standards and guidelines. Huge databases were searched for pertinent research publications in order to do this. Since practically all of the publications discovered in the Web of Science databases could also be located in the Scopus database, the SCOPUS database served as the review's primary data source (Meho & Sugimoto, 2009). The following terms and their combinations were entered into the search:

Search String Set 1 – ("Blended Learning" OR "Blended Learning Design") AND ("Blended Learning" OR "Blended Learning Strategy")

Search String Set 2 – ("Blended Learning") AND ("Technological Intervention")

Using the previously indicated keywords, the next step is to create search results. The method for choosing those results is covered in more detail in the section that follows.

Data Extraction and Synthesis

Following a stringent process for selecting articles for final evaluation is one of the most crucial prerequisites for completing a systematic literature review. The articles are initially evaluated according to the degree of relevance in the title. After the title makes a relationship to the subject, the abstract is carefully reviewed to determine whether the piece satisfies the standards. The final articles are chosen once the abstracts have been reviewed and evaluated. The factors that were discovered after the researches were properly evaluated are shown in a table for easy access.

A flow chart depicting the entire process is mentioned in the PRISMA created below:

Figure 1. PRISMA

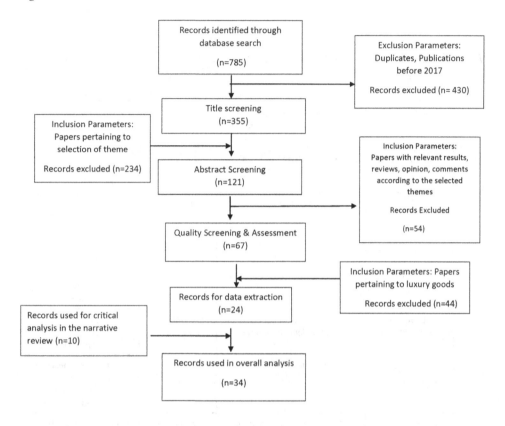

Quality Parameters and Mitigation of Threats to Validity

Dyba and Dingsoyr (2008) developed a series of questions to ensure the quality of publications included in systematic reviews. These questions are based on three main criteria: credibility, rigour, and relevancy. The nominated articles are assigned a score of either 1 or 0, depending on how closely they meet each of the three quality standards. Review content is considered to be of extraordinary quality if it scores four or higher. To help you understand the process, the appendix has a table with the appropriate scores. Prior to performing a review, the construct and external validity components must be investigated. Making use of the checklist for quality assurance parameters (Dyba & Dingsoyr, 2008), discrepancies or risks arising from article validity concerns are addressed. Second, the best method to reduce authenticity concerns is to finally arrive at the articles using the PRISMA methodology.

RESULTS AND DISCUSSION

Table 1. Summary of the literature review

Sl. No.	Authors	Objective	Research Methodology	Factors
1.	Aji, et al., (2020)	To analyse the perceptions of students and teachers on blended learning.	Quantitative	Blended learning, perception, learning experience
2.	Anthonysamy, et al., (2020)	To analyse the use of blended learning in higher education.	Qualitative	Self-regulated learning, learning strategies, blended learning
3.	Apandi & Raman, (2020)	To identify the factors influencing in the implementation of blended learning.	Qualitative	Behavioural intention, actual usage, blended learning
4.	Azizi, et al., (2020)	To analyse the factors influencing the blended learning in medical education.	Quantitative	Blended Learning, UTAUT2, social influence, price value, habit
5.	Bouilheres, et al., (2020)	To analyse student experiences through blended learning.	Quantitative	Blended learning, engagement, online experience, flexibity
6.	Jin, et al., (2020)	To explore the blended learning design.	Qualitative	Augmentative learning, Student perception, perceived benefits, perceived challenges
7.	Kaliisa, et al., (2020)	To identify the potential of Learning Analytics to inform Learning Design based on a blended learning course.	Qualitative	Learning Analytics, Learning Decision
8.	Resien, et al., (2020)	To determine the effect of blended learning strategy and creative thinking of students.	Quantitative	Blended learning, creative thinking,
9.	Vallee, et al., (2020)	To compare traditional learning and blended learning.	Quantitative	Blended learning, online learning, traditional learning
10.	Venkatesh, et al., (2020)	To evaluate the experiences of students on blended learning.	Quantitative	Blended learning, learner satisfaction, performance expectations, learning climate
11.	Huang, (2021)	To explore the factors influencing learning satisfaction in blended learning.	Quantitative	Blended learning, perceived usefulness, learning satisfaction, learning motivation

continued on following page

Table 1. Continued

Sl. No.	Authors	Objective	Research Methodology	Factors
12.	Bruggeman, et al., (2021)	To implement blended learning in higher education	Qualitative	Blended learning, teaching attributes, teaching change
13.	Kumar, et al., (2021)	To identify blended learning tools and practices	Qualitative	Blended learning, active learning, learning tools
14.	Lockee, (2021)	To evaluate the teaching performance for online and blended learning.	Qualitative	Online learning, blended learning, performance
15.	Musdalifah, et al., (2021)	To develop a community based approach on the use of blended learning.	Qualitative	Learning styles, learning, teaching, blended learning
16.	Rasheed, et al., (2021)	To develop an approach for scaffolding students peer-learning self-regulation strategy in the online component of blended learning.	Qualitative	Learning potential, blended learning, norm setting
17.	Antwi-Boampong & Bokolo, (2022)	To analyse the adoption of blended learning in institution.	Quantitative	Institutional adoption, blended learning, learning assistance
18.	Megahed & Hassan, (2022)	To develop blended learning strategy.	Qualitative	Online learning, technology, blended learning
19.	Li & Phongsatha, (2022)	To identify the factors affecting student's satisfaction and intention of blended learning.	Quantitative	Self-efficacy, information quality, continuance intention
20.	Topping, et al., (2022)	To analyse the effectiveness of online and blended learning.	Qualitative	Blended learning, effectiveness, self-efficacy
21.	Widjaja & Aslan, (2022)	To evaluate blended learning method in higher education	Qualitative	Blended learning, transformation learning, conventional learning
22.	Zhang et al., (2022)	To identify key factors affecting students in blended learning environment.	Quantitative	System quality, social influence, behavioural intention, information quality, blended learning
23.	Makovec Radovan & Radovan, (2023)	To analyse the integration of blended learning.	Quantitative	Teaching approaches, perceived workload, student learning, student motivation
24.	Ritz, et al., (2023)	To analyse the intervention of blended learning for self-regulated learning	Quantitative	Self-assessment, learning outcome, blended learning

A lot of emphasis has been paid to blended learning as a means of raising the standard of instruction at institutions. It's stated that nearly all courses at universities can now be classified as "blended." Blended learning is expected to become the "new normal" in higher education, according to researchers. "Enhanced, student-centered learning experiences made possible by the harmonious integration of various strategies, achieved by combining face-to-face interaction with ICT" is how Torrisi-Steele, (2011) characterised blended learning. Blended learning is becoming more and more popular since it offers new ways to maximise students' learning. Through structured teaching and learning activities, less congested classrooms, and flexible online information and communication technology, blended learning integrates online learning experiences and supports students in learning meaningfully (Goyal, 2015).

Research indicates that incorporating blended learning into instruction can raise student achievement. This is why it is thought that the adoption of blended learning will make all the difference in how well the technology is implemented. The incorporation of technology into educational establishments is revolutionising the field of education and promoting inventive methods of instruction. Around the world, scholars and researchers at Higher Education Institutions (HEIs) have come to use the term Blended Learning (BL). Universities have been able to switch from providing only face-to-face instruction to becoming BL institutions for more than thirty years thanks to the benefits of BL (Suprabha & Subramonian, 2015). The purpose of this study's research is to gain an understanding of the effects of student involvement and experiences that are provided through the university's Blended Learning model. In blended learning (BL), in-person and virtual delivery techniques are combined in the best possible ways to create flexible, effective, and efficient learning environments that raise student achievement levels. BL is renowned for being the "new normal" that will replace the face-to-face, conventional delivery method that colleges already employ (Johry, et al., 2019). According to research studies, an institution's decision to accept or reject blended learning is impacted by how much it wants to adopt blended learning and how much it intends to adopt blended learning.

An increasingly common strategy is blended learning, which combines technology and conventional teaching methods. With blended learning, technology may be fully integrated into the educational process while circumventing the drawbacks of being used only as a tool. varying teaching strategies produced varying results in terms of learning objectives (Aisha & Ratra, 2023), motivation, and workload for the students. It was discovered that pupils had varying degrees of difficulty when exposed to various instructional styles. Greater problems were offered, for instance, by live sessions and the integration of virtual reality/augmented reality (VR/AR) technologies. On the other hand, online courses that emphasise professional skill development and cooperative group work were discovered to be advantageous (Knoblauch, et al., 2021).

The process of debating and defending points in writing is known as argumentative writing. The introduction of blended learning design into argumentative writing teaching coincided with the emergence of the Web 2.0 era. Students might not be open to refuting the opinions of others, though. Furthermore, the lack of exposure that students have to digital technologies and lengthy argumentative writing may have a detrimental effect on their learning outcomes. The findings of these empirical investigations suggest that further investigation is warranted about the successful amalgamation of conventional offline learning methodologies and online technology in the teaching of argumentative writing. The relationship between learning design (LD) and learning analytics (LA) has drawn attention from practitioners and scholars in educational technology. Teachers typically base their pedagogical decisions on summative assessments, course evaluations, and personal experience (Lakhl & Meyer, 2020). However, LA may be able to provide teachers with timely feedback about student learning, which may help them make more informed decisions and improve student performance in educational programmes. This has been partly caused by higher education providers' increasing demands that teachers apply evidence-based approaches and provide better quality and customised learning experiences to their students. Therefore, it is crucial for researchers in educational technology to investigate how LA and LD might be combined to help teachers make timely and well-informed decisions about teaching and learning. But even with all of the advancements and interest in tying these two fields of study together, there is still a lot to learn about how LA might help LD (Kharb & Samanta, 2016).

Despite the fact that students utilise digital devices for nearly everything, recent research indicates that kids struggle with digital learning because they lack the self-regulation skills necessary for high performance. Students are assisted in learning effectively through the application of self-regulated learning techniques (SRLS). Little is known about the use of SRLS towards non-academic outcomes, which are as crucial to support university students' learning development, despite the fact that numerous academics have examined SRLS towards academic outcomes like grades. Therefore, it's important to comprehend how to use SRLS to improve non-academic results in digital learning in a blended learning setting. Higher education is adopting blended learning at an increasing rate due to the rapid growth of information technology (Shrivastava & Shrivastava, 2022).

Students have possibilities for timely, continuous, and flexible learning through blended learning, which blends e-learning and in-person instruction. It improves the e-learning activities' interaction, aids in students' information acquisition, and supports their independent and group learning. On the one hand, enhanced student learning and lower teaching costs are directly related to the successful design and execution of blended learning (Badre, 2020). Nonetheless, there are still certain issues with the application of blended learning. When e-learning is not required for students, it is a common grievance among university teachers that many, if not most, of their students do not actively participate in the blended learning component.

Even in cases when it is required, students' participation in online courses and the calibre of their online education fall short of expectations, even in cases of well-designed blended learning courses. Online deep interactions are uncommon, and students' excitement for using the e-learning platform for distance learning is low. The poor motivation of blended learning participants will make it difficult to address students' needs and accomplish educational goals, despite research showing that real use of the virtual learning environment improves student performance (Naik & Agarwal, 2021).

A blended learning approach combines traditional classroom instruction with online learning activities offered by teachers. Unlike fully integrated eLearning, the online portion of the training complements in-person teacher instruction by having teachers use technology to help students learn more effectively and broaden their subject-matter expertise. The method of combining online and in-person training is known as blended learning. As a result, following a lecture in class, students can instantly complete an online exam from home or another location. The purpose of this study is to determine the variables influencing blended learning. With the aid of the literature review, a few themes were found.

The themes that were discovered, are shown in table 2. These topics are focus of this work.

Table 2. Identified key themes ad categories

Key Themes	Categories
Blended Learning design	Design
Blended learning as a strategy	Strategy
Learners factors influencing Blended Learning	Factors
Institutional factors influencing Blended Learning	
Teachers' factors influencing Blended Learning	
Technological intervention in blended learning	
Evaluation	Evaluation
Implementation	
Benefits and barriers	
Comparative Study	Methodology
Case Study	

continued on following page

Table 2. Continued

Key Themes	Categories
Literature Review	Review
Overall Introduction	

CONCEPTUAL MODEL

The literature review conducted in this study was used to form a conceptual model. The factors influencing successful blended learning were identified through the literature study and it was observed that the factors – institutional factors, technological intervention, learners factors and teachers' factors influence the implementation of successful blended learning.

The roles that academic institutions play in developing proactive technology policies and legal frameworks, purchasing new equipment, scheduling frequent faculty and student training, establishing novel avenues for faculty professional growth, recruiting teaching assistants, and handling all other course-related logistics are referred to as institutional factors. The leadership of universities must have the right perspectives on technology and its application to education, research, and learning. The capabilities of technologies and unrestricted access to them are referred to as technological factors. The perceived qualities and the media synchronicity theory's concepts of feedback immediacy, symbol variety, parallelism, and rehearsability are reflected in these elements. The functions that technologies play in teaching, learning, and knowledge creation are also considered technological elements, even though these functions are not adequately explained by current frameworks. Each of the components associated with teaching practice are referred to as teachers' factors, including pedagogy, feedback, supervision, course design, and real teaching. Success is influenced in part by the beliefs of the faculty about education, learning, knowledge creation, and technology; it is also influenced by their prior technological experiences, level of proficiency, and workload. Successful blended learning is also influenced by students' perceptions of teaching, learning, knowledge construction, and technology; it is also influenced by their prior technological experiences, technological proficiency, needs, and expectations from the courses.

Thus, all these stakeholders (as mentioned in the conceptual model) play a crucial role in the success of blended learning. Learners must be proactive and adaptable, engaging with both digital and face-to-face components. Teachers need to be skilled in both traditional and digital pedagogies, providing support and motivation. Institutional support is essential for providing the necessary infrastructure, resources, and training. Technological intervention ensures access to reliable and user-friendly platforms that facilitate seamless integration of online and offline activities. Collaboration among these stakeholders creates a supportive ecosystem, fostering effective blended learning experiences that are responsive to diverse needs and contexts.

Figure 2. Conceptual model

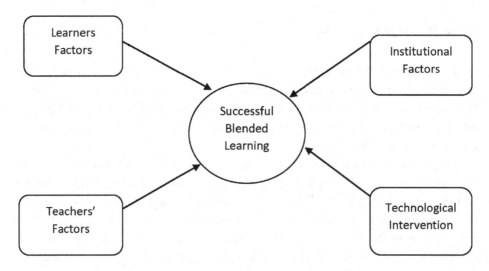

It is essential to take into account the preferences, skills, and learning styles of the learners. While some students may benefit from in-person instruction, others might prefer self-paced, online learning. Comprehending the reasons behind and objectives of students taking part in blended learning can influence their involvement and achievement. Learners who are driven are more likely to engage in the process of learning and persist with it. By evaluating students' past knowledge and abilities, teachers can adjust their lessons to fit each student's needs and provide the right kind of learning scaffold.

To support blended learning, educational institutions must have a sufficient technology infrastructure, including learning management systems (LMS), dependable internet connectivity, and technical support. For consistency and quality control, clear regulations and procedures governing the use of blended learning—including requirements for course design, methods of evaluation, and student support services—are crucial. Providing teachers with training and assistance on blended learning pedagogy, technology, and instructional tactics boosts their competency and self-assurance when teaching hybrid courses. Educators need to possess a strong grasp of instructional tactics and pedagogical ideas that complement mixed learning environments. This covers methods for active learning, procedures for assessments, and efficient use of technology. In both in-person and virtual environments, teachers are essential in helping students engage and communicate with one another. Establishing a collaborative environment, fostering conversations, and giving prompt feedback are all crucial components of a supportive learning community. In blended learning contexts, educators must be flexible and sensitive to the varied requirements and interests of their students. To accommodate varying learning styles and paces, instructional delivery, content presentation, and evaluation methods must be flexible.

Blended learning courses are better organised and managed when LMS systems are used to track student progress, promote communication, and provide course materials. Multimedia resources like interactive simulations, movies, and multimedia presentations can be incorporated to enhance the learning process and accommodate different learning styles. Using online collaboration tools like wikis, discussion boards, and virtual classrooms encourages student participation, peer communication, and cooperative learning.

The factor identified and the association of the factors are shown in figure 1. These relationships are needed to be tested empirically to further, confirm the conceptual model. According to this conceptual model, these factors must interact and line up for blended learning to be implemented successfully. Through the consideration of several aspects such as learners, teachers, institutions, and technology interventions, educators can create and implement blended learning programmes that maximise student engagement, enhance learning outcomes, and promote overall student happiness. Table 3 encapsulates the essential best practices for implementing blended learning effectively, ensuring a balanced and enriching educational experience.

Table 3. Best practices for blended learning

Category	Best Practice
Course Design	Integrate face-to-face and online activities seamlessly.
	Define clear objectives and outcomes for both online and offline components.
	Use diverse multimedia resources to cater to different learning styles.
Content Delivery	Provide pre-recorded lectures or tutorials for self-paced learning.
	Use interactive elements such as quizzes, discussions, and simulations.
	Ensure content is accessible on various devices (desktop, mobile, tablet).
Engagement	Facilitate regular interaction between students and instructors.
	Encourage collaborative projects and peer-to-peer learning.
	Use discussion forums and social media for continuous engagement.

continued on following page

Table 3. Continued

Category	Best Practice
Assessment	Implement formative assessments to monitor ongoing progress.
	Use a mix of assessments: quizzes, projects, peer reviews, and participation.
	Provide timely and constructive feedback.
Technology	Choose a reliable Learning Management System (LMS) that supports both online and offline modes.
	Ensure all students have access to necessary technology and internet connectivity.
	Provide training for both students and instructors on using digital tools effectively.
Support	Offer technical support and resources for troubleshooting.
	Provide academic support such as tutoring and mentoring.
	Establish clear communication channels for queries and support.
Flexibility	Allow flexible scheduling to accommodate diverse student needs.
	Adapt teaching methods based on student feedback and performance data.
	Consider asynchronous options to cater to different time zones and personal commitments.
Evaluation	Continuously evaluate and refine the blended learning strategy.
	Gather feedback from students on their learning experiences.
	Analyze data to identify areas for improvement and to measure the effectiveness of the approach.

CONCLUSION

One strategy that shows great potential for use in vocational and technical education is blended learning (BL). Just as BL demands a fundamental shift in viewpoint towards students, who must be positioned at the centre of educational planning in connection with the desired learning objectives, similar to how it is implemented at many other educational levels. The specifics of the classroom, as well as the students' individual interests and past knowledge, should all be taken into account when choosing a teaching strategy.

Blended learning is an instructional technique that combines digital or virtual components with in-person instruction. Since computers and other linked devices are necessary for modern business and communication, using them in the classroom helps students prepare for success in the real world. Students in mixed learning environments acquire sophisticated technological skills in addition to mastering the subject matter they are studying. Blended learning offers advantages and uses in the classroom. During the teaching and learning process, this approach offers a strong basis for connecting theory and practice. Blended learning, also referred to as hybrid learning, is the deliberate combination of online and in-person training. In a blended learning setting, the deliberate blending of online and in-person components is crucial. In regional contexts, blended learning can leverage local languages and culturally relevant content to enhance engagement, using community centers for group activities and digital hubs. Nationally, a centralized Learning Management System (LMS) can standardize curriculum delivery while allowing regional adaptations. Hybrid models can incorporate both synchronous and asynchronous learning, balancing live interactions with self-paced study. Partnerships with local organizations can provide resources and support, ensuring technology access. Regular feedback loops and professional development for educators will be essential to tailor approaches effectively, catering to diverse regional needs and promoting inclusivity in the national education landscape.

REFERENCES

Aisha, N., & Ratra, A. (2023). NEP 2020: Blended Learning-The Road Ahead for Higher Education in India. *Global Journal of Enterprise Information System*, 15(3), 42–46.

Aji, W. K., Ardin, H., & Arifin, M. A. (2020). Blended learning during pandemic corona virus: Teachers' and students' perceptions. *IDEAS: Journal on English Language Teaching and Learning. Linguistics and Literature*, 8(2), 632–646.

Anthonysamy, L., Koo, A. C., & Hew, S. H. (2020). Self-regulated learning strategies and non-academic outcomes in higher education blended learning environments: A one decade review. *Education and Information Technologies*, 25(5), 3677–3704. 10.1007/s10639-020-10134-2

Antwi-Boampong, A., & Bokolo, A. J. (2022). Towards an institutional blended learning adoption model for higher education institutions. *Technology. Knowledge and Learning*, 27(3), 765–784. 10.1007/s10758-021-09507-4

Apandi, A. M., & Raman, A. (2020). Factors affecting successful implementation of blended learning at higher education. *International Journal of Instruction, Technology, and Social Sciences*, 1(1), 13–23.

Azizi, S. M., Roozbahani, N., & Khatony, A. (2020). Factors affecting the acceptance of blended learning in medical education: Application of UTAUT2 model. *BMC Medical Education*, 20(1), 1–9. 10.1186/s12909-020-02302-233066768

Badre, P. (2020). Blended Learning a New Normal in Higher Education. *COVID–19: Crisis, Effects, Challenges and Innovations*, 152-159.

Bordoloi, R., Das, P., & Das, K. (2021). Perception towards online/blended learning at the time of Covid-19 pandemic: An academic analytics in the Indian context. *Asian Association of Open Universities Journal*, 16(1), 41–60. 10.1108/AAOUJ-09-2020-0079

Bouilheres, F., Le, L. T. V. H., McDonald, S., Nkhoma, C., & Jandug-Montera, L. (2020). Defining student learning experience through blended learning. *Education and Information Technologies*, 25(4), 3049–3069. 10.1007/s10639-020-10100-y

Bruggeman, B., Tondeur, J., Struyven, K., Pynoo, B., Garone, A., & Vanslambrouck, S. (2021). Experts speaking: Crucial teacher attributes for implementing blended learning in higher education. *The Internet and Higher Education*, 48, 100772. 10.1016/j.iheduc.2020.100772

Dangwal, K. L. (2017). Blended learning: An innovative approach. *Universal Journal of Educational Research*, 5(1), 129–136. 10.13189/ujer.2017.050116

Demillo, R. A. (2019). *Blended learning in practice: A guide for practitioners and researchers*. MIT Press.

Dybå, T., & Dingsøyr, T. (2008). Empirical studies of agile software development: A systematic review. *Information and Software Technology*, 50(9-10), 833–859. 10.1016/j.infsof.2008.01.006

Gecer, A., & Dag, F. (2012). A blended learning experience. *Educational Sciences: Theory & Practice*, 12(1), 438–442.

Graham, C. R. (2018). Current research in blended learning. *Handbook of distance education*, 173-188.

Hilliard, A. T. (2015). Global blended learning practices for teaching and learning, leadership and professional development. *Journal of International Education Research*, 11(3), 179–188. 10.19030/jier.v11i3.9369

Hrastinski, S. (2019). What do we mean by blended learning? *TechTrends*, 63(5), 564–569. 10.1007/s11528-019-00375-5

Huang, C. H. (2021). Using PLS-SEM model to explore the influencing factors of learning satisfaction in blended learning. *Education Sciences*, 11(5), 249. 10.3390/educsci11050249

Jin, T., Su, Y., & Lei, J. (2020). Exploring the blended learning design for argumentative writing.

Johry, G. S., Kant, U., & Asgar, A. (2019). Blended learning approach and students' satisfaction: A case study of IGNOU programmes. *Indian Journal of Open Learning*, 28(1), 3–22.

Kaliisa, R., Kluge, A., & Mørch, A. I. (2020). Combining Checkpoint and Process Learning Analytics to Support Learning Design Decisions in Blended Learning Environments. *Journal of Learning Analytics*, 7(3), 33–47. 10.18608/jla.2020.73.4

Kaur, M. (2013). Blended learning-its challenges and future. *Procedia: Social and Behavioral Sciences*, 93, 612–617. 10.1016/j.sbspro.2013.09.248

Kharb, P., & Samanta, P. P. (2016). Blended learning approach for teaching and learning anatomy: Students' and teachers' perspective. *Journal of the Anatomical Society of India*, 65(1), 43–47. 10.1016/j.jasi.2016.06.001

Knoblauch, C., Keßler, J. U., & Jakobi, M. (2021). Schools of education as agents of change: coping with diversity in India and Germany through a collaborative, interactive and blended-learning environment–a pre-test study. In *Cross Reality and Data Science in Engineering:Proceedings of the 17th International Conference on Remote Engineering and Virtual Instrumentation 17* (pp. 866-876). Springer International Publishing. 10.1007/978-3-030-52575-0_71

Kumar, A., Krishnamurthi, R., Bhatia, S., Kaushik, K., Ahuja, N. J., Nayyar, A., & Masud, M. (2021). Blended learning tools and practices: A comprehensive analysis. *IEEE Access : Practical Innovations, Open Solutions*, 9, 85151–85197. 10.1109/ACCESS.2021.3085844

Kundu, A., Bej, T., & Nath Dey, K. (2021). Time to Achieve: Implementing blended learning routines in an indian elementary classroom. *Journal of Educational Technology Systems*, 49(4), 405–431. 10.1177/0047239520984406

Lakhal, S., & Meyer, F. (2020). Blended learning. *Encyclopedia of education and information technologies*, 234-240.

Lockee, B. B. (2021). Shifting digital, shifting context:(re) considering teacher professional development for online and blended learning in the COVID-19 era. *Educational Technology Research and Development*, 69(1), 17–20. 10.1007/s11423-020-09836-833041603

Makovec Radovan, D., & Radovan, M. (2023). Teacher, think twice: About the importance and pedagogical value of blended learning design in VET. *Education Sciences*, 13(9), 882. 10.3390/educsci13090882

Megahed, N., & Hassan, A. (2022). A blended learning strategy: Reimagining the post-Covid-19 architectural education. *Archnet-IJAR: International Journal of Architectural Research*, 16(1), 184–202. 10.1108/ARCH-04-2021-0081

Meho, L. I., & Sugimoto, C. R. (2009). Assessing the scholarly impact of information studies: A tale of two citation databases—Scopus and Web of Science. *Journal of the American Society for Information Science and Technology*, 60(12), 2499–2508. 10.1002/asi.21165

Moskal, P., Dziuban, C., & Hartman, J. (2013). Blended learning: A dangerous idea? *The Internet and Higher Education*, 18, 15–23. 10.1016/j.iheduc.2012.12.001

Musdalifah, M., Baharuddin, B., Jabri, U., Elihami, E., & Mustakim, M. (2021, February). Building The Management System: Designs on the use of Blended Learning Environment. [). IOP Publishing.]. *Journal of Physics: Conference Series*, 1783(1), 012120. 10.1088/1742-6596/1783/1/012120

Naik, S., & Agarwal, V. (2021). A Study on Scope of Blended Learning in India. *IBA JOURNAL OF MANAGEMENT & LEADERSHIP*, 12(2), 28.

Picciano, A. G. (2013). Introduction to blended learning: research perspectives. *Taylor & Francis Ltd.*

Ranjan, P. (2020). Is Blended Learning Better than Online Learning for B. Ed Students? *Journal of Learning for Development*, 7(3), 349–366. 10.56059/jl4d.v7i3.412

Rasheed, R. A., Kamsin, A., & Abdullah, N. A. (2021). An approach for scaffolding students peer-learning self-regulation strategy in the online component of blended learning. *IEEE Access : Practical Innovations, Open Solutions*, 9, 30721–30738. 10.1109/ACCESS.2021.3059916

Resien, C., Sitompul, H., & Situmorang, J. (2020). The effect of blended learning strategy and creative thinking of students on the results of learning information and communication technology by controlling prior knowledge. *Budapest International Research and Critics in Linguistics and Education (BirLE). Journal*, 3(2), 879–893.

Ritz, E., Rietsche, R., & Leimeister, J. M. (2023). How to support students' self-regulated learning in times of crisis: An embedded technology-based intervention in blended learning pedagogies. *Academy of Management Learning & Education*, 22(3), 357–382. 10.5465/amle.2022.0188

Shrivastava, A., & Shrivastava, M. (2022). An Exploration of Students' Perceptions on the Blended Learning Mode in Management Education: A Case of Selected Colleges in India. *International Journal of Education and Development Using Information and Communication Technology*, 18(2), 207–214.

Suprabha, K., & Subramonian, G. (2015). Blended Learning Approach for Enhancing Students' Learning Experiences in a Knowledge Society. *Journal of Educational Technology, 11*(4), 1-7.

Tayebinik, M., & Puteh, M. (2013). Blended Learning or E-learning? *arXiv preprint arXiv:1306.4085.*

Topping, K. J., Douglas, W., Robertson, D., & Ferguson, N. (2022). Effectiveness of online and blended learning from schools: A systematic review. *Review of Education*, 10(2), e3353. 10.1002/rev3.3353

Torrisi-Steele, G. (2011). This thing called blended learning–a definition and planning approach. *Research and Development in Higher Education: Reshaping Higher Education*, 34, 360–371.

Vallée, A., Blacher, J., Cariou, A., & Sorbets, E. (2020). Blended learning compared to traditional learning in medical education: Systematic review and meta-analysis. *Journal of Medical Internet Research*, 22(8), e16504. 10.2196/1650432773378

Venkatesh, S., Rao, Y. K., Nagaraja, H., Woolley, T., Alele, F. O., & Malau-Aduli, B. S. (2020). Factors influencing medical students' experiences and satisfaction with blended integrated E-learning. *Medical Principles and Practice*, 29(4), 396–402. 10.1159/00050521031801145

Widjaja, G., & Aslan, A. (2022). Blended learning method in the view of learning and teaching strategy in geography study programs in higher education. *Nazhruna: Jurnal Pendidikan Islam*, 5(1), 22–36. 10.31538/nzh.v5i1.1852

Zhang, Z., Cao, T., Shu, J., & Liu, H. (2022). Identifying key factors affecting college students' adoption of the e-learning system in mandatory blended learning environments. *Interactive Learning Environments*, 30(8), 1388–1401. 10.1080/10494820.2020.1723113

Chapter 17
Enhancing Guest Loyalty in the Hotel Industry Through Artificial Intelligence-Drive Personalization

Sanjeev Kumar Saxena
https://orcid.org/0000-0002-2139-9255
Assam University, India

Vandana Gupta
https://orcid.org/0009-0007-1655-1172
LM College of Science and Technology, Jodhpur, India

Sunil Kumar
Institute of Hospitality Management, Kotdwar, India

ABSTRACT

This chapter is a product of the author's extensive first-hand experience gained during their professional journey and as well as their interactions with colleagues who are occupying the role of senior management in various hotels. Personalization has become the key factor for enhancing the experiences of the guest and also to foster loyalty in the hotel industry. The industry has witnessed a significant shift towards artificial intelligence (AI) that plays a pivotal role in providing various opportunities that tailor the guests' preferences accordingly. Through this chapter, the researcher aims to identify the influence of AI on guest loyalty, guest profiling and service customization within the hospitality sector. In addition to examining guest

DOI: 10.4018/979-8-3693-2272-7.ch017

profiling and customized services, this study examines the challenges and ethical considerations related to AI-powered personalization and guest loyalty.

INTRODUCTION

In recent years, the hospitality industry has experience a significant transformation and progress, largely driven by AI. Personalization guest experiences stands out as a key area profoundly influenced by AI, encompassing the customization of services to meet individual needs and preferences. This tailored approach has emerged as a pivotal factor in enhancing guest satisfaction and fostering loyalty within hotels.

The hospitality industry is undergoing a rapid transformation through the widespread adoption of artificial intelligence which aimed at delivering a WOW experiences that are customized. At the forefront of this revolution are the algorithms and machine learning models that are crucial for analyzing extensive datasets on guest behaviors, preferences and interactions. This advance technological development surpasses the traditional approaches, enabling the hotels not to just understand but predict individual guest preference. The outcome of these advances is a precisely tailored and seamless guest experiences, starting from taking up the booking to the end of their stay.

Harnessing algorithms, hotels can process extensive data of the guest, unveiling patterns and trends not easily discernible through manual analysis. Machine learning models, in particular, have the capacity to predict guest preferences by leveraging historical data, creating a proactive framework for anticipating and meeting individual needs. This predictive capability spans across diverse facets, encompassing room preferences, amenities, and personalized service recommendations

The interaction dynamics between hotels and guests reflect the transformative impact of AI, redefining the guest experiences. AI's influence extends beyond just personalization room settings to providing tailored dining recommendations, enhancing the overall guest interaction journey. Intelligent algorithms consider a guest's dietary preferences, past dining experiences and even the real-time factors like the current food trends or local events, crafting personalized dining suggestions that resonate with the tastes of every individual.

Furthermore, integrating AI-driven personalization enhances loyalty among guests and hotels. By consistently surpassing guest expectations with personalized services, hotels can forge a profound emotional bond with their clientele. The personalized/tailored approach not only increases guest satisfaction but also plays a vital role in cultivating strong brand loyalty. Hotels that understand and accommodate guest preferences are more likely to attract repeat guests, fostering a mutually beneficial relationship between guests and the hotels.

Through this paper, the author's aims to explore the implementation of AI-powered personalization in the hotel industry and its impact on guest loyalty, aspects of AI powered personalization, including guest profiling and customization of services within the hotel industry drawing from the authors firsthand work experience and interaction with their colleagues who are occupying senior level positions in various hotel groups and also from the available secondary sources. Additionally, the author's also tried to identify the challenges and ethical consideration related of AI-powered personalization and guest loyalty. The paper will provide a valuable insight for hoteliers, researchers and stakeholders who are interested in the intersection of AI and guest loyalty in the hospitality industry.

OBJECTIVES

1. To identify AI powered personalization in the hotels
2. To analyze AI's Utilization of Guest Data and Examine Customization of Services with AI.
3. To Identify Challenges and Ethical Considerations in AI-powered Personalization and Guest Loyalty.

LITERATURE REVIEW

Technological advancements have significantly transformed various sides of society as the industrial revolution started. Numerous assistance to humanity has been offered as many labor-intensive tasks have been replaced by innovative technological solutions. Among these innovations, Artificial Intelligence (AI)which was designed to replace manual labor across diverse fields is a stand out (Fetzer, 1990)

AI is a fusion of "artificial" and "intelligence" that denotes human creation and independent thought respectively, symbolizing a form of cognitive caplibility that are crafted by humans (Limna et al., 2021). Especially in computer systems, AI includes the emulation of human intelligence that processes through the computers (Wang et at., 2020).

Across the various aspects of life, there is a pervasive transformation on its way. While ensuring that the processes are seamless, many industries are now embracing technological progress that incorporates artificial intelligence and automation so as to enhance product and service quality. In industries like the hospitality, serious concerns regarding the introduction of artificial intelligence has arisen as this sector is very much reliant with human resources and AI might lead to the loss of human touch and human resources in the industry (Saini & Bhalla, 2022).

The success of the hospitality industry plays a very important role in the economic prosperity of numerous countries, emphasizing the importance of crafting welcoming and enjoyable experience for guest (Martínez et al., 2019). Globally, the hospitality and tourism sector is rapidly growing, providing substantial revenue and opportunities for employment with the ability to create further job (Ruel & Njoku, 2021).

Artificial Intelligence (AI) demonstrates the capability to replace human talent with technology in various specific scenarios as the hospitality industry experience growth, these prompt the need for businesses in the hospitality and tourism sector the restructure (Saini & Bhalla, 2022). Furthermore, leveraging digital analytics and AI tools for human talent performance management enhances talent attraction, development, deployment and overall productivity in human resource management (Hecklau et al., 2017; Nocker & Sena, 2019). As AI continues to integrate, there is a growing curiosity about its influence on employee engagement, retention, and productivity in the field of hospitality and tourism research (Ruel & Njoku, 2021).

The integration of Artificial Intelligence in the Hospitality industry is anticipated to lead the shift towards increased digitization in work methods, management, organization and instigate change across various organizational processes (Rosario & Dias, 2022). With the advancement in technological domains like AI, robotics and big data, the industry is undergoing a rapid and dynamic evolution (Reis et al., 2020). This metamorphosis is restructuring the sector, improving operational efficiency and introducing intelligent systems for enhanced decision-making and personalized services.

The incorporation of AI, robotics, and big data plays a crucial role in streamlining operational processes and cultivating a more intelligent and responsive approach to the services of the customer. Robotics enhances automation, optimization tasks from customer services to back-end operations, and big data facilitates data-driven decision-making and personalized services tailored to individual preferences. These technological advancements collectively propel the hospitality sector into a new era marked by innovation, efficiency and heightened customer-centric approaches (Reis et al., 2020). This ongoing evolution emphasizes the industry's dedication to staying at the forefront of technological progress to meet the evolving demands and expectations of contemporary travelers.

DISCUSSION AND RESULT

AI-Powered Personalization in the Hotel Industry

The dynamic hospitality industry has witnessed a transformative shift with the incorporation of AI-driven personalization. This technological leap has not just redefined guest interactions but has also markedly improved operational efficiency. In an age where customers crave distinctive, tailored experiences, hotels have harnessed artificial intelligence to provide personalized services that go beyond traditional norms.

An essential element of this evolution lies in the adoption of AI driven guests profiling. Unlike conventional approaches that center around the basic details like age and location, AI has elevated this practice to a heightened level of sophistications. The contemporary guest profiling, fueled by AI, goes beyond mere demographics, intricately exploring guest behavior, preferences, and even feedbacks. This results in holistic and nuanced comprehensions of each individual.

A significant facet of AI-driven guest profiling revolves around a thorough analysis of the guest's historical booking patterns. This involves a detailed scrutiny of elements such as the duration of their stays, the variety of rooms booked-spanning from the standard to suits and themed rooms- and any specific requests made in previous visits. By processing this historical data, AI equips hotels with invaluable insights, empowering them to deliver consistent and highly personalized experiences tailored to each guest's distinct preferences.

AI algorithms excel at recognizing patterns in a guest's booking behavior, pinpointing preferred room types, amenities, or specific services. This heightened level of insights enables hotels to seamlessly anticipate and fulfill individual preferences, crafting a personalized environment that resonates with each guest. Additionally, AI's proficiency in analyzing guest feedback ensures hotels can proactively address concerns or suggestions, continuously enhancing the overall guest experiences.

In summary, AI-driven personalization, particularly through sophisticated guest profiling, has revolutionized how the hospitality industry interacts with its patrons. Harnessing artificial intelligence to comprehend and predict guest needs at a detailed level, hotels have achieved a degree of personalization that not only elevates guest satisfaction but also plays a pivotal role in fostering enduring loyalty in an industry where delivering memorable and tailored experiences is of utmost important.

Past Booking History: Incorporating AI to analyze the historical booking records of hotel guests signifies a notable progression in the hospitality sector. AI algorithms can now delve deep into the past interaction of the guest with the hotel that offers a substantial insight beyond the superficial. This thorough analysis encompasses essential details that include the duration of the guest's previous stays, the particular type of room booked and any other specific requests made during their visits.

The number of days a guest stayed in the hotel over multiple visits is one of the crucial aspect that the AI has scrutinized. This data provides valuable insights into the guest's travel behavior that reveals whether they are frequent visitors, occasional travelers or seasonal guests. Acknowledging and analyzing these patterns empowers hotels to customize their approach for individual guests. This may involve offering loyalty rewards, personalized promotions or even anticipating specific needs based on their historical engagement.

Another key facet of past booking history critically examined by AI is the specific types of rooms a guest has previously reserved, spanning standard rooms, suites, or themed rooms. Hotels can optimize room assignments by ensuring that accommodations align with the individual preferences through grasping a guest's room preferences. For instance, if a guest consistently chooses suites, the hotel prioritizes offering suite options in subsequent stays, enhancing the overall personalized and enjoyable experience.

Moreover, AI considers previous special requests from the guests, spanning dietary preferences for in-room dining to specific amenity or service requests. Through cataloging and analyzing these preferences, AI empowers hotels to proactively meet and exceed expectations, showcasing a dedication to personalized service beyond conventional offerings.

A uniform and tailored experience for every guest can be delivered by utilizing AI to analyze previous booking history. With these insights hotels guarantee services and amenities that match individual preferences, fostering an environment where guests feel acknowledged and esteemed. This personalized approach not only elevates guest satisfaction but also cultivates loyalty, as patrons are inclined to return to establishments consistently surpassing their unique expectations.

Dining Preferences: In the modern hospitality realm, AI emerged as a potent tool for grasping and accommodation guests' dining preferences, signifying a notable transition towards a more individualized and customized culinary experience. AI effectively analyzes a guest's culinary inclinations, offering valuable insights into their dining habits within the hotel.

One of the important aspect of AI scrutiny involves the guest's inclination for dining within the hotel premises. Through the analysis of historical data, encompassing dining reservations and the frequency of room service orders, AI determines whether a guest favors the hotel's restaurants or leans towards the convenience of in-room dining. This insight plays a crucial role in customizing recommendations and services to harmonize with the guest's specific dining preferences.

Moreover, AI has surpassed the basic binary distinctions and delved more into the intricate details of the specific cuisine a guest favors. AI has constructed a comprehensive profile of the guest's culinary preferences through an analysis of historical data on the guest's dining choices, encompassing cuisine types, preferred dishes and special requests from prior visits. For example, if a guest frequently opts for vegetarian dishes or expresses a penchant for a particular cuisine, AI leverages this information to suggest pertinent dining options during their stay.

The overall guest experience has been enhanced by the capability of AI to understand the dining preferences that has extended to personalized recommendations. Suggestions on dining options that go along with the guest's culinary preferences can be served by hotels that are equipped with AI systems and this ensures that the guest has a seamless and enjoyable dining experiences. This options varies from vegetarian or vegan-friendly to fine dining experiences according to the past preferences of the guest.

The overarching objective has been to craft a dining experience that deeply connects with the guest on a personal level, surpassing their expectations. AI-driven insights into dining preferences have enabled hotels to provide customized recommendations, thereby elevating guest satisfaction and enriching their overall stay experience. With a growing embrace of AI- powered personalization in dining, the industry is advancing toward a future where each guest's culinary journey is meticulously tailored to cater to their individual tastes and preferences.

Room Amenity Preferences: The incorporation of AI in the hospitality sector has expanded to encompass the capture and comprehension of guest's preferences for room amenities, marking a notable stride in personalized services. AI now adeptly collects intricate details about a guest's individual preferences, spanning the type of bed they favor, the desired view, to special amenities that augment their overall comfort and satisfaction.

The type of bed preference by the guest is one of the fundamental aspect where AI examine. To understand the patterns in the guest's preference of the bed whether king size, queen or twin bed, AI uses historical data. This information helps the hotels in ensuring that the guests are assigned with their preferred type of bed. Promotion of a more restful and enjoyable stay is possible because of this level of customization as it contributes to the comfort of the guest.

AI now considers guest's preferred views. By taking factors into account like the city spaces or the waterfronts, that tailors the room assignments accordingly. Whether guests desire a bustling city space or a serene waterfront setting, this personalized approach enhances their stay, providing a more immersive and satisfying experience.

Further, special amenities like the spa baths or the in-room fitness equipment has been delved by the AI. AI is also able to understand whether the guest has a strong liking for any specific amenities that goes beyond the standard offerings of the hotel by studying the past preferences. The overall experience of the guest in the hotel can be elevated and create a personalized environment that exceeds the expectations of the guest from the information that has been gathered.

To enhance the guest's comfort and satisfaction has been the ultimate goal for any AI-powered personalization for room amenity preferences. Hotels have created an environment for the guest that feels like each of their unique tastes and requirements are tailored by aligning the room assignments with every individual preference.

Leisure Activities and Interests: In the domain of personalized hospitality, AI has broadened its capacities to take into account the leisure activities of guest and their interests, thereby deepening the comprehension of their needs and preferences. This approach empowers hotels not just to offer customized services on-site but also to suggest leisure activities that resonate with the guest's interests.

Monitoring guests' past bookings, allowing for the analysis of historical data to recognize patterns in preferred activities is a pivotal role of AI in this setting. These encompass spa treatments, guided tours, recreational classes, and other leisure pursuits offered by the hotel. Hotels can proactively recommend similar experiences during the guests' ongoing stay by grasping these preferences and crafting them a smooth and delightful leisure itinerary.

AI has further explored guest's inclinations towards local attractions. Through the analysis of data on excursions or visits to nearby landmarks in prior stays, AI has identified the kinds of attractions that captivated the interest of the guest. Whether it involves exploring the museums, historical sites, or natural landmarks, this insight has empowered hotels to recommend pertinent local attractions that align with the guest's preferences.

Furthermore, AI has take into account the recreational activities guests engage in during their stay, spanning participation on fitness classes, sports activities, or other on-site recreational offerings. By comprehending the guest's involvement in these activities, AI aids hotels in suggesting comparable experiences that enhance the overall enjoyment of their leisure time.

The main goal has been to ensure that the guest enjoys a relaxed and enjoyable experience throughout their stay. By utilizing AI to analyze guests' past leisure activities and interests, hotels have tailored their recommendations to match individual preferences. This has not only enhanced guest satisfaction but has also been instrumental in crafting a more memorable and personalized stay.

At its core, AI-driven personalization in leisure activities has propelled hotels beyond traditional hospitality services. By catering to the diverse interests of guests and suggesting experiences that align with their preferences, hotels have created an environment where leisure seamlessly integrates into the overall guest experience, fostering deeper connections. This meticulous attention to individual preferences enhances satisfaction, consequently boosting the likelihood of repeat visits.

Feedback from the previous stays: Feedback from previous stays has become a valuable asset in the realm of AI-driven personalization within the hospitality industry. AI algorithms play a crucial role in collecting, analyzing and extracting insights from guest reviews, ratings, compliments, complaints and suggestions. This wealth of information has proven instrumental in identifying areas for improvement, consistently enhancing guest satisfaction.

Hotels have systematically analyzed and decoded feedback of the guest using AI algorithms. Positive reviews and compliments have highlighted aspects valued by guests, while complaints and suggestions have pinpointed areas needing attention or refinement. This data-driven approach has empowered hotels to adeptly respond to the specific needs and expectations of their guests.

Formulation of the detailed profiles of guest is a significant result of the feedback analysis The data harnessed through AI has been utilized to create comprehensive profiles that encapsulate a guest's preferences, habits and specific points of satisfaction or dissatisfaction. This personalized approach has permeated various aspects of the guest experiences, ranging from personalized room assignments to customized dining recommendations and tailored leisure activities.

The importance of AI-driven guest profiling cannot be overstated, as it has enabled hotels to comprehend and cater to guests on an individual level. By consolidating data from various sources, hotels have successfully captured each guest's distinct preferences, guaranteeing that their stay is not only comfortable but also aligns seamlessly with their personal choices and habits.

Fundamentally, the integration of AI in guest profiling has significantly impacted the contemporary hotel industry's dedication to enhancing the journey of the guest. The capacity to establish detailed and precise profiles has empowered hotels to provide exceptionally personalized services that surpass conventional hospitality norms. Consequently, guest experiences have been elevated, satisfaction heightened, and guest loyalty fostered. This commitment to personalization mirrors the evolving landscape of the hotel industry, where technology-driven solutions have elevated the overall guest journey and played a pivotal role in fostering lasting, positive relationships between guests and establishments.

Customization of Services With AI

The hotel industry has experienced a transformative shift with the incorporation of artificial intelligence (AI), facilitating the provision of personalized services tailored to each guest's distinct preferences and requirements. This tailored approach has spanned multiple facets of the guest's stay, such as room configurations and dining experiences, and has been expanded to streamline the check-in and check-out processes. In this exploration, we delve into how AI has enabled these customized services and offer real-world examples of hotels effectively leveraging AI in this aspect.

Personalized Room Settings and Dining Experiences: AI has effectively assisted hotels in crafting setting of rooms and dining experiences that surpass traditional standards and here's how it is achieved:

Room setting: Guest have been granted with the ability to customized their room environment based on their preferences through the AI driven room automation. For instance, smart thermostats adjust the room temperature according to the preferences of the guest. Voice-activated systems allow guests to control lighting and window shades, while entertainment systems can be managed through voice commands or mobile apps. Consequently, AI has played a pivotal role in enhancing guest comfort, contributing to a more enjoyable and personalized stay.

Dining Experience: AI recommendations in the hotel industry have expanded to dining experiences, with the system suggesting restaurants and cuisines based on the guest's preferences stored in their profiles. AI goes a step further by making reservations according to the guest's history. For example, if a guest has a track record of ordering vegetarian meals, the hotel recommends vegetarian dining options to ensure the culinary experience aligns seamlessly with their preferences.

Streamlining Check-In/Check-Out and Anticipating Guest Needs: In optimizing the check-in and check-out processes, AI has played a pivotal role, foreseeing and addressing guest's needs effectively. The implementation of AI systems has streamlined and elevated the efficiency of these procedures. For Example, hotels have incorporated AI powered kiosks and mobile apps, facilitating seamless check in and checkout experience for the guests, thereby by reducing the wait time and enhancing the overall guest satisfaction.

Examples of AI-Enhanced Customized Services

The Taj Group of Hotels one of the leading Indian hotels chain has embraced AI and various other technology driven solution to improve the guest service experience and also enhance operational efficiency across all the properties. It exemplifies the potential to harness guest experience in the country by creating more personalized and convenient interactions through AI such as AI catbots on the websites and mobile apps to promptly address the guest request and queries, smart room controls having a features of control over room lighting, temperature and entertainment vis voice command, contact less check-in and checkout procedures to minimizing the physical interaction between the guest and staff, etc.

The hotel industry is undergoing significant transformation through AI, enabling personalized services in room settings, dining experiences and check-in/check-out processes. Hotels now offer a level of customization that not only boosts guest satisfaction but also cultivates guests' loyalty by leveraging AI's capabilities to anticipate guest needs and preferences. Additionally, as technology progresses, AI's role in delivering customized services in the industry continuous to expand, shaping the gesture of hospitality.

CHALLENGES AND ETHICAL CONSIDERATIONS IN AI-POWERED PERSONALIZATION AND GUEST LOYALTY

In the hotel industry, leveraging AI to elevate personalization and cultivates guest loyalty poses various challenges and ethical dilemmas. Foremost among these challenges is the meticulous handling of guest privacy. Hotels face intricacies in adhering to rigorous data privacy regulations while gathering and employing extensive guest data to fuel AI systems. Compliance with these regulations is vital to uphold guest trust and minimized legal ramifications. Essential measures entail maintaining transparency in data collection and utilization practices, securing explicit guest consent and implementing robust data security protocols.

Ethical considerations emerges as a significant challenge, underscoring the importance of ensuring AI algorithms are free from bias and discrimination Biased recommendations or profiling can negatively impact guest experiences and harm the hotel's reputation. Ethical data collection practices, including obtaining informed consent from guest regarding data use, are essential. Striking the right balance between personalization and ethics is crucial for maintaining guest trust, satisfaction and loyalty. To achieve the benefits of personalization without compromising ethical standards, hotels should invest in ethical AI development, conduct regular bias audits, and establish avenues for addressing AI-related issues.

CONCLUSION

In summary, the integration of AI in the hotel industry has inaugurated a new era of personalized services, reshaping the guest experience and nurturing enduring loyalty. The strides made in AI-powered personalization, notably through intricate guest profiling, enable hotels to comprehend and predict individual preferences at a granular level.

Through the analysis of past booking history, dining preferences, room amenity choices, leisure activities, and feedback from prior stays, hotels have constructed detailed guest profiles. This abundance of information has enabled establishments to customize services, accommodations and recommendations to harmonize with each guest's distinct tastes and preferences. The outcome is a hospitality experience that surpasses conventional standards, delivering a degree of personalization that elevates guest satisfaction that elevates guest satisfaction and fosters enduring loyalty.

The integration of AI extends customization to multiple facets of a guest's stay, encompassing personalized room settings, dining experiences, and streamlined check-in/check-out processes. Real-world instances, like the Taj Group of Hotels' adoption of AI-driven solutions, exemplify successful integration. Instant responses through AI-powered Chatbots, smart room control and contactless check-in/check-out procedures are also included, contributing in enhancing the experience of the guest.

Despite its advantages, the hotel industry faces challenges and ethical considerations when integrating AI-powered personalization. It's essential to navigate guest privacy in alignment with data protection regulations like GDPR and CCPA to maintain trust. Addressing ethical considerations, such as mitigating bias in AI algorithms and obtaining informed consent, becomes paramount to uphold personalized and ethical standards.

As hospitality industry embraces AI more extensively, success relies on responsibly navigating these challenges. By investing in ethical AI development, conducting frequent bias audits, and adhering to transparent data practices, hotels can harness the full potential of AI-powered personalization while upholding guest trust and satisfaction. In this evolving landscape, the integration of technology-driven solutions and ethical considerations will shape the future of the hotel industry, offering guests truly personalized and, memorable experiences.

Scope for Future Research

The future research landscape in AI-powered personalization within the hotel industry offers promising avenues for exploration. Firstly, researchers can advance AI algorithms for guest profiling, integrating additional data sources like social media and exploring real-time machine learning technique. Secondly, examining the feasibility and impact of dynamic personalization during a guest's stay, utilizing location-based services and IoT devices, presents areas of interests. Lastly, comprehending the economic and competitive implications of AI-powered personalization, such as its impact on revenue growth and market competitiveness, is crucial for shaping the industry's future. In summary, future research can significantly contribute to refining algorithms, implementing dynamic personalization, fostering collaborations, addressing ethical concerns, and assessing economic impacts in the evolving landscape of AI in hotel personalization.

REFERENCES

Al-Hyari, H. S. A., Al-Smadi, H. M., & Weshah, S. R. (2023). the impact of artificial intelligence (ai) on guest satisfaction in hotel management: An empirical study of luxury hotels. *Geo Journal of Tourism and Geosites*, 48(2 supplement), 810–819. 10.30892/gtg.482spl15-1081

Ameen, N., Tarhini, A., Reppel, A., & Anand, A. (2021). Customer experiences in the age of artificial intelligence. *Computers in Human Behavior*, 114, 106548. 10.1016/j.chb.2020.10654832905175

Ameen, N., Tarhini, A., Reppel, A., & Anand, A. (2021). Customer experiences in the age of artificial intelligence. *Computers in Human Behavior*, 114, 106548. 10.1016/j.chb.2020.10654832905175

Attaran, M. (2020, July). Digital technology enablers and their implications for supply chain management. In *Supply Chain ForumInternational Journal (Toronto, Ont.)*, 21(3), 158–172.

Banjac, I., & Palić, M. (2021). Analysis of best practice of artificial intelligence implementation in digital marketing activities. *CroDiM: International Journal of Marketing Science*, 4(1), 45–56.

Bulchand-Gidumal, J., William Secin, E., O'Connor, P., & Buhalis, D. (2023). Artificial intelligence's impact on hospitality and tourism marketing: Exploring key themes and addressing challenges. *Current Issues in Tourism*, 1–18.

Carev, D. (2008). *Guest satisfaction and guest loyalty study for hotel industry*. Rochester Institute of Technology.

. Chaturvedi, R., &Verma, S. (2023). Opportunities and challenges of AI-driven customer service. *Artificial Intelligence in customer service: The next frontier for personalized engagement*, 33-71.

Fetzer, J. H., & Fetzer, J. H. (1990). *What is Artificial Intelligence?* Springer.

Hecklau, F., Orth, R., Kidschun, F., & Kohl, H. (2017, December). Human resources management: Meta-study-analysis of future competences in Industry 4.0. In *Proceedings of the International Conference on Intellectual Capital, Knowledge Management & Organizational Learning* (pp. 163-174). Research Gate.

Ikumoro, A. O., & Jawad, M. S. (2019). Assessing intelligence conversation agent trends-chatbots-ai technology application for personalized marketing. *TEST Engineering and Management*, 81, 4779–4785.

Jaiswal, G. (2020). A quantitative evaluation of customer marketing impact by artificial intelligence in hospitality industry. *Pranjana: The Journal of Management Awareness*, 23(2), 40–44. 10.5958/0974-0945.2020.00011.4

Kapiki, S. (2012). Current and future trends in tourism and hospitality: The case of Greece. *International Journal of Economic Practices and Theories*, 2(1).

Kariru, A. N. (2023). *Contemporary Trends and Issues in The Hospitality and Tourism Industry.*

Kishen, R., Upadhyay, S., Jaimon, F., Suresh, S., Kozlova, N., Bozhuk, S., & Matchinov, V. A. (2021). Prospects for artificial intelligence implementation to design personalized customer engagement strategies. *Pt. 2 J.Legal Ethical &Regul. Isses*, 24, 1.

Kumar, V., Rajan, B., Venkatesan, R., & Lecinski, J. (2019). Understanding the role of artificial intelligence in personalized engagement marketing. *California Management Review*, 61(4), 135–155. 10.1177/0008125619859317

Limna, P. (2022). Artificial Intelligence (AI) in the hospitality industry: A review article. *Int. J. Comput. Sci. Res*, 6, 1–12.

Limna, P., Siripipatthanakul, S., & Phayaphrom, B. (2021). The role of big data analytics in influencing artificial intelligence (AI) adoption for coffee shops in Krabi, Thailand. *International Journal of Behavioral Analytics*, 1(2), 1–17.

Lu, T. L. (2019). Opportunities of Artificial Intelligence in Hospitality Industry for Innovative Customer Services. Case: Hotels in Ho Chi Minh City, Vietnam.

Martínez-Martínez, A., Cegarra-Navarro, J. G., Garcia-Perez, A., & Wensley, A. (2019). Knowledge agents as drivers of environmental sustainability and business performance in the hospitality sector. *Tourism Management*, 70, 381–389. 10.1016/j.tourman.2018.08.030

Nagar, K., Meghana, Y. G., & Rout, A. (2024). Artificial Intelligence in Tourism and Advertising. In *Artificial Intelligence for Business* (pp. 71–85). Productivity Press.

Nagar, K., Meghana, Y. G., & Rout, A. (2024). Artificial Intelligence in Tourism and Advertising. In *Artificial Intelligence for Business* (pp. 71–85). Productivity Press.

Nam, K., Dutt, C. S., Chathoth, P., Daghfous, A., & Khan, M. S. (2021). The adoption of artificial intelligence and robotics in the hotel industry: Prospects and challenges. *Electronic Markets*, 31(3), 553–574. 10.1007/s12525-020-00442-3

Nam, K., Dutt, C. S., Chathoth, P., Daghfous, A., & Khan, M. S. (2021). The adoption of artificial intelligence and robotics in the hotel industry: Prospects and challenges. *Electronic Markets*, 31(3), 553–574. 10.1007/s12525-020-00442-3

Nguyen, T. M., Quach, S., & Thaichon, P. (2022). The effect of AI quality on customer experience and brand relationship. *Journal of Consumer Behaviour*, 21(3), 481–493. 10.1002/cb.1974

Poku, K., Zakari, M., & Soali, A. (2013). Impact of service quality on customer loyalty in the hotel industry: An empirical study from Ghana. *International Review of Management and Business Research*, 2(2), 600–609.

Prentice, C., Dominique Lopes, S., & Wang, X. (2020). The impact of artificial intelligence and employee service quality on customer satisfaction and loyalty. *Journal of Hospitality Marketing & Management*, 29(7), 739–756. 10.1080/19368623.2020.1722304

Prentice, C., & Nguyen, M. (2020). Engaging and retaining customers with AI and employee service. *Journal of Retailing and Consumer Services*, 56, 102186. 10.1016/j.jretconser.2020.102186

. Rane, N. (2023). Enhancing Customer Loyalty through Artificial Intelligence (AI), Internet of Things (IoT), and Big Data Technologies: Improving Customer Satisfaction, Engagement, Relationship, and Experience. *Internet of Things (IoT), and Big Data Technologies: Improving Customer Satisfaction, Engagement, Relationship, and Experience (October 13, 2023)*.

. Rathore, B. (2016). Revolutionizing the Digital Landscape: Exploring the Integration of Artificial Intelligence in Modern Marketing Strategies. *Eduzone: International Peer Reviewed/Refereed Multidisciplinary Journal, 5*(2), 8-13.

Reis, J., Melão, N., Salvadorinho, J., Soares, B., & Rosete, A. (2020). Service robots in the hospitality industry: The case of Henn-na hotel, Japan. *Technology in Society*, 63, 101423. 10.1016/j.techsoc.2020.101423

Rosário, A. T., & Dias, J. C. (2022). Sustainability and the digital transition: A literature review. *Sustainability (Basel)*, 14(7), 4072. 10.3390/su14074072

Roslan, F. A. B. M., & Ahmad, N. B. (2023). The Rise of AI-Powered Voice Assistants: Analyzing Their Transformative Impact on Modern Customer Service Paradigms and Consumer Expectations. *Quarterly Journal of Emerging Technologies and Innovations*, 8(3), 33–64.

Ruel, H., & Njoku, E. (2021). AI redefining the hospitality industry. *Journal of Tourism Futures*, 7(1), 53–66. 10.1108/JTF-03-2020-0032

Saini, A., & Bhalla, R. (2022). Artificial intelligence and automation: transforming the hospitality industry or threat to human touch. In *Handbook of Research on Innovative Management Using AI in Industry 5.0* (pp. 88–97). IGI Global. 10.4018/978-1-7998-8497-2.ch006

Salazar, A. (2018). Hospitality trends: Opportunities and challenges. *Worldwide Hospitality and Tourism Themes*, 10(6), 674–679. 10.1108/WHATT-07-2018-0047

Sharma, S. (2023). Ethical Considerations in AI-Based Marketing: Balancing Profit and Consumer Trust. *TuijinJishu/Journal of Propulsion Technology, 44*(3), 1301-1309.

Štilić, A., Nicić, M., &Puška, A. (2023). Check-in to the future: Exploring the impact of contemporary information technologies and artificial intelligence on the hotel industry. *Turističkoposlovanje*, (31).

Trawnih, A., Al-Masaeed, S., Alsoud, M., & Alkufahy, A. (2022). Understanding artificial intelligence experience: A customer perspective. *International Journal of Data and Network Science*, 6(4), 1471–1484. 10.5267/j.ijdns.2022.5.004

Wang, C. X., Di Renzo, M., Stanczak, S., Wang, S., & Larsson, E. G. (2020). Artificial intelligence enabled wireless networking for 5G and beyond: Recent advances and future challenges. *IEEE Wireless Communications*, 27(1), 16–23. 10.1109/MWC.001.1900292

Wang, Y. C., & Uysal, M. (2023). Artificial intelligence-assisted mindfulness in tourism, hospitality, and events. *International Journal of Contemporary Hospitality Management*.

Chapter 18
Digitally Transforming Learning Campuses While Achieving SDGs

Sanjeev Kumar Ningombam
https://orcid.org/0000-0003-0449-7926
Indian Institute of Management, Shillong, India

ABSTRACT

This chapter provides examples of how technology and creative thinking can transform the context of higher education in India. It looks at how technology may bridge the gap between urban and rural communities, increase learning results, and improve access to education. It also emphasises how digital tools and online platforms can offer individualised learning experiences and promote cooperation between teachers and students. By mapping the sustainable development goals, it also aims to address sustainability-related issues. Focus has been made to underline and address the spirit and intent on education reforms as envisaged under the National Education Policy 2020 of India. Students, teachers, and higher education institutions would all benefit from this chapter while planning and creating online courses.

INTRODUCTION

Digital transformation is an important process for reforms in the education landscape. It is also a complex and multifaceted approach. Digital transformation of education requires technology upgradation and integration with effective methods and practices (Alenezi, 2021). The transformation faces challenges such as a lack of a holistic vision, digital transformation competency, and inadequate data structure and processing (Adam Marks, 2020). The COVID-19 pandemic has accelerated

DOI: 10.4018/979-8-3693-2272-7.ch018

digital transformation, emphasizing the need for future managers to possess digital skills and enhance higher education for a technology-rich society. A major force behind this change is the application of information and communication technologies (ICT), which can improve operational procedures and save costs (Petkovics, 2018). It has emerged as a significant phenomenon affecting the education system bringing varied opportunities and challenges at the same time. Research has highlighted various aspects related to the integration of digital technologies in education. (O V Bondarenko, 2023) discusses challenges in implementing digital technologies in geographic disciplines in higher education, emphasizing the need for proper technological support and educational resources. (Undheim, 2021) emphasises the significance of comprehending patterns and important viewpoints in this context as it focuses on how early children and teachers interact with digital technologies in early childhood education. (Tina Štemberger, 2021) emphasize the significance of attitudes towards digital technologies in education as a predictor of proficiency in using digital tools for educational purposes. (Pluzhnikova, 2022) forecasts the development of digitalization in education, highlighting the need for improved methods of integrating information technologies and adapting knowledge assessment methods. Rahman (2020) suggests that digital technology can have a positive impact on higher education in the long and short term, benefiting learners, educators, and nations.

LITERATURE REVIEW

The creation of electronic textbooks, Internet portals, and online courses are just a few examples of the ways that digital technologies are being widely used in education (Ordov, 2019) These technological advancements are revolutionizing the education sector by increasing classroom interaction and giving students access to new educational opportunities (Zain, 2021). Higher education still has to undergo additional digital transformation, with an emphasis on virtual learning and the use of digital tools (Monisha. M, 2022). Digitisation of education is necessary for meeting the emerging trend in the global educational landscape, navigating communication networks, and mitigating modern days challenges. This shift is influenced by the digital generation, who are immersed in digital communication, mobile devices, and social networks. The transition to a digital environment is predicted to be a turning point in education history. Digitisation of education is leading trend in transforming teaching and learning information to digital repositories (Rybchuk, 2022). (Minina, 2020) highlights four trends related to the integration of digital technologies and tools in higher education: the development of a blended learning model, the transition to online education, and the creation of a virtual educational environment. Digital technologies in education enhance interaction between teachers, students, and lecturers, enhancing effectiveness, efficiency, and personalized learning. They introduce new cooperation models and innovative strategies for students (V. Dzobelova, 2020). The education of university students on sustainable development is among the educational goals of the 2030 Agenda.

The fourth industrial revolution in the context of education known as Education 4.0 aims to equip students with cognitive, social, interpersonal and technical skills. These are required to address global challenges including climate change. (Oliveira, 2021) introduces TADEO method for guiding the design and application of teaching and learning experiences using digital transformation drivers to achieve Education 4.0 goals. TADEO was applied in elementary and higher education classes to enhance students' understanding of climate change through projects aimed at mitigating environmental problems caused by human actions. This approach also helps students develop the soft and hard skills needed for 21st-century learning and work. Evaluations from students and educators indicate that TADEO successfully achieved its intended outcomes.

The education system is evolving with technological advancements, and Education 4.0 signifies both the contextual and technological changes in learning; (Esin Mukul, 2023) article reviews the current state-of-the-art literature on Education 4.0, identifies the most commonly used approaches, explores recent trends, and highlights knowledge gaps and limitations for future development.

The 2030 Agenda sets out seventeen Sustainable Development Goals (SDGs). SDG – 4 aims to quality education. Educating today's digital citizens on sustainability means training them for justice and social activism, commitment and political engagement. However, research into the subject shows a lack of consistency in the education of university students (Lozano-Díaz & Fernández-Prados, 2020). The theme "Digital Education, Information and Communication Technology (ICT), and Education for Sustainable Development (ESD)" is part of a three-pronged approach that involves teaching sustainable development, mobilizing digital technologies, and changing teacher and learner behaviours. This approach aims to develop a structured framework to address education, communication, and learning issues, promoting lifelong learning and policy institutions of knowledge (Ricard, 2020).

Understanding Sustainable Development Goals (SDGs)

The Open Working Group on Sustainable Development Goals (SDGs) of the United Nations General Assembly put forth a list of 17 objectives, 169 targets, and 304 indicators known as the "Sustainable Development Goals," which are anticipated to be completed by 2030 (Nations, 2016). SDGs calls for collective action towards end of poverty, safeguarding environment and assuring peace and prosperity for every individual. The SDGs aim to address issues related to sustainability and advance economic empowerment and equal opportunity (Leal Filho, 2018). SDG - 4 seeks to foster lifelong learning opportunities for all individuals and guarantee inclusive and fair access to education of excellent quality. The incorporation of digital intervention in the teaching and learning process can significantly contribute to addressing these sustainable goals. Through the use of technology, educators may develop interactive and captivating educational experiences that have a broader reach. Moreover, digital platforms have the capability to ensure equitable access to educational resources, irrespective of geographic location or socio-economic status, hence fostering inclusiveness and fairness in education. SDG 4 aims to promote social inclusion, economic growth, and environmental sustainability by ten goals. These goals ensure quality education for all, address gender equality, improve literacy rates, and enhance educational infrastructure, fostering a world where education is crucial for sustainable development. Under the goal of SDG 4, there is a significant possibility to promote and participate in free online courses. Digital technology has created many alternative ways to get an education besides the traditional way of going to college (The Global Goals, 2023).

India is implementing innovative programs to achieve SDG 4 on education, with a focus on quality education (Singh, 2022). The National Education Policy (NEP, 2020) of India acknowledges the transformative potential of digital education, aiming to make it more inclusive, flexible, and 21st-century-aligned. NEP 2020 aims to integrate technology in education, creating a robust digital infrastructure for online and technology-enabled learning. It emphasises digital literacy for students, teachers, and administrators. The policy encourages the development of online and blended learning modules, high-quality e-content, and a National Educational Technology Forum (NETF) for collaboration. It also emphasises the importance of teacher training, assessment reforms, open and distance learning, and technology in higher education. The policy supports the use of digital tools for assessment, evaluation, and open and distance learning and encourages the adoption of online courses and credit transfer mechanisms (National Education Policy, 2020).

Digital Transformation in Higher Education

Digital technology is revolutionizing education by improving teaching, learning, research, and governance. India's higher education institutions are utilizing ICT, cloud computing, artificial intelligence, robotics, and virtual reality to enhance competencies and align with industry-based skills (Shailaj Kumar Shrivastava, The Impact of Digitalization in Higher Educational Institutions, 2022). (Marta Pinto, 2020) highlights the importance of digital technologies in fostering student participation and engagement, as well as the cultural shift towards more dynamic and flexible learning environments. He also emphasizes the necessity of striking a

•

balance between collaborative and transmissive teaching approaches. In general, the integration of digital technology in higher education has promise for revolutionizing conventional methods of instruction and learning; nonetheless, its successful implementation necessitates meticulous arrangement and backing. By implementing a participatory pedagogical approach and combining formal and informal learning, digital technologies have the potential to offer a more dynamic and adaptable educational experience (Lai, 2011). The use of digital technologies in the educational process increases by 1%, resulting in a 1% increase in the rate at which students learn (E.A. Voykina, 2019). (Michael Henderson, 2017) digital technology have a significant impact on how students interact with their learning process, but some contend that this isn't "transforming" university teaching and learning. Consequently, university instructors might need to temper their enthusiasm about the possible advantages of technology-enabled learning and have a better understanding of the realities of students' digital technology interactions. Digitalization in education has increased transparency and accountability, leading to the establishment of virtual, smart, digital, e-universities, and university 4.0. During the COVID-19 crisis, online teaching tools acted as a major facilitator for academic institutions in India (Shailaj Kumar Shrivastava, The Impact of Digitalization in Higher Educational Institutions, 2022). Digital India Program strongly encourage digitalisation of higher education. These digital tools have also allowed for greater accessibility to education for students in remote areas, bridging the gap between urban and rural learning opportunities. Additionally, the integration of technology in education has helped in personalizing learning experiences and catering to individual student needs. According to a study by (Vicente Díaz-Garcia, 2023), internal stakeholders believe that the following five ideas best support the process of digital transformation in higher education institutions: leadership, data-driven management, culture change, internal communication, and the teaching process. According to a survey conducted by EY Parthenon (Kasia Lundy, 2022), 93% of institutions believe that over the next ten years, teacher preparation and student success initiatives will undergo significant or extremely significant changes in digital tool and technology use.

Figure 1. Technology utilisation percentage of partnerships during the COVID-19 pandemic in 2020 in Indian higher education institutions (FICCI, 2021)

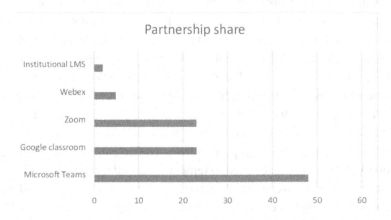

Source: Statistita 2024

Integration of SDGs Into Learning Campus Strategies

The NEP 2020 has set an ambitious goal of achieving a 50% Gross Enrolment Ratio (GER) in higher education by 2035, which would require the addition of 3.5 crore seats in higher education (Mumbai, 2020). The 'Digital India' campaign was launched by the Government of India with the aim of transforming the nation into a digitally empowered society and knowledge-based economy. The Ministry of Education provides top-notch educational programmes via DTH channels and digital platforms as part of the PM e-Vidya initiative. Key endeavours encompass DIKSHA, a platform that offers high-quality electronic content for primary and secondary education, as well as QR-coded textbooks that have been infused with energy for students across all grade levels. Currently, there are 12 DTH channels available for school education and 22 SWAYAM PRABHA channels for higher education. These channels are presently operational, and there are intentions to increase the number to 200 PM e-Vidya DTH TV channels. SWAYAM is the official Massive Open Online Course (MOOC) portal in India for higher education courses, offering a wide selection of over 10,000 courses (PIB, 2023). The Ministry of Education (MoE), Government of India, has developed the Study Webs of Active Learning for Young Aspiring Minds (SWAYAM) project. This initiative provides a centralised online platform for students from high school to higher education, using information and communication technology (ICT) to facilitate comprehensive learning. SWAYAM encompasses the creation of Massive Open Online Courses (MOOCs) that adhere to e-content standards, including video and text materials, as well as the construction of a resilient IT platform (Guidelines for Development of MOOCs). The Indian government has announced to establish a Digital University in its 2022-2023 budget, offering world-class, universally applicable education in multiple languages and ICT forms. The university will be built using a networked hub-spoke paradigm, with top-tier public colleges and institutions collaborating. The Department of Higher Education, UGC, AICTE, and other parties are collaborating to establish the digital university. BharatNet initiative aims to provide broadband connectivity to rural areas (PIB, 2023). Technologies like extended realities, AI, blockchain, digital twins, and the Metaverse can enhance education by providing immersive experiences through visors or glasses. These digital spaces enhance student-teacher connectivity, increasing attention and interaction. Additionally, immersive workspaces can be designed for larger groups, requiring only an internet connection and glasses (Vicente Díaz-Garcia, 2023).

Top EdTech unicorns globally by valuation in 2023 (measured in US dollars per billion)

ByJu, an Indian startup, was the highest valued EdTech unicorn globally as of January 2023, with a valuation of 22 billion US dollars. Out of the nine firms that are still listed here, two are from India, and one each from Austria and Canada is an EdTech unicorn that ranks among the top 10 in terms of valuation. Five of the companies are from the United States.

Figure 2. EdTech unicorns worldwide 2023

Source: Statista, 2024

India's online education sector has grown significantly in the last several years. The market for online education is projected to bring in US$6.71 billion by 2024. It is anticipated that sales will increase at a compound annual growth rate (CAGR) of 23.06% by 2029, reaching a market volume of US$18.94 billion. The online learning platform market is projected to bring in US$5.50 billion by 2024. In 2024, the United States is expected to generate the highest income internationally, amounting to $87.51 billion in US dollars. The average revenue per user (ARPU) in the online education market is projected to reach US$35.36 in 2024. By 2029, 309.1 million people are expected to be using online schooling. By 2024, the percentage of users in the online education market will reach 13.2% (Online Education - India, n.d.).

Figure 3. Market: Online Education, Region: India, Currency: USDs, 2024

Source: Statista Market Insights

The enrolment ratio of online education in India witnessed a significant rise with a record increase in enrolment of 170% between 2021 and 2022. From 42 HEIs in the 2020–21 academic year to 58 HEIs in the 2021–22 academic year, there was a 38% increase in the number of higher education institutions providing online programmes (Online, 2022)

India's Leading MOOC Platforms

1. Coursera: Coursera is a popular platform that offers a wide range of courses, with some being free, while others offer paid options for certificates and additional features.

2. edX: edX, an educational platform established by MIT and Harvard, offers anyone the opportunity to enrol in courses provided by prestigious colleges and institutions worldwide. Similar to Coursera, it provides both complimentary and paid courses.
3. NPTEL: The Indian Institutes of Technology (IITs) and the Indian Institute of Science (IISc) have launched the National Programme on Technology Enhanced Learning (NPTEL) to offer top-notch science and engineering education via online courses.
4. SWAYAM is an educational programme initiated by the Indian government. It provides online courses for both school and higher education. It encompasses a broad spectrum of topics.
5. Udacity is a company that focuses on offering courses in technology, with a particular emphasis on programming, data science, and artificial intelligence. Although a majority of courses require payment, there are other complimentary resources accessible.
6. Udemy is a worldwide website that offers a wide range of courses on many subjects. Although the majority of courses on Udemy require payment, the platform often provides promotional offers, allowing certain courses to be accessed without any cost.
7. FutureLearn partners with universities and institutions around to provide courses on a wide range of topics. It offers both complimentary and premium choices.
8. Khan Academy: This non-profit offers free educational resources, mainly in the fields of science, math, economics, and the humanities.
9. Skillshare provides a diverse range of courses, primarily emphasising creative abilities such as design, photography, and writing. Although its main business model is based on subscriptions, there are also some courses that may be accessed without charge.
10. LinkedIn Learning, previously known as Lynda.com, provides comprehensive courses covering a diverse array of professional and technical abilities. The service operates on a subscription-based model, typically offering a complimentary trial period.

Addressing Sustainability Through Digital Intervention in Education

An online "platform" is a digital architecture that may be programmed and used to manage interactions between users, including public and corporate entities in addition to end users. It is designed with the systematic collection, algorithmic processing, distribution, and commercialization of user data in mind (Decuypere,

Grimaldi, & Landric, 2021). With the advent of new technology-assisted learning tools, education in schools and institutions has changed. Examples of these tools include mobile devices, tablets, laptops, smartboards, MOOCs, simulations, dynamic visualisations, and virtual laboratories (Abid Haleem, 2022). Educators must embrace technology and integrate it into curriculum meaningfully, focusing on its purpose rather than a technical approach, to create innovative learning environments (Fullan, 2013).

Way Forward for Digital Education in India

India's educational landscape has a lot of potential for transformation. With the availability of technology and mediums, India has the potential to leverage digital education to bridge the gap between urban and rural areas, improve access to quality education, and enhance learning outcomes for students across the country. Transformation of India's Higher Education can happen through the following interventions:

1. **Online Courses:** India's higher education institutions should support online learning for their students and offer online classes to students who can't be on campus. This approach would not only ensure accessibility and inclusivity for all students but also provide flexibility in learning schedules. Moreover, it would enable institutions to leverage technology and reach a wider audience, fostering a culture of lifelong learning in the country.
2. **Virtual Classrooms:** Higher education institutions (HEIs) may implement virtual classrooms as it diminishes the necessity for physical infrastructure, hence reducing the environmental consequences linked to the construction and upkeep of conventional classrooms. Simultaneously, it will decrease commuting, eliminating the necessity of travelling to educational institutions, resulting in a decline in emissions associated with transportation.
3. **Hybrid Events:** HEIs should prioritize organising hybrid events like conferences, seminars, and workshops to enhance participation, reduce resource usage, and promote inclusivity. These events allow remote attendees to attend and benefit from shared knowledge, thereby enhancing event accessibility.
4. **Online Training:** Online training provides a versatile and convenient method for acquiring new skills, improving knowledge, and pursuing professional growth. Students and professionals can greatly benefit from pursuing value-added courses or engaging in upskilling activities.
5. **Curriculum development:** HEIs should promote the creation of high-quality digital content, such as e-textbooks, interactive modules, and multimedia resources, to enhance learning experiences, cater to different learning styles, and provide flexibility.

6. **Integration of technology in teaching:** HEIs should equip teachers with technology skills to create interactive, engaging classrooms, cater to different learning styles, and promote student engagement. This will help bridge the digital divide and ensure equal access to educational opportunities.

7. **Digital library and e-resources:** HEIs should prioritise the establishment of a comprehensive digital library that encompasses a vast digital repository and abundant materials. Higher education institutions (HEIs) may gradually phase out the practice of distributing physical printed books and instead promote the use of electronic books and study resources. Digital resources reduce printing and distribution costs, enhance accessibility, and facilitate sharing among students and researchers. HEIs can also collaborate with publishers to provide diverse e-resources.

8. **Community Engagement:** As part of their mission for institutional social responsibility, higher education institutions can strengthen their social commitment by providing digital platforms for community projects. These digital platforms can act as an intermediary between the institution and the community, facilitating collaboration and involvement on diverse social matters. Through the utilisation of technology, higher education institutions have the ability to enable individuals and organisations to collaborate, exchange resources, and collaborate towards the advancement of good transformation within their communities.

Few Best Practices of Digital Transformation in Higher Education

1. The Ministry of Education and Training of Vietnam has connected its database to the national population database, integrating over 24 million teachers and students. The database includes information from 53,000 establishments and profiles of 1.6 million teachers. The ministry is piloting electronic learning records and establishing MOET-MOOC, an open online training platform (Dharmaraj, 2024).

2. G20 presidency allowed the nation to showcase its higher education system globally. The G20 Education Ministers' Meeting in Pune approved a comprehensive report and policies, focusing on four priority themes: foundational literacy, digital technology, future workforce relevance, and cross-border collaboration. The report also introduced five key elements for inclusive, qualitative, and collaborative tech-enabled learning, aiming for a more accessible and impactful educational landscape. The G20 recognizes the critical role that digital transformation will play in accomplishing the SDGs (Banerjee, 2023).

3. Automated Permanent Academic Account Registry (APAAR) ID (APAAR, 2024) initiative launched by Government of India aims to digitally consolidate the complete academic records, including degrees, scholarships, rewards, and other credits into a unified ID. It also aims to reduce fraud and duplicate educational certificates by providing a single, trusted reference for educational institutions.

4. The National Educational Technology Forum (NETF) (NETF, 2024) is a platform that the Indian government developed to facilitate the free exchange of ideas about how to use technology to improve planning, administration, assessment, and learning for both higher education and schools. The goal of the NETF is to make decision-making about the introduction, implementation, and use of technology easier by giving leaders of educational institutions, state and federal governments, and other stakeholders access to the most recent information and research, as well as the chance to discuss and exchange best practices.

5. Government of India launched "Bhashini" under the national language translation mission. As an AI-powered language translation tool, Bhashini facilitates communication between speakers of various Indian languages by removing obstacles based on language. This platform will facilitate in translating digital content and AI content into regional languages thereby enhancing accessibility, improving educational outreach and addressing language barriers. The user-friendly platform can be accessed through applications specifically designed for iOS and Android devices (Bhashini, 2024). Nasscom Foundation and Digital India Bhashini entered into an MoU which aimed to serve as a cornerstone in translating digital literacy and accelerating in addressing SDGs (Mediawire, 2024).

6. In a significant move towards enhancing multilingualism in education, the central government has launched the 'Anuvadini' app, an AI-based platform. This innovative initiative aims to provide digital study materials for all school and higher education courses in Indian languages listed in the 8th Schedule of the Indian Constitution. Aligning with the National Education Policy (NEP) 2020, which underscores the importance of learning in one's mother tongue, the Anuvadini app represents a major step towards inclusive and accessible education for all linguistic communities in Bharat (Piyush, 2024).

Impact of Digital Education

1. Inclusive and Accessible: As envisioned by NEP 2020, digital education can bring about a systematic change in the provision of education to people from all walks of life, regardless of their socioeconomic status.

2. Economic Means: Digital learning is a great method to save money, make better use of available resources, encourage sustainability, and reach and impact more students and teachers. It has numerous advantages, including the reduction of paper usage for books and handouts, time savings, and ease of research.

3. Enhanced Productivity: By using cutting-edge technological tools that enable better planning, simple and practical learning, speedy assessment, better resources, new skills, etc., teaching productivity can be increased.

4. Continuous and lifelong learning: Digital education fosters ongoing learning outside of regular class hours by giving students access to tools and information around the clock. Professionals can participate in online learning programmes to advance their careers without having to quit, supporting lifelong learning. Additionally, adults who stopped their education for any reason have a plethora of chances to resume and finish their education at their convenience, thanks to digital education.

5. Better student engagement: Digital teaching involves interactive methods like discussion forums, quizzes, and collaborative projects, enhancing student engagement and making complex topics more accessible through multimedia elements.

6. Business opportunities: Future trends indicate that educational technology firms of all sizes, small and large, are starting to proliferate and are providing academic institutions with a wide range of innovative digital solutions (Abid Haleem, 2022).

REFERENCES

Abid Haleem, M. J. (2022). Understanding the role of digital technologies in education: A review. *Sustainable Operations and Computers*, 3, 275–285. 10.1016/j. susoc.2022.05.004

Adam Marks, M. A.-A. (2020). Digital Transformation in Higher Education: A Framework for Maturity Assessment. [IJACSA]. *International Journal of Advanced Computer Science and Applications*, 11(12). 10.14569/IJACSA.2020.0111261

Alenezi, M. (2021). *Deep Dive into Digital Transformation in Higher Education Institutions*. Semantic Scholar. 10.3390/educsci11120770

APAAR. (2024, March 02). *APAAR*. APAAR. https://apaar.education.gov.in/

Banerjee, S. (2023, September 18). G20's role in shaping online higher education. *Financial Express*. https://www.financialexpress.com/jobs-career/education-g20s -role-in-shaping-online-higher-education-3246128/

Bhashini. (2024, April 02). *Bhashini*. Bhashini. https://bhashini.gov.in/

Bondarenko, O. V., Hanchuk, O. V., Pakhomova, O. V., & Varfolomyeyeva, I. M. (2023). Digitalization of geographic higher education: Problems and prospects. *Journal of Physics: Conference Series*, 2611(1), 012015. 10.1088/1742-6596/2611/1/012015

Decuypere, M., Grimaldi, E., & Landric, P. (2021). Introduction: Critical studies of digital education platforms. *Critical Studies in Education*, 62(1), 1–16. 10.1080/17508487.2020.1866050

Dharmaraj, S. (2024, 03 30). https://opengovasia.com/. Retrieved from OpenGovAsia: https://opengovasia.com/2023/10/07/vietnams-quest-for-digital-transformation -in-education/

Dzobelova, L. A. (2020). Digital Technologies in Education and Their Influence on Modern Society. *New Silk Road: Business Cooperation and Prospective of Economic Development (NSRBCPED 2019)*. Research Gate.

Esin Mukul, G. B. (2023). Digital transformation in education: A systematic review of education 4.0. *Technological Forecasting and Social Change*, 194, 122664. Advance online publication. 10.1016/j.techfore.2023.122664

Ficci, E. (2021, February). *Partnership share of technology used in higher education institutions across India during COVID-19 pandemic in 2020*. Statista. https:// www.statista.com/statistics/1290694/india-technology-partnership-share-of-higher -education-institutions-during-covid-19/

Fullan, M. (2013). *Stratosphere: Integrating Technology, Pedagogy, and Change Knowledge*. Pearson.

Guidelines for Development of MOOCs. (n.d.). AICTE. https://www.aicte-india.org/downloads/MHRD%20moocs%20guidelines%20updated.pdf

Kasia Lundy, H. L. (2022). *How digital's impact on higher education can be improved*. EY Parthenon.

Lai, K.-W. (2011). Digital technology and the culture of teaching. *Australasian Journal of Educational Technology*, 1263–1275.

Leal Filho, W. T.-G. (2018). Using the sustainable development goals towards a better understanding of sustainability challenges. *International Journal of Sustainable Development and World Ecology*, 179–190.

Lozano-Díaz, A., & Fernández-Prados, J. (2020). Educating Digital Citizens: An Opportunity to Critical and Activist Perspective of Sustainable Development Goals. *Sustainability 2020*. 10.20944/preprints202008.0208.v1

Market: Online Education, Region: India, Currency: USDs. (2024, March). Statista Market Insights. https://www.statista.com/outlook/emo/online-education/india#revenue

Marta Pinto, C. L. (2020). Digital technologies in support of students learning in Higher. *Digital Education Review*, 343-360.

Mediawire. (2024). Accelerating India's SDG goals demands tech intervention. *Times of India*.

Michael Henderson, N. S. (2017). What works and why? Student perceptions of 'useful' digital technology in university teaching and learning. *Studies in Higher Education*, 42(8), 1567–1579. 10.1080/03075079.2015.1007946

Minina, V. N. (2020). Digitalization of higher education and its social outcomes. *Bulletin of St. Petersburg University.Sociology*, 84–101.

Monisha. M, V. D. (2022). Digital Transformation in Education. *EPRA International Journal of Economic and Business Review-Peer Reviewed Journal*, 58-64.

Mumbai, P. (2020, July 29). National Education Policy 2020 announced. Mumbai. (n.d.). *National Education Policy 2020*. New Delhi: Minstry of Human Resource Development, Government of India.

NETF. (2024, March 02). *NETF*. NETF. https://netf.aicte-india.org/

Oliveira, K. (2021). *Digital Transformation towards Education 4.0*. Informatics in Education., 10.15388/infedu.2022.13

Online, T. (2022). Students enrolment in online education programmes increased 170% between 2021 and 2022: UGC Chairman. *Times of India.*https://timesofindia .indiatimes.com/education/online-schooling/students-enrolment-in-online -education-programmes-increased-170-between-2021-and-2022-ugc-chairman/ articleshowprint/95197476.cms?val=3728

Online Education - India. (n.d.). Statista. https://www.statista.com/outlook/emo/ online-education/india

Ordov, K. A. (2019). New Trends in Education as the Aspect of Digital Technologies. *International Journal of Mechanical Engineering and Technology*, (pp. 1319-1330).

Petkovics, I. (2018). Digital Transformation in Higher Education. *Journal of Applied Technical and Educational Sciences,* 77-89. 10.24368/jates.v8i4.55

PIB. (2023, August). *Digital India initiative of Government has revolutionized education access in rural areas*. PIB.

PIB. (2023). Retrieved from PIB: https://www.education.gov.in/sites/upload_files/ mhrd/files/LU5163.pdf

Piyush. (2024, January 23). Central Government Launches 'Anuvadini' App for Multilingual Education. *Adda247 Current Affairs*.

Pluzhnikova, N. N. (2022). Digitalization of education and information technologies as a factor of agribusiness development. *BIO Web Conference, 53*, 7. 10.1051/ bioconf/20225307001

Ricard, M. Z. (2020). Digital Education, Information and Communication Technology, and Education for Sustainable Development. In Burgos, D. (Ed.), *Radical Solutions and eLearning* (pp. 27–39). Springer. 10.1007/978-981-15-4952-6_2

Rybchuk, A. Z. (2022). Digital Transformation of the Global Educational Environment. *Herald of Khmelnytskyi National University.*, 262-268.

Shailaj Kumar Shrivastava, C. S. (2022). *The Impact of Digitalization in Higher Educational Institutions. International Journal of Soft Computing and Engineering*. IJSCE. 10.35940/ijsce.B3536.0111222

Shailaj Kumar Shrivastava, C. S. (2022). The Impact of Digitalization in Higher Educational Institutions. [IJSCE]. *International Journal of Soft Computing and Engineering*, 7-11(2), 7–11. Advance online publication. 10.35940/ijsce.B3536.0111222

Singh, A. K. (2022). Role of Education in Sustainable Development Goals. *The Electrochemical Society*. Retrieved from 10.1149/10701.11685ecst

The Global Goals. (2023, December). Global Goals. https://www.globalgoals.org/goals/4-quality-education/

Tina Štemberger, S. Č. (2021). Attitudes Towards using Digital Technologies in Education as an Important Factor in Developing Digital Competence: The Case of Slovenian Student Teachers. *International Journal of Emerging Technologies in Learning*, 16(14), 83–98. 10.3991/ijet.v16i14.22649

Undheim, M. (2021). Children and teachers engaging together with digital technology in early childhood education and care institutions: A literature review. *European Early Childhood Education Research Journal*, 472–489.

Vicente Díaz-Garcia, A. M.-N.-L.-S. (2023). Managing Digital Transformation: A Case Study in a Higher Education Institution. *Electronics (Basel)*, 12(11), 2522. 10.3390/electronics12112522

Voykina, E. A., N. G. (2019). The impact of digital technologies on the effectiveness of learning material by students in the educational process. *Proceedings of the 1st International Scientific Conference "Modern Management Trends and the Digital Economy: from Regional Development to Global Economic Growth" (MTDE 2019)*. Atlantis Press. 10.2991/mtde-19.2019.135

Zain, S. (2021). Digital transformation trends in education. *Future Directions in Digital Information*, 223-234.

Chapter 19
Navigating the Data–Driven Future of Virtual and Hybrid Events

Rajeev Semwal
https://orcid.org/0000-0003-4572-5411
Amity University Uttar Pradesh, Greater Noida Campus, India

Pankaj Kumar Tyagi
https://orcid.org/0000-0001-9504-541X
Chandigarh University, India

Nandita Tripathi
Amity University Uttar Pradesh, Greater Noida Campus, India

Udit Kumar Pandey
https://orcid.org/0000-0003-2117-4117
Graphic Era Hill University, Haldwani, India

ABSTRACT

Data analytics is transforming virtual and hybrid event planning with quantifiable goals, real-time analytics, and many data sources. Modern technologies like emotional analytics, AI-driven predictive analytics, quantum computing, and others boost customization, engagement, and event immersion. Extended reality (XR) analytics, edge AI, and hyper-personalization provide unmatched participant experiences. An analytical attitude, coordinated leadership, and extensive team training are necessary. Participants' privacy is protected by data security and ethics. Data analytics affects decision-making, customization, innovation, and technology adoption, making virtual and hybrid events more engaging. It signals a shift toward a flexible, life-changing event experience in the data-driven future.

DOI: 10.4018/979-8-3693-2272-7.ch019

INTRODUCTION

In the dynamic panorama of digital and hybrid occasions, the heartbeat that propels innovation, strategic planning, and extraordinary player reviews is none aside from data. The technology of activities is now not restricted to bodily areas by myself; it extends into the realms of the virtual, the augmented, and the hybrid. Within this expansive domain, the function of statistics and analytics emerges as a guiding force, navigating event organizers through a sea of information to unveil insights that form the very essence of their techniques.

Data analytics stands as the silent architect behind the scenes, meticulously collecting, processing, and decoding a wealth of information generated by every digital interaction and bodily presence. This chapter delves into the essential function played by using data in shaping event techniques, supplying organizers with a compass to navigate the problematic landscapes of attendee engagement, content relevance, and universal occasion effectiveness. Beyond the traditional measures of success, the effectiveness of a modern event hinges on its potential to conform, evolve, and resonate with its target audience. Here, facts serve as the compass, revealing styles, possibilities, and traits that could, in any other case, remain hidden inside the vast expanse of occasional interactions. We explore how the strategic usage of statistics analytics transcends the bounds of mere statistical analysis, fostering an environment where decisions aren't simply knowledgeable but optimized for optimum impact.

As we embark on this journey into the world of event analytics, we unravel the layers of its significance and witness how it transforms occasions from static occurrences to dynamic, data-pushed reports that leave lasting impressions. Join us in decoding the language of statistics and uncovering the keys to unlocking the total capability of virtual and hybrid activities.

THE LANDSCAPE OF EVENT ANALYTICS

The analysis of events in the dynamic landscape of virtual and hybrid events offers valuable insights that influence future encounters(Schulte-Römer & Gesing, 2022). This chapter examines the various types of data and essential metrics and performance indicators in event analytics, which aid in making informed decisions.

Types of Data Collected

1. **Registration Data:** Registration data, including names, affiliations, and contact information, is the first stop on the data voyage. Event planners may target outreach and see all attendees using this initial dataset. By gathering this in-

formation upfront, organizers may better understand their participants' diverse backgrounds and modify their approach.

2. **Engagement Metrics:** Virtual platform engagement indicators include session attendance, booth visits, and content downloads. Event organizers may use these statistics to determine which sessions, exhibitors, and content were most popular, improving future events. Data-driven content curation may ensure that future events are tailored to the audience's choices and interests by examining participant engagement patterns.

3. **Polls and Surveys:** Polls and questionnaires distributed to attendees throughout the event provide rich qualitative data. By capturing participants' ideas, feelings, and preferences, organizers may gain a more detailed picture of how they feel. This data is essential for assessing participant satisfaction, improving things, and influencing future occurrences.

4. **Networking Data:** Participants' networking actions, such as connections made, messages exchanged, and virtual meetings attended, might reveal networking features' performance. Networking data may help event organizers develop meaningful relationships, community, and long-term engagement.

5. **Social Media Engagement:** Social media indicators like hashtags, mentions, and shares improve event visibility and indicate audience sentiment. The event's reach outside digital may be measured by tracking social media involvement, which provides organic marketing data. Keeping an eye on these metrics helps event organizers understand online discussions and identify strategic improvements.

6. **Session Interaction:** Participation may be tracked in real time using chat logs, questions, and replies during virtual sessions. Adapting courses based on user participation keeps the material fresh and entertaining. The event becomes more engaging and focused on the attendees when data guides session involvement.

7. **Technical Metrics:** Technical measures include platform speed, load times, and participant connectivity. These data enable proactive troubleshooting to provide a seamless virtual experience by immediately identifying and addressing technological issues. Organizers may improve the event experience and reduce disruptions by monitoring technical data and fixing issues in real time.

8. **Post-Events Surveys:** Surveys are given afterward to assess satisfaction, improvement ideas, and future event expectations. For analysis done after an event, which enhances and informs future occurrences, this data is priceless. Event planners may learn a lot about what works and what doesn't by conducting surveys with attendees.

Figure 1. Key metrics and performance indicators

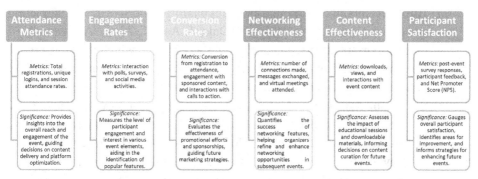

Source: Author's own compilation

To comprehend the event analytics ecosystem, one must go beyond the mere act of gathering data. To uncover significant insights that impact upcoming virtual and hybrid events, one must analyze participant narratives, grasp the complexities of involvement, and apply acquired knowledge. By thoroughly analyzing data and crucial clues, event planners may boost both present and future events.

TOOLS AND TECHNOLOGIES SHAPING THE FUTURE OF EVENT ANALYTICS

For interesting and smooth virtual and hybrid events, analytics systems must be effective. This chapter examines the features and capabilities of event industry analytics tools. Technology that might transform data collection and processing is also examined.

Analytics Tools in the Events Industry

a) **Event Management Platforms**: A comprehensive event management platform simplifies event planning, implementation, and analysis (Vasudavan et al., 2023). They offer real-time analytics, registration tracking, and centralized data administration. With this connection, event planners can see the entire picture and make wise decisions at every stage.

b) **Google Analytics** Online interactions may be tracked with Google Analytics, which measures and reports on website visitors (Pakkala et al., 2012). It helps analyze audience activities and attribute them to sources because it works with event websites. Event organizers may improve their digital strategy, user experience, and visibility with Google Analytics.

C) **Hubspot:** Inbound marketing and sales platform HubSpot tracks interaction and correspondence via analytics (Duke & Ashraf, 2019). Additionally, it gives important advertising campaign success data, which is a huge bonus. HubSpot can track engagement, audience interactions, and marketing strategy to help event planners maximize their events.

d) **Zoom Analytics:** Zoom Analytics meets virtual event demands by delivering detailed session engagement, participant interactions, and attendance data (Meyer et al., 2021). Zoom Analytics may let you discover how participants are acting throughout your virtual event, which can help you enlighten particular audiences and improve their experience. This tool lets event planners improve virtual gatherings based on data.

e) **Cvent:** Cvent stands out as a cloud-based event management software with built-in analytics. Event registration, planning, and analysis may be easier with it. Cvent's robust reporting lets organizers make data-driven decisions. Technology ensures a smooth planning-to-analysis process and excellent event administration (Lee et al., 2003).

f) **Aventri:** Aventri's event management and analytics software analyzes attendees, reports after events, and organizes events using data. Aventri is essential since it can illuminate numerous events. This software lets organizers assess event success, demographics, and planning, creating a cycle of improvement.

Table 1. Emerging technologies impacting event analytics

Emerging technologies	Impact on Data Collection	Impact on Data Analytics
Artificial Intelligence	AI algorithms can automate sentiment analysis, participant profiling, and trend spotting, improving speed and accuracy.	Improves decision-making with real-time data, personalized suggestions, and predictive analytics.
Augmented Reality (AR) and Virtual Reality (VR)	AR/VR immersive experiences reveal how users use and prefer virtual environments.	Improves virtual space participant behavior research by revealing how well immersive material and surroundings work.
Machine Learning (ML)	ML systems explore vast databases for trends, patterns, and outliers to acquire more detailed data.	Analyzes participant behaviors and uses predictive modeling to adjust event components to shifting patterns.
Blockchain for Data Security	All participant data is securely captured and cannot be manipulated using blockchain technology.	Validates analytics outcomes by providing a reliable data collection and storage basis.

continued on following page

Table 1. Continued

Emerging technologies	Impact on Data Collection	Impact on Data Analytics
Edge Computing	Processing data closer to the source reduces latency and enables real-time data collection.	Increases real-time data processing efficiency for faster, more accurate judgments.
Internet of Things (IoT)	IoT devices collect data on participant movements, booth visits, and interactions.	Enriches data sets for a more comprehensive understanding of participant behavior, preferences, and engagement.
5G Connectivity	Improved data transfer rates and reliability enable real-time data collection.	Optimizes data streaming for faster analytics reporting and smoother virtual events.
Cloud Computing	Enables scalable and flexible storage of vast amounts of event data.	Supports efficient processing and retrieval of data, ensuring event organizers can handle large volumes of information

Source: Author's own Compilation

A rich event data analytics ecosystem supports both traditional analytics tools and emerging technologies. These tools help event managers improve participant experiences, gain useful insights, and make industry-advancing decisions. Event professionals should examine current analytics tools and the revolutionary potential of emerging technologies to create more immersive, engaging, and data-informed events. When combined, these tools and technologies improve hybrid and virtual event dynamics and provide new opportunities.

DATA DRIVEN DECISION MAKING -MAKING IN EVENT PLANNING: UNLOCKING INSIGHTS FOR SUCCESS

The utilization of data in decision-making has improved the process of event planning, strategic planning, and overall achievement. This chapter employs case studies to analyze the impact of data-driven strategies on decision-making in event planning.

Illustrative Examples of Data-Informed Decision-Making

1. **Agenda Optimization**: The organizers of an annual business conference used data analysis to find out why attendees weren't actively participating during certain times (Cao et al., 2021). They found certain time slots with lower participation rates in the past by looking at session attendance statistics from prior years. With this data in hand, organizers were able to make educated judgments about the schedule, shifting high-impact programs to those hours with traditionally

low attendance. As a consequence, participation and happiness skyrocketed as people were able to enjoy programs that were more tailored to their schedules and passions.

2. **Sponsorship ROI Enhancement:** In order to increase the return on investment (ROI) for sponsors, organizers of a trade exhibition used data utilization tactics (A. Jensen et al., 2018). The goal was to make the most of sponsorship opportunities. They identified the most popular networking spots, exposition booths, and sponsored material downloads by evaluating engagement numbers. Sponsors were positioned in high-traffic locations, and attendees were offered bespoke sponsorship packages depending on their interests, thanks to this knowledge. As a result of sponsors' enhanced exposure in the most attention-grabbing regions, sponsor satisfaction rose and return on investment (ROI) improved.

3. **Content Personalization:** Using information gathered from registrations and engagement metrics, the organizers of a virtual conference were able to tailor the material to different demographics of participants (Fischl et al., 2020). They were able to learn about the demographics and preferences of the attendees by analyzing this data. Using this information, the event planners created individualized content tracks, giving each participant something unique according to their interests and the sector in which they worked. Participants were more satisfied, and the number of sessions attended went up because they thought the content was tailored to their interests and requirements.

4. **Real-time Agenda Adjustments:** Using real-time analytics techniques, organizers of a multi-day hybrid conference were able to swiftly resolve unanticipated technical difficulties in individual sessions (Li et al., 2023). During the sessions that were impacted, these technologies monitored engagement metrics and participant drop-offs. Using this information, organizers quickly changed things up by rearranging sessions or adding new content. Participants' involvement and general happiness were maintained by this proactive strategy, which guaranteed a flawless experience despite technological issues.

5. **Marketing Effectiveness Evaluation:** Event planners wanted to see how different forms of advertising fared at a product launch (Cooper, 1994). Google Analytics, social media analytics, and registration data were used to find out where people were signing up and how engaged they were. With this information in hand, the organizers redirected marketing funds to the platforms that had the greatest number of registrations and interactions, making data-driven decisions. As a result of this data-driven modification of the marketing plan, the event reach increased, proving once and for all the efficacy of data-driven marketing.

Table 2. Examples of successful data-driven strategies

Example	Objective	Data Driven Approach	Implementation	Outcome
1. Dreamforce	Dreamforce's annual conference aimed to enhance attendee satisfaction and optimize session content.	Dreamforce utilized AI-powered analytics to analyze past attendee behavior, session ratings, and engagement metrics.	Personalized recommendations were provided to attendees, guiding them to sessions aligning with their interests. Session content was adjusted based on historical engagement data.	Attendee satisfaction increased with higher session attendance and positive feedback, demonstrating the efficacy of data-driven personalization.
2. Web Summit	*The* Web Summit, one of the largest tech conferences globally, sought to improve networking opportunities for participants.	*Approach:* Salesforce utilized AI-powered analytics to analyze past attendee behavior, session ratings, and engagement metrics.	: Personalized recommendations were provided to attendees, guiding them to sessions aligning with their interests. Session content was adjusted based on historical engagement data.	Attendee satisfaction increased with higher session attendance and positive feedback, demonstrating the efficacy of data-driven personalization.
3. SXSW	:SXSW, a renowned music, film, and tech festival, aimed to optimize the festival schedule for diverse attendee interests.	Analysis of historical attendance data and participant feedback informed decisions on content curation and scheduling.	The festival schedule was diversified to cater to different audience segments, with data-driven recommendations for personalized experiences.	Increased attendance across a variety of sessions and a positive impact on participant satisfaction, showcasing the success of data-driven content planning.
Example	Objective	Data Driven Approach	Implementation	Outcome
4. IBM Think	IBM Think sought to enhance the effectiveness of sponsored content and exhibition booths.	Engagement metrics from previous events were analyzed to identify the most visited booths and popular sponsored sessions.	Sponsorship packages were redesigned, offering prime locations based on engagement data. Sponsored content was strategically integrated into the agenda.	Sponsors reported increased lead generation and participant interaction, demonstrating the value of data-driven sponsorship strategies.

Source: Author's own Compilation

The power of Decision Making

The provided examples and case studies highlight the significant impact of data-driven decision-making in event planning. By utilizing the knowledge obtained from participant data, event managers may customize experiences, optimize schedules, and strategically distribute resources, eventually resulting in more participant contentment, enhanced involvement, and the overall triumph of events. The utilization of data-driven decision-making has significantly improved the processes of event planning, strategic planning, and overall success. This chapter employs case studies to analyze the impact of data-driven strategies on decision-making in event planning.

NAVIGATING THE CHALLENGES OF EVENT ANALYTICS: STRATEGIES AND SOLUTIONS

Event analytics, where data drives decision-making, has several issues that require novel solutions. This chapter addresses the most frequent event analytics issues and offers ways to keep data useful.

Common Challenges in Event Analytics

1. **Data Overload:** The volume of data produced during events is a major hurdle. Event planners should use metrics that support the event's goals and use effective data filtering (Wu et al., 2006). Analytics tools with customizable dashboards let them analyze data and develop conclusions.
2. **Lack of Standardization:** Data formats and standards vary among systems, making data integration and analysis difficult (Schwinn & Schelp, 2005). A data integration platform and common data collection methods can overcome this challenge. Data sources should be checked routinely for reliability and consistency.
3. **Privacy Concerns:** Data privacy is becoming increasingly essential; therefore, many worry about whether collecting and using participant data is ethical (Favaretto et al., 2020). Event organizers should enforce strict privacy restrictions, seek participants' agreement, and anonymize sensitive data whenever possible to allay these concerns. Secure data transport and storage help protect participant data.
4. **Technical Issues:** Platform unavailability and network issues might affect data collection and real-time analytics (Dubuc et al., 2021). Event planners should employ several systems, prepare backup plans, and check for issues in real time to address this challenge. Interruptions need open and honest communication with participants.
5. **Integration Challenges:** Registration sites, social media, and online event management systems are among the data sources that may be challenging to combine (Bello-Orgaz et al., 2016). Investing in data integration technologies that make it simpler to integrate data sources and ensuring platforms can connect easily through APIs and protocols are important answers

6. **Limited Resources:** Due to manpower and budgetary constraints, smaller event firms may struggle to include significant analytics (Stam et al., 2014). To overcome this, event organizers might stress measurements that support event goals. They may also employ cost-effective analytics tools, outsource specialized tasks, and maximize team member potential.

7. **Resistance to Change:** Organizational opposition to new analytics tools and procedures may limit adoption (Ghaleb et al., 2021). We need an atmosphere that invites new ideas and makes evidence-based judgments to overcome this challenge. Training, instructional materials, and success stories demonstrate the benefits of analytics adoption.

8. **Inadequate Skill Sets:** Event crews without data analytics capabilities may struggle to embrace (Pidgeon & O'Leary, 2000). Funding skill-building programs, hiring specialists, and partnering with outside consultants or experts for analytics projects are among the options.

Strategies and Solutions

Addressing event analytics difficulties requires a comprehensive strategy involving many important approaches and solutions. Establish the objectives of the event beforehand. Clearly define event objectives and organize data gathering to utilize data for measuring success indicators. Another crucial approach is to prioritize data quality over quantity. Regular audits, validation testing, and data quality assurance may accomplish this. Implementing proactive privacy measures, including clear data usage rules, obtaining consent, and encryption, safeguards participant privacy. Investing in reliable technology, particularly in data integration and analytics, is another important option. To do this, it is essential to keep abreast of current technology and utilize analytics tools that align with the objectives of the event. Collaboration across cross-functional teams, facilitated by open communication and information sharing, is crucial for the coordination of event, marketing, and IT departments. Continuous improvement involves analyzing data post-event, soliciting input, and making incremental adjustments based on insights gained. Strategic outsourcing involves hiring external specialists to handle certain activities in order to make the most of internal resources. Instructional activities should encompass training, seminars, and instructional resources to enhance the abilities of team members. Event analytics necessitates an intentional and forward-thinking mindset. Companies need to pinpoint problems, devise solutions, and cultivate a growth mindset to thrive in the dynamic realm of data analytics in events.

NAVIGATING THE ETHICAL LANDSCAPE

Amidst the prevalence of data-driven decision-making, event planners and attendees are concerned about data ethics. The ethical issues in this chapter stress the need for data protection and transparency in the events industry.

Ethical Considerations in Data Collection

Informed Consent:

Consideration: Participants should know what data is collected, how it will be used, and how their privacy is protected.

Implementation: Clearly articulate data usage policies in registration forms and event communications. Obtain explicit consent for data collection, ensuring participants have the option to opt in or opt out.

Data Minimization:

Consideration: Collect only the data necessary for the intended purpose, avoiding the unnecessary collection of sensitive information.

Implementation: Define clear data collection objectives and limit the scope to information directly relevant to event planning. Avoid the collection of extraneous or unrelated personal details.

Anonymization and pseudonymization:

Consideration: Protecting participant identities requires anonymizing or pseudonymizing data, especially sensitive content.

Implementation: Encrypt, pseudonym, or anonymize data to remove participant identification.

Data Security:

Consideration: Guard participant data against misuse.

Implementation: Protect against cyberattacks with encrypted data storage and access restrictions. Update security to combat new threats.

5Participant Empowerment:

Consideration: Empower participants with control over their data and the ability to manage their privacy settings.

Implementation: Provide participants with clear options to manage their data preferences, including the ability to modify or delete their information. Communicate privacy features in the event app or platform.

Ensuring Privacy and Transparency

Clear Privacy Policies:

Consideration: Communicate transparent and concise privacy policies to participants.

Implementation: Create and share a clear privacy policy that explains data collection, why, and protections. Give participants easy access to this policy.

Transparent Data Usage:

Consideration: Be transparent about how the collected data will be utilized.

Implementation: Clearly communicate the intended use of data to participants during the registration process and within event communications. Highlight any analytics, marketing, or research purposes.

Participant Education:

Consideration: Make sure event attendees understand how data collection improves things.

Implementation: Educational items like FAQs and video courses may explain data-driven advances and privacy safeguards. Openness and honesty build trust.

Secure Data Sharing Practices:

Consideration: If sharing data with third parties, ensure secure and responsible data sharing practices.

Implementation: Create clear data-sharing agreements. Third parties must meet data processing ethics and privacy laws. They must obey these guidelines.

Consistent Communication:

Consideration: Maintain ongoing communication with participants about privacy measures.

Implementation: Provide periodic updates on privacy practices, especially if there are changes to data collection or usage policies. Address participant queries promptly and transparently.

Privacy by Design:

Consideration: Embed privacy considerations into the design and development of data systems from the outset.

Implementation: Event platforms and apps should offer privacy-focused features. Privacy impact evaluations help identify and address issues.

Compliance with Regulations:

Consideration: Adhere to relevant data protection regulations and frameworks.

Implementation: Ensure all data handling processes comply with changing privacy laws like CCPA or GDPR. Consult a lawyer to ensure compliance with local, national, and international laws.

Striking the Ethical Balance:

Collecting valuable event data requires rigorous ethical consideration and balancing openness with participant privacy. Event organizers must handle ethical issues to reassure attendees and improve public perceptions of fact-based decision-making. Event planners may follow the law and build confidence by implementing ethical and transparent practices. This ethical underpinning underpins data processing to empower and respect participants in digital events. The events industry can demonstrate that new data methods can be inventive, ethical, and participant-friendly.

HARNESSING THE POWER OF REAL-TIME ANALYTICS: ADAPTING AND OPTIMIZING EVENTS ON THE FLY

The Importance of Real-Time Data in Event Dynamics

Figure 2. Importance of real-time data in event dynamics

Source: Author's own Compilation

The impact of real-time data on several aspects of event organization highlights its significance in shaping event dynamics. Real-time analytics enables event managers to make prompt decisions by utilizing up-to-the-minute data. This ability is extremely helpful in dynamic event scenarios when quick reactions to participant actions, technological problems, and unforeseen obstacles are necessary. Another advantage is heightened participant involvement. Organizers may utilize real-time data to monitor the level of involvement of attendees in seminars, virtual booths, and networking activities. Event managers have the ability to modify the event based on popular aspects in order to enhance participation and pleasure. Event organizers have the ability to modify the program in response to participant preferences or unforeseen circumstances by utilizing up-to-date data. An adaptable and participant-focused schedule permits the inclusion of additional resources or adjustments to the timetable in case some sessions garner greater popularity than anticipated. Timely analytics are crucial for diagnosing and resolving technological problems. Swiftly addressing platform or connection issues minimizes participant interruption and guarantees a smooth event experience. Maximizing networking possibilities is achieved through the visibility of real-time participant networking activities. Organizers can identify popular networking areas and assist in facilitating immediate interactions to enhance networking and cultivate significant relationships. The utilization of real-time data in event dynamics can enhance decision-making, increase participant involvement, facilitate agenda adaptability, address technical challenges, and foster networking opportunities.

NAVIGATING THE HORIZON: FUTURE TRENDS AND ADVANCEMENTS IN EVENT ANALYTICS

The dynamic nature of virtual and hybrid events necessitates constant innovation in the field of event analytics. Numerous upcoming changes will impact how event planners collect, analyze, and utilize data to enhance their services to guests. This chapter explores upcoming advancements in event analytics and predicts the future of data analytics in the context of virtual and hybrid events.

Upcoming Trends in Event Analytics

1. AI-Driven Predictive Analytics:

Trend: The integration of AI-driven predictive analytics will become more sophisticated.
Prediction: AI algorithms will not only forecast attendance patterns but also predict participant preferences, enabling organizers to proactively tailor content and experiences based on anticipated interests.

2. Emotional Analytics:

Trend: Emotional analytics will gain prominence, capturing participant sentiments during virtual and hybrid events.
Prediction: Advanced sentiment analysis tools will be integrated into event platforms, allowing organizers to gauge participant emotions in real time. This data will inform adjustments to content and interactions to ensure a more emotionally resonant experience.

3. Quantum Computing for Complex Analysis:

Trend: The adoption of quantum computing for complex data analysis tasks will rise.

Prediction: Quantum computing's ability to process vast datasets and perform intricate calculations will revolutionize the depth and speed of event analytics. This advancement will enable more nuanced insights and complex modeling for event optimization.

4. Extended Reality (XR) Analytics:

Trend: XR analytics will expand beyond VR and AR to include mixed reality (MR) and other immersive technologies.

Prediction: The integration of XR analytics will enable organizers to track participant interactions in a mixed reality environment. This data will be leveraged to refine immersive experiences, enhancing the synergy between the physical and virtual realms.

5. Edge AI for Real-Time Processing:

Trend: Edge AI will be increasingly utilized for real-time data processing during events.

Prediction: Edge AI, combined with IoT devices and sensors, will enable immediate data processing at the source. This trend will enhance the immediacy and accuracy of event analytics, facilitating on-the-fly adjustments and optimizations.

6. Hyper-Personalization through Advanced Segmentation:

Trend: Hyper-personalization will be achieved through more advanced participant segmentation.

Prediction: Granular participant segmentation based on behavioral patterns, preferences, and engagement histories will enable organizers to deliver highly tailored content and experiences. This level of personalization will elevate participant satisfaction and engagement.

Evolution of Data Analytics in Virtual and Hybrid Events

1. Integrated Data Ecosystems:

Evolution: Data analytics will be seamlessly integrated into comprehensive event ecosystems.

Prediction: Event platforms will evolve to incorporate end-to-end data analytics capabilities. This integration will provide organizers with a holistic view of participant interactions, allowing for more informed decision-making across all facets of the event.

2. Real-Time Collaboration and Communication Analytics:

Evolution: Real-time collaboration and communication analytics will become integral for virtual and hybrid events.

Prediction: Analytics tools will extend beyond participant behaviors to analyze communication dynamics during virtual sessions, workshops, and networking events. This evolution will enable organizers to optimize engagement and foster meaningful connections.

3. Blockchain for Enhanced Data Security and Transparency:

Evolution: Blockchain technology will play a greater role in securing and transparently managing event data.

Prediction: Blockchain will be integrated into event analytics systems to enhance data security, prevent tampering, and provide participants with verifiable insights into how their data is utilized. This evolution will strengthen trust and compliance.

4. Neuroanalytics for Cognitive Engagement Measurement:

Evolution: Neuroanalytics will be utilized to measure cognitive engagement during virtual and hybrid events.

Prediction: By leveraging neuroscientific principles, organizers will gain insights into participant attention, focus, and cognitive load. This evolution will enable the optimization of content delivery and event pacing for enhanced participant engagement.

5. Robust Data Governance and Compliance Frameworks:

Evolution: Data governance and compliance frameworks will evolve to meet the increasing regulatory demands.

Prediction: As data privacy regulations continue to evolve globally, event organizers will implement more robust governance frameworks. This evolution will prioritize ethical data practices and ensure compliance with regional and international regulations.

6. Continuous Integration with Emerging Technologies:

Evolution: Event analytics will be continuously integrated with emerging technologies.

Prediction: As new technologies emerge, event analytics will adapt and integrate seamlessly. The evolution will involve staying at the forefront of technological trends and ensuring that analytics capabilities remain at the cutting edge of innovation.

Navigating the Future Landscape

As virtual and hybrid events continue to gain prominence, the trajectory of event analytics points towards a future defined by innovation, personalization, and real-time adaptability. The integration of AI, emotional analytics, quantum computing, extended reality, edge AI, and hyper-personalization will shape the landscape of event analytics, offering organizers unprecedented insights and capabilities.

To navigate this future landscape successfully, event organizers must stay agile, embrace technological advancements, and prioritize ethical data practices. The convergence of these trends will not only redefine how events are analyzed but will also pave the way for a new era of immersive, participant-centric experiences that set the standard for the events industry.

MAXIMIZING EVENT SUCCESS: BEST PRACTICES FOR EVENT ANALYTICS OPTIMIZATION

In the dynamic world of virtual and hybrid events, the effective utilization of data analytics is pivotal for achieving success. This chapter outlines actionable tips for event organizers to maximize the benefits of data analytics and provides guidance on fostering a data-driven culture within event teams.

Best Practices for Event Analytics Optimization

1. **Define clear objectives:** Clearly define the objectives of your event analytics strategy from the outset. Identify the key performance indicators (KPIs) that align with your event goals. Whether it's increasing participant engagement, optimizing session content, or improving networking, having well-defined objectives sets the foundation for effective analytics.
2. **Utilize comprehensive data sources:** Collect data from diverse sources to gain a holistic view of participant interactions. Integrate data from registration platforms, event apps, virtual booths, and social media. Combining data sources

provides a comprehensive understanding of participant behavior, preferences, and engagement across different touchpoints.

3. **Implement real-time analytics:** Prioritize real-time analytics for on-the-fly decision-making. Utilize platforms that offer live dashboards and real-time reporting. This enables organizers to adapt event elements dynamically, addressing issues promptly and capitalizing on emerging trends during the event.

4. **Focus on data quality assurance**: Prioritize data quality over quantity to ensure accurate insights.Regularly audit data sources, implement validation checks, and establish data quality assurance protocols. Clean and reliable data is essential for making informed decisions and optimizing event experiences.

5. **Implement Participant Feedback Mechanisms:** Actively seek participant feedback to enhance future events. Incorporate surveys, polls, and feedback forms within the event platform. Analyzing participant responses provides valuable insights into satisfaction levels, preferences, and areas for improvement, guiding future event planning.

Event organizers need to categorize people to enable focused analysis and interaction. Segmenting participants based on industry, job function, or level of commitment allows organizers to customize content, marketing strategies, and engagement for distinct groups. By focusing on certain demographics, we can provide tailored information to enhance their event experience. Predictive analytics may contribute to the success of an event. AI-powered predictive analytics can anticipate attendance, session popularity, and networking preferences. Prior planning allows organizers to refine several event aspects and fulfill participant expectations. Sustained success necessitates a culture of ongoing evolution guided by insights from analytics. Event organizers should analyze analytics data post-event to evaluate successful strategies and areas for enhancement. Organizations utilize data-driven insights to enhance event strategies and ensure continuous improvement, with each event surpassing the previous one. This dedication to enhancement results in more impactful future occurrences.

Creating a Data-Driven Culture Within Event Teams

Leadership alignment and support are essential for implementing a successful data-driven strategy in event planning. Leaders should advocate for the importance of data analytics, highlighting its significance in accomplishing event objectives. This assistance establishes a basis for implementing data-driven approaches throughout the whole event crew. Team training investment is equally crucial. Offering seminars, online courses, and tools may improve team members' data analytics abilities, allowing them to utilize analytics more efficiently in event planning and decision-making. Promote cross-functional cooperation by eliminating barriers between various departments in the event team, including marketing, operations, and technology. This partnership guarantees that data analytics is smoothly incorporated into every facet of event planning and implementation. It is essential to provide clear communication channels for topics connected to data. Establishing a communication strategy that promotes open sharing of insights helps ensuring that all team members are in sync with the data-driven goals. It is crucial to acknowledge and incentivize achievements based on data analysis to strengthen the value of a data-oriented environment and inspire others to adopt analytics in their positions. Incorporating analytics into planning meetings as a recurring agenda item guarantees that data is included into decision-making processes and becomes a fundamental aspect of event planning conversations. It is essential to give team members access to analytics tools to empower them to make proactive and self-reliant decisions. Encouraging the development of a culture that promotes experimentation and innovation backed by data is recommended. Team members should be authorized to investigate new ideas, experiment with hypotheses, and create innovations using insights from analytics. This environment of experimentation promotes creativity and a readiness to investigate new methods guided by data, eventually enhancing the effectiveness of data-driven event design.

Nurturing Success Through Data Excellence

Adopting these data-driven culture best practices will help event organizers create meaningful and productive events. Using advanced data approaches helps event organizers handle the present event world accurately and foresightedly. First, all event-lifetime choices benefit from data. Use registration data, engagement metrics, polls, surveys, and other data to understand participant behavior and preferences. With this information, event planners may ensure content, session scheduling, and event design fulfill participant expectations. Using new technology and analytical techniques helps organizers adapt to changing event settings. Using interaction data and participant feedback, organizers may use real-time analytics and predictive modeling to address patterns, rectify technical issues, and fine-tune event features. Data-driven event organizers may provide attendees with a flexible and tailored experience due to their agility. Creating a data-driven event team culture is equally groundbreaking. After this mindset adjustment, team members are more inclined to take the initiative and work collaboratively, seeing data as an inspiration for new ideas rather than merely an analytical instrument. Event organizers provide teams with analytics tools, incorporate analytics into planning sessions, and award data-driven wins. Constant data utilization helps event techniques evolve. Iterative analysis and post-event surveys promote organization-wide continuous improvement.

Every event builds on the successes and lessons acquired from the previous ones, allowing for continual advancement. Event organizers that embrace a data-driven culture will be pioneers, in addition to the obvious benefits. As the events industry evolves, data quality becomes a differentiator. Using data, organizers may meet and exceed audiences' growing expectations for engaging and tailored experiences.

CONCLUSION

Finally, data analytics is driving the virtual and hybrid event industry's transformation. This lengthy analysis has stressed the relevance of data analytics in predicting future occurrences. A complex network of data-driven breakthroughs, new ideas, and social shifts is shaping virtual and hybrid events. These proven strategies for boosting event analytics can help event planners maximize their data. A data-driven event planning approach may be created by using vast data sources, setting clear goals, using real-time analytics, and promoting continuous improvement. AI, AR, VR, and quantum computing will also transform event experiences. Predictive, emotive, and extended reality can enhance event personalization, engagement, and immersion. Event analytics' future depends on current technology, data governance frameworks, and ethical issues; therefore, data management must be responsible and safe. Most importantly, patterns and breakthroughs illuminated the future. AI-driven predictive analytics, emotional analytics, and quantum computing promise a data-driven, emotionally resonant, technologically advanced future. Integrating XR analytics, edge AI, and hyper-personalization shows the ever-changing analytics landscape, helping organizers stay ahead.

Event teams need a data-driven culture to succeed. To embrace and incorporate data into all aspects of event planning, leadership must be on the same page, team training must be invested in, and cross-functional cooperation must be encouraged. Organizations should recognize and incentivize data-driven triumphs, include analytics in planning discussions, and offer analytics tools to achieve exceptional event success. Future virtual and hybrid events will depend on data analytics. Data-driven insights aid decision-making, customization, innovation, and technology adoption. Event immersion and participant-centricity depend on data analytics applied strategically. By following these trends, best practices, and data-driven culture, event planners may shape virtual and hybrid events. Events will be more interesting, inventive, and successful than ever. As we progress toward a data-driven future, cultural and strategic changes define events as ever-changing, flexible, and possibly life-changing experiences.

REFERENCES

Bello-Orgaz, G., Jung, J. J., & Camacho, D. (2016). Social big data: Recent achievements and new challenges. *Information Fusion*, 28, 45–59. 10.1016/j.inffus.2015.08.00532288689

Cao, H., Lee, C. J., Iqbal, S., Czerwinski, M., Wong, P., Rintel, S., Hecht, B., Teevan, J., & Yang, L. (2021). Large scale analysis of multitasking behavior during remote meetings. *Conference on Human Factors in Computing Systems - Proceedings*. ACM. 10.1145/3411764.3445243

Cooper, R. G. (1994). New Products: The Factors that Drive Success. *International Marketing Review*, 11(1), 60–76. 10.1108/02651339410057527

Dubuc, T., Stahl, F., & Roesch, E. B. (2021). Mapping the Big Data Landscape: Technologies, Platforms and Paradigms for Real-Time Analytics of Data Streams. *IEEE Access : Practical Innovations, Open Solutions*, 9, 15351–15374. 10.1109/ACCESS.2020.3046132

Duke, L., & Ashraf, A. (2019). *Aligning Analytics with Marketing Strategy: Using Analytics to Drive Marketing Strategy with New Media Applications*. Springer. 10.1007/978-3-319-93299-6_11

Favaretto, M., De Clercq, E., Gaab, J., & Elger, B. S. (2020). First do no harm: An exploration of researchers' ethics of conduct in Big Data behavioral studies. *PLoS One*, 15(11), e0241865. 10.1371/journal.pone.024186533152039

Fischl, C., Blusi, M., Lindgren, H., & Nilsson, I. (2020). Tailoring to support digital technology-mediated occupational engagement for older adults – a multiple case study. *Scandinavian Journal of Occupational Therapy*, 27(8), 577–590. 10.1080/1 1038128.2020.176034732396419

Ghaleb, E. A. A., Dominic, P. D. D., Fati, S. M., Muneer, A., & Ali, R. F. (2021). The Assessment of Big Data Adoption Readiness with a Technology–Organization–Environment Framework: A Perspective towards Healthcare Employees. *Sustainability, 13*(15), 8379. 10.3390/su13158379

Jensen, , A., Walsh, P., & Cobbs, J. (2018). The moderating effect of identification on return on investment from sponsor brand integration. *International Journal of Sports Marketing & Sponsorship*, 19(1), 41–57. 10.1108/IJSMS-10-2016-0077

Lee, C., Nordstedt, D., & Helal, S. (2003). Enabling smart spaces with OSGi. *IEEE Pervasive Computing*, 2(3), 89–94. 10.1109/MPRV.2003.1228530

Li, B., Soma, T., Springle, N., & Shulman, T. (2023). Reflections From Implementing a Virtual Social Innovation Lab. *International Journal of Qualitative Methods*, 22. Advance online publication. 10.1177/16094069221149871

Meyer, M. F., Ladwig, R., Dugan, H. A., Anderson, A., Bah, A. R., Boehrer, B., Borre, L., Chapina, R. J., Doyle, C., Favot, E. J., Flaim, G., Forsberg, P., Hanson, P. C., Ibelings, B. W., Isles, P., Lin, F. P., Lofton, D., Moore, T. N., Peel, S., & Weathers, K. C. (2021). Virtual Growing Pains: Initial Lessons Learned from Organizing Virtual Workshops, Summits, Conferences, and Networking Events during a Global Pandemic. *Limnology and Oceanography Bulletin*, 30(1), 1–11. 10.1002/lob.10431

Pakkala, H., Presser, K., & Christensen, T. (2012). Using Google Analytics to measure visitor statistics: The case of food composition websites. *International Journal of Information Management*, 32(6), 504–512. 10.1016/j.ijinfomgt.2012.04.008

Pidgeon, N., & O'Leary, M. (2000). Man-made disasters: Why technology and organizations (sometimes) fail. *Safety Science*, 34(1–3), 15–30. 10.1016/S0925-7535(00)00004-7

Schulte-Römer, N., & Gesing, F. (2022). Online, offline, hybrid: Methodological reflection on event ethnography in (post-)pandemic times. *Sage Journals,* 23(6), 1620–1646. 10.1177/14687941221110172

Schwinn, A., & Schelp, J. (2005). Design patterns for data integration. *Journal of Enterprise Information Management*, 18(4), 471–482. 10.1108/17410390510609617

Stam, W., Arzlanian, S., & Elfring, T. (2014). Social capital of entrepreneurs and small firm performance: A meta-analysis of contextual and methodological moderators. *Journal of Business Venturing*, 29(1), 152–173. 10.1016/j.jbusvent.2013.01.002

Vasudavan, H., Razali, N. F., & Shah, D. A. (2023). Event Management Systems (EMS). *Article in Journal of Applied Research and Technology,* 7(2), 2600–7304. https://www.researchgate.net/publication/371874293

Wu, E., Diao, Y., & Rizvi, S. (2006). High-performance complex event processing over streams. *Proceedings of the ACM SIGMOD International Conference on Management of Data*, (pp. 407–418). ACM. 10.1145/1142473.1142520

Chapter 20
Virtual Reality Rehabilitation and Artificial Intelligence in Healthcare Technology

Nitin Sahai
https://orcid.org/0000-0001-7916-4363
North Eastern Hill University, India

Prabhat Kumar
University of Pécs, Hungary

Megha Sharma
Faculty of Health Sciences, University of Pécs, Hungary

ABSTRACT

The benefit of virtual rehabilitation is that it helps the patient increase their engagement and motivation. Another advantage is that it allows patient specific. A third utility is that the therapist can make the sessions more efficient and productive. A feature of virtual reality (VR) rehabilitation is that it is possible to create virtual environments which are more realistic than those in a video game and in which the patients can perform exercises. As a result, the patients are more immersed and motivated to avoid the boredom from which patients in standard therapy usually suffer. The features of artificial intelligence (AI) in biomedicine are the optimisation of diagnostics, treatment, and patient monitoring. AI allows for the analysis to have the potential to detect subtle deviations. In this chapter, the application of virtual reality and artificial intelligence in healthcare was discussed.

DOI: 10.4018/979-8-3693-2272-7.ch020

VIRTUAL REALITY TECHNOLOGY IN HEALTH CARE SYSTEM

At this point, it is necessary to start a new book chapter, which will analyze the history and development of VR technology in general, and its impact on the healthcare sector in particular. The chapter must present the way VR technology has evolved and its use in the present world (Mistry et al., 2023).

Historical Evolution of VR Technology

The history of VR technology, along with the devices constructed in the past, and even systems such as Holodeck from Star Trek that was produced in the twenty-third century, as noted by Sabine. Therefore, it was not until the mid-20th century that VR technology began to develop, and inventors and researchers such as Morton Heilig were at the forefront of this development. He called his film-like reality generator the Sensorama and developed the idea in the 1950s, creating the first device to produce sensation cinema. Over the years, there were improvements in VR technology, which handled both the hardware and software aspects of Sabine. Nevertheless, the most notable progress was made in the 1980s and 1990s (Hershberger et al., 2022).

One of the major developments introduced during this time was the standardisation of the 3D computer graphics representation on the Web through the creation of Virtual Reality Modelling Language (VRML). VPL Research and Other companies also tried to commercialize the VR systems, however, there were various technological issues at that time also the cost of creating such systems was high (Hershberger et al., 2022).

Advancements and Applications of the Turn of the Century

Interest in VR technology among the general public was re-kindled at the turn of the century when recent improvements in the technologies for use in VR headsets occurred such as open standard VRML or X3D, programming (e.g. the Combine) even the Atom and multimedia. In this context, this comeback paved the way for deeper and more realistic virtual reality experiences, rendering them increasingly useful for uses other than entertainment - in essence, a practical application near-to-real-lifeoutcome (Nishchyk et al., 2021).

The benefits of VR caught the attention of the healthcare world because they look to change medical teaching, patient care, and therapeutic interventions. Virtual Reality Simulation in Medical Training: VR surgical training, anatomic education, and phobia therapy are currently in the trial phase at medical institutions and research centres (Kane, 2018).

In addition, due to its versatility in addressing a variety of healthcare challenges, VR has been applied in pain management, rehabilitation, and psychiatric therapy. The potential of VR to supplement standard therapy methods as well as to enhance outcomes for patients has been recognized by scientists and experts (Castillo-Martinez et al., 2020).

In recent decades, the trend of VR technology in the healthcare industry has been increasing so much and will grow more and more in the future. The executive of the Emory Healthcare Veterans Programme, Barbara Rothbaum, had also been the first to deploy VR in healthcare in 1993, to treat phobias. It turned out that VR had even more medical applications like using it to treat Post-traumatic stress disorder (PTSD) in hospitals (Frewen et al., 2020).

Exploring the Modern Landscape: The Impact of Virtual Reality in the Healthcare

VR technology has rustled up and arrived in the healthcare delivery sphere of the world. Over the last few years, the use of VR solutions in healthcare has seen a substantial rise. Such growth may be due to its more affordable, easier-to-use, and more consumer-friendly technologies (Scherschinski et al., 2022).

Here is where VR simulations in medical education come into the picture and offer a virtual learning experience to students and professionals, where they can practice procedures, observe detailed anatomical hangings and have hands-on experience without the need to put the patients at risk. Educational programmes at universities worldwide now include training with VR technology to help students in the healthcare professional group hone their skills (Dy et al., 2023).

Furthermore, there have been high expectations for the application of VR in therapy for various psychological disorders like post-traumatic stress disorder (PTSD), anxiety disorder and phobias. Virtual reality therapy helps desensitize individuals and strengthens exposure therapy by allowing patients to be gradually introduced to their triggers in a controlled, safe manner through the use of controlled environments (Cerasa et al., 2024).

Clinical settings are making use of VR technology to assist patients with their pain and anxiety management, and to enhance their comfort levels during several medical procedures ranging from wound care to dental treatments, to chemotherapy sessions. These entertaining distractions, soothing methods, and tactile exercises help patients learn how to manage their symptoms to improve their experience with treatment as a whole (Taveira et al., 2022).

Prospects and Obstacles for the Future

In the future, VR in healthcare seems to be quite promising. This optimistic forecast is further supported due to technological advancements and an increased interest among healthcare professionals and patients in remote monitoring (Hadley et al., 2023; Ogdon & Crumpton, 2020). However, there are several hurdles to be cleared to truly realize the benefits of VR as a technology in healthcare. At the top of the list of course are the interoperability and standardisation challenges that are still a feature of the VR space. Most of these solutions are proprietary and do not interface with current healthcare systems or electronic health records (EHR) (McLean et al., 2023). Establishing integration and effective data transfer, between VR platforms and clinical processes is vital for the widespread acceptance of this technology. Additionally addressing issues surrounding data confidentiality, security and compliance with regulations is essential to guarantee the responsible use of VR in healthcare. Maintaining the confidentiality and security of data plays a role, in building trust and fostering belief in the effectiveness of VR healthcare solutions (Chang et al., 2021; Selim et al., 2022).

Virtual reality technology has changed, over the years evolving from a concept to a tool utilized in various healthcare applications (Ertl et al., 2021). Through its engaging experiences, scenarios and therapeutic solutions VR holds the promise of revolutionizing training, patient treatment and therapeutic approaches. Given the progress, in technology and the overcoming of implementation hurdles virtual reality is poised to make a mark on the healthcare landscape in the future (Schleider et al., 2019). Given the fact that it is at all possible, it seems that the ability of healthcare professionals to utilize virtual reality to improve clinical outcomes, patient experiences and thus the fact of healthcare as such is a complete marvel. Currently, there are several uses and modern technologies that are making this new shift to VR technology in the healthcare sector a dream of the past, maturing every day in profound ways. This concludes the work. The growing technology has an unbelievable potential to revolutionize training in the medical profession. When summarizing how virtual reality technology has had an impact on the medical industry, several advantages and uses are evident. The advancement of this technology is bound to shape and alter patient care and therapy, making it quite beneficial to the field of healthcare (Marcum et al., 2018).

BENEFITS OF VIRTUAL REALITY IN REHABILITATION

The modern world requires the application of modern technology. Virtual reality emerged as a popular trend a few years ago, starting with gaming and gradually making its way into various industries. Humans embraced VR and its usage grew steadily until it revolutionized healthcare, where it began to be utilized for the betterment of patients. VR is all about creating immersive computer-generated environments that transport users into artificial 3-dimensional worlds, stimulating their senses for a truly captivating experience (Torner et al., 2019). VR has extensive applications in the healthcare industry and offers numerous benefits, including also shown in Figure 1:

Figure 1. Medical application of virtual reality

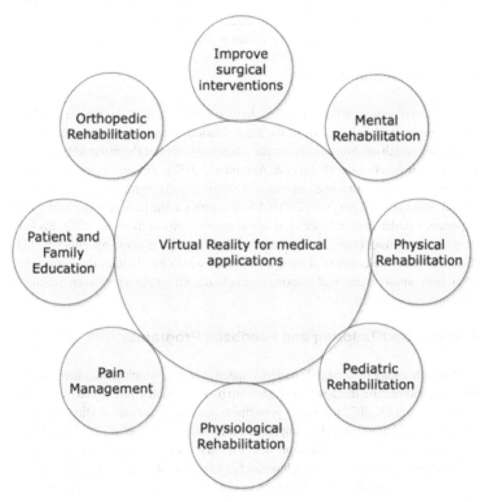

Cognitive and Mental Rehabilitation

VR has proven to be a valuable tool in aiding patients with neuro-cognitive and mental illnesses. Recent research has demonstrated positive outcomes, with patients who underwent VR rehabilitation experiencing significant improvements in their condition (Yasini & Marchand, 2016).VR is a versatile and effective tool for rehabilitating the brain, providing innovative solutions for addressing cognitive, emotional, and functional impairments resulting from neurological disorders or traumas. Virtual reality therapy harnesses the power of immersive technology to enhance engagement, promote neuroplasticity, and facilitate meaningful recovery for individuals undergoing neuropsychological rehabilitation (Zhou et al., 2022). VR enables patients to confront and gradually become less sensitive to anxiety-inducing stimuli in a controlled virtual environment. This technology greatly aids in exposure therapy for anxiety disorders, phobias, and PTSD. Virtual reality simulations manage to provide coping skills (Pedroli et al., 2022). Neuro-cognitive and psychological aspects patients are in direct need of virtual reality rehabilitation (Dy et al., 2023).

Physical Rehabilitation

The best outcome of this kind of evaluation is the health of the person involved. Virtual reality technology aids in the rehabilitation of patients with various forms of injuries and disabilities as they regain their strength and the affected body parts resume their functioning (Palozzi & Antonucci, 2022). Virtual reality is a type of exercise that ensures that one can customise the difficulty, complexity, and intensity of individual needs (Gao et al., 2020). VR also provide the patient with a real-world experience under the guidance of medical experts (Ntakakis et al., 2023; Szekely et al., 2024; Weiner et al., 2010). Teleconsultation helps provide patient care at far distances from the comfort of their own homes which emphasises the importance of giving consistent care and empowering patients, all within a virtual environment (Chiamulera et al., 2021).

Personalized Tailoring and Feedback Programs

VR technology understands patients' specific needs, which allows them to customise rehabilitation therapy that aligns with patient-specific individual treatments. (Ceccariglia et al., 2022). Patients participate actively in various challenging tasks and enjoy the therapy, which to improved outcomes (Usmani et al., 2022). VR therapy engages the patients in multiple activities that may be repetitive in comparison to conventional rehabilitation techniques (Z. Liu et al., 2022; Zhang & Ho, 2017). Virtual reality devices offer immediate feedback on patient performance, allowing physicians to continuously track progress and modify rehabilitation regimens as needed. Timely feedback improves the process of learning and helps to fix errors, hence enhancing the efficiency of rehabilitative interventions (Krpic et al., 2013). While VR equipment and software may need initial investment, VR rehabilitation eliminates the need for expensive physical therapy equipment and facilities. Healthcare providers and facilities may find VR setups cheaper than traditional rehabilitation equipment and this makes them a viable option. VR rehab facilitates faster recovery times, reducing the risk of complications, and minimizing the need for hospital readmissions or long-term care, VR rehab can result in significant cost savings for healthcare systems and payers (Breed et al., 2023). VR immersive and realistic rehabilitation simulators allow medical students and healthcare workers to experience clinical conditions in a supervised virtual environment. Medical students can practice clinical skills and interventions in VR simulations without harming patients. This lets students make mistakes, try new methods, and learn in a controlled environment. VR lets medical students practice rehabilitation skills like gait analysis, muscle testing, range of motion assessments, and therapeutic activities (Nicola et al., 2017).

APPLICATIONS OF VR REHABILITATION IN HEALTHCARE

VR is an emerging way of providing rehabilitative care to patients and it has a wide range of domains for its applications, transforming conventional rehabilitation methods and improving patient results (Obeid & Wolf, 2004). The applications of VR in healthcare are mentioned below: **Care for the elderly-** VR rehabilitation has the potential to address age-related deficits in physical and cognitive function among older persons. Additionally, old age people are more prone to the risk of falling or getting themselves injured during exercise routines, mobility and balance training and using VR ensures their safety this improves the overall well-being of elderly individuals and decreases the likelihood of age-related impairments (Pawassar & Tiberius, 2021). **Cardiovascular rehabilitation**: Cardiac patients require a strict regime in their rehabilitation due to their increased susceptibility to falling ill. VR provides an immersive and stimulating simulated workout environment for the patient recovering from myocardial infarction, coronary artery disease or congestive heart failure. By using VR, activities can be customized to enhance cardiovascular fitness, track vital signs, and encourage compliance with cardiac rehabilitation procedures (Shrestha et al., 2024). **Cognitive rehabilitation**: Virtual reality rehabilitation is especially advantageous for persons who have neurological disorders including stroke, traumatic brain injury (TBI), Alzheimer's disease, Parkinson's disease, or multiple sclerosis. VR settings can replicate real-life activities and difficulties, offering a secure and captivating platform for neurorehabilitation interventions that target the enhancement of balance, coordination, and cognitive function (Krupitzer et al., 2022). **Psychological rehabilitation**: VR rehabilitation includes not just neurological health therapies but also mental health interventions, such as psychological therapy and exposure therapy for anxiety disorders, phobias, bipolar disorders, depression, and post-traumatic stress disorder (PTSD). VR environments can replicate anxiety-inducing scenarios or traumatic events within a controlled environment, enabling patients to safely confront and conquer their phobias (Rizzo & Shilling, 2017). **Physical rehabilitation**: VR technology is extensively utilized in the field of physical rehabilitation to enhance motor function, mobility, and strength after accidents, surgeries, disabilities, and long hospitalization. VR exercises can focus on certain muscle groups or movements, making it easier to engage in repetitive repetition and improve motor learning (Palozzi & Antonucci, 2022). **Pain management**: VR technology is beneficial in pain management and encourages relaxation for those suffering from chronic pain disorders, such as fibromyalgia or complex regional pain syndrome (CRPS) (Donisi et al., 2023; Dy et al., 2023). VR also provide Patient and family education for pain management. VR helps patients and their nearby relatives learn about equipment and therapy environments (Kane, 2018; Padilla et al., 2018). VR also helps individuals have sensations and limitations belonging to a disability (Hauze et al., 2019; Kane, 2018). **Pediatric rehabilitation**: Virtual rehabilitation plays a crucial role in child rehabilitation by making it more interactive, enjoyable and stimulating. Virtual programmable games and simulations can help young individuals with neurological impairments enhance motor abilities. VR can help change the attention away from uncomfortable medical therapeutic sessions, and rehabilitation anxiety (Alanazi et al., 2022; Goktas & Avci, 2023). Virtual reality helps in various post-surgical interventions which include Orthopaedic rehabilitation and post-surgical traumas. It provides exercises and simulations to increase the range of motion following orthopaedic surgery additionally, it works well for orthopaedic surgery planning and rehabilitation (Bian et al., 2024) (Bhatia et al., 2020; Saikia et al., 2022; Sen et al., 2020). Also in the case of general post-surgical interventions simulations can direct patients on techniques for handling scars and caring for wounds. VR rehabilitation helps in re-educating the motor control and neuromuscular function of patients (Grajek et al., 2024; Khor et al., 2016). VR has the potential to help patients manage symptoms of anxiety and sadness, immersive VR settings have a calming and soothing effect, that helps in decreasing levels of stress and enhances the emotional well-being of patients (Kenngott et al., 2022).

PRINCIPLES OF VIRTUAL REALITY REHABILITATION

The pictorial representation of the basic principles of Virtual Reality rehabilitation is provided in Figure 2

Figure 2. Principle of virtual rehabilitation

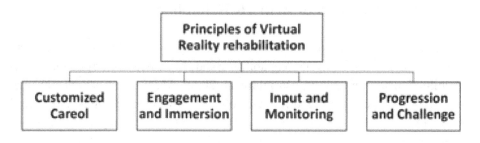

Customized Care: Adapting virtual reality experiences to meet the unique requirements, capabilities, and objectives of the patient. Individualized progress is ensured by focused and successful rehabilitation efforts thanks to personalized interventions.

Engagement and Immersion: Creating virtual reality activities and surroundings that draw patients in and make them feel present and immersed. Engaging activities improve rehabilitative protocol adherence, motivation, and focus.

Input and Monitoring: Giving users immediate input on how they're doing and where they're going in the virtual world. Through feedback systems, therapists and patients can monitor development, pinpoint areas for growth, and modify interventions as necessary.

Progression and its Challenge: This will help to encourage skill development rehabilitative results, and VR increase in complexity and difficulty.

IMPLEMENTATION OF AI INTO VR REHABILITATION

The combination of AI and VR has made significant advancements in various industries, which include mainly healthcare. Artificial intelligence with a combination of virtual reality plays a significant role in rehabilitation (Chawdhary &

Shoman, 2021). In this chapter, we examine the current ways they are being used and discuss the obstacles they face.

AI plays a major role in VR rehabilitation by applying algorithms to tailor and improve the rehabilitation process. By analysing patient data, AI algorithms can dynamically change VR environments to create unique requirements to patient-specific (Chen et al., 2021).

Current Applications of AI in VR Rehabilitation

AI in VR Rehabilitation use advanced algorithms to analyse the patient data, such as medical history; physical capabilities; and progress, to create patient-specific rehabilitation programmes (Ceccariglia et al., 2022). AI can detect patient movement help in virtual interactions and provide solutions whenever required (Krpic et al., 2013a) (M. Liu et al., 2021)(Xue et al., 2021). AI also reacts to patients' emotions while they are immersed in the VR domain (Saffaryazdi et al., 2022).

Obstacles and Factors to Take Into Consideration

Privacy and data protection are the main concerns in VR. It is important to establish strong measures to safeguard patient confidentiality (Catania et al., 2023). It is also important to have an ethical safeguard of patient data (Gutierrez-Martinez et al., 2021) (Asakawa et al., 2019). the expenses involved in data securities should be lowered and also it should be ensured fair access to cutting-edge rehabilitation technologies (Ahmed et al., 2022).

Future Directions

The application of AI with virtual reality makes the patient more realistic, this will help in a seamless integration of virtual and physical reality, and increase the overall experience (Kim et al., 2023)(Cunha et al., 2023; Lydakis et al., 2017). Encouraging collaboration among AI engineers, VR developers, healthcare professionals, and researchers will fuel innovation in rehabilitation technology, promoting interdisciplinary approaches to patient care (Parton, 2006). AI programming can help in monitoring patient health and provide feedback simultaneously (Bai et al., 2022).

With the application of the latest algorithms and virtual environments, healthcare experts can provide tailored, efficient, and captivating rehabilitation experiences (Khalid et al., 2024). As the patient experiences increase streamlining healthcare services provided by AI and VR increases patient recovery. These innovative technologies like AI and VR are revolutionising the global healthcare landscape (Zhao et al., 2023).

CURRENT APPLICATION OF AI AND VR IN MEDICAL TOURISM

AI and VR place a crucial role in medical tourism as they provide the patient with a much specific environment which is suitable to patients and it seems real to the patient and helps in their recovery (McCartney & Wang, 2024). This part of the chapter discusses the application of VR and AI in the field of medical tourism

VR technology helps to release stress from patients as it provides the local environment to them. The patient got the opportunity to see the virtual environment of the hospital and prepare his mind for any type of medical intervention (Agalarova et al., 2023). In addition, VR helps the doctor set up a hospital environment as per patient requirements (Xu et al., 2023).

AI helps the patient with specific treatment and helps in planning the various surgical interventions as per the requirement of the patient. They can create a medical environment as per the disease of the patient also AI can suggest the specific time and date of surgical intervention (Killela et al., 2023). AI offer 24/7 support to patientsand optimise solution to patient (Youssef et al., 2023).

AI and VR play a crucial role in telemedicine and remote consultation of patient to their required doctor which is inaccessible to them (Chirra et al., 2019). VR and AI will create a realistic environment so that the patient will feel that the doctor is near to him although he is far from him (Thai-Van et al., 2021) this technology of telemedicine integrated with AI and VI helps shorten the distance and fast recovery of patient (Wilson et al., 2010).

VI and AI-powered modules help in training the health care professionals and improve their learning experiences this will help in decreasing their mistakes in any surgical interventions (Savir et al., 2023). The AI-based algorithm helps the medical professional to learn the various latest medical tools virtually well in advance which is to be used on patients directly (Hsieh & Lin, 2017). AI algorithms with VR help to analyze patient data, including crucial signs patient, lifestyle factors, and genetic health, which helps identify potential health risks and predict future health conditions which helps to do predictive analytics also health condition monitoring (Krpic et al., 2013b).

AI and VR provide data accuracy and data security facility which is important in medical ethics, with the help of AI the healthcare professional can provide safe and ethical practices in the field of medical tourism (Maynard & Scragg, 2019). It is well known that advancements in technologies cause fast processing of data and high security As these technologies progress, stakeholders must work together to develop guidelines and best practices for VR-enhanced medical tourism to provide quality, privacy, and accountability medical tourism (Vuilleumier et al., 2014).

FUTURE PROSPECTS OF VR AND AI IN MEDICAL TOURISM

Virtual reality (VR) rehabilitation and artificial intelligence (AI) combine to provide solutions quickly to medical problems. AI-integrated VR helps the patients in faster rehabilitation. In future, there will be no need to go to a doctor physically and the specialised doctor and hospital treatment containing rehabilitation will be available online at a very low cost. Also, customized and adaptable rehabilitation programs are made possible by the convergence of VR and AI algorithms. Recent Medical Tourism Index (MTI) 2023-24 speaks that India's revenue surge in the healthcare area is expected to reach Rs 2,670.37 Bn by 2027.

CONCLUSION

To sum up, with the addition of the latest innovative and new generation artificial intelligence tools integrated with VR healthcare rehabilitation will become more advanced and the the patient will be more aware of his physical and mental condition. Efficiency in the delivery of the outcome of any medication and rehabilitation to the patient will be increased due to the application of AI as it will be more patient-specific.

REFERENCES

Agalarova, L. S., Rozanova, T. P., Stytsiuk, R. Y., & Tavakov, A. A. (2023). The problems of development of medical health-improving tourism in modern conditions. *Problemy Sotsial'noi Gigieny, Zdravookhraneniia i Istorii Meditsiny*, 31(1), 44–50. . 10.32687/0869-866X-2023-31-1-44-5036801873

Ahmed, S., Archambault, P., Auger, C., Durand, A., Fung, J., Kehayia, E., Lamontagne, A., Majnemer, A., Nadeau, S., Pineau, J., Ptito, A., & Swaine, B. (2022). Biomedical Research and Informatics Living Laboratory for Innovative Advances of New Technologies in Community Mobility Rehabilitation: Protocol for Evaluation and Rehabilitation of Mobility Across Continuums of Care. *JMIR Research Protocols*, 11(6), e12506. . 10.2196/1250635648455

Alanazi, A., Ashour, F., Aldosari, H., & Aldosari, B. (2022). The Impact of Virtual Reality in Enhancing the Quality of Life of Pediatric Oncology Patients. *Studies in Health Technology and Informatics*, 289, 477–480. . 10.3233/SHTI21096135062194

Asakawa, T., Sugiyama, K., Nozaki, T., Sameshima, T., Kobayashi, S., Wang, L., Hong, Z., Chen, S., Li, C., & Namba, H. (2019). Can the Latest Computerized Technologies Revolutionize Conventional Assessment Tools and Therapies for a Neurological Disease? The Example of Parkinson's Disease. *Neurologia Medico-Chirurgica*, 59(3), 69–78. . 10.2176/nmc.ra.2018-004530760657

Bai, Y., Liu, F., & Zhang, H. (2022). Artificial Intelligence Limb Rehabilitation System on Account of Virtual Reality Technology on Long-Term Health Management of Stroke Patients in the Context of the Internet. *Computational and Mathematical Methods in Medicine*, 2022, 2688003. . 10.1155/2022/268800335651925

Bhatia, D., Sahai, N., & Sarma, J. (2020). Recent advances on ankle foot orthosis for gait rehabilitation: A review. *International Journal of Biomedical Engineering and Technology*, 33(2), 159. Advance online publication. 10.1504/IJBET.2020.107711

Bian, D., Lin, Z., Lu, H., Zhong, Q., Wang, K., Tang, X., & Zang, J. (2024). The application of extended reality technology-assisted intraoperative navigation in orthopedic surgery. *Frontiers in Surgery*, 11, 1336703. . 10.3389/fsurg.2024.133670338375409

Breed, H. J., Jones, E., & Cubitt, J. (2023). Use of immersive virtual reality to reduce anxiety during complex paediatric dressing changes. *BMJ Case Reports*, 16(2), e252998. . 10.1136/bcr-2022-25299836764742

Castillo-Martinez, I. D., Bremer-Aztudillo, A. L., Velazquez-Marmolejo, L., Moreno-Gonzalez, A. M., & Belmont-Sanchez, J. (2020).. . *Acta Ortopédica Mexicana*, 34(5), 298–302. [REMOVED HYPERLINK FIELD]. 10.35366/9799233634633

Catania, V., Rundo, F., Panerai, S., & Ferri, R. (2023). Virtual Reality for the Rehabilitation of Acquired Cognitive Disorders: A Narrative Review. *Bioengineering (Basel, Switzerland)*, 11(1), 35. . 10.3390/bioengineering1101003538247912

Ceccariglia, F., Cercenelli, L., Badiali, G., Marcelli, E., & Tarsitano, A. (2022). Application of Augmented Reality to Maxillary Resections: A Three-Dimensional Approach to Maxillofacial Oncologic Surgery. *Journal of Personalized Medicine*, 12(12), 2047. . 10.3390/jpm1212204736556268

Cerasa, A., Gaggioli, A., Pioggia, G., & Riva, G. (2024). Metaverse in Mental Health: The Beginning of a Long History. *Current Psychiatry Reports*.

Chang, S.-L., Kuo, M.-J., Lin, Y.-J., Chen, S.-A., Yang, Y.-Y., Cheng, H.-M., Yang, L.-Y., Kao, S.-Y., & Lee, F.-Y. (2021). Virtual reality informative aids increase residents' atrial fibrillation ablation procedures-related knowledge and patients' satisfaction. *Journal of the Chinese Medical Association*, 84(1), 25–32. . 10.1097/JCMA.00000000000046433230060

Chawdhary, G., & Shoman, N. (2021). Emerging artificial intelligence applications in otological imaging. *Current Opinion in Otolaryngology & Head & Neck Surgery*, 29(5), 357–364. . 10.1097/MOO.00000000000075434459798

Chen, Z., Zhang, Y., Yan, Z., Dong, J., Cai, W., Ma, Y., Jiang, J., Dai, K., Liang, H., & He, J. (2021). Artificial intelligence assisted display in thoracic surgery: Development and possibilities. *Journal of Thoracic Disease*, 13(12), 6994–7005. . 10.21037/jtd-21-124035070382

Chiamulera, C., Mantovani, E., & Tamburin, S. (2021). Remote clinical trials: A timely opportunity for a virtual reality approach and its potential application in neurology. *British Journal of Clinical Pharmacology*, 87(10), 3639–3642. . 10.1111/bcp.1492234041779

Chirra, M., Marsili, L., Wattley, L., Sokol, L. L., Keeling, E., Maule, S., Sobrero, G., Artusi, C. A., Romagnolo, A., Zibetti, M., Lopiano, L., Espay, A. J., Obeidat, A. Z., & Merola, A. (2019). Telemedicine in Neurological Disorders: Opportunities and Challenges. *Telemedicine Journal and e-Health*, 25(7), 541–550. 10.1089/tmj.2018.010130136898

Cunha, B., Ferreira, R., & Sousa, A. S. P. (2023). Home-Based Rehabilitation of the Shoulder Using Auxiliary Systems and Artificial Intelligence: An Overview. *Sensors (Basel)*, 23(16), 7100. . 10.3390/s2316710037631637

Donisi, V., De Lucia, A., Pasini, I., Gandolfi, M., Schweiger, V., Del Piccolo, L., & Perlini, C. (2023). e-Health Interventions Targeting Pain-Related Psychological Variables in Fibromyalgia: A Systematic Review. *Healthcare (Basel, Switzerland), 11*(13).

Dy, M., Olazo, K., Lyles, C. R., Lisker, S., Weinberg, J., Lee, C., Tarver, M. E., Saha, A., Kontson, K., Araojo, R., Brown, E., & Sarkar, U. (2023). Usability and acceptability of virtual reality for chronic pain management among diverse patients in a safety-net setting: A qualitative analysis. *JAMIA Open*, 6(3), ooad050. . 10.1093/jamiaopen/ooad05037449058

Ertl, S., Steinmair, D., & Loffler-Stastka, H. (2021). Encouraging communication and cooperation in e-learning: Solving and creating new interdisciplinary case histories. *GMS Journal for Medical Education*, 38(3), Doc62. 33824898

Frewen, P., Mistry, D., Zhu, J., Kielt, T., Wekerle, C., Lanius, R. A., & Jetly, R. (2020). Proof of Concept of an Eclectic, Integrative Therapeutic Approach to Mental Health and Well-Being Through Virtual Reality Technology. *Frontiers in Psychology*, 11, 858. . 10.3389/fpsyg.2020.0085832581898

Gao, Z., Lee, J. E., McDonough, D. J., & Albers, C. (2020). Virtual Reality Exercise as a Coping Strategy for Health and Wellness Promotion in Older Adults during the COVID-19 Pandemic. *Journal of Clinical Medicine*, 9(6), 1986. . 10.3390/jcm906198632630367

Goktas, N., & Avci, D. (2023). The effect of visual and/or auditory distraction techniques on children's pain, anxiety and medical fear in invasive procedures: A randomized controlled trial. *Journal of Pediatric Nursing*, 73, e27–e35. . 10.1016/j.pedn.2023.07.00537455147

Grajek, J. S., Rettschlag, S., Schneider, A., Schraven, S. P., Mlynski, R., & van Bonn, S. M. (2024). *Multidimensional formats of surgical anatomy in otorhinolaryngology student teaching-a comparison of effectivity.* HNO.

Gutierrez-Martinez, J., Mercado-Gutierrez, J. A., Carvajal-Gamez, B. E., Rosas-Trigueros, J. L., & Contreras-Martinez, A. E. (2021). Artificial Intelligence Algorithms in Visual Evoked Potential-Based Brain-Computer Interfaces for Motor Rehabilitation Applications: Systematic Review and Future Directions. *Frontiers in Human Neuroscience*, 15, 772837. 10.3389/fnhum.2021.77283734899220

Hauze, S. W., Hoyt, H. H., Frazee, J. P., Greiner, P. A., & Marshall, J. M. (2019). Enhancing Nursing Education Through Affordable and Realistic Holographic Mixed Reality: The Virtual Standardized Patient for Clinical Simulation. *Advances in Experimental Medicine and Biology*, 1120, 1–13. . 10.1007/978-3-030-06070-1_130919290

Hershberger, P. J., Pei, Y., Crawford, T. N., Neeley, S. M., Wischgoll, T., Patel, D. B., Vasoya, M. M., Castle, A., Mishra, S., Surapaneni, L., Pogaku, A. A., Bositty, A., & Pavlack, T. (2022). An Interactive Game with Virtual Reality Immersion to Improve Cultural Sensitivity in Health Care. *Health Equity*, 6(1), 189–197. . 10.1089/heq.2021.012835402778

Hsieh, M.-C., & Lin, Y.-H. (2017). [VR and AR Applications in Medical Practice and Education]. *Hu Li Za Zhi. Journal of Nursing (Luton, England)*, 64(6), 12–18. 29164542

Kane, P. (2018). Simulation-based education: A narrative review of the use of VERT in radiation therapy education. *Journal of Medical Radiation Sciences*, 65(2), 131–136. . 10.1002/jmrs.27629654661

Kenngott, H. G., Pfeiffer, M., Preukschas, A. A., Bettscheider, L., Wise, P. A., Wagner, M., Speidel, S., Huber, M., Nickel, F., Mehrabi, A., & Muller-Stich, B. P. (2022). IMHOTEP: Cross-professional evaluation of a three-dimensional virtual reality system for interactive surgical operation planning, tumor board discussion and immersive training for complex liver surgery in a head-mounted display. *Surgical Endoscopy*, 36(1), 126–134. . 10.1007/s00464-020-08246-433475848

Khalid, U. B., Naeem, M., Stasolla, F., Syed, M. H., Abbas, M., & Coronato, A. (2024). Impact of AI-Powered Solutions in Rehabilitation Process: Recent Improvements and Future Trends. *International Journal of General Medicine*, 17, 943–969. . 10.2147/IJGM.S45390338495919

Khor, W. S., Baker, B., Amin, K., Chan, A., Patel, K., & Wong, J. (2016). Augmented and virtual reality in surgery-the digital surgical environment: Applications, limitations and legal pitfalls. *Annals of Translational Medicine*, 4(23), 454. . 10.21037/atm.2016.12.2328090510

Killela, M., Biddell, C., Keim-Malpass, J., Schwartz, T. A., Soto, S., Williams, J., & Santacroce, S. (2023). The Use of Medical Crowdfunding to Mitigate the Personal Costs of Serious Chronic Illness: Scoping Review. *Journal of Medical Internet Research*, 25, e44530. . 10.2196/4453038048149

Kim, K., Yang, H., Lee, J., & Lee, W. G. (2023). Metaverse Wearables for Immersive Digital Healthcare: A Review. *Advanced Science (Weinheim, Baden-Wurttemberg, Germany)*, 10(31), e2303234. . 10.1002/advs.20230323437740417

Krpic, A., Savanovic, A., & Cikajlo, I. (2013a). Telerehabilitation: Remote multimedia-supported assistance and mobile monitoring of balance training outcomes can facilitate the clinical staff's effort. *International Journal of Rehabilitation Research. Internationale Zeitschrift fur Rehabilitationsforschung. Revue Internationale de Recherches de Readaptation*, 36(2), 162–171. . 10.1097/MRR.0b013e32835dd63b23337324

Krpic, A., Savanovic, A., & Cikajlo, I. (2013b). Telerehabilitation: Remote multimedia-supported assistance and mobile monitoring of balance training outcomes can facilitate the clinical staff's effort. *International Journal of Rehabilitation Research. Internationale Zeitschrift fur Rehabilitationsforschung. Revue Internationale de Recherches de Readaptation*, 36(2), 162–171. . 10.1097/MRR.0b013e32835dd63b23337324

Krupitzer, C., Naber, J., Stauffert, J.-P., Mayer, J., Spielmann, J., Ehmann, P., Boci, N., Burkle, M., Ho, A., Komorek, C., Heinickel, F., Kounev, S., Becker, C., & Latoschik, M. E. (2022). CortexVR: Immersive analysis and training of cognitive executive functions of soccer players using virtual reality and machine learning. *Frontiers in Psychology*, 13, 754732. 10.3389/fpsyg.2022.75473236081714

Liu, M., Wilder, S., Sanford, S., Saleh, S., Harel, N. Y., & Nataraj, R. (2021). Training with Agency-Inspired Feedback from an Instrumented Glove to Improve Functional Grasp Performance. *Sensors (Basel)*, 21(4), 1173. 10.3390/s2104117333562342

Liu, Z., Ren, L., Xiao, C., Zhang, K., & Demian, P. (2022). Virtual Reality Aided Therapy towards Health 4.0: A Two-Decade Bibliometric Analysis. *International Journal of Environmental Research and Public Health*, 19(3), 1525. . 10.3390/ijerph1903152535162546

Lydakis, A., Meng, Y., Munroe, C., Wu, Y.-N., & Begum, M. (2017). A learning-based agent for home neurorehabilitation. *IEEE. International Conference on Rehabilitation Robotics : [Proceedings], 2017*, (pp. 1233–1238). IEEE.

Marcum, C. S., Goldring, M. R., McBride, C. M., & Persky, S. (2018). Modeling Dynamic Food Choice Processes to Understand Dietary Intervention Effects. *Annals of Behavioral Medicine : A Publication of the Society of Behavioral Medicine*, 52(3), 252–261.

Maynard, A. D., & Scragg, M. (2019). The Ethical and Responsible Development and Application of Advanced Brain Machine Interfaces. *Journal of Medical Internet Research*, 21(10), e16321. . 10.2196/1632131674917

McCartney, G., & Wang, C. F. (2024). Medical tourism and medical tourists: providing a sustainable course to integrating health treatments with tourism. *Journal of Travel Medicine*.

McLean, E., Cornwell, M. A., Bender, H. A., Sacks-Zimmerman, A., Mandelbaum, S., Koay, J. M., Raja, N., Kohn, A., Meli, G., & Spat-Lemus, J. (2023). Innovations in Neuropsychology: Future Applications in Neurosurgical Patient Care. *World Neurosurgery*, 170, 286–295. . 10.1016/j.wneu.2022.09.10336782427

Mistry, D., Brock, C. A., & Lindsey, T. (2023). The Present and Future of Virtual Reality in Medical Education: A Narrative Review. *Cureus*, 15(12), e51124. 10.7759/cureus.5112438274907

Nicola, S., Virag, I., & Stoicu-Tivadar, L. (2017). VR Medical Gamification for Training and Education. *Studies in Health Technology and Informatics*, 236, 97–103. [REMOVED HYPERLINK FIELD]28508784

Nishchyk, A., Chen, W., Pripp, A. H., & Bergland, A. (2021). The Effect of Mixed Reality Technologies for Falls Prevention Among Older Adults: Systematic Review and Meta-analysis. *JMIR Aging*, 4(2), e27972. . 10.2196/2797234255643

Ntakakis, G., Plomariti, C., Frantzidis, C., Antoniou, P. E., Bamidis, P. D., & Tsoulfas, G. (2023). Exploring the use of virtual reality in surgical education. *World Journal of Transplantation*, 13(2), 36–43. . 10.5500/wjt.v13.i2.3636908307

Obeid, I., & Wolf, P. D. (2004). Evaluation of spike-detection algorithms for a brain-machine interface application. *IEEE Transactions on Biomedical Engineering*, 51(6), 905–911. . 10.1109/TBME.2004.82668315188857

Padilla, J. J., Diallo, S. Y., & Armstrong, R. K. (2018). Toward Live Virtual Constructive Simulations in Healthcare Learning. *Simulation in Healthcare : Journal of the Society for Simulation in Healthcare, 13*, S35–S40.

Palozzi, G., & Antonucci, G. (2022). Mobile-Health based physical activities co-production policies towards cardiovascular diseases prevention: Findings from a mixed-method systematic review. *BMC Health Services Research*, 22(1), 277. 10.1186/s12913-022-07637-835232456

Parton, B. S. (2006). Sign language recognition and translation: A multidisciplined approach from the field of artificial intelligence. *Journal of Deaf Studies and Deaf Education*, 11(1), 94–101. . 10.1093/deafed/enj00316192405

Pawassar, C. M., & Tiberius, V. (2021). Virtual Reality in Health Care: Bibliometric Analysis. *JMIR Serious Games*, 9(4), e32721. . 10.2196/3272134855606

Pedroli, E., Mancuso, V., Stramba-Badiale, C., Cipresso, P., Tuena, C., Greci, L., Goulene, K., Stramba-Badiale, M., Riva, G., & Gaggioli, A. (2022). Brain M-App's Structure and Usability: A New Application for Cognitive Rehabilitation at Home. *Frontiers in Human Neuroscience*, 16, 898633. . 10.3389/fnhum.2022.89863335782042

Rizzo, A. & Shilling, R. (2017). Clinical Virtual Reality tools to advance the prevention, assessment, and treatment of PTSD. *European Journal of Psychotraumatology, 8*, 1414560.

Saffaryazdi, N., Wasim, S. T., Dileep, K., Nia, A. F., Nanayakkara, S., Broadbent, E., & Billinghurst, M. (2022). Using Facial Micro-Expressions in Combination With EEG and Physiological Signals for Emotion Recognition. *Frontiers in Psychology*, 13, 864047. . 10.3389/fpsyg.2022.86404735837650

Saikia, A., Mazumdar, S., Sahai, N., Paul, S., & Bhatia, D. (2022). Performance Analysis of Artificial Neural Network for Hand Movement Detection from EMG Signals. *Journal of the Institution of Electronics and Telecommunication Engineers*, 68(2), 1074–1083. Advance online publication. 10.1080/03772063.2019.1638316

Savir, S., Khan, A. A., Yunus, R. A., Rehman, T. A., Saeed, S., Sohail, M., Sharkey, A., Mitchell, J., & Matyal, R. (2023). Virtual Reality: The Future of Invasive Procedure Training? *Journal of Cardiothoracic and Vascular Anesthesia*, 37(10), 2090–2097. 10.1053/j.jvca.2023.06.03237422335

Scherschinski, L., McNeill, I. T., Schlachter, L., Shuman, W. H., Oemke, H., Yaeger, K. A., & Bederson, J. B. (2022). Augmented reality-assisted microsurgical resection of brain arteriovenous malformations: Illustrative case. *Journal of Neurosurgery. Case Lessons*, 3(25), CASE21135. . 10.3171/CASE2113535733837

Schleider, J. L., Mullarkey, M. C., & Weisz, J. R. (2019). Virtual Reality and Web-Based Growth Mindset Interventions for Adolescent Depression: Protocol for a Three-Arm Randomized Trial. *JMIR Research Protocols*, 8(7), e13368. . 10.2196/1336831290406

Selim, A. J., Rothendler, J. A., Qian, S. X., Bailey, H. M., & Kazis, L. E. (2022). The History and Applications of the Veterans RAND 12-Item Health Survey (VR-12). *The Journal of Ambulatory Care Management*, 45(3), 161–170. . 10.1097/JAC.0000000000000042035612387

Sen, D., Srivastava, R., Sahai, N., Tewari, R. P., & Kumar, B. (2020). Development of IoT Enabled Low Cost Management System for m-Cardiology. SSRN *Electronic Journal*. 10.2139/ssrn.3573502

Shrestha, A. B., Taha, A. M., Siddiq, A., Shrestha, S., Thakur, P., Chapagain, S., Sharma, S., Halder, A., Rajak, K., & Shah, V. (2024). Virtual and augmented reality in cardiovascular care in low and middle income country. *Current Problems in Cardiology*, 49(3), 102380. . 10.1016/j.cpcardiol.2024.10238038191103

Szekely, R., Mason, O., Frohlich, D., & Barley, E. (2024). "It's not everybody's snapshot. It's just an insight into that world": A qualitative study of multiple perspectives towards understanding the mental health experience and addressing stigma in healthcare students through virtual reality. *Digital Health*, 10, 20552076231223800. . 10.1177/2055207623122380138188857

Taveira, M. C., de Sa, J., & da Rosa, M. G. (2022). Virtual Reality-Induced Dissociative Symptoms: A Retrospective Study. *Games for Health Journal*, 11(4), 262–267. . 10.1089/g4h.2022.000935648035

Thai-Van, H., Bakhos, D., Bouccara, D., Loundon, N., Marx, M., Mom, T., Mosnier, I., Roman, S., Villerabel, C., Vincent, C., & Venail, F. (2021). Telemedicine in Audiology. Best practice recommendations from the French Society of Audiology (SFA) and the French Society of Otorhinolaryngology-Head and Neck Surgery (SFORL). *European Annals of Otorhinolaryngology, Head and Neck Diseases*, 138(5), 363–375. . 10.1016/j.anorl.2020.10.00733097467

Torner, J., Skouras, S., Molinuevo, J. L., Gispert, J. D., & Alpiste, F. (2019). Multi-purpose Virtual Reality Environment for Biomedical and Health Applications. *IEEE Transactions on Neural Systems and Rehabilitation Engineering : A Publication of the IEEE Engineering in Medicine and Biology Society*, 27(8), 1511–1520.

Usmani, S. S., Sharath, M., & Mehendale, M. (2022). Future of mental health in the metaverse. *General Psychiatry*, 35(4), e100825. . 10.1136/gpsych-2022-10082536189180

Vuilleumier, P., Sander, D., & Baertschi, B. (2014). Changing the brain, changing the society: Clinical and ethical implications of neuromodulation techniques in neurology and psychiatry. *Brain Topography*, 27(1), 1–3. . 10.1007/s10548-013-0325-724158724

Weiner, E., McNew, R., Trangenstein, P., & Gordon, J. (2010). Using the virtual reality world of second life to teach nursing faculty simulation management. *Studies in Health Technology and Informatics*, 160(Pt 1), 615–619. [REMOVED HYPERLINK FIELD]20841760

Wilson, L. S., Stevenson, D. R., & Cregan, P. (2010). Telehealth on advanced networks. *Telemedicine Journal and E-Health : The Official Journal of the American Telemedicine Association, 16*(1), 69–79.

Xu, A., Johari, S. A., Khademolomoom, A. H., Khabaz, M. T., Umurzoqovich, R. S., Hosseini, S., & Semiromi, D. T. (2023). Investigation of management of international education considering sustainable medical tourism and entrepreneurship. *Heliyon*, 9(1), e12691. . 10.1016/j.heliyon.2022.e1269136685466

Xue, X., Yang, X., Deng, Z., Tu, H., Kong, D., Li, N., & Xu, F. (2021). Global Trends and Hotspots in Research on Rehabilitation Robots: A Bibliometric Analysis From 2010 to 2020. *Frontiers in Public Health*, 9, 806723. . 10.3389/fpubh.2021.80672335087788

Yasini, M., & Marchand, G. (2016). Adoption and Use of a Mobile Health Application in Older Adults for Cognitive Stimulation. *Studies in Health Technology and Informatics*, 221, 13–17. [REMOVED HYPERLINK FIELD]27071867

Youssef, A., Lashley, E. E. L. O., Vermeulen, N., & van der Hoorn, M. L. P. (2023). Identifying discrepancies between clinical practice and evidence-based guideline in recurrent pregnancy loss care, a tool for clinical guideline implementation. *BMC Pregnancy and Childbirth*, 23(1), 544. . 10.1186/s12884-023-05869-y37507697

Zhang, M. W. B., & Ho, R. C. M. (2017). Smartphone applications for immersive virtual reality therapy for internet addiction and internet gaming disorder. *Technology and Health Care : Official Journal of the European Society for Engineering and Medicine, 25*(2), 367–372.

Zhao, L., Zhao, Y., Bu, L., Sun, H., Tang, W., Li, K., Zhang, W., Tang, W., & Zhang, Y. (2023). Design Method of a Smart Rehabilitation Product Service System Based on Virtual Scenarios: A Case Study. *IEEE Transactions on Neural Systems and Rehabilitation Engineering : A Publication of the IEEE Engineering in Medicine and Biology Society, 31*, 4570–4579.

Zhou, H., Gao, J.-Y., & Chen, Y. (2022). The paradigm and future value of the metaverse for the intervention of cognitive decline. *Frontiers in Public Health*, 10, 1016680. . 10.3389/fpubh.2022.101668036339131

Chapter 21
Impacts of COVID–19 on the Customers´ Review Behavior Towards Hotel and Travel Organizations:
A Netnography Approach

Maximiliano Emanuel Korstanje
https://orcid.org/0000-0002-5149-1669
University of Palermo, Argentina

ABSTRACT

The COVID-19 pandemic has generated an unparalleled crisis in the circles of tourism industries and beyond. The overcrowded cities associated with the technological revolution applied on transport has contributed directly to disseminating the virus worldwide. The tourism industry has been the main victim and spreader of COVID19. Though originally the consequences of the pandemic remain obscured or at the best uncertain no less true seems to be that scholars have devoted their attention to describing the economic effects in the tourism industry. The cOVID-19 has interrogated deeply the epistemology of tourism alluding to a world without tourists. In this vein, the present chapter discusses the question of entnography a new ethnographic method based on hybridity and hybridized methods of information gathering.

DOI: 10.4018/979-8-3693-2272-7.ch021

INTRODUCTION

Not surprisingly, the turn of the twentieth century has brought uncontemplated and global risks that placed the tourism industry in jeopardy. These risks included the radicalization of political violence, if not terrorism (Saha & Yap, 2014; Korstanje, 2023), followed by the ecological crisis and climate change (Pang, McKercher & Prideaux, 2013), without mentioning the recent COVID-19 pandemic (Sigala, 2020). Tourism security occupied a central place in the academic debate just after the 2000s (Seabra & Korstanje, 2023). The SARS-COv2, originally dubbed as COVID-19 was supposedly reported by the last days of December in 2019 in the Chinese city of Wuhan. In question of weeks, the virus has rapidly spread to other regions in Asia and Europe jumping to the US later. The overcrowded cities, as well as the fast transport, means which today connect distant cities in hours, have directly contributed to the virus dissemination (Nepal 2020; Lu et al., 2022). As Baum & Hai put it, tourism was the main carrier and victim of COVID-19 globally (Baum & Hai, 2020). At a closer look, the economic effects on the service sectors and the tourism industry have been devastating and long-lasting. Governments took the lead to implement some restrictive measures originally designed to stop the pandemic. These steps ranged from the border and airspace closure to strict lockdowns in free circulation, travel, and public spectacles (only to name a few). Underdeveloped economies or economies subject to tourism dependency experienced more major losses than developed ones (Rogerson & Baum, 2020). Of course, the literature discussing the economic effects of the COVID-19 pandemic on tourism simply abounds (Bakar & Rosbi, 2020; Gossling, Scott & Hall, 2020; Higgins-Desbiolles, 2020) but less attention was paid to the sociological and psychological effects on tourist behavior (Korstanje & George, 2022). The new normal witnessed how societies recovered but at a snail's pace. The new normal has some serious implications that changed leisure practices as never before. These changes encompassed geopolitical tensions, racist or chauvinist expressions (above all against Asian tourists), health passports or biological certificates, or simply the rise of new forms like vaccine tourism have come to stay (Mostafanezhad, Cheer & Sin, 2020). However, applied research in this direction is necessary. To fill the gap, the present research is centered on a netnography applied to tourists on specific websites regarding customer review behavior for hotels and travel organizations in a post-COVID-19 context. Since the method is not statistically representative nor the sample, the obtained results -though promising- should not be extrapolated to other universes.

COVID-19 AND TOURISM: A SHORT COMPANION

As stated in the introduction, the COVID-19 pandemic has brought unparalleled disastrous consequences for the tourism industry as well as for hospitality and global trade. Scholars who preliminary theorized on this have divided into two groups. On one hand, some voices applauded the opportunity to restore sustainable practices that solve the ecological crisis, giving a new opportunity for mankind (Higgins-Desbiolles, Bigby & Doening, 2022; Ratten, 2023), while -on another- other studies alerted on the obstacles to studying tourism in a world without tourists (Liu et al 2022). Quite aside from any discrepancy, the COVID-19 pandemic accelerated a deep economic crisis that whipped the Western capitalist societies in 2008 but now with uncertain consequences in the long run (Romagosa, 2020). In this respect, Sharma & Nicolau (2020) offer a set of assessments that allows a credible diagnosis of the real impacts of COVID-19 on the tourism industry. Governments have assisted the sector at different levels and stages in which case, which include tax reductions, financial bailouts or different programs to incentive consumption during the lockdown. As the authors conclude, the sectors associated with hotels, travel agencies, airlines and car rentals have been notably affected, but doubtless cruise industry is the most damaged one. This happens because business travel (which needs tour operators, hotels, aeroplanes and car rentals) recovers quicker than leisure travel. What is more important, the cruise industry seems to be essentially limited to a private space where contagion spreads easier and faster. The highly publicized ads on Diamond Princes, as well as the tragedy of thousands of tourists stranded on the cruises without authorization to land, is an example of the manifest fear of consumers buying these services. The evaluation of the impacts of the pandemic varies on the nation and level of economic maturation. In consonance with this, Pham et al. (2021) argue that policy responses are very specific according to country and health contexts. Having said this, the industry will be gradually recovering after 2024 at the least. Among the economic consequences, the authors enumerate the job losses, the destruction of the tourism value chain, the reduction of national GDP, the decline of investment, depressed rates of return, as well as serious disruption in the economy of scale. Rogerson & Rogerson (2020a; 2020b) reported that developed nations have further opportunities for rapid recovery than underdeveloped countries. Besides, those rural areas which are dependent on tourism have fewer odds to be recovered than urban areas. National and health authorities should make mix-balanced diagnoses that contemplate public health as well as the future of the economy in the long run. This is particularly important because not all governments have the same capacity for answer or recovery timeframe; some sub-services sectors unless assisted are slumped down into disastrous contexts. Some studies have reported social conflicts among stakeholders in the recovery facet or simply are subject to discrepancies in the used methods to forecast the recovery time (Fotiadis, Polyzos & Huan, 2021; Jin, Bao & Tang, 2022). S. S Yeh (2021) explores the figure of travel as the main important component of the industry. Crisis and disaster management should co-ordinate efforts to understand travel behavior to forecast the real intricacies of the current crisis; above all management should work actively to placate the post-crisis effects. The government-sponsored loans (or bailout) are essential to protect the industry but the communication process plays a major role in the configuration of more resilient destinations in the years to come. Also, the future research direction should be gone to the social impacts of the pandemic on travel behavior. This point will be addressed with accuracy in the next section.

SOCIOLOGICAL EFFECTS ON TRAVEL BEHAVIOR

Not surprisingly, the literature suggests the negative effects generated by COVID-19 will last for several months. As hotly debated in the earlier section, the consequences are evaluated by experts from an economic lens (Mann 2020). Little evidence or studies is focusing on the sociocultural effects of the pandemic in so-ciety as well as in the tourism industry. Some works emphasized the multiplication of psychological syndromes, or mental illnesses derived from prolonged periods of isolation or lockdown (Xiao 2020). The rise of depression or even suicidal acts has been reported in several works (Lakhan, Agrawal & Sharma 2020). What is more important, there are manifest geopolitical tensions among states and between authorities and citizens who are not in agreement with the restrictive measures (Korstanje & George 2021). Social protests against unemployment or the lockdown have been reported in Europe and the US. At the same time, emerging national expression against strangers has been documented by experts as well (Korstanje & George 2021; Kock et al, 2020; Mostafanezhad, Cheer & Sin, 2020). In the con-stellations of tourism research, these studies do not abound. Although there is little understanding of how the COVID-19 pandemic altered our travel behavior, some preliminary studies can be discussed. One of the negative effects associated with the suspension of the right to travel or tourism right was creating a state of anxiety and constant protest in social imagination (Baum & Hai 2020; Tremblay-Huet 2020). Phillipe Wassler has illustrated very well a durable state of conflict between hosts and guests derived from some travel anxieties. Under some contexts, the anti-tourist sentiment has been potentiated by the pandemic. For this instance, Tremblay-Huet (2020) alerts that even if the crisis resulted from the pandemic has certainly changed not only travel behavior but how leisure practices appropriate from the territorial spaces, it is beneficial for host communities. Given the problem in these terms, the tourism right should be re-interpreted along with the local initiatives, hosts´

identity and their preferences. In the name of tourism, many destinations have been gradually degraded, in the case that domestic or degrowth tourism will signify a great advancement for sustainable practices in future. It is not difficult to resist the impression the figure of the tour which was originally esteemed as an ambassador of economic prosperity has been in the centre-storm of critics during the pandemic. As Korstanje & George (2022) describe, unfortunately, the industry was not only affected by the COVID-19 pandemic but also the figure of the tourists received a notable demonization, considering most of them as potential carriers of a lethal virus. The act of touring was penalized as a criminal act that was confronted directly by health authorities and public order. From that moment onwards, tourists are considered undesired guests. Similar remarks are found in Mostafanezhad, Cheer & Sin (2020) who analyze the expression of hostility against Asian tourists in social media. Per these authors, there is an underlying anxiety (if not xenophobia) directed against Asian (Chinese) tourists who are blamed as "spreaders that are being part of the problem". It seems not to be difficult to resist the impression that a type of aversion to strangers has plausibly led to new forms of domestic tourism (Luo & Lam, 2020; Hoque et al. 2020). The opposite is equally true, anxiety to travel because of the risk to be infected accelerated the rise of new domestic forms of consumption and touring (Sengel et al 2023; Kamata 2022). In consonance with this, Gymothy, Braun & Zenker (2022) hold that the state of panic, which took place during the pandemic, was supported and disseminated by social media. As a result of this, lay-persons developed an "assortative sociality" which means an out-group avoidance or so to speak ethnocentric discourses. These sentiments resulted from the higher levels of anxiety and fear ignited by the pandemic and the strict lockdowns. The incipient ethnocentrism has invariably changed the travel behavior and the derivative decision-making process. Domestic tourism, to some extent, can be explained by the change of new patterns oriented to avoid strangers or unknown situations. Unless duly regulated, these dispositions may very well usher in ethnocentric traits undermining the opportunities for destinations to accommodate foreign visitors.

As the previous argument was given, customer review behavior has suffered some changes in the new normal (Haryanto, 2020; Cakmak, Issac & Butler, 2023). Domestic tourism or proximity tourism is situated as a leading niche worldwide. Tourists preferred nearby areas instead of international off-the-beaten-track-destinations (Jeon & Yang, 2021). In parallel, some travel restrictions and health passports have been implemented as security measures oriented to make safer travels (Koh 2020; Wen, Wang & Kozak, 2021). Digital technology was re-employed to monitor potential sick passengers as well as vehicles of sanitization and control (Serrano & Kazda, 2020). Domestic destinations, anyway, requested extensive migratory requirements such as medical (PCR) tests, health passports or even vaccination certificates. In a few words, the new normal changed travel behavior as well as security and safety protocols in transport hubs, hotels and tourist destinations (Nagai & Kurahashi, 2020; Korstanje & George 2022). Here two assumptions should be made. At first glimpse, travel patterns and leisure practices have mutated to more virtual forms which have been widely supported by artificial intelligence (AI) (Zhang et al 2022; Talwar et al., 2022). Secondly, not only consumers embraced enthusiastically virtual tourism as a form of mental displacement during the lockdown but also tour operators, air companies and hotels adopted digital platforms to optimize their sales. Consumers held mobile phones in their pockets as well as other devices while accessing vital information to improve their decision-making process (Chakravarty, Chand & Singh, 2021). At the same time, the internet has played a leading role in assisting consumers to consult the best tourist information for their travels. In the pre-pandemic days, word-of-mouth (WOM) was the most relied source for information. In the new normal, this tendency triplicated and e-wom represented a driver towards more efficient forms of information and travel organization globally (Toubes, Araujo-Vila & Fraiz-Brea, 2021).

NETNOGRAPHY AS THE SCIENTIFIC METHOD

The term netnography has been originally coined by Robert Kozinets to denote a qualitative method -derived from ethnography- using social media research. The recent technological breakthrough in the field of digital communications called for ethnography to work as a new method associated to data collection, research guidelines and ethics, as well as analysis and active participation engulfed into participant observation. Netnography is a combination of words such as internet + network. Unlike classic ethnography, it is important to add, netnography mainly emphasizes on reflections or data exposed in online communities. In so doing, netnography does not need fieldworkers in the site (Kozinets 2002; 2012). In the time, this method has received supporters and detractors but it was mainly applied in the constellations of tourism research. As Langer & Beckman eloquently note, one of the ethical dilemmas revolving around netnography seems to be the lack of consent of some users to take part of the research (Langer & Beckman, 2005). What is more important to discuss, exegetes of netnography hold that it is less time-consuming and less intrusive as a method (Kozinets, 2002).

A FRESH STUDY-CASE

The present study case is based on the commentaries posted by consumers in TripAdvisor in the post COVID19 context. Since the sample is not statistically representative, the obtained outcomes cannot be extrapolated to other universes or cases. TripAdvisor is a global platform that offers hotel, air ticket and tours to a wide range of audience or net of consumers. Its section *Travel Review (travel stories)* is a helpful instrument to thousands of tourists who need advice on a certain tourist destination. We have selected three different cities: Buenos Aires, Rio de Janeiro and Madrid. The selection criteria were based on the profile of visitors to these cities is similar and they represent a similar-centered niche. TripAdvisor is an American company that operates with hotels, air-companies and travel agencies globally. Founded by Stephen Kaufer, this group inspired millions of consumers to compare and buy cheaper rates while the travel reviews give some snapshot on the targeted destination. This review system was subject to a great controversy in the recent years due to "false" reviews or unsubstantiated anonymous reviews posted to discredit certain destination or company. Fake reviews have the potential to threaten a destination or a product if the necessary forms of controls are not duly implemented.

In each case, cities are pretty different or at least in large writ, so reviews vary considerably. For example, in the case of Buenos Aires, Sandy76 said *"When we arrived in Buenos Aires it was extremely hot, so we decided to take the bus to get a feel for the city and determine which sites we wanted to view first. Our cruise ship was here for 3 days but we only had 1-1/2 days since we booked an all-day tour to Iguazu Falls. The city is huge and spread out, so you really need to plan the sites based on the bus stops. I recommend going to the first 2 sites on your list. Have lunch in the area and then continue riding to the next stop on your list"*. At the same time, Robert12 wrote: *"I loved Buenos Aires city I visited several Latin American cities and nothing is comparable to Buenos Aires city, even is larger than Madrid or Rio de Janeiro. At time, I flew from London to Buenos Aires directly and all Argentinians are great lovely persons"*.

About Puerto Madero neighborhood, Mr. Smith claimed *"Puerto Madero is the best part of Buenos Aires, it's clean, spacious and beautiful. You can find a natural reserve which has walking, cycling trails which transport you into a quiet natural retreat within a bustling city"*. Of course, Puerto Madero is a new neighborhood offered for dwellers of high-power purchase. Regarding tourism security, Max22 writes *"Buenos Aires city is splendid and very secure. Its streets are replete of police and guards and Argentinian are very nice with foreigners. Of course, avoid to speak or make a joke on Malvinas-Falklands. Unlike Rio, we travelled and walked through the streets of this city at the nights"*.

Rom19 had the opportunity to visit the three cities earlier and later the COVID-19 pandemic. She said that cities have changed a lot because of COVID-19. "*I worked over years as tour operator in Madrid, Spain. I love traveling abroad and meeting with new cultures and landscapes. During the pandemic I suffered crisis of anxiety because my job was in jeopardy. Once the lockdown was released, I made the decision to fly Buenos Aires and Rio where I have good friends. Things changed a lot after the pandemic, if you ask me. Buenos Aires witnessed an unparalleled crisis while Rio de Janeiro a political turmoil just former President Bolsonaro leaves the presidency. Anyway, Buenos Aires had some bad areas (known as villas de emergencia) which you should avoid. The pandemic associated to the current economic turndown has accelerated a socio-economic crisis in the country*". Some testimonies have alerted on the anti-British sentiment resulted from the Malvinas-Falklands War, as well as the chauvinist expressions during the final World Cup match between Argentina and France. Stelladora laments "*being British in Buenos Aires during the FIFA world Cup was not a good idea, they shouted el que no salta es un ingles those who do not jump are British people to denote a sentiment of hostility against Britons. This sentiment is based on the last war between both countries for Malvinas-Falkland's. Paradoxically this hostility is extended to all English native speakers including Americans, Canadians or New Zealanders but not to those cultures occupied by the British Empire, for example la India or Bangladesh. As an ethnicity the Anglo-Saxons are put as enemies of the Spanish culture for Buenos Aires dwellers. I do not know if the same replies in other parts of the country. The Spanish imprint situates as superior (purer) than Anglo-Saxons who are compared to pirates. I do believe this happens because of the complicity of British crowns with pirates in the colonial past*".

At the same time, Madrid and Rio have suffered the economic crisis resulted from the lockdown and the restrictive measures over the COVID-19 pandemic. Alex27 who lives in Madrid posted "*the pandemic has taught two important things. Firstly, the tourism is very vulnerable to these types of crises. And secondly, the states of emergencies suspend given rights we all thought they were inalienable. The right to touring or traveling was suddenly suspended by the government leaving tourists and conational stranded abroad. The new normal is mainly moved by proximity tourism, though I must confess the tourism industry is gradually recovering in these years*".

Maxim59 goes to similar conclusion in his post "*in the pandemic I experienced a great fear. The implementations of lockdowns surprised me visiting Rio de Janeiro, I was sleeping three nights at the airport without assistance or food. This was a complete chaos and decontrol; we have not received assistance from the Embassy nor any national authority. People like me stayed at airport for days till I have been repatriated by a flight of Aerolineas Argentinas. From that moment on, I opted not* to travel long distances, I make only proximity tourism, just in case, nobody knows when a new pandemic will knock on our doors".

Maria56 recognizes that *"Rio de Janeiro is beauty but not the best destination to travel. At least, foreigner tourists are often targeted of robbing and often the city shows the higher levels of crime in Brazil, similarly to some cities in South Africa. The best places of Rio are situated at the south, in tourist friendly beaches like Copacabana or Ipanema who are safer during the day"*. Albert21 writes *"Rio is not the city people often believe, criminality and violence coexist but they are in a specific region of the city. What anyone can do is to avoid "the problematic areas" or not to accept or do not trust in anyone who can offer a free ride from Airport to the hotel. Criminality was certainly reduced over the recent years but still remains higher in comparison with other destinations as Buenos Aires or Montevideo"*.

The question of xenophobia or chauvinist expression for Chinese (Asian) tourists is of vital importance to understand the changes in consumers after the pandemic. By the way, lay-people see in Asian tourists the potential spreaders or carriers of a lethal virus. Originally reported in Wuhan, China, this country is targeted as the cradle of the COVID-19. Because of international travels and tourism as well as by the overcrowds in cities have spread the virus in questions of months. Some studies have alerted on the rise of chauvinist expression or hostility against Asian tourists globally. Chrales11 posted his opinion saying *"I am Japanese and experienced great levels of mistreatments in the New Normal. Front desk staff treated me differently or I felt that also; what is important, I have heard opinion like the Virus was an invention of Chinese or something alike. As an invention, this suggests that China fabricated and infected the world causing thousand and millions of victims. Donald Trump echoed the thing of Chinese virus to blame Asian tourists, what do you think? Ignorant people will say yes this is a problem of Chinese tourists"*. Similarly Rebecca12 made public her discontent how she was treated in Brazil in 2021. *"Asian tourists like me suffer daily discrimination in hotels and their travels as never before because of COVID-19. These acts range from verbal abuse to explicit discrimination. Many travel writers have alerted on this increasing problem. I believed this would disappear once the new normal but I was mistaken. This racism has been potentiated in the recent months. Many Asian are native from other countries like the US or Spain while speaking a perfect English or Spanish but they are discriminated as well. In some cases, I know of persons whose reservations have been unilaterally cancelled because they were Asian tourists. I am very sad incident like these happen even today. Asian tourists are targeted because of fear and ignorance, a tragic combination. The opposite is equally true, since the fear leads persons to discriminate Chinese visitors, the same happen in China respecting Western tourists who are seen with mistrust"*.

Mary-ann72 confessed she returned to China, after years of living in San Francisco, and she was put in quarantine over more than one month. *"The coronavirus challenged the lives of persons but altered serious geopolitical tensions among states. Tourists suffer part of this tension bearing and sharing a certain blame for the pandemic"*. In other cases, Asian tourists are blamed as "rule-brakers". Phillipland exclaimed *"I am not a racist but I have been treated very bad by Chinese front desk workers in my stay in China. In some instances, they refused to speak me in English. One boy told me here we speak Chinese, English is spoken in the UK and US. what do you feel on that? I feel this is a result of the racism Chinese have experienced in the US regarding the COVID19, this is for sure a blowback"* In a similar line of inquiry, Ciro22 writes *"I remind a curious case in Buenos Aires, days after the first lockdown was imposed by President Alberto Fernandez. This was a sad moment where thousand of Argentinian stranded abroad without assistance or workers lost their jobs. In the mid of this mayhem, a group of Korean tourists not only violated the quarantine they were assigned to make at a specific hotel, but also wandered by the streets of Buenos Aires city. This is a clear sign on the lack of engagement in Asian minds for Western culture"*. Last but not least, the pandemic has prompted radical shifts in travel behavior but what is more relevant, it created a symbolic chams between Western and Eastern cultures. This point is coincidental with other studies such as Korstanje & George 2022; Mostafanezhad, M., Cheer, J. M., & Sin, H. L. 2020 or Wassler 2023.

CONCLUSION

The COVID-19 pandemic has generated an unparalleled crisis in the circles of tourism industries and beyond. The overcrowding cities associated to the technological revolution applied on transport, has contributed directly to disseminate the virus worldwide. The tourism industry has been the main victim and spreader of COVID19. Though originally the consequences of the pandemic remain obscured or at the best uncertain no less true seems to be that scholars have devoted their attention to describe the economic effects in the tourism industry. For some reason, which is very hard to precise here, the sociological effects are unexplored in the specialized literature. These consequences include the geopolitical tensions, the cultural hostility against strangers or even the rise of new forms of consumption associated to virtual tourism and IA. This paper is centered to discuss the host-guest encounters while basing conclusions on a netnography. Since the sample was not statistically represented the obtained results cannot be extrapolated to other universes. Netnography has received some criticism in the recent years, but it remains as a fertile ground to understand certain issues related to discrimination.

REFERENCES

Bakar, N. A., & Rosbi, S. (2020). Effect of Coronavirus disease (COVID-19) to tourism industry. *International Journal of Advanced Engineering Research and Science*, 7(4), 189–193. 10.22161/ijaers.74.23

Baum, T., & Hai, N. T. T. (2020). Hospitality, tourism, human rights and the impact of COVID-19. *International Journal of Contemporary Hospitality Management*, 32(7), 2397–2407. 10.1108/IJCHM-03-2020-0242

Butcher, J. (2023). Covid-19, tourism and the advocacy of degrowth. *Tourism Recreation Research*, 48(5), 633–642. 10.1080/02508281.2021.1953306

Çakmak, E., & Isaac, K. R., & Butler, R. (2023). *Changing Practices of Tourism Stakeholders in Covid-19 Affected Destinations*. Bristol, Goodfellows.

Chakravarty, U., Chand, G., & Singh, U. N. (2021). Millennial travel vlogs: Emergence of a new form of virtual tourism in the post-pandemic era? *Worldwide Hospitality and Tourism Themes*, 13(5), 666–676. 10.1108/WHATT-05-2021-0077

Fotiadis, A., Polyzos, S., & Huan, T. C. T. (2021). The good, the bad and the ugly on COVID-19 tourism recovery. *Annals of Tourism Research*, 87, 103117. 10.1016/j.annals.2020.10311733518847

Gössling, S., Scott, D., & Hall, C. M. (2020). Pandemics, tourism and global change: A rapid assessment of COVID-19. *Journal of Sustainable Tourism*, 29(1), 1–20. 10.1080/09669582.2020.1758708

Gowreesunkar, V. G., Maingi, S. W., & Korstanje, M. E. (2024). Introduction: The Changing Landscape of Tourist Behavior—Navigating from the New Normal to the Next Normal. In *Tourist Behaviour and the New Normal, Volume I: Implications for Tourism Resilience* (pp. 1-7). Cham: Springer Nature Switzerland.

Haryanto, T. (2020). COVID-19 pandemic and international tourism demand. *Journal of Developing Economies*, 5(1), 1–5. 10.20473/jde.v5i1.19767

Hoque, A., Shikha, F. A., Hasanat, M. W., Arif, I., & Hamid, A. B. A. (2020). The effect of Coronavirus (COVID-19) in the tourism industry in China. *Asian Journal of Multidisciplinary Studies*, 3(1), 52–58.

Jeon, C. Y., & Yang, H. W. (2021). The structural changes of a local tourism network: Comparison of before and after COVID-19. *Current Issues in Tourism*, 24(23), 3324–3338. 10.1080/13683500.2021.1874890

Jin, X., Bao, J., & Tang, C. (2022). Profiling and evaluating Chinese consumers regarding post-COVID-19 travel. *Current Issues in Tourism*, 25(5), 745–763. 10.1080/13683500.2021.1874313

Kamata, H. (2022). Tourist destination residents' attitudes towards tourism during and after the COVID-19 pandemic. *Current Issues in Tourism*, 25(1), 134–149. 10.1080/13683500.2021.1881452

Kock, F., Nørfelt, A., Josiassen, A., Assaf, A. G., & Tsionas, M. G. (2020). Understanding the COVID-19 tourist psyche: The evolutionary tourism paradigm. *Annals of Tourism Research*, 85, 103053. 10.1016/j.annals.2020.10305332921847

Koh, E. (2020). The end of over-tourism? Opportunities in a post-Covid-19 world. *International Journal of Tourism Cities*, 6(4), 1015–1023. 10.1108/IJTC-04-2020-0080

Korstanje, M. E. (2020). Passage from the tourist gaze to the wicked gaze: A case study on COVID-19 with special reference to Argentina. In *International case studies in the management of disasters* (pp. 197–211). Emerald Publishing Limited. 10.11 08/978-1-83982-186-820201012

Korstanje, M. E. (2023). The Janus Face of Terrorism and Tourism: Terrorism as a Risk, as a Danger and as a Worry. In Seabra, C., & Korstanje, M. (Eds.), *Safety and Tourism* (pp. 103–115). Emerald Publishing Limited. 10.1108/978-1-80382-81 1-420231006

Korstanje, M. E., & George, B. (2021). *Mobility and globalization in the aftermath of COVID-19: Emerging new geographies in a locked world*. Palgrave Macmillan. 10.1007/978-3-030-78845-2

Korstanje, M. E., & George, B. (2022). *The nature and future of tourism: A post-COVID-19 context*. CRC Press. 10.1201/9781003277507

Korstanje, M. E., & George, B. (2022). *The nature and future of tourism: A post-COVID-19 context*. Apple Academic Press. 10.1201/9781003277507

Korstanje, M. E., Gowreesunkar, V. G., & Maingi, S. W. (2024). Conclusion: Tourist Behavior in the New Normal—Emerging Frontiers Toward Tourism Resilience. In *Tourist Behaviour and the New Normal, Volume I: Implications for Tourism Resilience* (pp. 273-278). Cham: Springer Nature Switzerland.

Korstanje, M. E., Séraphin, H., & Maingi, S. W. (Eds.). (2022). *Tourism through troubled times: Challenges and opportunities of the tourism industry in the 21st century*. Emerald Publishing Limited. 10.1108/9781803823119

Kozinets, R. V. (2002). The field behind the screen: Using netnography for marketing research in online communities. *JMR, Journal of Marketing Research*, 39(1), 61–72. 10.1509/jmkr.39.1.61.18935

Kozinets, R. V. (2012). Marketing netnography: Prom/ot (ulgat) ing a new research method. *Methodological Innovations Online*, 7(1), 37–45. 10.4256/mio.2012.004

Lakhan, R., Agrawal, A., & Sharma, M. (2020). Prevalence of depression, anxiety, and stress during COVID-19 pandemic. *Journal of Neurosciences in Rural Practice*, 11(04), 519–525. 10.1055/s-0040-171644233144785

Langer, R., & Beckman, S. C. (2005). Sensitive research topics: Netnography revisited. *Qualitative Market Research*, 8(2), 189–203. 10.1108/13522750510592454

Liu, X., Wen, J., Kozak, M., Jiang, Y., & Li, Z. (2022). Negotiating interdisciplinary practice under the COVID-19 crisis: Opportunities and challenges for tourism research. *Tourism Review*, 77(2), 484–502. 10.1108/TR-01-2021-0034

Lu, J., Xiao, X., Xu, Z., Wang, C., Zhang, M., & Zhou, Y. (2022). The potential of virtual tourism in the recovery of tourism industry during the COVID-19 pandemic. *Current Issues in Tourism*, 25(3), 441–457. 10.1080/13683500.2021.1959526

Luo, J. M., & Lam, C. F. (2020). Travel anxiety, risk attitude and travel intentions towards "travel bubble" destinations in Hong Kong: Effect of the fear of COVID-19. *International Journal of Environmental Research and Public Health*, 17(21), 7859. 10.3390/ijerph1721785933120949

Maingi, S. W., Gowreesunkar, V. G., & Korstanje, M. E. (2024). *Tourist Behaviour and the New Normal* (Vol. I). Springer.

Mann, C. L. (2020). Real and financial lenses to assess the economic consequences of COVID-19. *Economics in the Time of COVID-19, 81*, 85.

Mostafanezhad, M., Cheer, J. M., & Sin, H. L. (2020). Geopolitical anxieties of tourism:(Im) mobilities of the COVID-19 pandemic. *Dialogues in Human Geography*, 10(2), 182–186. 10.1177/2043820620934206

Nagai, H., & Kurahashi, S. (2022). Measures to prevent and control the spread of novel coronavirus disease (COVID-19) infection in tourism locations. *SICE Journal of Control, Measurement, and System Integration*, 15(2), 1–12. 10.1080/18824889.2021.2012398

Nepal, S. K. (2020). Adventure travel and tourism after COVID-19–business as usual or opportunity to reset? *Tourism Geographies*, 22(3), 646–650. 10.1080/14616688.2020.1760926

Pang, S. F., McKercher, B., & Prideaux, B. (2013). Climate change and tourism: An overview. *Asia Pacific Journal of Tourism Research*, 18(1-2), 4–20. 10.1080/10941665.2012.688509

Pham, T. D., Dwyer, L., Su, J. J., & Ngo, T. (2021). COVID-19 impacts of inbound tourism on Australian economy. *Annals of Tourism Research*, 88, 103179. 10.1016/j. annals.2021.10317936540369

Ratten, V. (2023). The post COVID-19 pandemic era: Changes in teaching and learning methods for management educators. *International Journal of Management Education*, 21(2), 100777. 10.1016/j.ijme.2023.100777

Rogerson, C. M., & Baum, T. (2020). COVID-19 and African tourism research agendas. *Development Southern Africa*, 37(5), 727–741. 10.1080/0376835X.2020.1818551

Rogerson, C. M., & Rogerson, J. M. (2020). COVID-19 tourism impacts in South Africa: Government and industry responses. *Geo Journal of Tourism and Geosites*, 31(3), 1083–1091. 10.30892/gtg.31321-544

Saha, S., & Yap, G. (2014). The moderation effects of political instability and terrorism on tourism development: A cross-country panel analysis. *Journal of Travel Research*, 53(4), 509–521. 10.1177/0047287513496472

Seabra, C., & Korstanje, M. E. (Eds.). (2023). *Safety and Tourism: A Global Industry with Global Risks*. Emerald. 10.1108/9781803828114

Şengel, Ü., Genç, G., Işkın, M., Çevrimkaya, M., Zengin, B., & Sarıışık, M. (2023). The impact of anxiety levels on destination visit intention in the context of COVID-19: The mediating role of travel intention. *Journal of Hospitality and Tourism Insights*, 6(2), 697–715. 10.1108/JHTI-10-2021-0295

Seraphin, H., & Maingi, S. W. (2023). The luxury yacht charter market and sustainable brand image: The case of Sunreef. *Worldwide Hospitality and Tourism Themes*, 15(4), 386–397. 10.1108/WHATT-03-2023-0045

Serrano, F., & Kazda, A. (2020). The future of airports post COVID-19. *Journal of Air Transport Management*, 89, 101900. 10.1016/j.jairtraman.2020.10190032834696

Sharma, A., & Nicolau, J. L. (2020). An open market valuation of the effects of COVID-19 on the travel and tourism industry. *Annals of Tourism Research*, 83, 102990. 10.1016/j.annals.2020.10299032834220

Talwar, S., Kaur, P., Nunkoo, R., & Dhir, A. (2022). Digitalization and sustainability: Virtual reality tourism in a post pandemic world. *Journal of Sustainable Tourism*, 1–28.

Toubes, D. R., Araújo Vila, N., & Fraiz Brea, J. A. (2021). Changes in consumption patterns and tourist promotion after the COVID-19 pandemic. *Journal of Theoretical and Applied Electronic Commerce Research*, 16(5), 1332–1352. 10.3390/jtaer16050075

Tremblay-Huet, S. (2020). COVID-19 leads to a new context for the "right to tourism": A reset of tourists' perspectives on space appropriation is needed. *Tourism Geographies*, 22(3), 720–723. 10.1080/14616688.2020.1759136

Wassler, P. (2023). Covid-19 and the Host Community: Towards an Uncertain Future? In *Changing Practices of Tourism Stakeholders in Covid-19 Affected Destinations* (pp. 1-12). Channel View Publications.

Wen, J., Wang, C. C., & Kozak, M. (2021). Post-COVID-19 Chinese domestic tourism market recovery: Potential influence of traditional Chinese medicine on tourist behaviour. *Anatolia*, 32(1), 121–125. 10.1080/13032917.2020.1768335

Xiao, C. (2020). A novel approach of consultation on 2019 novel coronavirus (COVID-19)-related psychological and mental problems: Structured letter therapy. *Psychiatry Investigation*, 17(2), 175–185. 10.30773/pi.2020.004732093461

Yang, Y., Zhang, C. X., & Rickly, J. M. (2021). A review of early COVID-19 research in tourism: Launching the Annals of Tourism Research's Curated Collection on coronavirus and tourism. *Annals of Tourism Research*, 91, 103313. 10.1016/j.annals.2021.10331334611371

Yeh, S. S. (2021). Tourism recovery strategy against COVID-19 pandemic. *Tourism Recreation Research*, 46(2), 188–194. 10.1080/02508281.2020.1805933

Zhang, S. N., Li, Y. Q., Ruan, W. Q., & Liu, C. H. (2022). Would you enjoy virtual travel? The characteristics and causes of virtual tourists' sentiment under the influence of the COVID-19 pandemic. *Tourism management, 88*, 104429.

KEY TERMS AND DEFINITIONS

COVID-19: A new ARN virus originally reported in Wuhan China.

Lockdown: A sanitary restriction imposed to stop the contagion during pandemics.

Netnography: It is a new method that combines classic ethnography with digital technologies and media information gathering.

Pandemics: An epidemic or infectious disease that often affects large regions.

Tourism Industry: A service-related industry dedicated to boost pleasurable travels.

Conclusion

This book was created in response to a perception that there is a demand for a focused academic work that would be of interested to students, scholars, and practitioners. We hope that we were able to work in ways to create an effective response to this perception of the demand. Even if we have missed producing an effective book to fill the perception of the need, many readers will have found some value in some of the twenty-one chapters contributed by highly esteemed and insightful authors who we were fortunate enough to attract to this project. So, we feel confident that we have, in the end, created a book that has value because of the interesting topic and the strength of the talent we were able to attract.

The book gives critical insight into the way that the events industry is moving. One thing that readers will notice is that while technologies are a major influence and driver for innovation in events, technology is not the only issue. Authors highlighted how 5G, AI, virtual reality, the metaverse, robots, and other technologies will play a role in the expansion of virtual and hybrid events. But the technology is not the only driver nor topic of interest pertaining to virtual events, there are also other considerations and concerns. For example, several authors made reference to gamification, a concept that does not require very much technology but does require a change of mindset, changing meetings and events into something more interactive to maintain the interest of the participants.

We hope that readers have seen the value of the book and that they will encourage others to read the chapters from the book. Additionally, we hope that this book is a book that will increase awareness and interest in the academic study of virtual and hybrid events. We feel that the greatest reward from working to make such a book come to fruition is to see that it is cited widely in the academic literature and that practitioners write to us to tell us how the book has given them insight to make their events more effective or profitable. Since this book was not designed to just sit on bookshelves and remain unread, we will be thrilled to see how widely chapters are sighted and look forward to feedback from readers throughout the world.

While this edited work is not the definitive book on the topic and we recognize that there is a great deal of potential for others to build upon this work, we are very happy that we were able to attract great authors and insightful chapters. We feel that future works will be able to give greater insight into social, economic, and political changes that will lead to an expansion of virtual and hybrid events. As this tome has shown, technological advances play a major role in advancing virtual events, although technology is not the only driver.

Our ultimate hope, beyond filling a need in the market of ideas, is to also work as a catalyst for future research. Future research should not just concentrate upon the technological issues but also look at managerial concerns and concerns linked with the bottom-line. Future research should look more at developing ideas that are of use to the event manager, showing managers clearly how to make online and hybrid events interesting, effective, and lucrative. To some extent, this may require the utilization of technologies to keep participants engaged in a virtual environment, but it may also eventually be linked with simple low-tech solutions and design choices that are appealing to the eye and ensure greater participation and engagement by participants. In the end, what really matters is not that an event takes place on a virtual platform but also that participants are happy with the event and remain engaged in the event.

At any rate, this book is now in your hands and we hope that you find what you are looking for in the book while at the same time find something else in the book that captivates you, even if you were not looking for it.

Sharad Kumar Kulshreshtha
North-Eastern Hill University, India

Craig Webster
Ball State University, USA

Compilation of References

. Chaturvedi, R., & Verma, S. (2023). Opportunities and challenges of AI-driven customer service. *Artificial Intelligence in customer service: The next frontier for personalized engagement*, 33-71.

. Jin, T., Su, Y., & Lei, J. (2020). Exploring the blended learning design for argumentative writing.

. Rane, N. (2023). Enhancing Customer Loyalty through Artificial Intelligence (AI), Internet of Things (IoT), and Big Data Technologies: Improving Customer Satisfaction, Engagement, Relationship, and Experience. *Internet of Things (IoT), and Big Data Technologies: Improving Customer Satisfaction, Engagement, Relationship, and Experience (October 13, 2023)*.

. Rathore, B. (2016). Revolutionizing the Digital Landscape: Exploring the Integration of Artificial Intelligence in Modern Marketing Strategies. *Eduzone: International Peer Reviewed/Refereed Multidisciplinary Journal, 5*(2), 8-13.

Abid Haleem, M. J. (2022). Understanding the role of digital technologies in education: A review. *Sustainable Operations and Computers*, 3, 275–285. 10.1016/j.susoc.2022.05.004

Aburbeian, A. M., Owda, A. Y., & Owda, M. (2022). A technology acceptance model survey of the metaverse prospects. *AI, 3*(2), 285–302. 10.3390/ai3020018

Adam Marks, M. A.-A. (2020). Digital Transformation in Higher Education: A Framework for Maturity Assessment. [IJACSA]. *International Journal of Advanced Computer Science and Applications, 11*(12). 10.14569/IJACSA.2020.0111261

Adam, T. (2019). Digital neocolonialism and massive open online courses (MOOCs): Colonial pasts and neoliberal futures. *Learning, Media and Technology, 44*(3), 365–380. 10.1080/17439884.2019.1640740

Adu-Ampong, E. A., & Dillette, A. (2024). Commemoration and commodification: Slavery heritage, Black travel and the #YearofReturn2019 in Ghana. *Tourism Geographies, 26*(1), 120–139. 10.1080/14616688.2023.2275731

Agalarova, L. S., Rozanova, T. P., Stytsiuk, R. Y., & Tavakov, A. A. (2023). The problems of development of medical health-improving tourism in modern conditions. *Problemy Sotsial'noi Gigieny, Zdravookhraneniia i Istorii Meditsiny, 31*(1), 44–50. . 10.32687/0869-866X-2023-31-1-44-5036801873

Aggarwal, V., & Ansari, N. (2014). *Emerging trends: apps in event management.* ACM. 10.1145/2593761.2593767

Ahmad, F., Draz, M. U., Su, L., & Rauf, A. (2019). Taking the bad with the good: The nexus between tourism and environmental degradation in the lower middle-income Southeast Asian economies. *Journal of Cleaner Production*, 233, 1240–1249. 10.1016/j.jclepro.2019.06.138

Ahmad, H., Islam, M. Z., Ali, R., Haider, A., & Kim, H. S. (2021). Intelligent stretch optimization in information centric Networking-Based tactile internet applications. *Applied Sciences (Basel, Switzerland)*, 11(16), 7351. 10.3390/app11167351

Ahmed, A. M., Qiu, T., Xia, F., Jedari, B., & Abolfazli, S. (2014). Event-Based Mobile Social Networks: Services, Technologies, and Applications. *IEEE Access : Practical Innovations, Open Solutions*, 2, 500–513. 10.1109/ACCESS.2014.2319823

Ahmed, S., Archambault, P., Auger, C., Durand, A., Fung, J., Kehayia, E., Lamontagne, A., Majnemer, A., Nadeau, S., Pineau, J., Ptito, A., & Swaine, B. (2022). Biomedical Research and Informatics Living Laboratory for Innovative Advances of New Technologies in Community Mobility Rehabilitation: Protocol for Evaluation and Rehabilitation of Mobility Across Continuums of Care. *JMIR Research Protocols*, 11(6), e12506. . 10.2196/1250635648455

Airey, D. (2013). Forty years of tourism education and research. *Poznan university of economics review, 13*(4), 1-15.

Airey, D., & Tribe, J. (Eds.). (2006). *An international handbook of tourism education*. Routledge. 10.4324/9780080458687

Airey, D., Tribe, J., Benckendorff, P., & Xiao, H. (2015). The managerial gaze: The long tail of tourism education and research. *Journal of Travel Research*, 54(2), 139–151. 10.1177/0047287514522877

Aisha, N., & Ratra, A. (2023). NEP 2020: Blended Learning-The Road Ahead for Higher Education in India. *Global Journal of Enterprise Information System*, 15(3), 42–46.

Aji, W. K., Ardin, H., & Arifin, M. A. (2020). Blended learning during pandemic corona virus: Teachers' and students' perceptions. *IDEAS: Journal on English Language Teaching and Learning. Linguistics and Literature*, 8(2), 632–646.

Akour, I. A., Al-Maroof, R. S., Alfaisal, R., & Salloum, S. A. (2022). A conceptual framework for determining metaverse adoption in higher institutions of gulf area: An empirical study using hybrid SEM-ANN approach. *Computers and education: artificial intelligence, 3*, 100052.

Aksentyeva, N., Aminov, D. S., Cayenne, J., Foo, J., Kammogne, G., Lum, A., & Zhou, H. (2020). Technology Use in Meetings. NIH.

Al Fararni, K., Nafis, F., Aghoutane, B., Yahyaouy, A., Riffi, J., & Sabri, A. (2021). Hybrid recommender system for tourism based on big data and AI: A conceptual framework. *Big Data Mining and Analytics*, 4(1), 47–55. 10.26599/BDMA.2020.9020015

Compilation of References

Al-Adwan, A. S., & Al-Debei, M. M. (2023). The determinants of Gen Z's metaverse adoption decisions in higher education: Integrating UTAUT2 with personal innovativeness in IT. *Education and Information Technologies*, 1–33.37361794

Alananzeh, O. A. (2022). Drivers and Challenges for Future Events and their Impact on Hotel Industry. *African Journal of Hospitality, Tourism and Leisure*, 11(3), 1273–1287.

Alanazi, A., Ashour, F., Aldosari, H., & Aldosari, B. (2022). The Impact of Virtual Reality in Enhancing the Quality of Life of Pediatric Oncology Patients. *Studies in Health Technology and Informatics*, 289, 477–480. . 10.3233/SHTI21096135062194

Alarcón, D. M., & Cole, S. (2019). No sustainability for tourism without gender equality. *Journal of Sustainable Tourism*, 27(7), 903–919. 10.1080/09669582.2019.1588283

Albaom, M. A., Sidi, F., Jabar, M. A., Abdullah, R., Ishak, I., Yunikawati, N. A., Priambodo, M. P., Nusari, M. S., & Ali, D. A. (2022). The moderating role of personal innovativeness in tourists' intention to use web 3.0 based on updated information systems success model. *Sustainability (Basel)*, 14(21), 13935. 10.3390/su142113935

Alenezi, M. (2021). *Deep Dive into Digital Transformation in Higher Education Institutions*. Semantic Scholar. 10.3390/educsci11120770

Alhusban, H. A. (2022). A Novel Synchronous Hybrid Learning Method: Voices from Saudi Arabia. *Electronic Journal of e-Learning*, 20(4), 400–418. 10.34190/ejel.20.4.2340

Al-Hyari, H. S. A., Al-Smadi, H. M., & Weshah, S. R. (2023). the impact of artificial intelligence (ai) on guest satisfaction in hotel management: An empirical study of luxury hotels. *Geo Journal of Tourism and Geosites*, 48(2 supplement), 810–819. 10.30892/gtg.482spl15-1081

Ali, A., Rasoolimanesh, S. M., & Cobanoglu, C. (2020). Technology in tourism and hospitality to achieve sustainable development goals (SDGs). *Journal of Hospitality and Tourism Technology*, 11(2), 177–181. 10.1108/JHTT-05-2020-146

Ali, N., & Ullah, S. (2020). Review to analyze and compare virtual chemistry laboratories for their use in education. *Journal of Chemical Education*, 97(10), 3563–3574. 10.1021/acs.jchemed.0c00185

Alina, D. M., Miguel, F. L., Marian, N., Mihail, B., & Vanesa, V. M. (2021). The Challenges of the Higher Education Sector. The Impact of COVID-19 Crisis on the Educational Process—Case of Romania. *Springer Proceedings in Business and Economics*, 37–58. Springer. 10.1007/978-3-030-86641-9_3

Aljuhani, K., Sonbul, M., Althabiti, M., & Meccawy, M. (2018). Creating a virtual science lab (VSL): The adoption of virtual labs in Saudi schools. *Smart Learn Environ*, 5(1), 16. 10.1186/s40561-018-0067-9

Al-Kfairy, M., Alomari, A., Al-Bashayreh, M., Alfandi, O., & Tubishat, M. (2024). Unveiling the Metaverse: A survey of user perceptions and the impact of usability, social influence and interoperability. *Heliyon*, 10(10), 1–16. 10.1016/j.heliyon.2024.e3141338826724

Alkhwaldi, A. F. (2023). Understanding learners' intention toward Metaverse in higher education institutions from a developing country perspective: UTAUT and ISS integrated model. *Kybernetes*, ●●●, 1–12. 10.1108/K-03-2023-0459

Allam, Z., Sharifi, A., Bibri, S. E., Jones, D. S., & Krogstie, J. (2022). The metaverse as a virtual form of smart cities: Opportunities and challenges for environmental, economic, and social sustainability in urban futures. *Smart Cities*, 5(3), 771–801. 10.3390/smartcities5030040

Alonso-Muñoz, S., Torrejón-Ramos, M., Medina-Salgado, M.-S., & González-Sánchez, R. (2023). Sustainability as a building block for tourism – future research: Tourism Agenda 2030. *Tourism Review*, 78(2), 461–474. 10.1108/TR-12-2021-0568

Alroy, A., Ben-Shushan, E., & Katz, B. (2022). *Event Success: Maximizing the Business Impact of In-person, Virtual, and Hybrid Experiences*. John Wiley & Sons.

Alston, E. (2024). When Digital Carnival? Distributed Control of the Metaverse Asset Layer to Enable Creative Digital Expression to Flourish. In *Defining Web3: A Guide to the New Cultural Economy* (pp. 105-113). Emerald Publishing Limited. 10.1108/S0733-558X20240000089009

Alvarez-Risco, A., Del-Aguila-Arcentales, S., Rosen, M. A., & Yáñez, J. A. (2022). Social Cognitive Theory to Assess the Intention to participate in the Facebook Metaverse by citizens in Peru during the COVID-19 pandemic. *Journal of Open Innovation*, 8(3), 142. 10.3390/joitmc8030142

Ameen, N., Tarhini, A., Reppel, A., & Anand, A. (2021). Customer experiences in the age of artificial intelligence. *Computers in Human Behavior*, 114, 106548. 10.1016/j.chb.2020.10654832905175

Amoah, V. A., & Baum, T. (1997). Tourism education: Policy versus practice. *International Journal of Contemporary Hospitality Management*, 9(1), 5–12. 10.1108/09596119710157531

Andresen, M., & Bergdolt, F. (2021). Individual and job-related antecedents of a global mindset: An analysis of international business travelers' characteristics and experiences abroad. *International Journal of Human Resource Management*, 32(9), 1953–1985. 10.1080/09585192.2019.1588349

Andronas, D., Kampourakis, E., Papadopoulos, G., Bakopoulou, K., Kotsaris, P. S., Michalos, G., & Makris, S. (2023). Towards seamless collaboration of humans and high-payload robots: An automotive case study. *Robotics and Computer-integrated Manufacturing*, 83, 102544. 10.1016/j.rcim.2023.102544

Ansah, A. A., Vivacqua, A. S., Zhong, S., Boll, S., Constantinides, M., Verma, H., El Ali, A., Lushnikova, A., Alavi, H., Rintel, S., Kun, A. L., Shaer, O., Cox, A. L., Gerling, K., Muller, M., Rusnak, V., Machado, L. S., & Kosch, T. (2023). Reflecting on Hybrid Events: Learning from a Year of Hybrid Experiences. *Extended Abstracts of the 2023 CHI Conference on Human Factors in Computing Systems*, (pp. 1–4). ACM. 10.1145/3544549.3583181

Ansari, A. I., & Singh, A. (2023). Application of Augmented Reality (AR) and Virtual Reality (VR) in Promoting Guest Room Sales: A Critical Review. Z. Tučková, S. Dey, H. Thai, & S. Hoang. (Ed.) *Impact of Industry 4.0 on Sustainable Tourism*. Emerald Publishing Limited, Leeds. 10.1108/978-1-80455-157-820231006

Compilation of References

Antchak, V., & Adams, E. (2020). Unusual venues for business events: Key quality attributes of museums and art galleries. *International Journal of Tourism Cities*, 6(4), 847–862. 10.1108/IJTC-09-2019-0156

Anthonysamy, L., Koo, A. C., & Hew, S. H. (2020). Self-regulated learning strategies and non-academic outcomes in higher education blended learning environments: A one decade review. *Education and Information Technologies*, 25(5), 3677–3704. 10.1007/s10639-020-10134-2

Antwi-Boampong, A., & Bokolo, A. J. (2022). Towards an institutional blended learning adoption model for higher education institutions. *Technology. Knowledge and Learning*, 27(3), 765–784. 10.1007/s10758-021-09507-4

Anwar, M. S., Alhalabi, W., Choi, A., Ullah, I., & Alhudali, A. (2024). Internet of metaverse things (IoMT): Applications, technology challenges and security consideration. In *Future Communication Systems Using Artificial Intelligence, Internet of Things and Data Science* (pp. 133–158). CRC Press.

APAAR. (2024, March 02). *APAAR*. APAAR. https://apaar.education.gov.in/

Apandi, A. M., & Raman, A. (2020). Factors affecting successful implementation of blended learning at higher education. *International Journal of Instruction, Technology, and Social Sciences*, 1(1), 13–23.

Araújo, J., & Pestana, G. (2017). A framework for social well-being and skills management at the workplace. *International Journal of Information Management*, 37(6), 718–725. 10.1016/j.ijinfomgt.2017.07.009

Arcese, G., Valeri, M., Poponi, S., & Elmo, G. C. (2021). Innovative drivers for family business models in tourism. *Journal of Family Business Management*, 11(4), 402–422. 10.1108/JFBM-05-2020-0043

Arcos, R., & Smith, H. (2021). Digital communication and hybrid threats. In *Icono14*. 10.7195/ri14.v19i1.1662

Arpaci, I., Karatas, K., Kusci, I., & Al-Emran, M. (2022). Understanding the social sustainability of the Metaverse by integrating UTAUT2 and big five personality traits: A hybrid SEM-ANN approach. *Technology in Society*, 71, 102–120. 10.1016/j.techsoc.2022.102120

Artjukhov, A. (2019). Roadmap for the development of education quality assurance systems in higher education institutions: educational and socio-economic aspects. *Prychornomorsjki Ekonomichni Studiji, 37*, 243-247. http://bses.in.ua/journals/2019/37_2019/48.pdf

Asakawa, T., Sugiyama, K., Nozaki, T., Sameshima, T., Kobayashi, S., Wang, L., Hong, Z., Chen, S., Li, C., & Namba, H. (2019). Can the Latest Computerized Technologies Revolutionize Conventional Assessment Tools and Therapies for a Neurological Disease? The Example of Parkinson's Disease. *Neurologia Medico-Chirurgica*, 59(3), 69–78. . 10.2176/nmc.ra.2018-004530760657

Ateljevic, I., Morgan, N., & Pritchard, A. (Eds.). (2013). *The critical turn in tourism studies: Creating an academy of hope* (Vol. 22). Routledge. 10.4324/9780203806586

Atrakchi-Israel, B., & Nahmias, Y. (2022). Metaverse, Competition, and the Online Digital Ecosystem. *Minnesota Journal of Law, Science & Technology*, 24, 235.

Attaran, M. (2020, July). Digital technology enablers and their implications for supply chain management. In *Supply Chain ForumInternational Journal (Toronto, Ont.)*, 21(3), 158–172.

Atzori, L., Iera, A., & Morabito, G. (2017). Understanding the Internet of Things: Definition, potentials, and societal role of a fast-evolving paradigm. *Ad Hoc Networks*, 56, 122–140. 10.1016/j.adhoc.2016.12.004

Awad, I., Salah, R., & Saleh, R. (2021). Using virtual platforms in architectural education to manage the Corona virus crisis: An applied study on the Microsoft platform at Horus University - Egypt. *Journal of Architecture, Arts and Humanities*. 10.21608/mjaf.2020.44838.1885

Azizi, S. M., Roozbahani, N., & Khatony, A. (2020). Factors affecting the acceptance of blended learning in medical education: Application of UTAUT2 model. *BMC Medical Education*, 20(1), 1–9. 10.1186/s12909-020-02302-233066768

Backman, K. F., Backman, S. J., Uysal, M., & Sunshine, K. M. (1995). Event tourism: An examination of motivations and activities. *Festival Management & Event Tourism*, 3(1), 15–24.

Badre, P. (2020). Blended Learning a New Normal in Higher Education. *COVID–19: Crisis, Effects, Challenges and Innovations*, 152-159.

Bailenson, J. N. (2021). Nonverbal Overload: A Theoretical Argument for the Causes of Zoom Fatigue. *Technology, Mind, and Behavior*, 2(1). 10.1037/tmb0000030

Bai, Y., Liu, F., & Zhang, H. (2022). Artificial Intelligence Limb Rehabilitation System on Account of Virtual Reality Technology on Long-Term Health Management of Stroke Patients in the Context of the Internet. *Computational and Mathematical Methods in Medicine*, 2022, 2688003. . 10.1155/2022/268800335651925

Bakar, N. A., & Rosbi, S. (2020). Effect of Coronavirus disease (COVID-19) to tourism industry. *International Journal of Advanced Engineering Research and Science*, 7(4), 189–193. 10.22161/ijaers.74.23

Ball, M. (2022). *The metaverse: and how it will revolutionise everything*. Liveright Publishing Corporation. www.matthewball.vc/all/forwardtothemetaverseprimer

Banda, H. J., & Nzabahimana, J. (2023). The impact of physics education technology (PhET) interactive simulation-based learning on motivation and academic achievement among malawian physics students. *Journal of Science Education and Technology*, 32(1), 127–141. 10.1007/s10956-022-10010-336569225

Banerjee, S. (2023, September 18). G20's role in shaping online higher education. *Financial Express*. https://www.financialexpress.com/jobs-career/education-g20s-role-in-shaping-online-higher-education-3246128/

Compilation of References

Banjac, I., & Palić, M. (2021). Analysis of best practice of artificial intelligence implementation in digital marketing activities. *CroDiM: International Journal of Marketing Science*, 4(1), 45–56.

Bansal, R., Martinho, C., Pruthi, N., & Aggarwal, D. (2023). From virtual observations to business insights: A bibliometric review of netnography in business research. *Heliyon*, 10(1), e22853. Advance online publication. 10.1016/j.heliyon.2023.e2285338163120

Barrera, K. G., & Shah, D. (2023). Marketing in the metaverse: Conceptual understanding, framework, and research agenda. *Journal of Business Research*, 15, 113420. 10.1016/j.jbusres.2022.113420

Bassyiouny, M., & Wilkesmann, M. (2023). Going on workation – Is tourism research ready to take off? Exploring an emerging phenomenon of hybrid tourism. *Tourism Management Perspectives*, 46, 101096. 10.1016/j.tmp.2023.101096

Basurto-Cedeno, E., & Pennington-Gray, L. (2018). An Applied Destination Resilience Model. *Tourism Review International*, 22(3), 293–302. 10.3727/154427218X15369305779092

Batth, R. S., Nayyar, A., & Nagpal, A. (2018, August). Internet of robotic things: driving intelligent robotics of future-concept, architecture, applications and technologies. In *2018 4th international conference on computing sciences (ICCS)* (pp. 151-160). IEEE. 10.1109/ICCS.2018.00033

Bauer, T., Law, R., Tse, T., & Weber, K. (2008). Motivation and satisfaction of mega-business event attendees: The case of ITU Telecom World 2006 in Hong Kong. *International Journal of Contemporary Hospitality Management*, 20(2), 228–234. 10.1108/09596110810852195

Baum, T., & Hai, N. T. T. (2020). Hospitality, tourism, human rights and the impact of COVID-19. *International Journal of Contemporary Hospitality Management*, 32(7), 2397–2407. 10.1108/IJCHM-03-2020-0242

Becken, S., & Loehr, J. (2022). Asia–Pacific tourism futures emerging from COVID-19 recovery responses and implications for sustainability. *Journal of Tourism Futures*, 9(1), 35–48. 10.1108/JTF-05-2021-0131

Behringer, W. (2006). Communications revolutions: A historiographical concept. *German History*, 24(3), 333–374. 10.1191/0266355406gh378oa

Bellini, H., Chen, W., Sugiyama, M., Shin, M., Alam, S., & Takayama, D. (2016). Virtual & Augmented Reality: Understanding the race for the next computing platform. *Profiles in Innovation,* 1-58. https://www.gspublishing.com/content/research/en/reports/2016/01/13/eb9acad9-3db9-485c-864d-321372a23726.pdf

Bello-Orgaz, G., Jung, J. J., & Camacho, D. (2016). Social big data: Recent achievements and new challenges. *Information Fusion*, 28, 45–59. 10.1016/j.inffus.2015.08.00532288689

Benet, D., & Pellicer-Valero, O. J. (2022). *Metaverse in Ophthalmology: The Convergence of Virtual and Physical Space in Eye Care.* Digital Medicine and Healthcare Technology., 10.5772/dmht.10

Berger, J. (2012). What makes online content viral? *Strategic Direction*, 28(8). 10.1108/sd.2012.05628haa.014

Bevolo, M., & Amati, F. (2024). The future of business events in the "phygital" age: development of a generative tool: A qualitative research project combining Design Research and foresight principles to co-design and develop a futures matrix for potential implementation by business event designers and managers. *World Leisure Journal*, 66(1), 92–115. 10.1080/16078055.2023.2238275

Bhalla, A., Singh, P., & Singh, A. (2023). Technological Advancement and Mechanization of the Hotel Industry. In Tailor, R. (Ed.), *Application and Adoption of Robotic Process Automation for Smart Cities* (pp. 57–76). IGI Global. 10.4018/978-1-6684-7193-7.ch004

Bhamra, R., Dani, S., & Burnard, K. (2011). Resilience: The Concept, A Literature Review and Future Directions. *International Journal of Production Research*, 49(18), 5375–5393. 10.1080/00207543.2011.563826

Bhanot, L., Shyam, R., Khan, M. A., Bahadur, P., & Ali, S. (2024). Even to: An Android App for Event Planners. *International Research Journal of Modernization in Engineering Technology and Science*. 10.56726/IRJMETS53489

Bhashini. (2024, April 02). *Bhashini*. Bhashini. https://bhashini.gov.in/

Bhatia, D., Sahai, N., & Sarma, J. (2020). Recent advances on ankle foot orthosis for gait rehabilitation: A review. *International Journal of Biomedical Engineering and Technology*, 33(2), 159. Advance online publication. 10.1504/IJBET.2020.107711

Bian, D., Lin, Z., Lu, H., Zhong, Q., Wang, K., Tang, X., & Zang, J. (2024). The application of extended reality technology-assisted intraoperative navigation in orthopedic surgery. *Frontiers in Surgery*, 11, 1336703. . 10.3389/fsurg.2024.133670338375409

Biasutti, M. (2017). A comparative analysis of forums and wikis as tools for online collaborative learning. *Computers & Education*, 111, 158–171. 10.1016/j.compedu.2017.04.006

Bibri, S. E. (2022). The social shaping of the metaverse as an alternative to the imaginaries of data-driven smart Cities: A study in science, technology, and society. *Smart Cities*, 5(3), 832–874. 10.3390/smartcities5030043

Bignell, J., & Fickers, A. (Eds.). (2008). *A European television history*. Wiley-Blackwell.

Binh Nguyen, P. M., Pham, X. L., & To Truong, G. N. (2023). A bibliometric analysis of research on tourism content marketing: Background knowledge and thematic evolution. *Heliyon*, 9(2), e13487. 10.1016/j.heliyon.2023.e1348736816254

Birkeland, H., Khalil, M., & Wasson, B. (2022). *Learning analytics in collaborative online lab environments: A systematic scoping review*.

Bladen, C., Kennell, J., Abson, E., & Wilde, N. (2022). *Events management: An introduction*. Routledge. 10.4324/9781003102878

Compilation of References

Boluk, K. A., Cavaliere, C. T., & Higgins-Desbiolles, F. (2019). A critical framework for interrogating the United Nations Sustainable Development Goals 2030 Agenda in tourism. *Journal of Sustainable Tourism*, 27(7), 847–864. 10.1080/09669582.2019.1619748

Bondar A., Komarovsky, V., Shobik, V., & Yatsenko, V. (2021). Management of digital transformation processes in socio-cultural sphere. *Actual problems of Public Administration, 3*(84), 66-72. _[in Ukrainian]10.35432/1993-8330appa3842021246259

Bondarenko, O. V., Hanchuk, O. V., Pakhomova, O. V., & Varfolomyeyeva, I. M. (2023). Digitalization of geographic higher education: Problems and prospects. *Journal of Physics: Conference Series*, 2611(1), 012015. 10.1088/1742-6596/2611/1/012015

Bordoloi, R., Das, P., & Das, K. (2021). Perception towards online/blended learning at the time of Covid-19 pandemic: An academic analytics in the Indian context. *Asian Association of Open Universities Journal*, 16(1), 41–60. 10.1108/AAOUJ-09-2020-0079

Boshnakova, D., & Goldblatt, J. (2017). *The 21st century meeting and event Technologies: Powerful tools for better planning, marketing, and evaluation.* CRC Press.

Bosse, S., & Pournaras, E. (2017). An ubiquitous multi-agent mobile platform for distributed crowd sensing and social mining. *Proceedings - 2017 IEEE 5th International Conference on Future Internet of Things and Cloud, FiCloud 2017.* IEEE. 10.1109/FiCloud.2017.44

Bouarar, A. C., Mouloudj, S., & Mouloudj, K. (2022). Digital Transformation: Opportunities and Challenges. In Mansour, N., & Ben Salem, S. (Eds.), *COVID-19's Impact on the Cryptocurrency Market and the Digital Economy* (pp. 33–52). IGI Global. 10.4018/978-1-7998-9117-8.ch003

Bouarar, A. C., Stojczew, K., & Mouloudj, K. (2023). An Analytical Study on Digital Transformation in the Poland Hospitality Industry. In Fernandes, G., & Melo, A. (Eds.), *Handbook of Research on Innovation, Differentiation, and New Technologies in Tourism, Hotels, and Food Service* (pp. 32–50). IGI Global. 10.4018/978-1-6684-6985-9.ch002

Bouilheres, F., Le, L. T. V. H., McDonald, S., Nkhoma, C., & Jandug-Montera, L. (2020). Defining student learning experience through blended learning. *Education and Information Technologies*, 25(4), 3049–3069. 10.1007/s10639-020-10100-y

Bovsh, L. A., Hopkalo, L. M., & Rasulova, A. M. (2023). Digital Relationship Marketing Strategies of Medical Tourism Entities. In Bouarar, A., Mouloudj, K., & Martínez Asanza, D. (Eds.), *Integrating Digital Health Strategies for Effective Administration* (pp. 133–150). IGI Global. 10.4018/978-1-6684-8337-4.ch008

BR, S. R. (2022). Information and communication technology application in tourism events, fairs and festivals in India. *Technology Application in Tourism Fairs, Festivals and Events in Asia, 209.*

Bradaric, B. D., & Tresselt, D. B. (2022). Factors influencing undergraduate education in an expanding virtual world during COVID-19. *Education and Information Technologies*, 27(9), 11991–12002. 10.1007/s10639-022-11104-635645596

Bran, E., Nadoleanu, G., & Popovici, D. M. (2022). Towards an Accessible Platform for Multimodal Extended Reality Smart Environments. *Information (Basel)*, 13(9), 439. 10.3390/info13090439

Bravo, R., Catalán, S., & Pina, J. M. (2021). Gamification in tourism and hospitality review platforms: How to R.A.M.P. up users' motivation to create content. *International Journal of Hospitality Management*, 99, 103064. 10.1016/j.ijhm.2021.103064

Breed, H. J., Jones, E., & Cubitt, J. (2023). Use of immersive virtual reality to reduce anxiety during complex paediatric dressing changes. *BMJ Case Reports*, 16(2), e252998. . 10.1136/bcr-2022-25299836764742

Broderick, M., Bender, S. M., & McHugh, T. (2018). *Virtual Trauma: Prospects for Automediality*. M/C Journal. 10.5204/mcj.1390

Brossillon, B., & Ferjani, C. (2023). Metaverse and Video Game: Brand Development in the Sport Industry. In *Digital Marketing in Sports* (pp. 252-272). Routledge.

Brown, T., & Drakeley, C. (2023). *Designing the virtual and hybrid event experience*. Goodfellow Publishers eBooks. 10.23912/978-1-915097-34-7-5400

Brown, A., & Davis, M. (2021). The role of financial management tools in event planning applications: A user perspective. *Proceedings of the IEEE International Conference on Computer Vision*, (pp. 486-499). IEEE.

Brown, T., & Drakeley, C. (Eds.). (2023). *Virtual Events Management: Theory and Methods for Event Management and Tourism*. Goodfellow Publishers Ltd. 10.23912/978-1-915097-03-3-4967

Bruggeman, B., Tondeur, J., Struyven, K., Pynoo, B., Garone, A., & Vanslambrouck, S. (2021). Experts speaking: Crucial teacher attributes for implementing blended learning in higher education. *The Internet and Higher Education*, 48, 100772. 10.1016/j.iheduc.2020.100772

Buckley, P., & Doyle, E. (2017). Individualising gamification: An investigation of the impact of learning styles and personality traits on the efficacy of gamification using a prediction market. *Computers & Education*, 106, 43–55. 10.1016/j.compedu.2016.11.009

Bueno, A. R., Urbistondo, P. A., & Martínez, B. A. (2020). The MICE Tourism Value Chain: Proposal of a Conceptual Framework and Analysis of Disintermediation. *Journal of Convention & Event Tourism*, 21(3), 177–200. 10.1080/15470148.2020.1740851

Buhalis, D., Harwood, T., Bogicevic, V., Viglia, G., Beldona, S., & Hofacker, C. (2019). Technological disruptions in services: Lessons from tourism and hospitality. *Journal of Service Management*, 30(4), 484–506. 10.1108/JOSM-12-2018-0398

Buhalis, D., Leung, D., & Lin, M. (2023). Metaverse as a disruptive technology revolutionising tourism management and marketing. *Tourism Management*, 97, 104724. 10.1016/j.tourman.2023.104724

Compilation of References

Buhalis, D., & Moldavska, I. (2022). Voice assistants in hospitality: Using artificial intelligence for customer service. *Journal of Hospitality and Tourism Technology*, 13(3), 386–403. 10.1108/JHTT-03-2021-0104

Bui, V., Pandey, S. R., Chiariotti, F., & Popovski, P. (2023, January 1). Game Networking Principles for Real-Time Social Networking in the Metaverse. Cornell University. https://doi.org//arxiv.2302.0167210.48550

Bukovska, G., Mezgaile, A., & Klepers, A. (2021). The pressure of technological innovations in meeting and event industry under the COVID-19 influence. *Vide. Tehnologija. Resursi - Environment, Technology. Resources*, 2, 44–50. 10.17770/etr2021vol2.6623

Bulchand-Gidumal, J., William Secin, E., O'Connor, P., & Buhalis, D. (2023). Artificial intelligence's impact on hospitality and tourism marketing: Exploring key themes and addressing challenges. *Current Issues in Tourism*, 1–18.

Burnard, K., Ran, B., & Christos, T. (2018). Building Organisational Resilience: Four Configurations. *IEEE Transactions on Engineering Management*, 65(3), 351–362. 10.1109/TEM.2018.2796181

Butcher, J. (2023). Covid-19, tourism and the advocacy of degrowth. *Tourism Recreation Research*, 48(5), 633–642. 10.1080/02508281.2021.1953306

Butnaru, G. I., Ni ă, V., Anichiti, A., & Brînză, G. (2021). The effectiveness of online education during covid 19 pandemic–a comparative analysis between the perceptions of academic students and high school students from romania. *Sustainability (Basel)*, 13(9), 5311. 10.3390/su13095311

Çakar, K. (2022). The Use of Qualitative Content Analysis in Hospitality and Tourism. In Okumus, F., Rasoolimanesh, S. M., & Jahani, S. (Eds.), *Contemporary Research Methods in Hospitality and Tourism* (pp. 143–155). Emerald Publishing. 10.1108/978-1-80117-546-320221010

Cakir, A. E. (2002). Virtual Communities – A Virtual Session on Virtual Conferences. *Behaviour & Information Technology*, 21(5), 365–371. 10.1080/0144929021000048439

Çakmak, E., & Isaac, K. R., & Butler, R. (2023). *Changing Practices of Tourism Stakeholders in Covid-19 Affected Destinations*. Bristol, Goodfellows.

Campbell, M., Greated, C. A., & Myers, A. (2004). *Musical instruments: history, technology, and performance of instruments of western music*. OUP Oxford. 10.1093/acprof:oso/9780198165040.001.0001

Canva, (2024). How best to make a content plan: instructions, templates and examples. Available at: https://surl.li/pkrrw

Cao, H., Lee, C. J., Iqbal, S., Czerwinski, M., Wong, P., Rintel, S., Hecht, B., Teevan, J., & Yang, L. (2021). Large scale analysis of multitasking behavior during remote meetings. *Conference on Human Factors in Computing Systems - Proceedings*. ACM. 10.1145/3411764.3445243

Carev, D. (2008). *Guest satisfaction and guest loyalty study for hotel industry*. Rochester Institute of Technology.

Carswell, J., Jamal, T., Lee, S., Sullins, D. L., & Wellman, K. (2023). Post-Pandemic Lessons for Destination Resilience and Sustainable Event Management: The Complex Learning Destination. *Tourism and Hospitality*, 4(1), 91–140. 10.3390/tourhosp4010007

Cassar, J., Whitfield, J., & Chapman, A. (2020). Contemporary Factors Influencing Association Conference Attendance. *Journal of Convention & Event Tourism*, 21(1), 57–90. 10.1080/15470148.2020.1719948

Castillo-Martinez, I. D., Bremer-Aztudillo, A. L., Velazquez-Marmolejo, L., Moreno-Gonzalez, A. M., & Belmont-Sanchez, J. (2020).. . *Acta Ortopédica Mexicana*, 34(5), 298–302. [REMOVED HYPERLINK FIELD]. 10.35366/9799233634633

Catania, V., Rundo, F., Panerai, S., & Ferri, R. (2023). Virtual Reality for the Rehabilitation of Acquired Cognitive Disorders: A Narrative Review. *Bioengineering (Basel, Switzerland)*, 11(1), 35. . 10.3390/bioengineering1101003538247912

Caton, K. (2014). Underdisciplinarity: Where are the humanities in tourism education? *Journal of Hospitality, Leisure, Sport and Tourism Education*, 15, 24–33. 10.1016/j.jhlste.2014.03.003

Cavallin Toscani, A., Vendraminelli, L., & Vinelli, A. (2024). Environmental sustainability in the event industry: A systematic review and a research agenda. *Journal of Sustainable Tourism*, 1–35. 10.1080/09669582.2024.2309544

Cavallo, M., Dholakia, M., Havlena, M., Ocheltree, K., & Podlaseck, M. (2019, March). Dataspace: A reconfigurable hybrid reality environment for collaborative information analysis. In *2019 IEEE conference on virtual reality and 3D user interfaces (VR)* (pp. 145-153). IEEE. 10.1109/VR.2019.8797733

Cavana, R., Delahaye, B., & Sekeran, U. (2001). *Applied business research: Qualitative and quantitative methods*. John Wiley & Sons.

Ceccariglia, F., Cercenelli, L., Badiali, G., Marcelli, E., & Tarsitano, A. (2022). Application of Augmented Reality to Maxillary Resections: A Three-Dimensional Approach to Maxillofacial Oncologic Surgery. *Journal of Personalized Medicine*, 12(12), 2047. . 10.3390/jpm1212204736556268

Celuch, K., & Neuhofer, B. (2023). Towards Transformative Event Experiences: State of the Art and Future Research. *Event Management*. Advance online publication. 10.3727/15259952 3X16990639314792

Cerasa, A., Gaggioli, A., Pioggia, G., & Riva, G. (2024). Metaverse in Mental Health: The Beginning of a Long History. *Current Psychiatry Reports*.

Chakravarty, U., Chand, G., & Singh, U. N. (2021). Millennial travel vlogs: Emergence of a new form of virtual tourism in the post-pandemic era? *Worldwide Hospitality and Tourism Themes*, 13(5), 666–676. 10.1108/WHATT-05-2021-0077

Compilation of References

Chamola, V., Hassija, V., Gupta, V., & Guizani, M. (2020). A Comprehensive Review of the COVID-19 Pandemic and the Role of IoT, Drones, AI, Blockchain, and 5G in Managing its Impact. *IEEE Access : Practical Innovations, Open Solutions*, 8, 90225–90265. 10.1109/ACCESS.2020.2992341

Chandiwala, M., Patel, P., & Mehta, A. (2023). Advertising and branding with Metaverse. *Dogo Rangsang Research Journal*, 13(6), 95–99.

Chang, M., Walimuni, A. C. S. M., Kim, M., & Lim, H. (2022). Acceptance of tourism blockchain based on UTAUT and connectivism theory. *Technology in Society*, 71, 102027. 10.1016/j.techsoc.2022.102027

Chang, S.-L., Kuo, M.-J., Lin, Y.-J., Chen, S.-A., Yang, Y.-Y., Cheng, H.-M., Yang, L.-Y., Kao, S.-Y., & Lee, F.-Y. (2021). Virtual reality informative aids increase residents' atrial fibrillation ablation procedures-related knowledge and patients' satisfaction. *Journal of the Chinese Medical Association*, 84(1), 25–32. . 10.1097/JCMA.00000000000046433230060

Chawdhary, G., & Shoman, N. (2021). Emerging artificial intelligence applications in otological imaging. *Current Opinion in Otolaryngology & Head & Neck Surgery*, 29(5), 357–364. . 10.1097/MOO.000000000000075434459798

Chen, Y., & Lu, H. (2018). Leveraging AI in event planning applications: Opportunities and challenges. *International Conference on Human-Computer Interaction*, (pp. 482-495). Research Gate.

Chen, C. F. (2023). Literary Theory and Cultural Practice of "Metaverse" in China. *Critical Arts*, 1–15. 10.1080/02560046.2023.2269238

Cheng, X., Zhang, S., Liu, W., & Mou, J. (2023). *Understanding visitors' metaverse and in-person tour intentions during the COVID-19 pandemic: A coping perspective.*

Cheng, S. (2023). Metaverse. In *Metaverse: Concept, Content and Context* (pp. 1–23). Springer Nature Switzerland.

Cheng, Y., Sharma, S., Sharma, P., & Kulathunga, K. M. M. C. B. (2020). Role of Personalization in Continuous Use Intention of Mobile News Apps in India: Extending the UTAUT2 Model. *Information (Basel)*, 11(1), 33. 10.3390/info11010033

Chen, L. (2020). Online Education in the Post-epidemic Era. *International Journal of Social Science and Education Research*, 3(10), 332–335. 10.6918/IJOSSER.202010_3(10).0052

Chen, S., Chan, I. C. C., Xu, S., Law, R., & Zhang, M. (2023). Metaverse in tourism: Drivers and hindrances from stakeholders' perspective. *Journal of Travel & Tourism Marketing*, 40(2), 169–184. 10.1080/10548408.2023.2227872

Chen, Z. (2024). Beyond boundaries: Exploring the metaverse in tourism. *International Journal of Contemporary Hospitality Management*. 10.1108/IJCHM-06-2023-0900

Chen, Z., Zhang, Y., Yan, Z., Dong, J., Cai, W., Ma, Y., Jiang, J., Dai, K., Liang, H., & He, J. (2021). Artificial intelligence assisted display in thoracic surgery: Development and possibilities. *Journal of Thoracic Disease*, 13(12), 6994–7005. . 10.21037/jtd-21-124035070382

Cherednichenko, A. (2020). *Invited dinners, press brunches, gastronomic apartments and restaurant festivals.* SURLI. https://surl.li/pkrrw

Chetty, K., & Motala, S. (2021). Working from Anywhere: Is South Africa Ready? *HSRC Review*, 19(1), 14–16.

Cheung, W. S., & Hew, K. F. (2011). Design and evaluation of two blended learning approaches: Lessons learned. *Australasian Journal of Educational Technology*, 27(8), 1–15. 10.14742/ajet.896

Chiamulera, C., Mantovani, E., & Tamburin, S. (2021). Remote clinical trials: A timely opportunity for a virtual reality approach and its potential application in neurology. *British Journal of Clinical Pharmacology*, 87(10), 3639–3642. . 10.1111/bcp.1492234041779

Chikusvura, N., Nkomo, S., & Sibanda, L. (2022). Transition to Virtual Graduation: Experiences of 2021 University Graduates in Zimbabwe. *Randwick International of Education and Linguistics Science Journal*, 3(3), 497–503. 10.47175/rielsj.v3i3.537

Chirra, M., Marsili, L., Wattley, L., Sokol, L. L., Keeling, E., Maule, S., Sobrero, G., Artusi, C. A., Romagnolo, A., Zibetti, M., Lopiano, L., Espay, A. J., Obeidat, A. Z., & Merola, A. (2019). Telemedicine in Neurological Disorders: Opportunities and Challenges. *Telemedicine Journal and e-Health*, 25(7), 541–550. 10.1089/tmj.2018.010130136898

Choi, J.-S., Kim, D.-M., Kim, Y., Jin, S., & Ha, J.-Y. (2021). An Analysis of College Students. *Journal of the Korea Academia-Industrial Cooperation Society*, 22(7), 68–76. 10.5762/KAIS.2021.22.7.6834762060

Choi, U., & Choi, B. (2020). The effect of augmented reality on consumer learning for search and experience products in mobile commerce. *Cyberpsychology, Behavior, and Social Networking*, 23(11), 800–805. 10.1089/cyber.2020.005732799542

Chua, K. H., & Bong, W. K. (2022). Providing inclusive education through virtual classrooms: A study of the experiences of secondary science teachers in Malaysia during the pandemic. *International Journal of Inclusive Education.* 10.1080/13603116.2022.2042403

Cirisano, T. (2020). Getting in the game: With his record-setting (and eye-popping) performance in Fortnite, Travis Scott proved that limitless creative potential—and a captive, merch mad audience could make video games the most lucrative new frontier for the live music business. *Billboard*, 132(11), 36–43.

Cobanoglu, C., Doğan, S., & Güngör, M. Y. (2021). Emerging technologies at the events. In *Impact of ICTs on Event Management and Marketing* (pp. 53–68). IGI Global. 10.4018/978-1-7998-4954-4.ch004

Compilation of References

Colombo, A., & Marques, L. (2020). Motivation and experience in symbiotic events: An illustrative example grounded in culture and business events. *Journal of Policy Research in Tourism, Leisure & Events*, 12(2), 222–238. 10.1080/19407963.2019.1657437

Cooper, R. G. (1994). New Products: The Factors that Drive Success. *International Marketing Review*, 11(1), 60–76. 10.1108/02651339410057527

Corne, A., Massot, V., & Merasli, S. (2023). The determinants of the adoption of blockchain technology in the tourism sector and metaverse perspectives. *Information Technology & Tourism*, 25(4), 605–633. 10.1007/s40558-023-00263-y

Cudny, W. (2014). The phenomenon of festivals: Their origins, evolution, and classifications. *Anthropos*, (H. 2), 640-656.

Cui, C., Wu, X., Liu, L., & Zhang, W. (2020). The spatial-temporal dynamics of daily intercity mobility in the Yangtze River Delta: An analysis using big data. *Habitat International*, 106, 102174. 10.1016/j.habitatint.2020.102174

Cunha, B., Ferreira, R., & Sousa, A. S. P. (2023). Home-Based Rehabilitation of the Shoulder Using Auxiliary Systems and Artificial Intelligence: An Overview. *Sensors (Basel)*, 23(16), 7100. . 10.3390/s2316710037631637

Cuomo, M. T., Tortora, D., Foroudi, P., Giordano, A., Festa, G., & Metallo, G. (2021). Digital transformation and tourist experience co-design: Big social data for planning cultural tourism. *Technological Forecasting and Social Change*, 162, 120345. 10.1016/j.techfore.2020.120345

CVENT. (2024). *Metrics That Matter: 68 Event Statistics You Need to Know in 2024*. CVENT. https://www.cvent.com/en/blog/events/event-statistics

da Silva, M. P. (2021). *The Age of Hybrid Events: Amplifying the Power of Culture Through Digital Experiences (Music Festivals Feat. Technology)* [Doctoral dissertation, Instituto Politecnico do Porto, Portugal].

Dagnaw, G. (2020). *Artificial intelligence towards future industrial opportunities and challenges*.

Dahles, H., & Susilowati, T. P. (2015). Business Resilience in Times of Growth and Crisis. *Annals of Tourism Research*, 51, 34–50. 10.1016/j.annals.2015.01.002

Daif, R., & Elsayed, K. (2019). Viral marketing impact on tourism and hospitality industry. *International Journal of Research in Tourism and Hospitality*, 5(3). 10.20431/2455-0043.0503004

Dalgarno, B., Bishop, A., & Bedgood, D. (2003). The potential of virtual laboratories for distance education science teaching: reflections from the initial development and evaluation of a virtual chemistry laboratory. In *Improving Learning Outcomes Through Flexible Science Teaching Symposium* (pp. 90-95). Uniserve Science, University of Sydney.

Dalgic, A., & Birdir, K. (2021). Which Key Factors Will Be Effective in the Success of Festivals?: An Evaluation in the Context of Information and Communication Technology. In *Impact of ICTs on Event Management and Marketing* (pp. 1-17). IGI Global.

Dangwal, K. L. (2017). Blended learning: An innovative approach. *Universal Journal of Educational Research*, 5(1), 129–136. 10.13189/ujer.2017.050116

Davenport, T. H., & Ronanki, R. (2018). Artificial intelligence for the real world. *Harvard Business Review*, 96(1), 108–116.

David, B., & Chalon, R. (2023, July). Digitalization and Virtual Assistive Systems in Tourist Mobility: Evolution, an Experience (with Observed Mistakes), Appropriate Orientations and Recommendations. In *International Conference on Human-Computer Interaction* (pp. 125-141). Cham: Springer Nature Switzerland. 10.1007/978-3-031-35908-8_10

Davis, A., Murphy, J., Owens, D., Khazanchi, D., & Zigurs, I. (2009). Avatars, people, and virtual worlds: Foundations for research in metaverses. *Journal of the Association for Information Systems*, 10(2), 90–117. 10.17705/1jais.00183

Davis, K., & Singh, S. (2015). Digital badges in afterschool learning: Documenting the perspectives and experiences of students and educators. *Computers & Education*, 88, 72–83. 10.1016/j.compedu.2015.04.011

Deci, E. L., Ryan, R. M., Gagné, M., Leone, D. R., Usunov, J., & Kornazheva, B. P. (2001). Need Satisfaction, Motivation, and Well-Being in the Work Organizations of a Former Eastern Bloc Country: A Cross-Cultural Study of Self-Determination. *Personality and Social Psychology Bulletin*, 27(8), 930–942. 10.1177/0146167201278002

Decuypere, M., Grimaldi, E., & Landric, P. (2021). Introduction: Critical studies of digital education platforms. *Critical Studies in Education*, 62(1), 1–16. 10.1080/17508487.2020.1866050

Demillo, R. A. (2019). *Blended learning in practice: A guide for practitioners and researchers.* MIT Press.

Deriba, F., Saqr, M., & Tukiainen, M. (2023). Exploring Barriers and Challenges to Accessibility in Virtual Laboratories: A Preliminary Review. In *Proceedings of the Technology-Enhanced Learning in Laboratories CEUR workshop (TELL 2023),* (Vol. 27). IEEE.

Deri, M. N., Zaazie, P., & Singh, A. (2024). Digital Future of the Hospitality Industry and Hospitality Education Globally. In Sharma, A. (Ed.), *International Handbook of Skill, Education, Learning, and Research Development in Tourism and Hospitality. Springer International Handbooks of Education.* Springer. 10.1007/978-981-99-3895-7_14-1

Desheng, L., Jiakui, C., & Ning, Z. (2021). Political connections and green technology innovations under an environmental regulation. *Journal of Cleaner Production*, 298, 126778. 10.1016/j.jclepro.2021.126778

Deterding, S., Dixon, D., Khaled, R., & Nacke, L. (2011). From game design elements to gamefulness. *Proceedings of the 15th International Academic MindTrek Conference on Envisioning Future Media Environments - MindTrek '11, 11,* (pp. 9–15). ACM. 10.1145/2181037.2181040

Compilation of References

Deyshappriya, N. P. R. (2020). Dynamics of Travel Behaviour and Mode of Travelling during COVID-19 Outbreak. Evidence from South Asian Countries. SSRN *Electronic Journal*. https://doi.org/10.2139/SSRN.3725681

Dharmaraj, S. (2024, 03 30). https://opengovasia.com/. Retrieved from OpenGovAsia: https://opengovasia.com/2023/10/07/vietnams-quest-for-digital-transformation-in-education/

Diestro Mandros, J., Garcia Mercado, R., & Bayona-Oré, S. (2021). Virtual reality and tourism: visiting Machu Picchu. In *New Perspectives in Software Engineering:Proceedings of the 9th International Conference on Software Process Improvement (CIMPS 2020)* (pp. 269-279). Springer International Publishing. 10.1007/978-3-030-63329-5_18

Dillette, A., & Ponting, S. S. (2021). Diffusing Innovation in Times of Disasters: Considerations for Event Management Professionals. *Journal of Convention & Event Tourism*, 22(3), 197–220. 10.1080/15470148.2020.1860847

Dimitrovski, D., Seočanac, M., & Luković, M. (2021). Business events at a spa destination: An insight into senior participant motivation. *International Journal of Tourism Cities*, 7(1), 13–31. 10.1108/IJTC-04-2019-0054

Diodato, R. (2021). Ontology of the Virtual. In *Philosophy of Engineering and Technology*. 10.1007/978-3-030-54522-2_15

Disimulacion, M. A. T. (2020). MICE tourism during Covid-19 and future directions for the new normal. *Asia Pacific International Events Management Journal*, 1(2), 11–17.

Do, H., Budhwar, P., Shipton, H., Nguyen, H.-D., & Nguyen, B. (2022). Building Organisational Resilience, Innovation through Resource-Based Management Initiatives, Organisational Learning and Environmental Dynamism. *Journal of Business Research*, 141, 808–821. 10.1016/j.jbusres.2021.11.090

Dohale, V., Akarte, M., Gunasekaran, A., & Verma, P. (2022). Exploring the role of artificial intelligence in building production resilience: Learnings from the COVID-19 pandemic. *International Journal of Production Research*, 1–17.

Donisi, V., De Lucia, A., Pasini, I., Gandolfi, M., Schweiger, V., Del Piccolo, L., & Perlini, C. (2023). e-Health Interventions Targeting Pain-Related Psychological Variables in Fibromyalgia: A Systematic Review. *Healthcare (Basel, Switzerland), 11*(13).

Dowson, R., Albert, B., & Lomax, D. (2022). *Event planning and management: Principles, planning and practice*. Kogan Page Publishers.

Dragin-Jensen, C., Kwiatkowski, G., Hannevik Lien, V., Ossowska, L., Janiszewska, D., Kloskowski, D., & Strzelecka, M. (2022). Event innovation in times of uncertainty. *International Journal of Event and Festival Management*, 13(4), 387–405. 10.1108/IJEFM-07-2021-0063

Dubuc, T., Stahl, F., & Roesch, E. B. (2021). Mapping the Big Data Landscape: Technologies, Platforms and Paradigms for Real-Time Analytics of Data Streams. *IEEE Access : Practical Innovations, Open Solutions*, 9, 15351–15374. 10.1109/ACCESS.2020.3046132

Duchek, S., Raetze, S., & Scheuch, I. (2020). The Role of Diversity in Organisational Resilience: A Theoretical Framework. *Business Research*, 13(2), 387–423. 10.1007/s40685-019-0084-8

Duffy, C., & McEuen, M. B. (2010). *The future of meetings: The case for face-to-face.* Cornell Hospitality Industry Perspectives.

Du, J. (2003). Reforms and development of higher tourism education in China. *Journal of Teaching in Travel & Tourism*, 3(1), 103–113. 10.1300/J172v03n01_07

Duke, L., & Ashraf, A. (2019). *Aligning Analytics with Marketing Strategy: Using Analytics to Drive Marketing Strategy with New Media Applications.* Springer. 10.1007/978-3-319-93299-6_11

Durans, A. de A., & Sousa, W. S de., Costa, N. P. de M., Vale, C., & Macedo, C. J. T. (2023a) Novo petróleo mundial? Guia de aplicação prática em privacidade de dados pessoais. *3° Business Technology Congress* (B-TECH). https://fucape.br/btechcongress

Durans, A. de A., Macedo, C. J. T., Vale, C., Cisneiros, G. P. O., & Patwardhan, A. A. (2021a). Boas e más práticas da privacidade de dados pessoais na visão dos consumidores do Brasil e da Índia. *XLV EnANPAD*. https://anpad.org.br

Durans, A. de A., d'Angelo, M. J., Macedo, C. J. T., & Vale, C. (2021b). *Líder, você é a força motriz da sua organização? Como a responsabilidade social e os comportamentos contraprodu- centes podem impactar o desempenho dos colaboradores e das organizações. 1.* Appris.

Durans, A. de A., Silva, F. P. B., Costa, K. C. S., Franco, J. P., & Kran, F. S. (2023b). Satisfação e insatisfação no trabalho: Estudo de caso com trabalhadores brasileiros. *Revista Saúde, Ambiente. Sustentabilidade & Tecnologia*, 1(1), 90–108. 10.5281/zenodo.10042373

Dwivedi, Y. K., Hughes, L., Baabdullah, A. M., Ribeiro-Navarrete, S., Giannakis, M., Al-Debei, M. M., Dennehy, D., Metri, B., Buhalis, D., Cheung, C. M. K., Conboy, K., Doyle, R., Dubey, R., Dutot, V., Felix, R., Goyal, D. P., Gustafsson, A., Hinsch, C., Jebabli, I., & Wamba, S. F. (2022). Metaverse beyond the hype: Multidisciplinary perspectives on emerging challenges, opportunities, and agenda for research, practice and policy. *International Journal of Information Management*, 66, 102542. 10.1016/j.ijinfomgt.2022.102542

Dwivedi, Y. K., Hughes, L., Wang, Y., Alalwan, A. A., Ahn, S. J., Balakrishnan, J., Barta, S., Belk, R., Buhalis, D., Dutot, V., Felix, R., Filieri, R., Flavián, C., Gustafsson, A., Hinsch, C., Hollensen, S., Jain, V., Kim, J., Krishen, A. S., & Wirtz, J. (2023). Metaverse marketing: How the metaverse will shape the future of consumer research and practice. *Psychology and Marketing*, 40(4), 750–776. 10.1002/mar.21767

Dwivedi, Y. K., Kshetri, N., Hughes, L., Slade, E. L., Jeyaraj, A., Kar, A. K., Baabdullah, A. M., Koohang, A., Raghavan, V., Ahuja, M., Albanna, H., Albashrawi, M. A., Al-Busaidi, A. S., Balakrishnan, J., Barlette, Y., Basu, S., Bose, I., Brooks, L., Buhalis, D., & Wright, R. (2023). "So what if ChatGPT wrote it?" Multidisciplinary perspectives on opportunities, challenges and implications of generative conversational AI for research, practice and policy. *International Journal of Information Management*, 71, 102642. 10.1016/j.ijinfomgt.2023.102642

Compilation of References

Dybå, T., & Dingsøyr, T. (2008). Empirical studies of agile software development: A systematic review. *Information and Software Technology*, 50(9-10), 833–859. 10.1016/j.infsof.2008.01.006

Dy, M., Olazo, K., Lyles, C. R., Lisker, S., Weinberg, J., Lee, C., Tarver, M. E., Saha, A., Kontson, K., Araojo, R., Brown, E., & Sarkar, U. (2023). Usability and acceptability of virtual reality for chronic pain management among diverse patients in a safety-net setting: A qualitative analysis. *JAMIA Open*, 6(3), ooad050. . 10.1093/jamiaopen/ooad05037449058

Dyrberg, N. R., Treusch, A. H., & Wiegand, C. (2017). Virtual laboratories in science education: Students' motivation and experiences in two tertiary biology courses. *Journal of Biological Education*, 51(4), 358–374. 10.1080/00219266.2016.1257498

Dziabenko, O., & Budnyk, O. (2019). Go-Lab ecosystem: Using online laboratories in a primary school. In *EDULEARN19 Proceedings* (pp. 9276-9285). IATED.

Dzobelova, L. A. (2020). Digital Technologies in Education and Their Influence on Modern Society. *New Silk Road: Business Cooperation and Prospective of Economic Development (NSRBCPED 2019)*. Research Gate.

Ehrlich, P., & Ehrlich, A. (1968). *The Population Bomb*. Sierra Club/Ballantine Books.

Elmoazen, R., Saqr, M., Khalil, M., & Wasson, B. (2023). Learning analytics in virtual laboratories: A systematic literature review of empirical research. *Smart Learning Environments*, 10(1), 23. 10.1186/s40561-023-00244-y

Elshaer, I., Moustafa, M., Sobaih, A. E., Aliedan, M., & Azazz, A. M. (2021). The impact of women's empowerment on sustainable tourism development: Mediating role of tourism involvement. *Tourism Management Perspectives*, 38, 100815. 10.1016/j.tmp.2021.100815

Elston, K., & Draper, J. (2012). A Review of Meeting Planner Site Selection Criteria Research. *Journal of Convention & Event Tourism*, 13(3), 203–220. 10.1080/15470148.2012.715269

Ertl, S., Steinmair, D., & Loffler-Stastka, H. (2021). Encouraging communication and cooperation in e-learning: Solving and creating new interdisciplinary case histories. *GMS Journal for Medical Education*, 38(3), Doc62. 33824898

Esin Mukul, G. B. (2023). Digital transformation in education: A systematic review of education 4.0. *Technological Forecasting and Social Change*, 194, 122664. Advance online publication. 10.1016/j.techfore.2023.122664

Estanyol, E. (2022). Traditional festivals and COVID-19: Event management and digitalization in times of physical distancing. *Event Management*, 26(3), 647–659. 10.3727/152599521X16 288665119305

EUAM. (2020). *Посібник з питань використання соціальних мереж*. EUAM. https://surl.li/ewfil

Fang, J., Zhao, Z., Wen, C., & Wang, R. (2017). Design and performance attributes driving mobile travel application engagement. *Elsevier BV, 37*(4), 269-283. 10.1016/j.ijinfomgt.2017.03.003

Fatima Samer, S., Jahan, Y., & Abrar Hassan, M. (2023). A STUDY ON CHANGE IN LEARN-ING PATTERN FROM OFFLINE TO ONLINE MODE DURING COVID-19 PANDEMIC. *International Journal of Advanced Research*, 11(02), 636–642. 10.21474/IJAR01/16291

Favale, T., Soro, F., Trevisan, M., Drago, I., & Mellia, M. (2020). Campus traffic and e-Learning during COVID-19 pandemic. *Computer Networks*, 176, 107290. 10.1016/j.comnet.2020.10729038620622

Favaretto, M., De Clercq, E., Gaab, J., & Elger, B. S. (2020). First do no harm: An exploration of researchers' ethics of conduct in Big Data behavioral studies. *PLoS One*, 15(11), e0241865. 10.1371/journal.pone.024186533152039

Fernandes, J., Duarte, D., Ribeiro, C., Farinha, C., Pereira, J. M., & da Silva, M. M. (2012). iThink: A Game-Based Approach Towards Improving Collaboration and Participation in Requirement Elicitation. *Procedia Computer Science*, 15, 66–77. 10.1016/j.procs.2012.10.059

Fesenmaier, D. R., & Xiang, Z. (2017). *Design Science in Tourism: Foundations of Destinations Management*. Springer. 10.1007/978-3-319-42773-7

Fetzer, J. H., & Fetzer, J. H. (1990). *What is Artificial Intelligence?* Springer.

Feulner, S., Sedlmeir, J., Schlatt, V., & Urbach, N. (2022). Exploring the use of self-sovereign identity for event ticketing systems. *Electronic Markets*, 32(3), 1759–1777. 10.1007/s12525-022-00573-935965736

Ficci, E. (2021, February). *Partnership share of technology used in higher education institutions across India during COVID-19 pandemic in 2020*. Statista. https://www.statista.com/statistics/1290694/india-technology-partnership-share-of-higher-education-institutions-during-covid-19/

Filimonau, V., Ashton, M., & Stankov, U. (2022). Virtual spaces as the future of consumption in tourism, hospitality and events. *Journal of Tourism Futures*.

Filimonau, V., & Brown, L. (2018). 'Last hospitality' as an overlooked dimension in contemporary hospitality theory and practice. *International Journal of Hospitality Management*, 74, 67–74. 10.1016/j.ijhm.2018.02.019

Fischl, C., Blusi, M., Lindgren, H., & Nilsson, I. (2020). Tailoring to support digital technology-mediated occupational engagement for older adults – a multiple case study. *Scandinavian Journal of Occupational Therapy*, 27(8), 577–590. 10.1080/11038128.2020.176034732396419

Flavián, C., Ibáñez-Sánchez, S., Orús, C., & Barta, S. (2024). The dark side of the metaverse: The role of gamification in event virtualization. *International Journal of Information Management*, 75, 102726. 10.1016/j.ijinfomgt.2023.102726

Florido-Benítez, L. (2024). Metaverse cannot be an extra marketing immersive tool to increase sales in tourism cities. *International Journal of Tourism Cities*.

Compilation of References

Flowers, A. A., & Gregson, K. (2012). Decision-making factors in selecting virtual worlds for events: Advocacy, computer efficacy, perceived risks, and collaborative benefits. *Event Management*, 16(4), 319–334. 10.3727/152599512X13539583375054

Fotiadis, A., Polyzos, S., & Huan, T. C. T. (2021). The good, the bad and the ugly on COVID-19 tourism recovery. *Annals of Tourism Research*, 87, 103117. 10.1016/j.annals.2020.10311733518847

Francis, R. S., Anantharajah, S., Sengupta, S., & Singh, A. (2024). Leveraging ChatGPT and Digital Marketing for Enhanced Customer Engagement in the Hotel Industry. In Bansal, R., Ngah, A., Chakir, A., & Pruthi, N. (Eds.), *Leveraging ChatGPT and Artificial Intelligence for Effective Customer Engagement* (pp. 55–68). IGI Global. 10.4018/979-8-3693-0815-8.ch004

Francis, R., Wan Zainodin, W. H., Saifuddin, A. H., & Ahmadrashidi, N. (2023). The Role of Social Media Platforms in Promoting Kaamatan Festival During Covid-19 Pandemic. *International Journal of Academic Research in Business & Social Sciences*, 13(5). 10.6007/IJARBSS/v13-i5/16729

Fremdling, R. (1997). Industrial revolution and scientific and technological progress. *Jahrbuch für Wirtschaftsgeschichte/Economic History Yearbook, 38*(2), 147-168.

Frewen, P., Mistry, D., Zhu, J., Kielt, T., Wekerle, C., Lanius, R. A., & Jetly, R. (2020). Proof of Concept of an Eclectic, Integrative Therapeutic Approach to Mental Health and Well-Being Through Virtual Reality Technology. *Frontiers in Psychology*, 11, 858.. 10.3389/fpsyg.2020.0085832581898

Fullan, M. (2013). *Stratosphere: Integrating Technology, Pedagogy, and Change Knowledge.* Pearson.

Fusté-Forné, F., & Jamal, T. (2021). Co-creating new directions for service robots in hospitality and tourism. *Tourism and Hospitality*, 2(1), 43–61. 10.3390/tourhosp2010003

Gao, Z., Lee, J. E., McDonough, D. J., & Albers, C. (2020). Virtual Reality Exercise as a Coping Strategy for Health and Wellness Promotion in Older Adults during the COVID-19 Pandemic. *Journal of Clinical Medicine*, 9(6), 1986. . 10.3390/jcm906198632630367

Gao, Z., & Lyu, X. (2023). Planet Anima: A virtual graduation experience in the metaverse. *Digital Creativity (Exeter)*, 34(3), 248–263. 10.1080/14626268.2023.2254750

García Revilla, R., Martinez Moure, O., & Einsle, C. S. (2023). Advances in event management using new technologies and mobile applications. *International Journal of Event and Festival Management*, 14(1), 56–72. 10.1108/IJEFM-05-2022-0039

Gaur, A., & Kumar, M. (2018). A systematic approach to conducting review studies: An assessment of content analysis in 25 years of IB research. *Journal of World Business*, 53(2), 280–289. 10.1016/j.jwb.2017.11.003

Gecer, A., & Dag, F. (2012). A blended learning experience. *Educational Sciences: Theory & Practice*, 12(1), 438–442.

Gegenfurtner, A., & Ebner, C. (2019). Webinars in higher education and professional training: A meta-analysis and systematic review of randomized controlled trials. In *Educational Research Review*. 10.1016/j.edurev.2019.100293

Ghaleb, E. A. A., Dominic, P. D. D., Fati, S. M., Muneer, A., & Ali, R. F. (2021). The Assessment of Big Data Adoption Readiness with a Technology–Organization–Environment Framework: A Perspective towards Healthcare Employees. *Sustainability, 13*(15), 8379. 10.3390/su13158379

Giddings, G. (2008). Humans versus computers: Differences in their ability to absorb and process information for business decision purposes — and the implications for the future. *Business Information Review*, 25(1), 32–39. 10.1177/0266382107088211

Gidhagen, M., Helkkula, A., Löbler, H., Jonas, J., Sörhammar, D., & Tronvoll, B. (2017). Human-to-nonhuman value co-creation and resource integration: parasocial actors in a service ecosystem. In E. Gummesson, C. Mele, & F. Polese (Eds.), *Service Dominant Logic, Network and Systems Theory and Service Science: Integrating three Perspectives for a New Service Agenda*. Youcanprint Self-Publishing.

Girma, L. L. (2023). Travel Will Represent a $15.5 Trillion Economy by 2033. *Bloomberg News*. https://www.bloomberg.com/news/articles/2023-08-21/global-travel-and-tourism-will-represent-a-15-5-trillion-economy-by-2033

Glavič, P. (2021). Evolution and current challenges of sustainable consumption and production. *Sustainability (Basel)*, 13(16), 9379. 10.3390/su13169379

Glennie, P., & Thrift, N. (2009). *Shaping the day: a history of timekeeping in England and Wales 1300-1800*. OUP Oxford. 10.1093/acprof:oso/9780199278206.001.0001

Go, H., & Kang, M. (2023). Metaverse tourism for sustainable tourism development: Tourism agenda 2030. *Tourism Review*, 78(2), 381–394. 10.1108/TR-02-2022-0102

Goktas, N., & Avci, D. (2023). The effect of visual and/or auditory distraction techniques on children's pain, anxiety and medical fear in invasive procedures: A randomized controlled trial. *Journal of Pediatric Nursing*, 73, e27–e35. . 10.1016/j.pedn.2023.07.00537455147

Goldblatt, J. (2010). *Special events: A new generation and the next frontier* (Vol. 13). John Wiley & Sons.

Gómez-Rey, P., Fernández-Navarro, F., & Vázquez-De Francisco, M. J. (2021). Identifying Key Variables on the Way to Wellbeing in the Transition from Face-to-Face to Online Higher Education due to COVID-19: Evidence from the Q-Sort Technique. *Sustainability (Basel)*, 13(11), 6112. 10.3390/su13116112

Gonzalez, T., De la Rubia, M. A., Hincz, K. P., Comas-Lopez, M., Subirats, L., Fort, S., & Sacha, G. M. (2020). Influence of COVID-19 confinement on students' performance in higher education. *PLoS One*, 15(10), e0239490. 10.1371/journal.pone.023949033035228

Gössling, S., Scott, D., & Hall, C. M. (2020). Pandemics, tourism and global change: A rapid assessment of COVID-19. *Journal of Sustainable Tourism*, 29(1), 1–20. 10.1080/09669582.2020.1758708

Compilation of References

Gowreesunkar, V. G., Maingi, S. W., & Korstanje, M. E. (2024). Introduction: The Changing Landscape of Tourist Behavior—Navigating from the New Normal to the Next Normal. In *Tourist Behaviour and the New Normal, Volume I: Implications for Tourism Resilience* (pp. 1-7). Cham: Springer Nature Switzerland.

Gowreesunkar, V. G., Maingi, S. W., & Korstanje, M. E. (2024). Introduction: The Interplay Between Tourism Resilience and Sustainability in the New Normal. In *Tourist Behaviour and the New Normal, Volume II: Implications for Sustainable Tourism Development* (pp. 1-6). Cham: Springer Nature Switzerland.

Graham, C. R. (2018). Current research in blended learning. *Handbook of distance education*, 173-188.

Grajek, J. S., Rettschlag, S., Schneider, A., Schraven, S. P., Mlynski, R., & van Bonn, S. M. (2024). *Multidimensional formats of surgical anatomy in otorhinolaryngology student teaching-a comparison of effectivity*. HNO.

Grua, E. M., De Sanctis, M., Malavolta, I., Hoogendoorn, M., & Lago, P. (2022). An evaluation of the effectiveness of personalization and self-adaptation for e-Health apps. *Information and Software Technology*, 146, 106841. 10.1016/j.infsof.2022.106841

Guerreiro, C., Wang, Z., & Nguyen, H. (2020). *New Avenues in Mobile Tourism*. IEEE. 10.1109/IJCNN48605.2020.9207561

Guevara, L., & Cheein, F. A. (2020, August 11). The Role of 5G Technologies: Challenges in Smart Cities and Intelligent Transportation Systems. *Sustainability (Basel)*, 12(16), 6469–6469. 10.3390/su12166469

Guidelines for Development of MOOCs. (n.d.). AICTE. https://www.aicte-india.org/downloads/MHRD%20moocs%20guidelines%20updated.pdf

Guidotti, A., Vanelli-Coralli, A., Conti, M., Andrenacci, S., Chatzinotas, S., Maturo, N., Evans, B., Awoseyila, A., Ugolini, A., Foggi, T., Gaudio, L., Alagha, N., & Cioni, S. (2019, March 1). Architectures and Key Technical Challenges for 5G Systems Incorporating Satellites. *IEEE Transactions on Vehicular Technology*, 68(3), 2624–2639. 10.1109/TVT.2019.2895263

Guo, R., Lv, S., Liao, T., Xi, F., Zhang, J., Zuo, X., Cao, X., Feng, Z., & Zhang, Y. (2020). Classifying green technologies for sustainable innovation and investment. *Resources, Conservation and Recycling*, 153, 104580. 10.1016/j.resconrec.2019.104580

Gupta, P. (2023). *International Conference on Business, Innovation and Sustainability in Digital Era*. Research Gate.

Gursoy, D., Malodia, S., & Dhir, A. (2022). The metaverse in the hospitality and tourism industry: An overview of current trends and future research directions. *Journal of Hospitality Marketing & Management*, 31(5), 527–534. 10.1080/19368623.2022.2072504

Gutierrez-Martinez, J., Mercado-Gutierrez, J. A., Carvajal-Gamez, B. E., Rosas-Trigueros, J. L., & Contreras-Martinez, A. E. (2021). Artificial Intelligence Algorithms in Visual Evoked Potential-Based Brain-Computer Interfaces for Motor Rehabilitation Applications: Systematic Review and Future Directions. *Frontiers in Human Neuroscience*, 15, 772837. 10.3389/fnhum.2021.77283734899220

Hadi, R., Melumad, S., & Park, E. S. (2024). The Metaverse: A new digital frontier for consumer behaviour. *Journal of Consumer Psychology*, 34(1), 142–166. 10.1002/jcpy.1356

Haleem, A., Javaid, M., Qadri, M. A., Singh, R. P., & Suman, R. (2022). Artificial intelligence (AI) applications for marketing: A literature-based study. *International Journal of Intelligent Networks*, 3, 119–132. 10.1016/j.ijin.2022.08.005

Hall, M. A. (2015). *Radio After Radio: Redefining radio art in the light of new media technology through expanded practice* [Doctoral dissertation, University of the Arts London].

Hamari, J. (2013). Transforming homo economicus into homo ludens: A field experiment on gamification in a utilitarian peer-to-peer trading service. *Electronic Commerce Research and Applications*, 12(4), 236–245. 10.1016/j.elerap.2013.01.004

Hamari, J. (2017). Do badges increase user activity? A field experiment on the effects of gamification. *Computers in Human Behavior*, 71(71), 469–478. 10.1016/j.chb.2015.03.036

Hamari, J., Koivisto, J., & Sarsa, H. (2014). Does gamification work? - A literature review of empirical studies on gamification. *Proceedings of the Annual Hawaii International Conference on System Sciences*, (pp. 3025–3034). IEEE. 10.1109/HICSS.2014.377

Han, D. I. D., Weber, J., Bastiaansen, M., Mitas, O., & Lub, X. (2019). Virtual and augmented reality technologies to enhance the visitor experience in cultural tourism. *Augmented reality and virtual reality: The power of AR and VR for business*, 113-128.

Hanaei, S., Takian, A., Majdzadeh, R., Maboloc, C. R., Grossmann, I., Gomes, O., Milosevic, M., Gupta, M., Shamshirsaz, A. A., Harbi, A., Burhan, A. M., Uddin, L. Q., Kulasinghe, A., Lam, C. M., Ramakrishna, S., Alavi, A., Nouwen, J. L., Dorigo, T., Schreiber, M., & Rezaei, N. (2022). Emerging Standards and the Hybrid Model for Organizing Scientific Events during and after the COVID-19 Pandemic. *Disaster Medicine and Public Health Preparedness*, 16(3), 1172–1177. 10.1017/dmp.2020.40633100253

Hanus, M. D., & Fox, J. (2015). Assessing the effects of gamification in the classroom: A longitudinal study on intrinsic motivation, social comparison, satisfaction, effort, and academic performance. *Computers & Education*, 80, 152–161. 10.1016/j.compedu.2014.08.019

Hartmann, I. (2023). *Bridging the hybridity gap: connecting online and onsite participants through peer learning circles at hybrid events.*

Haryanto, T. (2020). COVID-19 pandemic and international tourism demand. *Journal of Developing Economies*, 5(1), 1–5. 10.20473/jde.v5i1.19767

Hashimoto, S. (2022). Technology Application in the Asian Tourism Industry: The Future. In *Handbook of Technology Application in Tourism in Asia* (pp. 1299–1310). Springer Nature Singapore. 10.1007/978-981-16-2210-6_59

Hassan, L., & Hamari, J. (2020). Gameful civic engagement: A review of the literature on gamification of e-participation. *Government Information Quarterly*, 37(3), 101461. 10.1016/j.giq.2020.101461

Hauze, S. W., Hoyt, H. H., Frazee, J. P., Greiner, P. A., & Marshall, J. M. (2019). Enhancing Nursing Education Through Affordable and Realistic Holographic Mixed Reality: The Virtual Standardized Patient for Clinical Simulation. *Advances in Experimental Medicine and Biology*, 1120, 1–13. . 10.1007/978-3-030-06070-1_130919290

Hayes, S., & Tucker, H. (2021). Using synchronous hybrid pedagogy to nurture a community of inquiry: Insights from a tourism Master's programme. *Journal of Hospitality, Leisure, Sport and Tourism Education*, 29, 100339. 10.1016/j.jhlste.2021.100339

Hazira, M. N., Alagas, E. N., Amin, M., Zamzuri, N. H., & Zairul, M. M. (2022). The best practice of marketing strategies for the Malaysian business event industry from experts' perspective. *Journal of Hospitality and Tourism Insights*, 5(2), 413–434. 10.1108/JHTI-09-2020-0178

Heaton, H. (2017). Industrial revolution. In *The causes of the industrial revolution in England* (pp. 31–52). Routledge. 10.4324/9781315172163-2

Hecklau, F., Orth, R., Kidschun, F., & Kohl, H. (2017, December). Human resources management: Meta-study-analysis of future competences in Industry 4.0. In *Proceedings of the International Conference on Intellectual Capital, Knowledge Management & Organizational Learning* (pp. 163-174). Research Gate.

Hemmer, P., Schemmer, M., Vössing, M., & Kühl, N. (2021). Human-AI Complementarity in Hybrid Intelligence Systems: A Structured Literature Review. *PACIS*, 78.

Hennig-Thurau, T., Herting, A. M., & Jütte, D. (2024). EXPRESS: Adoption of Virtual-Reality Headsets: Role of Metaverse Trials for Consumers' Usage and Purchase Intentions. *Journal of Interactive Marketing*, 1–54. 10.1177/10949968241263353

Hernandez, F., Birke, J., & Bullinger, A. C. (2023, July). The Tribrid-Meeting-Setup–Improving Hybrid Meetings Using a Telepresence Robot. In *International Conference on Human-Computer Interaction* (pp. 347-361). Cham: Springer Nature Switzerland. 10.1007/978-3-031-34609-5_26

Hershberger, P. J., Pei, Y., Crawford, T. N., Neeley, S. M., Wischgoll, T., Patel, D. B., Vasoya, M. M., Castle, A., Mishra, S., Surapaneni, L., Pogaku, A. A., Bositty, A., & Pavlack, T. (2022). An Interactive Game with Virtual Reality Immersion to Improve Cultural Sensitivity in Health Care. *Health Equity*, 6(1), 189–197. . 10.1089/heq.2021.012835402778

He, Z., Sui, X., Jin, G., & Cao, L. (2019). Progress in virtual reality and augmented reality based on holographic display. *Applied Optics*, 58(5), 74–81. 10.1364/AO.58.000A7430873963

Hill, D. (2013). *A history of engineering in classical and medieval times*. Routledge. 10.4324/9781315800110

Hilliard, A. T. (2015). Global blended learning practices for teaching and learning, leadership and professional development. *Journal of International Education Research*, 11(3), 179–188. 10.19030/jier.v11i3.9369

Hoggenmüller, M. (2022). *Urban Robotic Interfaces: Designing for Encounters with Non-Humanoid Robots in Cities* [Doctoral dissertation, The University of Sydney].

Hollensen, S., Kotler, P., & Opresnik, M. O. (2022). Metaverse–the new marketing universe. *The Journal of Business Strategy*, 44(3), 119–125. 10.1108/JBS-01-2022-0014

Hoque, A., Shikha, F. A., Hasanat, M. W., Arif, I., & Hamid, A. B. A. (2020). The effect of Coronavirus (COVID-19) in the tourism industry in China. *Asian Journal of Multidisciplinary Studies*, 3(1), 52–58.

Hossain, M. I., Jamadar, Y., Alam, M. K., Pal, T., Islam, M. T., & Sharmin, N. (2024). Exploring the Factors Impacting the Intention to Use Metaverse in the Manufacturing Industry Through the Lens of Unified Technology Acceptance Theory. In *Research, Innovation, and Industry Impacts of the Metaverse* (pp. 43-61). IGI Global. 10.4018/979-8-3693-2607-7.ch003

Hossain, M. (2008). The extent of disclosure in annual reports of banking companies: The case of India. *European Journal of Scientific Research*.

Hradecky, D., Kennell, J., Cai, W., & Davidson, R. (2022). Organizational readiness to adopt artificial intelligence in the exhibition sector in Western Europe. *International Journal of Information Management*, 65, 102497. 10.1016/j.ijinfomgt.2022.102497

Hrastinski, S. (2019). What do we mean by blended learning? *TechTrends*, 63(5), 564–569. 10.1007/s11528-019-00375-5

Hsieh, M.-C., & Lin, Y.-H. (2017). [VR and AR Applications in Medical Practice and Education]. *Hu Li Za Zhi. Journal of Nursing (Luton, England)*, 64(6), 12–18. 29164542

Hsu, C. H. (2018). Tourism education on and beyond the horizon. *Tourism Management Perspectives*, 25, 181–183. 10.1016/j.tmp.2017.11.022

Huang, X., & Zhi, H. (2023). Factors Influencing Students' Continuance Usage Intention with Virtual Classroom during the COVID-19 Pandemic: An Empirical Study. *Sustainability 2023, Vol. 15, Page 4420, 15*(5), 4420. 10.3390/su15054420

Huang, C. H. (2021). Using PLS-SEM model to explore the influencing factors of learning satisfaction in blended learning. *Education Sciences*, 11(5), 249. 10.3390/educsci11050249

Huang, M. H., & Rust, R. T. (2022). A framework for collaborative artificial intelligence in marketing. *Journal of Retailing*, 98(2), 209–223. 10.1016/j.jretai.2021.03.001

Compilation of References

Huang, X. T., Wang, J., Wang, Z., Wang, L., & Cheng, C. (2023). Experimental study on the influence of virtual tourism spatial situation on the tourists' temperature comfort in the context of metaverse. *Frontiers in Psychology*, 13, 1062876. 10.3389/fpsyg.2022.106287636687952

Huang, X., Wu, Y., Kang, J., Nie, J., Zhong, W., Kim, D. I., & Xie, S. (2023). Service reservation and pricing for green metaverses: A Stackelberg game approach. *IEEE Wireless Communications*, 30(5), 86–94. 10.1109/MWC.014.2300095

Huff, T. E. (2010). *Intellectual curiosity and the scientific revolution: a global perspective.* Cambridge University Press. 10.1017/CBO9780511782206

Huggett, J. (2020). Virtually real or really virtual: Towards a heritage metaverse. *Studies in digital heritage, 4*(1), 1-15.

Huizinga, T., Lohuis, A., Zwerver-Bergman, J., & van der Meer, R. (2022). Student and teacher perceptions of community of inquiry in hybrid virtual classrooms. *Heliyon*, 8(12), e12549. Advance online publication. 10.1016/j.heliyon.2022.e1254936619452

Hutson, J., & Hutson, P. (2024). Immersive Technologies. In *Inclusive Smart Museums: Engaging Neurodiverse Audiences and Enhancing Cultural Heritage* (pp. 153–228). Springer Nature Switzerland. 10.1007/978-3-031-43615-4_5

Hutzler, A., Wagner, R., Pirker, J., & Gütl, C. (2017). MythHunter: Gamification in an Educational Location-Based Scavenger Hunt. *Communications in Computer and Information Science*, 725, 155–169. 10.1007/978-3-319-60633-0_13

Huynh-The, T., Gadekallu, T R., Wang, W., Yenduri, G., Ranaweera, P., Pham, Q., Costa, D B D., & Liyanage, M. (2023, June 1). *Blockchain for the metaverse: A Review*. Elsevier. 10.1016/j.future.2023.02.008

Hyatt, C. (2010). Facilitating quality in event management. In Mallen, C., & Adams, L. (Eds.), *Sport, Recreation and Tourism Event Management* (pp. 181–196). Routledge. 10.4324/9780080878768-15

Hyun, M., & Jordan, J. S. (2019). Athletic goal achievement: A critical antecedent of event satisfaction, re-participation intention, and future exercise intention in participant sport events. *Sport Management Review*. 10.1016/j.smr.2019.01.007

Iatsyshyn, A. V., Kovach, V. O., Lyubchak, V. O., Zuban, Y. O., Piven, A. G., Sokolyuk, O. M., Iatsyshyn, A. V., Popov, O. O., Artemchuk, V. O., & Shyshkina, M. P. (2020). Application of augmented reality technologies for education projects preparation. *CEUR Workshop Proceedings*. CEUR. 10.31812/123456789/3856

Ikumoro, A. O., & Jawad, M. S. (2019). Assessing intelligence conversation agent trends-chatbots-ai technology application for personalized marketing. *TEST Engineering and Management*, 81, 4779–4785.

Inoue, Y., & Havard, C. T. (2014). Determinants and Consequences of the Perceived Social Impact of a Sport Event. *Journal of Sport Management*, 28(3), 295–310. 10.1123/jsm.2013-0136

Ismail, S., Salam, A., & Hajriyanti, R. (2022). Event Management System for Webinars and Survey. *International Journal Software Engineering and Computer Science (IJSECS)*. 10.35870/ijsecs.v2i1.761

Ivanov, S. (2021). Robonomics: The rise of the automated economy. *ROBONOMICS: The Journal of the Automated Economy, 1*, 11. https://journal.robonomics.science/index.php/rj/article/view/11

Ivanov, S., Seyitoğlu, F., & Webster, C. (2024), Tourism, automation and responsible consumption and production: a horizon 2050 paper, *Tourism Review*. 10.1108/TR-12-2023-0898

Ivanov, S., Duglio, S., & Beltramo, R. (2023). Robots in tourism and Sustainable Development Goals: Tourism Agenda 2030 perspective article. *Tourism Review, 78*(2), 352–360. 10.1108/TR-08-2022-0404

Ivanov, S., & Webster, C. (2021). Willingness-to-pay for robot-delivered tourism and hospitality services – an exploratory study. *International Journal of Contemporary Hospitality Management, 33*(11), 3926–3955. 10.1108/IJCHM-09-2020-1078

Ivanov, S., Webster, C., & Berezina, K. (2017). Adoption of Robots and Service Automation by Tourism and Hospitality Companies. *Revista Turismo & Desenvolvimento, 27/28*, 1501-1517., Available at *SSRN*: https://ssrn.com/abstract=2964308

Jadán-Guerrero, J., Mendoza, M., & Alvites-Huamaní, C. (2023). Redefining the Museum Experiences in the Virtual Age. In *Intelligent Sustainable Systems: Selected Papers of WorldS4 2022* (Vol. 1, pp. 459–469). Springer Nature Singapore. 10.1007/978-981-19-7660-5_39

Jafari, J., & Ritchie, J. B. (1981). Toward a framework for tourism education: Problems and prospects. *Annals of Tourism Research, 8*(1), 13–34. 10.1016/0160-7383(81)90065-7

Jahn, K., Kordyaka, B., Machulska, A., Eiler, T. J., Gruenewald, A., Klucken, T., Brueck, R., Gethmann, C. F., & Niehaves, B. (2021). Individualized gamification elements: The impact of avatar and feedback design on reuse intention. *Computers in Human Behavior, 119*, 106702. 10.1016/j.chb.2021.106702

Jain, G., Kamble, S. S., Ndubisi, N. O., Shrivastava, A., Belhadi, A., & Venkatesh, M. (2022). Antecedents of Blockchain-Enabled E-commerce Platforms (BEEP) adoption by customers–A study of second-hand small and medium apparel retailers. *Journal of Business Research, 149*, 576–588. 10.1016/j.jbusres.2022.05.041

Jaiswal, G. (2020). A quantitative evaluation of customer marketing impact by artificial intelligence in hospitality industry. *Pranjana: The Journal of Management Awareness, 23*(2), 40–44. 10.5958/0974-0945.2020.00011.4

Jaramillo-Botero, A., Matta-Gomez, A., Correa-Caicedo, J. F., & Perea-Castro, W. (2006). Robomosp. *IEEE Robotics & Automation Magazine, 13*(4), 62–73. 10.1109/MRA.2006.250572

Jauhiainen, J. S. (2021). Entrepreneurship and Innovation Events during the COVID-19 Pandemic: The User Preferences of VirBELA Virtual 3D Platform at the SHIFT Event Organized in Finland. *Sustainability (Basel), 13*(7), 3802. 10.3390/su13073802

Compilation of References

Jensen, , A., Walsh, P., & Cobbs, J. (2018). The moderating effect of identification on return on investment from sponsor brand integration. *International Journal of Sports Marketing & Sponsorship*, 19(1), 41–57. 10.1108/IJSMS-10-2016-0077

Jeon, C. Y., & Yang, H. W. (2021). The structural changes of a local tourism network: Comparison of before and after COVID-19. *Current Issues in Tourism*, 24(23), 3324–3338. 10.1080/13683500.2021.1874890

Jia, S., Chi, O. H., Martinez, S. D., & Lu, L. (2023). When "Old" Meets "New": Unlocking the Future of Innovative Technology Implementation in Heritage Tourism. *Journal of Hospitality & Tourism Research (Washington, D.C.)*, 10963480231205767. 10.1177/10963480231205767

Jin, X., Bao, J., & Tang, C. (2022). Profiling and evaluating Chinese consumers regarding post-COVID-19 travel. *Current Issues in Tourism*, 25(5), 745–763. 10.1080/13683500.2021.1874313

Jo, H. (2023). Tourism in the digital frontier: A study on user continuance intention in the metaverse. *Information Technology & Tourism*, 25(3), 307–330. 10.1007/s40558-023-00257-w

Johry, G. S., Kant, U., & Asgar, A. (2019). Blended learning approach and students' satisfaction: A case study of IGNOU programmes. *Indian Journal of Open Learning*, 28(1), 3–22.

Jones, B. A., Madden, G. J., & Wengreen, H. J. (2014). The FIT Game: Preliminary evaluation of a gamification approach to increasing fruit and vegetable consumption in school. *Preventive Medicine*, 68, 76–79. 10.1016/j.ypmed.2014.04.01524768916

Jones, K., & Johnson, L. (2019). Task management features in event planning applications: A usability study of [Your Application Name Here]. *International Journal of Usability Studies*, 14(2), 87–101.

Jones, M. (2017). *Sustainable event management: A practical guide*. Routledge. 10.4324/9781315439723

Josephi, S. (2019). Adding value to the hospitality experience. *Hospitality Experience*, 38–65. 10.4324/9781003023814-2

Joy, M. M., & Chiramel, M. J. (2017). *Fun is The Future*. Educreation Publishing.

Juergensmeyer, M., & Adetunji, S. A. (2022). Safety in Chemical and Biomedical Laboratories: Guidelines for the Use of Head Covers by Female Muslim Scientists. *Applied Biosafety : Journal of the American Biological Safety Association*, 27(1), 1–6. 10.1089/apb.2021.001536032321

Jun, G. (2020). Virtual reality church as a new mission frontier in the metaverse: Exploring theological controversies and missional potential of virtual reality church. *Transformation (Durban)*, 37(4), 297–305. 10.1177/0265378820963155

Jung, S., Kim, Y. S., Malek, K., & Lee, W. (2016). Engaging attendees in environmental sustainability at trade shows: Attendees' perceptions and willingness to participate. *Anatolia*, 27(4), 540–542. 10.1080/13032917.2016.1193758

Jyotsna, J., & Madkaikar, S. (2020). Educational Repercussions due to Covid-19 in Hospitality Institutes. *JOURNAL OF TOURISM AND HOSPITALITY MANAGEMENT*, 8(2). 10.15640/jthm.v8n2a4

Kahiya, E. T. (2018). Five decades of research on export barriers: Review and future directions. *International Business Review*, 27(6), 1172–1188. 10.1016/j.ibusrev.2018.04.008

Kalaur, S. M., & Maksymyak, B. (2021). The potential of sociocultural animation in the organization of socio-pedagogical prevention of aggressive behavior of schoolchildren. *Social work: today's challenges: a collection of scientific works based on the materials of the 10th International Scientific and Practical Conference*. Ternopil: TNPU named after V. Hnatyuka. https://surl.li/pbncf

Kaliisa, R., Kluge, A., & Mørch, A. I. (2020). Combining Checkpoint and Process Learning Analytics to Support Learning Design Decisions in Blended Learning Environments. *Journal of Learning Analytics*, 7(3), 33–47. 10.18608/jla.2020.73.4

Kallou, S., & Kikilia, A. (2021). A transformative educational framework in tourism higher education through digital technologies during the COVID-19 pandemic. *Advances in Mobile Learning Educational Research*, 1(1), 37–47. 10.25082/AMLER.2021.01.005

Kamata, H. (2022). Tourist destination residents' attitudes towards tourism during and after the COVID-19 pandemic. *Current Issues in Tourism*, 25(1), 134–149. 10.1080/13683500.2021.1881452

Kane, P. (2018). Simulation-based education: A narrative review of the use of VERT in radiation therapy education. *Journal of Medical Radiation Sciences*, 65(2), 131–136. . 10.1002/jmrs.27629654661

Kapici, H. O., Akcay, H., & de Jong, T. (2019). Using hands-on and virtual laboratories alone or together–which works better for acquiring knowledge and skills? *Journal of Science Education and Technology*, 28(3), 231–250. 10.1007/s10956-018-9762-0

Kapiki, S. (2012). Current and future trends in tourism and hospitality: The case of Greece. *International Journal of Economic Practices and Theories*, 2(1).

Kapp, K. (2012). *The gamification of learning and instruction: Game-based methods and strategies for training and education*. Wiley.

Karaca, Y., Derias, D., & Sarsar, G. (2023). AI-Powered Procedural Content Generation: Enhancing NPC Behaviour for an Immersive Gaming Experience. *Available at SSRN* 4663382. 10.31234/osf.io/8pt4q

Kariru, A. N. (2023). *Contemporary Trends and Issues in The Hospitality and Tourism Industry*.

Kasia Lundy, H. L. (2022). *How digital's impact on higher education can be improved*. EY Parthenon.

Kaur, G., Pande, R., Mohan, R., Vij, S., Agrawal, P., Shobhane, P., & Bagane, P. (2024). A Comprehensive Review of Metaverse: Taxonomy, Impact, and the Hype around It. *Engineering Proceedings*, 62(1), 9.

Compilation of References

Kaur, M. (2013). Blended learning-its challenges and future. *Procedia: Social and Behavioral Sciences*, 93, 612–617. 10.1016/j.sbspro.2013.09.248

Kemp, S. (2023). *Digital 2023: Global Overview Report*. Data Reportal. https://datareportal .com/reports/digital-2023-global-overview-report

Kenngott, H. G., Pfeiffer, M., Preukschas, A. A., Bettscheider, L., Wise, P. A., Wagner, M., Speidel, S., Huber, M., Nickel, F., Mehrabi, A., & Muller-Stich, B. P. (2022). IMHOTEP: Cross-professional evaluation of a three-dimensional virtual reality system for interactive surgical operation planning, tumor board discussion and immersive training for complex liver surgery in a head-mounted display. *Surgical Endoscopy*, 36(1), 126–134. . 10.1007/s00464-020-08246-433475848

Khalid, U. B., Naeem, M., Stasolla, F., Syed, M. H., Abbas, M., & Coronato, A. (2024). Impact of AI-Powered Solutions in Rehabilitation Process: Recent Improvements and Future Trends. *International Journal of General Medicine*, 17, 943–969. . 10.2147/IJGM.S45390338495919

Khalilzadeh, J., Ozturk, A. B., & Bilgihan, A. (2017). Security-related factors in extended UTAUT model for NFC based mobile payment in the restaurant industry. *Computers in Human Behavior*, 70, 460–474. 10.1016/j.chb.2017.01.001

Kharb, P., & Samanta, P. P. (2016). Blended learning approach for teaching and learning anatomy: Students' and teachers' perspective. *Journal of the Anatomical Society of India*, 65(1), 43–47. .10.1016/j.jasi.2016.06.001

Kharouf, H., Biscaia, R., Garcia-Perez, A., & Hickman, E. (2020). Understanding online event experience: The importance of communication, engagement and interaction. *Journal of Business Research*, 121, 735–746. 10.1016/j.jbusres.2019.12.037

Khor, W. S., Baker, B., Amin, K., Chan, A., Patel, K., & Wong, J. (2016). Augmented and virtual reality in surgery-the digital surgical environment: Applications, limitations and legal pitfalls. *Annals of Translational Medicine*, 4(23), 454. . 10.21037/atm.2016.12.2328090510

Killela, M., Biddell, C., Keim-Malpass, J., Schwartz, T. A., Soto, S., Williams, J., & Santacroce, S. (2023). The Use of Medical Crowdfunding to Mitigate the Personal Costs of Serious Chronic Illness: Scoping Review. *Journal of Medical Internet Research*, 25, e44530. . 10.2196/4453038048149

Kim, D. Y., Lee, H. K., & Chung, K. (2023). Avatar-mediated experience in the metaverse: The impact of avatar realism on user-avatar relationship. *Journal of Retailing and Consumer Services*, 73, 103382. 10.1016/j.jretconser.2023.103382

Kim, J. (2021). Advertising in the metaverse: Research agenda. *Journal of Interactive Advertising*, 21(3), 141–144. 10.1080/15252019.2021.2001273

Kim, K., Yang, H., Lee, J., & Lee, W. G. (2023). Metaverse Wearables for Immersive Digital Healthcare: A Review. *Advanced Science (Weinheim, Baden-Wurttemberg, Germany)*, 10(31), e2303234. . 10.1002/advs.20230323437740417

Kishen, R., Upadhyay, S., Jaimon, F., Suresh, S., Kozlova, N., Bozhuk, S., & Matchinov, V. A. (2021). Prospects for artificial intelligence implementation to design personalized customer engagement strategies. *Pt. 2 J.Legal Ethical &Regul. Isses*, 24, 1.

Kitanov, S., Petrov, I., & Janevski, T. (2021). 6G MOBILE NETWORKS: RESEARCH TRENDS, CHALLENGES AND POTENTIAL SOLUTIONS. *Journal of Electrical Engineering and Information Technologies*, 6(2), 67–77. 10.51466/JEEIT2162186067k

Knoblauch, C., Keßler, J. U., & Jakobi, M. (2021). Schools of education as agents of change: coping with diversity in India and Germany through a collaborative, interactive and blended-learning environment–a pre-test study. In *Cross Reality and Data Science in Engineering:Proceedings of the 17th International Conference on Remote Engineering and Virtual Instrumentation 17* (pp. 866-876). Springer International Publishing. 10.1007/978-3-030-52575-0_71

Knossenburg, Y., Nogueira, R., & Chimenti, P. (2016). Contagious Content: Viral Video Ads Identification of Content Characteristics that Help Online Video Advertisements Go Viral. *Revista Brasileira de Marketing*, 15(4), 448–458. 10.5585/remark.v15i4.3385

Kock, F., Nørfelt, A., Josiassen, A., Assaf, A. G., & Tsionas, M. G. (2020). Understanding the COVID-19 tourist psyche: The evolutionary tourism paradigm. *Annals of Tourism Research*, 85, 103053. 10.1016/j.annals.2020.10305332921847

Koh, E. (2020). The end of over-tourism? Opportunities in a post-Covid-19 world. *International Journal of Tourism Cities*, 6(4), 1015–1023. 10.1108/IJTC-04-2020-0080

Koretsky, M. D., Amatore, D., Barnes, C., & Kimura, S. (2008). Enhancement of student learning in experimental design using a virtual laboratory. *IEEE Transactions on Education*, 51(1), 76–85. 10.1109/TE.2007.906894

Korstanje, M. E., Gowreesunkar, V. G., & Maingi, S. W. (2024). Conclusion: Tourist Behavior in the New Normal—Emerging Frontiers Toward Tourism Resilience. In *Tourist Behaviour and the New Normal, Volume I: Implications for Tourism Resilience* (pp. 273-278). Cham: Springer Nature Switzerland.

Korstanje, M. E. (2020). Passage from the tourist gaze to the wicked gaze: A case study on COVID-19 with special reference to Argentina. In *International case studies in the management of disasters* (pp. 197–211). Emerald Publishing Limited. 10.1108/978-1-83982-186-820201012

Korstanje, M. E. (2023). The Janus Face of Terrorism and Tourism: Terrorism as a Risk, as a Danger and as a Worry. In Seabra, C., & Korstanje, M. (Eds.), *Safety and Tourism* (pp. 103–115). Emerald Publishing Limited. 10.1108/978-1-80382-811-420231006

Korstanje, M. E., & George, B. (2021). *Mobility and globalization in the aftermath of COVID-19: Emerging new geographies in a locked world*. Palgrave Macmillan. 10.1007/978-3-030-78845-2

Korstanje, M. E., & George, B. (2022). *The nature and future of tourism: A post-COVID-19 context*. CRC Press. 10.1201/9781003277507

Compilation of References

Korstanje, M. E., Mustelier, L. C., & Herrera, S. (2016). Understanding the indiscipline of tourism: A radical critique to the current state of epistemology. In *Global dynamics in travel, tourism, and hospitality* (pp. 208–221). IGI Global. 10.4018/978-1-5225-0201-2.ch012

Korstanje, M. E., Séraphin, H., & Maingi, S. W. (Eds.). (2022). *Tourism through troubled times: Challenges and opportunities of the tourism industry in the 21st century.* Emerald Publishing Limited. 10.1108/9781803823119

Kozinets, R. V. (2002). The field behind the screen: Using netnography for marketing research in online communities. *JMR, Journal of Marketing Research*, 39(1), 61–72. 10.1509/jmkr.39.1.61.18935

Kozinets, R. V. (2012). Marketing netnography: Prom/ot (ulgat) ing a new research method. *Methodological Innovations Online*, 7(1), 37–45. 10.4256/mio.2012.004

Kraus, S., Li, H., Kang, Q., Westhead, P., & Tiberius, V. (2020). The sharing economy: A bibliometric analysis of the state-of-the-art. *International Journal of Entrepreneurial Behaviour & Research*, 26(8), 1769–1786. 10.1108/IJEBR-06-2020-0438

Kristiansen, E., Solem, B. A. A., Dille, T., & Houlihan, B. (2021). Stakeholder Management of Temporary Sport Event Organizations. *Event Management*, 25(6), 619–639. 10.3727/1525995 21X16106577965080

Krpic, A., Savanovic, A., & Cikajlo, I. (2013a). Telerehabilitation: Remote multimedia-supported assistance and mobile monitoring of balance training outcomes can facilitate the clinical staff's effort. *International Journal of Rehabilitation Research. Internationale Zeitschrift fur Rehabilitationsforschung. Revue Internationale de Recherches de Readaptation*, 36(2), 162–171. . 10.1097/MRR.0b013e32835dd63b23337324

Krupitzer, C., Naber, J., Stauffert, J.-P., Mayer, J., Spielmann, J., Ehmann, P., Boci, N., Burkle, M., Ho, A., Komorek, C., Heinickel, F., Kounev, S., Becker, C., & Latoschik, M. E. (2022). CortexVR: Immersive analysis and training of cognitive executive functions of soccer players using virtual reality and machine learning. *Frontiers in Psychology*, 13, 754732. 10.3389/fpsyg.2022.75473236081714

Kshetri, N., Dwivedi, Y. K., & Janssen, M. (2024). Metaverse for advancing government: Prospects, challenges and a research agenda. *Government Information Quarterly*, 41(2), 101931. 10.1016/j.giq.2024.101931

Kumar, D., & Pindoriya, N M. (2020, December 17). *A Review on 5G Technological Intervention in Smart Grid*. 10.1109/NPSC49263.2020.9331759

Kumar, N., & Sharma, S. (2024). *Demystifying the Technology Adoption by the Asian Cargo Industry*. 10.4018/979-8-3693-1602-3.ch006

Kumar, A., Krishnamurthi, R., Bhatia, S., Kaushik, K., Ahuja, N. J., Nayyar, A., & Masud, M. (2021). Blended learning tools and practices: A comprehensive analysis. *IEEE Access : Practical Innovations, Open Solutions*, 9, 85151–85197. 10.1109/ACCESS.2021.3085844

Kumar, A., Kumar, D. V. S., Khetarpal, M., & Megha, R. U. (2023). Customer Experience in the Magic World of Metaverse: Conceptual Framework of Customer Adoption of Metaverse. In *Immersive Technology and Experiences: Implications for Business and Society* (pp. 99–126). Springer Nature Singapore.

Kumar, A., Shankar, A., Shaik, A. S., Jain, G., & Malibari, A. (2023). Risking it all in the metaverse ecosystem: Forecasting resistance towards the enterprise metaverse. *Information Technology & People*. 10.1108/ITP-04-2023-0374

Kumar, N., Tandon, R., & Misra, N. (2022). Emotional Intelligence as Intangible Class Content for Effective Communication in Managing University Classes: A Bibliometric Analysis. *Journal of Content. Community and Communication*, 16(8), 26–36. 10.31620/JCCC.12.22/03

Kumar, V., Rajan, B., Venkatesan, R., & Lecinski, J. (2019). Understanding the role of artificial intelligence in personalized engagement marketing. *California Management Review*, 61(4), 135–155. 10.1177/0008125619859317

Kummitha, H. R., Kolloju, N., Chittoor, P., & Madepalli, V. (2021). Coronavirus disease 2019 and its effect on teaching and learning process in the higher educational institutions. *Higher Education for the Future*, 8(1), 90–107. 10.1177/2347631120983650

Kundu, A., Bej, T., & Nath Dey, K. (2021). Time to Achieve: Implementing blended learning routines in an indian elementary classroom. *Journal of Educational Technology Systems*, 49(4), 405–431. 10.1177/0047239520984406

Kuntsman, A., & Miyake, E. (2019). The paradox and continuum of digital disengagement: Denaturalising digital sociality and technological connectivity. *Media Culture & Society*, 41(6), 901–913. 10.1177/0163443719853732

Kusuma, R. R., Widianingsih, I., Ningrum, S., & Myrna, R. (2021). Five clusters of flood management articles in Scopus from 2000 to 2019 using social network analysis. *Science Editing*, 8(1), 85–92. 10.6087/kcse.234

Kuznetsova, A. (2023). *Why is posting time important for social media?* Web-promo. https://web-promo.ua/ua/blog/najkrashij-chas-dlya-postingu-u-socialnih-merezhah-u-2023-roci/

Ladkin, A. (2006). Conference tourism–MICE market and business tourism. In *Tourism business frontiers* (pp. 56–66). Routledge. 10.1016/B978-0-7506-6377-9.50014-6

Lai, K.-W. (2011). Digital technology and the culture of teaching. *Australasian Journal of Educational Technology*, 1263–1275.

Lakhal, S., & Meyer, F. (2020). Blended learning. *Encyclopedia of education and information technologies*, 234-240.

Lakhan, R., Agrawal, A., & Sharma, M. (2020). Prevalence of depression, anxiety, and stress during COVID-19 pandemic. *Journal of Neurosciences in Rural Practice*, 11(04), 519–525. 10.1055/s-0040-171644233144785

Compilation of References

Landers, R. N., & Landers, A. K. (2014). An Empirical Test of the Theory of Gamified Learning. *Simulation & Gaming*, 45(6), 769–785. 10.1177/1046878114563662

Langer, R., & Beckman, S. C. (2005). Sensitive research topics: Netnography revisited. *Qualitative Market Research*, 8(2), 189–203. 10.1108/13522750510592454

Langston, C. (2020). Entrepreneurial educators: Vital enablers to support the education sector to reimagine and respond to the challenges of COVID-19. *Entrepreneurship Education*, 3(3), 311–338. 10.1007/s41959-020-00034-4

Lau, J. X., Ch'ng, C. B., Bi, X., & Chan, J. H. (2024). Exploring attitudes of gen z towards metaverse in events industry. *International Journal of Sustainable Competitiveness on Tourism*, 3(01), 49–53.

Le, N T., Hossain, M A., Islam, A., Kim, D., Choi, Y., & Jang, Y M. (2016, January 1). *Survey of Promising Technologies for 5G Networks*. IOS Press. 10.1155/2016/2676589

Leal Filho, W. T.-G. (2018). Using the sustainable development goals towards a better understanding of sustainability challenges. *International Journal of Sustainable Development and World Ecology*, 179–190.

Lee, C., Nordstedt, D., & Helal, S. (2003). Enabling smart spaces with OSGi. *IEEE Pervasive Computing*, 2(3), 89–94. 10.1109/MPRV.2003.1228530

Lee, S. G., Trimi, S., Byun, W. K., & Kang, M. (2011). Innovation and imitation effects in Metaverse service adoption. *Service Business*, 5(2), 155–172. 10.1007/s11628-011-0108-8

Lee, S., & Kim, E. (2021). User experience design in event planning applications: A comparative study of [Your Application Name Here] and similar apps. *Journal of User Experience Design*, 8(1), 45–60.

Lee, U. K., & Kim, H. (2022). UTAUT in metaverse: An "Ifland" case. *Journal of Theoretical and Applied Electronic Commerce Research*, 17(2), 613–635. 10.3390/jtaer17020032

Lekgau, R. J., & Tichaawa, T. M. (2022). Exploring the Use of Virtual and Hybrid Events for MICE Sector Resilience: The Case of South Africa. *African Journal of Hospitality, Tourism and Leisure*, 11(4), 1579–1594. 10.46222/ajhtl.19770720.310

Lerner, J. S., Li, Y., Valdesolo, P., & Kassam, K. S. (2015). Emotion and decision making. *Annual Review of Psychology*, 66(1), 799–823. 10.1146/annurev-psych-010213-11504325251484

Leung, X. Y., Zhang, H., Lyu, J., & Bai, B. (2023). Why do hotel frontline employees use service robots in the workplace? A technology affordance theory perspective. *International Journal of Hospitality Management*, 108, 103380. 10.1016/j.ijhm.2022.103380

Liang, X., Liu, F., Wang, L., Zheng, B., & Sun, Y. (2023). Internet of Cultural Things: Current research, challenges and opportunities. *Computers, Materials & Continua*, 74(1), 469–488. 10.32604/cmc.2023.029641

Li, B., Soma, T., Springle, N., & Shulman, T. (2023). Reflections From Implementing a Virtual Social Innovation Lab. *International Journal of Qualitative Methods*, 22. Advance online publication. 10.1177/16094069221149871

Lichy, J., & McLeay, F. (2018). Bleisure: Motivations and typologies. *Journal of Travel & Tourism Marketing*, 35(4), 517–530. 10.1080/10548408.2017.1364206

Limna, P. (2022). Artificial Intelligence (AI) in the hospitality industry: A review article. *Int. J. Comput. Sci. Res*, 6, 1–12.

Limna, P., Siripipatthanakul, S., & Phayaphrom, B. (2021). The role of big data analytics in influencing artificial intelligence (AI) adoption for coffee shops in Krabi, Thailand. *International Journal of Behavioral Analytics*, 1(2), 1–17.

Limniou, M., & Hands, C. (2019, November). A critique of blended learning: Examples from an undergraduate psychology program. In *Proceedings Of The 18th European Conference On E-Learning (ECEL 2019)* (*Vol. 2019*, pp. 320-328). ACPI.

Lindström, S., & Pettersson, M. (2010). *Supporting ad-hoc re-planning and shareability at large-scale events*. 10.1145/1880071.1880113

Liu, C.-R., Wang, Y.-C., Huang, W.-S., & Tang, W.-C. (2019). Festival gamification: Conceptualization and scale development. *Tourism Management*, 74, 370–381. 10.1016/j.tourman.2019.04.005

Liu, D., Li, C., Zhang, J., & Huang, W. (2023). Robot service failure and recovery: Literature review and future directions. *International Journal of Advanced Robotic Systems*, 20(4), 17298806231191606. 10.1177/17298806231191606

Liu, F., Wang, T., Liu, X., & Fan, L. Z. (2021). Challenges and recent progress on key materials for rechargeable magnesium batteries. *Advanced Energy Materials*, 11(2), 2000787. 10.1002/aenm.202000787

Liu-Lastres, B., Bufkin, A., & Cecil, A. (2024). Developing a risk profile of female business travellers in pandemic times. *Routledge handbook on gender in tourism: Views on Teaching, Research and Praxis*, 178–192. 10.4324/9781003286721-18

Liu, M., Wilder, S., Sanford, S., Saleh, S., Harel, N. Y., & Nataraj, R. (2021). Training with Agency-Inspired Feedback from an Instrumented Glove to Improve Functional Grasp Performance. *Sensors (Basel)*, 21(4), 1173. 10.3390/s2104117333562342

Liu, R., Wang, L., Koszalka, T. A., & Wan, K. (2022). Effects of immersive virtual reality classrooms on students' academic achievement, motivation and cognitive load in science lessons. *Journal of Computer Assisted Learning*, 38(5), 1422–1433. 10.1111/jcal.12688

Liu, X., Wen, J., Kozak, M., Jiang, Y., & Li, Z. (2022). Negotiating interdisciplinary practice under the COVID-19 crisis: Opportunities and challenges for tourism research. *Tourism Review*, 77(2), 484–502. 10.1108/TR-01-2021-0034

Compilation of References

Liu, Z., Li, Q., Chen, X., Wu, C., Ishihara, S., Li, J., & Ji, Y. (2020). Point Cloud Video Streaming in 5G Systems and Beyond: Challenges and Solutions. IEEE Network. 10.36227/techrxiv.13138940.v1

Liu, Z., Ren, L., Xiao, C., Zhang, K., & Demian, P. (2022). Virtual Reality Aided Therapy towards Health 4.0: A Two-Decade Bibliometric Analysis. *International Journal of Environmental Research and Public Health*, 19(3), 1525. . 10.3390/ijerph1903152535162546

Lockee, B. B. (2021). Shifting digital, shifting context:(re) considering teacher professional development for online and blended learning in the COVID-19 era. *Educational Technology Research and Development*, 69(1), 17–20. 10.1007/s11423-020-09836-833041603

Looyestyn, J., Kernot, J., Boshoff, K., Ryan, J., Edney, S., & Maher, C. (2017). Does gamification increase engagement with online programs? A systematic review. *PLoS One*, 12(3), e0173403. 10.1371/journal.pone.017340328362821

López-Pernas, S., Munoz-Arcentales, A., Aparicio, C., Barra, E., Gordillo, A., Salvachúa, J., & Quemada, J. (2022). Educational Data Virtual Lab: Connecting the Dots Between Data Visualization and Analysis. *IEEE Computer Graphics and Applications*, 42(5), 76–83. 10.1109/MCG.2022.318955736194698

Lozano-Díaz, A., & Fernández-Prados, J. (2020). Educating Digital Citizens: An Opportunity to Critical and Activist Perspective of Sustainable Development Goals. *Sustainability 2020*. 10.20944/preprints202008.0208.v1

Lu, T. L. (2019). Opportunities of Artificial Intelligence in Hospitality Industry for Innovative Customer Services. Case: Hotels in Ho Chi Minh City, Vietnam.

Lu, J., Xiao, X., Xu, Z., Wang, C., Zhang, M., & Zhou, Y. (2022). The potential of virtual tourism in the recovery of tourism industry during the COVID-19 pandemic. *Current Issues in Tourism*, 25(3), 441–457. 10.1080/13683500.2021.1959526

Luo, J. M., & Lam, C. F. (2020). Travel anxiety, risk attitude and travel intentions towards "travel bubble" destinations in Hong Kong: Effect of the fear of COVID-19. *International Journal of Environmental Research and Public Health*, 17(21), 7859. 10.3390/ijerph1721785933120949

Luong, T. T., Huynh, V. N., & Kim, E. (2023). A Hybrid Use of Soft Systems Methodology for Developing a Framework of Evidence-Based Teaching for Hospitality and Tourism Instructors in Vietnam. *Systemic Practice and Action Research*, 36(2), 241–274. 10.1007/s11213-022-09609-936032693

Luxford, A., & Dickinson, J. E. (2015). The Role of Mobile Applications in the Consumer Experience at Music Festivals. *Event Management*, 19(1), 33–46. 10.3727/152599515X14229071392909

Lydakis, A., Meng, Y., Munroe, C., Wu, Y.-N., & Begum, M. (2017). A learning-based agent for home neurorehabilitation. *IEEE. International Conference on Rehabilitation Robotics : [Proceedings], 2017*, (pp. 1233–1238). IEEE.

Lynch, T., & Ghergulescu, I. (2017). Review of virtual labs as the emerging technologies for teaching STEM subjects. *INTED2017 proceedings*, 6082-6091.

Mahadewi, N. (2023). *Hybrid Event: Utilization of Digital Technology in Organizing Events during the COVID-19 Pandemic in Indonesia.* MDPI. 10.3390/proceedings2022083053

Mahanta, N. R., & Lele, S. (2022). Evolving Trends of Artificial Intelligence and Robotics in Smart City Applications: Crafting Humane Built Environment. *Trust-Based Communication Systems for Internet of Things Applications*, 195-241.

Mainardes, E. W., Cisneiros, G. P. de O., Macedo, C. J. T., & Durans, A. de A. (2022). Marketing capabilities for small and medium enterprises that supply large companies. *Journal of Business and Industrial Marketing*, 37(1), 47–64. 10.1108/JBIM-07-2020-0360

Maingi, S. W., Gowreesunkar, V. G., & Korstanje, M. E. (2024). *Tourist Behaviour and the New Normal* (Vol. I). Springer.

Majid, G. M., Tussyadiah, I., Kim, Y. R., & Pal, A. (2023). Intelligent automation for sustainable tourism: A systematic review. *Journal of Sustainable Tourism*, 31(11), 1–20. 10.1080/09669582.2023.2246681

Mäkelä, L., Bergbom, B., Saarenpää, K., & Suutari, V. (2015). Work-family conflict faced by international business travellers: Do gender and parental status make a difference? *Journal of Global Mobility*, 3(2), 155–168. 10.1108/JGM-07-2014-0030

Mäkelä, L., Bergbom, B., Tanskanen, J., & Kinnunen, U. (2014). The relationship between international business travel and sleep problems via work-family conflict. *Career Development International*, 19(7), 794–812. 10.1108/CDI-04-2014-0048

Mäkelä, L., & Kinnunen, U. (2018). International business travelers' psychological well-being: The role of supportive HR practices. *International Journal of Human Resource Management*, 29(7), 1285–1306. 10.1080/09585192.2016.1194872

Mäkelä, L., Tanskanen, J., Kangas, H., & Heikkilä, M. (2021a). International business travelers' job exhaustion: Effects of travel days spent in short-haul and long-haul destinations and the moderating role of leader-member exchange. *Journal of Global Mobility*, 9(3), 434–455. 10.1108/JGM-10-2020-0066

Makovec Radovan, D., & Radovan, M. (2023). Teacher, think twice: About the importance and pedagogical value of blended learning design in VET. *Education Sciences*, 13(9), 882. 10.3390/educsci13090882

Malek, K., Tanford, S., & Baloglu, S. (2018). Evaluating event effectiveness across alternate platforms. *Event Management*, 22(2), 135–151. 10.3727/152599518X15173355843307

Malik, A. A., & Brem, A. (2021). Digital twins for collaborative robots: A case study in human-robot interaction. *Robotics and Computer-integrated Manufacturing*, 68, 102092. 10.1016/j.rcim.2020.102092

Malik, A. A., Masood, T., & Bilberg, A. (2020). Virtual reality in manufacturing: Immersive and collaborative artificial-reality in design of human-robot workspace. *International Journal of Computer Integrated Manufacturing*, 33(1), 22–37. 10.1080/0951192X.2019.1690685

Compilation of References

Manas-Alvarez, F. J., Guinaldo, M., Dormido, R., & Dormido, S. (2023). *Robotic Park: Multi-Agent Platform for Teaching Control and Robotics*. IEEE., 10.1109/ACCESS.2023.3264508

Mangunsong, F. (2020). SENIOR TOURISM AND CHANCE FOR TOURISM BUSINESS PLAYERS. *Journal of Tourism, Hospitality and Environment Management, 5*(19), 01–13. 10.35631/JTHEM.519001

Mann, C. L. (2020). Real and financial lenses to assess the economic consequences of COVID-19. *Economics in the Time of COVID-19, 81,* 85.

Mansouri, S. (2022). Technology Application in Tourism Events: Reflections on a Case Study of a Local Food Festival in Thailand. In *Digital Transformation and Innovation in Tourism Events.* 10.4324/9781003271147-10

Marais, M., Du Plessis, E., & Saayman, M. (2017). Critical Success Factors of a Business Tourism Destination: Supply Side Analysis. *Acta Commercii, 17*(1), 1–12. 10.4102/ac.v17i1.423

Marcum, C. S., Goldring, M. R., McBride, C. M., & Persky, S. (2018). Modeling Dynamic Food Choice Processes to Understand Dietary Intervention Effects. *Annals of Behavioral Medicine : A Publication of the Society of Behavioral Medicine, 52*(3), 252–261.

Marker, B. (2022). *6 Keys To Success For Any Hybrid Event.* Big Maker. https://get.bigmarker .com/blog/6-keys-to-success-for-any-hybrid-event

Market: Online Education, Region: India, Currency: USDs. (2024, March). Statista Market Insights. https://www.statista.com/outlook/emo/online-education/india#revenue

Marta Pinto, C. L. (2020). Digital technologies in support of students learning in Higher. *Digital Education Review*, 343-360.

Martínez-Martínez, A., Cegarra-Navarro, J. G., Garcia-Perez, A., & Wensley, A. (2019). Knowledge agents as drivers of environmental sustainability and business performance in the hospitality sector. *Tourism Management*, 70, 381–389. 10.1016/j.tourman.2018.08.030

Martin-Rios, C., Hofmann, A., & Mackenzie, N. (2020). Sustainability-oriented innovations in food waste management technology. *Sustainability (Basel)*, 13(1), 210. 10.3390/su13010210

Martin, V., & Cazarré, L. (2016). *Technology and Events: Organizing an engaging event.* Goodfellow Publishers Ltd.

Maynard, A. D., & Scragg, M. (2019). The Ethical and Responsible Development and Application of Advanced Brain Machine Interfaces. *Journal of Medical Internet Research*, 21(10), e16321. . 10.2196/1632131674917

McCartney, G., & Wang, C. F. (2024). Medical tourism and medical tourists: providing a sustainable course to integrating health treatments with tourism. *Journal of Travel Medicine.*

McCullough, B. P., Collins, A., Roberts, J., & Villalobos, S. (2023). Sport Events and Emissions Reporting: An Analysis of the Council for Responsible Sport Standard in Running Events. *Sustainability, 15*(19), 14375. 10.3390/su151914375

McLean, E., Cornwell, M. A., Bender, H. A., Sacks-Zimmerman, A., Mandelbaum, S., Koay, J. M., Raja, N., Kohn, A., Meli, G., & Spat-Lemus, J. (2023). Innovations in Neuropsychology: Future Applications in Neurosurgical Patient Care. *World Neurosurgery, 170*, 286–295. . 10.1016/j.wneu.2022.09.10336782427

Mediawire. (2024). Accelerating India's SDG goals demands tech intervention. *Times of India.*

Medini, K., Wiesner, S., Poursoltan, M., & Romero, D. (2020). Ramping Up Customer-Centric Modular Design Projects: Mobile App Development for Pandemic Relief. *Systems, 8*(4), 40. 10.3390/systems8040040

Meeprom, S., & Fakfare, P. (2023). Blended learning: Examining must-have, hybrid, and value-added quality attributes of hospitality and tourism education. *Journal of Hospitality & Tourism Education,* •••, 1–15. 10.1080/10963758.2023.2172419

Megahed, N., & Hassan, A. (2022). A blended learning strategy: Reimagining the post-Covid-19 architectural education. *Archnet-IJAR: International Journal of Architectural Research, 16*(1), 184–202. 10.1108/ARCH-04-2021-0081

Mehla, L., Sheorey, P. A., Tiwari, A. K., & Behl, A. (2021). Paradigm shift in the education sector amidst COVID-19 to improve online engagement: Opportunities and challenges. *Journal of Global Information Management, 30*(5), 1–21. 10.4018/JGIM.290366

Meho, L. I., & Sugimoto, C. R. (2009). Assessing the scholarly impact of information studies: A tale of two citation databases—Scopus and Web of Science. *Journal of the American Society for Information Science and Technology, 60*(12), 2499–2508. 10.1002/asi.21165

Mei, Z., Shuheng, D., Guofang, L., Yazhen, X., Xinyuan, F., Wei, Z., & Ziqiang, X. (2021). Negativity bias in emergent online events: Occurrence and manifestation. *Acta Psychologica Sinica, 53*(12), 1361. 10.3724/SP.J.1041.2021.01361

Melissen, F. (2019). The concept of hospitality. *Hospitality Experience,* 10–36. 10.4324/9781003023814-1

Meyer, M. F., Ladwig, R., Dugan, H. A., Anderson, A., Bah, A. R., Boehrer, B., Borre, L., Chapina, R. J., Doyle, C., Favot, E. J., Flaim, G., Forsberg, P., Hanson, P. C., Ibelings, B. W., Isles, P., Lin, F. P., Lofton, D., Moore, T. N., Peel, S., & Weathers, K. C. (2021). Virtual Growing Pains: Initial Lessons Learned from Organizing Virtual Workshops, Summits, Conferences, and Networking Events during a Global Pandemic. *Limnology and Oceanography Bulletin, 30*(1), 1–11. 10.1002/lob.10431

Michael Henderson, N. S. (2017). What works and why? Student perceptions of 'useful' digital technology in university teaching and learning. *Studies in Higher Education, 42*(8), 1567–1579. 10.1080/03075079.2015.1007946

Microsoft. (2024). What are OKRs (Objectives and Key Results)? Definition of methodology of OKR. Microsoft. https://www.microsoft.com/uk-ua/microsoft-viva/what-is-okr-objective-key -results

Minina, V. N. (2020). Digitalization of higher education and its social outcomes. *Bulletin of St. Petersburg University.Sociology*, 84–101.

Mistry, D., Brock, C. A., & Lindsey, T. (2023). The Present and Future of Virtual Reality in Medical Education: A Narrative Review. *Cureus*, 15(12), e51124. 10.7759/cureus.5112438274907

Mitra, R N., & Marina, M K. (2021, January 26). *5G Mobile Networks Security Landscape and Major Risks*, 1-23. Wiley. 10.1002/9781119471509.w5GRef145

Mody, M., Gordon, S., Lehto, X., So, S. I., & Li, M. (2016). The Augmented Convention Offering: The Impact of Destination and Product Images on Attendees' Perceived Benefits. *Tourism Analysis*, 21(1), 1–15. 10.3727/108354216X14537459508739

Mohana. S, & Anbumani, P. (2022). Online Event Management System. *International Journal of Research Publication and Reviews Journal Homepage*.

Mokoena, P., & Hattingh, C. (2024, March). Unlocking the Potential of Hybrid Learning: Tourism Student Voices in South African Universities of Technology. In *International Conference on Tourism Research* (Vol. 7, No. 1, pp. 232-238). 10.34190/ictr.7.1.2184

Molins-Ruano, P., Sevilla, C., Santini, S., Haya, P. A., Rodríguez, P., & Sacha, G. M. (2014). Designing videogames to improve students' motivation. *Computers in Human Behavior*, 31, 571–579. 10.1016/j.chb.2013.06.013

Monaco, S., & Sacchi, G. (2023). Travelling the metaverse: Potential benefits and main challenges for tourism sectors and research applications. *Sustainability (Basel)*, 15(4), 3348. 10.3390/ su15043348

Monisha. M, V. D. (2022). Digital Transformation in Education. *EPRA International Journal of Economic and Business Review-Peer Reviewed Journal*, 58-64.

Morey, Y., Bengry-Howell, A., Griffin, C., Szmigin, I., & Riley, S. (2016). Festivals 2.0: Consuming, producing and participating in the extended festival experience. In *The festivalization of culture* (pp. 251-268). Routledge.

Morschheuser, B., Hamari, J., & Maedche, A. (2019). Cooperation or competition – When do people contribute more? A field experiment on gamification of crowdsourcing. *International Journal of Human-Computer Studies*, 127, 7–24. 10.1016/j.ijhcs.2018.10.001

Moskal, P., Dziuban, C., & Hartman, J. (2013). Blended learning: A dangerous idea? *The Internet and Higher Education*, 18, 15–23. 10.1016/j.iheduc.2012.12.001

Mostafanezhad, M., Cheer, J. M., & Sin, H. L. (2020). Geopolitical anxieties of tourism:(Im) mobilities of the COVID-19 pandemic. *Dialogues in Human Geography*, 10(2), 182–186. 10.1177/2043820620934206

Mukherjee, D., Kumar, S., Donthu, N., & Pandey, N. (2021). Research Published in Management International Review from 2006 to 2020: A Bibliometric Analysis and Future Directions. *MIR. Management International Review*, 61(5), 599–642. 10.1007/s11575-021-00454-x34658534

Mulder, J. (2013). *Making things louder: Amplified music and multimodality* [Doctoral dissertation, OPUS].

Mumbai, P. (2020, July 29). National Education Policy 2020 announced. Mumbai. (n.d.). *National Education Policy 2020*. New Delhi: Minstry of Human Resource Development, Government of India.

Munsch, A. (2021). Millennial and generation Z digital marketing communication and advertising effectiveness: A qualitative exploration. *Journal of Global Scholars of Marketing Science*, 31(1), 10–29. 10.1080/21639159.2020.1808812

Musdalifah, M., Baharuddin, B., Jabri, U., Elihami, E., & Mustakim, M. (2021, February). Building The Management System: Designs on the use of Blended Learning Environment. []. IOP Publishing.]. *Journal of Physics: Conference Series*, 1783(1), 012120. 10.1088/1742-6596/1783/1/012120

Nagai, H., & Kurahashi, S. (2022). Measures to prevent and control the spread of novel coronavirus disease (COVID-19) infection in tourism locations. *SICE Journal of Control, Measurement, and System Integration*, 15(2), 1–12. 10.1080/18824889.2021.2012398

Nagar, K., Meghana, Y. G., & Rout, A. (2024). Artificial Intelligence in Tourism and Advertising. In *Artificial Intelligence for Business* (pp. 71–85). Productivity Press.

Naik, S., & Agarwal, V. (2021). A Study on Scope of Blended Learning in India. *IBA JOURNAL OF MANAGEMENT & LEADERSHIP*, 12(2), 28.

Nam, K., Dutt, C. S., Chathoth, P., Daghfous, A., & Khan, M. S. (2021). The adoption of artificial intelligence and robotics in the hotel industry: Prospects and challenges. *Electronic Markets*, 31(3), 553–574. 10.1007/s12525-020-00442-3

Nanto, D., Agustina, R. D., Ramadhanti, I., Putra, R. P., & Mulhayatiah, D. (2022). The usefulness of LabXChange virtual lab and PhyPhox real lab on pendulum student practicum during pandemic. []. IOP Publishing.]. *Journal of Physics: Conference Series*, 2157(1), 012047. 10.1088/1742-6596/2157/1/012047

Naraine, M. L., Hayduk, T., & Doyle, J. P. (2022). *The Routledge Handbook of Digital Sport Management*. Taylor & Francis. http://books.google.ie/ books?id=gICUEAAAQBAJ&pg=PT73&d-q=digital+tarnsformation+not+for+profit+sport+organisation&hl=&cd=1&source=gbs_api

Nawarathna, D. B., & Arachchi, D. R. S. S. W. (2021). *A Study on Sustainable Event Management Practices in Sri Lanka; Event Managers' Perspective*. Tourism and Sustainable Development Review. 10.31098/tsdr.v2i1.40

Neate, R. (2020). Zoom Booms As Demand For Video-Conferencing Tech Grows. *The Guardian*. https://www.theguardian.com/technology/2020/mar/31/zoom-booms-as-demand-for-video-conferencing-tech-grows-in-coronavirus-outbreak

Nedjalkov, A., Meyer, J., Köhring, M., Doering, A., Angelmahr, M., Dahle, S., Sander, A., Fischer, A., & Schade, W. (2016). Toxic Gas Emissions from Damaged Lithium Ion Batteries—Analysis and Safety Enhancement Solution. *Batteries*, 2(1), 5. 10.3390/batteries2010005

Nepal, S. K. (2020). Adventure travel and tourism after COVID-19–business as usual or opportunity to reset? *Tourism Geographies*, 22(3), 646–650. 10.1080/14616688.2020.1760926

NETF. (2024, March 02). *NETF*. NETF. https://netf.aicte-india.org/

Nguyen, L. T., Duc, D. T. V., Dang, T. Q., & Nguyen, D. P. (2023). Metaverse Banking Service: Are We Ready to Adopt? A Deep Learning-Based Dual-Stage SEM-ANN Analysis. *Human Behavior and Emerging Technologies*, 2023(1), 1–23. 10.1155/2023/6617371

Nguyen, T. M., Quach, S., & Thaichon, P. (2022). The effect of AI quality on customer experience and brand relationship. *Journal of Consumer Behaviour*, 21(3), 481–493. 10.1002/cb.1974

Nicholson, S. (2014). A RECIPE for Meaningful Gamification. In *Gamification in Education and Business* (pp. 1–20). Springer. 10.1007/978-3-319-10208-5_1

Nicola, S., Virag, I., & Stoicu-Tivadar, L. (2017). VR Medical Gamification for Training and Education. *Studies in Health Technology and Informatics*, 236, 97–103. [REMOVED HYPERLINK FIELD]28508784

Nishchyk, A., Chen, W., Pripp, A. H., & Bergland, A. (2021). The Effect of Mixed Reality Technologies for Falls Prevention Among Older Adults: Systematic Review and Meta-analysis. *JMIR Aging*, 4(2), e27972. . 10.2196/2797234255643

Nižetić, S., Djilali, N., Papadopoulos, A., & Rodrigues, J. J. P. C. (2019). Smart technologies for promotion of energy efficiency, utilization of sustainable resources and waste management. In *Journal of Cleaner Production*. 10.1016/j.jclepro.2019.04.397

Ntakakis, G., Plomariti, C., Frantzidis, C., Antoniou, P. E., Bamidis, P. D., & Tsoulfas, G. (2023). Exploring the use of virtual reality in surgical education. *World Journal of Transplantation*, 13(2), 36–43. . 10.5500/wjt.v13.i2.3636908307

Obeid, I., & Wolf, P. D. (2004). Evaluation of spike-detection algorithms for a brain-machine interface application. *IEEE Transactions on Biomedical Engineering*, 51(6), 905–911. . 10.1109/TBME.2004.82668315188857

Ocaña, M., Khosravi, H., & Bakharia, A. (2019). *Profiling language learners in the big data era*. ASCILITE Publications.

Ochoa Jiménez, S., García García, A. R., Valdez del Río, S., & Jacobo Hernández, C. A. (2022). Entrepreneurship in Tourism Studies in the 21st Century: A Bibliometric Study of Wos and Scopus. *SAGE Open*, 12(2). 10.1177/21582440221102438

Ogbeide, G. C., Fenich, G. G., Scott-Halsell, S., & Kesterson, K. (2013). Communication Preferences for Attracting the Millennial Generation to Attend Meetings and Events. *Journal of Convention & Event Tourism*, 14(4), 331–344. 10.1080/15470148.2013.843480

Ogle, A., & Lamb, D. (2019). The role of robots, artificial intelligence, and service automation in events. In *Robots, artificial intelligence, and service automation in travel, tourism and hospitality* (pp. 255–269). Emerald Publishing Limited. 10.1108/978-1-78756-687-320191012

Olewski, T., & Snakard, M. (2017). Challenges in applying process safety management at university laboratories. *Journal of Loss Prevention in the Process Industries*, 49, 209–214. 10.1016/j.jlp.2017.06.013

Oliveira, Z., Teixeira, S., Teixeira, S., & Pratas, J. M. (2024). The Use of Social Media: Influence of Content Marketing for Brazilian Health Industry SMEs. In J. Remondes, P. Madeira, & C. Alves (Eds.), *Connecting With Consumers through Effective Personalization and Programmatic Advertising* (pp. 243-267). IGI Global. 10.4018/978-1-6684-9146-1.ch013

Oliveira, K. (2021). *Digital Transformation towards Education 4.0*. Informatics in Education., 10.15388/infedu.2022.13

Online Education - India. (n.d.). Statista. https://www.statista.com/outlook/emo/online-education/india

Online, T. (2022). Students enrolment in online education programmes increased 170% between 2021 and 2022: UGC Chairman. *Times of India*.https://timesofindia.indiatimes.com/education/online-schooling/students-enrolment-in-online-education-programmes-increased-170-between-2021-and-2022-ugc-chairman/articleshowprint/95197476.cms?val=3728

Onwuegbuzie, I. U. (2022). 5G: next generation mobile wireless technology for a fast pacing world. [JPAS]. *Journal for Pure and Applied Sciences*, 1(1), 1–9. 10.56180/jpas.vol1.iss1.57

Ooi, K. B., Tan, G. W. H., Al-Emran, M., Al-Sharafi, M. A., Arpaci, I., Zaidan, A. A., & Iranmanesh, M. (2023). The metaverse in engineering management: Overview, opportunities, challenges, and future research agenda. *IEEE Transactions on Engineering Management*.

Ordov, K. A. (2019). New Trends in Education as the Aspect of Digital Technologies. *International Journal of Mechanical Engineering and Technology*, (pp. 1319-1330).

Orthodoxou, D. L., Loizidou, X. I., Gavriel, A., Hadjiprocopiou, S., Petsa, D., & Demetriou, K. (2022). Sustainable Business Events: The Perceptions of Service Providers, Attendees, and Stakeholders in Decision-Making Positions. *Journal of Convention & Event Tourism*, 23(2), 154–178. 10.1080/15470148.2021.1964666

Oskam, J., & Zandberg, T. (2019). The hospitality industry. *Hospitality Experience*, 66–96. 10.4324/9781003023814-3

Padilla, J. J., Diallo, S. Y., & Armstrong, R. K. (2018). Toward Live Virtual Constructive Simulations in Healthcare Learning. *Simulation in Healthcare : Journal of the Society for Simulation in Healthcare, 13*, S35–S40.

Compilation of References

Pakanen, M., Alavesa, P., van Berkel, N., Koskela, T., & Ojala, T. (2022). "Nice to see you virtually": Thoughtful design and evaluation of virtual avatar of the other user in AR and VR based telexistence systems. *Entertainment Computing*, 40, 100457. 10.1016/j.entcom.2021.100457

Pakarinen, T., & Hoods, J. (2018). *From hybrid events to the next generation-interactive virtual events: Viewed from three different stakeholders' point of view*. Research Gate.

Pakkala, H., Presser, K., & Christensen, T. (2012). Using Google Analytics to measure visitor statistics: The case of food composition websites. *International Journal of Information Management*, 32(6), 504–512. 10.1016/j.ijinfomgt.2012.04.008

Pal, M. (2024). Effect of Virtual Lab-Enabled Active Learning Method on Academic Achievement of Secondary Stage Students in Physics. *Educational Administration: Theory and Practice*, 30(2), 709–717.

Palmatier, R. W., Houston, M. B., & Hulland, J. (2018). Review articles: Purpose, process, and structure. *Journal of the Academy of Marketing Science*, 46(1), 1–5. 10.1007/s11747-017-0563-4

Palmer, M. (2005). Industrial archaeology: Constructing a framework of inference. In *Industrial archaeology: Future directions* (pp. 59–75). Springer US. 10.1007/0-387-22831-4_3

Palozzi, G., & Antonucci, G. (2022). Mobile-Health based physical activities co-production policies towards cardiovascular diseases prevention: Findings from a mixed-method systematic review. *BMC Health Services Research*, 22(1), 277. 10.1186/s12913-022-07637-835232456

Pang, S. F., McKercher, B., & Prideaux, B. (2013). Climate change and tourism: An overview. *Asia Pacific Journal of Tourism Research*, 18(1-2), 4–20. 10.1080/10941665.2012.688509

Pappas, N. (2019). Crisis Management Communications For Popular Culture Events. *Event Management*, 23(4), 655–667. 10.3727/152599519X15506259855652

Park, E. (2024). Examining metaverse game platform adoption: Insights from innovation, behavior, and coolness. *Technology in Society*, 77, 102594. 10.1016/j.techsoc.2024.102594

Park, J. S., Kim, K. H., Hong, J., Jeong, S. H., Kim, S. D., Nduhura, D., & Mumporeze, N. (2023). *ICT Innovation and Korean Society: Industry*. Media, and Culture.

Park, J., & Bennis, M. (2018). URLLC-eMBB Slicing to Support VR Multimodal Perceptions over Wireless Cellular Systems. *IEEE Conference on Global Communications (GLOBECOM)*. IEEE. 10.1109/GLOCOM.2018.8647208

Parton, B. S. (2006). Sign language recognition and translation: A multidisciplined approach from the field of artificial intelligence. *Journal of Deaf Studies and Deaf Education*, 11(1), 94–101. . 10.1093/deafed/enj00316192405

Pasi, S. A., Altaf, P., Shah, T., Amol, P., & Kasture, B. (2018). A Study and Implementation of Event Management System Using Smartphone. *International Journal of Innovative Research in Engineering & Multidisciplinary Physical Sciences*, 6(5).

Pastrana, C. I., González, F. J. N., Ciani, E., Baena, S. N., & Bermejo, J. V. D. (2020). Camel Genetic Resources Conservation through Tourism: A Key Sociocultural Approach of Camelback Leisure Riding. *Animals (Basel)*, 10(9), 1–23. 10.3390/ani1009170332962294

Paul, J., & Shrivatava, A. (2016). Do young managers in a developing country have stronger entrepreneurial intentions? Theory and debate. *International Business Review*, 25(6), 1197–1210. 10.1016/j.ibusrev.2016.03.003

Paul, N. I., & Ali Amaran, M. (2023). The music events in Kuching, Sarawak post-pandemic times: Changes and perception. *International Journal of Applied and Creative Arts*, 6(1), 01–11. Advance online publication. 10.33736/ijaca.4825.2023

Pawassar, C. M., & Tiberius, V. (2021). Virtual Reality in Health Care: Bibliometric Analysis. *JMIR Serious Games*, 9(4), e32721. . 10.2196/3272134855606

Pearlman, D. M., & Gates, N. A. (2010). Hosting Business Meetings and Special Events in Virtual Worlds: A Fad or the Future? *Journal of Convention & Event Tourism, 11*(4).

Pearlman, D. M., & Gates, N. A. (2010, November). Hosting business meetings and special events in virtual worlds: A fad or the future? []. Taylor & Francis Group.]. *Journal of Convention & Event Tourism*, 11(4), 247–265. 10.1080/15470148.2010.530535

Pedroli, E., Mancuso, V., Stramba-Badiale, C., Cipresso, P., Tuena, C., Greci, L., Goulene, K., Stramba-Badiale, M., Riva, G., & Gaggioli, A. (2022). Brain M-App's Structure and Usability: A New Application for Cognitive Rehabilitation at Home. *Frontiers in Human Neuroscience*, 16, 898633. . 10.3389/fnhum.2022.89863335782042

Peng, W., Lin, J.-H., Pfeiffer, K. A., & Winn, B. (2012). Need Satisfaction Supportive Game Features as Motivational Determinants: An Experimental Study of a Self-Determination Theory Guided Exergame. *Media Psychology*, 15(2), 175–196. 10.1080/15213269.2012.673850

Peralta, A., & Salama, M. (2021). *Sustainable business model innovation for event management.* Event Project Management., 10.23912/9781911635734-4771

Pérez-Juárez, M. A., Aguiar-Pérez, J. M., Alonso-Felipe, M., & Del-Pozo-Velázquez, J. (2022). Exploring the Possibilities of Artificial Intelligence and Big Data Techniques to Enhance Gamified Financial Services. Next-Generation *Applications and Implementations of Gamification Systems*. IGI Global. 10.4018/978-1-7998-8089-9.ch010

Perumal, J. (2008). Student resistance and teacher authority: The demands and dynamics of collaborative learning. *Journal of Curriculum Studies*, 40(3), 381–398. 10.1080/00220270701724570

Petkovics, I. (2018). Digital Transformation in Higher Education. *Journal of Applied Technical and Educational Sciences,* 77-89. 10.24368/jates.v8i4.55

Petrescu, M., & Krishen, A. S. (2023). Hybrid intelligence: human–AI collaboration in marketing analytics. *Journal of Marketing Analytics*, 11(3), 263–274. 10.1057/s41270-023-00245-3

Compilation of References

Pham, C. T., & Thi Nguyet, T. T. (2023). Determinants of blockchain adoption in news media platforms: A perspective from the Vietnamese press industry. *Heliyon*, 9(1), e12747. Advance online publication. 10.1016/j.heliyon.2022.e1274736685429

Pham, T. D., Dwyer, L., Su, J. J., & Ngo, T. (2021). COVID-19 impacts of inbound tourism on Australian economy. *Annals of Tourism Research*, 88, 103179. 10.1016/j.annals.2021.10317936540369

PIB. (2023). Retrieved from PIB: https://www.education.gov.in/sites/upload_files/mhrd/files/LU5163.pdf

PIB. (2023, August). *Digital India initiative of Government has revolutionized education access in rural areas*. PIB.

Picciano, A. G. (2013). Introduction to blended learning: research perspectives. *Taylor & Francis Ltd*.

Pidgeon, N., & O'Leary, M. (2000). Man-made disasters: Why technology and organizations (sometimes) fail. *Safety Science*, 34(1–3), 15–30. 10.1016/S0925-7535(00)00004-7

Pilipczuk, O. (2021). A Conceptual Framework for Large-Scale Event Perception Evaluation with Spatial-Temporal Scales in Sustainable Smart Cities. *Sustainability (Basel)*, 13(10), 5658. 10.3390/su13105658

Pillai, R., Sivathanu, B., Rana, N. P., Preet, R., & Mishra, A. (2024). Factors influencing customers' apparel shopping intention in metaverse. *Journal of Computer Information Systems*, 1–16.

Piñeiro-Chousa, J., López-Cabarcos, M. Á., Romero-Castro, N. M., & Pérez-Pico, A. M. (2020). Innovation, entrepreneurship and knowledge in the business scientific field: Mapping the research front. *Journal of Business Research*, 115, 475–485. 10.1016/j.jbusres.2019.11.045

Pinho, M., & Marques, J. (2021). The bleisure tourism trend and the potential for this business-leisure symbiosis in Porto. *Journal of Convention & Event Tourism*, 22(4), 346–362. 10.1080/15470148.2021.1905575

Piyush. (2024, January 23). Central Government Launches 'Anuvadini' App for Multilingual Education. *Adda247 Current Affairs*.

Pluzhnikova, N. N. (2022). Digitalization of education and information technologies as a factor of agribusiness development. *BIO Web Conference, 53*, 7. 10.1051/bioconf/20225307001

Poku, K., Zakari, M., & Soali, A. (2013). Impact of service quality on customer loyalty in the hotel industry: An empirical study from Ghana. *International Review of Management and Business Research*, 2(2), 600–609.

Pop, A. M., Marian-Potra, A. C., & Hognogi, G. G. (2023). The COVID-19 Pandemic as Catalyst for Virtual Events. *Journal of Settlements & Spatial Planning*, 14(1), 13–23. 10.24193/JSSP.2023.1.02

Porobanyuk, V. (2024). *SMM 2024: improving strategies and latest trends*. Webpromo. https://surl.li/pnrnl

Post-up. (2023). *Content strategy for Instagram in 2023*. Post-Up. https://www.postup.com.ua/kontent-strategiya-dlya-instagram-v-2023/

Potkonjak, V., Gardner, M., Callaghan, V., Mattila, P., Guetl, C., Petrović, V. M., & Jovanović, K. (2016). Virtual laboratories for education in science, technology, and engineering: A review. *Computers & Education*, 95, 309–327. 10.1016/j.compedu.2016.02.002

Prayag, G. (2020). Time for reset? COVID-19 and tourism resilience. *Tourism Review International*, 24(2-3), 179–184. 10.3727/154427220X15926147793595

Prayogi, S. F., & Michael. (2022). Kajian Desain 3D Virtual Exhibition Ruang Pamer Karya Desain Produk Istts. *Prosiding SNADES*.

Prentice, C., Dominique Lopes, S., & Wang, X. (2020). The impact of artificial intelligence and employee service quality on customer satisfaction and loyalty. *Journal of Hospitality Marketing & Management*, 29(7), 739–756. 10.1080/19368623.2020.1722304

Prentice, C., & Nguyen, M. (2020). Engaging and retaining customers with AI and employee service. *Journal of Retailing and Consumer Services*, 56, 102186. 10.1016/j.jretconser.2020.102186

Qiu, H., Li, Q., & Li, C. (2021). How technology facilitates tourism education in COVID-19: Case study of Nankai University. *Journal of Hospitality, Leisure, Sport and Tourism Education*, 29, 100288. 10.1016/j.jhlste.2020.10028834720752

Quinn, B. (2009). Festivals, events and tourism. *The SAGE handbook of tourism studies*, 483-503. Sage.

Radhamani, R., Sasidharakurup, H., Kumar, D., Nizar, N., Achuthan, K., Nair, B., & Diwakar, S. (2015, November). Role of Biotechnology simulation and remotely triggered virtual labs in complementing university education. In *2015 International Conference on Interactive Mobile Communication Technologies and Learning (IMCL)* (pp. 28-32). IEEE. 10.1109/IMCTL.2015.7359548

Rady Mohamed, S. (2022). *Technological Innovation in Tourism and Events industry: A hybrid future of Events*. International Journal of Tourism, Archaeology and Hospitality., 10.21608/ijtah.2023.185020.1027

Ragab, H., & Salama, M. (2021). *Advanced Technology for Event Management*. Event Project Management. 10.23912/9781911635734-4774

Rajan, S., Bindu, G. V., & Mukherjee, S. (2021). Adopting Evolving Technologies to Aid Cognitive Abilities in Classroom Learning-Teaching. *Neuro-Systemic Applications in Learning*, 483–506. 10.1007/978-3-030-72400-9_24

Rajhans, V., Memon, U., Patil, V., & Goyal, A. (2020). Impact of COVID-19 on academic activities and way forward in Indian Optometry. *Journal of Optometry*, 13(4), 216–226. 10.1016/j.optom.2020.06.00232703749

Compilation of References

Ramos, C. M., Henriques, C., & Lanquar, R. (2016). Augmented reality for smart tourism in religious heritage itineraries: Tourism experiences in the technological age. In *Handbook of research on human-computer interfaces, developments, and applications* (pp. 245–272). IGI Global. 10.4018/978-1-5225-0435-1.ch010

Ranjan, P. (2020). Is Blended Learning Better than Online Learning for B. Ed Students? *Journal of Learning for Development*, 7(3), 349–366. 10.56059/jl4d.v7i3.412

Rasheed, R. A., Kamsin, A., & Abdullah, N. A. (2021). An approach for scaffolding students peer-learning self-regulation strategy in the online component of blended learning. *IEEE Access : Practical Innovations, Open Solutions*, 9, 30721–30738. 10.1109/ACCESS.2021.3059916

Rastegar, N., Flaherty, J., Liang, L., & Choi, H. C. (2021). The adoption of self-service kiosks in quick-service restaurants. *European Journal of Tourism Research*, 27, 2709. 10.54055/ejtr.v27i.2139

Ratten, V. (2023). Event Management and Social Entrepreneurship: An Overview. *Event Management*, 27(8), 1127–1134. 10.3727/152599523X16847420514782

Ratten, V. (2023). The post COVID-19 pandemic era: Changes in teaching and learning methods for management educators. *International Journal of Management Education*, 21(2), 100777. 10.1016/j.ijme.2023.100777

Rauschnabel, P. A., Babin, B. J., tom Dieck, M. C., Krey, N., & Jung, T. (2022). What is augmented reality marketing? Its definition, complexity, and future. *Journal of Business Research*, 142(1), 1140–1150. 10.1016/j.jbusres.2021.12.084

Reece, A. (2015). *An Investigation of the Impacts of Face-to-Face and Virtual Laboratories in an Introductory Biology Course on Students' Motivation to Learn Biology.*

Reinartz, W., Wiegand, N., & Imschloss, M. (2019). The impact of digital transformation on the retailing value chain. *International Journal of Research in Marketing*, 36(3), 350–366. 10.1016/j.ijresmar.2018.12.002

Reis, J., Melão, N., Salvadorinho, J., Soares, B., & Rosete, A. (2020). Service robots in the hospitality industry: The case of Henn-na hotel, Japan. *Technology in Society*, 63, 101423. 10.1016/j.techsoc.2020.101423

Remmel, A. (2021). Scientists want virtual meetings to stay after the COVID pandemic. *Nature*, 591(7849), 185–187. 10.1038/d41586-021-00513-133654258

Renieris, E. M. (2023). *Beyond data: Reclaiming human rights at the dawn of the metaverse.* MIT Press. 10.7551/mitpress/14119.001.0001

Resien, C., Sitompul, H., & Situmorang, J. (2020). The effect of blended learning strategy and creative thinking of students on the results of learning information and communication technology by controlling prior knowledge. *Budapest International Research and Critics in Linguistics and Education (BirLE). Journal*, 3(2), 879–893.

Ricard, M. Z. (2020). Digital Education, Information and Communication Technology, and Education for Sustainable Development. In Burgos, D. (Ed.), *Radical Solutions and eLearning* (pp. 27–39). Springer. 10.1007/978-981-15-4952-6_2

Richard, E., Tijou, A., Richard, P., & Ferrier, J. L. (2006). Multi-modal virtual environments for education with haptic and olfactory feedback. *Virtual Reality (Waltham Cross)*, 10(3-4), 207–225. 10.1007/s10055-006-0040-8

Richert, A., Shehadeh, M. A., Müller, S. L., Schröder, S., & Jeschke, S. (2016, July). Socializing with robots: Human-robot interactions within a virtual environment. In *2016 IEEE Workshop on Advanced Robotics and its Social Impacts (ARSO)* (pp. 49-54). IEEE. 10.1109/ARSO.2016.7736255

Richter, G., Raban, D. R., & Rafaeli, S. (2015). Studying gamification: The effect of rewards and incentives on motivation. *Gamification in Education and Business*, 21–46. 10.1007/978-3-319-10208-5_2

Richter, T., Boehringer, D., & Jeschke, S. (2011). Lila: A european project on networked experiments. In *Automation, Communication and Cybernetics in Science and Engineering 2009/2010* (pp. 307-317). Springer Berlin Heidelberg. 10.1007/978-3-642-16208-4_27

Richter, S., & Richter, A. (2023). What is novel about the metaverse? *International Journal of Information Management*, 73, 102684. 10.1016/j.ijinfomgt.2023.102684

Rieple, A., DeFillippi, R., & Schreiber, D. (2023). Trans formational Innovation in Ephemeral Experiences. *Transformational Innovation in the Creative and Cultural Industries*, 152.

Rigby, S., & Ryan, R. M. (2011). *Glued to games how video games draw us in and hold us spellbound.* Praeger. 10.5040/9798400658105

Ritz, E., Rietsche, R., & Leimeister, J. M. (2023). How to support students' self-regulated learning in times of crisis: An embedded technology-based intervention in blended learning pedagogies. *Academy of Management Learning & Education*, 22(3), 357–382. 10.5465/amle.2022.0188

Rizzo, A. & Shilling, R. (2017). Clinical Virtual Reality tools to advance the prevention, assessment, and treatment of PTSD. *European Journal of Psychotraumatology, 8*, 1414560.

Roberts, A., Goodman-Scott, E. C., & Edirmanasinghe, N. A. (2023). The Experiences of School Counselors Providing Virtual Services During COVID-19: A Phenomenological Investigation. *Professional School Counseling*, 27(1), 2156759X231199738. 10.1177/2156759X231199738

Rogerson, C. M., & Rogerson, J. M. (2021). The other half of urban tourism: Research directions in the global South. *Urban Tourism in the Global South: South African Perspectives*, 1-37.

Rogerson, C. M. (2019). Business Tourism Under Apartheid: The Historical Development of South Africa's Conference Industry. *Urbani Izziv*, 30(30, Supplement), 82–95. 10.5379/urbani-izziv-en-2019-30-supplement-006

Rogerson, C. M., & Baum, T. (2020). COVID-19 and African Tourism Research Agendas. *Development Southern Africa*, 37(5), 727–741. 10.1080/0376835X.2020.1818551

Compilation of References

Rogerson, C. M., & Rogerson, J. M. (2020). COVID-19 tourism impacts in South Africa: Government and industry responses. *Geo Journal of Tourism and Geosites*, 31(3), 1083–1091. 10.30892/gtg.31321-544

Rogerson, C. M., & Rogerson, J. M. (2021). COVID-19 and Changing Tourism Demand: Research Review and Policy Implications for South Africa. *African Journal of Hospitality, Tourism and Leisure*, 10(1), 1–21. 10.46222/ajhtl.19770720-83

Rojek, C. (2020). Event Management. In *Routledge Handbook of Leisure Studies*. Routledge. https://doi.org/10.4324/9781003074717-49

Rosário, A. T., & Dias, J. C. (2022). Sustainability and the digital transition: A literature review. *Sustainability (Basel)*, 14(7), 4072. 10.3390/su14074072

Roslan, F. A. B. M., & Ahmad, N. B. (2023). The Rise of AI-Powered Voice Assistants: Analyzing Their Transformative Impact on Modern Customer Service Paradigms and Consumer Expectations. *Quarterly Journal of Emerging Technologies and Innovations*, 8(3), 33–64.

Ruban, A. (2023). *The role of the government in metaverse development in China and South Korea: A Comparative Analysis*.

Ruel, H., & Njoku, E. (2021). AI redefining the hospitality industry. *Journal of Tourism Futures*, 7(1), 53–66. 10.1108/JTF-03-2020-0032

Rugman, A. M., Verbeke, A., & Nguyen, Q. T. K. (2011). Fifty Years of International Business Theory and Beyond. *MIR. Management International Review*, 51(6), 755–786. 10.1007/s11575-011-0102-3

Russo, E., Figueira, A. R., & Kogut, C. S., & Mello, R. D. C. D. (2022). The Tokyo 2020 Olympic Games: Impacts of COVID-19 and digital transformation. *Cadernos EBAPE.BR*, 20, 318–332. 10.1590/1679-395120210150

Rustana, C. E., Khalifah, S. N., & Sugihartono, I. (2021). The effect of the use of harmonic movement phet interactive simulation in online learning process on mastering the concept of high school students. *Journal of Physics: Conference Series*, 2019(1), 012022. 10.1088/1742-6596/2019/1/012022

Ryan, R. M., & Deci, E. L. (2000a). Intrinsic and Extrinsic motivations: Classic Definitions and New Directions. *Contemporary Educational Psychology*, 25(1), 54–67. 10.1006/ceps.1999.102010620381

Ryan, R. M., & Deci, E. L. (2000b). Self-determination theory and the facilitation of intrinsic motivation, social development, and well-being. *The American Psychologist*, 55(1), 68–78. 10.1037/0003-066X.55.1.6811392867

Ryan, R. M., Rigby, C. S., & Przybylski, A. (2006). The Motivational Pull of Video Games: A Self-Determination Theory Approach. *Motivation and Emotion*, 30(4), 344–360. 10.1007/s11031-006-9051-8

Ryan, W. G., Fenton, A., Ahmed, W., & Scarf, P. (2020). Recognizing events 4.0: The digital maturity of events. *International Journal of Event and Festival Management*, 11(1), 47–68. 10.1108/IJEFM-12-2019-0060

Rybchuk, A. Z. (2022). Digital Transformation of the Global Educational Environment. *Herald of Khmelnytskyi National University.*, 262-268.

Saffaryazdi, N., Wasim, S. T., Dileep, K., Nia, A. F., Nanayakkara, S., Broadbent, E., & Billinghurst, M. (2022). Using Facial Micro-Expressions in Combination With EEG and Physiological Signals for Emotion Recognition. *Frontiers in Psychology*, 13, 864047. . 10.3389/fpsyg.2022.86404735837650

Saha, S., & Yap, G. (2014). The moderation effects of political instability and terrorism on tourism development: A cross-country panel analysis. *Journal of Travel Research*, 53(4), 509–521. 10.1177/0047287513496472

Sahoo, N., Gupta, D., & Sen, K. Metaverse: The Pursuit to Keep the Human Element Intact in the Media and Entertainment Industry. In *The Business of the Metaverse* (pp. 156-167). Productivity Press.

Saikia, A., Mazumdar, S., Sahai, N., Paul, S., & Bhatia, D. (2022). Performance Analysis of Artificial Neural Network for Hand Movement Detection from EMG Signals. *Journal of the Institution of Electronics and Telecommunication Engineers*, 68(2), 1074–1083. Advance online publication. 10.1080/03772063.2019.1638316

Sailer, M., Hense, J. U., Mayr, S. K., & Mandl, H. (2017). How Gamification motivates: An Experimental Study of the Effects of Specific Game Design Elements on Psychological Need Satisfaction. *Computers in Human Behavior*, 69(69), 371–380. 10.1016/j.chb.2016.12.033

Sailer, M., Hense, J., Mandl, H., & Klevers, M. (2013). Psychological Perspectives on Motivation through Gamification. *Interaction Design and Architecture(S)*, 19(19), 28–37. 10.55612/s-5002-019-002

Saini, A., & Bhalla, R. (2022). Artificial intelligence and automation: transforming the hospitality industry or threat to human touch. In *Handbook of Research on Innovative Management Using AI in Industry 5.0* (pp. 88–97). IGI Global. 10.4018/978-1-7998-8497-2.ch006

Salazar, A. (2018). Hospitality trends: Opportunities and challenges. *Worldwide Hospitality and Tourism Themes*, 10(6), 674–679. 10.1108/WHATT-07-2018-0047

Salen, K., & Zimmerman, E. (2003). *Rules of Play: Game Design Fundamentals*. The Mit Press.

Santhanam, R., Liu, D., & Shen, W.-C. M. (2016). Research Note—Gamification of Technology-Mediated Training: Not All Competitions Are the Same. *Information Systems Research*, 27(2), 453–465. 10.1287/isre.2016.0630

Santos, L. L., Borini, F. M., & Oliveira Júnior, M. (2020). In search of the frugal innovation strategy. *Review of International Business and Strategy*, 30(2), 245–263. 10.1108/RIBS-10-2019-0142

Compilation of References

Savir, S., Khan, A. A., Yunus, R. A., Rehman, T. A., Saeed, S., Sohail, M., Sharkey, A., Mitchell, J., & Matyal, R. (2023). Virtual Reality: The Future of Invasive Procedure Training? *Journal of Cardiothoracic and Vascular Anesthesia*, 37(10), 2090–2097. 10.1053/j.jvca.2023.06.03237422335

Scherschinski, L., McNeill, I. T., Schlachter, L., Shuman, W. H., Oemke, H., Yaeger, K. A., & Bederson, J. B. (2022). Augmented reality-assisted microsurgical resection of brain arteriovenous malformations: Illustrative case. *Journal of Neurosurgery. Case Lessons*, 3(25), CASE21135. . 10.3171/CASE2113535733837

Schipper, F. (2008). *Driving Europe: Building Europe on roads in the twentieth century* (Vol. 3). Amsterdam University Press.

Schleider, J. L., Mullarkey, M. C., & Weisz, J. R. (2019). Virtual Reality and Web-Based Growth Mindset Interventions for Adolescent Depression: Protocol for a Three-Arm Randomized Trial. *JMIR Research Protocols*, 8(7), e13368. . 10.2196/1336831290406

Schöbel, S. M., Janson, A., & Söllner, M. (2020). Capturing the complexity of gamification elements: A holistic approach for analysing existing and deriving novel gamification designs. *European Journal of Information Systems*, 29(6), 1–28. 10.1080/0960085X.2020.1796531

Schönherr, S., Peters, M., & Kuščer, K. (2023). Sustainable tourism policies: From crisis-related awareness to agendas towards measures. *Journal of Destination Marketing & Management*, 27, 100762. 10.1016/j.jdmm.2023.100762

Schulte-Römer, N., & Gesing, F. (2022). Online, offline, hybrid: Methodological reflection on event ethnography in (post-)pandemic times. *Sage Journals, 23*(6), 1620–1646. 10.1177/14687941221110172

Schut, P. O., & Glebova, E. (2022). Sports Spectating in Connected Stadiums: Mobile Application Roland Garros 2018. *Frontiers in Sports and Active Living*, 4, 802852. 10.3389/fspor.2022.80285235368418

Schwinn, A., & Schelp, J. (2005). Design patterns for data integration. *Journal of Enterprise Information Management*, 18(4), 471–482. 10.1108/17410390510609617

Seabra, C., & Korstanje, M. E. (Eds.). (2023). *Safety and Tourism: A Global Industry with Global Risks*. Emerald. 10.1108/9781803828114

Selim, A. J., Rothendler, J. A., Qian, S. X., Bailey, H. M., & Kazis, L. E. (2022). The History and Applications of the Veterans RAND 12-Item Health Survey (VR-12). *The Journal of Ambulatory Care Management*, 45(3), 161–170. . 10.1097/JAC.00000000000042035612387

Semiz, M., & Čutović, M. (2023). Extracurricular activities during the COVID-19 pandemic: Teachers' experiences and lessons. *Zbornik Radova Pedagoskog Fakulteta Uzice*, 25(25), 165–182. 10.5937/ZRPFU2325141S

Sen, D., Srivastava, R., Sahai, N., Tewari, R. P., & Kumar, B. (2020). Development of IoT Enabled Low Cost Management System for m-Cardiology. SSRN *Electronic Journal*. 10.2139/ssrn.3573502

Şengel, Ü., Genç, G., Işkın, M., Çevrimkaya, M., Zengin, B., & Sarıışık, M. (2023). The impact of anxiety levels on destination visit intention in the context of COVID-19: The mediating role of travel intention. *Journal of Hospitality and Tourism Insights*, 6(2), 697–715. 10.1108/JHTI-10-2021-0295

SenthilKumar, G., Sommers, K. C., He, Y., Stark, K., Craig, T., Keval, A., Shah, N., Patel, K., & Meurer, J. (2023). Student Leadership Development Initiative for Medical Students: Lessons Learned From Transitioning to Virtual Modalities. *Journal of Medical Education and Curricular Development*, 10, 23821205231200731. 10.1177/23821205231200731137692559

Seo, S., & Kim, H. J. (2021). How COVID-19 influences hospitality and tourism education: Challenges, opportunities, and new directions. *Journal of Hospitality & Tourism Education*, 33(3), 147–147. 10.1080/10963758.2021.1929531

Seraphin, H., & Maingi, S. W. (2023). The luxury yacht charter market and sustainable brand image: The case of Sunreef. *Worldwide Hospitality and Tourism Themes*, 15(4), 386–397. 10.1108/WHATT-03-2023-0045

Serrano, F., & Kazda, A. (2020). The future of airports post COVID-19. *Journal of Air Transport Management*, 89, 101900. 10.1016/j.jairtraman.2020.10190032834696

Serrano-Perez, J. J., González-García, L., Flacco, N., Taberner-Cortés, A., García-Arnandis, I., Pérez-López, G., Pellín-Carcelén, A., & Romá-Mateo, C. (2023). Traditional vs. virtual laboratories in health sciences education. *Journal of Biological Education*, 57(1), 36–50. 10.1080/00219266.2021.1877776

Shah, P., Agrawal, S., Joby, J., Ansari, S., Bhandari, R., & Bhatt, I. (2023). Prevalence of Indian Culture over Western Culture in 21st Century. *Integrated Journal for Research in Arts and Humanities*, 3(5), 230–239. 10.55544/ijrah.3.5.21

Shailaj Kumar Shrivastava, C. S. (2022). *The Impact of Digitalization in Higher Educational Institutions. International Journal of Soft Computing and Engineering*. IJSCE. 10.35940/ijsce. B3536.0111222

Shal, T., Ghamrawi, N., & Ghamrawi, N. A. R. (2024). Webinars for teacher professional development: Perceptions of members of a virtual professional community of practice. *Open Learning*, 1–17. 10.1080/02680513.2023.2296645

Sharma, S. (2023). Ethical Considerations in AI-Based Marketing: Balancing Profit and Consumer Trust. *TuijinJishu/Journal of Propulsion Technology, 44*(3), 1301-1309.

Sharma, S. K., Dwivedi, Y. K., Metri, B., Lal, B., & Elbanna, A. (Eds.). (2023). Transfer, Diffusion and Adoption of Next-Generation Digital Technologies. *IFIP WG 8.6 International Working Conference on Transfer and Diffusion of IT, Proceedings, Part I* (Vol. 697). Springer Nature.

Sharma, A., & Nicolau, J. L. (2020). An open market valuation of the effects of COVID-19 on the travel and tourism industry. *Annals of Tourism Research*, 83, 102990. 10.1016/j.annals.2020.10299032834220

Sharma, M., & Singh, A. (2024). Enhancing Competitive Advantages Through Virtual Reality Technology in the Hotels of India. In Kumar, S., Talukder, M., & Pego, A. (Eds.), *Utilizing Smart Technology and AI in Hybrid Tourism and Hospitality* (pp. 243–256). IGI Global. 10.4018/979-8-3693-1978-9.ch011

Sharpley, R. (2021). On the need for sustainable tourism consumption. *Tourist Studies*, 21(1), 96–107. 10.1177/1468797620986087

Shekhar, G., Gupta, A., & Valeri, M. (2022a). Mapping research on family business in tourism and hospitality: A bibliometric analysis. *Journal of Family Business Management*, 12(3), 367–392. 10.1108/JFBM-10-2021-0121

Sheldon, P. J., Fesenmaier, D. R., & Tribe, J. (2011). The tourism education futures initiative (TEFI): Activating change in tourism education. *Journal of Teaching in Travel & Tourism*, 11(1), 2–23. 10.1080/15313220.2011.548728

Shen, B., Tan, W., Guo, J., Zhao, L., & Qin, P. (2021). How to promote user purchase in metaverse? A systematic literature review on consumer behavior research and virtual commerce application design. *Applied Sciences (Basel, Switzerland)*, 11(23), 11087. 10.3390/app112311087

Shih, C. (2010). *The Facebook era: Tapping online social networks to market, sell, and innovate.* Pearson Education.

Shih, N. J., Diao, P. H., Qiu, Y. T., & Chen, T. Y. (2020). Situated ar simulations of a lantern festival using a smartphone and lidar-based 3d models. *Applied Sciences (Basel, Switzerland)*, 11(1), 12. 10.3390/app11010012

Shin, H. H., Jeong, M., So, K. K. F., & DiPietro, R. (2022). Consumers' experience with hospitality and tourism technologies: Measurement development and validation. *International Journal of Hospitality Management*, 106, 103297. 10.1016/j.ijhm.2022.103297

Shkil, L. (2023). 63% of people are online now. *The Big Digital 2022 Report on Internet Users.* AIN. https://ain.ua/2022/04/30/zvit-digital-2022/

Shrestha, A. B., Taha, A. M., Siddiq, A., Shrestha, S., Thakur, P., Chapagain, S., Sharma, S., Halder, A., Rajak, K., & Shah, V. (2024). Virtual and augmented reality in cardiovascular care in low and middle income country. *Current Problems in Cardiology*, 49(3), 102380. . 10.1016/j.cpcardiol.2024.10238038191103

Shrivastava, A., & Shrivastava, M. (2022). An Exploration of Students' Perceptions on the Blended Learning Mode in Management Education: A Case of Selected Colleges in India. *International Journal of Education and Development Using Information and Communication Technology*, 18(2), 207–214.

Shukla, A., Mishra, A., Rana, N. P., & Banerjee, S. (2024). The future of metaverse adoption: A behavioral reasoning perspective with a text-mining approach. *Journal of Consumer Behaviour*, •••, 1–21. 10.1002/cb.2336

Sigala, M. (2021). A bibliometric review of research on COVID-19 and tourism: Reflections for moving forward. *Tourism Management Perspectives*, 40, 100912. 10.1016/j.tmp.2021.10091234804787

Silva, F., Ferreira, R., Correia, A., Pinto, P., & Ramos, J. (2021). Experiments on Gamification with Virtual and Augmented Reality for Practical Application Learning. *Springer EBooks*, 175–184. 10.1007/978-3-030-86618-1_18

Silver, D., & Rumsey, L. (2022). Going viral: Limited-purpose public figures, involuntary public figures, and viral media content. *Communication Law and Policy*, 27(1), 49–76. 10.1080/10811680.2021.2014297

Sim, A. J. X. (2023). *A study of metaverse acceptance among Malaysian undergraduate media students based on the technology acceptance model* [Doctoral dissertation, UTAR].

Simons, I. (2019). Events and online interaction: The construction of hybrid event communities. *Leisure Studies*, 38(2), 145–159. 10.1080/02614367.2018.1553994

Šímová, T., Zychová, K., & Fejfarová, M. (2024). Metaverse in the virtual workplace. *Vision (Basel)*, 28(1), 19–34. 10.1177/09722629231168690

Sing Yun, W. (2023). Digitalization challenges in education during COVID-19: A systematic review. *Cogent Education*, 10(1), 2198981. 10.1080/2331186X.2023.2198981

Singh, A., & Bathla, G. (2023). Fostering Creativity and Innovation: Tourism and Hospitality Perspective. In P. Tyagi, V. Nadda, V. Bharti, & E. Kemer (Eds.), *Embracing Business Sustainability Through Innovation and Creativity in the Service Sector* (pp. 70-83). IGI Global. 10.4018/978-1-6684-6732-9.ch005

Singh, A., Yadav, B., Kaushik, A., Raj, A., Yadav, J., & Hari, P. B. (2022). *3D Virtual Modelling and Its Future Scope-Metaverse.*

Singh, S. V. (2018). Study on impact of factors in employee retention and turnover in hospitality industry with special reference to hotels in Varanasi. *Development of Aspects in Tourism and Hospitality Sector*, 190-201.

Singh, A. K. (2022). Role of Education in Sustainable Development Goals. *The Electrochemical Society*. Retrieved from 10.1149/10701.11685ecst

Singh, A., & Hassan, S. C. (2024). Service Innovation Through Blockchain Technology in the Tourism and Hospitality Industry: Applications, Trends, and Benefits. In Singh, S. (Ed.), *Service Innovations in Tourism: Metaverse, Immersive Technologies, and Digital Twin* (pp. 205–214). IGI Global. 10.4018/979-8-3693-1103-5.ch010

Singh, S. V. (2018). An Analysis of Tourist Satisfaction in Varanasi as Destination Perspective through Important Performance Analysis. *Avahan. Journal of Hospitality and Tourism.*

Sisson, A. D., & Whalen, E. A. (2021). Exploratory study on the perceptions of event gamification on positive behavioral outcomes. *Journal of Hospitality and Tourism Insights*. 10.1108/JHTI-04-2021-0085

Compilation of References

Slocum, S. L., & Lee, S. (2014). Green ICT practices in event management: Case study approach to examine motivation, management and fiscal return on investment. *Information Technology & Tourism*, 14(4), 347–362. 10.1007/s40558-014-0019-3

Smil, V. (2005). *Creating the twentieth century: Technical innovations of 1867-1914 and their lasting impact.* Oxford University Press. 10.1093/0195168747.001.0001

Smith, C. H., Molka-Danielsen, J., Rasool, J., & Webb-Benjamin, J. B. (2023). *The world as an interface: exploring the ethical challenges of the emerging metaverse.*

Smith, J. (2018). Enhancing communication and collaboration in event planning through mobile applications: Insights from [Your Application Name Here]. *Journal of Event Technology and Communication*, 5(1), 18–32.

Somova, O. (2023). *How the rating of social networks in Ukraine and the world has changed: current statistics after February 24, 2022.* SURLI. https://surl.li/echar

Song, X., Li, Y., Leung, X. Y., & Mei, D. (2023). Service robots and hotel guests' perceptions: Anthropomorphism and stereotypes. *Tourism Review*, 79(2), 505–522. 10.1108/TR-04-2023-0265

Soni, V. (2023). Adopting Generative AI in Digital Marketing Campaigns: An Empirical Study of Drivers and Barriers. *Sage Science Review of Applied Machine Learning*, 6(8), 1–15.

Sorrentino, A., Fu, X., Romano, R., Quintano, M., & Risitano, M. (2020). Measuring event experience and its behavioral consequences in the context of a sports mega-event. *Journal of Hospitality and Tourism Insights*, 3(5), 589–605. 10.1108/JHTI-03-2020-0026

Sox, C. B., Crews, T. B., & Kline, S. F. (2014, April). Virtual and hybrid meetings for generation X: Using the Delphi method to determine best practices, opportunities, and barriers. []. Routledge.]. *Journal of Convention & Event Tourism*, 15(2), 150–169. 10.1080/15470148.2014.896231

Spencer, J. P., & Bavuma, Z. (2018). *How important are mice to the tourism economy?* The Business and Management Review.

Spoladore, E., Geri, M., & Widmann, V. (2023). Strategic Communication in a Transnational Project—The Interreg Alpine Space Project HEALPS2. In Spoladore, D., Pessot, E., & Sacco, M. (Eds.), *Digital and Strategic Innovation for Alpine Health Tourism. Springer Briefs in Applied Sciences and Technology* (pp. 117–127). Springer. 10.1007/978-3-031-15457-7_8

Spracklen, K. (2015). *Digital leisure, the internet and popular culture: Communities and identities in a digital age.* Springer. 10.1057/9781137405876

Sritong, C., Sawangproh, W., & Teangsompong, T. (2024). Unveiling the adoption of metaverse technology in Bangkok metropolitan areas: A UTAUT2 perspective with social media marketing and consumer engagement. *PLoS One*, 19(6), e0304496. 10.1371/journal.pone.030449638848432

Stam, W., Arzlanian, S., & Elfring, T. (2014). Social capital of entrepreneurs and small firm performance: A meta-analysis of contextual and methodological moderators. *Journal of Business Venturing*, 29(1), 152–173. 10.1016/j.jbusvent.2013.01.002

Ştefănescu, D. C., & Papoi, A. (2020). NEW threats to the national security of states ⇓ Cyber threat. *Scientific Journal of Silesian University of Technology. Series Transport.* 10.20858/sjsutst.2020.107.13

Štilić, A., Nicić, M., &Puška, A. (2023). Check-in to the future: Exploring the impact of contemporary information technologies and artificial intelligence on the hotel industry. *Turističko-poslovanje,* (31).

Strohm, R. (2005). *The rise of European music, 1380-1500.* Cambridge University Press.

Suh, A., Cheung, C. M. K., Ahuja, M., & Wagner, C. (2017). Gamification in the Workplace: The Central Role of the Aesthetic Experience. *Journal of Management Information Systems,* 34(1), 268–305. 10.1080/07421222.2017.1297642

Sultana, S., Parvez, M., Khan, R. S., & Jalil, M. S. (2020). PERCEPTION OF EVENT MANAGEMENT COMPANY TOWARDS GREEN EVENT: EVIDENCE FROM BANGLADESH. *Academy of Strategic Management Journal.*

Suprabha, K., & Subramonian, G. (2015). Blended Learning Approach for Enhancing Students' Learning Experiences in a Knowledge Society. *Journal of Educational Technology, 11*(4), 1-7.

Suzuki, S., Kanematsu, H., Barry, D. M., Ogawa, N., Yajima, K., Nakahira, K. T., Shirai, T., Kawaguchi, M., Kobayashi, T., & Yoshitake, M. (2020). Virtual Experiments in Metaverse and their Applications to Collaborative Projects: The framework and its significance. *Procedia Computer Science,* 176, 2125–2132. 10.1016/j.procs.2020.09.249

Syah, F., & Rajoendah, M. I. K. (2022). The Role Model of MICE Activities After the COVID-19 Pandemic in Indonesia. *Journal of Tourism Education.* 10.17509/jote.v2i1.48875

Szekely, R., Mason, O., Frohlich, D., & Barley, E. (2024). "It's not everybody's snapshot. It's just an insight into that world": A qualitative study of multiple perspectives towards understanding the mental health experience and addressing stigma in healthcare students through virtual reality. *Digital Health,* 10, 20552076231223800. . 10.1177/20552076231223801381 88857

Talantis, S., Shin, Y. H., & Severt, K. (2020). Conference mobile application: Participant acceptance and the correlation with overall event satisfaction utilizing the technology acceptance model (TAM). *Journal of Convention & Event Tourism,* 21(2), 100–122. 10.1080/15470148.2020.1719949

Talavera, A. M., Al-Ghamdi, S. G., & Koç, M. (2019). Sustainability in mega-events: Beyond qatar 2022. In *Sustainability (Switzerland).* MDPI. 10.3390/su11226407

Talwar, S., Kaur, P., Nunkoo, R., & Dhir, A. (2022). Digitalization and sustainability: Virtual reality tourism in a post pandemic world. *Journal of Sustainable Tourism,* 1–28.

Tambralli, K. (2021). Event Management. ITSM. https://www.itsm-docs.com/blogs/itil-concepts/itsm-event-management

Compilation of References

Tang, Q., Yu, F. R., Xie, R., Boukerche, A., Huang, T., & Liu, Y. (2022). Internet of Intelligence: A survey on the enabling technologies, applications, and challenges. *IEEE Communications Surveys and Tutorials*, 24(3), 1394–1434. 10.1109/COMST.2022.3175453

Tanyildizi, E., & Orhan, A. (2009). A virtual electric machine laboratory for synchronous machine application. *Computer Applications in Engineering Education*, 17(2), 187–195. 10.1002/cae.20133

Tavakoli, R., & Wijesinghe, S. N. (2019). The evolution of the web and netnography in tourism: A systematic review. *Tourism Management Perspectives*, 29, 48–55. 10.1016/j.tmp.2018.10.008

Taveira, M. C., de Sa, J., & da Rosa, M. G. (2022). Virtual Reality-Induced Dissociative Symptoms: A Retrospective Study. *Games for Health Journal*, 11(4), 262–267. . 10.1089/g4h.2022.000935648035

Tawfeeq, T., & Alabdullah, Y. (2023). THE ROLE OF AUDIT COMMITTEES IN OMANI BUSINESS CONTEXT: DO THEY AFFECT THE PERFORMANCE OF NON-FINANCIAL COMPANIES. *JOURNAL OF HUMANITIES, SOCIAL SCIENCES AND BUSINESS*, 2(4), 643–659. 10.55047/jhssb.v2i4.707

Tayal, S., Rajagopal, K., & Mahajan, V. (2022). Virtual Reality based Metaverse of Gamification. *2022 6th International Conference on Computing Methodologies and Communication (ICCMC)*, 1597–1604. 10.1109/ICCMC53470.2022.9753727

Tayebinik, M., & Puteh, M. (2013). Blended Learning or E-learning? *arXiv preprint arXiv:1306.4085*.

Teixeira, S., Mota Veiga, P., Figueiredo, R., Fernandes, C., Ferreira, J. J., & Raposo, M. (2020). A systematic literature review on family business: Insights from an Asian context. *Journal of Family Business Management*, 10(4), 329–348. 10.1108/JFBM-12-2019-0078

Tempel, P., Schnelle, F., Pott, A., & Eberhard, P. (2015). Design and programming for cable-driven parallel robots in the German Pavilion at the EXPO 2015. *Machines (Basel)*, 3(3), 223–241. 10.3390/machines3030223

Teng, Z., Cai, Y., Gao, Y., Zhang, X., & Li, X. (2022). Factors affecting learners' adoption of an educational metaverse platform: An empirical study based on an extended UTAUT model. *Mobile Information Systems*, 2022(1), 5479215. 10.1155/2022/5479215

Thai-Van, H., Bakhos, D., Bouccara, D., Loundon, N., Marx, M., Mom, T., Mosnier, I., Roman, S., Villerabel, C., Vincent, C., & Venail, F. (2021). Telemedicine in Audiology. Best practice recommendations from the French Society of Audiology (SFA) and the French Society of Oto-rhinolaryngology-Head and Neck Surgery (SFORL). *European Annals of Otorhinolaryngology, Head and Neck Diseases*, 138(5), 363–375. . 10.1016/j.anorl.2020.10.00733097467

The Global Goals. (2023, December). Global Goals. https://www.globalgoals.org/goals/4-quality-education/

The Instapreneurs. (2023). *We generate ideas: How to create a content plan and why it is needed*. The Instapreneurs. https://www.theinstapreneurs.com.ua/blog-posts/how-to-create-a-content-plan

Thomson, A., Proud, I., Goldston, A. L., & Dodds-Gorman, R. (2021). Virtual reality for better event planning and management. In *Impact of ICTs on event management and marketing* (pp. 177–198). IGI Global. 10.4018/978-1-7998-4954-4.ch011

Tina Štemberger, S. Č. (2021). Attitudes Towards using Digital Technologies in Education as an Important Factor in Developing Digital Competence: The Case of Slovenian Student Teachers. *International Journal of Emerging Technologies in Learning*, 16(14), 83–98. 10.3991/ijet.v16i14.22649

Tiwari, P., Séraphin, H., & Chowdhary, N. R. (2021). Impacts of COVID-19 on tourism education: Analysis and perspectives. *Journal of Teaching in Travel & Tourism*, 21(4), 313–338. 10.1080/15313220.2020.1850392

Tkachenko, V., & Tkachenko, K. (2019). Leisure as the area of socio-cultural activity. *Bulletin of the Cherkasy National University named after Bohdan Khmelnytskyi*. https://ped-ejournal.cdu.edu.ua/article/view/3460

Topping, K. J., Douglas, W., Robertson, D., & Ferguson, N. (2022). Effectiveness of online and blended learning from schools: A systematic review. *Review of Education*, 10(2), e3353. 10.1002/rev3.3353

Torner, J., Skouras, S., Molinuevo, J. L., Gispert, J. D., & Alpiste, F. (2019). Multipurpose Virtual Reality Environment for Biomedical and Health Applications. *IEEE Transactions on Neural Systems and Rehabilitation Engineering : A Publication of the IEEE Engineering in Medicine and Biology Society, 27*(8), 1511–1520.

Torres, K. P. (2021). A virus and viral content: The Vietnam government's use of TikTok for public health messages during the COVID-19 pandemic. In Hutchins, A. L., & Tindall, N. T. (Eds.), *Public Relations and Online Engagement* (pp. 70–77). Routledge. 10.4324/9780429327094-10

Torrisi-Steele, G. (2011). This thing called blended learning–a definition and planning approach. *Research and Development in Higher Education: Reshaping Higher Education*, 34, 360–371.

Toubes, D. R., Araújo Vila, N., & Fraiz Brea, J. A. (2021). Changes in consumption patterns and tourist promotion after the COVID-19 pandemic. *Journal of Theoretical and Applied Electronic Commerce Research*, 16(5), 1332–1352. 10.3390/jtaer16050075

Trawnih, A., Al-Masaeed, S., Alsoud, M., & Alkufahy, A. (2022). Understanding artificial intelligence experience: A customer perspective. *International Journal of Data and Network Science*, 6(4), 1471–1484. 10.5267/j.ijdns.2022.5.004

Tremblay-Huet, S. (2020). COVID-19 leads to a new context for the "right to tourism": A reset of tourists' perspectives on space appropriation is needed. *Tourism Geographies*, 22(3), 720–723. 10.1080/14616688.2020.1759136

Tribe, J. (1997). The indiscipline of tourism. *Annals of Tourism Research*, 24(3), 638–657. 10.1016/S0160-7383(97)00020-0

Compilation of References

Tribe, J. (2000). Indisciplined and unsubstantiated. *Annals of Tourism Research*, 27(3), 809–813. 10.1016/S0160-7383(99)00122-X

Tribe, J. (2001). Research paradigms and the tourism curriculum. *Journal of Travel Research*, 39(4), 442–448. 10.1177/004728750103900411

Tsai, S. P. (2022). Investigating metaverse marketing for travel and tourism. *Journal of Vacation Marketing*, 13567667221145715.

Tsaur, S. H., & Tsai, C. H. (2023). Bleisure travel experience: Scale development and validation. *Journal of Travel & Tourism Marketing*, 40(1), 21–37. 10.1080/10548408.2023.2199773

Tsiakali, K. (2018). User-generated-content versus marketing-generated-content: Personality and content influence on traveler's behavior. *Journal of Hospitality Marketing &amp. Journal of Hospitality Marketing & Management*, 27(8), 946–972. 10.1080/19368623.2018.1477643

Tuomi, A. I. (2021). *Designing Restaurants of the Future: Integrating Robots into Hospitality Service* [Doctoral dissertation, University of Surrey].

Udin, W. N., Ramli, M., & Muzzazinah, . (2020, April). Virtual laboratory for enhancing students' understanding on abstract biology concepts and laboratory skills: A systematic review. []. IOP Publishing.]. *Journal of Physics: Conference Series*, 1521(4), 042025. 10.1088/1742-6596/1521/4/042025

Undheim, M. (2021). Children and teachers engaging together with digital technology in early childhood education and care institutions: A literature review. *European Early Childhood Education Research Journal*, 472–489.

United Nations. (2022). *Fast Facts – What is Sustainable Development?* UN. https://www.un.org/sustainabledevelopment/blog/2023/08/what-is-sustainable-development/

Ünlü, S., Yaşar, L., & Bilici, E. (2023). Metaverse as a Platform for Event Management: The Sample of the Metaverse Türkiye E-Magazine. *TRT Akademi*, 8(17), 122–143. 10.37679/trta.1202057

Usmani, S. S., Sharath, M., & Mehendale, M. (2022). Future of mental health in the metaverse. *General Psychiatry*, 35(4), e100825. . 10.1136/gpsych-2022-10082536189180

Üyesi Gonca, Ö., Davras, M., Uygulamalı, I., Üniversitesi, B., Fakültesi, T., Üyesi, Ö., Baykul, A., & Yüksekokulu, I. M. (2019)... *Türk Turizm Araştırmaları Dergisi ARAŞTIRMA MAKALESİ Akdeniz Ülkelerinde Turizm Sektörünün Ekonomik Etkinliğinin Değerlendirilmesi.*, 2019(3), 791–804. 10.26677/TR1010.2019.192

Valipour, M., Krasilnikof, J., Yannopoulos, S., Kumar, R., Deng, J., Roccaro, P., Mays, L., Grismer, M. E., & Angelakis, A. N. (2020). The evolution of agricultural drainage from the earliest times to the present. *Sustainability (Basel)*, 12(1), 416. 10.3390/su12010416

Vallée, A., Blacher, J., Cariou, A., & Sorbets, E. (2020). Blended learning compared to traditional learning in medical education: Systematic review and meta-analysis. *Journal of Medical Internet Research*, 22(8), e16504. 10.2196/1650432773378 van Brakel, V., Barreda-Ángeles, M., & Hartmann, T. (2023). Feelings of presence and perceived social support in social virtual reality platforms. *Computers in Human Behavior*, 139, 107523. 10.1016/j.chb.2022.107523

Van den Beemt, A., Groothuijsen, S., Ozkan, L., & Hendrix, W. (2023). Remote labs in higher engineering education: Engaging students with active learning pedagogy. *Journal of Computing in Higher Education*, 35(2), 320–340. 10.1007/s12528-022-09331-435974997

Van Winkle, C., & Bueddefeld, J. (2020). Information and communication technology in event management. *Handbook of e-Tourism*, 1-22.

Vasudavan, H., Razali, N. F., & Shah, D. A. (2023). Event Management Systems (EMS). *Article in Journal of Applied Research and Technology, 7*(2), 2600–7304. https://www.researchgate.net/publication/371874293

Vegt, N., Visch, V., de Ridder, H., & Vermeeren, A. (2014). Designing Gamification to Guide Competitive and Cooperative Behavior in Teamwork. *Gamification in Education and Business*, 513–533. 10.1007/978-3-319-10208-5_26

Venkatesh, S., Rao, Y. K., Nagaraja, H., Woolley, T., Alele, F. O., & Malau-Aduli, B. S. (2020). Factors influencing medical students' experiences and satisfaction with blended integrated E-learning. *Medical Principles and Practice*, 29(4), 396–402. 10.1159/00050521031801145

Venkatesh, V., & Davis, F. D. (2000). Theoretical extension of the Technology Acceptance Model: Four longitudinal field studies. *Management Science*, 46(2), 186–204. 10.1287/mnsc.46.2.186.11926

Verezomska, I., Bovsh, L., Baklan, H., & Prykhodko, K. (2022). Cyber protection of hotel brands. *Restaurant and Hotel Consulting.Innovations*, 5(2), 190–210. 10.31866/2616-7468.5.2.2022.270089

Verma, R., Vinoda, K. S., Papireddy, M., & Gowda, A. N. S. (2016). Toxic pollutants from plastic waste-a review. *Procedia Environmental Sciences*, 35, 701–708. 10.1016/j.proenv.2016.07.069

Vicente Díaz-Garcia, A. M.-N.-L.-S. (2023). Managing Digital Transformation: A Case Study in a Higher Education Institution. *Electronics (Basel)*, 12(11), 2522. 10.3390/electronics12112522

Vieira, E., & Medeiros, F. (2023). Feasibility of immersive environments in the metaverse for remote practical education in computer networks. In *ICERI2023 Proceedings* (pp. 7301-7310). IATED. 10.21125/iceri.2023.1815

Vimala, D., Evangelin, M. R., & Vasantha, S. (2022). Sustainability and Green Technology Innovation. In *Remittances Review*. 10.47059/rr.v7i2.2408

Voykina, E. A., N. G. (2019). The impact of digital technologies on the effectiveness of learning material by students in the educational process. *Proceedings of the 1st International Scientific Conference "Modern Management Trends and the Digital Economy: from Regional Development to Global Economic Growth" (MTDE 2019)*. Atlantis Press. 10.2991/mtde-19.2019.135

Compilation of References

Vuilleumier, P., Sander, D., & Baertschi, B. (2014). Changing the brain, changing the society: Clinical and ethical implications of neuromodulation techniques in neurology and psychiatry. *Brain Topography*, 27(1), 1–3. . 10.1007/s10548-013-0325-724158724

Vychivskyi, P., Malanyuk, T., Orlova, V., & Drychak, S. (2023). Modern approaches to understanding the essence of socio-cultural activity management in scientific literature. *Scientific Perspectives*, 4(34), 204–214. 10.52058/2708-7530-2023-4(34)-204-214

Wallace, K., & Michopoulou, E. (2023). Building Resilience and Understanding Complexities of Event Project Stakeholder Management. *Event Management*, 27(4), 499–517. 10.3727/1525 99522X16419948695143

Wang, C. X., Di Renzo, M., Stanczak, S., Wang, S., & Larsson, E. G. (2020). Artificial intelligence enabled wireless networking for 5G and beyond: Recent advances and future challenges. *IEEE Wireless Communications*, 27(1), 16–23. 10.1109/MWC.001.1900292

Wang, G., & Shin, C. (2022). Influencing factors of usage intention of metaverse education application platform: Empirical evidence based on PPM and TAM models. *Sustainability (Basel)*, 14(24), 17037. 10.3390/su142417037

Wang, J., Makowski, S., Cieślik, A., Lv, H., & Lv, Z. (2023). Fake news in virtual community, virtual society, and metaverse: A survey. *IEEE Transactions on Computational Social Systems*.

Wang, W. X., & Zhou, F., Wan, Y. L., & Ning, H. S. (2022). A survey of metaverse technology. *Chinese Journal of Engineering*, 44(4), 744–756.

Wang, Y. C., & Uysal, M. (2024). Artificial intelligence-assisted mindfulness in tourism, hospitality, and events. *International Journal of Contemporary Hospitality Management*, 36(4), 1262–1278. 10.1108/IJCHM-11-2022-1444

Wassler, P. (2023). Covid-19 and the Host Community: Towards an Uncertain Future? In *Changing Practices of Tourism Stakeholders in Covid-19 Affected Destinations* (pp. 1-12). Channel View Publications.

WCED. (1987). *Our Common Future*. Oxford University Press.

Webster, C. & Cain, L. (2024) Regulation, Automated Technologies, and Competitiveness in the Hospitality Industry. *Journal of Hospitality and Tourism Research*. OnlineFirst.

Webster, C. (2021). Demography as a Driver of Robonomics. *ROBONOMICS: The Journal of the Automated Economy, 1*, 12. https://journal.robonomics.science/index.php/rj/article/view/12

Webster, C. (2022). War of the Default Settings. *ROBONOMICS: The Journal of the Automated Economy, 3*, 38. https://journal.robonomics.science/index.php/rj/article/view/38

Webster, C., & Ivanov, S. (2021). Attitudes towards robots in tourism: robophobes vs. robophiles. In Farmaki, A., & Pappas, N. (Eds.), *Emerging Transformations in Tourism and Hospitality* (pp. 66–82). Routledge. 10.4324/9781003105930-6

Wee, H., Mustapha, N. A., & Anas, M. S. (2021). Characteristic of green event practices in mice tourism: A systematic literature review. *International Journal of Academic Research in Business & Social Sciences*, 11(16), 271–291. 10.6007/IJARBSS/v11-i16/11234

Weiner, E., McNew, R., Trangenstein, P., & Gordon, J. (2010). Using the virtual reality world of second life to teach nursing faculty simulation management. *Studies in Health Technology and Informatics*, 160(Pt 1), 615–619. [REMOVED HYPERLINK FIELD]20841760

Wen, J., Wang, C. C., & Kozak, M. (2021). Post-COVID-19 Chinese domestic tourism market recovery: Potential influence of traditional Chinese medicine on tourist behaviour. *Anatolia*, 32(1), 121–125. 10.1080/13032917.2020.1768335

Wenzlhuemer, R. (2013). *Connecting the nineteenth-century world: The telegraph and globalization*. Cambridge University Press.

Werbach, K. (2014). (Re)Defining Gamification: A Process Approach. *Persuasive Technology*, 266–272. 10.1007/978-3-319-07127-5_23

Werbach, K., & Hunter, D. (2012). *For the win: how game thinking can revolutionize your business*. Wharton Digital Press.

Werner, K., Junek, O., & Wang, C. (2022). Event Management Skills In The Post-Covid-19 World: Insights From China, Germany, And Australia. *Event Management*, 26(4), 867–882. 10.3727/152599521X16288665119558

Westera, W., Prada, R., Mascarenhas, S., Santos, P. A., Dias, J., Guimarães, M., Georgiadis, K., Nyamsuren, E., Bahreini, K., Yumak, Z., Christyowidiasmoro, C., Dascalu, M., Gutu-Robu, G., & Ruseti, S. (2020). Artificial intelligence moving serious gaming: Presenting reusable game AI components. *Education and Information Technologies*, 25(1), 351–380. 10.1007/s10639-019-09968-2

Westmattelmann, D., Grotenhermen, J. G., Sprenger, M., & Schewe, G. (2021). The show must go on-virtualisation of sport events during the COVID-19 pandemic. *European Journal of Information Systems*, 30(2), 119–136. 10.1080/0960085X.2020.1850186

Wickham, M., Donnelly, T., & French, L. (2021). Strategic Sustainability Management in the Event Sector. *Event Management*, 25(3), 279–296. 10.3727/152599519X15506259856318

Widjaja, G., & Aslan, A. (2022). Blended learning method in the view of learning and teaching strategy in geography study programs in higher education. *Nazhruna: Jurnal Pendidikan Islam*, 5(1), 22–36. 10.31538/nzh.v5i1.1852

Wilson, L. S., Stevenson, D. R., & Cregan, P. (2010). Telehealth on advanced networks. *Telemedicine Journal and E-Health : The Official Journal of the American Telemedicine Association*, 16(1), 69–79.

Wood, L. C., & Reiners, T. (2014). *Gamification*. IGI Global. 10.4018/978-1-4666-5888-2.ch297

Compilation of References

Wu, E., Diao, Y., & Rizvi, S. (2006). High-performance complex event processing over streams. *Proceedings of the ACM SIGMOD International Conference on Management of Data*, (pp. 407–418). ACM. 10.1145/1142473.1142520

Xiao, C. (2020). A novel approach of consultation on 2019 novel coronavirus (COVID-19)-related psychological and mental problems: Structured letter therapy. *Psychiatry Investigation*, 17(2), 175–185. 10.30773/pi.2020.004732093461

Xie, X., Siau, K., & Nah, F. F. H. (2020). COVID-19 pandemic–online education in the new normal and the next normal. *Journal of information technology case and application research*, 22(3), 175-187.

Xie, T., Wang, X., Cifuentes-Faura, J., & Xing, Y. (2023). Integrating immersive experience into hybrid education: A case study in fintech experimental education. *Scientific Reports*, 13(1), 22762. 10.1038/s41598-023-50259-138123646

Xi, N., Chen, J., Gama, F., Korkeila, H., & Hamari, J. (2024). Acceptance of the metaverse: A laboratory experiment on augmented and virtual reality shopping. *Internet Research*, 34(7), 82–117. 10.1108/INTR-05-2022-0334

Xin, S., Tribe, J., & Chambers, D. (2013). Conceptual research in tourism. *Annals of Tourism Research*, 41, 66–88. 10.1016/j.annals.2012.12.003

Xu, A., Johari, S. A., Khademolomoom, A. H., Khabaz, M. T., Umurzoqovich, R. S., Hosseini, S., & Semiromi, D. T. (2023). Investigation of management of international education considering sustainable medical tourism and entrepreneurship. *Heliyon*, 9(1), e12691. . 10.1016/j.heliyon.2022.e1269136685466

Xue, X., Yang, X., Deng, Z., Tu, H., Kong, D., Li, N., & Xu, F. (2021). Global Trends and Hotspots in Research on Rehabilitation Robots: A Bibliometric Analysis From 2010 to 2020. *Frontiers in Public Health*, 9, 806723. . 10.3389/fpubh.2021.80672335087788

Xu, X. (2023). To social with social distance: A case study on a VR-enabled graduation celebration amidst the pandemic. *Virtual Reality (Waltham Cross)*, 27(4), 3319–3331. 10.1007/s10055-022-00646-235464641

Xu, Y., Liu, W., He, T., & Tsai, S. B. (2024). Buzzword or fuzzword: An event study of the metaverse in the Chinese stock market. *Internet Research*, 34(1), 174–194. 10.1108/INTR-07-2022-0526

Yang, D. (2021). RETRACTED: Online sports tourism platform based on FPGA and machine learning. *Microprocessors and Microsystems*, 80, 103584. 10.1016/j.micpro.2020.103584

Yang, K., Zhang, Z., Tian, Y., & Ma, J. (2023). A secure authentication framework to guarantee the traceability of avatars in metaverse. *IEEE Transactions on Information Forensics and Security*, 18, 3817–3832. 10.1109/TIFS.2023.3288689

Yang, Y., Zhang, C. X., & Rickly, J. M. (2021). A review of early COVID-19 research in tourism: Launching the Annals of Tourism Research's Curated Collection on coronavirus and tourism. *Annals of Tourism Research*, 91, 103313. 10.1016/j.annals.2021.10331334611371

Yasini, M., & Marchand, G. (2016). Adoption and Use of a Mobile Health Application in Older Adults for Cognitive Stimulation. *Studies in Health Technology and Informatics*, 221, 13–17. [REMOVED HYPERLINK FIELD]27071867

Yasin, N., Majid Gilani, S. A., & Nair, G. (2021). "Dump the paper quiz"—The PERI model for exploring gamification in student learning in the United Arab Emirates. *Industry and Higher Education*, 095042222110550. 10.1177/09504222211055067

Yassin, A. A. B. (2022). The Effect of Using Interactive Simulation (Phet) and Virtual Laboratories (Praxilabs) on Tenth-Grade Students' Achievement in Physics. *Britain International of Linguistics Arts and Education (BIoLAE). Journal*, 4(2), 58–72.

Ye, H., & Law, R. (2021). Impact of COVID-19 on hospitality and tourism education: A case study of Hong Kong. *Journal of Teaching in Travel & Tourism*, 21(4), 428–436. 10.1080/15313220.2021.1875967

Yeh, S. S. (2021). Tourism recovery strategy against COVID-19 pandemic. *Tourism Recreation Research*, 46(2), 188–194. 10.1080/02508281.2020.1805933

Yemenici, A. D. (2022). Entrepreneurship in the world of Metaverse: Virtual or real? *Journal of Metaverse*, 2(2), 71–82. 10.57019/jmv.1126135

Yen, T. H., Wey, P. S., & Sullivan, K. (2016, May). Classification of Event and Meeting Technology. In *International Interdisciplinary Business-Economics Advancement Conference* (p. 88).

Yeoman, I., Robertson, M., & Smith, K. (2014). A futurist's view on the future of events. In *The Routledge handbook of events* (pp. 518–536). Routledge.

Youssef, A., Lashley, E. E. L. O., Vermeulen, N., & van der Hoorn, M. L. P. (2023). Identifying discrepancies between clinical practice and evidence-based guideline in recurrent pregnancy loss care, a tool for clinical guideline implementation. *BMC Pregnancy and Childbirth*, 23(1), 544. . 10.1186/s12884-023-05869-y37507697

You, X., Zhang, C., Tan, X., Jin, S., & Wu, H. (2018, October 26). AI for 5G: Research directions and paradigms. *Springer Nature*, 62(2), 1589–1602. 10.1360/N112018-00174

Yung, R., Le, T. H., Moyle, B., & Arcodia, C. (2022). Towards a typology of virtual events. *Tourism Management*, 92, 104560. 10.1016/j.tourman.2022.104560

Zadro, L., Williams, K. D., & Richardson, R. (2004). How low can you go? Ostracism by a computer is sufficient to lower self-reported levels of belonging, control, self-esteem, and meaningful existence. *Journal of Experimental Social Psychology*, 40(4), 560–567. 10.1016/j.jesp.2003.11.006

Zagorski-Thomas, S. (2016). The Influence of Recording Technology and Practice on Popular Music Performance in the Recording Studio in Poland between 1960-1989. *Polish Sociological Review*, 196(4), 531–548.

Zain, S. (2021). Digital transformation trends in education. *Future Directions in Digital Information*, 223-234.

Compilation of References

Zhang, M. W. B., & Ho, R. C. M. (2017). Smartphone applications for immersive virtual reality therapy for internet addiction and internet gaming disorder. *Technology and Health Care : Official Journal of the European Society for Engineering and Medicine, 25*(2), 367–372.

Zhang, J., Quoquab, F., & Mohammad, J. (2024). Metaverse tourism and Gen-Z and Gen-Y's motivation: "will you, or won't you travel virtually?". *Tourism Review*, 79(2), 304–320. 10.1108/TR-06-2023-0393

Zhang, S. N., Li, Y. Q., Ruan, W. Q., & Liu, C. H. (2022). Would you enjoy virtual travel? The characteristics and causes of virtual tourists' sentiment under the influence of the COVID-19 pandemic. *Tourism management, 88*, 104429.

Zhang, Z., Cao, T., Shu, J., & Liu, H. (2022). Identifying key factors affecting college students' adoption of the e-learning system in mandatory blended learning environments. *Interactive Learning Environments*, 30(8), 1388–1401. 10.1080/10494820.2020.1723113

Zhao, L., Zhao, Y., Bu, L., Sun, H., Tang, W., Li, K., Zhang, W., Tang, W., & Zhang, Y. (2023). Design Method of a Smart Rehabilitation Product Service System Based on Virtual Scenarios: A Case Study. *IEEE Transactions on Neural Systems and Rehabilitation Engineering : A Publication of the IEEE Engineering in Medicine and Biology Society, 31*, 4570–4579.

Zhao, Z., Ma, Y., Mushtaq, A., Rajper, A. M. A., Shehab, M., Heybourne, A., Song, W., Ren, H., & Tse, Z. T. H. (2022). Applications of robotics, artificial intelligence, and digital technologies during COVID-19: A review. *Disaster Medicine and Public Health Preparedness*, 16(4), 1634–1644. 10.1017/dmp.2021.933413717

Zheng, X., Lin, F., & Cai, X. (2021). Exploration of Contextual Marketing Model Based on Mobile Apps. *Proceedings of the 6th Annual International Conference on Social Science and Contemporary Humanity Development (SSCHD 2020)*. Atlantis Press. 10.2991/assehr.k.210121.017

Zhou, H., Gao, J.-Y., & Chen, Y. (2022). The paradigm and future value of the metaverse for the intervention of cognitive decline. *Frontiers in Public Health*, 10, 1016680. . 10.3389/fpubh.2022.101668036339131

Zhou, Y., Huang, H., Yuan, S., Zou, H., Xie, L., & Yang, J. (2023). Metafi++: Wifi-enabled transformer-based human pose estimation for metaverse avatar simulation. *IEEE Internet of Things Journal*, 10(16), 14128–14136. 10.1109/JIOT.2023.3262940

Zuccoli, A., & Korstanje, M. E. (2023a). The Future of Tourism Education Just after the COVID-19. In *The Role of Pleasure to Improve Tourism Education* (pp. 93–107). Springer International Publishing. 10.1007/978-3-031-21580-3_6

Zuccoli, A., Seraphin, H., & Korstanje, M. (2022). The Role of Pleasure (Joy) in Enhancing Pregraduate Students' Creativity. In *Strategic Entrepreneurial Ecosystems and Business Model Innovation* (pp. 113–123). Emerald Publishing Limited. 10.1108/978-1-80382-137-520221008

About the Contributors

Sharad Kumar Kulshreshtha (b. 1978), is an Assistant Professor at the Department of Tourism and Hotel Management, North-Eastern Hill University, Shillong-Meghalaya (India). He has acclaimed publications research papers in various books, journals of national and international repute and participated in national and international Seminars and Conferences. including International Conference on Wine Market and Cultures of Consumption in SHTM the Hong Kong Polytechnic University, Hong Kong. His area of research interest is Event Management, Health & Wellness, Sustainable Tourism. He has also been invited as a resource person in various universities and business associations of India to deliver talks as subject experts. He has co-edited books on 'Emerging Dynamics of India Tourism & Hospitality: Transformation and Innovation' and Global Developments in Healthcare and Medical Tourism Advance in Hospitality, Tourism, and the Service Industry (AHTSI) Book Series, IGI Global, U.S.A., Virus Outbreaks, and Tourism Mobility: Strategy to Encounter Global Health Hazards, Publisher: Emerald Publishing Limited under Book Series: Tourism Security Safety and Post Conflict Destinations Series

Craig Webster (Ph.D.) is a Professor in the Department of Applied Business Studies at Ball State University, USA. He studied Government and German Literature at St. Lawrence University in New York State, received an MA and Ph.D. in Political Science from Binghamton University in New York State and an MBA Intercollege, Cyprus. He has taught at Binghamton University, Ithaca College, the College of Tourism and Hotel Management, and the University of Nicosia. His research interests include the political economy of tourism, event management, robots and artificial intelligence in tourism and hospitality, public opinion analysis, and human rights.

***

About the Contributors

Sunildro L.S. Akoijam is currently working as an Associate Professor in the area of Marketing and Strategy at the Department of Management, North-Eastern Hill University (NEHU), A Central University, Meghalaya (India). He is currently the secretary of North Eastern Management Association (NEMA), India. He has more than 13 years of teaching experience at university level. He teaches the students of both PG and PhD levels. He has presented research papers in 62 international and national seminars and conferences. He has published more than 50 research papers in various reputed international and national journals and 18 book chapters. He has published 12 books in various fields of management. He has completed 1 major research project sponsored by ICSSR, New Delhi. He has successfully guided two PhD research scholars and currently four research scholars are pursuing PhD under his supervision. He is associated with 22 premier journals as Editorial board member and Reviewer. He has reviewed more than 100 research papers of various premier journals published by Emerald (UK), Sage (US), Routledge (UK), Springer (US), Inderscience (Switzerland) etc. He has delivered lectures/sessions in more than 45 National and International academic programmes like Conference, Seminar, Refresher Course, Workshop, FDP, EDP, MTP etc. He has also participated in 106 workshops, symposiums, Faculty Development Programmes, short term certificate courses and academic related activities organized by premier management institutes in different parts of the country and abroad. He has visited foreign countries like South Korea, Singapore, Thailand, Malaysia, United Arab Emirates (UAE), Sri Lanka, Nepal, Bhutan, Mauritius, Indonesia and Myanmar for various academic programmes. He has also organized 34 academic events like seminars, conferences, workshops, training courses, symposium, management fest etc. He is a member of 21 International and National Associations and Bodies in various Management and allied disciplines.

Aarti Chopra is a seasoned academician with over 18 years of teaching and administrative experience in higher education. She is an admired teacher and an efficient administrator. Besides her Masters and Doctorate in Business Administration, she also holds a professional law degree. She is the national gold medalist in Public Relation Program. She is the author of several books and research papers on various topics related to commerce and management. She is also an active member of NGO working actively for the promotion of Khadi and sustainable fashion. She is the member of many professional organisations and the joint secretary of a leading research organisation. Dr Chopra is the former student union president of Kanoria Mahila Mahavidyalaya and vice president of KMM alumni association. She is the recipient of many awards as Education Icon Award, Excellence in Academics Award and Mahila Shakti Award. She is also SHRM certified corporate trainer.

Sarada Prasad Dakua currently serves as a Senior Research Scientist at the Department of Surgery, Hamad Medical Corporation, Qatar. Additionally, he holds a position as a Clinical Assistant Professor at Qatar University. With over 15 years of research experience, his expertise spans computer vision, image processing, simulation, augmented reality, virtual reality, and in vitro disease modelling of neurological diseases. He has successfully secured over 20 funded research grants totalling multimillion US dollars from institutions such as QNRF, MRC, AHS, IRGC, etc. He has authored over 115 peer-reviewed journal and conference papers in alignment with his research interests. Apart from his academic endeavours, he engages in activities like reviewing research proposals and articles, editing journal submissions, and mentoring master's and Ph.D. students. He earned his Ph.D. in medical image processing from the Indian Institute of Technology Guwahati and holds an MBA degree in finance, along with PMP certification.

Gaurav Kumar Gupta is currently the senior Lecturer serving at J.S. University, Shikohabad, Distt Firozabad. He did his Ph.D. (Commerce) from Dr. Bhimrao Ambedkar University, Agra. He has published research articles in journals and conference proceedings

Vandana Gupta, Ph.D, MBA, M.Com, B.Sc., UGC NET qualified, RSLET qualified. She is working as Head, Department of Commerce & Management Studies in L M College of Science & Technology (Autonomous), Jodhpur. She is having more than 15 years of teaching experience in both UG & PG. Her area of expertise is Strategic Management, Economics, Law, Project Management, Marketing and Finance. She is having more than 40 reputed National and International publications.

Ahdi Hassan is serving as a Researcher at Global Institute for Research Education & Scholarship, Amsterdam, Netherlands, Commissioning Editor, IGI Global publisher publishes more than 300 journals quarterly and semi-annually, Researcher, "Vanishing Languages and Cultural Heritage", Austrian Academy of Sciences, and representative of Imperial English UK-A Trusted British Brand in English Language, Independent Research International [IRI] and Advisor Scholarly Journal Management. He has been Associate or Consulting Editor of numerous journals and also served the editorial review board from 2013- to till now. He has a number of publications and research papers published in various domains. He invited as keynote speaker in International conferences more than 50. He has given contribution with the major roles such as using modern and scientific techniques to work with sounds and meanings of words, studying the relationship between the written and spoken formats of various Asian/European languages, developing the artificial languages in coherence with modern English language, and scientifically approaching the various ancient written material to trace its origin. He teaches topics connected but not limited to communication such as English for Young Learners, English for Academic Purposes, English for Science, Technology and Engineering, English for Business and Entrepreneurship, Business Intensive Course, Applied Linguistics, interpersonal communication, verbal and nonverbal communication, cross cultural competence, language and humor, intercultural communication, culture and humor, language acquisition and language in use.

Maximiliano E. Korstanje is editor in chief of International Journal of Safety and Security in Tourism (UP Argentina) and Editor in Chief Emeritus of International Journal of Cyber Warfare and Terrorism (IGI-Global US). Korstanje is Senior Researchers in the Department of Economics at University of Palermo, Argentina. In 2015 he was awarded as Visiting Research Fellow at School of Sociology and Social Policy, University of Leeds, UK and the University of La Habana Cuba. In 2017 is elected as Foreign Faculty Member of AMIT, Mexican Academy in the study of Tourism, which is the most prominent institutions dedicated to tourism research in Mexico. He had a vast experience in editorial projects working as advisory member of Elsevier, Routledge, Springer, IGI global and Cambridge Scholar publishing. Korstanje had visited and given seminars in many important universities worldwide. He has also recently been selected to take part of the 2018 Albert Nelson Marquis Lifetime Achievement Award. a great distinction given by Marquis Who´s Who in the world.

Chitra Krishnan, Ph.D.,Symbiosis Centre for Management Studies, Noida, Symbiosis International (Deemed University) India, Teaching professional with over 16 years of national and International experience. She possesses excellence in teaching and research. Before her academic career, she worked in industry in various positions of responsibility. She has been actively involved in rigorous academic pursuits in the field of higher professional education to enhance skill sets that promote the holistic development of learners. She has a number of publications in acclaimed journals at the National and International level and has also participated in many national and international conferences. She is passionate about writing and has six books to her credit with International publishers. She has been empaneled as a member of the review committee for conferences and journals of repute. Her area of interest includes Human Resource Management, Organization Behavior, Talent Management, Diversity Management, Employee Satisfaction, Knowledge Management, Artificial Intelligence, and Emotional Intelligence.

Narendra Kumar earned his Ph. D. from JS University, Shikohabad, India and currently working as Assistant Professor at Amity Institute of Travel & Tourism, Amity University, Noida. With 23 years of experience in travel & tourism, he has made significant contributions to the area of tourism education. Dr. Kumar has a strong interest in Business travel, tourist behaviour and visitor experiences in the field of tourism and has published extensively on related topics. In addition to his academic pursuits, Dr. Kumar is actively involved in helping young graduates of tourism and hospitality domain to help them in establishing their start-ups. He has been invited to speak at numerous conferences and seminars on tourism and related fields and his current research focuses on student mentoring. Dr. Kumar's previous works include one edited book on "Tourist Behaviour" published by Apple Academic Press, USA; one book on "Digital Marketing" and one on "Ethical Aspects of Business in Tourism".

About the Contributors

Sunil Kumar has a PhD. in Hospitality Management /CTU (2023. Master of Hotel Management/ UOU (2018) Diploma in Hotel Management & Catering Technology / (Boad of Technical Education, Lucknow (2004). Bachelor of Commerce/ CCSU (2003) Director Academics of Full time at Institute of Hospitality, Management and Sciences, Kotdwar, Uttarakhand.

Supriya Lamba Sahdev is is a certified trained academician, researcher, and a certified coach with 12+ years of experience in the field of Marketing and International Business, is currently working as Associate Professor + HOD Marketing and Head of International Office at ISBR Business School, Bengaluru, Karnataka, India. Prior to this she has worked with Amity University, Uttar Pradesh for 10+ years. She has done her double bachelors- in Commerce and Education and her double masters- in Commerce and Education. She has done Ph.D. in Management in the area of Open Innovation in Indian Food Processing SMEs. Having an enriched research portfolio with the peer-reviewed publication in International and National Journals, book chapters, and conference presentations across top tier journals in Management. Presently has to her credit more than 50 plus Research Papers in UGC and SCOPUS publications in reputed national and international journals accompanied with hundreds of Research participation in International/National Conferences. She is serving as a member ofreview/ editor committee for multiple conferences and journals. She has conducted more than 4 International Conferences as the Co-Convener. She had acted as the special session-conference chair for more than 6 International Conferences. She is also acting as the Lead Editor for 10 journals. She has also delivered several invited talks and seminars at several platforms of national and international repute. She got 3 patents published out of which 2 are granted. And has edited one book as the first author. Demonstrating exceptional leadership skills, Dr. Supriya Lamba Sahdev has held the position of Head of International Programs, underscoring her global outlook and commitment to fostering international partnerships. Her academic expertise traverses' various domains within Research Methodology, Digital Marketing, Service Marketing, Marketing Analytics, Gamification in Marketing, International Marketing, Open Innovation, International Business, Trade Analytics, International Documentation and Logistics, International Trade, Big data analytics, Artificial Intelligence in the area of International Business and Marketing. Throughout her illustrious career, Dr. Supriya has made significant contributions to the academic community, remaining at the forefront of technological advancements. With a comprehensive skill set, she is widely recognized as an authority in her field, making invaluable contributions to research, education, and international collaboration.

Vaniki Joshi Lohani is an Assistant Professor based at Atal Bihari Vajpayee School of Management and Entrepreneurship, Jawaharlal Nehru University, New Delhi, India. Her research area includes financial analyses, capital markets, technology adoption in the banking sector and financial inclusion.

Dalamchwami Chen Lyngdoh has completed his B.Tech degree in Biomedical Engineering from North-Eastern Hill University, Shillong, Meghalaya and completed his M.Tech degree in Biomedical Engineering from Vellore Institute of Technology, Vellore, Tamil Nadu. He has worked with PATH (Program for Appropriate Technology in Health) from June to December 2021. He is currently pursuing his Ph.D degree at the Department of Biomedical Engineering, North-Eastern Hill University, Shillong, Meghalaya. His areas of interest are Medical Image Processing, Artificial Intelligence and Deep Learning in Image Processing, and Biomedical Instrumentation.

Aarti Madan is a PhD candidate based at Atal Bihari Vajpayee School of Management and Entrepreneurship, Jawaharlal Nehru University, New Delhi, India. Her research area includes technology adoption, gamification, and consumer behaviour. She has numerous papers to her credit. She has presented her PhD work in various national and international conferences.

Ravi Kant Modi works as a Professor & Dean, at Nirwan University Jaipur. He is a distinguished faculty member with extensive 13years of teaching experience. His contribution to research solidifies his position as a highly accomplished researcher and scholar. Dr. Modi is an active member of several professional bodies, staying connected with the latest developments in his field. He has organized numerous online and offline conferences, seminars, FDP, workshops as Conference Secretary, showcasing his commitment to advancing knowledge and fostering intellectual exchange. As an author, Dr. Modi has contributed to the academic community through his textbooks and edited books. Moreover, he has published over 40 papers in renowned National and International journals, including notable Scopus journals. His expertise in research is further exemplified by his position as an editorial board member for reputable journals. Dr. Modi is an avid participant in academic conferences and seminars, having attended more than 50 events where he has presented his research. His comprehensive knowledge and rich academic background make him an invaluable Mentor.

Kamel Mouloudj is a Professor in the College of Economic at University of Medea (Algeria). His researches have focused primarily on studies predicting the behavior of individuals (including customers, employees, students, etc.). He earned her Bachelor of Science in Commercial Sciences and Master of Marketing from University of Blida, and Doctor of Marketing from University of Algiers 3. He has over 18 years of teaching experience and has over 35 publications. He participated in three research projects at the University of Medea on industrial marketing, energy, and green start-ups. He is Chair of Doctoral Training Committee at department of commercial sciences from 2019 to now (2024).

Gajendra Kumar Mourya is currently an Assistant Professor in the Department of Biomedical Engineering, School of Technology, North-Eastern Hill University (NEHU), Shillong. He completed his B.E. in Biomedical Engineering from Samrat Ashok Technological Institute (SATI) Vidisha 2007. He received his M.Tech degree in Biomedical Engineering from the Indian Institute of Technology-Banaras Hindu University (IIT-BHU), Varanasi. He completed his Ph.D (Biomedical Engineering) degree in field of Medical Image Processing from North-Eastern Hill University (NEHU), Shillong. His research interests are Biomedical Image Analysis, Medical Image Processing, Machine Learning and Artificial Intelligence, Deep Learning, Virtual Instrumentation, Augmented Reality, Biomedical Instrumentation, and Biomedical Signal Analysis and Processing.

Akshay Nain is working as an Assistant Professor at the Amity School of Hospitality in Amity University Haryana. He has teaching experience of ten years. His specialization is in Front Office and his credentials may be verified on various research platforms like Google Scholar, LinkedIn and Research Gate.

Mildred Deri is working as lecturer in Hospitality and Tourism at University of Energy and Natural Resources, Ghana.

Nitin Sahai completed M.Tech. degree in Biomedical Engineering from Motilal Nehru National Institute of Technology, India in 2010, Ph.D. degree in Biomedical Engineering from North Eastern Hill University (NEHU), India in 2022. Currently he is working as an Assistant Professor, Department of Biomedical Engineering, NEHU, India from 2012 also he completed his Visiting Post-Doctoral Fellow at 3D Printing and Visualisation Centre, University of Pecs, Hungary from March 2023 -24. His area of specialization are 3D Printing, Biomechanics & Rehabilitation Engineering, Tissue Engineering, Biomaterials and having 14 years of undergraduate, Postgraduate and PhD level of teaching experience

About the Contributors

Sanjeev Kumar Saxena currently holds the position of Associate Professor in the Department of Hospitality & Tourism Management at Assam University, a Central University located in Silchar. With a remarkable career spanning over 31 years in both the industry and academia, Dr. Saxena's journey in the field of hospitality began in 1992 when he joined The Taj Group of Hotels as a Kitchen Management Trainee. He dedicated more than five years to Taj Group before transitioning to the role of lecturer at the Institute of Hotel Management in Jodhpur, where he served for over nine years. In 2007, he embarked on a new chapter of his career by joining Jaypee Hotels as a Additional General Manager (Training), contributing five years of expertise to their team. Subsequently, he assumed the role of Principal at IHM Silvassa, affiliated with the National Council for Hotel Management, New Delhi. After a year at IHM Silvassa, Dr. Saxena returned to Jaypee Hotels & Resorts in 2013 and made significant contributions over the next eight years as Additional General Manager (HR,Learning & Development) and Head of Jaypee Hotel Training Centre Agra. Dr. Saxena's educational background is equally impressive, holding a three-year Diploma in Hotel Management from IHM Lucknow, B.Sc in Hotel & Hospitality Administration, B.Com, M.Com in Business Administration (earning him a Gold Medal), an MBA, and a PhD in Human Resource. He has also successfully completed leadership programs from renowned institutions such as IIT Kharagpur, as well as courses in Strategic Management, Essentials of Marketing, and Customer Relationship Management from IIM Bangalore, and Management of Field Sales and Management of New Product & Services from IIT Kanpur. As a scholar, Dr. Saxena has made significant contributions, with 24 research papers published in esteemed journals indexed in Scopus, UGC, and peer-reviewed databases. Additionally, he has authored seven books and provided guidance to two PhD scholars and one MPhil scholar in their research pursuits.

Rajeev Semwal, an accomplished academician, holds the position of Assistant Professor and Head of the Department at Amity Institute of Travel and Tourism, situated within the vibrant campus of Amity University in Greater Noida. His academic journey is marked by a Ph.D. and UGC Net in tourism, coupled with credentials including MTM, PGDTTM, B.A. (TTM), and a diploma in building design. Over the past 12 years, Dr. Semwal has made notable contributions to the industry, from community-based tourism to adventure marketing. At the Greater Noida campus, he passionately imparts knowledge, specializing in cultural heritage tourism, adventure tourism, sustainable tourism development, and strategic tourism marketing, shaping the future leaders of the tourism industry.

Swati Sharma earned her Ph.D. from Kurukshetra University, India and has qualified UGC NET twice. She is currently Associate Professor at Amity Institute of Travel & Tourism, Amity University, Noida. With 18 years of experience in travel & tourism academia and industry, she has made significant contributions to the area of tourism. Dr. Sharma has a strong interest in MICE Tourism and Destination Image and has published extensively on related topics. She has been invited to speak at numerous conferences and seminars on tourism and related fields. She keeps a track of the changing dimensions of business travel. Dr. Sharma's previous works include one edited book on "Tourist Behaviour" published by Apple Academic Press, USA; one book on "Research Methodology" and one on "Ethical Aspects of Business in Tourism". She brings a unique perspective to the current chapter, drawing on her extensive knowledge and experience in tourism and hospitality academia.

U N Shukla (b.1968) is a Professor in Institute of Tourism and Hotel Management Dr. Bhimrao Ambedkar University, Agra (U.P.). He has completed his qualifications M.Sc, M.T.A., Ph.D. in Tourism Management. He has twenty six years teaching experiences of university level and contributed in teaching as well as in research. He has been a Head in Department of Travel & Tourism Management, Department of Hotel Management and also the Director in Institute of Tourism and Hotel Management Dr. Bhimrao Ambedkar University, Agra. He has also been a Dean Faculty of Management, in his university. He is a member of Board of Studies- Academic committee's of tourism in various universities of the country. He has served as a member of Board of Studies-Academic committees, Academic Council as well as Court of this University. He has a vast experience of visiting the country of abroad such as Sri Lanka, Indonesia, Malaysia & Italy during presentation of research papers in many national and international conferences. He has been invited as an expert as well as resource person by many forums of academicians to deliver talks on Sustainable and Eco Tourism, Adventure Tourism, Personality Development and Spiritual Management. He has contributed his research articles in more than twenty five books, magazines and journals of national and international fame. He has guided many research scholars in the field of Tourism and Hospitality. He has been life time member of different tourism bodies, social organizations of the country. He has edited a book on 'Emerging Dynamics of Indian Tourism and Hospitality' while another book on Incredible Tourism of India: Potentials, Policies and Practices by Copal Publishing Group India is under publication.

Amrik Singh is working as Professor in the School of Hotel Management and Tourism at Lovely Professional University, Punjab, India. He obtained his Ph.D. degree in Hotel Management from Kurukshetra University, Kurukshetra. He started his academic career at Lovely Professional University, Punjab, India in the year 2007. He has published more than 40 research papers in UGC and peer-reviewed and Scopus/Web of Science) journals. He has published 12 patents and 01 patent has been granted in the inter-disciplinary domain. Dr. Amrik Singh participated and acted as a resource person in various national and international conferences, seminars, research workshops, and industry talks. His area of research interest is accommodation management, ergonomics, green practices, human resource management in hospitality, waste management, AR VR in hospitality, etc. He is currently guiding 8Ph.D. scholars and 2 Ph.D. scholars have been awarded Ph.D.

Kuldeep Singh currently serves as an Assistant Professor at Amity School of Hospitality, Amity University, Haryana, India. He completed his PhD in tourism from Maharishi Dayanand University (Rohtak) in India in 2020. He is also a UGC (Net- JRF qualified). Dr. Singh has also served the tourism industry for a couple of years and three years in academics. Dr. Singh has so far published more than 30 research articles in both international and national referred journals as well as in edited books in the field of Tourism. Currently, He is serving as an editor of book series in various reputed publications (Emerald, IIP series). Dr. Singh is passionate about the academic areas of Service Quality Management, Rural tourism, Ecotourism, and Sustainable tourism. He also won an aspiring researchers welcome award from Indian Hospitality Congress. His credentials may be verified on various research platforms like Google Scholar, SSRN, LinkedIn, Academia, and Research Gate.

Sujay Vikram Singh, a Senior Research Fellow currently pursuing a doctoral degree at Banaras Hindu University, completed his graduation and post-graduation from IHM Lucknow. His research interests encompass Hospitality, CRM, Service Marketing, Service Quality, and Systematic Literature reviews. He has authored papers featured in diverse handbooks and journals, with recent publications in reputable outlets such as the International Journal of Market Research (Sage publishing), ABDC-A, Scopus, and the Journal of Global Information Management (IGI Publishing), indexed in Scopus and ABDC-A. Additionally, he has presented papers at numerous conferences and seminars, earning recognition for the best papers at events like IHM Bhopal and Subharati University, with special mentions at Shaheed Bhagat Singh College, DU, and achieving the highest marks in special tracks at Wosxen University and AMU. His credential may be verified on various research platforms like Google Scholar, SSRN, LinkedIn, Academia, and Research Gate.

About the Contributors

Pravin Chandra Singh is Currently Working as an Assistant Professor at MSMSR, Mats University. Before Mats University, he was associated with Raffles University. He has done his Doctorate from IM-BHU in Marketing and published several research papers in the journals and publishers of repute Like IIM-S, Emerald, IGI-Global, and PBRI. His credential may be verified on various research platforms like Google Scholar, SSRN, LinkedIn, Academia, and Research Gate.

Jugnoo Thakur is a passionate, goal oriented, and skillful student. Currently, pursuing P.G.D.M from ISBR Business School Bangalore. Has various problem-solving skills. Currently is in 2nd semester of PGDM and have taken Marketing in specialization. Have done an internship at VIMUL COM LTD for 1 month. And is a keen learner and a avid researcher.

Anila Thomas is an accomplished researcher and educator with approximately 25 years of academic and research experience. Dr. Thomas is currently working as an Associate Professor and Head, Department of Tourism and Travel Management at Jyoti Nivas College Autonomous in Bengaluru, Karnataka. She has authored many research-based chapters/papers in journals and book publications, and acted as a resource person at numerous international and national conferences. In 2012, she received a Doctorate in Tourism Management from Mother Teresa Women's University in Kodaikanal, Tamil Nadu. Her research focuses on the Sustainable Development Goals (SDGs) and Tourism Destinations, AI Applications in Tourism & Hospitality Industry, Geographic relevance to various tourist destinations, Health and Wellness Tourism, women's participation in Ayurvedic Medical Tourism, and Community involvement in Tourism resource preservation.

Tetiana Tkachuk has a PhD in Economics, Associate Professor, Associate Professor of the Department of Hotel and Restaurant Business. Disciplines Startup training, Hotel business, Luxury service management, Communication management, Information technologies and E-commerce of hospitality and tourism.

Pankaj Kr. Tyagi is an accomplished academician, researcher, and consultant. He is presently working as Professor at Chandigarh University, Mohali, India. Dr. Tyagi is an alumnus of Hemwati Nandan Bahuguna Garhwal University (Central University) and Kurukshetra University. He has over 2 decades of experience in the industry, teaching, training, consultancy, and expertise in destination management, travel process and disruptive technologies. He has published over 40 research papers in international journals indexed in the quality database and authored/edited 15 books with premium publications Like IGI-GLOBAL, Emerald Publications, CRC, Apple Academic Press and many more. He is a reviewer for many international tourism, management, and technology journals. His area of expertise is Travel Technologies, Sustainable Development Goals, Disruptive Technologies, Community Based Tourism, Meaningful Tourism, Hospitality Operations, Events and Festivals, Digital Innovation in Service Sector etc.

Index

Symbols

5G technology 89, 90, 91, 92, 93, 94, 95, 96, 100, 101, 102, 103

A

Academia 140, 281, 292, 304, 307
Academic Achievements 282, 285, 287
Amity University 106, 164, 278, 285, 286, 287, 288, 289, 368
AR and VR 35, 41, 59, 98, 216, 224, 289
Artificial Intelligence 12, 13, 25, 26, 27, 29, 30, 32, 34, 36, 37, 39, 40, 41, 42, 43, 45, 46, 66, 68, 73, 74, 79, 91, 94, 100, 121, 130, 159, 179, 194, 216, 224, 233, 259, 262, 263, 264, 270, 335, 336, 337, 338, 339, 343, 347, 348, 349, 350, 354, 359, 372, 391, 399, 402, 403, 404, 405, 408, 417
Augmented Reality 12, 13, 16, 24, 35, 41, 43, 52, 56, 67, 72, 90, 93, 94, 95, 96, 97, 101, 102, 103, 121, 129, 130, 131, 136, 148, 149, 159, 164, 166, 180, 207, 216, 224, 225, 247, 248, 253, 254, 259, 262, 284, 285, 322, 372, 404, 409, 410
Automation Technologies 184, 185, 188, 189, 190, 191, 192, 193

B

Bleisure 106, 107, 109, 110, 112, 113, 114, 120, 121, 122, 125, 126, 127
Blended learning 263, 272, 273, 313, 314, 315, 316, 317, 318, 320, 321, 322, 323, 324, 325, 326, 327, 328, 329, 330, 331, 332, 333, 334, 352, 354
blended learning strategy 318, 320, 321, 328, 332, 333
Business Events 20, 35, 38, 49, 51, 69, 107, 108, 111, 112, 114, 115, 116, 123, 124, 142

Business Travel 109, 111, 112, 113, 114, 115, 125, 414

C

Communities 17, 37, 44, 67, 108, 128, 138, 140, 187, 230, 234, 236, 252, 281, 298, 316, 351, 361, 362, 415, 417, 424
connectivity 5, 7, 12, 13, 23, 24, 26, 36, 47, 48, 64, 89, 92, 93, 94, 95, 96, 97, 100, 101, 102, 103, 130, 141, 144, 151, 169, 217, 280, 282, 283, 287, 289, 326, 328, 357, 370, 373
content analysis 55, 114, 124, 231, 254
Covid-19 2, 3, 5, 6, 15, 16, 17, 18, 32, 40, 41, 44, 45, 46, 47, 48, 49, 50, 51, 57, 59, 60, 62, 64, 65, 66, 69, 72, 73, 87, 88, 90, 104, 108, 110, 111, 113, 123, 129, 143, 148, 179, 229, 231, 253, 254, 256, 258, 259, 261, 262, 266, 268, 269, 270, 271, 272, 273, 274, 275, 276, 279, 284, 285, 289, 290, 291, 292, 293, 294, 296, 297, 298, 308, 310, 311, 315, 317, 330, 332, 351, 355, 364, 405, 412, 413, 414, 415, 416, 419, 420, 421, 422, 423, 424, 425, 426
Crisis 4, 49, 50, 58, 67, 119, 196, 230, 255, 258, 259, 260, 261, 262, 283, 292, 308, 330, 333, 355, 412, 413, 414, 415, 419, 421, 424
customer experiences 347

D

Data Analytics 10, 12, 13, 57, 80, 84, 94, 122, 130, 348, 368, 369, 372, 373, 377, 382, 383, 384, 385, 386, 387, 388
Data-Driven Culture 385, 386, 387, 388
Determinants of Transformation in Global Events 20
Digital Education 353, 354, 360, 362, 363, 364, 365, 366
Digital Transformation 4, 44, 87, 88, 117, 143, 148, 229, 231, 236, 253, 351, 352, 353, 354, 355, 361, 364, 365, 366, 367

E

Education 16, 18, 25, 28, 32, 44, 45, 51, 55, 68, 89, 93, 96, 126, 127, 129, 146, 179, 183, 186, 192, 201, 222, 223, 224, 226, 233, 253, 258, 259, 260, 261, 262, 263, 264, 265, 269, 270, 271, 272, 273, 274, 275, 276, 279, 281, 290, 291, 292, 293, 294, 296, 297, 300, 301, 302, 305, 308, 309, 310, 311, 312, 314, 315, 316, 317, 320, 321, 322, 323, 324, 325, 328, 330, 331, 332, 333, 334, 351, 352, 353, 354, 355, 356, 357, 358, 359, 360, 361, 362, 363, 364, 365, 366, 367, 379, 392, 393, 398, 405, 406, 408, 411, 425

Effort Expectancy 165, 166, 167, 168, 170, 171, 172, 173, 175, 177, 178

E-Learning 15, 259, 273, 301, 308, 310, 314, 323, 324, 333, 334, 405

Emerging technologies 1, 6, 9, 12, 13, 39, 66, 95, 121, 182, 198, 215, 216, 221, 310, 349, 367, 372, 373, 385

Engagement 6, 9, 16, 19, 25, 26, 30, 31, 32, 48, 49, 61, 62, 63, 64, 65, 66, 68, 73, 74, 75, 76, 78, 79, 80, 83, 84, 86, 95, 99, 101, 102, 106, 107, 108, 109, 110, 115, 120, 121, 122, 136, 140, 147, 148, 165, 166, 167, 169, 177, 178, 183, 198, 199, 200, 201, 202, 204, 205, 206, 207, 208, 209, 210, 211, 212, 213, 214, 215, 216, 217, 218, 219, 220, 221, 223, 224, 226, 227, 239, 240, 242, 256, 263, 279, 280, 281, 282, 283, 284, 285, 286, 289, 290, 294, 317, 320, 327, 329, 338, 340, 347, 348, 349, 353, 354, 361, 363, 368, 369, 370, 372, 373, 374, 375, 383, 384, 385, 386, 387, 388, 389, 391, 396, 399, 421

Ethical Considerations 77, 132, 159, 198, 213, 215, 221, 336, 337, 345, 346, 350, 378

Event Experiences 1, 13, 24, 34, 49, 66, 80, 85, 89, 90, 92, 101, 103, 148, 166, 198, 200, 216, 217, 218, 219, 220, 221, 254, 386, 388

event industry 9, 11, 12, 13, 15, 32, 34, 49, 50, 58, 71, 72, 73, 82, 85, 124, 146, 147, 148, 149, 150, 151, 152, 153, 155, 160, 161, 164, 165, 166, 167, 168, 169, 173, 174, 175, 176, 177, 178, 194, 371, 388

Event Innovation 12, 124

Event Optimization 383

Event Planning 23, 34, 40, 45, 51, 66, 75, 76, 80, 83, 86, 87, 88, 166, 198, 199, 200, 208, 209, 211, 213, 215, 218, 220, 221, 368, 371, 373, 375, 376, 378, 386, 387, 388

Event Technology 1, 2, 52, 88

F

Facilitating Conditions 164, 165, 169, 170, 171, 172, 173, 175, 176, 177

Festivals 11, 12, 13, 21, 22, 23, 24, 36, 39, 40, 42, 43, 71, 72, 75, 77, 87, 128, 129, 130, 133, 134, 135, 137, 138, 139, 140, 141, 184, 188, 190, 229, 254, 259, 272

Future Trends 198, 215, 348, 363, 382, 406

G

Gamification 61, 72, 79, 83, 106, 107, 109, 110, 111, 112, 113, 114, 115, 116, 120, 121, 122, 124, 126, 127, 198, 199, 200, 201, 202, 203, 205, 208, 209, 210, 211, 212, 213, 214, 215, 216, 217, 218, 219, 220, 221, 222, 223, 224, 225, 226, 227, 231, 254, 258, 263, 265, 270, 408

Gamified Networking 200, 212, 218, 219, 227

H

Hospitality 15, 34, 38, 40, 42, 43, 45, 50, 55, 56, 68, 69, 70, 75, 77, 86, 87, 88, 118, 119, 123, 124, 125, 127, 142, 143, 144, 145, 180, 182, 183, 185, 188, 194, 195, 196, 197, 225, 228, 229, 230, 231, 232, 233, 234, 235, 236,

237, 238, 239, 240, 241, 242, 243,
244, 246, 249, 250, 251, 252, 253,
254, 255, 257, 263, 264, 272, 273,
274, 275, 276, 293, 335, 336, 337,
338, 339, 340, 341, 342, 343, 345,
346, 347, 348, 349, 350, 414, 422, 425
hotel industry 38, 67, 68, 335, 337, 339,
343, 344, 345, 346, 347, 348, 349, 350
hybrid events 1, 2, 3, 6, 7, 8, 9, 12, 13, 20,
34, 39, 41, 43, 47, 48, 49, 55, 56, 57,
58, 60, 61, 62, 63, 64, 65, 66, 69, 71,
75, 77, 87, 165, 166, 198, 199, 215,
217, 218, 227, 280, 282, 292, 360,
368, 369, 371, 382, 383, 384, 385, 388

I

Immersive Experience 26, 45, 56, 95, 96,
99, 101, 102, 107, 207, 283, 286
Immersive Experiences 31, 35, 80, 92, 94,
95, 97, 98, 102, 131, 140, 150, 165,
199, 211, 218, 284, 290, 357, 372, 383
immersive interactions 25, 89
Impact 4, 8, 9, 10, 21, 23, 26, 31, 32, 36,
38, 39, 44, 45, 48, 49, 54, 55, 62, 64,
65, 67, 73, 75, 78, 79, 81, 85, 88, 92,
104, 107, 108, 110, 111, 113, 118,
119, 121, 122, 124, 126, 131, 132,
139, 140, 144, 149, 151, 152, 155,
156, 158, 159, 162, 164, 175, 177,
178, 179, 182, 184, 185, 194, 200,
203, 210, 217, 220, 221, 222, 223,
227, 228, 231, 232, 253, 254, 260,
275, 281, 282, 287, 288, 292, 298,
305, 307, 309, 311, 315, 316, 332,
336, 337, 345, 346, 347, 348, 349,
350, 352, 354, 355, 362, 363, 365,
366, 367, 369, 371, 372, 373, 375,
376, 380, 381, 382, 392, 393, 394,
403, 406, 422, 425
India 1, 19, 20, 39, 47, 69, 71, 81, 82, 86,
89, 106, 113, 114, 128, 134, 135, 137,
138, 139, 146, 147, 148, 149, 151, 152,
155, 157, 160, 161, 164, 198, 278,
285, 289, 293, 295, 296, 298, 301,
305, 313, 330, 331, 332, 333, 335,
351, 354, 355, 356, 357, 358, 360,

362, 364, 365, 366, 368, 391, 402, 419
Innovation 1, 9, 12, 16, 18, 28, 30, 31, 43,
48, 49, 54, 56, 66, 68, 69, 70, 72, 76,
77, 78, 87, 88, 90, 102, 104, 108, 109,
113, 117, 118, 119, 121, 124, 126,
127, 131, 137, 140, 141, 147, 150,
159, 162, 179, 181, 182, 186, 218,
221, 253, 256, 259, 275, 279, 280,
284, 338, 368, 369, 382, 385, 387,
388, 390, 400
Interpretive Structural Modelling 148, 155
Intrinsic Motivation 201, 223, 225

L

Leisure Tourism 109

M

Machine Learning 24, 29, 44, 93, 122, 127,
130, 216, 336, 346, 372, 407
Marketing Event Industry 146, 147, 148,
149, 150, 151, 152, 153, 155, 160, 161
marketing innovation 140
Medical Tourism 253, 401, 402, 408, 411
Metaverse 10, 12, 15, 70, 93, 100, 104,
124, 128, 129, 130, 131, 132, 133,
134, 135, 136, 137, 139, 140, 141,
142, 143, 144, 145, 146, 147, 148,
149, 150, 151, 152, 153, 155, 156,
158, 159, 160, 161, 162, 163, 164,
165, 166, 167, 168, 169, 172, 173,
174, 175, 176, 177, 178, 179, 180,
181, 182, 183, 222, 226, 293, 357,
404, 407, 410, 411
MICE tourism 37, 40, 50, 55, 56, 67, 70
MOOCs 272, 296, 297, 357, 360, 365

N

NEP 2020 330, 354, 356, 362
Netnography 119, 123, 274, 412, 413, 417,
421, 424, 426
network capacity 89, 102
New Century 261

O

operational efficiency 79, 338, 339, 344

P

Participant Engagement 165, 218, 221, 289, 370, 384, 385
Performance Expectancy 165, 166, 167, 170, 171, 172, 173, 175, 177, 178

R

real-time communication 28, 89
Rehabilitation 234, 391, 393, 395, 396, 397, 398, 399, 400, 402, 403, 404, 405, 406, 407, 409, 410, 411
Robots 19, 20, 22, 23, 25, 28, 29, 30, 31, 32, 34, 35, 38, 40, 41, 42, 43, 44, 45, 188, 189, 193, 195, 196, 197, 261, 349, 411

S

SDG 184, 186, 188, 353, 354, 365
SDG12 187, 188, 189, 190
seamless streaming 100
Service Automation 25, 43, 184, 188, 189, 191, 195
Social Influence 164, 165, 168, 169, 170, 171, 172, 173, 175, 176, 177, 178, 179, 320, 321
social media 9, 23, 24, 57, 79, 80, 85, 87, 91, 118, 183, 217, 229, 231, 238, 239, 240, 242, 252, 255, 257, 283, 297, 327, 346, 370, 374, 376, 385, 416, 417
Students performance 276
Sustainability 5, 10, 11, 18, 25, 43, 45, 48, 49, 61, 62, 64, 65, 66, 68, 69, 104, 124, 131, 142, 144, 158, 162, 179, 183, 184, 185, 186, 187, 188, 189, 190, 192, 194, 195, 196, 235, 257, 272, 288, 289, 290, 293, 309, 348, 349, 351, 353, 354, 359, 363, 365, 389, 425

T

technological intervention 104, 318, 324, 325
Technology 1, 2, 4, 6, 9, 11, 12, 13, 15, 16, 17, 18, 19, 21, 22, 23, 24, 25, 28, 29, 30, 31, 32, 34, 35, 38, 39, 40, 41, 42, 44, 45, 46, 49, 50, 51, 52, 54, 56, 57, 59, 63, 64, 65, 66, 67, 69, 70, 71, 72, 73, 75, 78, 80, 81, 82, 84, 85, 86, 87, 88, 89, 90, 91, 92, 93, 94, 95, 96, 97, 98, 100, 101, 102, 103, 104, 105, 106, 107, 109, 110, 117, 124, 129, 130, 131, 132, 135, 136, 137, 139, 140, 141, 142, 147, 148, 149, 150, 151, 155, 159, 161, 162, 163, 164, 165, 166, 167, 168, 169, 172, 175, 176, 177, 178, 179, 180, 181, 182, 183, 187, 188, 191, 194, 195, 196, 209, 210, 211, 216, 218, 225, 226, 229, 246, 248, 256, 259, 261, 262, 272, 274, 276, 280, 281, 282, 283, 284, 285, 286, 287, 288, 289, 290, 291, 296, 300, 301, 302, 305, 306, 307, 308, 309, 310, 311, 313, 314, 315, 316, 317, 321, 322, 323, 324, 325, 326, 327, 328, 329, 330, 331, 332, 333, 335, 338, 343, 344, 345, 346, 347, 349, 350, 351, 352, 353, 354, 355, 356, 359, 360, 361, 362, 363, 364, 365, 366, 367, 368, 369, 371, 372, 377, 384, 387, 388, 389, 390, 391, 392, 393, 394, 395, 396, 398, 400, 401, 403, 405, 408, 410, 411, 416
Technology Adoption 124, 167, 176, 368, 388
Tourism 17, 18, 23, 24, 32, 34, 37, 38, 39, 40, 41, 42, 43, 44, 45, 50, 54, 55, 56, 58, 67, 68, 69, 70, 71, 72, 75, 77, 86, 87, 88, 109, 110, 111, 112, 116, 117, 118, 119, 123, 124, 125, 126, 127, 129, 131, 132, 133, 134, 139, 140, 141, 142, 143, 144, 145, 180, 181, 182, 183, 185, 188, 194, 195, 196, 197, 223, 224, 225, 226, 231, 253, 254, 256, 258, 259, 260, 261, 262, 263, 264, 265, 270, 271, 272, 273, 274,

275, 276, 277, 293, 338, 347, 348, 349, 350, 401, 402, 403, 408, 411, 412, 413, 414, 415, 416, 417, 418, 419, 420, 421, 422, 423, 424, 425, 426

U

ultra-low latency 92, 95
User Acceptance 150, 152, 153, 156, 157, 158, 160, 168, 169

V

virality 229, 231, 232, 242, 243, 244, 246, 247, 248, 249, 250, 251, 252
Virtual convocation 285, 286, 287, 288
virtual event experiences 80, 89, 90, 92, 101, 103, 217
virtual events 2, 3, 6, 9, 10, 17, 22, 23, 25, 30, 31, 32, 34, 35, 43, 49, 51, 56, 57,

58, 59, 62, 63, 64, 65, 91, 92, 93, 94, 95, 96, 97, 98, 99, 100, 101, 102, 103, 142, 150, 151, 164, 165, 221, 226, 236, 280, 281, 289, 290, 373
Virtual Experiences 19, 25, 26, 32, 91, 132, 165, 265, 285, 287
Virtual Laboratory 300, 306, 307, 310, 312
Virtual Reality 12, 13, 23, 24, 25, 34, 35, 39, 40, 41, 42, 45, 52, 56, 59, 62, 67, 69, 89, 90, 93, 94, 95, 96, 97, 99, 101, 102, 103, 121, 129, 130, 131, 133, 137, 159, 164, 165, 166, 168, 181, 183, 216, 226, 234, 246, 248, 254, 280, 282, 284, 285, 286, 293, 294, 311, 322, 354, 372, 391, 392, 393, 394, 395, 396, 397, 398, 399, 400, 402, 403, 404, 405, 406, 407, 408, 409, 410, 411, 425

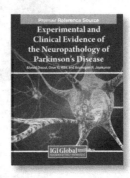

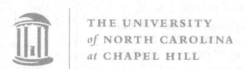

Printed in the United States
by Baker & Taylor Publisher Services